WORLD FASCISM

WORLD FASCISM

A HISTORICAL ENCYCLOPEDIA

VOLUME 2: L–Z

Cyprian P. Blamires, Editor
with Paul Jackson

A B C · C L I O

Santa Barbara, California • Denver, Colorado • Oxford, United Kingdom

Library of Congress Cataloging-in-Publication Data

World fascism : a historical encyclopedia / Cyprian P. Blamires, editor ; with Paul Jackson.
p.   cm
Includes bibliographical references and index.
ISBN 1-57607-940-6 (hard cover : alk. paper)—ISBN 1-57607-941-4 (ebook)
1. Fascism—History—Encyclopedias.   I. Blamires, Cyprian.   II. Jackson, Paul.
JC481.W67 2006
335.603—dc22
20006021588

10   09   08   07   06   05 / 10   9   8   7   6   5   4   3   2   1

This book is also available on the World Wide Web as an ebook.
Visit abc-clio.com for details.

ABC-CLIO, Inc.
130 Cremona Drive, P.O. Box 1911
Santa Barbara, California 93116–1911

Production Editor: Vicki Moran
Editorial Assistant: Alisha Martinez
Production Manager: Don Schmidt
Media Editor: Sharon Daughtery
Image Coordinator: Ellen Dougherty
Media Resources Manager: Caroline Price
File Manager: Paula Gerard

This book is printed on acid-free paper ∞ .
Manufactured in the United States of America

Contents

List of Entries

LA ROCQUE DE SEVERAC, FRANÇOIS, COMTE DE (1885–1946)

Leader of the Croix de Feu (CF) from December 1930 on, La Rocque, the son of a royalist general, transformed the movement from an association bringing former combatants together into the most feared extreme right *ligue* in interwar France. Following the dissolution of the leagues by the Popular Front government in 1936, La Rocque established the movement as the Parti Social Français. Rallying to Pétain during the war and named a member of the National Council (1941), La Rocque nevertheless refused to let the membership of the PSF (by now renamed the Progrès Social Français) join the Légion des Volontaires Français, or to take part in Pétain's Légion Française de Combattants. Indeed, despite public pronouncements in favor of the National Revolution, La Rocque is claimed by his supporters to have participated in the Resistance. La Rocque was arrested and deported by the Germans in 1943 to Ravensbrück for contacts with the Allies. Arrested on returning to France, he was first imprisoned, then put under house arrest in Croissy, where he died in 1946

Steve Bastow

See Also: ACTION FRANÇAISE; CONCENTRATION CAMPS; FARMERS; FRANCE; MAURRAS, CHARLES; MONARCHISM; PETAIN, MARSHAL HENRI PHILIPPE; VICHY; WAR VETERANS; WORLD WAR II

References
Coston, H. 1960. *Partis, journaux et homes politiques d'hier et d'aujourd'hui.* Special ed. *Lectures Françaises.* Paris: Librarie Française.
Soucy, Robert. 1997. *French Fascism: The Second Wave, 1933–1939.* New Haven: Yale University Press.

LABOR FRONT, THE (DEUTSCHE ARBEITSFRONT; DAF)

The sole trades union organization permitted under the Third Reich, headed by Robert Ley. It was envisaged as the means of establishing peaceful labor relations. Although the chairman of the existing Council of the Trades Unions proposed collaboration with the new regime in 1933, it was refused. Officials of the new organization were drawn from the ranks of the NSDAP. The funds of the trade unions were seized and devoted to the founding of the "Strength through Joy" movement. Initially the front included management and white-collar associations, the aim being to create a "community" of labor. Including the whole workforce of the Third Reich, the front enrolled more than 20 million individuals, and consequently it had a massive budget and considerable holdings of property. This attempt by the Nazis to win over workers to the philosophy of the Third Reich was not wholly successful, in the sense that industrial disputes continued, but the improved rates of employment certainly made the regime more attractive. It was one of the facets of the Third Reich to be imitated in Japan.

Cyprian Blamires

See Also: COMMUNITY; CORPORATISM; EMPLOYMENT; GERMANY; JAPAN; LEISURE; LEY, ROBERT; MASSES, THE ROLE OF THE; NAZISM; THIRD REICH, THE; TRADE UNIONS; WORK

References
Frese, M. 1991. *Betriebspolitik im "Dritten Reich": Deutsche Arbeitsfront, Unternehmer und Staatsbürokratie in der westdeutschen Grossindustrie, 1933–1939*. Paderborn: F. Schöningh.
Smelser, R. M. 1998. *Robert Ley: Hitler's Labor Front Leader*. New York: St. Martin's.

LABOR SERVICE, THE

The German Labor Service (Arbeitsdienst) started as a job creation scheme and developed into an obligatory work program for young Germans. In the years before the war the organization was one of the most important propaganda and educational tools of the Nazi regime. After World War I, many countries discussed the introduction of a labor service in order to organize their youth for work for the common good with an educational dimension. Bulgaria introduced a compulsory labor service in 1920. As a reaction to the Great Depression, several nations instituted such organizations on a voluntary basis in the fight against the economic and social consequences of unemployment, among them Germany (from 1931) and the United States (from 1933).

After their seizure of power, the Nazis coordinated the voluntary labor service. From 1933 until 1945, the organization was headed by *Reichsarbeitsführer* Konstantin Hierl (1875–1955). On 26 June 1935, the *Reichsarbeitsdienstgesetz* (Reich labor service law) was passed. From that point on the organization was called Reichsarbeitsdienst (RAD), and labor service became compulsory for all male Germans between the ages of eighteen and twenty-five. The duration of service was six months, normally directly prior to military service. Altogether, more than 3 million men passed through this organization. For women, obligatory service was formally instituted on 4 September 1939 but never fully translated into action. The Arbeitsdienst was an important ideological and educational instrument of the regime. Labor service was considered "honorary service." According to the ideological claim, it helped to build up the "national community" through the common work of Germans with different social backgrounds and through the shared living arrangements in camps far away from urban centers. The RAD for men was employed in forestry, soil improvement projects, and other forms of work-intensive manual labor, whereas the much smaller suborganization for women helped on farms and in homework. The economic effectiveness and efficiency of the institution was low. Primarily, the RAD served as a political symbol of integration and as a propaganda instrument for the Nazi regime aimed at the German population as well as at foreign observers.

Apart from their work, the enrollees were indoctrinated with Nazi ideology. In the male section of the RAD, the educational dimension lost influence in 1937–1938. From that point on, the efficient deployment of labor and premilitary training for the young men were considered to be more important, as part of the regime's effort of war preparation. In the less important RAD for women, whose history follows completely different lines, highly centralized education along Nazi concepts had been introduced only in 1936. During World War II, the RAD for men increasingly developed into an auxiliary troop of the German military. It also became involved in the regime's racist war of extermination. After 1940, several occupied and dependent countries of Nazi Germany built up similar organizations (for example, Croatia, The Netherlands, Norway, Slovakia). In May 1945, the RAD was demobilized as part of the Wehrmacht, and on 20 May 1945 the Allied Control Council abolished the organization.

Kiran Patel

See Also: CROATIA; EDUCATION; EMPLOYMENT; GERMANY; HOLOCAUST, THE; LABOR FRONT, THE; MILITARISM; NAZISM; NETHERLANDS, THE; NORWAY; NUREMBERG RALLIES, THE; PROPAGANDA; RACISM; RURALISM; SLOVAKIA; THIRD REICH, THE; TOTALITARIANISM; *VOLKSGEMEINSCHAFT*, THE; WALL STREET CRASH, THE; WEHRMACHT, THE; WORK; WORLD WAR II; YOUTH MOVEMENTS

References

Patel, Kiran Klaus. 2005. *"Soldiers of Work": Labor Services in New Deal America and Nazi Germany, 1933–1945*. New York: Cambridge University Press.

Seifert, Manfred. 1996. *Kulturarbeit im Reichsarbeitsdienst: Theorie und Praxis nationalsozialistischer Kulturpflege im Kontext historisch-politischer, organisatorischer und ideologischer Einflüsse*. Münster: Waxmann.

LAGARDE, PAUL DE (1827–1891)

One of those anti-Semitic Pangermanists and preachers of the need for a rebirth of the German nation whose theories helped to create the climate in which the Nazis could thrive. Born Paul Anton Boetticher, Lagarde was a theologian, professor of Oriental studies at Göttingen, cultural critic, and guiding force of the late-nineteenth-century conservative revolution. Lagarde's philosophy was a response to the "decay" of state and church in Germany in the second half of the nineteenth century. He preached an ideology composed of religious, mystical-romantic, chauvinistic, and anti-Semitic ideas that he claimed could inspire the rebirth of the German nation. The thrust of this ideology was Pangermanism, antiliberalism, hostility to the Enlightenment, and reformism. He set out his program in a series of writings that were brought together in the two-volume *Deutsche Schriften*, first published in 1878–1881 and subsequently re-edited and enlarged several times.

For Lagarde, religion was of central significance, both for individuals and for the nation. He criticized religious pluralism in Germany and upheld the view that the religious divisions of Christendom were outdated. Lagarde demanded the separation of church and state and called for a single national religion for each people, in order to avoid internal conflicts. He aimed to prepare the way for such a national religion through his scholarly researches. He rejected the Old Testament as morally dubious and not appropriate to the German being, and set out to purify the Gospel from all historical additions, so as to allow the Germans access to the real core of revelation. Politically Lagarde strove for a strong Central Europe ruled by Germany and Austria that would found colonies to the east and southeast. He argued for a corporative society in which a new and wider nobility formed from capable families would be entrusted with particular colonization tasks. Through colonization the new nobility, and with it the German people, would rediscover its essence, while the decay of values, alienation from Germanness, rootlessness, and weakness of character would be remedied. Lagarde rejected Judaism as outdated but repeatedly stressed that he was not a supporter of racially motivated anti-Semitism; however, he reproached the Jews with being profiteers and speculators on the stock exchange. He insinuated that they were striving for world domination and complained of a perceptibly increasing influence of Jews in universities, the legal system, the press, and politics. Lagarde also thought that he could establish a decline in standards in German education as a result of its "Judaization." In the Jews he saw both a cause of Germany's supposed decline and a power whose very existence was an expression of German weakness. Lagarde seems to have accepted assimilation as an option for the German Jews, although he wanted the Jews to leave the areas to be colonized in the East and found their own state. In spite of his superficial detachment from racial anti-Semitism, there are passages in Lagarde in which he describes Jews as "parasites," saying that negotiation with them was not possible; they must be eliminated quickly and thoroughly.

With his nationalist revival theology Lagarde exercised an influence on various individuals and groupings, including Julius Langbehn, Alfred Rosenberg, the Wagner circle, the Alldeutscher Verband, a part of the Youth Movement, and the German Christians.

Michael Schäbitz
(translated by Cyprian Blamires)

See Also: ANTI-SEMITISM; ARISTOCRACY; BANKS, THE; BAYREUTH; CHRISTIANITY; COLONIALISM; CORPORATISM; CULTURE; DECADENCE; ECONOMICS; ELITE THEORY; ENLIGHTENMENT, THE; GERMAN CHRISTIANS, THE; GERMANNESS (*DEUTSCHHEIT*); GERMANY; HITLER, ADOLF; LANGBEHN, JULIUS; LIBERALISM; NATIONALISM; NIETZSCHE, FRIEDRICH; NORDIC SOUL, THE; PALINGENETIC MYTH; PANGERMANISM; PLUTOCRACY; PROTOFASCISM; RELIGION; ROOTLESSNESS; ROSENBERG, ALFRED; SPENGLER, OSWALD; THEOLOGY; UNIVERSITIES (GERMANY); WAGNER, (WILHELM) RICHARD; YOUTH MOVEMENTS; ZIONISM

References

Lougee, P. 1962. *Paul de Lagarde, 1827–1891: A Study of Radical Conservatism in Germany*. Cambridge: Harvard University Press.

Stern, F. 1962. *The Politics of Cultural Despair: A Study in the Rise of the Germanic Ideology*. Berkeley: University of California Press.

LANGBEHN, JULIUS (1851–1907)

Cultural critic and anti-Semite, Pangermanist and hypernationalist, Langbehn was one of those who helped to create the kind of cultural climate in which Nazism could thrive. His *Rembrandt als Erzieher (Rembrandt as Educator)* aroused a furor at the time of its publication in 1890. Within a few months the book, published anonymously, ran through several editions. The author, after studies in art and classical archaeology culminating in a doctorate, had led an unstable, wandering life. Like many of his contemporaries, Langbehn felt disquiet in regard to the ambient culture. In a cryptic language full of metaphors and allegories, he called insistently for a cultural renewal of Germany. He took Rembrandt and his art for a model, arguing that reforms should be inspired by Rembrandt's outlook. Langbehn's critique was directed against a number of developments of his day, including materialism, naturalism, democracy, internationalism, specialization in science, and the growth of the big cities. He valued solitude, peace, individualism, aristocratism, and above all art as the means to the rebirth of the German spirit that he desired. He assigned to art and the mystical a role superior to science and technology, for art was rooted in the national, while science, technology, and industrialization were international. Art could penetrate existence where science could not. Science needed to undergo a mystical process that would make it truly national, and the association of mysticism, science, and art would be the driving force for a renewal of national life. Such a spiritual rebirth could, however, occur only when a people was healthy, and to that end Langbehn called for a return to the peasant way of life. He saw such a return as the only way to produce the education and character that would enable Germany to take the lead in the European life of the spirit. In the sphere of foreign policy, Langbehn argued for the creation of a united Europe under German leadership. He believed that Germans were called to mastery of the world by peaceful means and for purposes of harmony and peace among the peoples.

Langbehn hoped for the unification and renewal of the German peoples under a charismatic leader. He advocated a hierarchical order, and his aristocracy was to be rooted in the life of the people and recruited from all classes of the population. Langbehn's concept of self-education, his blood-and-soil philosophy, and his belief in a *Volksgemeinschaft* ("national community"), his romantically exaggerated reverence for the homeland, and his Pangermanic racist nationalism had a huge influence on the German youth movement. The first editions of *Rembrandt als Erzieher* contain few observations about the Jews, but from the thirty-seventh edition of 1891, a markedly anti-Semitic attitude became evident in his writing. Now the Jew appeared as the corrupter and destroyer of German culture; the Jews were exploiters, they were amoral, they were without character or homeland, and they were poisoning the German people. Germany must belong to the Germans, and the Jews could not be German because they are not Aryan by race. Particularly harsh expressions of anti-Semitism appeared in another anonymous writing of his, published in 1892, *Der Rembrandtdeutsche. Von einem Wahrheitsfreund (The Rembrandt-type German: By a Friend of Truth)*. In 1900, Langbehn was received into the Catholic Church.

Michael Schäbitz
(translated by Cyprian Blamires)

See Also: ANTI-SEMITISM; ARISTOCRACY; ART; ARYANISM; BLOOD AND SOIL; COSMOPOLITANISM; CULTURE; DEMOCRACY; EDUCATION; ELITE THEORY; EUROPE; GERMANNESS (*DEUTSCHHEIT*); GERMANY; IMPERIALISM; INDIVIDUALISM; LAGARDE, PAUL DE; LEADER CULT, THE; MATERIALISM; MYSTICISM; MYTH; NATIONALISM; NAZISM; NORDIC SOUL, THE; PALINGENETIC MYTH; PANGERMANISM; RACIAL DOCTRINE; RACISM; RURALISM; SCIENCE; SPENGLER, OSWALD; *VOLKSGEMEINSCHAFT*, THE; YOUTH MOVEMENTS

References
Carr, C. T. 1938. "Julius Langbehn—A Forerunner of National Socialism." *German Life and Letters* 3, no. 1: 45–54.
Stern, F. 1962. *The Politics of Cultural Despair: A Study in the Rise of the Germanic Ideology.* Berkley: University of California Press.

LANZ VON LIEBENFELS: *See* LIEBENFELS, JÖRG ADOLF JOSEF LANZ VON

LAPUA

The Lapua movement began as a reaction of Finnish farmers to communist agitation in the town of Lapua in 1929, and it quickly received the blessing of right-wing establishment figures. The authorities attempted to appease the movement by endorsing its main goal of eradicating communism and did little to stop its campaign of physical intimidation against political opponents on the Left. Although not engaging directly in electoral politics, Lapua succeeded in mobilizing broad popular support and pressuring the government into passing anticommunist legislation. However, Lapua alienated many of its bourgeois supporters through its continued lawlessness and escalating demands. Matters came to a head in February 1932 with a muddled rebellion at the town of Mäntsälä, subsequent to which the movement was outlawed.

Andres Kasekamp

See Also: "ANTI-" DIMENSION OF FASCISM, THE; BOLSHEVISM; CONSERVATISM; FINLAND; MARXISM; SOCIALISM

Reference
Rintala, Martin. 1962. *Three Generations: The Extreme Right Wing in Finnish Politics.* Bloomington: Indiana University Press.

LAROUCHE, LYNDON HERMYLE (born 1922)

U.S. former Quaker and former far-left activist who shifted to the far Right in the 1970s and attracted a following through his writing, speaking, and propagandistic activities. His movement generally operates under front groups such as Food for Peace and the Schiller Institute, and it publishes journals like the *New Federalist* and the *Executive Intelligence Review.* LaRouche is associated in particular with anti-Semitic conspiracy theories—in which the British royal family often plays a leading role—and he has developed an extensive intelligence-gathering service. The LaRouchite ideology contains elements of populist antielitism and hostility to a range of targets, including the Left in general, environmentalism, feminism, homosexuality, and organized labor. LaRouchites have called for a dictatorship led by a "humanist" elite.

Cyprian Blamires

See Also: "ANTI-" DIMENSION OF FASCISM, THE; ANTI-SEMITISM; CONSPIRACY THEORIES; DICTATORSHIP; ECOLOGY; FEMINISM; HOMOSEXUALITY; KÜHNEN, MICHAEL; NATURE; NEOPOPULISM; TRADES UNIONS; UNITED STATES, THE (POSTWAR); WOMEN

References
Gilbert, Helen. 2003. *Lyndon LaRouche: Fascism Restyled for the New Millennium.* Seattle, WA: Red Letter.
King, Dennis. 1989. *Lyndon LaRouche and the New American Fascism.* New York: Doubleday.

LAROUCHITES, THE: *See* LAROUCHE, LYNDON HERMYLE
LATERAN PACTS, THE: *See* CATHOLIC CHURCH, THE

LATVIA

The most significant of the various extremist nationalist groups to emerge in Latvia in the interwar years was the Thunder Cross (Perkonkrusts), which was founded in 1933 after its predecessor, the Fire Cross (Ugunskrusts), was banned. The guiding slogan of the Thunder Cross was "Latvia for the Latvians." Led by Gustavs Celmiņš (1899–1968), the movement was most popular among young, urban, university-educated men. In particular, it channeled resentment of the continued predominance of Germans and Jews in certain professions, such as law and medicine. The Thunder Cross adopted paramilitary attributes and appeared to be gaining popularity, but it never had an opportunity to contest elections. Following the example of Päts in Estonia, Prime Minister Kārlis Ulmanis declared a state of emergency on 15 May 1934 and arrested the leaders of the Thunder Cross, as well as communists. While claiming to save democracy from the threat of extremism, Ulmanis erected his own authoritarian regime. In 1936 he united the offices of president and prime minister in his own person. Although banned, cells of the Thunder Cross continued to operate underground. Celmiņš was exiled. Despite Ulmanis's adoption of nationalist policies favored by the Thunder Cross, the latter continued to view him as beholden to the business interests of the ethnic minorities. In 1939 the Soviet Union issued an ultimatum to Latvia to authorize the establishment of military bases on her territory, and the following year Latvia was annexed to the USSR. Ulmanis and thousands of his countrymen were deported to Russia, where most perished. In their thirst for revenge against the Soviets, many former members of the

Thunder Cross collaborated with the Nazis when they invaded in 1941, though Celmiņš was later arrested for opposing German rule. After the restoration of independence from the Soviet Union in 1991, a small extremist nationalist group revived the name of the Thunder Cross and blew up a few Soviet monuments. Other acts of political violence in Latvia have come from Russian extremists, particularly the National Bolsheviks.

Andres Kasekamp

See Also: ANTI-SEMITISM; AUTHORITARIANISM; BOLSHEVISM; ESTONIA; LITHUANIA; NATIONAL BOLSHEVISM; NATIONALISM; NAZISM; PARAMILITARISM; PÄTS, KONSTANTIN; SOVIET UNION, THE; ULMANIS, KĀRLIS

References
Ezergailis, Andrew. 1996. *The Holocaust in Latvia: The Missing Center.* Riga: Historical Institute of Latvia.
Kasekamp, Andres. 1999. "Radical Right-Wing Movements in the North-East Baltic." *Journal of Contemporary History* 34, no. 4 (October), pp. 587–600.
Von Hehn, Jürgen. 1957. "Lettland zwischen Demokratie und Diktatur." *Jahrbücher für Geschichte Osteuropas, Beiheft* 3. München.

LAVAL, PIERRE (1883–1945)

Leading minister, Vichy France (July–December 1940, April 1942–August 1944). Elected to parliament as a socialist (1914), Laval evolved opportunistically to become a centrist prime minister (1931–1932, 1935–1936). In July 1940, he engineered Petain's assumption of power. Ideologically agnostic, Laval made unilateral concessions to the German occupiers with confidence that clever bargaining would win counter-concessions. Pétain dismissed him on 10 December 1940, possibly for excessive concessions but more likely for failing to consult, for his unpopularity as an unprincipled politician, and for an absence of promised results. Reinstated under German pressure (April 1942), Laval continued with his policy of collaboration. He was executed in 1945.

Robert O. Paxton

See Also: FRANCE; MUNICH AGREEMENT/PACT, THE; PETAIN, MARSHAL HENRI PHILIPPE; VICHY; WORLD WAR II

Reference
Warner, Geoffrey. 1968. *Pierre Laval and the Eclipse of France, 1931–1945.* London: Macmillan.

LAW

The role played by law in interwar Italy and Germany was ambivalent, multifaceted, and variable. On the one hand, the political theory and practice of Italian Fascism and German Nazism were antagonistic to the role assigned to law in modern liberal societies—that is, social integration through general and public common action norms that assign subjective rights to individuals. Italian Fascist and German Nazi authors advocated alternative means of achieving social integration—namely, by means of the rule of the charismatic leader who would articulate the will of the masses in his ad hoc decisions or commands. The irrationalistic and antiliberal tenor of the two regimes was at odds with modern law, and very especially with the rule of law. In addition, their opposition to liberal democracy entailed the firm rejection of the representative and participatory procedures of law-making. On the other hand, Mussolini and Hitler did not abolish law and legal orders when they came to power; instead, they made ample use of law as a means of their rule. This allowed them to retain the form of law while attempting a substantial transformation of the very idea of law. "Fascist" law can be said to have been characterized by three main features. First, both the law-making procedures and the system of sources of law were dramatically simplified. The will of the leader was affirmed as the ultimate source of law, and that will was said not to be limited or framed by any legal constraint, which implied emancipating the political will from law. Not only were formal constitutional norms alien to Italian Fascist and German Nazi conceptions of law but, in addition, the very idea of judicial review of executive and administrative action and regulation was foreign to them. Second, the legal order was conceived as composed of objective rules, to the exclusion of subjective rights and principles. Indeed, the legal theory of the two regimes aimed at explicating subjective rights as the mere reflex of objective legal norms, while legal principles were regarded as mere devices of rhetoric. This curtailed the potential of legal norms to serve as limits of state (and private) power. Third, the regulative ideal of the legal order was formally retained but substantially instrumentalized, with a view to increasing the social legitimacy of the regimes. This was done in three main ways: (a) formal law kept on playing a visible role in integrating society in certain domains (for example, private property regimes and contractual relationships), even if systematically subject to potential exceptions stemming from the will of the leader. This reflected the dual character of the political orders in Mussolinian Italy and Hitlerite Germany, wherein the *prerogative state* (ad hoc commands or decisions) overlapped with and constrained the *normative state,* the remnants of social relations still integrated through law; (b) the most oppressive and exploitative objectives of these regimes (such as the physical suppression of the opposition or Nazism's genocidal crimes against classes of individuals) required the enaction of general norms of sorts, the efficiency of which was increased by their transmission in a legal vest. Racial laws and (in the case of Germany) the rules governing the functioning of concentration camps constitute paramount examples; (c) these regimes made extensive use of laws as a propaganda tool. They indulged in the production of legal norms that were not intended to be actually applied but to serve as window-dressing for a social reality that clearly contradicted their own rhetoric. This was especially true for what concerned labor and industrial relationships. Indeed, the Italian Charter of Labor (1927) and the German National Labor Law (1934), like the parallel pieces of legislation instituted by the dictatorial regimes in Portugal (the Portuguese Charter of National Labor,1935) and Spain (the Spanish Charter of Labor, 1938), were conceived, drafted, publicized, and diffused as pieces of propaganda.

The resiliency of the legal form, even if emptied of most of its legal substance, can be explained on both functional and normative grounds. Complex societies based on the division of labor and modern forms of economic production simply could not do away with a certain element of normative predictability. Positive morality is bound to be ineffective as an alternative to law, and it was dysfunctional even in the organization of racial discrimination and mass violations of rights. Moreover, social legitimacy could not be exclusively dependent on the charisma of the supreme leader or on physical coercion and violence. It needed to be supplemented with the appearance of the *formal* observance of legal norms if ample sectors of the legal profession, of the agents of the regime, and of the population in general were to acquiesce in the rule of such governments.

The extent to which actual legal systems were made to correspond to the core characteristics of Italian Fascist and German Nazi law was variable in time and space. The most relevant explanatory variables of such differences are the extent to which political systems actually complied with the central tenets of the two regimes and the way in which the Nazi and Fascist parties gained a grip on power. The evolution of Italian law toward a Fascist paradigm was slow, and came hand in hand with the progressive consolidation of Fascist rule. In contrast, the decisive and quick way in which the Nazi party managed to monopolize power in Germany explains why the Reichstag Fire Decree marked a clear break with the liberal legal order in a short period of time.

LAWYERS, SCHOLARS, AND THE ITALIAN FASCIST AND GERMAN NAZI REGIMES

Practitioners, judges, and legal scholars played a prominent role in the establishment and consolidation of Italian Fascist and Nazi German rule. Firstly, the active or passive acquiescence of judges and legal professionals rendered possible the affirmation of the dual state: that is, the coexistence of areas or domains in which state power was ruled by and subject to law with areas or domains in which state power operated apart from the law in reality, with the law serving as a fig leaf. This provided decisive credibility to the claim that ad hoc decisions were to be regarded as part of the legal order. Secondly, many lawyers and jurists lent their legal credentials to exceptional jurisdictions through which the political prosecution and oppression of the opponents of the regimes were conducted. An example of this was, among others, the "courts of honor" and the courts through which political opponents were deprived of their freedom and wealth. Once again, the legal vest supplied an appearance of legitimacy to repressive measures. Thirdly, a good number of legal scholars assumed as their own the task of "fascistizing" the legal field in which they were specialized—that is, figuring out a new conceptual and normative framework with which to offer a systematic reconstruction of a sector of the legal order in line with the basic assumptions of Italian Fascist or German Nazi law. Numerous treatises on Fascist/Nazi penal law, economic law, family law, or even tax law were produced. As the number of countries under the rule of the regimes increased, we can even talk of the emergence of an "international fascist academia," in which scholars from Italy and Germany played a leading role. Fourthly and finally, legal scholars tended to play an outstanding role as ideologues of the regimes. The irrationalistic and antitheoretical stance of Italian Fascism and German Nazism as political movements created the conditions under which political theorists and legal scholars became ideologues of the regimes. The underdeveloped theoretical foundations of the movements were in great need of being supplemented once the parties got hold of power. This explains the opportunities offered to Carl Schmitt in Germany or Giovanni Gentile in Italy to become leading court ideologues despite the suddenness of their respective conversions to Nazism and to Italian Fascism.

DEALING WITH ITALIAN FASCIST/ GERMAN NAZI LAW AFTER THE DEFEAT OF THE REGIMES

The defeat of Italy and Germany in World War II resulted in the demise of their legal orders. That opened up a wide debate on the criminal responsibility of those enforcing their laws, which in its turn raised deeper questions about the legality of German Nazi and Italian Fascist law, and consequently, about the very concept and conception of law. The key practical question was whether blatant violations of human rights committed in compliance with such laws should give rise to criminal liability, or whether they should instead go unpunished because they were legal at the time at which they were committed. That was one of the central questions at the core of the Nuremberg Trials—and indeed, of all trials aiming at establishing the responsibility of those implicated in the actions of Italian Fascism, German Nazism, or governments elsewhere that imitated them. As indicated, such practical questions were tightly related to theoretical debates on the question of whether extremely unjust legal orders should be regarded as law at all, and whether specific extremely unjust norms should be regarded as legal. These debates revolved around the formula put forward by leading German jurist Gustav Radbrüch in 1946, according to which those norms that were "intolerably unjust" should not be regarded as legal. A harsh debate followed concerning the practical implications of adopting one or another conception of law when faced with totalitarian political systems.

THE DARK LEGACY OF LAW AS UNDERSTOOD BY ITALIAN FASCISM AND GERMAN NAZISM

Increasing attention is being paid to the analysis of the hidden, dark legacies of the fascistization of legal orders and scholarship. Not only was there a remarkable continuity of personnel in the composition of the judiciary, the legal profession, and academia in postwar Italy and Germany, but there were remarkable (even if generally unnoticed) positive and theoretical continuities as well. Some pieces of legislation elaborated under Italian Fascist and German Nazi rule were left virtually untouched after the war (an outstanding example being the Italian Civil Code of 1942), and the intellectual foundations of certain disciplines (such as labor law) established under Mussolini and Hitler remained insufficiently explored and challenged afterward.

Agustín J. Menéndez

See Also: INTRODUCTION; ACERBO LAW, THE; ARENDT, HANNAH; CANADA; COMMUNITY; CONCENTRATION CAMPS; DECADENCE; DEMOCRACY; EMPLOYMENT; ENABLING ACT (*ERMÄCHTIGUNGSGESETZ*), THE; FASCIST PARTY, THE; FRANCE; FRICK, WILHELM; GENTILE, GIOVANNI; GERMANY; HITLER, ADOLF; HOLOCAUST, THE; HOLOCAUST DENIAL; HOMOSEXUALITY; IRVING, DAVID JOHN CAWDELL; ITALY; LEADER CULT, THE; LIBERALISM; MILITARISM; MUSSOLINI, BENITO ANDREA; NAZISM; NUREMBERG LAWS, THE; NUREMBERG TRIALS, THE; PALINGENETIC MYTH; PARLIAMENTARISM; PORTUGAL; PROPAGANDA; RACIAL DOCTRINE; RATIONALISM; REICHSTAG FIRE, THE; RELIGION; REVOLUTION; ROCCO, ALFREDO; SCHMITT, CARL; SEXUALITY; SPAIN; SPANN, OTHMAR; STATE, THE; TOTALITARIANISM; TRADES UNIONS; UNIVERSITIES; VICHY; *VOLKSGERICHT*, THE; WORLD WAR II

References

On the general relationships between law and fascism:

Broszat, M. 1981. *The Hitler State: The Foundation and Development of the Internal Structure of the Third Reich.* London: Longman.

Fraenkel, E. 1941. *The Dual State: A Contribution to the Theory of Dictatorship.* New York: Oxford University Press.

Jackson, J. 2001. *France: The Dark Years.* Oxford: Oxford University Press.

Neumann, F. 1942. *Behemoth: The Structure and Practice of National-Socialism.* Oxford: Oxford University Press.

Sofsky, W. 1996. *The Order of Terror: The Concentration Camp.* Princeton: Princeton University Press.

Weisberg, R. H. 1996. *Vichy Law and the Holocaust in France.* New York: New York University Press.

On the role of the legal profession, judges, and scholars:

Balakrishnan, G. 2000. *The Enemy: An Intellectual Portrait of Carl Schmitt.* London: Verso.

Bendersky, J. W. 1983. *Carl Schmitt, Theorist for the Reich.* Princeton: Princeton University Press.

Special issue of *Le genre humain.* 1994. *Juger sous Vichy* no 28 (summer–autumn).

Stolleis, M. 1998. *The Law under the Swastika.* Chicago: Chicago University Press.

———. 2004. *A History of Public Law in Germany 1914–45.* Oxford: Oxford University Press.

On adjudication on fascist law in the postwar period:

Alexy, R. 2003. *An Argument from Injustice.* Oxford: Oxford University Press.

Fuller, L. 1958. "Positivism and Fidelity to Law." *Harvard Law Review* 71 (1958): 630.

Hart, H. L. A. 1961. *The Concept of Law.* Oxford: Oxford University Press.

Santiago, Nino C. 1996. *Radical Evil on Trial.* New Haven: Yale University Press.

On the legacy of fascist law and legal theory:

Joerges, C. 2003. "The Darker Side of a Pluralist Heritage: Anti-liberal Traditions in European Social Theory and Legal Thought." *Law and Critique* (special issue) 14, no. 3, pp. 225–228.

Joerges, C., and N. S. Ghaleigh, eds. 2003. *Darker Legacies of Law in Europe.* Oxford: Hart.

Müller, Jan-Werner. 2003. *A Dangerous Mind: Carl Schmitt in Post-war European Thought.* New Haven: Yale University Press.

LE BON, GUSTAVE (1841–1931)

French social theoretician whose ideas on the behavior of crowds uncannily anticipated and perhaps influenced the manipulation of mass audiences by interwar Italian Fascist and German Nazi leaders. Le Bon started out as a doctor, but later his intellectual interests widened to the study of physiology, psychology, sociology, politics, and archaeology; he became the founder of crowd psychology. His convictions about the role of race in human societies were also very influential in fascist thinking. Le Bon attributed the workings of society to the overwhelming power of physiological determinism, and that hypothesis was for him the primary causal mechanism to explain the operation and character of history. Nineteenth-century evolutionary science, he believed, demonstrated that human beings were unambiguously separated into clearly defined racial groups, and that the many different societies that arose during the course of evolution manifested uniquely original racial souls that reflected intrinsically varied psychological and physical characteristics. According to Le Bon, the different racial soul peculiar to every nation and people could be empirically investigated like any other branch of science.

Le Bon's ideas are not largely traceable to indigenous French intellectual traditions but rather show clear parallels to the vitalistic and racial assumptions of the evolutionary monist science of the German zoologist Ernst Haeckel. The commonly held belief that it was the tradition of Italian and French scientific materialism and positivism, as seen in the writings of such figures as B. A. Morel, Hippolyte Taine, Scipio Sighele, J. M. Charcot, Paul Broca, and Gabriel Tarde, that decisively shaped Le Bon's thinking, has to be revised. Those authors, for the most part, were also influenced by Haeckel's science, so that all of them, including Le Bon, shared a common intellectual milieu. Anticipating fascist social theory, Le Bon held a pessimistic view of the intellectual capacity of the ordinary person, necessitating the cultivation of political elites who could provide society with meaningful leadership and control. In his view, the regrettable democratic tradition of the Enlightenment and the French Revolution, which had confused modern political life, had to be recast so as to harmonize with the antidemocratic implications of evolutionary science. The laws of society, Le Bon argued, directly parallel the laws of nature, and therefore any attempt, as proposed by liberalism and socialism, to subvert the natural laws of struggle, social hierarchy, and human inequality would undermine the antiegalitarian, scientifically established axioms of evolution.

Of particular interest was Le Bon's theory of crowd behavior, a sociological analysis of mass society that consciously influenced the manipulative strategies employed by Mussolini and Hitler in their drive for political ascendancy. Based for the most part on the psychological monism of Haeckel, Le Bon published in 1904 what was to become his most famous book, *The Psychology of Crowds.* The book offered practical advice on how to control the collective mind of the masses and was geared to political programs that deliberately challenged the basic assumptions of liberal and democratic society. Crowds, for Le Bon, manifested an irrational psychological unity, and he pointed out that at decisive moments all ethical restraints among people dissolve and violence takes over. At such times, leaders have the capacity to gain power over vast numbers of individuals, literally to captivate them hypnotically, their words and ideas spreading among the people like a "contagion"—a highly prophetic formulation that uncannily anticipated the magiclike powers of persuasion that Hitler and Mussolini exercised over the thought and mass behavior of multitudes of people in Germany and Italy.

Daniel Gasman

See Also: DEMOCRACY; ELITE THEORY; ENLIGHTENMENT, THE; FRENCH REVOLUTION, THE; GERMANY; GOEBBELS, (PAUL) JOSEPH; HITLER, ADOLF; ITALY; LEADER CULT, THE; MASSES, THE ROLE OF THE; MATERIALISM; MUSSOLINI, BENITO ANDREA; MYSTICISM; MYTH; NUREMBERG RALLIES, THE; POSITIVISM; PROPAGANDA; PSYCHOANALYSIS; PSYCHODYNAMICS OF PALINGENETIC MYTH, THE; PSYCHOLOGY; RACIAL DOCTRINE; RATIONALISM;

SCIENCE; SOCIAL DARWINISM; SOCIOLOGY; THEATER; VITALISM

References

Gasman, Daniel. 1998. *Haeckel's Monism and the Birth of Fascist Ideology.* New York: Lang.

Marpeau, Benoît. 2000. *Gustave Le Bon: Parcours d'un intellectuel.* Paris: CNRS.

Widener, Alice, ed. 1979. *Gustave Le Bon: The Man and His Works.* Indianapolis, IN: Liberty Fund.

LE PEN, JEAN-MARIE
(born 1928)

Leader of the Front National in France, who has presided over the development of the most important extreme-right-wing party in present-day Europe. Le Pen has played an essential part in making the FN a significant force in French politics. He is the son of a Breton fisherman who was killed in 1940. Part of the mythology created around him by his followers and himself holds that the role of head of the family assumed by Le Pen as a teenager gave him a personal authority that made him a natural leader of the French nation. Whatever the truth behind his disputed claims to have taken part in the Resistance, Le Pen subsequently showed himself eager for military experience. In 1954, after finishing his law degree in Paris, he enlisted to serve in Indo-China with the First Parachute Battalion of the Foreign Legion but arrived too late to see action before the French defeat, though he gained journalistic experience on an army magazine instead. Later, after re-enlisting in 1956, he took part in the Suez episode before serving in Algeria, where he was accused of using torture, a charge that he has continued to deny. Having returned to France in 1957, he continued to campaign for *Algérie française* and to use the rhetoric of revolt against the government. His political career, as well as his capacity for verbal and physical violence, had been foreshadowed by his activity while an undergraduate, as he became president of the law students' union but also gained a reputation for brawling.

In 1956, at the age of twenty-seven, Le Pen became the youngest deputy in the National Assembly, elected to a Paris constituency as part of Pierre Poujade's virulently anticommunist, populist, nationalistic movement, the UDCA, representing small shopkeepers and artisans who considered their interests to have been abandoned by the self-serving elites of the Fourth Republic. Le Pen's relationship with Poujade rapidly soured, but not before he had established himself as the group's most powerful orator in parliament. Following his time in Algeria he was re-elected as an Independent in 1958 but lost his seat in 1962. For more than two decades afterward he was on the margin of French politics but remained prominent in the turbulent microcosm of the extreme Right. His organizational flair was evident in his management of Tixier-Vignancour's campaign for the presidency in 1965, although the candidate's score of 5.3 percent in the first round did not herald the revival of the far Right for which Le Pen had hoped. As leader of the FN from its inception in 1972, and supported by a fortune inherited from a wealthy sympathizer under disputed circumstances, he weathered the early years of in-fighting and factionalism to create an effective party run on top-down, authoritarian lines under his very personal control. He showed himself astute at balancing the rival currents within the party and neutralizing their potential for division until the late 1990s, when his distrust of the rising popularity of Bruno Mégret, his presumed deputy, led him to force a confrontation that split the party in the winter of 1998–1999, damaging it severely through loss of cadres, grass-roots activists, and electoral supporters but eliminating the internal challenge and maintaining his own supremacy.

Le Pen was and is a curious mixture. He is brazenly nationalist and a peddler of offensive public comments about immigrants and Jews. He is an educated, articulate self-publicist and polemicist. He is a charismatic leader and effective organizer who succeeded in uniting most of the extreme Right and taking it from the margins of political life to a position where it could at least influence national political debates, implant itself in local government, and hold a handful of seats in the European Parliament (where Le Pen himself has held a seat since 1984, except during a one-year ban in 2000–2001 for assaulting a socialist politician), even if the electoral system kept it out of the National Assembly except from 1986 to 1988. The widespread revulsion caused by his score of nearly 17 percent in the French presidential election of 2002 despite reduced support for the FN itself since the 1999 split was a fitting apotheosis for such a deeply flawed but in some ways remarkable political actor.

Christopher Flood

See Also: ANTI-SEMITISM; AUTHORITARIANISM; EUROPE; FRANCE; IMMIGRATION; NATIONAL FRONT (FRANCE), THE; NATIONALISM; POSTWAR FASCISM; POUJADE, PIERRE MARIE RAYMOND

References

Arnold, E. J. ed. 2000. *The Development of the Radical Right in France: From Boulanger to Le Pen.* Basingstoke: Macmillan.

Atkin, N. 2003. *The Right in France: From Revolution to Le Pen.* London: I. B. Taurus.

Davies, P. 2002. *The Extreme Right in France, 1789 to the Present: From de Maistre to Le Pen.* London: Routledge.

LEADER CULT, THE

The leader cult was a marked feature of the regimes of Hitler and Mussolini; as official Italian fascist propaganda put it, *Il duce* [Mussolini] *ha sempre ragione* ("Mussolini is always right"). Forged by regime propaganda and expressed in multiple ways by ceremonies, chants, speeches, symbols, and myths, the leader cult became in fascist regimes a characteristic feature of what Walter Benjamin has called the "aesthetics" of fascism. The presence of a leader enjoying an immense personal popularity and adulation from his people that, moreover, often possessed a pseudo-religious dimension thus served a double function: it provided the fascist regimes with both charismatic legitimacy and a strong organizational principle for coordinating the activities and internal life of the regime.

Interwar fascism developed in environments characterized by crisis, uncertainty, and fear. For the early-twentieth-century European citizen, the Great War meant much more than the collapse of the old world order, the Russian Revolution, and the sweeping away of the old empires. At the micro level of participant societies, the long years of sacrifice had caused personal disaster, social dislocation, and horror at the collapse of community and its values. Overwhelmed by a general crisis and having lost faith in the old liberal ideal and the leaders associated with it, many European peoples turned to fascist or quasi-fascist leaders who promised to confront the crisis with both workable solutions and new ideological visions. Elevated to superhuman status relevant to the crisis dimensions and the importance of the mission they were expected to carry out, fascist leaders were considered "charismatic" in the purest Weberian sense, thus enjoying the full surrender and unquestioned adoration of their faithful. The quest for strong and charismatic leadership found a solid ideological and psychological foundation in the contemporary elite theories of Gaetano Mosca and Vilfredo Pareto about the importance of a ruling oligarchy holding power over a majority, as well as the theses about collective psychology advanced especially by Scipio Sighele (1868–1913) and Gustave Le Bon, assuming that crowds are naturally susceptible to manipulation by strong leaders. Some have argued that the leader cult was in fact an element in fascism's distinctive core ideology, that which set it apart as a creed. But the fact is that the cult of Stalin in the Soviet Union and other leadership cults in places such as postwar Iraq, Romania, Albania, and North Korea (where it remains in place) show that the leadership cult is in no way unique to fascism.

Takis Pappas

See Also: ARENDT, HANNAH; CARLYLE, THOMAS; ELITE THEORY; HERO, THE CULT OF THE; GERMANNESS (*DEUTSCHHEIT*); GERMANY; HITLER, ADOLF; INFLATION; ITALY; LE BON, GUSTAVE; MICHELS, ROBERTO; MOSCA, GAETANO; MUSSOLINI, BENITO ANDREA; MYSTICISM; MYTH; NORDIC SOUL, THE; PARETO, VILFREDO; PROPAGANDA; RATIONALISM; SOVIET UNION, THE; STALIN, IOSIF VISSARIONOVICH; STYLE; TOTALITARIANISM; WALL STREET CRASH, THE; WAR VETERANS; WARRIOR ETHOS, THE; WORLD WAR I

References

Bullock, Alan. 1998. *Hitler and Stalin: Parallel Lives.* London: Fontana.

Falasca-Zamponi, Simonetta. 1997. *Fascist Spectacle: The Aesthetics of Power in Mussolini's Italy.* Berkeley: University of California Press.

Kershaw, Ian. 1987. *The "Hitler Myth": Image and Reality in the Third Reich.* Oxford: Oxford University Press.

Mangan, J. A. 2000. *Superman Supreme: Fascist Body as Political Icon—Global Fascism.* London: Frank Cass.

———, ed. 1999. *Shaping the Superman: Fascist Body as Political Icon—Aryan Fascism.* London: Frank Cass.

Struve, W. 1973. *Elites against Democracy: Leadership Ideals in Bourgeois Political Thought in Germany, 1890–1933.* Princeton: Princeton University Press.

LEAGUE OF NATIONS, THE

Founded after World War I, forerunner of the United Nations, by which it was replaced after World War II. Like the other defeated nations, Germany was not allowed to take up membership until 1926; thus for the defeated nations, the League of Nations was seen as a tool of the victors. The first true tests for the League were the Japanese invasion of Manchuria in September 1931 and the creation of the satellite state of Mand-

The opening session of the League of Nations in 1920. Established out of a desire to prevent any recurrence of war on the scale of World War I, the League was held in contempt by Hitler, for whom it was the embodiment of the pacifist spirit; he and Mussolini consciously promoted militarism and a warrior ethos. (Corel)

schukuo in March 1932. In the face of this open aggression the League reacted hesitantly, eventually sending a commission of inquiry under Lord Lytton that took three months for the journey alone. Its report came out in September 1932, a year after the Japanese attack. Following that the League of Nations Assembly of 24 February 1933 decided not to recognize Mandschukuo, with the result that Japan left the League on 27 March 1933. On 19 October 1933, Hitler's Germany also withdrew, having abandoned the Geneva Disarmament Conference a few days earlier, leaving it to collapse definitively a few months later after eight years of work. Hitler had already announced to the Reichstag on 17 May 1933 that, for him, the League had been an irrelevance from the start. He had in fact denounced it several years earlier in *Mein Kampf*, in which he asserted that it belonged to "Jewish world finance," "Jewish world domination," and "Jewish world Bolshevization."

The League failed to halt the aggression of Italy at the beginning of 1935 against Ethiopia, one of its own members. Great Britain and France had no interest in thwarting Mussolini because they saw in him a potential ally against Hitler, who was considered more immediately dangerous. Because the League Assembly resolved on only half-hearted economic sanctions and implemented them even more half-heartedly (an oil embargo was rejected, and the Suez Canal was not closed to Italian supplies), Mussolini could interpret the entry of his troops into Addis Ababa (5 May 1936)—a military success due in part to the use of poison gas—as a victory over the League (especially in his Milan Speech of 1 November 1936). The departure of Japan (March 1933), Germany (October 1933), and Italy (December 1937) sounded the death knell of the League of Nations. The increasingly impotent organization could do nothing to prevent the military buildup in Europe and Asia, nor the *Anschluss* of Austria, Hitler's annexation of the Sudetenland, Mussolini's occupation of Albania, the Japanese invasion of China beginning on 7 July 1937, nor above all the European war unleashed on 1 September 1939 by Hitler. The organization remained formally in existence until the end of World War II, when it was replaced by the United Nations. It was officially dissolved on 18 April 1946 in Geneva.

Carlo Moos
(translated by Cyprian Blamires)

See Also: ALBANIA; *ANSCHLUSS*, THE; ANTI-SEMITISM; AUSTRIA; BOLSHEVISM; CONSPIRACY THEORIES; CORFU; COSMOPOLITANISM; CZECHOSLOVAKIA; ETHIOPIA; GERMANY; HITLER, ADOLF; ITALY; JAPAN; JAPAN AND WORLD WAR II; *MEIN KAMPF*; MUNICH AGREEMENT/PACT, THE; MUSSOLINI, BENITO ANDREA; NATIONALISM; SUDETENLAND, THE; UNITED NATIONS, THE; VERSAILLES, THE TREATY OF; WORLD WAR I; WORLD WAR II

References
Barros, J. 1965. *The Corfu Incident of 1923: Mussolini and the League of Nations.* Princeton: Princeton University Press.
Bendiner, A. 1975. *A Time for Angels: The Tragicomic History of the League of Nations.* London: Weidenfeld and Nicholson.
Kimmich, C. K. 1976. *Germany and the League of Nations.* Chicago: University of Chicago Press.
Stone, R. 1973. *Irreconcilables: The Fight against the League of Nations.* New York: W. W. Norton.

LEBENSBORN HOMES, THE: *See* EUGENICS; SS, THE

LEBENSRAUM

Roughly translates from German as "living space"; particularly associated with the imperialistic ideology and population policies of Nazism, although there was an equivalent expression in Italian Fascism (*spazio vitale*). In policy and prosecution, the Nazi pursuit of *Lebensraum* involved the massive transfer—and violent uprooting—of indigenous populations in Central Eastern Europe. Forming a significant aspect of Hitler's *Weltanschauung* as illustrated in *Mein Kampf,* and put into violent practice during World War II, the quest for *Lebensraum* can be seen to underpin a number of actions undertaken by the Third Reich: the invasions of Poland and Soviet Russia, massive population resettle-

ments and "evacuations," and the Holocaust. All were defended as a means to secure Germanic hegemony in Europe by control of natural resources (such as grain and oil) as well as forcible depopulation of vast territories—including some 50 million Eastern Europeans—construed as indispensable to the resettlement and functioning of a European "New Order," or "thousand-year Reich," dreamed of by Nazi planners.

On the eve of World War I, *völkisch* Pangermanism, military expansionism, and increasingly explicit racism became more closely associated with the doctrine of the established idea of *Lebensraum,* which had generally been used to cover colonial expansionism such as was practiced by all the major European powers in the nineteenth century. Friedrich von Bernhardi in particular explicitly advocated territorial seizures to the east of Germany, and the issue of the progression from Bernhardi via German militarism in World War I to Nazi conceptions of *Lebensraum* has been hotly debated, especially after the so-called Fischer Controversy in the 1960s concerning the continuity (or otherwise) of postunification German expansionism. Although the Third Reich's expansionist policies between 1933 and 1939 in areas such as Czechoslovakia and Austria may be viewed as the first shots in the battle for *Lebensraum,* that battle is generally considered to have begun with the onset of World War II in Europe. Following the conquest of Poland, massive population transfers of ethnic Germans and "non-Aryans" alike were prioritized by Nazi functionaries, and following the invasion of the Soviet Union efforts were made to depopulate vast areas through murdering millions in Central Eastern Europe.

Matt Feldman

See Also: *ANSCHLUSS*, THE; ARYANISM; AUSTRIA; BARBAROSSA, OPERATION; CZECHOSLOVAKIA; *DRANG NACH OSTEN* ("DRIVE TO THE EAST"), THE; EXPANSIONISM; FASCIST PARTY, THE; GERMANNESS (*DEUTSCHHEIT*); GERMANY; HAUSHOFER, KARL ERNST; HITLER, ADOLF; HOLOCAUST, THE; HOLY ROMAN EMPIRE, THE; IMPERIALISM; ITALY; *MEIN KAMPF;* NEW ORDER, THE; PANGERMANISM; POLAND AND NAZI GERMANY; RACIAL DOCTRINE; RACISM; SLAVS, THE (AND GERMANY); SOVIET UNION, THE; THIRD REICH, THE; *VOLK, VÖLKISCH;* WORLD WAR I; WORLD WAR II

References
Burleigh, Michael. 2000. *The Third Reich.* Basingstoke: Macmillan.
Fischer, Fritz. 1986. *From Kaiserreich to Third Reich: Elements of Continuity in German History, 1871–1945.* London: Unwin Hyman.
Housden, Martyn. 2003. *Hans Frank: Lebensraum and the Holocaust.* Basingstoke: Palgrave Macmillan.

LEESE, ARNOLD SPENCER (1877–1956)

Leading adherent to fascist ideas in 1920s Britain and fanatical anti-Semite. Leese was a veterinarian who spent periods living both in India and in East Africa. After serving in World War I, he became convinced that there was a Jewish and Masonic threat to the British Empire and was elected to a local council as a British Fascist in 1924. Four years later he became one of the founding members of the Imperialist Fascist League, and his anti-Semitism grew so extreme that he openly called for the extermination of the Jewish race: in 1936 he was imprisoned on charges relating to articles he had published in his newspaper, *The Fascist.* He had no time for his fellow fascist Oswald Mosley, whom he regarded as insufficiently alert to the Jewish menace. Leese was interned during World War II until December 1943, and he was again imprisoned in 1947 for having assisted members of the Waffen-SS to escape punishment. He handed on the baton of his brand of British fascism after the war to Colin Jordan.

Cyprian Blamires

See Also: ANTI-SEMITISM; BRITISH FASCISTI/BRITISH FAS-CISTS, THE; CONSPIRACY THEORIES; GREAT BRITAIN; HOLOCAUST, THE; MOSLEY, SIR OSWALD; POSTWAR FAS-CISM; WAFFEN-SS, THE; WAR VETERANS; WORLD WAR I; WORLD WAR II

Reference
Linehan, Thomas. 2001. *British Fascism 1918–1939: Parties, Ideology, and Culture.* Manchester: Manchester University Press.

LEGION OF THE ARCHANGEL MICHAEL, THE

Romanian fascist movement (also known as the Iron Guard) founded in 1927 and named after a famous Orthodox icon of the Archangel Michael. The legion claimed to be neither a political party nor a sect but a "school," aimed at the creation of a "new man." The legion was based on a strong belief in communion with the departed and in spiritual rebirth for its members through a cult of death—including political assassination. It was organized, on its lowest level, in "nests," counting three to thirteen members each. The legion ruled Romania between September 1940 and January 1941, after which it was definitively banned.

Philip Vanhaelemeersch

See Also: CODREANU, CORNELIU ZELEA; CULTS OF DEATH; NEW MAN, THE; ORTHODOX CHURCHES, THE; PALIN-GENETIC MYTH; ROMANIA

References
Ioanid, R. 1990. *The Sword of the Archangel Michael: Fascist Ideology in Romania.* Boulder, CO: Eastern European Monographs.
Nagy-Talavera, N. 1970. *The Green Shirts and Others.* Stanford: Stanford University Press.

LEISURE

In addition to organized sport, a range of other leisure activities were promoted by fascist regimes and movements to keep their followers loyal. The provision of leisure opportunities was part of a paternalistic attitude toward the general population. In addition to policies that sought to improve the conditions of the people—such as the reduction of unemployment through large-scale public works and armament programs—the provision and control of leisure time through organized activities aimed to produce a more compliant and satisfied populace. General leisure-time activities, such as visits to theaters, concerts, the cinema, art galleries, and sports grounds were all used by fascist regimes to expose audiences to nationalistic and ideologically slanted messages. In addition to those activities of choice, bodies such as Kraft durch Freude (KDF: "Strength through Joy"), established in 1933, also organized and controlled the leisure time of the individual. The leader of the KDF, Dr. Robert Ley, had worked out that the average German worker had 3,740 hours of free time each year. If that were left unfilled by the state, he argued, workers would become bored, disloyal, and open to degenerate ideas. The KDF coordinated a massive leisure program for loyal Nazi workers, including cruise ships that visited the Canary Islands for two-week holidays. Other organized holidays—including skiing trips to Bavaria, and tours to Italy and Switzerland—were also offered. The KDF had a touring orchestra that entertained workers and Nazi party groups across Germany, and it also organized sports days, and theater and opera outings. By 1937 the KDF had thirty touring theater companies that performed a program of opera, comedy, cabaret, and variety shows. In 1937 alone the companies performed to a total national audience exceeding 30 million.

For the children of Nazi Germany, the Hitler Youth, which had been established as early as 1926, was the cornerstone of their leisure time. It was led from 1934 by Baldur von Schirach, and membership in it was made compulsory for all boys between the ages of sixteen and eighteen from 1936. In addition to meetings and rallies, the members of the Hitler Youth were provided with day trips, holidays, magazines, and comics, as well as cultural excursions.

In Italy compulsory youth organizations such as the Balilla were used to teach young Italians what their role in society was: boys as defenders of the country, girls as wives and mothers. For adults the *dopolavoro* was established to provide Italians with leisure pursuits that were based around an adherence to Fascism. Radio was a key tool in Mussolini's Italy. With more than a million radio sets in the country by 1939, many of which had been distributed free, a large number of Italians built their life around *dopolavoro*-sponsored programming. Additionally, *dopolavoro* supported cinema and theater attendance by providing its members with discount admission. Like the KDF, the *dopolavoro* encouraged and organized country marches, day trips, and tours, and provided a program of holidays throughout the country for its members with subsidized rates of travel and accommodation.

Meredith Carew

See Also: BERLIN OLYMPICS, THE; BODY, THE CULT OF THE; BOOKS, THE BURNING OF THE; EDUCATION; FASCIST PARTY, THE; FILM; FOOTBALL/SOCCER; HEALTH; HITLER, ADOLF; LEY, ROBERT; MASSES, THE ROLE OF THE; MUSSOLINI, BENITO ANDREA; NATIONALISM; NAZISM; NUREMBERG RALLLIES, THE; PROPAGANDA; RADIO; RELIGION; SCHIRACH, BALDUR VON; SPORT; THEATER; TOTALITARIANISM; *WANDERVÖGEL,* THE; YOUTH

References
Baranowski, Shelley. 2004. *Strength through Joy: Consumerism and Mass Tourism in the Third Reich.* Cambridge: Cambridge University Press.
DeGrazia, Victoria. 2002. *The Culture of Consent: Mass Organization of Leisure in Fascist Italy.* Cambridge: Cambridge University Press.
Schnapp, Jeffrey T. 1996. "Fascinating Fascism." *Journal of Contemporary History* 31, no. 2: 235–244.

LEY, ROBERT (1890–1945)

Head of the Labor Front under the Third Reich. A Rhinelander and a chemist by profession, Ley became an early member of the NSDAP. He was elected to the Reichstag in 1930. On 2 May 1933, Ley ordered the occupation of the offices of all Trade Unions at the head of a "committee of action for the protection of German labor." Soon afterward Ley became the supreme arbiter in labor matters in Germany at the head of the Labor Front. He was also involved in the nazification of leisure through the construction of mass leisure organizations, and was responsible for the special elite schools for young adult men that were to be the matrices of the Nazi elite of the future. Ley's administrative empire eventually attained gigantic proportions. He committed suicide in prison in 1945.

Cyprian Blamires

See Also: EDUCATION; GERMANY; LABOR FRONT, THE; LEISURE; MASSES, THE ROLE OF THE; NAZISM; TRADES UNIONS; WARRIOR ETHOS, THE; YOUTH MOVEMENTS

Reference
Smelser, Ronald. 1992. *Robert Ley: Hitler's Labour Front Leader.* Oxford: Berg.

LIBERALISM (Germany)

The wholesale condemnation of liberalism by German Nazis had to do with the fact that it was associated with a hated political reality, the Weimar Republic, which for them was an embodiment of things they associated with liberalism: parliamentarism, individualism, and pacifism, along with symptoms of German shame and weakness such as hyperinflation and the imposition of the humiliating terms of the Versailles Treaty. For them liberalism above all implied weakness and represented the polar opposite of the heroic and powerful destiny of conquest that they considered appropriate for the German people.

Universal law, one of the pillars of liberalism, was anathema to Nazi nationalism. The Nazi legal expert

Werner Best rejected every form of codified rights of nations that was in some way based on universal values. Instead of an "effete" universalism, Nazis valued reality (*Wirklichkeit*), by which was meant the existence of actual power differences within society and among nations. And on those actual power differences they based their morality of "might is right." The Treaty of Versailles was intended to humiliate the Germans and succeeded in doing so. Versailles—as both Jan Smuts and John Maynard Keynes observed—sanctioned the plundering of German resources, territory, colonies, and self-respect. Not surprisingly, bright German youths soon saw themselves as the victims of liberal modernism. Young conservative Germans took pride in unmasking liberal universalist claims, which they saw as cloaking mere power politics and economic greed in a very present and concrete situation of despair.

Seeing universalism as an abstraction intended to serve arbitrarily special interests, the Nazis rejected it out of hand. Nazism was ultimately mythological in character. It despaired of any absolute or ultimate truth, disowned abstract metaphysical truth, and instead embraced concrete, organic, and personal truth as epitomized by the myth of a race-specific culture and a personal faith in its leader, Hitler. Rosenberg, Hauer, and Goebbels tied together scientific and religious dogma and biologized religious language until the Darwinian biological struggle became a racial struggle, and the political goal became a new Nazi religion, one that was particularistic rather than universalistic.

Karla Poewe

See Also: INTRODUCTION; ABSTRACTION; "ANTI-" DIMENSION OF FASCISM, THE; ARENDT, HANNAH; ARISTOCRACY; AUTARKY; AUTHORITARIANISM; CAPITALISM; COMMUNITY; COSMOPOLITANISM; DEMOCRACY; DICTATORSHIP; ECONOMICS; EGALITARIANISM; FREEDOM; GERMANY; GOEBBELS, (PAUL) JOSEPH; HAUER, JAKOB WILHELM; HITLER, ADOLF; INDIVIDUALISM; INFLATION; LEADER CULT, THE; LIBERALISM (IN THEOLOGY); MYTH; NATIONALISM; NAZISM; NOVEMBER CRIMINALS/*NOVEMBERBRECHER*, THE; ORGANICISM; PACIFISM; PALINGENETIC MYTH; PARLIAMENTARISM; PSYCHODYNAMICS OF PALINGENETIC MYTH, THE; PSYCHOLOGY; RACIAL DOCTRINE; RATIONALISM; RELIGION; ROSENBERG, ALFRED; SPANN, OTHMAR; STATE, THE; TOTALITARIANISM; VERSAILLES, THE TREATY OF; *VOLKSGEMEINSCHAFT*, THE; WAR; WAR VETERANS; WARRIOR ETHOS, THE; WEIMAR REPUBLIC, THE; WORLD WAR I

References

Barnes, K. C. 1991. *Nazism, Liberalism, and Christianity: Protestant Social Thought in Germany and Great Britain 1925–1937.* Lexington: University Press of Kentucky.

Jarausch, K. H., and L. E. Jones, eds. 1990. *In Search of a Liberal Germany: Studies in the History of German Liberalism from 1789 to the Present.* Oxford: Berg.

Jones, L. E. 1998. *German Liberalism and the Dissolution of the Weimar Party System.* London: University of North Carolina Press.

Krieger, Leonard. 1973. *The German Idea of Freedom.* Chicago: University of Chicago Press.

Langewiesche, D. 2000. *Liberalism in Germany.* Basingstoke: Macmillan.

LIBERALISM (Italy)

Mussolini and the movement he founded were as hostile to liberalism as were the Nazis. But the first serious questioning of liberalism in Italy had in fact come from pre–World War I nationalists like Enrico Corradini and Alfredo Rocco. Speaking in 1919, Corradini, whose ideas were ultimately to furnish the ideological core of Italian Fascism, condemned Italy's "individualistic parliamentarism" as outdated. Rocco, who as Mussolini's minister of justice was to invent much of the legislative basis of both the Fascist police state and corporative institutions, in the *Politica* manifesto of December 1918 provided a scathing critique of the failure of liberalism. The early Fascists, despite their commitment to Wilsonian ideals of democracy—including votes for women and the demand for a constituent assembly—sharply criticized the whole liberal parliamentary system in the Manifesto of the First Fascio of March 1919: in particular they rejected political parties as corrupt, eschewing even the label "party" for their movement until 1921.

Mussolini's "carrot and stick" political strategy from the spring of 1921 onward, balancing the destructive effects of squadrist violence in the provinces against attempts to woo leading members of the liberal political elite, was in itself damaging to the liberal state. In his first speech to the Chamber of Deputies as prime minister in November 1922, Mussolini expressed his contempt for the key institution of liberal Italy, the parliament: "Gentlemen! What I am doing now in this hall is an act of formal deference to you, for which I ask no special sign of gratitude. . . . I could have transformed this drab, silent hall into a bivouac for my squads" (Delzell 1970, 45). The Acerbo electoral reform law of July 1923, while providing the basis for the Fascists' two-thirds majority in the March 1924 general elections, could not suffice as a basis for normalization.

The murder of opposition leader Giacomo Matteotti two years later, and the subsequent outcry, demonstrated that Fascism could not comfortably govern inside the existing, albeit modified, liberal parliamentary system.

Mussolini's speech in January 1925, in which he accepted responsibility for all Fascist violence, and therefore implicitly for the murder of Matteotti, marked the beginning of a process that transformed Italy into a one-party police state in which Mussolini himself as head of the government enjoyed wide executive powers, unfettered by responsibility to parliament. The final rejection of liberalism, tout court, came in the "Doctrine of Fascism" published in the *Enciclopedia Italiana* in 1932. In that article, originally written by the idealist philosopher and leading Fascist intellectual Giovanni Gentile but reshaped in substantial part by Mussolini himself, the classical liberal concept was replaced by Gentile's idea of the "Ethical State." In the parts written by him, Mussolini emphatically rejected the theory and practice of liberalism: "It (Fascism) is opposed to classical liberalism which arose as a reaction to absolutism and exhausted its historical function when the State became the will and conscience of the people. Liberalism denied the State in the name of the individual; Fascism re-asserts the rights of the State as expressing the real essence of the individual." And in a clear enunciation of the new doctrine of "totalitarianism," Mussolini proclaimed: "The Fascist concept of the State is all-embracing; outside of it no human or spiritual values can exist, much less have value. Thus understood, Fascism is totalitarian, and the Fascist State—a synthesis and a unit inclusive of all values—interprets, develops, and potentiates the whole life of the people. No individuals or groups (political parties, cultural associations, economic unions, social classes) outside the State" (ibid., 93–94).

In 1934, at the height of the Great Depression, and in the year that the system of corporations had been established as governing bodies for all sectors of the economy, Mussolini turned his fire on economic liberalism: "[It] can now be confidently asserted that the capitalist mode of production is superseded, and with it the theory of economic liberalism that has in reality brought about the end of free competition. . . . Corporatism supersedes both socialism and liberalism." (*Il Popolo D'Italia,* 24 February 1934, p. 3). Lest it should be thought that the development of Mussolini's political theory was yet another example of his pragmatic, opportunistic improvisation in response to events, it is worth remembering that from the very beginning of his political career Mussolini had supported ideologies and organizations that were intrinsically antiliberal and anticapitalist. From revolutionary socialism to the "revolutionary," totalitarian, and corporatist state was not, therefore, a great intellectual journey for Il Duce.

John Pollard

See Also: INTRODUCTION; ABSTRACTION; ACERBO LAW, THE; ACTUALISM; "ANTI-" DIMENSION OF FASCISM, THE; ARISTOCRACY; AUTARKY; AUTHORITARIANISM; AVENTINE SECESSION, THE; CAPITALISM; COMMUNITY; CORPORATISM; COSMOPOLITANISM; CORRADINI, ENRICO; DEMOCRACY; DICTATORSHIP; ECONOMICS; EGALITARIANISM; ELITE THEORY; *ENCICLOPEDIA ITALIANA,* THE; FASCIO, THE; FASCIST PARTY, THE; GENTILE, GIOVANNI; INDIVIDUALISM; ITALY; MARXISM; MATTEOTTI, GIACOMO; MUSSOLINI, BENITO ANDREA; NATIONALISM; ORGANICISM; PACIFISM; PALINGENETIC MYTH, THE; PSYCHODYNAMICS OF PALINGENETIC MYTH; PSYCHOLOGY; RATIONALISM; RELIGION; ROCCO, ALFREDO; SOCIALISM; *SQUADRISMO;* STATE, THE; TOTALITARIANISM; WALL STREET CRASH, THE; WARRIOR ETHOS, THE; WORLD WAR I

References

Delzell, C. F. 1970. *Mediterranean Fascism 1919–1945.* London: Macmillan.

Gentile, G., ed. 1951. *Enciclopedia Italiana,* vol. 14. Rome: Istituto Treccani.

Lyttelton, A., ed. 1973. *Italian Fascisms: From Pareto to Gentile.* London: Jonathan Cape.

Robson, M. 2000. *Italy: Liberalism and Fascism 1870–1945.* London: Hodder and Stoughton.

LIBERALISM (in Theology)

Scholars are now only beginning to recognize the importance of German liberal theology to the worldview of numerous leading Nazis, and particularly to its anti-Semitic dimension. Dietrich Klagges (1891–1971) took liberal theology to its ultimate conclusion by reducing the Bible to the Gospel of Mark, in the belief of having stripped it of all "Jewish" distortion. He blended politics and religion to postulate that the Gospel of Mark was the *Ur*-gospel. Klagges was inspired by Houston Stewart Chamberlain, who in turn was inspired by the Old Testament scholar and Orientalist Julius Wellhausen. In order to make his free-thinking acceptable, Klagges also drew on the works of such philologists as Lachmann, Wilke, Weisse, and Holtzmann. As the original Gospel, Mark appeared to be innocent of "Jewish" distortion and was therefore considered worthy of being the foundation of a new German faith. In a manner analogous to Hauer, Klagges then founded the Working Community of German Christians (Deutsch-Christliche Arbeitsgemeinschaft), whose task it was to show that the real Jesus was un-Jewish and Indo-Germanic and that his true identity was distorted by later apostles who were under the spell of Jewish intellectual power (*jüdischen Geistesmacht*). The aim of the German Christians was to unite Christianity with National Socialism, turning it into a "positive Christianity" as per Article 24 of the NSDAP party program. While the German Christians became a popular phenomenon in the 1930s, the idea is older. Ernst Moritz Arndt (1769–1860) talked about *deutsches Christentum* and *eine deutsche Kirche* (German Church) in 1815, following the Napoleonic wars.

Propagandists like Walther Darré and numerous literary figures including Hans F. Blunck (1888–1961), Gustav Frenssen (1863–1945), and Hans Grimm (1875–1959), among others, were directly or indirectly connected to Jakob Wilhelm Hauer (founder of the German Faith Movement) and the SS. All walked the path from liberal theology to freeing Germany from the imperialism of Jewish-Christianity. Together they harnessed enormous listening and reading audiences, addressing anywhere from 100 to more than 20,000 people at any one time. For example, Reventlow, the editor of *Reichswart* and co-founder of the German Faith Movement, mentioned that about 2.5 million people declared themselves to be its followers in 1935. In that year, too, the movement referred to itself as a "movement of millions." A large membership increase occurred after the Sports Palace meeting in Berlin on 26 April 1935. Because the crowd crushed the Sports Palace even after its 20,000 seats were filled, it had to be closed by the police. Apparently vigorous propaganda had preceded the meeting, with as many as ninety talks per month being given all over Germany.

When in 1934 the Nazi Uniate Reichsbishop argued that "Christianity is not an outgrowth of Jewishness but originated from the constant battle with it, and for the first time since the emergence of Christianity has a *Volk* dared to declare war on the Jews," J. W. Hauer responded that the "thoughts that the Uniate Reichsbishop developed here are a typical result of liberal theology." Likewise, Gloege (1934, 393–415, 464–505) and Hutten (1934, 506–533) argued that *deutsch-germanisch* religions and worldviews have their origins in liberal theology. They categorized Rosenberg's ruminations as liberalism dressed in *völkisch* garb. Walter Künneth, who edited the volume with chapters by Gloege and Hutten, was a controversial Protestant theologian who initially approved of National Socialism and only later turned to criticizing it. Liberal theology was used to divest Christianity of its Jewish elements.

Karla Poewe

See Also: ANTI-SEMITISM; ARYANISM; CHAMBERLAIN, HOUSTON STEWART; CHRISTIANITY; DARRÉ, RICHARD WALTHER; GERMAN CHRISTIANS, THE; GERMAN FAITH MOVEMENT, THE; GERMANIC RELIGION; GERMANY; HAUER, JAKOB WILHELM; HIMMLER, HEINRICH; MÜLLER, BISHOP LUDWIG; NAZISM; NORDIC SOUL, THE; PROTESTANTISM; ROSENBERG, ALFRED; SS, THE; THEOLOGY; *VOLK, VÖLKISCH*

References
Barnes, K. C. 1991. *Nazism, Liberalism, and Christianity: Protestant Social Thought in Germany and Great Britain 1925–1937.* Lexington: University Press of Kentucky.
Feige, Franz G. M. 1990. *The Varieties of Protestantism in Nazi Germany: Five Theopolitical Positions.* Lewiston: Edwin Mellen.
Germann, Holger. 1995. *Die politische Religion des Nationalsozialisten Dietrich Klagges.* Frankfurt/M: Peter Lang.
Gloege, Gerhard. 1934. "*Die Deutschkirche.*" Pp. 393–415 in *Die Nation vor Gott,* edited by Walter Künneth and Helmuth Schreiner. Berlin: Wichern.
Goebbels, Joseph. 1927. *Wege ins Dritte Reich.* München: Frz. Eher.
Herbert, Ulrich. 1996. *Best: Biographische Studein über Radikalismus, Weltanschauung und Vernunft 1903–1989.* Bonn: J. H. W. Dietz.
Hutchinson, George P. 1977. "The Nazi Ideology of Alfred Rosenberg: A Study of His Thought 1917–1946. Ph.D. dissertation. Oxford: University of Oxford.
Hutten, Kurt. 1934. "Die Deutsche Glaubensbewegung." Pp. 506–533 in *Die Nation vor Gott,* edited by Walter Künneth and Helmuth Schreiner. Berlin: Wichern.
Klagges, Dietrich. 1926. *Das Urevangelium Jesu, der deutsche Glaube.* Wilster: Meister Ekkehart.
Poewe, Karla. 2005. *New Religions and the Nazis.* London: Routledge.

LIBERTY LOBBY, THE: *See* CARTO, WILLIS; UNITED STATES, THE

LIBYA

Libya figures in the history of fascism first as an Italian colony between the wars and then, in the postwar era, as the scene for the implementation of Mu'ammar Qadhafi's philosophy, regarded by some commentators as having certain fascistic traits. Libya was seen as a terrain for Italian expansion and domination from the early twentieth century. Initially commercial interests were involved, but the Italians were also ambitious for colonies in Africa. At that time Libya was a part of the Ottoman Empire. In September 1911, Italy declared war on Turkey, and in October Italian troops landed in Tripoli. The Turks and Libyans together organized armed resistance to the invaders, and the Italians failed to gain the anticipated military successes; when the Turks were defeated in the Balkan War, however, a peace treaty was arranged between the two sides. According to that treaty, Libya was to come under Italian rule on condition of its being granted "administrative autonomy"—a condition never honored. The Libyans, however, did not succumb, and, in spite of the pacification of some parts of the country, many areas (for example, Fezzan and Tripolitania) organized resistance against Italian occupation. By the beginning of World War I, Italy controlled only some coastal areas, including Tripoli, Benghazi, and Tobruk.

Resistance headed by the Sanusiya clan (represented at the time by Amir Muhammad Idris) to foreign troops continued both during and after the war. The seizure of power by the Fascists in Italy in 1922 was accompanied in Libya by harsh measures, the pacification of rebellious provinces, and the disarming of the population. This time, on behalf of the Amir, resistance was organized in Cyrenaica by the legendary Libyan national leader Omar al-Mukhtar. From that time onward, the Italians concentrated their efforts on liquidating Sanusiya bases in the south of the country. In 1928 the Italian government appointed Marshal Pietro Badoglio as governor-general of Libya. Concentration camps were built for insurgent tribes, in addition to the installation of a barbed-wire fence on the border with Egypt. In 1931, Omar al-Mukhtar was isolated, captured, and hanged.

In September 1940, Italian troops encroached from Libyan territory into Egypt up to Sidi Barrani, only to be defeated at the end of the same year. Thereafter German troops joined the Italians, both under the command of Rommel, and they again entered Egyptian territory in April 1941. The Axis forces were, however, driven out of Egypt once more. A concerted offensive in the direction of Alexandria by German-Italian forces at the beginning of 1942 came to nothing. The U.S.-British Operation "Torch"—a landing on the North African coast (November 1942)—then liquidated the Axis presence there, including in Libya.

Hassan Jamsheer

See Also: AXIS, THE; BADOGLIO, PIETRO; COLONIALISM; IMPERIALISM; EL ALAMEIN; ITALY; MUSSOLINI, BENITO ANDREA; QADHAFI (GADDHAFI), MU'AMMAR; WORLD WAR I; WORLD WAR II

References
Liddell Hart, B. H., ed. 1953. *The Rommel Papers.* London: Collins.
Montgomery, Viscount. 1958. *The Memoirs of Field-Marshall The Viscount Montgomery of Alamein, K.G.* London: Collins.

LIEBENFELS, JÖRG ADOLF JOSEF LANZ VON (1874–1954)

Former Cistercian monk and founder of the Ordo Novi Templi (ONT), the purpose of which was to foster the "pure" racial foundations of Aryanism. After renouncing his monastic vows, Lanz elaborated Ariosophy, a religion based on a heretical Manichaean form of Christianity combined with the racial anthropology that was in vogue at the turn of the century. The German Aryans were regarded as the closest living descendants of erstwhile semidivine prehistoric beings, while the various non-Aryan races—identified with the Slav and Latin nationalities of the Habsburg Empire—represented the demonic principle. Eugenic restoration of Aryan purity led to salvation, while miscegenation was the triumph of chaos and evil. There is some evidence that Hitler read Lanz's journal *Ostara* (named after the Teutonic god of beauty) during his Vienna years before 1914.

Nicholas Goodrick-Clarke

See Also: ANTHROPOLOGY; ARYANISM; AUSTRO-HUNGARIAN EMPIRE, THE; CHRISTIANITY; EUGENICS; GERMANNESS (*DEUTSCHHEIT*); GERMANY; HITLER, ADOLF; MYSTICISM; MYTH; NORDIC SOUL, THE; OCCULTISM; RACIAL DOCTRINE, SLAVS, THE (AND GERMANY)

References
Daim, Wilfried. 1985. *Der Mann, der Hitler die Ideen gab.* Vienna: Hermann Böhlau.
Goodrick-Clarke, Nicholas. 2004. *The Occult Roots of Nazism: Secret Aryan Cults and Their Influence on Nazi Ideology.* New York: New York University Press.

LINDBERGH, CHARLES AUGUSTUS (1902–1974)

World-famous U.S. aviation pioneer of the interwar era who was strongly pro-Nazi and anti-Semitic in the 1930s and who agitated for the United States to stay out of World War II. He had connections with U.S. Nazi propagandist Lawrence Dennis, whom he admired, as well as with agents of the German government in the United States. Like his friend Alexis Carrel, he was worried about the apparent decadence of the West and looked for salvation to the establishment in power of elites rather than to democracy. In his introduction to his journals, which were published long after World War II, Lindbergh expressed confidence that his prewar stance had been right, arguing that the war was the start of the breakdown of Western civilization, in that it opened the door to the expansionism of Soviet and Chinese communism.

Cyprian Blamires

See Also: ANTI-SEMITISM; BOLSHEVISM; CARREL, ALEXIS; CHINA; DECADENCE; DEMOCRACY; DENNIS, LAWRENCE; ELITE THEORY; GERMANY; HEARST, WILLIAM RANDOLPH; INTERVENTIONISM; MARXISM; NAZISM; SOCIALISM; SOVIET UNION, THE; SPENGLER, OSWALD; UNITED STATES, THE (PRE-1945); WORLD WAR II

References

Cole, Wayne S. 1974. *Charles A. Lindbergh and the Battle against Intervention in World War II.* New York: Harcourt Brace.

Wallace, Max. 2003. *The American Axis.* New York, St. Martin's Griffin.

LINTORN-ORMAN, ROTHA (1895–1935)

Founder of the first fascist movement in Britain, the British Fascisti, renamed in 1924 the British Fascists. She was from a military family, the granddaughter of a famous field marshal, Sir John Lintorn Arabin-Simmons, and she served in an ambulance unit during World War I. Support for her movement was mainly

Mrs. Rotha Lintorn-Orman, who founded the first British openly fascist movement in 1923, some years before the celebrated Sir Oswald Mosley came to prominence as the leading British fascist. (Topical Press Agency/Hulton Archive/Getty Images)

middle and upper class, with most members coming from a services or "county" background. The aims of the movement were vague; it chiefly supported the monarchy, promoted class friendship and the eradication of slum housing, encouragement of empire trade, restrictions on immigration, antisocialism, and anti-Bolshevism. It did not have an anti-Semitic dimension until later, and hardened anti-Semites soon split off to form the British National Fascisti in 1925. Lintorn-Orman was motivated by a keen desire to save Britain from socialism. Her attitude to women's issues was not "feminist" in the modern sense, but one scholar has described her as a believer in "fascist feminism." Among the strong-minded women who joined her movement were the prominent conspiracy theorist and anti-Semite Nesta Webster. Lintorn-Orman's views about the role of women led her into conflict with at least one other contemporary fascist party founder: that was

Lieutenant-Colonel Oscar Boulton, who set up the Unity Band in 1930 and also contributed material to the British Fascist newspaper *British Lion* before breaking with the BF in 1932.

Cyprian Blamires

See Also: "ANTI-" DIMENSION OF FASCISM, THE; ANTI-SEMITISM; BOLSHEVISM; BRITISH FASCISTI/BRITISH FASCISTS, THE; CONSERVATISM; CONSPIRACY THEORIES; FEMINISM; GREAT BRITAIN; IMMIGRATION; MARXISM; MONARCHISM; SOCIALISM; WEBSTER, NESTA; WOMEN; WORLD WAR I

Reference

Linehan, T. 2001. *British Fascism, 1918–1939: Parties, Ideology and Culture*. Manchester: Manchester University Press.

LITERATURE: *See* ART; BARRES, AUGUSTE MAURICE; BENN, GOTTFRIED; BLANCHOT, MAURICE; BRASILLACH, ROBERT; BOOKS, THE BURNING OF THE; CELINE, LOUIS FERDINAND; D'ANNUNZIO, GABRIELE; DRIEU LA ROCHELLE, PIERRE; FUTURISM; GEORGE, STEFAN; HAMSUN, KNUT; INTERNATIONAL BRIGADES, THE; JÜNGER, ERNST; MALAPARTE, CURZIO; MARINETTI, FILIPPO TOMMASO; MISHIMA, YUKIO; MODERNISM; ORWELL, GEORGE; POUND, EZRA; REBATET, LUCIEN; SARFATTI-GRASSINI, MARGHERITA; SOUTH AFRICA; SOVIET UNION, THE; SPANISH CIVIL WAR, THE; YEATS, WILLIAM BUTLER

LITHUANIA

Lithuania's parliamentary democracy was cut short by a military coup d'etat in December 1926, when Antanas Smetona, leader of the Nationalist Union (Tautininkai), was made president and his younger collaborator, Augustinas Voldemaras, became prime minister. They altered the constitution to strengthen the presidency and sideline the parliament and proceeded to erect an authoritarian nationalist regime. Smetona became known as *Tautas Vados* ("leader of the nation"). Smetona feared Voldemaras's ambitions and replaced him in 1929 with his brother-in-law, Juozas Tubelis. The issue that dominated Lithuania foreign policy and strongly influenced domestic policy as well was the recovery of the ancient Lithuanian capital, Vilnius, which the Poles had annexed in 1920. Lithuanian nationalists and right-wing extremists were wholly preoccupied with this issue. Younger members of the Nationalist Union grew restless with Smetona, whom they viewed as too conservative. Those desiring a more robust nationalist authoritarian regime formed a semiofficial paramilitary group, registered as a sports club, known as the Iron Wolf. In 1934 a group of officers aligned with the Iron Wolf unsuccessfully attempted a coup to return Voldemaras to power. The main opposition to the regime, however, came from the Christian Democrats, the former governing party. After a Polish ultimatum in 1938 humiliated the regime, opposition party representatives were included in the cabinet.

In 1939 the Soviet Union issued an ultimatum to Lithuania to be allowed to establish military bases on her territory. The following year Lithuania was annexed to the USSR, and thousands of Lithuanians were deported. The Lithuanian population included a high percentage of Jews, the majority of whom were killed during the Nazi occupation, 1941–1944. While Lithuanian collaborators played a significant role in carrying out the Holocaust, propensity for collaboration was not necessarily determined by links with prewar radical nationalist organizations. Since the restoration of independence from the Soviet Union in 1991, extreme right parties have had no role in Lithuanian politics.

Andres Kasekamp

See Also: ANTI-SEMITISM; AUTHORITARIANISM; DEMOCRACY; ESTONIA; GERMANY; HOLOCAUST, THE; LATVIA; LEADER CULT, THE; NATIONALISM; NAZISM; PARAMILITARISM; PARLIAMENTARISM; POLAND; SMETONA, ANTANAS; SOVIET UNION, THE; WORLD WAR II

References

Eidintas, Alfonsas, and Vytautas Žalys. 1998. *Lithuania in European Politics: The Years of the First Republic, 1918–1940*. New York: St. Martin's.

Misiunas, Romuald J. 1970. "Fascist Tendencies in Lithuania." *Slavonic and East European Review* 48, pp. 88–109.

Von Rauch, Georg. 1970. *The Baltic States: The Years of Independence, 1918–1940*. London: C. Hurst.

LIVING SPACE: *See LEBENSRAUM*

LJOTIĆ, DIMITRIJE (1891–1945)

Leader of the Serbian fascistic organization Zbor ("Rally"). He began his political career in 1930 as regional deputy for the Smederevo district. In 1931 he briefly held the post of minister of justice. In 1935 he founded Zbor, whose political program consisted of a blend of Italian Fascism, German Nazism, and Orthodox Christian fundamentalism. During the German occupation (1941–1945), he supported the occupying forces and the collaborationist government of Milan Nedić. He masterminded the establishment of a pro-Nazi militia, the Srpski Dobrovoljački Korpus (Serbian Volunteer Force), and founded the Radna Služba (National Service), a youth organization that closely resembled the Hitler Youth. He was the author of numerous anti-Semitic and profascist articles, books, and pamphlets.

Jovan Byford

See Also: ANTI-SEMITISM; FASCIST PARTY, THE; GERMANY; ITALY; NAZISM; ORTHODOX CHURCHES, THE; SERBS, THE; WORLD WAR II; YOUTH MOVEMENTS; YUGOSLAVIA

References
Avakumović, I. 1971. "Yugoslavia's Fascist Movements." In *Native Fascism in the Successor States,* edited by P. F. Sugar. Santa Barbara, CA: ABC-CLIO.
Martić, Miloš. 1980. "Dimitrije Ljotić and the Yugoslav National Movement Zbor, 1935–1945." *East European Quarterly* 16, no. 2: 219–239.
Stefanović, Mladen. 1984. *Zbor Dimitrija Ljotića, 1934–1945.* Beograd: Narodna Knjiga.

LONDON NAIL BOMBINGS, THE

Between 17 and 30 April 1999, three nail bombs targeting London's black, Asian, and homosexual communities exploded in Brixton, Brick Lane, and Soho, leaving 110 injured and 3 people dead, including a pregnant woman. The day after the final bomb, police arrested David Copeland, a semiliterate, mentally disturbed Christian Identity adherent who had hoped that his bombing campaign would be the spark to ignite a "race war." Although Copeland admitted sole responsibility for the bombings, he was greatly influenced by the ideas of several fascist parties, including the British National Party, which he had joined in 1997. Copeland received six life sentences for his crime.

Graham Macklin

See Also: BRITISH NATIONAL PARTY, THE; CHRISTIAN IDENTITY; CYBERFASCISM; GREAT BRITAIN; HOMOSEXUALITY; IMMIGRATION; POSTWAR FASCISM; RACIAL DOCTRINE; RACISM; XENOPHOBIA

Reference
McLagan, Graeme, and Nick Lowles. 2000. *Mr. Evil: The Secret Life of Racist Bomber and Killer David Copeland.* London: John Blake.

LORENZ, KONRAD (1903–1989)

Austrian ethologist who used explicitly pro-Nazi terminology to commend the Nazi regime for advocating policies to preserve racial purity. He was one of the founders of ethology, which examines how animals behave in their natural environment. Lorenz showed how animals inherit patterns of behavior that are triggered by stimuli in the environment. In his later popular writings, Lorenz expressed concern that humans were becoming "domesticated" and losing touch with their own biological nature. He won the Noble Prize in Physiology and Medicine in 1973 (jointly with two other specialists in animal behavior). At that time Lorenz expressed regret for his wartime pro-Nazi writings.

Michael Billig

See Also: ANIMALS; BLOOD; NATURE; NAZISM; PSYCHOLOGY; RACIAL DOCTRINE; SOCIAL DARWINISM

Reference
Evans, R. I. 1975. *Konrad Lorenz: The Man and His Ideas.* New York: Harcourt Brace Jovanovich.

LUDENDORFF, ERICH (1865–1937)

Early collaborator with Hitler who took part with the Nazi leader in the Munich putsch but who turned against him for a period after the Nazis took power. Ludendorff acquired a reputation for heroism early in World War I and became chief of staff to General Paul von Hindenburg. In 1916 he became von Hindenburg's senior quartermaster general when the latter was promoted to chief of the general staff of the army. After the Armistice, Ludendorff fled to Sweden but returned to Munich in 1919. At the trial after the Munich putsch the celebrated war hero was acquitted. In 1924 he was elected to the Reichstag as a National Socialist delegate. Together with his second wife, Dr. Mathilde Spiess Ludendorff, whose right-wing ideas he found increasingly attractive, he established the Tannenbergbund, dedicated to the battle with forces considered to be above the state—Jews, Jesuits, Freemasons, and Marxists.

Cyprian Blamires

See Also: "ANTI-" DIMENSION OF FASCISM, THE; ANTI-SEMITISM; CONSPIRACY THEORIES; FREEMASONRY/FREEMASONS, THE; GERMANY; HINDENBURG, PAUL VON BENECKENDORFF UND VON; HITLER, ADOLF; JESUITS, THE; LUDENDORFF, MATHILDE SPIESS; MARXISM; MUNICH (BEER-HALL) PUTSCH, THE; NAZISM; WEIMAR REPUBLIC, THE; WORLD WAR I

References

Goodspeed, D. J. 1966. *Ludendorff: Soldier, Dictator, Revolutionary.* London: Rupert Hart-Davis.
Steigmann-Gall, R. 2003. *The Holy Reich: Nazi Conceptions of Christianity, 1919–1945.* Cambridge: Cambridge University Press.

LUDENDORFF, MATHILDE SPIESS (1877–1966)

Second wife of Erich Ludendorff and advocate of a worldview that combined an allegedly "scientific" new religion with extreme-right views close to National Socialism. Mathilde Ludendorff was the daughter of a Lutheran minister, Dr. Bernhard Spiess of Wiesbaden. In 1904 she married the zoologist Gustav Adolf von Kemnitz. Two years later she withdrew officially from the Lutheran Church, and in 1913 she received a doctorate in neurology. With this science background, she criticized both the occult and Christianity and prepared "a new religion." In 1916, Mathilde von Kemnitz (by now a widow) married a Major Kleine, whom she later divorced in order to marry General Erich Ludendorff in 1926. While Mathilde Ludendorff held extreme-right-wing views, she was a champion of gender equality. The book that made her name was *Triumph des Unsterblichkeitwillens,* published in 1921. In 1925, Erich Ludendorff founded an umbrella organization called the Tannenbergbund (recalling a famous German World War I victory at Tannenberg in which he was involved) that had approximately 100,000 members, many of them war veterans. This movement combined a fierce nationalism with opposition to the range of "enemies" classically opposed by fascists. Part of the umbrella organization was the German Volk Society (Verein Deutschvolk), founded in 1930. Its purpose was to disseminate Mathilde Ludendorff's science-based religious views called "God-knowledge" (*Gotterkenntnis*). These two organizations were prohibited in 1933. The Ludendorff publishing house survived. What also survived is the pattern of combining "elitist" metapolitics with subliminal common-people organicist spirituality. In 1937, Ludendorff founded the Society for German God-knowledge (Verein Deutsche Gotterkenntnis). Its members were Mathilde's followers. Between 1945 and 1951 it was dormant, only to be reactivated under the new name of League for God-cognition (Bund für Gotterkenntnis). It had some 12,000 members when the Bavarian Administrative Court banned it in 1961 because it was judged hostile to the constitution (*verfassungsfeindlich*).

Karla Poewe

See Also: ARISTOCRACY; ARYANISM; CHRISTIANITY; ELITE THEORY; FEMINISM; GERMAN CHRISTIANS, THE; GERMANIC RELIGION; GERMANNESS (*DEUTSCHHEIT*); GERMANY; HITLER, ADOLF; LUDENDORFF, ERICH; LUTHERAN CHURCHES, THE; NATIONALISM; NAZISM; NORDIC SOUL, THE; OCCULTISM; ORGANICISM; PROTESTANTISM AND NAZISM; SCIENCE; SEXUALITY; THEOLOGY; *VOLK, VÖLKISCH*; WAR VETERANS; WOMEN; WORLD WAR I

References

Ludendorff, Mathilde. 1921. *Triumph des Unsterblichkeitwillens.* Stuttgart: Hohe Warte.

Mecklenburg, Jens. 1996 *Handbuch Deutscher Rechts Extremismus.* Berlin: Elefanten.

Poewe, Karla. 2005. *New Religions and the Nazis.* London: Routledge.

LUEGER, KARL (1844–1910)

Radical populist anti-Semite, Viennese politician for thirty years from 1875, and an important influence on Adolf Hitler. In his *Fin de Siècle Vienna,* historian Carl Schorske describes a "politics in a new key": the mobilization by skilled demagogues of masses newly enfranchised but aggrieved by the abuses or shortcomings of the liberal political and economic order. Making use of modern extraparliamentary tactics of mass action, and holding out a vision combining both a mythic past and a utopian future, these nineteenth-century movements were the seedbed and prototype of twentieth-century fascism. It was in Karl Lueger's Vienna that the young Adolf Hitler first witnessed the political effectiveness of mass action and of anti-Semitism as a tool in forging cross-class coalitions. Karl Lueger rose from lower-middle-class origins. He attended the elite Theresianum Preparatory School and then the University of Vienna, where he earned a law degree. He established a legal practice in 1874, serving lower-middle-class and working-class clients, often charging no fee but earning a popular following upon which he built his political career. Lueger joined the democratic wing of the Liberal Party, advocating universal manhood suffrage and fighting fiscal corruption in city government. Elected to Vienna's city council in 1875, he won a seat in parliament in 1885. Already Lueger had joined with followers of Karl von Vogelsang, the Catholic theoretician of corporatism whose anticapitalist, anti-Liberal, and anti-Semitic program attracted a diverse following: lower-middle-class artisans, bureaucrats, and property owners; peasants; and workers. Also drawn to Vogelsang's ideas were younger members of the clergy with their own political and economic grievances against the hierarchy, priests who were seeking new ways of engaging a popular following for the Church in an era of growing secularism.

The Christian Social Party came into existence between 1889 and 1891 out of this amalgam of disaf-fected Liberals, anti-Semites, Catholic intellectuals, and activist clergy. Lueger's fortunes rose with those of the party. In 1890 he was elected to the Lower Austrian provincial assembly. In 1895 a Christian Social majority on the city council elected him mayor. Emperor Franz Joseph—who along with the hierarchy and the Vatican mistrusted mass politics and found Lueger's anti-Semitism distasteful—repeatedly vetoed Lueger's election, capitulating only in 1897 after the city council had selected Lueger five times. As mayor from 1897 until his death in 1910, Lueger moderated his populist radicalism and anti-Semitic rhetoric. He was the model, indeed the exemplar, "gas and water socialist," building public utilities and Vienna's tram and electrified railway, and preserving from developers the green belt of the Vienna Woods. Famously declaring "I decide who is a Jew," Lueger "blunt[ed] the explosive and subversive potential of anti-Semitism in the interests of the monarchy, the Catholic church, and even the capitalism he professed to fight" (Schorske 1981, 146).

Laura Gellott

See Also: ANTI-SEMITISM; AUSTRIA; CAPITALISM; CATHOLIC CHURCH, THE; CORPORATISM; HITLER, ADOLF; LIBERALISM; MASSES, THE ROLE OF THE; PAPACY, THE; POLITICAL CATHOLICISM; PROTOFASCISM; SCHÖNERER, GEORG RITTER VON; SECULARIZATION; SOCIALISM

References
Boyer, John W. 1981. *Political Radicalism in Late Imperial Vienna: Origins of the Christian Social Movement 1848–1897.* Chicago: University of Chicago Press.

Pulzer, P. G. 1988 [1964]. *The Rise of Political Anti-Semitism in Germany and Austria.* London: Peter Halban.

Schorske, Carl E. 1981. *Fin-de-Siecle Vienna: Politics and Culture.* New York: Vintage.

LUFTWAFFE, THE

The name for the German air force during the Third Reich, a potent and terrifying symbol of Nazi technological power and superiority from the time of its first operations in 1936. Germany had already developed a very effective aircraft industry before Hitler came to power, and German aircraft technology was soon at the leading edge. Hitler put Goering in charge of the Luftwaffe, and he set up its basic structures in collaboration with Erhard Milch, a former director of Lufthansa, the civil aviation arm. By March 1935 there were already nearly 2,000 operational aircraft. In 1936 the Luftwaffe intervened to powerful effect in the Spanish Civil War. German planes were used as troop transports for Franco's side; by November of that year the number of aircraft involved had reached 200, and they had been named the Condor Legion. They were responsible for the infamous bombing of Guernica, which shocked the world. They also ran bombing raids on Barcelona that provided a foretaste of what was to come in Poland and elsewhere. Up to the summer of 1940, the Luftwaffe was a potent and seemingly invincible symbol of Nazi military might, with the Stuka dive-bombers playing a particularly potent role in the lightning conquest of Poland, Denmark, The Netherlands, and France. But the turning point came with the Battle of Britain, which began on 13 August 1940. Hitler's attempt to destroy the RAF in preparation for an invasion led to very damaging aircraft losses for the Luftwaffe. From 15 September 1940, when Hitler abandoned the costly struggle with the RAF, the Luftwaffe went into decline. By early 1945 the substantial numbers of aircraft still remaining were largely grounded through fuel and pilot shortages.

Cyprian Blamires

See Also: BATTLE OF BRITAIN, THE; BLITZKRIEG; CHURCHILL, SIR WINSTON LEONARD SPENCER; GOERING, HERMANN; GUERNICA; SPANISH CIVIL WAR, THE; WORLD WAR II

References
Hayward, Joel S. A. 2001. *Stopped at Stalingrad: The Luftwaffe and Hitler's Defeat in the East, 1942–1943.* Lawrence: University Press of Kansas.
Murray, W. 1985. *Luftwaffe.* London: Allen and Unwin.

LUTHER, MARTIN (1483–1546)

Initiator of the Reformation in Germany, portrayed by the Nazis as an authentically German cultural hero whose teachings were consistent with the nationalism, totalitarian principles, and anti-Semitism of the Third Reich. In his attacks on "Catholic internationalism" and the "Jewish spirit" of modernity and secularism, Nazi propagandist Alfred Rosenberg cited Luther's writings as proof that the Nazi worldview was inherited from that of the father of the Reformation.

Luther's anti-Jewish polemic "Of the Jews and Their Lies" was used to give theological credibility to Nazi ideology, and the Nazis authorized and distributed the government publication of the tract in 1935, following the passage of the Nuremberg Laws. In 1937 the city of Nuremberg gave a rare edition of Luther's polemic to Julius Streicher on the occasion of his birthday. This ideological appropriation of Luther, the historical figure who personified German Protestantism, met with little protest from prominent Lutheran leaders at the time, despite Protestant tensions with the Nazi regime over issues of church independence. Mainstream Protestants were far more concerned about the theological extremism of the German Christians, a pro-Nazi Protestant faction within the church that called for such steps as the removal of the Old Testament from Christian Scriptures. Yet the German Christians themselves traced much of their thinking to Luther's anti-Jewish writings. The more outspoken Protestant apologists for Nazism even viewed the rise of Nazism as the historical culmination of some of the cultural trends that began in the Reformation, and they argued that, because of Luther's anti-Catholicism, German Protestantism was more inherently aligned with National Socialist ideology than was Catholicism. In their support for the regime, leading Lutheran theologians such as Paul Althaus, Gerhard Kittel, and Emanuel Hirsch drew upon Luther's other writings to portray the Lutheran *Geist* as antimodern, antisecular, antiecumenical, and pronationalist.

Victoria Barnett

See Also: ANTI-SEMITISM; ARYANISM; CATHOLIC CHURCH, THE; CHAMBERLAIN, HOUSTON STEWART; CHRISTIANITY; COSMOPOLITANISM; GERMAN CHRISTIANS, THE; GERMANIC RELIGION; GERMANNESS (*DEUTSCHHEIT*); GERMANY; LIBERALISM (IN THEOLOGY); LUTHERAN CHURCHES, THE; MODERNITY; NATIONALISM; NAZISM; NORDIC SOUL, THE; NUREMBERG LAWS, THE; PROTESTANTISM AND NAZISM; RELIGION; ROSENBERG, ALFRED; SECULARIZATION; THEOLOGY; THIRD REICH, THE; TOTALITARIANISM

References
Ericksen, Robert P. 1985. *Theologians under Hitler: Gerhard Kittel, Paul Althaus, and Emanuel Hirsch.* New Haven: Yale University Press.
Erikson, Eric H. 1993. *Young Man Luther: A Study in Psychoanalysis and History.* New York: Norton.
Gerlach, Wolfgang. 2000. *And the Witnesses were Silent: The Confessing Church and the Jews.* Lincoln: University of Nebraska Press.
Oberman, Heiko A. 1986. *The Roots of Anti-Semitism: In the Age of Renaissance and Reformation.* Philadelphia: Fortress.

LUTHERAN CHURCHES, THE

Responses among Lutheran churches to fascist movements (which they have encountered more or less exclusively in its Nazi or neo-Nazi form) have varied widely, determined as much by the historical background, institutional attitudes, different cultural and social traditions, and the ideological alliances of the respective churches as by actual Lutheran theological teachings and doctrine. There are different theological streams in Lutheranism, but the predominant aspects of Lutheran theology are situated within the individual's relationship to faith and the direct reception of the word of God through Scripture. These theological tenets constitute an antiauthoritarian effect; but that exists in tension with an institutional tradition that in some nations, notably Germany, led to a pronounced alliance between the Lutheran Church and state authority. From the time of Martin Luther, the Protestant church in Germany was under the jurisdiction of the regional princes and landed nobility, who served as patrons of their parishes by naming and supporting clergy. The German Protestant church's institutional ties to the landed nobility laid the foundation for the "throne and altar" mentality in German Protestantism, symbolized by the church's alliance with governmental authority. This patronage system remained in some regions of Germany until the 1930s. Yet the decisive break in Prussia came in 1817, when Frederick William III united the Lutheran and Reformed churches of Prussia into the Church of the Old Prussian Union, creating a new "united" church that was a less hierarchical institution and more Reformed in its theology. The legacy of these historical developments became evident under Nazism, when the Church of the Old Prussian Union became the heart of the Confessing Church movement, which sought to preserve the church's freedom from Nazi ideology and which became a critical force in Nazi society. In contrast, the three purely Lutheran regional churches of Bavaria, Hanover, and Württemberg were far more cautious and compromising in their dealings with Nazi authorities, and other predominantly Lutheran regions such as Thuringia and Schleswig-Holstein became strongholds of the German Christian movement, which embraced Nazi ideology and sought a Germanic Reich church.

Under the Hitler regime, prominent German Lutheran theologians such as Gerhard Kittel offered theological apologetics for Nazism, drawing upon Martin Luther's anti-Judaic writings, his critique of Catholicism, and his support for authority. Nonetheless, differences among Lutherans emerged, primarily over the issue of church independence from state ideology and faithfulness to Scripture, as well as in response to the Nazi state's pressures on the churches. When the church asked the theological faculties of Marburg and Erlangen to offer *Gutachten* (expert opinions) on the application of Nazi racial law to the churches, the two faculties rendered opposing judgments. The three German Lutheran bishops were briefly arrested by Nazi authorities in October 1934, and all of them signed the 1934 Barmen declaration, the founding document of the Confessing Church, which declared the Protestant church's independence from all worldly ideologies and rejected church allegiance to any worldly Fuehrer whose dictates contradicted church teachings. The Lutherans who supported Barmen, however, emphasized that their concerns were with church issues, not challenges against the Nazi state itself. Their support for the Confessing Church soon dissipated as some sectors within the confessional movement became more clearly opposed to the state. During the course of the 1930s the Lutheran regional churches in Germany became increasingly quiescent toward the Nazi regime, and their loyalty to the state became virtually absolute once war broke out.

In other parts of Europe, the Lutheran church's response to Nazism differed. Despite the fact that the Lutheran churches of Denmark, Norway, and (until 2000) Sweden are state churches, the emergence of Lutheranism in those countries coincided historically with struggles for independence. Confronted by the Nazi occupation, leaders of these churches joined many of their compatriots in fighting against the Germans, and there were strong Lutheran-based resistance movements against Nazism in all three of those countries. In Denmark, for example, where 90 percent of the population were members of the Lutheran Church, a large sector of the population aided in the rescue of the Danish Jews, and the Danish Lutheran Church publicly condemned anti-Semitism and protested other measures taken by the Nazi occupation forces. The question that arises, then, is the degree to which the Lutheran churches' response was shaped by Lutheran theological doctrine as opposed to other factors, such as institutional patterns and traditions of obedience to state authority. In Lutheran churches such as the Danish one, Lutheran teachings were interpreted to allow for political activism and protest. Thus the variation in the responses of Lutheran churches in Europe during the Nazi era tends to reflect the historically based differences among those churches both in theological emphasis and in the relationship between church leaders and authority. Similar dynamics are evident in other historical encounters between Lutheran churches and authoritarian or fascist regimes. In Eastern Europe, for example, there are significant minority Lutheran communities in Estonia, Lithuania, and parts of Russia, most of them consisting of people of German descent. Both before and after the fall of communism, these diaspora communities were denied the privileges accorded the Russian Orthodox Church and suffered actual persecution by state authorities; they therefore viewed themselves as a dissident force under communism. During the 1930s and 1940s, however, their identity as part of the German diaspora led to a strong sense of German nationalism that led many of them to collaborate with the Nazi occupation forces.

The Lutheran experience under National Socialism led to a wide range of responses in the postwar period as well. As early as 1941, the confrontation with Nazi Germany led prominent U.S. Lutheran theologian Reinhold Niebuhr to call for a rethinking of Lutheran theology and repudiate the evangelization of Jews. In Germany, the Lutheran bishops joined other German church leaders in 1945 to issue the Stuttgart Declaration of Guilt, an apology directed toward other European churches that included the German church's admission of its own complicity in Nazism. This sparked a widespread debate within German Protestantism, in which the critique of most Lutheran bishops and theologians of their country's past was more guarded than that which emerged from other sectors in the church. Yet other prominent Lutherans such as Martin Niemoeller were outspoken in their criticism of the church's complicity in Nazism, and pushed for church debates not only about the church's subservience to the state but also about its theological support for the Nazi persecution of the Jews and other groups. The issue of theological anti-Judaism was first raised at the 1950 national synod of the German church in Weissensee, where the church acknowledged its guilt to the Jewish people for the first time.

In the decades since then, the debate about the Lutheran Church's attitudes toward Judaism and its relationship to state authority has continued, particularly in Germany, where a strong postwar antiauthoritarian movement within German Protestantism, led by for-mer Confessing Christians such as Niemoeller, significantly changed that church's relationship to the state. The German Protestant church has joined other German institutions in condemning instances of neo-Nazism in that country. In Europe and in North America, Lutheran churches have also focused particularly on the Holocaust and the church's relationship to Judaism. In 1980, the Church of the Rhineland in Germany officially acknowledged the theological and covenantal validity of the Jewish faith, and the Evangelical Church of Germany, which includes the regional Lutheran churches, has issued a similar statement. In the United States, the Evangelical Lutheran Church in America made a "Declaration to the Jewish Community" in 1994 that repudiated the anti-Jewish writings of Martin Luther and repented of Christian complicity in the persecution of the Jews.

Victoria Barnett

See Also: ANTIFASCISM; ANTI-SEMITISM; ARYANISM; BONHOEFFER, DIETRICH; CATHOLIC CHURCH, THE; CHAMBERLAIN, HOUSTON STEWART; CHRISTIANITY; CONFESSING (OR CONFESSIONAL) CHURCH, THE; DINTER, ARTUR; EDUCATION; ESTONIA; GERMAN CHRISTIANS, THE; GERMAN FAITH MOVEMENT; GERMANIC RELIGION; GERMANY; JULY PLOT, THE; KREISAU CIRCLE, THE; LAGARDE, PAUL DE; LANGBEHN, JULIUS; LEISURE; LIBERALISM (IN THEOLOGY); LITHUANIA; LUDENDORFF, ERICH; LUDENDORFF, MATHILDE; LUTHER, MARTIN; MÜLLER, BISHOP LUDWIG; MYSTICISM; NAZISM; NEO-NAZISM; NIEMOELLER, MARTIN; NUREMBERG LAWS, THE; OCCULTISM; ORTHODOX CHURCHES, THE; PACIFISM; PROTESTANTISM AND NAZISM; RELIGION; ROSENBERG, ALFRED; SECULARIZATION; SOVIET UNION, THE; STATE, THE; THEOLOGY; TOTALITARIANISM; UNITED STATES, THE (POSTWAR); WEIMAR REPUBLIC, THE; WORLD WAR II; YOUTH MOVEMENTS

References

Ericksen, Robert P., and Susannah Heschel, editors. 1999. *Betrayal: German Churches and the Holocaust.* Minneapolis, MN: Fortress.

Helmreich, Ernst Christian. 1979. *The German Churches under Hitler: Background, Struggle, and Epilogue.* Detroit: Wayne State University Press.

Rittner, Carol, Stephen D. Smith, and Irena Steinfeldt, eds. 2000. *The Holocaust and the Christian World: Reflections on the Past, Challenges for the Future.* London: Kuperard.

Stumme, John R., and Robert W. Tuttle. 2003. *Church and State: Lutheran Perspectives.* Minneapolis, MN: Fortress.

Walker, Williston, et al. 1986. *A History of the Christian Church.* 4th ed. Edinburgh: T. and T. Clark.

MACHIAVELLI, NICCOLÒ (1469–1527)

Certain aspects of the philosophies of both Mussolini and Hitler strongly recall the kind of thinking to be found in the notorious political tract authored by Machiavelli under the title *The Prince* and in his *Discourses.* In Italy, some of the ideas of the celebrated Renaissance political thinker were being propagated again in the early part of the twentieth century by ideologues of the "Machiavelli" school of elite theorists (Michels, Mosca, Pareto). Although the true nature of Machiavelli's political philosophy is hotly debated, there are certain clear themes that are likely to have pleased and probably influenced the two fascist dictators. In particular, Machiavelli boldly attacks Christian morality for teaching virtues that are not compatible with a successful state. Moreover, for Machiavelli political "virtue" has nothing to do with the traditional ideas of morality; it resides particularly in boldness and courage, and that doctrine of "heroism" is reflected in the lives and policies of Hitler and Mussolini, as well as in at least one of their mentors, Carlyle. Machiavelli is also celebrated for his encouragement of the idea that the kind of qualities required of the political leader include cunning and a readiness to deceive, as well as flexibility in the face of events. This mentality was supremely demonstrated by Hitler, for example, in his orchestra-tion of the Hitler-Stalin Pact, which shocked so many of his own followers as well as the rest of the world. But it was an act of pure and deliberate duplicity perpetrated on Stalin. Hitler would have found in Machiavelli encouragement for the notion that the issue was not the intrinsic rightness or wrongness of this kind of action, but whether or not his people would "forgive" him for it and tolerate it.

Cyprian Blamires

See Also: BARBAROSSA, OPERATION; CARLYLE, THOMAS; CHRISTIANITY; ELITE THEORY; HERO, THE CULT OF THE; HITLER, ADOLF; HITLER-STALIN PACT, THE; MICHELS, ROBERTO; MOSCA, GAETANO; MUSSOLINI, BENITO ANDREA; PARETO, VILFREDO; SCHMITT, CARL; STALIN, IOSIF VISSARIONOVICH; WAR

References

Fontana, B. 1993. *Hegemony and Power: On the Relation between Gramsci and Machiavelli.* London: University of Minnesota Press.

Mead, Edward, et al., eds. 1972. *Makers of Modern Strategy: Military Thought from Machiavelli to Hitler.* Princeton: Princeton University Press.

Rees, E. A. 2004. *Political Thought from Machiavelli to Stalin: Revolutionary Machiavellism.* Basingstoke: Palgrave Macmillan.

MAISTRE, COMTE JOSEPH DE: *See* TRADITIONALISM

McVEIGH, TIMOTHY (1968–2001)

A mechanized infantry gunner in the Gulf War and an admirer of neo-Nazi ideologist William Pierce, McVeigh showed increasing hostility to the U.S. government, which came to a head after the FBI siege of the Branch Davidian sect in Waco, Texas. The siege, which culminated on 19 April 1993 in the deaths of 76 adults and children, led McVeigh to decide upon a revenge attack on a federal building in Oklahoma City. On the second anniversary of Waco, a truck bomb devastated the building and killed 168 people. McVeigh was arrested shortly after the bombing, found guilty of murder, and executed in June 2001.

Martin Durham

See Also: NEO-NAZISM; OKLAHOMA BOMBING, THE; PIERCE, WILLIAM; *TURNER DIARIES, THE;* UNITED STATES, THE (POSTWAR)

Reference
Michel, L. 2001. *American Terrorist: Timothy McVeigh and the Oklahoma City Bombing.* New York: Regan.

MALAPARTE, CURZIO (real name, Kurt Erich Suckert) (1898–1957)

One of the most influential Italian writers of the twentieth century and an active member of the Fascist Party. He was born in Prato of an Italian mother and a German Protestant father. After serving in World War I he became a journalist, joining the Fascist Party in 1922. In 1924 he founded *La Conquista dello stato,* a periodical based in Rome, and in 1926 he and Massimo Bontempelli established a literary quarterly entitled *900.* This pursued a policy of encouragement for progress and technology. In the late 1920s, Malaparte joined the staff of *La Stampa,* which he turned into a Fascist paper. But he lost that job as a result of enmities incurred within the Fascist Party. He published a number of novels in the 1920s and 1930s and in 1931 was sent into internal exile on the island of Lipari af-

ter the publication in French of *Technique du coup d'état* (1931), in which he attacked both Hitler and Mussolini. Galeazzo Ciano's intervention eventually led to his release. He went on to found *Prospettive* in 1937, a cultural and literary journal. During World War II he was employed as a correspondent for *Corriere della Sera* and was able to report on the German advance into the Soviet Union. After the fall of Mussolini he endured periods of incarceration, though he ended the war working with the Allied Command in Italy. After the war Malaparte published further novels and also plays, one of which was turned into a film that was released in the United States under the title of *Strange Deception.* He converted to Catholicism on his deathbed.

Cyprian Blamires

See Also: BARBAROSSA, OPERATION; CATHOLIC CHURCH, THE; CIANO, COUNT GALEAZZO; FASCIST PARTY, THE; GERMANY; HITLER, ADOLF; ITALY; LITERATURE; MUSSOLINI, BENITO ANDREA; PROGRESS; SOVIET UNION, THE; TECHNOLOGY; WORLD WAR I; WORLD WAR II

References
Arndt, Astrid. 2005. *Aberration and Greatness: Malaparte—Céline—Benn. Valuation Problems in French, German, and Italian Literary Criticism.* Tübigen-Lustnau: Max Niemeyer.
De Grand, A. 1972. "Curzio Malaparte: The Illusion of the Fascist Revolution." *Journal of Contemporary History* 7, nos. 1–2.
Hope, W. 2000. *Curzio Malaparte: The Narrative Contract Strained.* Market Harborough: Troubador.

MAN, HENDRIK/HENRI DE (1885–1953)

A left-wing activist in the Belgian Workers Party whose attempt to go "beyond" Marxism was followed by his collaboration with the Nazis during the war. Hendrik de Man was one of the leading left-wing intellectuals of the early twentieth century. His theoretical revision of Marxism in the 1920s marked him down as the "cosmopolitan heir to more widely known political thinkers such as Bernstein, Jaurès, and Sorel," as "the true systematizer of the ethical and cultural strand in the European revisionist tradition" (Pels 2002, 283). In his 1926 *Zur Psychologie des Sozialismus,* de Man attacked the philosophical roots of Marxism—defined as "summarized in the catchwords determinism, causal mechanism, historicism, rationalism and economic hedonism" (de Man 1928, 23)—and reinterpreted the evolution of the workers' movement in the light of the methods of social psychology, seeking the foundations of socialist "faith" in sentimental and ethical motivations. The practical political outcome of this revisionism was the *Plan du Travail* adopted by the Belgian Workers Party in 1933, which articulated a model of economic intervention seeking to develop a mixed economy between capitalism and socialism as a stage on the way to socialism, but that was also to act as a symbol or myth uniting forces against capitalism and fascism. De Man's authorship of the *Plan* "made him the main ideological founding father of postwar social democracy" (Pels 2002, 283). In the subsequent period, following the relative failure of the *Plan* to be implemented, de Man would come to develop ideas about "authoritarian democracy"—in 1936 he would state: "It is a fact that the masses have a desire to believe in authoritarian and responsible leaders and especially to love them. They get disgusted with parliamentary democracy because it tends to prevent the formation of personages of heroic stature" (de Man, cited in Burrin 1986, 87). He also flirted with elements of fascist ideology and political style, articulating the slogan *socialisme national* in 1937, and would collaborate, albeit briefly, as chairman of the Belgian Workers' Party, with the Nazi occupants of Belgium during 1940–1941. Nonetheless, as Burrin notes, de Man refused to launch a political movement of his own during the occupation, and there were limits to his willingness to cooperate with the Nazis. He retired to France in November 1941 but continued to pledge allegiance to the occupation regime. Convicted of treason in September 1944, de Man fled to Switzerland, where he settled. There is considerable debate regarding whether de Man's collaboration and flirtation with authoritarian and fascist ideology was or was not a direct outcome of the ideological affinity between de Man's "ethical socialism" and national socialism.

Steve Bastow

See Also: AUTHORITARIANISM; BELGIUM; BOLSHEVISM; CAPITALISM; DEMOCRACY; ECONOMICS; EGALITARIANISM; FRANCE; GERMANY; HERO, THE CULT OF THE; MARXISM; MASSES, THE ROLE OF THE; MYTH; NAZISM; PARLIAMENTARISM; RATIONALISM; SOCIALISM; SOREL, GEORGES; STYLE; SWITZERLAND; SYMBOLS; WORLD WAR II

References
Burrin, Philippe. 1986. *La dérive fasciste: Doriot, Déat, Bergery 1933–1945*. Paris: Editions du Seuil.
Man, Hendrik de. 1928. *The Psychology of Socialism*. London: George Allen.
Pels, D. 1987. "Henri de Man and the Ideology of Planism." *International Review of Social History* 32, no. 3: 206–229.
———. 1993. "The Dark Side of Socialism: Hendrik de Man and the Fascist Temptation." *History of the Human Sciences* 6, no. 2: 75–95.
———. 2002. "Socialism between Fact and Value: From Tony Blair to Hendrik de Man and Back." *Journal of Political Ideologies* 6, no. 2: 281–300.
Sternhell, Z. 1986. *Neither Right, nor Left*. Princeton: Princeton University Press.
White, D. S. 1992. *Lost Comrades: Socialists of the Front Generation 1918–1945*. Cambridge: Harvard University Press.

MANIFESTO OF FASCIST INTELLECTUALS, THE
and
MANIFESTO OF ANTI-FASCIST INTELLECTUALS, THE

In the spring of 1925, Giovanni Gentile convened a Conference on Fascist Culture in Bologna with the aim of demonstrating that culture was perfectly compatible with Fascism. Around 250 delegates attended and at the end produced a Manifesto of Fascist Intellectuals, published in April 1925. Among the signatories were Corradini, Marinetti, Panunzio, Rocco, Spirito, and Volpe. Less than a fortnight later a countermanifesto was published on the inspiration of Croce and Amendola, and that came to be known as the Manifesto of Anti-Fascist Intellectuals. It had forty-one signatories initially, but many others added their names later, and the list came to include many of Italy's intellectual elite.

Cyprian Blamires

See Also: CORRADINI, ENRICO; CROCE, BENEDETTO; FASCIST PARTY, THE; FUTURISM; GENTILE, GIOVANNI; ITALY; MARINETTI, FILIPPO TOMMASO; ROCCO, ALFREDO; SPIRITO, UGO; UNIVERSITIES (ITALY); VOLPE, GIOACHINNO

References
Cannistraro, Philip V., and Brian R. Sullivan. 1993. *Il Duce's Other Woman: The Untold Story of Margherita Sarfatti, Benito Mussolini's Jewish Mistress, and How She Helped Him Come to Power*. New York: William Morrow.
Papa, Emilio R. 1974. *Fascismo e cultura*. Padua: Marsilio.

MARCH ON ROME, THE

The March on Rome was the operation organized by the leading Italian Fascist chiefs to converge Fascist "squads" on the capital at the end of October 1922 as a means of seizing power. The squads had already effectively taken control of several provinces of northern and central Italy in the previous months, but the march was essentially used by Mussolini to put pressure on King Victor Emmanuel to bring him into the government. Mussolini did not in fact participate in the march but stayed behind in Milan, and when the squads eventually arrived in Rome, he had already been appointed prime minister.

John Pollard

See Also: FASCIST PARTY, THE; ITALY; MUSSOLINI, BENITO ANDREA; *SQUADRISMO;* VICTOR EMMANUEL/VITTORIO EMANUELE III, KING

Reference
Lyttelton, A. 1973. *Seizure of Power: Fascism in Italy, 1919–1929.* London: Weidenfeld and Nicolson.

MARCONI, GUGLIELMO (1874–1937)

Italian pioneer in the development of wireless telegraphy and an active member of the Fascist Party, which he first joined in 1923. In 1930, Mussolini made him president of the Accademia d'Italia, overriding a law that prevented Marconi, by then a member of the Italian senate, from serving. This automatically made Marconi a member of the Grand Council of Fascism.

Cyprian Blamires

See Also: FASCIST PARTY, THE; GRAND COUNCIL OF FASCISM, THE; ITALY; MUSSOLINI, BENITO ANDREA; RADIO

Reference
Jolly, W. P. 1972. *Marconi.* London: Constable.

MARINETTI, FILIPPO TOMMASO (1876–1944)

Writer, poet, and founder and theoretician of Futurism. Born in Alexandria in Egypt, he completed his studies in Paris and in Italy, where in 1899 he graduated in jurisprudence at the University of Genoa. But his true passion was literature: his first volume of verse, *La conquête des étoiles,* appeared in 1902. He also involved himself in the political and social life of the day, and was particularly attracted by the revolutionary dynamism of socialism, by the rhetoric of political assemblies, by great political mass demonstrations, and by party meetings. He was especially interested in Sorel's anarcho-syndicalism. On 20 February 1909, Marinetti published his *Manifesto of Futurism* on the first page of the French daily *Figaro.* This marked the beginning of a profound aesthetic, artistic, but also political revolution. Gifted with an innate propensity for propaganda, publicity, and showmanship, Marinetti began to publicize his program, looking for supporters and proselytes. He dreamed up the idea of "Futurist parties," preceded by the distribution of fliers and publicity and involving poetry readings, musical performances, and exhibitions. The public flocked to these events, which almost always ended in arguments, egg-throwing, and fistfights. Despite the mockery of critics and newspapers, Marinetti's energy and charm were such that he managed to attract a whole array of enthusiasts to his side within the space of a year. Among them were poets, writers, painters, composers, musicians, and theater folk.

Espousing a political position halfway between anarchism and syndicalism, Marinetti gave lectures to working men's societies in which he proposed an alliance between the proletariat and the Futurists in the name of "beauty" and "the necessity for violence." The myth of "war as the only hygiene for the world" was a theme that began to creep into his writings. His ideology was an assemblage of elements of the most diverse provenance: anarchism, syndicalism, nationalism, imperialism, patriotism, and idealism, resulting in something very similar to what would become, ten years later, the ideology of Italian Fascism. In March 1915, Marinetti was arrested together with Mussolini during a demonstration in favor of Italian participation in World War I. With the outbreak of war he volunteered for the call-up. When the war was over Marinetti thought about the creation of a Futurist Party of national-revolutionary inspiration, to bring together former soldiers and tap the healthy energies of the nation on the basis of a radical program of "Futurist democracy," taking as its enemies the "parasitic" bourgeoisie and degenerate socialism: it was the same idea to which Mussolini gave shape with the creation of the Fasci di combattimento in March 1919. Marinetti immediately gave his support to Mussolini's political program. In November 1919 he was a candidate for the elections on the list sanctioned by the future dictator. In 1920 he published *Al di là del comunismo,* a text in which he criticized egalitarianism and the bureaucratic spirit that had thwarted the Russian Revolution and advocated putting art and artists into power.

With the conquest of power by Fascism in October 1922, a new phase opened for Marinetti; he became somewhat disillusioned with politics and recovered an anarchical individualistic vein (though still violently antibourgeois and antiliberal). Although disappointed by the compromises that Fascism was accepting with respect to the old monarchical and liberal ruling class, Marinetti nonetheless sought to get involved in the cultural policy of the regime, with the intention of keeping alive the revolutionary spirit of the Futurist Movement. In March 1929, Marinetti—recognized by Mussolini himself as a precursor of Fascism—was admitted to the Accademia d'Italia. The politico-military alliance between Italy and Hitlerite Germany was not to his liking, however, and his relations with the regime became increasingly strained. He was equally opposed to Nazi polemics against "degenerate art" and anti-Semitism. In the official press he began to be accused of "anti-Fascism." A rapprochement with Fascism and Mussolini took place only with the outbreak of World War II. In 1942, Marinetti, now old and ill, asked to be allowed to join up with the Italian troops fighting in Russia. After the fall of Fascism in July 1943 he moved to Venice, giving his support to the Salò Republic out of a sense of honor and patriotism.

Alessandro Campi
(translated by Cyprian Blamires)

See Also: ANTIFASCISM; ANTI-SEMITISM; ARCHITECTURE; ART; AXIS, THE; BARBAROSSA, OPERATION; BOURGEOISIE, THE; DECADENCE; DEGENERACY; DEMOCRACY; FASCIST PARTY, THE; FUTURISM; GERMANY; HITLER, ADOLF; INTERVENTIONISM; ITALY; MODERNISM; MUSIC (ITALY); NATIONALISM; NAZISM; MUSSOLINI, BENITO ANDREA; PROPAGANDA; REVOLUTION; SALÒ REPUBLIC, THE; SARFATTI-GRASSINI, MARGHERITA; SOCIALISM; SOREL, GEORGES; SOVIET UNION, THE; SYNDICALISM; TECHNOLOGY; VIOLENCE; WAR; WAR VETERANS; WORLD WAR I; WORLD WAR II

References
Berghaus, G. 1995. *The Genesis of Futurism: Marinetti's Early Career and Writings 1899–1909.* Leeds: Society for Italian Studies.
———. 1996. *Futurism and Politics: Between Anarchist Rebellion and Fascist Reaction, 1909–1944.* Oxford: Berghahn.
Gentile, E. 2003. *The Struggle for Modernity: Nationalism, Futurism and Fascism.* London: Praeger.
Joll, J. 1960. *Intellectuals in Politics: Three Biographical Essays.* London: Weidenfeld and Nicholson.
Special Issue. 1994. "Marinetti and the Futurists." *Modernism/Modernity* 1, no. 3.

MARRIAGE: *See* FAMILY, THE; SEXUALITY; WOMEN

MARXISM

Italian Fascists and German Nazis usually spoke of Marxism contemptuously as "Bolshevism," which had become a common expression of anxiety at the "red menace" felt throughout Western Europe. In this way they tapped into a widespread fear of a revolution from below, an insurgency of the proletariat, such as had developed since the October Revolution in Russia in 1917. The Germans had their own brush with Marxism at close quarters when in April 1919 power was seized briefly in Bavaria by communists and anarchists, and the "Bavarian Soviet Republic" was founded. It was overthrown in the following month by armed forces of the Right including a force of 30,000 members of the Freikorps. In Italy, left-wing working-class militancy reached such a pitch after World War I that for a period in 1920 (largely inspired, in fact, by anarchists and revolutionary syndicalists) workers forcibly took over and ran certain factories for themselves. The fear of the "red menace" was, of course, intensified by Soviet propaganda, according to which communism held a universal message of salvation for all the world and not just for Russians. Both Italian Fascists and German Nazis saw themselves as offering a radical and healthier alternative message of revolutionary change to that of Soviet Marxism. Marxism called on the workers of the world to unite across national borders in a global battle against their oppressors, treating nation-states and national pride as tools in the arsenal of bourgeois propaganda intended to lull the workers to sleep; interwar fascists, on the other hand, gave priority back to national (and, for the Nazis) racial pride as the source of all good and rejected all forms of universalism that would aim to downgrade or destroy nation-states as dangerous abstractions and pipe dreams.

The Nazis in particular associated such universalism with the Jews and spoke of Marxism as a Jewish world conspiracy. (A confusing factor was that they also spoke of capitalism as a Jewish conspiracy and denounced the "Jewish" plutocrats of world finance and banking who were holding the world to ransom.) Marxism was furthermore denounced by interwar fascists for its materialist theory of historical development. The Nazis believed themselves to be the bearers of a "spiritual" interpretation of reality and of history, which they connected with the concept of "soul"; the Italian Fascists also rejected Marxist (dialectical) materialism, in the name of the heroic values of courage, nobility, and military valor. They, like the Nazis, believed that people and "destiny" were the motors of history, rather than (as the Marxists supposed) economic factors, and in particular the social relations of production; the influence of Machiavelli and Carlyle can be discerned in their thinking. Italian Fascists and Nazis alike scorned Marxist egalitarianism, to which they preferred the elitism that went with a belief that "fortune favors the brave." Their program was unashamedly oriented toward the production of a hierarchical, top-down, authoritarian society run by an elite ("revolution from above"), and Hitler's plans included special academies to train the brutally purposeful elite cadres who would spearhead the forward drive of Nazism. Both the Italian Fascist and German Nazi movements included a great number of war veterans who had learned to admire outstanding courage and endurance in the trenches of World War I. (This idea of a revolutionary elite did, of course, have a counterpart in the thought of Lenin and his successors, who saw the need for an elite to drive the proletarian revolution forward.)

On this question of revolution there were similarities and divergences. The Marxists called for a global revolution powered by the proletariat, and that fascists rejected out of hand. Although they did call for revolution themselves, it was a "national" revolution—with "national" understood in terms of an "ideal expanded nation" rather than of the nation considered within existing boundaries. Mussolini's revolution was aimed at restoring Italy to the greatness of ancient Rome, with the expansionism that this implied. Hitler's revolution was a Pangermanic one that envisaged a single German nation comprising all populations of Germanic (or "Aryan") racial stock. Furthermore, Hitler aimed for an imperialistic drive to increase existing Germanic territory by invading Russia in order to subject the Slav lands and colonize them. Attempts were made by Italian Fascism to promote a world movement of nationalists, but these foundered, partly on divisions between Italian Fascist and German Nazi perspectives. Where German occupying forces encountered fascist movements in occupied territories, their response was ambivalent; they sometimes banned such movements (as in Hungary) and sometimes encouraged them (as in Denmark), but the Germans had no intention of letting ultimate power fall into the hands of their hypernationalist fellow travelers in the countries they occupied. Although fascism claimed to be a "new" political creed, its practice by Germany and Italy in their foreign policy seemed to be tantamount to the old imperialism in a new guise.

For Marxists, the chief social evil to be eradicated was the oppression by the capitalists and their allies of the working class. Insofar as their utopia was theorized, it was that of a classless egalitarian society in which there were no oppressors and oppressed, but a society of equals in which government had given way to administration. There would be universal peace once the source of conflict—that is, capitalist oppression—had been abolished. For interwar fascists the glaring evil was something that they called "decadence," which they associated with many of the things that Marxism stood for, such as internationalism, egalitarianism, materialism, and pacifism (for Marxists considered that nationalistic wars like World War I had nothing to do with them); fascists also, however, opposed other things that Marxism also opposed, such as liberalism, individualism, and parliamentarism. Where fascism and Marxism agreed was in the need for bloody revolution to inaugurate a new era. In the fascist utopia, however, the struggles endemic to nations would continue, so that universal peace was a chimera.

During the Cold War, postwar fascism continued to see itself as having a mission to destroy communism. But in the 1960s and 1970s, there were some fascist movements that seemed prepared to absorb insights from such Marxist writers as Gramsci. With the collapse of communism in Eastern Europe after 1989, the focus shifted to such targets as immigration, Americanization, and sometimes globalization as the major threats in the modern world.

Cyprian Blamires

See Also: INTRODUCTION; ABSTRACTION; AMERICANIZATION; "ANTI-" DIMENSION OF FASCISM, THE; ANTI-COMINTERN PACT, THE; ANTI-SEMITISM; AXIS, THE; BANKS, THE; BENOIST, ALAIN DE; BOLSHEVISM; CAPITALISM; CARLYLE, THOMAS; COLD WAR, THE; COMINTERN, THE; CONSPIRACY THEORIES; COSMOPOLITANISM; DECADENCE; EGALITARIANISM; ELITE THEORY; EUROPEAN NEW RIGHT, THE; EXPANSIONISM; FASCIST PARTY, THE; FREIKORPS, THE; GERMANY; GLOBALIZATION; GRAMSCI, ANTONIO; HERO, THE CULT OF THE; HITLER, ADOLF; IMMIGRATION; IMPERIALISM; IRREDENTISM; ITALY; MACHIAVELLI, NICCOLÒ; MARXIST THEORIES OF FASCISM; MATERIALISM; MUSSOLINI, BENITO ANDREA; NATIONALISM; NAZISM; NEW MAN, THE; NEW ORDER, THE; PACIFISM; PANGERMANISM; PLUTOCRACY; POSTWAR FASCISM; RACIAL DOCTRINE; REVOLUTION; SOCIAL DARWINISM; SOCIALISM; SOUL; SYNDICALISM; VIOLENCE; WAR; WAR VETERANS; WARRIOR ETHOS, THE; WORLD WAR I

References

Griffin, R. 1991. *The Nature of Fascism*. London: Routledge.
Payne, S. 1995. *A History of Fascism 1914–1945*. London: University College London Press.

MARXIST THEORIES OF FASCISM

The rise of the interwar fascist parties represented an urgent challenge to their opponents on the Left. Existing liberal, socialist, feminist, and other radical traditions were charged with explaining how the tragedy had been possible. Given that the interwar European Left was dominated by two traditions that had both emerged from Marxism (social democracy and communism), it is no surprise that the first and most important antifascist theories were developed under that banner. The Marxist legacy was felt in terms of certain key insights, an interpretative stress placed on such concepts as class, class fractions, and class dynamics. The history of Marxist theories of fascism can be seen in terms of the changing weight given to each insight.

Born in the German Rhineland, Karl Marx (1818–1883) was a revolutionary socialist and an advocate of workers' rule. His followers described him as having synthesized the best insights of English economic theory, French political science, and German philosophy. Such ideas were integrated to make a total narrative of human history. The history of all previous societies was one of class struggle. A minority had owned or controlled the wealth of society. Dispossessed groups had challenged them for power. Each new rising class had represented a revolutionary force in its own day. Either the new class had triumphed, or both the new and old classes had been ruined. In the *Communist Manifesto* (1848), Marx argued that this cycle could be brought to an end. Unlike all previous class societies, capitalism had solved the relationship of inequality between mankind and the environment. Industry was transforming life. World trade was bringing together goods across vast distances. The challenge now was to resolve the imbalance of power between the classes. The rule of capital depended on the productive labor of the masses (the proletariat). Unlike all previous classes, the urban working class was a majority, and had the potential to rule in behalf of all humanity. After capitalism, the next order would be an equal, communist society.

When antifascists used these insights to explain the rise of fascism, there were different parts of Marx's theory that appealed to them. Some writers treated Marx as if he had been just a radical sociologist. They searched for evidence that the fascist parties had recruited disproportionately from one class or from a set of classes. Some writers linked fascism to the big bourgeoisie, the capitalist ruling class. Others argued that fascism had in fact received its most significant support from the classes between the working class and the ruling class: civil servants, small owners and producers, the middle peasantry. The term usually given to these intermediate layers was the "petty bourgeoisie." Some Marxists maintained that the real source of fascism's mass backing had been in significant class minorities. Thus Daniel Guérin argued that fascism's rise had been dependent on a previous story: the displacement of nineteenth-century free trade capitalism by a new order based on heavy industry organized in trusts and monopolies. The politics of the new society were more closed, militaristic, and bureaucratic. Even nonfascist societies were tending to become more fascistic. Fascism depended on the triumph of a set of grand industrialists, a fraction within the capitalist class. Other writers understood Marx to have argued that as societies developed, their components entered into antagonistic relationships with each other. Social forces rose and fell. Class should not be treated as some timeless formula, as in the possible equation "bosses = fascists." A number of theories emerged that explained fascism in terms of the total conjuncture of the interwar years. One such was

Antonio Gramsci's argument that fascism represented "Caesarism." Mussolini's personal rule was said to depend on the incompleteness of the workers' revolution of 1919–1921. The proletariat had been strong enough to match the Italian bourgeoisie, but not to overcome it. Fascism emerged from the exhaustion of two greater forces.

From the arguments so far, it would follow that fascism was a faithful reflection of trends immanent to capitalism. Yet not all present-day historians would accept such a grand claim. For while it would be difficult to separate Nazi goals in regard to working hours and productivity from the usual patterns of capitalist interest, the same direct link cannot be found as easily when it comes to other aspects of state policy. This debate has in turn been associated with a second question, of whether there was any economic rationality lying behind the Holocaust. Many writers have portrayed the Nazi genocide as a murderous act that cannot be explained on the basis of ordinary human rational thinking: something so grand and so terrible that it contravenes normal historical rules of explanation. By the late 1960s, even a number of Marxist historians had begun to argue that capitalism acted more as an indirect influence on Nazi racial policy, a background factor, rather than a constant, determining cause.

One of the most important writers to discuss these issues was the left-wing British historian Tim Mason. In an important article first published in 1968, Mason argued that the task of understanding fascism required historians to grasp what he called "the primacy of politics." The Holocaust could not be understood as following the logic of capitalist interests. Nazi Germany wasted money, people, resources, and skills on the Holocaust that could have been spent on the war effort. The Holocaust could be understood only in light of Nazi ideology, and not in economic terms. In a later book, Mason tells the story of one firm caught in wartime bombing raids: "In March 1945 the deputy head of one of the largest heavy industrial combines in the Ruhr reported to the head of the firm that the factories and offices had been destroyed; production had ceased, and he was writing from the cellars of the old administration building, where the board's grand piano and some of the wine had been saved; the workers no longer clocked on to clear the debris, but tried to save what they could of their own homes; in the preceding quarter, however, profits had remained satisfactory at five per cent" (Mason 1993, 10). This accountant may have thrived, but the majority of business owners would surely have noticed that fascism was bringing them to ruin.

There are potential problems with the sort of argument that Mason gives for the primacy of politics. In order to square the circle between his general belief in material explanation and the rules of the particular society that he was studying, Tim Mason argued a form of historical exceptionalism. In all industrial capitalist societies with the sole exception of Nazi Germany, he maintained, economics had been the vital explanatory factor. Only Germany was different. Mason also downplayed the significance of a broad literature that existed already by then, listing the involvement of such businesses as IG Farben, Siemens, Krupp, Volkswagen, and IBM in the execution of the Nazis' racial war. By cutting the links between the economic base of society and its political superstructure, Tim Mason also tended to describe the latter as a discrete entity that existed according to rules of its own. Such an approach is at least potentially awkward. It breaks the analytical link between politics and economic interest. The argument also contradicts the sort of detailed research to which the rest of Mason's life was committed, in which class relationships were often seen as crucial. A number of interwar and postwar Marxists did believe that they had succeeded in establishing a link between the Holocaust and capitalism. Important figures in that literature have included Abram Leon and Enzo Traverso. Leon in particular argued that the Jews had been trapped in a dual crisis of capitalism and feudalism. In late-nineteenth-century Eastern Europe, where societies continued to follow older feudal patterns, the Jews had continued to hold distinct roles in society. The decline of the Polish and Russian economies had forced the Jews to flee. Arriving in the developed capitalist West they were treated as something new, economic migrants competing with the salaries of local workers. These two different patterns of anti-Semitism reinforced each other, giving Hitler his lead.

Several liberal critics of fascism observed the willingness of the far Right to define themselves in terms of mass politics. They concluded that the age of fascism was itself shaped by broader social processes, including the rise of mass production and mass media. Both of these phenomena had the tendency to reduce society to a condition of individual isolation. Older habits of collective working and discussion were being eroded. It was only in this context that a mass, antidemocratic politics could flourish. This whole question looked rather different from the perspective of militant antifascists. Such writers could not accept the self-description of the fascists. But neither could they endorse the pessimistic conclusions of mass theory, which seemed to suggest that class politics belonged to an already fading past. Fascism's opponents recognized two challenges facing them. The first was an intellectual one: to realize that fascism was in fact a new force, an independent and radical party capable of winning mass support. The second was a practical one: to work in a way that would detach the supporters of fascism from that party. For left-wing critics of fascism, both were difficult, alarming tasks. The masses were supposed to provide backing for the parties of the revolutionary Left. Something had evidently gone wrong. In the 1920s, many leftist activists were tempted to minimize the novelty of this new force. They tended to assume that it was just another strand of conservatism, limited like the others by its inability to speak of the radical changes that the masses demanded. Thus, in one of his first articles on fascism, Antonio Gramsci compared this new movement to the reactionary armies made up of former czarist officers, which had come together to oppose the Russian October Revolution. Fascism was the "white guard" of capitalism, he wrote (Renton 1999, 54). Similar ideas appeared in the early work of other prominent Italian leftists, including Amadeo Bordiga, the first leader of the Italian Communist Party. They were also expressed in the famous montage picture of John Heartfield, showing Hitler with his arm outstretched (to accept a bribe): "Behind me, there are millions."

Over time, however, a number of fascism's critics came to realize that their antagonist was a large and powerful enemy, capable of enjoying mass support. The realization of fascism's plebeian backing was the major theme of Daniel Guérin's eyewitness accounts of Germany in 1933. Guérin toured Nazi Germany recording everything he saw and hiding documents in the frame of his bicycle, before returning to his native France. He described the defeat of the German Left in even such former bastions as "Red" Wedding, a poor area of Berlin. The same phrases that working-class communists had used to criticize socialist inertia now appeared on Nazi lips. British communist MP Phil Piratin recorded a similar moment of unpleasant recognition. In his book *Our Flag Stays Red,* Piratin described attending a fascist march through London in 1936. He was astonished to see the extent of Mosley's support among ordinary working-class people, "I knew some of these people, some of the men wore trade-union badges." Piratin describes local communists asking themselves, "Why are these ordinary working-class people supporting Mosley?"

One of the most important of the practical strategies for confronting fascism began from the fact of the fas-

cists' support. The fascist alliance of bosses, small producers, and unemployed workers was said to be unstable: while unemployed workers might temporarily be persuaded to march for campaigns that were against their direct economic interests, such a situation could surely not continue indefinitely. At a certain point, it was argued, such working-class people would have to confront the inequalities implied in the fascist program. There was a potential contradiction between the reactionary character of the fascist programs and the popular nature of their mass support. The fascist parties showed a constant tendency to break down under the pressure of their own internal contradictions. The tactic most associated with this argument was that of the "united front," the argument that socialist parties should ally both to stop fascism and also to demand significant reforms of the capitalist system. In Italy, Germany, and Spain, the supporters of this argument maintained that the consistent use of this approach would contribute to the defeat of fascism. Such perspectives were partly confirmed by events. The fascist parties did indeed prove fissiparous, and bitter rivalries did flare up.

Since 1945 it has been hard to discern any single direction in the evolution of Marxist analysis. Such writers as Erich Fromm, Wilhelm Reich, and Theodor Adorno blamed fascism on the rise of an authoritarian personality. Others, including David Lewis, have argued for a revived notion of fascism as the socialism of the petty bourgeoisie. Ralph Miliband restored the Marxist conception of a link between the state and fascism. One school has explained fascism in terms of its sexism and antifeminism and its reactionary attitude toward sexuality. Nicos Poulantzas explained fascism using notions of the state derived from Gramsci and Althusser. Herbert Marcuse described fascism as the culmination of idealism in philosophy. Ernest Laclau has stressed the importance of ideas to fascism as an ideology. Martin Kitchen has argued for something like the Comintern theories of 1936. A number of arguments have been put in a space between liberal and Marxist concepts. Some recent Marxists have argued for a return to Trotsky's insights, linking them to the practice of contemporary antifascist movements. In 1945, say, or 1950, Marxism was regarded as the most important, serious, and creative tradition from which antifascist theories had been drawn. More than fifty years later, its hegemony has largely been lost. The idea of a single Marxist theory of fascism also seems more elusive than ever. The challenge facing academics still tied to the tradition is dual: first to persuade their contemporaries that fascism remains a threat to democracy, and second to convince them also that analyses rooted in material conditions have something to offer in explaining the continued existence of the far Right.

David Renton

References

Beetham, D. 1983. *Marxists in Face of Fascism: Writings on Fascism from the Inter-War Period.* Manchester: Manchester University Press.

Benjamin, W. 1992. *Illuminations.* London: Fontana.

Gramsci, A. 1976. *Selections from the Prison Notebooks.* London: Lawrence and Wishart.

Gluckstein, D. 1999. *The Nazis, Capitalism and the Working Class.* London: Bookmarks.

Griffin, R. 1995. *Fascism.* Oxford: Oxford University Press.

Guérin, D. 1973. *Fascism and Big Business.* New York: Monad.

———. 1994. *The Brown Plague: Travels in Late Weimar and Early Nazi Germany.* Durham: Duke University Press.

Mason, T. 1993. *Social Policy in the Third Reich: The Working Class and the National Community.* Oxford: Berg.

Piratin, Phil. 1948. *Our Flag Stays Red.* London: Thames.

Renton, D. 1999. *Fascism, Theory and Practice.* London: Pluto.

Trotsky, L. 1971. *The Struggle against Fascism in Germany.* New York: Pathfinder.

———. 1989. *Fascism, Stalinism and the United Front.* London: Bookmarks.

MASCULINITY: *See* WARRIOR ETHOS, THE

MASSES, THE ROLE OF THE

One of the features of fascism that singled it out from conservatism, of which it was often considered an extreme right-wing version, was its direct and unashamed appeal to the masses. Hitler and Mussolini both liked to talk overtly about their preference for simple, muscular peasant types over "effete" intellectuals or snobbish aristocrats; it must be admitted, however, that they also sometimes spoke privately in derogatory terms about the masses as being easily led and "lamblike." They were themselves of humble birth, and even a fellow hypernationalist like Moeller van den Bruck found Hitler impossible to stomach on account of his "primitive proletarian" character. Hitler relied on the rugged strength of his brownshirts and Mussolini of his blackshirts to establish and maintain power. The ethos of masculinity and virility that fascism preached had moreover an obvious appeal to a mass audience whom the elevation of intellect or piety would not greatly attract. That, combined with the hypernationalist appeal to patriotism, was a powerful elixir indeed in the hands of the skilled fascist propagandists. One fact demonstrated abundantly by World War I was the extraordinary power of patriotism to engage vast numbers in suicidal combat. Hypernationalist fervor played on some very deeply ingrained and universal instincts. The Marxists appealed to workers in the name of a vague and seemingly utopian hypothetical internationalism yet to be achieved; the fascists told them that they could achieve hope and pride through the nation, a concrete existent entity.

Once in power, both dictators understood the need to indoctrinate the masses through education and leisure activities. But it was the Hitlerite regime under the inspiration of the likes of Goebbels and Speer that created the most powerful and lasting bond with its people through its orchestration of such events as the Nuremberg Rallies. In place of the civic rights proposed by liberal democracy, Nazism offered the masses exhilarating quasi-liturgical events in which they could lose themselves in the sheer excitement, the color, and the drama of majestic public rituals. The net result was to bond huge numbers of people emotionally to the regime and to make them feel proud to belong to it. Drawing on all the resources of modern technology—loudspeakers, electric floodlighting, the provision of mass transportation to bring participants to the shows—the Nazi regime literally bewitched a populace that had been mired in the slough of despond of a nightmare four years of war followed by a nightmare "defeat" that many of them believed to have been an illusion, a falsehood, a deceitful trick played on the nation: the German soldiers were undefeated; it was the German bourgeois who had stabbed the heroes of the trenches in the back and sold Germany down the river.

Both Fascist Italy and Nazi Germany sought further to entice and control the masses through their creation of national leisure organizations and youth movements that were vehicles for both socialization and indoctrination. Offering alluring opportunities for travel and sporting activities, these organizations had some success in endearing the masses to the regimes. In the meantime Hitler offered the German masses through his aggressive foreign policy of expansion a rebirth from the shame of her defeat in 1918 and the terrible oppression of the terms of the Versailles Treaty. What he gave to them was a restored sense of pride in being German after a horrendous experience of humiliation and bewilderment. This injection of fresh hope and vigor left them desensitized to the dark side of the regime.

The ability to win the support of millions was what enabled the Italian Fascists and German Nazis to attain to power and hold on to it; fascist movements in other countries were never able to imitate this to the same degree, even though they might rack up impressive numbers of supporters for a while. Its interaction with the masses was not, however, ultimately a distinguishing mark of fascism, for it was in a sense "stolen" from Bolshevism. It was, in other words, something that fascism and Bolshevism had in common. At the same time fascism, unlike Bolshevism, combined the appeal to the masses with an unashamed elitism. In this the fascists perhaps showed themselves to be better psychologists than the Bolshevists, absorbing the lessons to be found in Le Bon and others about how crowds love to be led (echoing an old tradition going back to Aristotle and Machiavelli). The fascist leadership elite was not, however, to be the intellectual elite proposed by the Enlightenment but the master class of battle-hardened, courageous, and resolute warriors— as embodied by the SS—in alliance with the most productive.

Cyprian Blamires

See Also: ARISTOCRACY; BODY, THE CULT OF THE; BOLSHEVISM; CONSERVATISM; COUNTER-REVOLUTION; DEMOCRACY; EDUCATION; ELITE THEORY; ENLIGHTENMENT, THE; FASCIST PARTY, THE; GOEBBELS, (PAUL) JOSEPH; HITLER, ADOLF; LE BON, GUSTAVE; LEISURE; MACHIAVELLI, NICCOLÒ; MARXISM; MARXIST THEORIES OF FASCISM; MICHELS, ROBERTO; MOELLER VAN DEN BRUCK, ARTHUR; MUSSOLINI, BENITO ANDREA; MYSTICISM; NATIONALISM; NAZISM; NOVEMBER CRIMINALS/ *NOVEMBERBRECHER*, THE; NUREMBERG RALLIES, THE; PALINGENETIC MYTH; PROPAGANDA; REICH, WILHELM; RELIGION; SPEER, ALBERT; SPORT; SS, THE; TECHNOLOGY; THEATER; TOTALITARIANISM; VERSAILLES, THE TREATY OF; WAR VETERANS; WARRIOR ETHOS, THE; WORK; WORLD WAR I; YOUTH MOVEMENTS

References

Germani, G. 1978. *Authoritarianism, Fascism, and National Populism*. New Brunswick, NJ: Transaction.

Koon, T. 1985. *Believe, Obey, Fight: The Political Socialisation of Youth in Fascist Italy*. London: University of North Carolina Press.

Mosse, George L. 1980. *Masses and Man: Nationalist and Fascist Perceptions of Reality*. New York: H. Fertig.

Reich, Wilhelm. 1997. *The Mass Psychology of Fascism*. London: Souvenir.

Schnapp, Jeffrey T. 1996. *Staging Fascism: 18BL and the Theater of Masses for the Masses*. Stanford: Stanford University Press.

MASTER RACE, THE: *See* ARYANISM

MATERIALISM

"The basic idea of fascism is the spiritual interpretation of history," wrote the British fascist and one-time secretary-general of the International Centre of Fascist Studies in Lausanne, James Strachey Barnes (1931, 43). And both Italian Fascism and Nazism were inclined to use a "spiritual" rhetoric in their propaganda. There was a clear intent in this to put themselves forward as the polar opposites of the Bolsheviks in their thinking. The "materialism" they had in mind to oppose was often the dialectical materialism that formed the basis of Marxism. They put themselves forward as having a much fuller and more satisfying view of humanity than their Bolshevik opponents, casting scorn on the materialist view of man as determined by his economic needs. They denied that economic improvements were the only motor of history and the only goal of human progress. As the *Enciclopedia italiana* article on the doctrine of fascism put it, "Fascism believes, now and always, in holiness and heroism, that is in acts in which no economic motive—remote or immediate—plays a part." The same article makes it clear that this kind of statement was also aimed at varieties of liberalism like utilitarianism that equated prosperity with happiness, "which would transform men into animals with one sole preoccupation: that of being well-fed and fat, degraded in consequence to a merely physical existence." For many Italian Fascists and German Nazis, this kind of materialism was one of the symptoms of decadence, which some of them identified with city life as opposed to the healthy life of the countryman.

Such "spiritual" rhetoric was calculated to allay the anxieties of those for whom religion was something to be treasured, or at least approved of. But the truth was that in Italian Fascist thinking the only physical manifestation of the spiritual "reality" was the state, which Fascism saw as a spiritual as well as a moral fact that made concrete "the political, juridical, economic organization of the nation." The author of the *Enciclopedia italiana* article went on to say that "such an organization is . . . a manifestation of the spirit. . . . The State is the . . . guardian and transmitter of the spirit of the people as it has been elaborated through the centuries in language, custom, faith." Individuals live and die, their existence is evanescent, but the state goes on; the state "transcends the brief limit of individual lives, represents the immanent conscience of the nation." In fascist thinking the state took over from the church or churches as the one transcendent body to which spiritual allegiance was owed. By presenting the state in this "spiritual," ethereal light, fascists were able to persuade individual citizens to channel their religious instincts into nationalistic fervor.

Although German Nazism was as much opposed to communist materialism as was Italian Fascism, it was also opposed to another type of "materialism," which it associated with Judaism and with the Catholic Church. Following in the footsteps of a strong tradition within Protestantism, it located the contrast between the Old Testament and the New as a polarity between a "materialistic" religion that focused on outward symbols and rituals and a "spiritual" religion of inwardness taught by Jesus. It believed that the Catholic Church had unfortunately lost sight of this new revelation very quickly and had been subjected to a Jewish takeover, so that it too had become a "materialistic" religion of rituals and externals. The Reformation had begun to bring this to light, but it was still contaminated by reverence for the Old Testament and by a belief in the need for a positive religion. Not until the elaboration of a truly Germanic religion of inwardness would the "materialistic" legacy finally be cast off. Unsurprisingly, this kind of thinking did not have much appeal to Italian Fascism, which came out of a totally different history and tradition.

There was a different version of the "materialism" thesis in Nazi thinking about aesthetics that drew inspiration from the likes of Richard Wagner, who praised German art and music for its depth and seriousness, contrasting it with French "materialism" and shallowness.

Cyprian Blamires

See Also: ACTUALISM; "ANTI-" DIMENSION OF FASCISM, THE; ANTI-SEMITISM; BOLSHEVISM; CATHOLIC CHURCH, THE; CHAMBERLAIN, HOUSTON STEWART; CHRISTIANITY; CULTURE (GERMANY); DECADENCE; ECONOMICS; FASCIST PARTY, THE; GENTILE, GIOVANNI; GERMANIC RELIGION; GERMANNESS; HERO, THE CULT OF THE; LIBERALISM (IN THEOLOGY); MARXISM; MUSIC (GERMANY); MYSTICISM; NAZISM; NORDIC SOUL, THE; RELIGION; ROSENBERG, ALFRED; RURALISM; SOUL; STATE, THE; UTILITARIANISM; WAGNER, (WILHELM) RICHARD; VITALISM; WAR; WARRIOR ETHOS, THE

References
Barnes, J. S. 1931. *Fascism.* London: Thornton Butterworth.
Griffin, R. 1991. *The Nature of Fascism.* London: Routledge.
Hughes, S. H. 1979. *Consciousness and Society: The Reorientation of European Social Thought, 1880–1930.* Brighton: Harvester.
Sternhell, Z. 1994. *The Birth of Fascist Ideology: From Cultural Rebellion to Political Revolution.* Princeton: Princeton University Press.

MATTEOTTI, GIACOMO (1885–1924)

Italian Socialist Party leader abducted and murdered by Fascist thugs in June 1924. As a parliamentary representative from northern Italy, Matteotti had witnessed at first hand the brutality of the Fascist squads. He denounced the outcome of the 1924 election, in which the Fascists won a two-thirds majority thanks to the use of widespread violence and intimidation. The discovery of Matteotti's body led to a wave of revulsion, and allegations of Mussolini's complicity provoked the "Matteotti Crisis," during which the Fascist government came close to being overthrown.

John Pollard

See Also: AVENTINE SECESSION, THE; FASCIST PARTY, THE; ITALY; MUSSOLINI, BENITO ANDREA; SOCIALISM; *SQUADRISMO;* VIOLENCE

References

Cannistraro, P. V. 1982. *Historical Dictionary of Fascist Italy.* Westport, CT: Greenwood.

Lyttelton, Adrian. 1973. *The Seizure of Power.* London: Weidenfeld and Nicholson.

MAURRAS, CHARLES (1868–1952)

Leading figure in the French Action Française movement in early twentieth-century France, often considered a forerunner or inspiration for Italian Fascism. After graduating he moved to Paris, where he collaborated on numerous newspapers and reviews, during which time he met Barrès, who became his friend. Maurras supported Boulangism and was impressed by Drumont, contributing to his *La Libre Parole.* In the wake of the Dreyfus Affair, Maurras co-founded the Action Française movement, which became the vehicle for the articulation of his integral nationalism.

The system of ideas propagated by Maurras was an original synthesis of elements drawn from the counterrevolutionary tradition of Bonald, Maistre, and Le Play, from Comtean positivism, and from the scientism of Taine, articulating a fusion of nationalism and traditionalism in which the nation was united around the figure of the king. In the period up to and including World War I, Maurras's integral nationalist ideas were expounded in a plethora of books, most notably the *Enquête sur la Monarchie* (1900), which had a major influence on nationalist milieux, as well as a number published during World War I. Maurras also produced a number of studies of Catholicism during this period: *La Politique religieuse* (1912) and *L'Action française et la religion catholique,* which increased Maurras's difficulties with Rome. Conflict with the Catholic hierarchy reached a peak in 1926, when Rome forbade all Catholics to have anything to do with the organization, a sanction that was lifted only in 1939 by Pope Pius XII.

The violent actions of the AF led to several of the leadership being taken to court. Maurras was no exception, being condemned to eight months in prison in 1912, given a one-year suspended sentence in 1929 for death threats aimed at the home office minister, Abraham Schrameck, and being given a further eight-month prison term in 1936 for threatening reprisals against the 140 MPs that had voted for sanctions against Italy for invading Abyssinia. He entered the Académie Française in 1938. The following year, opposed to a war that he judged France to be in no position to win, Maurras rallied to Pétain after the Armistice, publishing a number of books in which the same ideas continued to be expounded. Arrested after the liberation, Maurras was condemned on 27 January 1945 by the Court of Justice in Lyons to "solitary confinement for life" and national degradation for having "intelligence with the enemy." He was expelled from the Académie Française.

Steve Bastow

See Also: ACTION FRANÇAISE; BARRES, AUGUSTE MAURICE; BOULANGISM; CATHOLIC CHURCH, THE; DREYFUS CASE, THE; DRUMONT, EDOUARD ADOLPHE; ETHIOPIA; FASCIST PARTY, THE; FRANCE; INTEGRAL NATIONALISM; ITALY; MONARCHISM; MONARCHY; NATIONALISM; PETAIN, MARSHAL HENRI PHILIPPE; PIUS XII, POPE; POSITIVISM; PROTOFASCISM; TRADITIONALISM; WORLD WAR I

References

Carroll, D. 1995. *French Literary Fascism.* Princeton: Princeton University Press.

Nolte, E. 1969. *Three Faces of Fascism: Action Française, Italian Fascism, National Socialism.* New York: Signet.

Weber, E. 1962. *Action Française: Royalism and Reaction in Twentieth Century France.* Palo Alto: Stanford University Press.

MECHANISTIC THINKING

The adjective "mechanistic"—for which there is no equivalent commonly used abstract noun in English—was a term of abuse in the vocabulary of interwar fascism. It was associated with ideas such as abstraction, rationalism, individualism, and positivism. It was associated with scientism as an attitude of mind embodied in nineteenth-century positivism, according to which science understood in a narrow empiricist sense should provide the pattern and the template for the procedures of all our knowing and thinking. There was a general turn away from scientistic philosophies in the years after World War I, and fascism was a part of that movement. In place of mechanistic thought fascist ideologues preferred philosophies marked by organicism and vitalism. The Nazis were undoubtedly influenced by the voluntarism of Schopenhauer and Nietzsche and the Italian Fascists by the actualism of Gentile.

Cyprian Blamires

See Also: ABSTRACTION; ACTUALISM; COSMOPOLITANISM; FASCIST PARTY, THE; GENTILE, GIOVANNI; INDIVIDUALISM; MATERIALISM; NAZISM; NIETZSCHE, FRIEDRICH; NORDIC SOUL, THE; ORGANICISM; POSITIVISM; RATIONALISM; SCHOPENHAUER, ARTHUR; SCIENCE; SOUL; VITALISM; VOLUNTARISM

References

Gregor, A. James. 2005. *Mussolini's Intellectuals: Fascist Social and Political Thought.* Princeton: Princeton University Press.

Hughes, S. H. 1961. *Consciousness and Society.* New York: Vintage.

MEDIA, THE: *See* FILM; PRESS, THE; PROPAGANDA; RADIO; *VÖLKISCHER BEOBACHTER,* THE

MEDICINE (Germany)

Nazism had a deep impact on German medicine: medical organizations were reconstructed on a nazified basis, and physicians were expected to research, teach, and practice medicine on a racial basis. The process of *Gleichschaltung* meant appointing Nazi medical activists to influential positions in the administration and organization of medicine. It also meant the segregation and (at first) expulsion of those deemed to be Jewish, and discriminatory measures against persons of part-Jewish ancestry or persons simply married to Jews. Political opponents of National Socialism were liable to arrest and persecution. *Gleichschaltung* was extended to annexed areas of the Saar, Czechoslovakia, and Austria, where some degree of autonomy was maintained by authorities that were enthusiastically Nazi. Medicine contributed to the identification and extermination of racial undesirables in the Holocaust.

Doctors were enthusiastic Nazis. By 1937 more than 40 percent of physicians had joined the NSDAP; some 7 percent joined the SS. While women's participation in the medical profession had greatly increased to more than 10 percent by 1939, they too supported Nazism.

Nazification of public health meant ending the divide between state and municipal health organizations. The new health offices took a key role in pressing for sterilization and other racial aspects of health policy. A high proportion of German doctors were expelled for racial reasons (primarily for Jewish ancestry), or politics. Left-wing doctors and advocates of birth control and unorthodox forms of eugenics went into exile. Few non-Jewish Germans left voluntarily. Among the academics were the pharmacologist Otto Krayer and the embryologist Johannes Holtfreter. Jewish physicians holding a university post were dismissed. Exceptionally, the half-Jewish biochemist Otto Warburg was retained in office throughout the Third Reich. Jewish doctors were rapidly excluded from sickness insurances. They were forced to treat only Jewish patients, and were redesignated *Krankenbehaendler* ("therapists of the sick"). Some Jewish medical and dental students were allowed to complete their degrees on condition that they emigrated. About 10 percent had their medical degrees abolished. Some 4,500 to 6,000 German Jewish doctors were forced to emigrate, an estimated 5 percent committed suicide, and approximately 2,000 were killed in the Holocaust. France and Belgium were important countries in assisting medical refugees, although to date that has not been studied. The largest numbers of medical refugees reached the United States, where they had to overcome professional resistance. Palestine and the United Kingdom took a higher proportion per head of population, although Britain played a negative role in curbing immigration to Palestine. Approximately 850 German physicians settled in the United Kingdom, and about 420 Austrians. All medical refugees had difficulties in obtaining permission to practice abroad. Britain recognized all foreign degrees from late 1941.

Race became a central category of medicine, applied to physiology, genetics, mind, and metabolism. Eugenic racism assisted a shift toward chronic degenerative diseases. Thus Nazis gave increased attention to cancer, establishing a new Reich organization for cancer research. Epidemiological analysis of the correlation between tobacco consumption and lung cancer was an example of a successful piece of research that at the time gained little attention. At the same time, cancer research was a cover for biological warfare research. The Nazis prioritized early diagnosis of tuberculosis by means of mobile X-ray units. Despite the expulsion of Jewish and dissident researchers, medical research was intensified during the 1930s. However, when war was declared, research was seriously weakened. Nazi medicine remained pluralistic, with strong lobbies for nature therapy and homeopathy. Himmler was renowned for his support for alternative medicine such as homeopathy and nature therapy, and he was also interested in anthroposophy and ideas of reincarnation. Unconventional areas of medicine received increased official recognition from the Nazi state, notably with qualifications for nature therapists. But all types of health care were subject to Nazi racism and to ideas of racial biology.

University medical faculties offered allegiance to the regime but retained some autonomy. Tensions arose with incursions of the SS. The University of Jena was heavily nazified, but the process was uneven. This is seen with the difficulties of the SS researcher Rascher, who undertook murderous physiological experiments in concentration camps to secure a *Habilitation* (higher degree). The universities of Munich and Marburg declined to accept Rascher, although the Reich University of Strassburg was prepared to accept him. That was where medical professors carried out experiments at the concentration camp of Natzweiler. The numbers of medical students remained high. Students were exposed to strong dosages of Nazi propaganda, most universities had lectures in racial hygiene, and students were attracted into organizations such as the SA and SS. There were some foreign medical students: Norwegian medical students were held hostage in Buchenwald.

Physicians' organizations were consolidated and nazified. Karl Haedenkamp was a veteran of the antisocialist Hartmannbund and the Deutschnationale Volkspartei (German National People's Party), and an activist in purging Jews from the medical profession. He was himself ousted by Nazis in 1939. The National Socialist Physicians' League recruited Nazi activists. Resistance was more limited. Certain doctors used the cover of their practices for illegal meetings. The psychoanalyst John Rittmeister and the "White Rose" medical students Hans and Sophie Scholl were among those executed. Other physicians refused to comply with regulations such as the exclusion of Jewish patients or the registration of cases of hereditary disease.

By 1940 many researchers had been dispatched to frontline units. A shortage of laboratory animals and a willingness to exploit human material deemed surplus meant that the human experiments in concentration camps rapidly increased in 1941, reaching a high point in 1944. Researchers shifted from military to general scientific problems, and especially in 1944–1945, a large number of women and children were victims. Since the pioneering reconstruction by Schwarberg of how twenty children previously used for tuberculosis

research were killed in April 1945, there has been an increasing amount of historical research on German medicine under National Socialism. Yet many interpretative issues and quantitative dimensions remain open. We lack a definitive number of victims of human experiments and associated atrocities, although the number must amount to more than 10,000. The Allies were left with an immense historical puzzle in terms of reconstructing what happened in German medicine under the Nazis. This was made more difficult by restrictions on access to archives and widespread indifference in the 1950s and 1960s. Despite a steady increase of historical research since 1977 on medicine under National Socialism, we still lack much information about the medical perpetrators of racial atrocities, the victims of various categories of Nazi medical war crimes and racial atrocities, and health conditions in the Third Reich.

Paul Weindling

See Also: ANTI-SEMITISM; AUSTRIA; CZECHOSLOVAKIA; CONCENTRATION CAMPS; DEMOGRAPHIC POLICY; EUGENICS; EUTHANASIA; FAMILY, THE; GERMANY; *GLEICHSCHALTUNG;* HEALTH; HIMMLER, HEINRICH; HOLOCAUST, THE; HOMOSEXUALITY; MENGELE, JOSEF; NAZISM; RACIAL DOCTRINE; RACISM; SEXUALITY; SOCIAL DARWINISM; SS, THE; THIRD REICH, THE; UNIVERSITIES (GERMANY); WHITE ROSE; WOMEN

References
Gumpert, M. 1940. *Heil Hunger! Health under Hitler.* London: Allen and Unwin.
Kater, M. 1989. *Doctors under Hitler.* London: North Carolina University Press.
Leibfried, S., and F. Tennstedt. 1979. *Berufsverbote und Sozialpolitik 1933.* Bremen: University Press.
Lilienthal, G. 1985. *Der "Lebensborn e.V." Ein Instrument nationalsozialistischer* Rassenpolitik. Stuttgart: G. Fischer.
Schwarberg, G. 1984. *The Murders at Bullenhuser Damm.* Bloomington: Indiana University Press.
Weindling, P. 1989. *Health, Race and German Politics between National Unification and Nazism 1870–1945.* Cambridge: Cambridge University Press.

MEDICINE (Italy)

The Italian Fascist government made some significant changes to the medical system inherited from its Liberal predecessors. It created many governmental and parastatal organizations, and it centralized and standardized the system to a greater extent. However, despite the regime's propagandistic boasts, the health sector remained fragmented, chaotic, and poorly funded. There was considerable continuity from the Liberal period to the Fascist era. Little medical care was offered by the state directly; communes, provinces, mutual aid societies, and charities were responsible for most services. Communes ran hospitals, employed general practitioners, and provided free or subsidized assistance to their poorest residents. Religious orders and charities also ran many hospitals. The prevention and treatment of "social diseases" became a top priority for the regime. Malaria and tuberculosis were the most deadly of these, particularly afflicting peasants and urban workers. Fascism continued the Liberal antimalaria campaign but limited the distribution of quinine and instead focused on marshland drainage. Grand schemes around Rome and in northern Italy were prioritized over assisting the malaria-plagued south. The proclaimed victory over malaria was partial at best. Many clinics and dispensaries were established for the treatment of social diseases such as syphilis and trachoma. These were run by communes but were at least partly state funded, offering free care and medicines.

The Fascists introduced a greater degree of compulsion into the health system. Word of the incidence of certain infectious diseases had to be communicated to authorities, and the 1934 *Testo Unico* (new health laws) allowed for the mandatory hospitalization of patients with such diseases. The regime claimed to be especially concerned with the health of workers. Many new organizations were established to insure workers against accident and illness. In reality, the multitude of organizations and the complexity of the regulations meant that relatively few workers received the care that they were entitled to. Under Fascism, doctors gained greater prominence as important players in the demographic and social welfare campaigns. Both specialists and general practitioners were required to join Fascist syndicates, but some existing professional bodies flourished with regime support. Since Italian Fascism was not burdened with a powerful racial doctrine of the kind adopted by German Nazism, there was not the same ideological impact on the field of medicine in Italy that there was in Germany.

Meredith Carew

See Also: DEMOGRAPHIC POLICY; EUGENICS; FASCIST PARTY, THE; HEALTH; ITALY; MEDICINE (GERMANY); RACIAL DOCTRINE; WELFARE

References
Cosmacini, Giorgio. 1989. *Medicina e Sanità in Italia nel Ventesimo Secolo: dalla "Spagnola" alla II Guerra Mondiale.* Bari: Laterza.
Snowden, Frank. 1999. "Fields of Death: Malaria in Italy, 1861–1962." *Modern Italy* 4 (1999): 25–57.
Zamagni, Vera. 1993. *The Economic History of Italy, 1860–1990: Recovery after Decline.* Oxford: Clarendon.

MEIN KAMPF

The title (*My Struggle*) of the work in which Adolf Hitler set out his philosophy and his vision for Germany. It was published in two volumes, the first on 19 July 1925, the second on 11 December 1926. By 1929 the first volume had sold about 23,000 copies and the second about 13,000. In 1930 the publisher, Max Amann (a sergeant-major in Hitler's regiment in World War I), brought out the work in a single volume that sold 62,000 in one year. By the end of 1933, more than 1.5 million copies had been sold. By 1934 the book figured among school primers, and in 1936 the Ministry of the Interior recommended that registrars present a copy to every bridal couple. Total sales in Hitler's lifetime were probably around 8 to 9 million. The first English translation was an abridgement, and the complete text did not become available until 1938. Versions appeared in the 1920s, 1930s, and early 1940s in at least ten European languages, as well as in Arabic, Chinese, and Japanese.

The title was actually Max Amann's idea—the author's projected title was *Four and a Half Years of Struggle against Lies, Stupidity and Cowardice.* The book consists of autobiographical recollections intermingled with reflections on political and social principles. Hitler begins by noting the significance of his birthplace, Braunau on the Inn, on the boundary between Bavaria and Austria. The importance of this becomes clear when he gives an account of his student years in Vienna. It was in Vienna that he discovered the reality of the Austro-Hungarian Empire, an empire in decay, an empire crippled by centrifugal forces of its constituent parts, an empire in which the German peoples were downtrodden and victimized. It was this experience that first developed his German nationalistic feelings. It was also Vienna that converted him into an anti-Semite, since he witnessed what seemed to him Jewish control of Social Democratic agitation, of the world of the press, and of prostitution in the city. His experience of the Social Democrats showed him the power of fanatical determination allied to a readiness to use violence, and he grew cynical about the purposes of the leaders. He found that although he could have rational arguments with almost anybody from whatever class, his attempts to debate with Jews were always a waste of time and got him nowhere. He realized that part of the success of the Social Democrats had to do with their mastery of oratory and their readiness to address the masses. He noted that liberal leaders tended to be middle class and to rely on the printed word, which was read only by other bourgeois.

Then came the crucial wartime experience. Hitler noted that his generation, who set out for the front in 1914, soon turned from youngsters to old soldiers. He observed the power of Allied propaganda and grew enraged by the feebleness of what was produced by his own side. He sensed that the Allies understood that you must exaggerate one negative fact about the enemy to the utmost—in this case, the atrocities of the Hun. This gave steel to the Allied troops and also prepared them to fight a vicious enemy. His own side used the weapon of mockery, but the troops in the field discovered that their opponents were extremely tough and consequently felt let down by what they had been told. As the war progressed, Hitler also saw the effectiveness of the Allied thrust to drive a wedge between Prussia and the rest—putting all the blame on the one side in order to embitter the other. He received news of the German capitulation when in the hospital after a gas attack and was shocked to the core. He accepted the popular explanation of betrayal by Jewish propagandists and intellectuals who sapped the will of the government and the middle classes to continue the war, but he also acknowledged the underlying decay that allowed all this to happen. Germany was being undermined by the Jews, and the governing classes were cowardly and irresolute.

After the war he became increasingly drawn to politics and increasingly convinced of the centrality of the racial question. Following a well-established type of racial ideology that went back at least to the French nineteenth-century thinker Gobineau, he argued that a superior race that allowed itself to interbreed would decay, and the preservation of the purity of the German race was the prime responsibility of the German state. This truth was not widely admitted, and the failure to face it was one of the main reasons for the defeat. Racial theory must be the foundation of a new political order. Young Germans must be indoctrinated in their role in the preservation of racial purity. There should be no truck with compassion for cripples or mental defectives. The birth rate had been declining since the previous century because people were having fewer children by deliberate policy; one result was that they fussed too much about the survival of the few children they did have—hence a reluctance to deal with defective offspring.

Western-style democracy with its electoral and parliamentary obsessions was a sham. Hitler had been inoculated against parliamentarism by his experiences of observing political debates in Vienna, which had induced in him nothing but contempt for the parliamentary system. He believed that great things come from great individual personalities, not from assemblies. The aristocratic mode was the only one appropriate for Germanic peoples, and that involved individual rulers surrounded by advisers. Trade unions were certainly allowable, but only to prevent abuses in the workplace. Germany's future rulers needed to realize that the masses must be won over, and on two occasions in the book Hitler writes of them as being like women who respond to a strong man better than to a weak one. Marxism was the big enemy of the day, but it could not be put down simply by force. A philosophy can be defeated only by another force that also has a philosophy. Hitler joyfully describes the way in which he defeated Marxist provocateurs who attempted to break up his meetings by good preparation and the disciplined use of force. This method was often able to get the better of a much larger number of opponents. One of the things he stresses in the book is the role of conviction, will, and resolve, which can enable a well-organized and well-motivated minority to topple a majority. He has a poor opinion of his German contemporaries but sees them as victims of Jewish manipulators. He does not elaborate a systematic anti-Semitic theory but dismisses the Jews as aliens who can simply never become Germans. The old religious anti-Judaism is feeble; what is needed is a frank recognition that the Jews are an enemy that cannot be accommodated or allowed into a Germanic society. They are unstable, dishonest, greedy, and manipulative. Their aim is world domination, and the Jewish religion is simply a tool to enable them to achieve this.

Unlike Rosenberg, Hitler shows a grudging respect for the Catholic Church, whose inner strength he respects. He notes that celibacy rules require the Church to replenish herself in every generation, which she does from the ranks of the poor, and that creates a sympathy between the poor and the Church that is one of the foundations of her influence. He is, however, very clear about the need to keep politics and religion entirely separate, and disclaims any intention to interfere in ecclesiastical affairs. Hitler is very aware of the crucial role of the masses in politics, but not simply as fodder for exploitation. His time in Vienna showed him the horror of the daily life of the laboring poor in a big city and sensitized him to the big social issues. He saw that any serious political party must plan to address these if it was to have any success.

A study of *Mein Kampf* is very helpful for an understanding of how Hitler came to power. It shows an astonishing combination of ruthless logic, awareness of political realities, and powers of organization. It leaves a distinct impression that the war experience of Hitler and his contemporaries was of the utmost importance for what came after the war. Battle-hardened veterans felt that parliamentarism had betrayed them and could not bring themselves to support the republic. They looked for something to believe in after the shock of the defeat, and Hitler offered them pride in their nation, a set of simple principles they could understand, and organizations to join that offered some semblance of the camaraderie of the trenches.

Markus Hattstein (translated by Cyprian Blamires)

See Also: ANTI-SEMITISM; ARISTOCRACY; ARYANISM; AUSTRIA; AUSTRO-HUNGARIAN EMPIRE/HABSBURG EMPIRE, THE; BLOOD; BOLSHEVISM; BOURGEOISIE, THE; CATHOLIC CHURCH, THE; CONSPIRACY THEORIES; COSMOPOLITANISM; DEMOCRACY; DEMOGRAPHIC POLICY; ELITE THEORY; EUGENICS; GERMANNESS (*DEUTSCHHEIT*); GERMANY; GOBINEAU, COMTE ARTHUR DE; HERO, THE CULT OF THE; HITLER, ADOLF; LIBERALISM; LIEBENFELS, JÖRG ADOLF JOSEF LANZ VON; LUEGER, KARL; MACHIAVELLI, NICCOLÒ; MARXISM; MASSES, THE ROLE OF THE; NATIONALISM; NAZISM; NOVEMBER CRIMINALS/*NOVEMBERBRECHER*, THE; PARLIAMENTARISM; PROPAGANDA; RACIAL DOCTRINE; ROSENBERG, ALFRED; SLAVS, THE (AND GERMANY); SOCIAL DARWINISM; TRADES UNIONS; VERSAILLES, THE TREATY OF; WAR VETERANS; WARRIOR ETHOS, THE; WORLD WAR I

References

Caspar, C. 1958. "Mein Kampf: A Best Seller." *Jewish Historical Studies* 20, no. 1, pp. 3–16.
Kershaw, Ian. 1998. *Hitler, 1889–1936: Hubris.* London: Allen Lane.
Watt, D. C. 1974. *Hitler's Mein Kampf.* Trans. Ralph Mannheim. London: Hutchinson.

MENGELE, JOSEF (1911–1979)

Nazi doctor nicknamed the "Angel of Death," notorious for his medical experiments on concentration camp inmates. His name has gone down in history as the embodiment of the terrifyingly amoral inhumanity generated by the Nazi philosophy and view of life in the sphere of the perversion of medicine. He was born in Günzburg in Bavaria, where his father had founded a farm machinery factory. Mengele studied philosophy and medicine and later joined the SS. He focused on the study of (supposed) racial characteristics and genetics. In 1943, after having served as the doctor of the SS *Viking* division (1941), he became senior consultant in Auschwitz where, together with other doctors, he was responsible for selecting victims for his barbarous human experiments from those arriving on deportation trains, and for sending many others straight to the gas chambers. He was especially interested in conducting medical experiments on twins, and one of his projects involved sewing together two Gypsy children to create Siamese twins. The completely inhuman brutality of his behavior at Auschwitz was remembered by witnesses as outstanding. After the war Mengele escaped via Rome to Latin America and took an assumed name. Information from friends and family led in 1985 to the exhumation of the remains of a man drowned in Brazil six years earlier; an international team of forensic experts unanimously concluded that this had been Mengele.

Fabian Virchow and Cyprian Blamires

See Also: AUSCHWITZ; CONCENTRATION CAMPS; EUGENICS; EUTHANASIA; GERMANY; HOLOCAUST, THE; MEDICINE; NAZISM; RACIAL DOCTRINE; ROMA AND SINTI, THE; SS, THE

References

Cefrey, Holly. 2001. *Dr. Josef Mengele: The Angel of Death.* New York: Rosen.
Grabowski, John F. 2004. *Heroes & Villains: Josef Mengele.* San Diego, CA: Lucent.
Posner, Gerald, and John Ware. 1986. *Mengele: The Complete Story.* London: Macdonald.

MESKÓ, ZOLTÁN (1883–1959)

Fascist leader in interwar Hungary. Meskó attended a military academy in Vienna and became an MP supported by the Independence Party in 1917. In 1919 he assisted in organizing the National Army, a move that later earned him various high-level positions in different ministries (Agriculture, Internal Affairs). Meskó's populist idea was to elevate the peasantry by solving rural misery, and in order to achieve this, on 16 June 1932 he organized his fascist party, the Hungarian National Socialist Agrarian and Workers' Party (Magyar Nemzeti Szocialista Földmuves és Munkás Párt). He published the party's newspaper, the *National Word* (*Nemzet Szava*), and can also be credited with the implementation of the arrow cross symbol to be used together with the green shirt in Hungary. Meskó was a chief architect of the Society for Name Hungarianization, a racist intellectual association. In 1933 he was able to have a meeting with Hitler. He was a fervent supporter of Regent Horthy, and in his party the greeting was: "With God for the Fatherland. Loyalty to the Regent!" In 1946 he was sentenced to life imprisonment but was eventually pardoned; he died soon after his release. (Meskó should not be confused with another politician and physician of the same name who was a member of Hungary's upper house during the interwar period.)

László Kürti

See Also: ARROW CROSS, THE; FARMERS; GERMANY; HITLER, ADOLF; HORTHY DE NAGYBÁNYA, MIKLÓS; HUNGARY; NATIONALISM; NAZISM; RACIAL DOCTRINE; RURALISM

References

Braham, R. L. 1981. *The Politics of Genocide.* New York: Columbia University Press.
Lackó, Miklós. 1966. *Nyilasok, nemzetiszocialisták 1935–1944* [*Arrow Cross Members, National Socialists 1935–1944*]. Budapest: Kossuth.
Macartney, C. A. 1961. *October Fifteenth.* Edinburgh: Edinburgh University Press.
Nagy-Talavera, N. M. 1970. *The Green Shirts and Others.* Stanford: Stanford University Press.
Szirmai, Rezso. 1993 [1946]. *Fasiszta lelkek. Pszihoanalitikus beszélgetések a háborús fobunösökkel a börtönben* [*Fascist Souls: Psychoanalytical Conversations with Major War Criminals in Jail*]. Budapest: Pelikán.

METAXAS, GENERAL IOANNIS (1871–1941)

Fascistic dictator of Greece in the late 1930s (the Fourth of August regime). Growing up in a conservative, proroyalist family, Metaxas followed a military career. In 1913 he was promoted to the rank of chief of staff and served as advisor to King Constantine during the Balkans Wars (1912–1913) and World War I

(1914–1917). His patrician background and personal attachment to the Gluecksburg royal family of Greece, as well as his admiration for Prussian military values, were in sharp contrast to the new, modernizing, and decidedly bourgeois political style of Eleftherios Venizelos, who dominated Greek politics from the years following 1910 until the early 1930s. Metaxas opposed the latter's expedition in Asia Minor (1919–1922), and in 1924 he became the leader of the small conservative/royalist party Eleftherofrones. In April 1936, Metaxas was appointed prime minister by the palace and subsequently plotted with King George the suspension of the parliamentary system. On 4 August 1936 he established a dictatorship with strong fascist tendencies. He resisted the temptation to align Greece to the Axis powers, however, upholding King George's pro-British outlook in foreign affairs but also striving to follow an equidistant policy vis-à-vis the two emerging coalitions in Europe. In October 1940 he responded to the Italian ultimatum (demand for occupation of strategic points in Greece by the Italian army) by declaring war on Italy.

Aristotle Kallis

See Also: AXIS, THE; CONSERVATISM; DICTATORSHIP; GREECE; ITALY; MONARCHISM; MONARCHY; PARLIAMENTARISM; WORLD WAR I; WORLD WAR II

References

Higham, R., and T. Veremis. 1993. *The Metaxas Dictatorship: Aspects of Greece 1936–1940.* Athens: Hellenic Foundation for Defense and Foreign Policy.
Kofas, J. V. 1983. *Authoritarianism in Greece: The Metaxas Regime.* Boulder, NY: Eastern European Monographs.
Vatikiotis, P. J. 1998. *Popular Autocracy in Greece, 1936–41: A Political Biography of General Ioannis Metaxas.* London: Frank Cass.

MEXICO

During the interwar years and World War II, the fascist phenomenon impacted in Mexico in three areas: opposition to the most radical tendencies in the Mexican Revolution, the search for a new political model by the national ruling class, and the activities of the fascist states—above all in the organization of the Italian and German expatriate communities. The urban and rural middle classes opposed to socialism and agrarian reform looked early for a model in European fascism. In 1922, Gustavo Sáenz de Sicilia founded the Partido

Fascista Mexicano (Mexican Fascist Party), a conservative, Catholic, antirevolutionary but not violent political movement. International circumstances (the Depression, the Spanish Civil War, and the leftist radical shift in the country during *cardenismo,* from 1934 to 1940) impelled the formation of several nationalist and anticommunist movements with fascist tendencies, such as the Unión Nacional de Veteranos de la Revolución (National Union of Veterans of the Revolution, 1935), the Confederación de la Clase Media (Middle Class Confederation, 1936), the Partido Social Democrático Mexicano (Mexican Social Democratic Party, 1937), and, mainly, the Acción Revolucionaria Mexicanista (Mexicanist Revolutionary Action, 1934) of Nicolás Rodríguez, openly violent and anti-Semitic, whose members were known as "golden shirts." In 1937 was founded the most important opposition movement: the Unión Nacional Sinarquista, inspired by the Spanish Falange, with a half-million members in 1941, mostly radical Catholic and nationalist peasants with urban middle-class leaders.

Fascism also had an impact on some intellectuals and artists, such as José Vasconcelos and Gerardo Murillo, and on politicians such as the president and *Jefe Máximo,* Plutarco Elías Calles, the governor of Sonora, Román Yocupicio, and General Saturnino Cedillo. Meanwhile the Mexican government sought in fascist corporatism an inspiration for the reactivation of the economy and the reorganization of the state.

German and Italian politics in Mexico was focused on commercial relationships, propaganda, protection of nationals, and monitoring antifascist and U.S. activities. Rumors of Axis conspiracies and a subversive fascist "fifth column" mostly lacked foundation. The small Italian and German colonies grouped around the local sections of their own national fascist parties, coordinated with the respective legations, consulates, and other community organizations. Among the Spaniards the Falange had an important presence.

Franco Savarino

See Also: "ANTI-" DIMENSION OF FASCISM, THE; ANTI-SEMITISM; AXIS, THE; BOLSHEVISM; CATHOLIC CHURCH, THE; CONSPIRACY THEORIES; CORPORATISM; FALANGE; FARMERS; FASCIST PARTY, THE; GERMANY; ITALY; MARXISM; NATIONALISM; NAZISM; SOCIALISM; SPANISH CIVIL WAR, THE; WALL STREET CRASH, THE; WORLD WAR II

References
Savarino, Franco. 2002. "The Sentinel of the Bravo: Italian Fascism in Mexico, 1922–35." Pp. 97–120 in *International Fascism,* edited by Gert Sorensen and Robert Mallet. London: Frank Cass.
Schuler, Friedrich E. 1998. *Mexico between Hitler and Roosevelt: Mexican Foreign Politics in the Age of Lázaro Cárdenas, 1934–1940.* Albuquerque: University of New Mexico Press.
Sherman, John W. 1997. *The Mexican Right.* Westport, CT: Praeger.

MICHELS, ROBERTO (1876–1936)

Leading sociologist and economist and supporter of Mussolini whose belief in an "iron law of oligarchy"—that organizations competing for power will tend to develop in an oligarchical direction—offered clear justification for dictatorships. Michels was born in Cologne into a well-to-do business family. He studied at the French lycée in Berlin, then in England and France, and finally in Munich. He graduated at Halle in 1900 with the historian Droysen. From his youth he was a militant in the Socialist Party, which brought on him the hostility of the academic authorities and made it difficult for him to acquire a university teaching position. In 1901, thanks to the support of Max Weber, he obtained his first post as professor at the University of Marburg.

Michels had very close contacts with socialist circles in Belgium, Italy, and France. Between 1904 and 1908 he collaborated in the monthly Le Mouvement Socialiste and participated as a delegate in various social democratic congresses. At this period his encounter with Georges Sorel, Edouard Berth, and the Italian revolutionary syndicalists Arturo Labriola and Enrico Leone was decisive. It was under the influence of syndicalism that he began to rethink theoretical Marxism and to propose a critique of the reformism of the socialist leaders. The activistic, voluntaristic, and antiparliamentarian conception that Michels had of socialism could not be reconciled with the parliamentaristic, legalitarian, and bureaucratic development of the social democratic movement. He was particularly influenced by the critique of democracy put forward by Gaetano Mosca and Vilfredo Pareto, the two chief exponents of the Italian "Machiavelli" school.

In 1905, Max Weber invited Michels to collaborate with the prestigious review *Archiv fur Sozialwissenschaft und Sozialpolitik.* In 1907 he obtained a chair at the University of Turin, where he became personally acquainted with Mosca and came into contact with the economist Luigi Einaudi and the positivist anthropologist Cesare Lombroso. In the years that followed, Michels was working on his fundamental *Sociologie des parteiwesens* (1911). Also in 1911, during the war in Libya, Michels took up a position in favor of the imperial projects of Italy and against German expansionism. He began to draw close to the Italian nationalist movement, and his relations with Weber deteriorated irremediably. Before the outbreak of World War I in 1914, he transferred to the University of Basle in Switzerland. In 1922, Michels greeted the victory of Mussolini and Fascism and the destruction of the liberal system sympathetically. He returned to Italy for good in 1928 to take up the chair of political economy at the University of Perugia. At this time he gave numerous lectures and courses, publishing a great number of books and articles, both in Italy and abroad, in which he gave his open support for the dictatorship of Mussolini. Michels came to a position of support for Fascism as a result of his revision of Marxist determinism and his belief in the inevitably oligarchical and bureaucratic degeneration of democracy. Together with Sorel, Lagardelle, and de Man, he contributed to demolish from the theoretical point of view the mechanistic, reductionistic, and economistic foundation of Marxist thought, proposing a conception of political action based on the idea of the nation (instead of on class) and on the will to power of minorities. On the sociological level, he contributed to the formulation of a "law" according to which every social organization—for example, parties and syndicates—involves the risk of an oligarchical degeneration: the larger and more complex the organization, the more decisive becomes the role of organized minorities. In other words, mass democracy and organization are technically incompatible.

An internationalist in his youth, Michels also understood the propulsive role assumed at the start of the twentieth century by the myth of the nation, a sentiment capable much more than humanitarian universalism of mobilizing the masses and favoring their integration into the structure of the state. He also noted, again following Weber, the fundamental role in history and politics of charisma and great personalities. From the point of view of economic analysis, Michels's rigorously historical and antiformalistic approach led him to criticize the theoretical inconsistency of the liberal *Homo economicus;* according to Michels there do not in fact exist abstract rational economic subjects but only concrete social actors, bearers of specific historically determined interests. At the same time he criti-

cized the radically conflictual interpretation of economic dynamisms typical of Marxism, arguing for the regulatory and equilibratory role of the state and the necessity for a close collaboration between the various social categories. For this reason he came to support the practical utility and doctrinal foundedness of the corporatism encouraged by Fascism. Perhaps his most important text in the years of his militant Fascism was the *Corso di sociologia politica* ("Political Sociology Course"), published in 1926. In this volume, developing his elitist vision of politics, he theorized the figure of the "charismatic leader" who draws his strength directly from investiture by the people, and is thus in a position to extend his own legitimacy to the whole political order.

Alessandro Campi
(translated by Cyprian Blamires)

See Also: ABSTRACTION; ACTUALISM; CLASS; CORPORATISM; COSMOPOLITANISM; ECONOMICS; EGALITARIANISM; ELITE THEORY; FASCIST PARTY, THE; HERO, THE CULT OF THE; INDIVIDUALISM; ITALY; LAW; LEADER CULT, THE; LIBERALISM; LIBYA; MACHIAVELLI, NICCOLÒ; MAN, HENDRIK/HENRI DE; MARXISM; MASSES, THE ROLE OF THE; MATERIALISM; MECHANISTIC THINKING; MOSCA, GAETANO; MUSSOLINI, BENITO ANDREA; NATIONALISM; PARETO, VILFREDO; PARLIAMENTARISM; SOCIALISM; SOCIOLOGY; SOREL, GEORGES; STATE, THE; SYNDICALISM; WORLD WAR I

References

Ghiringhelli, R. 1992. *Elitism and Democracy: Mosca, Pareto and Michels.* Milan: Cisalpino.
Hughes, S. H. 1979. *Consciousness and Society: The Reorientation of European Social Thought, 1880–1930.* Brighton: Harvester.
Nye, R. A. 1977. *The Anti-Democratic Sources of Elite Theory: Pareto, Mosca, Michels.* London: Sage.

MIDDLE EAST, THE

After World War I, Arab nationalists and pan-Arabists became increasingly radicalized, anti-British, and anti-French. A mandate system had been set up by the terms of the Treaty of Versailles to administer the former overseas possessions of Turkey, and that was treated as a betrayal of wartime promises given by the British and the French to their Arab wartime allies (among them, the McMahon Pledge to create a united Arab state after the war). Another example of betrayal was considered

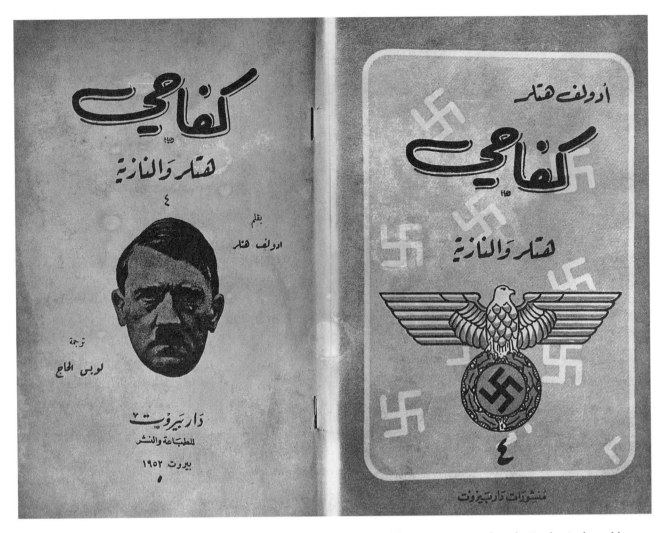

Arabic edition of Hitler's Mein Kampf. *Anti-Semitism gave the ideology of the Nazis a particular edge in the Arab world, where the infamous 'Protocols of the Elders of Zion' continues to circulate. (Hulton-Deutsch Collection/Corbis)*

to be the Balfour Declaration to bring about a Jewish homeland in Palestine at the cost of its Arab inhabitants. In 1919 there was an insurrection in Egypt, in 1920 an uprising in Iraq (both anti-British), and also the establishment of an Arab government in Damascus (toppled by the French in July 1920). In the case of Palestine, and in the atmosphere of the pro-Jewish Balfour Declaration, one of the dominant Palestinian families, al-Husaini, inclined toward Fascist Italy. Fascist and—later—Nazi ideas became an alternative among such radical organizations as the Egyptian Jam'iat Misr al-Fatat (Young Egypt Society), headed by Ahmad Husain, and the National Syrian Party, headed by Antun Sa'ada.

Italy, being among the victorious World War I powers, desired to consolidate its relations and position in Arab Mediterranean countries. As a consequence of centuries of trade exchange between Italian ports and the ports of the region, there were in many North African and Levantine ports and towns large Italian communities with their schools, hospitals, clergy, churches, and other institutions. Italy began to conquer Libya in 1911 and later received the East Mediterranean Dodecanese islands as part of the World War I settlements; she also had control of African colonies on the Red Sea. The Italian presence in Libya and consequent repression of Libyan Arabs could scarcely create much sympathy for Italy among the Arab nations. At the same time, the Italian invasion of Ethiopia caused much anxiety in the Middle East. However, anti-British and anti-French sentiments induced some Arab countries (Yemen, Saudi Arabia, and Iraq) to seek Italian armaments. With the rise of the German menace the capacity of Britain to supply arms to Arab countries dwindled, for British home demand had to be satisfied first. Through her armaments and her military instructors, Italy consolidated her position in the Arab world, and a new channel for her influence was an Arabic radio transmission from Bari.

After World War I, Germany was interested mainly in European affairs. Egypt was an important German trade partner during the 1920s, however, including a substantial movement through the Suez Canal by German ships (16.5 percent of the total tonnage in 1929). Among other Arab countries, Iraq was a second trade partner. However, trade with Arab countries did not play a significant part in Germany's trade exchange. The situation was different with Iran and Turkey, where steady rises in the volume of trade with Germany were noted during both the Weimar Republic and the Third Reich (in the case of Turkey, it amounted to 50 percent of that country's trade). Of particular interest for Germans among the Arab countries was Iraq, and to a lesser extent Egypt. Germany followed the opinions of Arab politicians and government circles closely. However, Germans could exert less influence than could the Italians upon the Middle Eastern political scene. Nationalist and national independence ideas were gaining ground in the 1930s, when the racism and anti-Semitism of the Nazis could count on some limited sympathy in the Islamic world. Typical movements were the radical Muslim Brotherhood, founded in the late 1920s, and the Young Egypt Society, founded by Cairo students in 1933 and popularly known as the "Green Shirts." Negative attitudes toward the British meant sympathizing with their rivals and enemies. During World War II leading members of the society distanced themselves from Germany and fascism. In Algeria, when the French authorities banned the Parti du People Algérien in September 1939, an insignificant minority of its members organized the secret Comité d'Action Revolutionaire Nord-Africaine with a program echoing the ideas of Italian Fascism.

In general terms we can trace two tendencies among Islamists: one left-oriented in the social spectrum (that the evolution of Islamic society is a historical process) and the second right-oriented (that a glorified state is the requirement of the time). The Nazi vision, including anti-Semitism, did not have many advocates within Islamic ideological movements. It cannot be said that such organizations as the Muslim Brotherhood or Young Egypt Society had a fascist concept of state and society, but only that the general atmosphere in the Arab and Islamic world was favorable to fascist programs.

Meanwhile, German interest in the Islamic and Arab world started to show a spectacular rise from 1937 onwards: the strategic significance of the area was reassessed, agitation and propaganda publications were enhanced, organizations dealing with the Orient were revived, visits were paid to Middle Eastern countries. A spectacular event in this field was the visit by Baldur von Schirach (as leader of German youth) to Damascus, Baghdad, and Tehran at the end of 1937. Paramilitary youth organizations in the Middle East became a popular phenomenon. Their authoritarian structure, fascist slogans, and contacts with Germans and Italians, as well as their presence in NSDAP rallies (together with politicians) in Nuremberg were certainly a source of anxiety for the British and the French. Moreover, a widening range of German circles were calling for a more active German role in the Middle East, a view shared by Alfred Rosenberg, head of the Aussenpolitisches Amt NSDAP.

The occasion for implementing Rosenberg's proposal was the increasing tension around the Palestine question in connection with mass Jewish immigration. Since the late 1920s many Islamic politicians, intellectuals, and journalists had started to attach great importance to, and have many reservations about, Jewish immigration to Palestine. The fourth wave of immigrants of 1924–1928, mainly from Poland, was alarming. The world economic crisis aggravated matters. The Palestinian uprising of 1936 lasting for three years differed from earlier ones (of 1921 and 1929), taking the form of a long-lasting Arab strike against the British, and uniting Arab organizations around the leadership of Jerusalem's mufti Haj Amin al-Husseini. The British government attached great significance to the Palestine problem; it sent a special commission headed by Earl Peel to investigate the matter. In its report (July 1937), the commission proposed termination of the mandate and partition of Palestine (one-fifth of the land to go as a Jewish state, an Arab state in the rest of the country, and minor areas remaining under British mandate, in addition to Transjordan). The Arab uprising and the Royal Commission Report had a great impact in Palestine and the Middle East. The entire Arab world was moved by events: popular committees emerged spontaneously in support of Palestinian Arabs, diplomatic conferences were held, resolutions were adopted against "the Zionist menace," and the partition plan was rejected. Naturally, the British—having their imperial interests involved—were aware of the pressure from both the Arabs and rival Axis states.

At first, the Nazis, forcing their own Jews to emigrate, were in favor of the establishment of a Jewish state in Palestine. Later, however, they distanced themselves from such an idea. The Palestinian question was utilized by the Nazis in a dual manner. On the one hand, by their persecution of Jews and pressure upon their allies to do likewise, they gave an impetus to the immigration movement into Palestine, and thereby aggravated the situation still further. On the other, Nazi anti-Semitic propaganda coincided with Arab anti-Jewish agitation, both directed against the British, who were seen as part of the conspiracy to deprive Palestinians of their homeland; this propaganda was directed through the Arab press, paid advertisements, diplomatic and personal channels, and after the spring of 1939 through radio transmissions. The revised German foreign policy in connection with these events could be summarized as follows: the creation of a Jewish state under British domination would not be in the interest of Germany, because the new state would not absorb all world Jews, but merely create for them an additional international legal base; international Jewry would always be an ideological option politically contrary to the National Socialist Third Reich. Germany ought to be interested in the existence of an Arab counterbalance to Jewish power; hence, Germany rejected the idea of the establishment of a Jewish Palestinian state. German missions in some Arab countries received instructions to make clear the Reich's support for Arab aspirations in Palestine. A similar role was assigned to the Aussenpolitisches Amt NSDAP, which maintained relations with Middle Eastern parties and organizations.

Hassan Jamsheer

See Also: ANTI-SEMITISM; ARYANISM; AXIS, THE; CONSPIRACY THEORIES; ETHIOPIA; FASCIST PARTY, THE; GERMANY; IMMIGRATION; IRAN; IRAQ; ITALY; LIBYA; NATIONALISM; NAZISM; NUREMBERG RALLIES, THE; PALESTINE; PARAMILITARISM; *PROTOCOLS OF THE ELDERS OF ZION, THE;* RACIAL DOCTRINE; RACISM; RADIO; ROSENBERG, ALFRED; SCHIRACH, BALDUR VON; THIRD REICH, THE; TURKEY; VERSAILLES, THE TREATY OF; WALL STREET CRASH, THE; WEIMAR REPUBLIC, THE; WORLD WAR I; WORLD WAR II; YOUTH MOVEMENTS; ZIONISM

References
Cleveland, William L. 1994. *A History of the Modern Middle East.* Boulder: Westview.
Hirszowicz, Lukasz. 1966. *The Third Reich and the Arab East.* London: Routledge and Kegan Paul.
Mansfield, Peter. 1992. *A Modern History of the Middle East.* London: Penguin.
Schultze, Reinhardt. 2000. *A Modern History of the Muslim World.* London: I. B. Tauris.
The Middle East and North Africa 2000: A Survey and Reference Book. London: Europa.

MILITARISM

There are two senses in which the interwar fascist regimes were militaristic: in the sense that the Italian Fascists and the German Nazis each aimed at the militarization of their entire society, and in the sense that both regimes focused on national military achievement as their chief foreign policy goal. The latter goal was a traditional one in Europe, the former rather more unusual.

Based on a Social-Darwinistic belief in the endemic nature of struggle in the world, and on the glorification of war as a means of building heroic character, interwar fascism was orientated to an unusual degree toward the militarization of society. Both Fascist Italy and Nazi Germany pursued the militarization of their own countries domestically through the establishment of mass movements devoted to the creation of alert, physically fit, warlike populations. This was not about increasing the control of the military in society—which neither Hitler nor Mussolini aspired to do—but about developing a warrior people with a warrior ethos. The idea was also propounded (by Werner Daitz) of organizing economic life along the lines of the chains of command in the military. Meanwhile, Hitler in particular devoted himself to building up his armed forces (whose numbers had been severely limited by the terms of the Versailles Treaty) from the moment he came to power in 1933, with the aim of raising Germany from the humiliations of 1918 to the status of a world power—which he achieved very quickly. But while the Wehrmacht that Hitler created proved a potent weapon for Nazism, Mussolini was never able to create an Italian armed force to match, something that he himself realized when he postponed entry into World War II. Both Mussolini and Hitler broke onto the world stage through their militaristic adventurism—Mussolini in Corfu and Ethiopia, Hitler with his bombing of Guernica, his remilitarization of the Rhineland, and his massive troop parades at the Nuremberg Rallies. But while militarism was a key aspect of interwar fascism, it was not, of course, a distinctive one, for it was and is a feature of many other kinds of regime: the hugely bellicose May Day parades in Soviet Russia were a symbol of Soviet militarism. Nor did fascist militarism amount to the same thing as military dictatorship, which was not at all the intention or practice of either Hitler or Mussolini.

Cyprian Blamires

References

Bracher, K. D. 1973. *The German Dictatorship: The Origins, Structure, and Consequences of National Socialism.* Harmondsworth: Penguin University Books.

Broszat, M. 1981. *The Hitler State.* London: Longman.

Germino, D. L. 1971. *The Italian Fascist Party in Power: A Study in Totalitarian Rule.* Minneapolis: University of Minnesota Press.

Koon, Tracy H. 1985. *Believe, Obey, Fight: Political Socialization of Youth in Fascist Italy, 1922–1943.* Chapel Hill: University of North Carolina Press.

Alfredo Stroessner, commander-in-chief of the Paraguayan army, seized power in 1954 and ruled for thirty-five years. He was an admirer of Hitler and his regime is sometimes labeled 'fascist', but Hitler and Mussolini themselves always kept the military at arms' length. (Horacio Villalobos/ Corbis)

MILITARY, THE: *See* MILITARISM; MILITARY DICTATORSHIP; WEHRMACHT, THE

MILITARY DICTATORSHIP

Most modern military dictatorships have been called "fascist" by their opponents, since they have had in common with fascism a thoroughgoing militarization of society, an extreme nationalist phraseology, a massive limitation and infringement of human rights and extension of police powers, the gagging of freedom of thought, and the "institutionalization" of a state of emergency. Nonetheless, most military dictatorships have showed only a very selective association with Italian Fascism and National Socialism. That has certainly been true of the military dictatorships of Latin America, whose leading generals have often encouraged adulation of themselves in fascistoid terms as "national saviors" from communism and the influence of "decadent" Western democracy—for example, Augusto Pinochet in Chile (1973–1990) or Jorge Rafael Videla in Argentina (1976–1981). The most clearly fascist would seem to be the military dictatorship of Hitler-admirer General Alfredo Stroessner in Paraguay (1954–1989). While military dictatorships in Africa have generally come down to "kleptocracies" of the leading tribes, those with mass support in the Arab world—Egypt under Gamal Abd-el-Nasser (1954–1970) or Libya under Muammar al-Ghaddafi—are more difficult to evaluate.

Hitler and Mussolini expressly refused to see themselves as military dictators. They admired the discipline, readiness for sacrifice, and obedience of the military, yet Hitler considered government by the military to be a reactionary form of state without political "vision," and he distrusted the military all his life. In November 1932 he warned President von Hindenburg about the dangers of a military dictatorship, which would be likely with a presidial regime under General von Schleicher, and in March 1938 he dissolved the Soldatenbund of retired front soldiers that had been formed in 1935 after it became clear that this was aiming to install a military dictatorship in Germany. Both Italian Fascism and National Socialism subjected the military to the ends of the state and party, which an intensive ideological education of the soldiers was also to serve. With the "military statute" in Italy of 1926 and the Wehrmacht's oath of loyalty to the person of Adolf Hitler instituted in 1934, Mussolini and Hitler both assured themselves of command over the military. If in World War II both dictators presented themselves as military leaders of their respective countries, it was in order to demonstrate a united front of state, party, and military leadership and to prevent a gulf developing between political and military requirements.

Parallel with the emergence of Italian Fascism and National Socialism, many countries of Europe after 1920 suffered a temporary or lasting seizure of power by the military. European military dictatorship manifested in general as nationalistic, anti-Semitic, and hostile to democracy and flirted in one way or another with the organizational forms and goals of the fascist movements. The earliest such fascistic military dictatorship was manifested in the Spain of the "Caudillo" Francisco Franco in its earlier period (1936/1939–1945), after the country had previously had a nationalistic right-wing military dictatorship under General Miguel Primo de Rivera (1923–1930). Attaining power with the help of the fascists, Franco had at his disposal with the Falange a fascistic mass organization, but his dominance was built mainly on an alliance of Falange, army chiefs, and the Catholic Church. In neighboring Portugal, by contrast, after a military dictatorship was first established in 1926 under General Gomes da Costa, it gradually turned into a personal dictatorship under Antonio Salazar after 1928.

A profascist military dictatorship allied with Italy and Germany was to be found in Romania under Marshal Ion Antonescu, whose power base was the fascist "Iron Guard," but he went on to eliminate their leadership. The "royal dictatorship" of Czar Boris III of Bulgaria (1935–1944) also had a power base in the military and came in on the side of the Axis. The regimes in Poland and Hungary were military regimes of a very particular kind that were often called "fascist" by Marxists. In Poland, Marshal Józef Pilsudski led an extreme authoritarian nationalistic regime (1926–1935) that developed increasingly into a personal dictatorship; the attempt by Pilsudski to bring all the parties together in an alliance in conformity with the regime may have modeled itself on fascist forms of organization. Even more tricky to assess is Hungary under the "Regent of the Empire," Admiral Miklós Horthy (1920–1944), whose personal rule was more of a "liberal dictatorship," while his minister president, Colonel Gyula Gömbös, with his "Szegeder Fascists" took over Ger-

many's race laws and aimed to transform the state into a "nationalistic dictatorship" (1936–1941). Eventually, power was taken in 1944/1945 by the ultrafascist "Arrow Cross," a movement that Horthy had for a long time kept out of power. The military dictatorship in Greece was also shot through with fascist elements: General Ioannis Metaxas (1936–1941) introduced the *Heil* greeting and propagated a radical nationalism of the "Hellenes" (which he understood, however, as cultural rather than racist), but he also avoided the creation of a fascist mass party just as did the later Junta of the Colonels (1967–1974), who presented their coup as a "national revolution" against communism.

Markus Hattstein
(translated by Cyprian Blamires)

See Also: INTRODUCTION; ANTI-SEMITISM; ARGENTINA; ARROW CROSS, THE; BOLIVIA; CATHOLIC CHURCH, THE; CHILE; DECADENCE; DEMOCRACY; FALANGE; FASCIST PARTY, THE; FRANCO Y BAHAMONDE, GENERAL FRANCISCO; GERMANY; GÖMBÖS, GYULA; GREECE; *HEIL HITLER!*; HINDENBURG, PAUL VON BENECKENDORFF UND VON; HITLER, ADOLF; HORTHY DE NAGYBÁNYA, MIKLÓS; HUNGARY; IRON GUARD, THE; ITALY; LIBYA; METAXAS, GENERAL IOANNIS; MILITARISM; MUSSOLINI, BENITO ANDREA; NATIONALISM; NUREMBERG LAWS, THE; PARAGUAY; PILSUDSKI, MARSHAL JOZEF; PINOCHET UGARTE, GENERAL AUGUSTO; POLAND; PORTUGAL; QADHAFI (GADDHAFI), MU'AMMAR; ROMANIA; SALAZAR, ANTÓNIO DE OLIVEIRA; SPAIN; SPANISH CIVIL WAR, THE; WAR; WAR VETERANS; WARRIOR ETHOS, THE; WEHRMACHT, THE; WORLD WAR I; WORLD WAR II

References

De Meneses, F. R. 2004. *Portugal 1914–1926: From the First World War to Military Dictatorship.* Bristol: HiPLAM.
Griffin, R. D. 1991. *The Nature of Fascism.* London: Routledge.
Kofas, J. V. 1983. *Authoritarianism in Greece: The Metaxas Regime.* Boulder: Eastern European Monographs.
Macartney, C. A. 1957. *October Fifteenth: A History of Modern Hungary, 1929–1945.* Edinburgh: Edinburgh University Press.
Payne, S. 1995. *A History of Fascism 1914–1945.* London: University College London Press.

MILIZIA VOLONTARIA PER LA SICUREZZA NAZIONALE (MVSN)

The MVSN (Voluntary Militia for National Security) was the Italian state security force, which Mussolini created out of the *squadristi* who had enabled him to come to power with their violence against his opponents. The army saw the MVSN as a potential rival, and even though Mussolini appointed army generals to high posts, the military remained keen to see the organization suppressed. There was a conflict also between some local groups that remained loyal to their local commandants and the central leadership. The MVSN was encouraged to participate in the war in Ethiopia, where it proved a complete disaster, and Mussolini then gave more power over it to the army. Four MVSN divisions were crushed by Allied Forces in Libya between late 1940 and early 1941. The force was formally abolished by the monarch on 6 December 1943. It was briefly revived under the Salò Republic as the Guardia Nazionale Repubblicana (Republican National Guard) and finally dissolved in the spring of 1945.

Cyprian Blamires

See Also: ETHIOPIA; FASCIST PARTY, THE; ITALY; LIBYA; MUSSOLINI, BENITO ANDREA; SALÒ REPUBLIC, THE; *SQUADRISMO*

References
Cannistraro, Philip V. 1982. *Historical Dictionary of Fascist Italy.* Westport, CT: Greenwood.
Hite, J., and C. Hinton. 1998. *Fascist Italy.* London: John Murray.
Lyttelton, Adrian. 1973. *The Seizure of Power: Fascism in Italy, 1919–1929.* London: Weidenfeld and Nicholson.

MILLENARIANISM

Fascism has been studied as a form of modern millenarianism. Millenarian movements pursue an apocalyptic confrontation with the status quo in hopes of creating a future utopian society established through metaphysical deliverance, political revolution, or both. The terms *apocalyptic, millenarian,* or *millennialist* are sometimes used interchangeably, although some argue for fine distinctions among them. Apocalyptic belief anticipates an upcoming social transformation of immense scale that signals a new historical epoch. In the Christian Bible, the Apocalypse is prophesied as a global battle between righteous believers and Satanic forces that must take place before the return of their Messiah, Jesus Christ. This Battle of Armageddon results in God's triumph over evil, followed by one thousand years of rule by righteous Christians. The word *millennialism* was originally tied to some measure of a one-thousand-year time span, but is now used to discuss diverse apocalyptic movements. Apocalyptic prophecy appears not only in Christianity but also in many other religious traditions, including Zoroastrianism, Judaism, and Islam.

Cohn traces the roots of Hitler's Nazi vision to the millenarian Christian apocalyptic mystics of the Middle Ages. According to Cohn, millenarian movements see their anticipated salvation as collective, imminent, total, miraculous, and occurring on earth rather than in some heavenly venue. Rhodes describes "the Hitler movement" as a "millenarian-Gnostic revolution" complete with apocalyptic metaphors and anticipating a "modern battle of Armageddon for a worldly New Jerusalem" (Rhodes 1980, 18). For example, the Nazi Thousand Year Reich echoed the Christian idea of the approaching millennium. Ellwood also calls Nazism a modern form of millenarianism, and argues that "Nazi belief in the superior qualities and destiny of the Aryans took on the nature of nonrational, transcendentally sanctioned, self-validating faith" (Ellwood 2000, 243). Two other theories are complementary to the view that fascism is a form of apocalyptic millenarianism. Griffin calls fascism a form of revolutionary populist nationalism that promotes palingenesis, the heroic rebirth of the society after a period of decline or decadence. Gentile argues that fascism involves the sacralization of politics, with roots in millenarian and messianic traditions drawn from Christianity. As Eatwell explains, the monotheistic and Christian roots of Western culture helped to shape an apocalyptic worldview in which conflict is sometimes framed as a dualistic "struggle between God and Satan, a tendency which encourages a belief in the existence of a hidden, evil, hand" (Eatwell 1990, 72). This helps to explain the tendency in fascist and other extreme right movements and groups to engage in demonization, scapegoating, and conspiracism. For example, the Nazis picked Jews as their primary scapegoat, but other groups were listed for extermination in what was seen as the necessary purification of society before the anticipated millenarian transformation.

Chip Berlet

See Also: INTRODUCTION; ANTI-SEMITISM; ARYANISM; CHRISTIAN IDENTITY; CHRISTIANITY; CONSPIRACY THEORIES; HITLER, ADOLF; MYSTICISM; MYTH; NATIONALISM; NAZISM; OCCULTISM; PALINGENETIC MYTH; PSYCHODYNAMICS OF PALINGENETIC MYTH, THE; RELIGION; REVOLUTION; SECULARIZATION; THIRD REICH, THE; UTOPIA, UTOPIANISM

References

Cohn, Norman. 1977 [1957]. *The Pursuit of the Millennium: Revolutionary Millenarians and Mystical Anarchists of the Middle Ages.* Rev. and enl. 3d ed. New York: Oxford University Press.

Eatwell, Roger. 1990 [1989]. "The Nature of the Right, 2: The Right as a Variety of 'Styles of Thought.'" Pp. 62–76 in *The Nature of the Right: American and European Politics and Political Thought since 1789,* edited by Eatwell and Noël O'Sullivan. Boston: Twayne.

Ellwood, Robert. 2000. "Nazism as a Millennialist Movement." Pp. 241–260 in *Millennialism, Persecution, and Violence: Historical Cases,* edited by Catherine Wessinger. Syracuse, NY: Syracuse University Press.

Rhodes, James M. 1980. *The Hitler Movement: A Modern Millenarian Revolution.* Stanford: Hoover Institution Press, Stanford University.

MISCEGENATION: *See* ARYANISM; RACIAL DOCTRINE; RACISM

MISHIMA, YUKIO (pseudonym for Hiraoka Kimitake) (1925–1970)

The most celebrated novelist and intellectual associated with ultranationalism in postwar Japan. Although Mishima eulogized historical right-wing protagonists in many of his writings, he is best remembered for the bizarre manner in which his death was linked to rightist politics. Mishima embraced right-wing causes with the publication of his short story "Patriotism" in 1960. This work addressed the abortive coup d'etat of nationalistic junior officers in February 1936. Mishima later enacted the hero's part in a film based on the story. Mishima's finest and most subtle political novel is *Runaway Horses*. Set in the 1930s, the story's protagonist is a patriotic youth who assassinates a business leader and then commits ritual suicide. The book criticizes not only the political establishment but also the hypocrisy of many organized rightist groups of the period, and it expresses Mishima's despair that Japan will ever reconcile its traditional values with its modern development. In the late 1960s, Mishima took his politics from literature into life. He founded a rightist organization of young men who mixed their blood and drank it in a loyalty pledge. In 1970, he and several followers kidnapped a Japanese general and demanded that he

muster the troops to hear Mishima speak. When the soldiers scoffed at Mishima's demand that they overthrow the constitution in the emperor's name, he damned them as "American mercenaries." He then committed ritual suicide by cutting open his belly. Mishima's vague political ideas, which included restoring the samurai sword to Japan, resist easy categorization. He never identified himself with Japan's wartime military government, and he criticized Emperor Hirohito for renouncing his divinity after the war. Nonetheless, his ambiguous exaltation of a selfless nationalism, "a value which is greater than respect for life," typifies the worldview of many modern Japanese rightists.

Gregory Kasza

See Also: AMERICANIZATION; CULTS OF DEATH; FILM; HIROHITO, EMPEROR; JAPAN; JAPAN AND WORLD WAR II; MODERNITY; NATIONALISM; WORD WAR II

Reference

Scott-Stokes, Henry. 1974. *The Life and Death of Yukio Mishima.* New York: Farrar, Straus, and Giroux.

MITFORD FAMILY, THE

The two most notorious out of the six celebrated British Mitford sisters, Lady Diana Mosley (1910–2003) and Unity Mitford (1911–1948), were heavily involved in the world of fascism in Britain and Germany. But long before that their grandfather, Algernon Bertram Mitford (1st Lord Redesdale, 1837–1916) had provided an extensive and enthusiastic introduction in 1910 to the English translation of the proto-Nazi racist and anti-Semitic work *Foundations of the Nineteenth Century* by Houston Stewart Chamberlain. He also helped with the translation of that text, which he called "a work of the highest importance." Redesdale also translated Chamberlain's book on Kant. He was very musical and had a special admiration for German composers, and Wagner in particular. This admiration he shared with Chamberlain, who was Wagner's son-in-law, and indeed Redesdale became so much a part of the inner circle at Bayreuth that his photograph could be seen on Siegfried Wagner's desk. The pro-German sympathies that Redesdale possessed re-emerged in his grandchildren: his grandson Tom completed his education in Germany, loved German culture, and saw fascism as the only bulwark against communism. As a soldier in World War II he was so distressed at the

Unity Mitford, whose grandfather Lord Redesdale provided an enthusiastic introduction to the translation of one of the classic works of proto-Nazi ideology into English— The Foundations of the Nineteenth Century, *written in German by the expatriate Englishman Houston Stewart Chamberlain. Unity's public adulation of Hitler (who treated her as a friend) aroused much comment in the British press. (Hulton-Deutsch Collection/Corbis)*

prospect of having to join the invasion forces in Germany that he volunteered for service in the Far East, where he was killed. But it was Redesdale's granddaughters Diana and Unity whose Nazi sympathies caused the most uproar. Diana left her first husband, Bryan Guinness, for the notorious British fascist leader Sir Oswald Mosley and was interned for a while (as was he) during World War II. During the interwar years they had become so close to the Nazi regime that their marriage actually took place in the Goebbels family drawing room. Diana's sister Unity was baptized with the middle name Valkyrie, in honor of her grandfather's love of Wagner; she went to live in Germany in the 1930s, becoming a devotee (literally) of Hitler and a member of his close circle of acquaintances. She pre-

sented herself as "a British fascist woman" and was openly anti-Semitic. She met Hitler regularly, spoke of him as "sweet," and was well treated by him. She was also much attached to Julius Streicher. Unity and Diana waxed so enthusiastic about Nazism that their parents were attracted to it, too. Her father, Lord Redesdale, became a very active member of a Nazi front organization called the Link, founded by Sir Barry Domvile in 1937, making frequent speeches about the beauties of Hitlerism. Lady Redesdale wrote in the *Daily Sketch* that National Socialism had eradicated the problem of class warfare, improved living standards, and was a support to religion. When war was declared between Germany and Great Britain in 1939, she attempted to kill herself but survived. Hitler saw to it that she was sent back to England, where she lived on for several years in poor health. The activities of these two high-profile aristocratic sisters were of great interest to the British press, and when Unity was brought back to England on a stretcher, the ambulance taking her from the ferry was pursued by a procession of press vehicles.

Cyprian Blamires

See Also: ANTI-SEMITISM; BAYREUTH; CHAMBERLAIN, HOUSTON STEWART; GERMANNESS; GERMANY; GOEBBELS, (PAUL) JOSEPH; GREAT BRITAIN; HITLER, ADOLF; MOSLEY, SIR OSWALD; NAZISM; NORDIC SOUL, THE; SWASTIKA, THE; WAGNER, (WILHELM) RICHARD; WAGNER AND GERMANNESS; WORLD WAR II

References
Courcy, Anne de. 2003. *Diana Mosley.* London: Chatto and Windus.
Dalley, Jan. 2000. *Diana Mosley: A Life.* London: Faber and Faber.
Guinness, Jonathan, with Catherine Guinness. 1984. *The House of Mitford.* London: Hutchinson.
Mosley, Diana. 2003. *A Life of Contrasts: The Autobiography of Diana Mosley.* London: Gibson Square.
Pryce-Jones, David. 1995. *Unity Mitford: A Quest.* London: Weidenfeld and Nicholson.

MODERNISM

When considering the relationship of modernism to fascism, we must contextualize both in terms of modernity—that is, first the socioeconomic transformation of Europe and the world following the Industrial Revolution of the eighteenth and nineteenth centuries;

second, the birth of democracy in the wake of the Enlightenment and the French Revolution of 1789; and third, the subsequent globalization of capitalism. Scholars now recognize the role of fascism and modernist aesthetics in the emergence of anti-Enlightenment movements opposed to the democratic tradition that was the heritage of Enlightenment thought; indeed, the rise of fascism in Europe amounted to a widespread search for spiritual values and "organic" institutions able to counteract what many thought were the corrosive effects of rationalism and capitalism on the body politic. Thus fascists posited ethnic, regional, and religious forms of national identity that were antithetical to capitalism's and democracy's universalist and rationalist precepts. Fascists were eager to absorb those aspects of modernity (and modernist aesthetics) that could be reconfigured within their antirational, anticapitalist concept of nationhood, and many practitioners of modernism—for example, Ezra Pound and Marinetti—endorsed fascist aims and ideals.

Among the pantheon of fascist values conducive to modernist aesthetics were notions of regeneration, primitivism, and avant-gardism; these paradigms were equally relevant to the primitivist and *völkisch* art of such fascists as German expressionist Emil Nolde and Italian painter Ardengo Soffici, the "antimaterialist" aesthetics of the one-time Futurist Mario Sironi and the modernist architect Guiseppe Terragni, and to the use of photo-montage and other new media by those Italian modernists who designed the groundbreaking Exhibition of the Fascist Revolution of 1932. In like fashion, historians have documented the Nazis' thorough acceptance of modern design and industrialism, which has led some to coin the term "reactionary modernism" to describe those thinkers and ideologues under the Weimar Republic and the Third Reich who disdained liberal democracy and Enlightenment values while nonetheless embracing the modern technology of the Industrial Revolution. This configuration accounts for the Nazis' simultaneous embrace of "blood and soil" tribalism, manifest in a celebration of indigenous, preindustrial "folk" culture, and the ultramodernism signaled by newly created autobahns and Bauhaus-inspired aircraft factories. Before 1934 a debate occurred in Nazi circles over whether German Expressionism should be regarded as a regenerative expression of Germany's Nordic roots, or as a style tainted by artistic miscegenation. Thus the Nazis' subsequent condemnation of modern art was not the product of an absolute rejection of modernism in and of itself but a strategic choice, stemming from aesthetic debates within the Nazi Party. Historians have reached similar conclusions with regard to Italian Fascism, noting that Mussolini's modernist allies among the Futurist, Novecento, Romanità, and Strapaese (Supercountry) movements promoted competing aesthetics that nevertheless expressed spiritual values they deemed antithetical to the Enlightenment project. As a result, Italian Fascists eulogized the art and culture of Roman antiquity and preindustrial peasant society even as they endorsed the Italian Futurist movement with its cult of urbanism, speed, and modern technology, as well as such aesthetic signifiers of modernism as montage in film and photography.

In both Nazi Germany and Fascist Italy, the past—whether in the guise of the seemingly timeless seasonal cycles of peasant culture or the legacy of Graeco-Roman civilization—was evoked to remind citizens of the spiritual values that could serve as building blocks for a fascist future, as manifest in a millennial Third Reich or Mussolini's creation of a new Italian empire. To underscore this Janus-faced ideology, artists and architects incorporated past styles and imagery that they associated with fascist values with modernist methods and materials they deemed conducive to a future society still in the making. For instance, in the interwar period Soffici painted images of Tuscan peasants that combined stylistic features derived from the Trecento artist Giotto with those developed by the French modernist (and regionalist) Paul Cézanne; while in 1938, the architect Vittorio Ballio Morporgo encased the newly restored Ara Pacis in a glass and steel Bauhaus-inspired structure. Similarly, Albert Speer's Hitler-approved plans for the rebuilding of Berlin envisioned a central axis composed of classicizing monumental structures anchored at its extremities by railway stations, an airport, and an outer autobahn ring road. Thus images culled from a mythical past and indicative of a mythogenetic future were marshaled to overcome a degenerative present, to help purge society of those values and institutions associated with capitalism and the Enlightenment. The fascist embrace of modernism represented the forward-looking thrust of this palingenetic project.

Mark Antliff

See Also: INTRODUCTION; ARCHITECTURE; ART; ARYANISM; CAPITALISM; COSMOPOLITANISM; DECADENCE; DEGENERACY; DEMOCRACY; ENLIGHTENMENT, THE; FASCIST PARTY, THE; FILM; FRENCH REVOLUTION, THE; FUTURISM; GERMANNESS (*DEUTSCHHEIT*); GERMANY; HITLER, ADOLF; ITALY; MARINETTI, FILIPPO TOMMASO; MODERNITY; MUSSOLINI, BENITO ANDREA; NATIONALISM;

NAZISM; NORDIC SOUL, THE; ORGANICISM; POUND, EZRA; RATIONALISM; ROME; SARFATTI-GRASSINI, MARGHERITA; SCIENCE; SOUL; SPEER, ALBERT; TECHNOLOGY; THIRD REICH, THE; TRADITION; *VOLK, VÖLKISCH;* WEIMAR REPUBLIC, THE

References

Antliff, Mark. 2002. "Fascism, Modernism, and Modernity." *Art Bulletin* 84, no. 1 (March): 148–169.

Braun, Emily. 2000. *Mario Sironi and Italian Modernism: Art and Politics under Fascism.* Cambridge: Cambridge University Press.

Griffin, Roger. 1994 [1991]. *The Nature of Fascism.* London: Routledge.

Sternhell, Zeev, ed. 1996. *The Intellectual Revolt against Liberal Democracy, 1870–1945.* Jerusalem: Israel Academy of Sciences and Humanities.

MODERNITY

Because of its traditional classification as a doctrine of the Right and the "reactionary" label attached to it by its opponents, interwar fascism can easily be viewed as a nostalgic creed, but nothing would be further from the truth, for it adopted a resolutely "modern" stance. In Italy the Futurists were quickly attracted to Fascism, and with reason. Fascism in Italy was founded as a revolutionary movement that embraced new technologies and exploited with alacrity opportunities provided by new media. Mussolini loved flying, and similarly there was nothing that Hitler liked better than to drive at speed in a powerful car down a straight road. He pioneered not only the autobahns but also the idea of a car for the masses, the Volkswagen (literally, "car of the people"). Hitler's technologically advanced army was vastly superior to the French and the British forces at the start of the war. The Blitzkrieg military strategy employed by the Nazis involved a highly sophisticated combination of advanced aviation and ground movement technologies, and at the end of the war the Nazis provided further evidence of their ability to exploit modern techniques in their rocketry and flying bombs.

At the same time, confusion was generated by the fact that interwar fascists did also condemn what they called "modernity." What they meant by this were a set of values commonly associated with modernity, the values associated with the French Revolution: socialism, democracy, and liberalism. But the *Enciclopedia italiana* article on the doctrine of Fascism that appeared

under Mussolini's name was quite clear that "one does not go backwards." From the beginning, fascists did not reject socialism, democracy, and liberalism because they believed them to be symptomatic of modernity, but precisely because they believed these doctrines to be outmoded—belonging to the nineteenth century rather than to the twentieth, demonstrably shown up as bankrupt by World War I. The interwar fascist attitude toward "liberal" modernity echoes the thinking of French positivists like Saint-Simon and Auguste Comte, for whom democratic egalitarianism made no sense: the truth of politics could no more be ascertained by majority vote than could the truth of chemistry. What was needed was for the best minds to be put in charge of the social and political order. Their objection to liberalism was a "scientific" one.

Another aspect of their thinking that made fascists look "nostalgic" was their emphasis on the spiritual, oddly out of kilter with a determinedly "scientific" and "secular" age. However, to some extent the "spiritual" language they favored had a chiefly rhetorical value and was brandished as yet another weapon against Bolshevism. Bolshevism rested on the basis of the doctrine of historical materialism, and the fascists' resolve to present themselves as believers in the spiritual nature of man and his spiritual destiny was "one in the eye for the Reds." On the positive side, it equally served to legitimize them in the eyes of persons with existing religious beliefs who might be reconciled to supporting them by this comforting-sounding language. At least they sounded less antipathetic to the religious view of the world than did the Bolsheviks. On the other hand, it would not be fair to apply this rather cynical assessment to someone like Gentile, whose "spiritual" philosophy of actualism sprang from decided philosophical convictions. Moreover, fascism's "spiritual" rhetoric did represent a genuine desire to discover an alternative modernity as a reaction to both Marxist and capitalist materialism. In this sense they were predecessors to today's radical movement of protest against capitalism, consumerism, globalization, and McDonaldization, which are regarded as forms of a materialism that is bad for the human race and the cause of a looming ecological disaster.

From the perspective of the Left, of course, Fascism was reactionary and "antimodern" because for all of its talk of "national revolution" there was no intention to provoke a global revolution with the purpose of installing the proletariat in the seat of power. Property ownership was not attacked as such, and although there was much inveighing against "plutocracy" and

"Jewish capital" by the Nazis in particular, there was no serious program to strip the rich of their wealth for the benefit of the poor. However, from outside the ranks of the Left it is quite possible to see the corporatist ideal—whatever the failure to implement it—as a utopian attempt to revolutionize the economic order. And again there are definite echoes in interwar fascism of the protosocialist Saint-Simonian critique of the French Revolution from the Left: Saint-Simon said that while the eighteenth century had been a century of criticism and destruction culminating in the events of 1789, the nineteenth century would be the century of association, and the corporatist state was one way of attempting to fulfill that prophecy—like the Cooperative Movement that began in England in the early nineteenth century.

Among the Nazis there were some who advocated ruralism and a return to peasant values, most notably Walther Darré, but they were never allowed to influence policy in a substantive way. Both Mussolini's Italy and Hitler's Germany did employ traditional ancient symbols such as the *fasces* from Ancient Rome or the ancient emblem of the swastika, but that was for the purposes of validating their regimes by claiming ownership of signs with powerful historical associations. The same was true of the attempts to associate Nazism with the Teutonic Knights. For all the historical echoes of their pageantry, the Nuremberg Rallies were marvels of modern technological organization and accomplishment that demonstrated Nazi mastery of the communications and propaganda skills of the contemporary age.

Alongside their resolute embrace of technological innovation and scientific advance, interwar fascists also embraced the cult of youth. They portrayed themselves as the party of youth, and their philosophy laid great emphasis on physical fitness and athleticism. The staging of the Berlin Olympics was another opportunity for this. It was also exploited as a propaganda opportunity in typical modern fashion, with cheering crowds lined up to welcome the runner with the Olympic torch on his way through Germany for the benefit of the newsreel cameras.

Cyprian Blamires

See Also: INTRODUCTION; ACTUALISM; AMERICANIZATION; ANTI-SEMITISM; AUTOBAHNS, THE; BERLIN OLYMPICS, THE; BLITZKRIEG; BODY, THE CULT OF THE; BOLSHEVISM; CORPORATISM; DARRE, (RICHARD) WALTHER; DEMOCRACY; ECOLOGY; ECONOMICS; EGALITARIANISM; *ENCICLOPEDIA ITALIANA*, THE; FASCIO, THE; FASCIST PARTY, THE; FILM; FRENCH REVOLUTION, THE; FUTURISM; GENTILE, GIOVANNI; GERMANY; GLOBALIZATION; HIMMLER, HEINRICH; HITLER, ADOLF; ITALY; LIBERALISM; MOD-ERNISM; MUSSOLINI, BENITO ANDREA; MYTH; NAZISM; NUREMBERG RALLIES, THE; PARLIAMENTARISM; PLUTOCRACY; PROGRESS; PROPAGANDA; REVOLUTION; RURALISM; SCIENCE; SOCIALISM; SPORT; SS, THE; SWASTIKA, THE; SYMBOLS; TECHNOLOGY; UTOPIA, UTOPIANISM; VOLKSWAGEN; WORLD WAR I; WORLD WAR II; YOUTH MOVEMENTS

References
Alpher, J., ed. 1986. *Nationalism and Modernity: A Mediterranean Perspective.* London: Praeger.

Bauman, Z. 1989. *Modernity and the Holocaust.* Cambridge: Polity.

———. 1991. *Modernity and Ambivalence.* Cambridge: Polity.

Ben-Ghiat, R. 2001. *Fascist Modernities: Italy, 1922–1945.* Berkeley: University of California Press.

Cobley, Evelyn. 2002. *Temptations of Faust: The Logic of Fascism and Postmodern Archaeologies of Modernity.* Toronto: University of Toronto Press.

Gentile, E. 2003. *The Struggle for Modernity: Nationalism, Futurism and Fascism.* London: Praeger.

Griffin, R. 1991. *The Nature of Fascism.* London: Routledge.

Herf, G. 1984. *Reactionary Modernism: Technology, Culture and Politics in Weimar and the Third Reich.* Cambridge: Cambridge University Press.

MOELLER VAN DEN BRUCK, ARTHUR (1876–1925)

German nationalist ideologue and historian of culture, author of the famous tract *Das dritte Reich,* which was the inspiration for the Nazis' title for their regime. He dropped out of high school in Düsseldorf early and left for Paris in 1902 to avoid military service. While living in France and Italy, Moeller continued his studies and published various books, including the massive eight-volume *Die Deutschen, unsere Menschengeschichte* (1904–1910), in which he classified his countrymen according to psychological types (drifting, dreaming, decisive, and so forth). At the outbreak of World War I, Moeller volunteered for the German army. Besides completing the editing of the first German edition of the works of Fyodor Dostoyevsky, Moeller joined the propaganda division of the army command in 1916. There he started writing his nationalistic tract *Das Recht der jungen Völker* (1919), in which he glorified the state, patriotism, and being Prussian (*Preußentum*). His theme was clearly anti-Western and anti-imperialistic, his focus what he called Germany's cultural decline. He called for a new Germanic faith to save the country from the disintegration and vulgarity of modern industrial society, Western capitalism, and especially liberalism.

In June 1919, Moeller co-founded the *völkisch*-elitist circle Juniklub, which agitated against the Treaty of Versailles and which had a profound influence on the emerging Young Conservatives. He also edited the club's magazine *Gewissen*. In 1922, Moeller met the young Adolf Hitler but rejected him because of his "proletarian primitiveness." One year later, Moeller's most famous book, *Das dritte Reich* was published (1923), and despite his distancing himself from Hitler, the Nazis later adopted the title. In the book Moeller drew up his counterprogram to democracy, socialism, and communism. He called for the transfer of power to a small elite and for a medieval-type German empire under the term "German socialism." *Das dritte Reich* was a huge success and sold at least 100,000 copies in countless editions. One of its early admirers was the young Joseph Goebbels, and it is even said that a signed copy of the book was discovered in Hitler's underground bunker where he and Eva Braun took their lives in 1945. Since the end of the war the New Right has taken up Moeller's writing and ideas, including among others the highly influential French author and theorist Alain de Benoist.

Thomas Grumke

See Also: ARYANISM; BARBAROSSA, FREDERICK, HOLY ROMAN EMPEROR; BARBAROSSA, OPERATION; BENOIST, ALAIN DE; BOLSHEVISM; CAPITALISM; DECADENCE; DEMOCRACY; *DRANG NACH OSTEN* ("DRIVE TO THE EAST"), THE; ELITE THEORY; EUROPEAN NEW RIGHT, THE; EXPANSIONISM; GERMANNESS (*DEUTSCHHEIT*); GERMANY; GOEBBELS, (PAUL) JOSEPH; HITLER, ADOLF; HOLY ROMAN EMPIRE, THE; IMPERIALISM; LAGARDE, PAUL DE; LANGBEHN, JULIUS; MASSES, THE ROLE OF THE; MODERNITY; NATIONALISM; NAZISM; NORDIC SOUL, THE; PANGERMANISM; POSTWAR FASCISM; PROTOFASCISM; RURALISM; SLAVS, THE (AND GERMANY); SOCIALISM; SPENGLER, OSWALD; THIRD REICH, THE; WORLD WAR I; WORLD WAR II

References

Breuer, Stefan. 1993. *Anatomie der Konservativen Revolution.* Darmstadt: Wissenschaftliche Buchgesellschaft.
Goeldel, Denis. 1984. *Moeller van den Bruck (1876–1925), un nationaliste contre la révolution.* Frankfurt: Peter Lang.
Grunewald, Michel. 2001. *Moeller van den Brucks Geschichtsphilosophie.* Bern: Peter Lang.
Klemperer, K. von. 1957. *Germany's New Conservatism.* Princeton: Princeton University Press.
Lauryssens, Stan. 1999. *The Man Who Invented the Third Reich: The Life and Times of Arthur Moeller van den Bruck.* Stroud: Sutton.

Mosse, G. L. 1964. *The Crisis of German Ideology: The Intellectual Origins of the Third Reich.* New York: Schocken.
Stackelberg, Roderick. 1981. *Idealism Debased: From Völkisch Ideology to National Socialism.* Kent, OH: Kent State University Press.

MOHLER, ARMIN (1920–2003)

Extreme right-wing Swiss philosopher and journalist, known for his work on the "conservative revolution." He went to the University of Basle in 1938 to study art history, German studies, and philosophy. In 1942 he deserted the Swiss Army to join the Waffen-SS. He reported being much influenced by the writings of Spengler and Jünger. He published *Die Konservative Revolution* in 1950 as the product of his doctoral research under Karl Jaspers, and gave a widespread popularity to the concept of a "conservative revolution" (though he did not invent it) as a descriptive term to denote the antidemocratic movement of ideas under the Weimar Republic. The book remains in print today. From 1949 to 1953 he acted as Jünger's private secretary. In the 1950s, Mohler was in Paris as a journalist. He later used a pseudonym, Michael Hintermwald, to publish in Frey's *Deutschen National-Zeitung*. In 1961 he moved to Munich to work for the Carl-Friedrich von Siemens Stiftung and studied political science at the University of Innsbruck. In the 1980s he actively promoted Alain de Benoist. He remained an unrepentant fascist to the end of his life.

Cyprian Blamires

See Also: BENOIST, ALAIN DE; CONSERVATISM; DEMOCRACY; FREY, DR. GERHARD; GERMANY; HEIDEGGER, MARTIN; JÜNGER, ERNST; NEO-NAZISM; NIHILISM; POSTWAR FASCISM; SPENGLER, OSWALD; SWITZERLAND; WAFFEN-SS, THE; WEIMAR REPUBLIC, THE

References

Willms, Thomas. 2004. *Armin Mohler.* Papyrossa.
Woods, Roger. 1996. *The Conservative Revolution in the Weimar Republic.* Basingstoke: Palgrave-Macmillan.

MOLOTOV-RIBBENTROP PACT, THE: *See* HITLER-STALIN PACT, THE

MONARCHISM

Generally speaking, interwar fascist regimes and movements were hostile to monarchism, although for pragmatic reasons Mussolini had to compromise with Italy's monarchical establishment. Fascism's palingenetic myth did not have any space for monarchy in its desired utopia. Monarchy was part of the old order—along with aristocracy—that fascist leaders saw themselves as destined to sweep away. There was a royalist protofascist movement in France called Action Française, but that arose out of the specifics of French history—the current of traditionalist antirepublicanism that had emerged from the French Revolution. In Spain there were monarchists who supported Franco, and in countries with an Eastern Orthodox tradition such as Russia and Romania there were fascistic promonarchy movements.

Cyprian Blamires

See Also: ACTION FRANÇAISE; ARISTOCRACY; FRANCO Y BAHAMONDE, GENERAL FRANCISCO; FRENCH REVOLUTION, THE; INTEGRAL NATIONALISM; ITALY; LEGION OF THE ARCHANGEL MICHAEL, THE; MAURRAS, CHARLES; MODERNITY; MONARCHY; MUSSOLINI, BENITO ANDREA; ORTHODOX CHURCHES, THE; PALINGENETIC MYTH; PROTOFASCISM; REVOLUTION; ROMANIA; RUSSIA; SPAIN; SPANISH CIVIL WAR, THE; TRADITIONALISM; UTOPIA, UTOPIANISM; VICTOR EMMANUEL/VITTORIO EMANUELE III, KING

References

Judd, Denis. 1976. *Eclipse of Kings: European Monarchies in the Twentieth Century.* New York: Stein and Day.
Kiste, John van der. 1996. *Crowns in a Changing World: British and European Monarchies 1901–1936.* Rochester, Kent: Grange.

MONARCHY

The relationship between interwar fascisms and the monarchs in their respective countries is a complex one. In Britain, Sir Oswald Mosley and his British Union of Fascists were formally deferential toward the monarchy, for to have launched a full-frontal attack upon it would have been as suicidal as for Mussolini to have taken on the papacy. But the British monarchy was, of course, at the very heart of the conservative political establishment that so successfully managed the effects of the Great Depression—thus marginalizing the BUF—and it was the very epitome of the "civic patriotism" that made Mosely's aggressive nationalism look so false and foreign. During the course of World War II, Quisling in Norway could no more assert governmental legitimacy against the government-in-exile of King Haakon than Mussert and the Dutch Nazis could compete with the formidable Queen Wilhelmina and her government in London. What all these examples demonstrate is that where monarchy survived under relatively dynamic personalities (not the rather mediocre Victor Emmanuel III of Italy), fascist movements often saw it as a dangerous alternative center of popular loyalty. Even in Fascist Italy, the king, insignificant though he was, remained, like the pope, a rival to Mussolini's "cult of Il Duce," and the dictator chafed under the constraints that the "Dyarchy" (the theoretical sharing of power between Mussolini and the monarch) imposed on his regime; he threatened to abolish it once he had been successful in World War II. In the end it was the monarch, as representative of the Italian establishment, who dismissed Mussolini and abolished Fascism. Adolf Hitler, on the other hand, carefully ensured that there would never be any restoration of the monarchy in Nazi Germany.

John Pollard

See Also: ARISTOCRACY; BRITISH FASCISTI/BRITISH FASCISTS, THE; CONSERVATISM; FASCIST PARTY, THE; GERMANY; GREAT BRITAIN; HITLER, ADOLF; ITALY; LEADER CULT, THE; MODERNITY; MONARCHISM; MOSLEY, SIR OSWALD; MUSSERT, ANTON ADRIAAN; MUSSOLINI, BENITO ANDREA; NAZISM; NETHERLANDS, THE; NORWAY; PAPACY, THE; QUISLING, VIDKUN; REVOLUTION; TRADITION; VICTOR EMMANUEL/VITTORIO EMANUELE III, KING; WINDSOR, EDWARD DUKE OF; WORLD WAR II

References

Blinkhorn, M., ed. 1990. *Fascists and Conservatives: The Radical Right and the Establishment in Twentieth-century Europe.* London: Unwin Hyman.
Griffin, R. 1993. *The Nature of Fascism.* London: Routledge.
Morgan, P. 2003. *Fascism in Europe, 1919–1945.* London: Routledge.

MONISM: *See* ORGANICISM AND NAZISM

MOSCA, GAETANO
(1858–1941)

Italian jurist, social scientist, and politician whose elite theory—according to which the development of a minority ruling class is unavoidable in social and political systems—offered the Italian Fascists support for their own position. Mosca was born in Palermo, where, in 1881, he graduated in jurisprudence with a thesis on the theme of nationality. After having moved to Rome to complete his politico-administrative studies, in 1884 he published his first important work, *Sulla teorica dei governi e sul governo parlamentare,* in which appeared the two concepts that constitute the heart of his scientific theory: that of "political class" and that of "political formula." Appointed professor of constitutional law at the University of Palermo in 1885, he published *Le constituzioni moderne* in 1887. In 1896 he published the *Elementi di scienza politica,* the source of his posthumous fame and the work that immediately won him an appointment as professor at the University of Turin, where he taught up to 1923. In this work Mosca gave a systematic exposition of his idea that the history of human societies is characterized by structural divisions between the "governors" (those who hold power and who always represent an organized minority) and the "governed" (those who are the objects of power). According to a definition that has become famous, the former constitute the "political class," which is accessed only by men moved by a natural passion for power and for the symbolic and material advantages connected to it. In order to exercise rule, the political class cannot, however, base itself solely on force and physical coercion: it needs an abstract principle that justifies it from the moral point of view and that gives a historical foundation to the exercise of its authority. According to Mosca, that principle constitutes the "political formula" (or ideology) through which every political class seeks to justify and legitimate its own power over the majority.

Mosca's ambition, typically positivist, was to construct a scientific theory of politics on the basis of the constants of history and the regularities that characterize human behavior. His best-known thesis, regarding the impossibility of democracy and the belief that all political regimes are by definition oligarchies, is not, however, simply a scientific formulation; it constitutes the basis for his ideological critique of socialism, liberalism, and parliamentary democracy, typical of the conservative tradition with which Mosca identified and which Italian Fascism took over, accentuating its antidemocratic and authoritarian nature. In 1909, Mosca entered the Italian political scene: he was elected a parliamentary deputy, a post that he was to hold for ten years. After 1919 he was appointed "senator of the kingdom." For a short period between 1914 and 1916 he also held the position of undersecretary for the colonies in the government of Antonio Salandra.

Toward Fascism, Mosca initially maintained an attitude of sympathetic interest: in the rise of the movement founded by Mussolini he saw both the confirmation of his scientific predictions as to the structural crisis of parliamentary and democratic-representative regimes, and also a political brake on socialism and social anarchy. In 1923, the year when the second and definitive edition of the *Elementi di scienza politica* was published, he voted in favor of the Acerbo Law, the majoritarian electoral reform with which Mussolini was to ensure for himself a landslide parliamentary majority in the elections of April 1924. Subsequently, with the spread of violence against political opponents and the strengthening of the dictatorship, Mosca moved toward a more critical attitude that led him gradually to reevaluate the principles of liberal democracy; and eventually he found himself in a position of total political and intellectual isolation. In May 1925 he signed the Manifesto of Antifascist Intellectuals put together by the philosopher Benedetto Croce, and in December of that same year he intervened in parliament with a famous speech in which he opposed the bill on the prerogatives of the head of the government. His final parliamentary speech was delivered on 21 May 1926, and afterward he abandoned political life for good.

Alessandro Campi
(translated by Cyprian Blamires)

See Also: ACERBO LAW, THE; ARISTOCRACY; CONSERVATISM; CROCE, BENEDETTO; DEMOCRACY; EGALITARIANISM; ELITE THEORY; FASCIST PARTY, THE; HERO, THE CULT OF THE; ITALY; LEADER CULT, THE; LIBERALISM; MACHIAVELLI, NICCOLÒ; MANIFESTO OF FASCIST INTELLECTUALS, THE; MICHELS, ROBERTO; MUSSOLINI, BENITO ANDREA; PARETO, VILFREDO; PARLIAMENTARISM; POSITIVISM; SOCIALISM; SOCIOLOGY; SOREL, GEORGES

References
Albertoni, E. A. 1987. *Mosca and the Theory of Elitism.* Oxford: Basil Blackwell.

Sir Oswald Mosley and his second wife Diana, one of the six celebrated Mitford sisters. Mosley was the best-known British fascist of the twentieth century, and continued to be active as influential fascist propagandist and politician into the postwar era. Diana was a staunch supporter. (Chris Ware/Keystone/Hulton Archive/Getty Images)

Ghiringhelli, R. 1992. *Elitism and Democracy: Mosca, Pareto and Michels.* Milan: Cisalpino.

Nye, R. A. 1977. *The Anti-Democratic Sources of Elite Theory: Pareto, Mosca, Michels.* London: Sage.

MOSLEY, SIR OSWALD (1896–1980)

Leader of the British Union of Fascists (BUF) during the 1930s. Born in 1896, the scion of a wealthy Staffordshire family, Mosley was educated at Winches-ter before attending Sandhurst Military School in January 1914 at the age of seventeen. During World War I, Mosley served briefly in the 16th Queen's Light Dragoons before joining the Royal Flying Corps (RFC), injuring his leg during a crash (while performing for his mother) that left him with a permanent limp. Invalided out, in 1918 Mosley stood for Parliament and was elected Conservative MP for Harrow. In 1920 he married Lady Cynthia Curzon, daughter of Lord Curzon, the foreign secretary. Gradually disillusioned with the lack of "dynamism" displayed by the government, and disgusted at Black and Tan paramilitaries in Northern Ireland, Mosley "crossed the floor" on 27 March 1924 and joined the Labour Party, to which he submitted a series of Keynsian economic proposals for solving unemployment, culminating with the *Mosley*

Memorandum (1930). When this was rejected Mosley abandoned the Labour Party and formed the New Party in 1931 to challenge the ossified "Old Gang" of British politics. Roundly trounced during the 1931 general election, Mosley consulted Mussolini before founding the BUF in October 1932; it became increasingly anti-Semitic and pro-Nazi, although Mosley claimed to eschew the "Continental approach." Despite the initial enthusiasm of the Rothermere press, potential support ebbed away following the shockingly brutal Olympia meeting in June 1934. A further symbolic defeat occurred in October 1936 at the "Battle of Cable Street," when the BUF was prevented from marching through the East End by widespread working-class opposition. The subsequent passing of the Public Order Act (1936) prohibiting fascist uniforms and the lamentable performance of the BUF in the 1937 local elections exacerbated internal problems that were further intensified when Mussolini withdrew his secret subsidy, crippling the BUF financially and leading to the departure of William Joyce and others. Membership of the BUF recovered slowly throughout 1939 as Mosley campaigned against a "Jews' War," until he and his chief lieutenants were interned in May 1940 under Defence Regulation 18B, which destroyed the BUF as a political force. In November 1943, Mosley and his second wife, Diana, were released from prison (due to illness) amid near universal protest. After 1945, Mosley published his apologia, *My Answer* (1946), followed by *The Alternative* (1947), outlining his pan-European philosophy: "Europe-a-Nation." In February 1948, Mosley formed the Union Movement before moving to Ireland in 1951 and then to France, where he lived for the remainder of his life. He returned to England to stand as candidate for South Kensington in 1959, in order to exploit fears surrounding mass immigration following race riots there. He gained only 8 percent of the vote and lost his deposit. Intimately involved in the postwar international fascist network, Mosley became the driving force behind the (failed) initiative to form a pan-European fascist party at the Conference of Venice in 1962.

Graham Macklin

See Also: ANTI-SEMITISM; BRITISH FASCISTI/BRITISH FASCISTS, THE; EUROPE; EUROPEANIST FASCISM/RADICAL RIGHT, THE; FASCIST PARTY, THE; FINANCE; GREAT BRITAIN; IMMIGRATION; JOYCE, WILLIAM; ITALY; MITFORD FAMILY, THE; MUSSOLINI, BENITO ANDREA; NAZISM; POSTWAR FASCISM

References
Courcy, Anne de. 2003. *Diana Mosley.* London: Chatto and Windus.
Dorril, Stephen. 2006. *Blackshirt: Sir Oswald Mosley and British Fascism.* London: Viking.
Hawkey, Andrew, ed. 1997. *Revolution by Reason and Other Essays by Sir Oswald Mosley.* Lampeter: Edwin Mellen.
Skidelsky, Robert. 1990. *Oswald Mosley.* London: Macmillan.

MOŢA, ION I. (1902–1937)

Founder of a Romanian version of the Action Française (Actiunea Românesca) in 1923. He studied in Grenoble, France, with Codreanu and was one of the founding members of the Legion of the Archangel Michael. He fought as a volunteer in the Spanish Civil War and was killed in Majadahonda (near Madrid) on 13 January 1937, together with his friend Vasile Marin. Moţa and Marin were buried in the Mausoleum of the Green House (the headquarters of the Legion of the Archangel Michael) in Bucharest. The tour that their coffins made throughout Romania drew hundreds of thousands of people and was the first public display of the enormous support that the legion enjoyed among the Romanian population.

Philip Vanhaelemeersch

See Also: ACTION FRANÇAISE; CODREANU, CORNELIU ZELEA; FRANCE; INTEGRAL NATIONALISM; LEGION OF THE ARCHANGEL MICHAEL, THE; MAURRAS, CHARLES; ROMANIA; SPANISH CIVIL WAR, THE

References
Ioanid, R. 1990. *The Sword of the Archangel Michael: Fascist Ideology in Romania.* Boulder: Eastern European Monographs.
Nagy-Talavera, N. 1970. *The Green Shirts and Others.* Stanford: Stanford University Press.

MOVIMENTO SOCIALE ITALIANO (MSI; ITALIAN SOCIAL MOVEMENT), THE

Neofascist party established in Italy in 1946 by former associates and supporters of Mussolini under the leadership of Giorgio Almirante. Forcefully hostile to communism but not in the name of liberalism, it saw itself as a third way between capitalism and communism. Its rejection of the party system and belief in a strong executive, together with its advocacy of proactive government involvement in the social arena, gave it the appearance of having taken on the mantle of its celebrated forebear. Other prominent figures associated with the MSI have included Giuseppe ("Pino") Rauti and Alessandra Mussolini, Il Duce's granddaughter. In 1995 the leader, Gianfranco Fini, dissolved the MSI to found the Alleanza Nazionale (AN), a movement that was committed to parliamentarism and officially opposed to anti-Semitism, xenophobia, and racism. At that point hardline members of the MSI left to found the Fiamma Tricolore.

Cyprian Blamires

See Also: ALMIRANTE, GIORGIO; ANTI-SEMITISM; BOLSHEVISM; CAPITALISM; FASCIST PARTY, THE; ITALY; LIBERALISM; MARXISM; MUSSOLINI, ALESSANDRA; MUSSOLINI, BENITO ANDREA; PARLIAMENTARISM; POSTWAR FASCISM; RACISM; RAUTI, GIUSEPPE ("PINO"); SOCIALISM; THIRD WAY, THE; XENOPHOBIA

References
Ferraresi, Franco. 1996. *Threats to Democracy: The Radical Right in Italy after the War.* Princeton: Princeton University Press.
Weinberg, Leonard. *After Mussolini: Italian Neo-Fascism and the Nature of Fascism.* Washington, DC: University Press of America.

MÜLLER, BISHOP LUDWIG (1883–1946)

Hitler's appointee as head of the German Christians. Müller was born at Gütersloh and became a Protestant army chaplain, known for his extreme nationalism and anti-Semitism. Soon after Hitler became chancellor, he appointed Müller as his personal adviser in Lutheran Church matters. On 23 July 1933, Müller was elected Reich bishop by a national synod in Wittenberg. However, that was only a titular position, and it gave Müller no political or ecclesiastical influence. Moreover, many Lutherans went with the Confessing Church and rejected the extreme nationalistic and anti-Semitic positions of the German Christians. Hitler soon lost interest in Müller, who was arrested at the end of the war and committed suicide in March 1946 in a Berlin prison.

Cyprian Blamires

See Also: ANTI-SEMITISM; CHRISTIANITY; CONFESSING (OR CONFESSIONAL) CHURCH, THE; GERMAN CHRISTIANS, THE; GERMANY; HITLER, ADOLF; LUTHERAN CHURCHES, THE; NATIONALISM; NAZISM; NIEMOELLER, MARTIN; PROTESTANTISM AND NAZISM

Reference
Barnett, Victoria. 1992. *For the Soul of the People: Protestant Protest against Hitler.* New York: OUP.

MULTICULTURALISM

Multiculturalism (the doctrine that different cultures, rather than one national culture, can coexist peacefully and equitably in a single country) has proved to be a favorite target of postwar fascists in Europe. Following in the footsteps of interwar fascism, all contemporary right-wing extremist groups in the United States and Western and Eastern Europe are opposed to multiculturalism, even where there would be adjustment to the one dominant culture. Equally, there has been a far-right current of thought in more recent years that opposes globalization in the name of the preservation of indigenous cultures. The philosophy is to defend the national culture against an all-conquering homogeneous U.S. culture.

Ekkart Zimmermann and Cyprian Blamires

See Also: AMERICANIZATION; EUROPEAN NEW RIGHT, THE; GLOBALIZATION; IMMIGRATION; NATIONALISM; POSTWAR FASCISM

References
Deutsch, Karl W. 1966. *Nationalism and Social Communication: An Inquiry into the Foundations of Nationality.* Cambridge: MIT Press.
Fearon, James D., and David D. Laitin. 2003. "Ethnicity, Insurgency, and Civil War." *American Political Science Review* 97: 75–89.
Hechter, Michael. 2000. *Containing Nationalism.* Oxford: Oxford University Press.
Kitschelt, Herbert. 1998. *The Radical Right in Western Europe: A Comparative Analysis.* Ann Arbor: University of Michigan Press.

MUNICH AGREEMENT/PACT, THE

An agreement ceding part of the Sudetenland in Czechoslovakia to the Third Reich, signed on 30 September 1938, chiefly between Neville Chamberlain of

Britain, Edouard Daladier of France, Adolf Hitler of Germany, and Benito Mussolini of Italy. Usually regarded as the high point in the "appeasement" of Nazi expansionism, the Munich Pact was principally intended to avoid another European war twenty years after World War I. However, in March 1939, Nazi Germany occupied the remainder of Czechoslovakia, provoking French and British security guarantees to Poland, and triggering World War II in Europe when that country was invaded by the Wehrmacht on 1 September 1939.

Matt Feldman

See Also: APPEASEMENT; CZECHOSLOVAKIA; GERMANY; HITLER, ADOLF; MUSSOLINI, BENITO ANDREA; NAZISM; POLAND AND NAZI GERMANY; SUDETENLAND, THE; WEHRMACHT, THE; WORLD WAR I; WORLD WAR II

References
Kee, Robert. 1988. *Munich: The Eleventh Hour.* London: Hamish Hamilton.
Latynski, Maya, ed. 1992. *Reappraising the Munich Pact: Continental Perspectives.* Baltimore: Johns Hopkins University Press.
McDonough, Frank. 2002. *Hitler, Chamberlain and Appeasement.* Cambridge: Cambridge University Press.

MUNICH (BEER-HALL) PUTSCH, THE

Failed attempt by Adolf Hitler to seize power with his new Nazi Party. On the evening of 8 November 1923, a number of dignitaries gathered in the Bürgerbräu Keller in Munich on the occasion of a speech by Gustav Ritter von Kahr, the state commissioner of Bavaria. They included the commander of the armed forces in Bavaria and the chief of the Bavarian state police. During the talk, which was attended by an audience of some 3,000, Hitler's forces surrounded the building; Hitler jumped on a chair and shouted, "The national revolution has begun!," firing a gunshot at the ceiling. He took the eminent figures on the dais prisoner and announced that he was forming a new government together with General Erich Ludendorff. The prisoners managed to escape. The next morning the Nazis set out with swastika banners on a march toward the center of Munich, headed by Hitler, Ludendorff, Goering, and Streicher. At the Odeonplatz, near the Felherrn Halle, they were faced with 100 police; Hitler called on them

to surrender, but they answered with gunfire. Sixteen Nazis and three policemen were killed, and Goering was wounded. On 24 February ten defendants were put on trial as leaders of the putsch, including Ernst Roehm and Wilhelm Frick, along with Hitler and Ludendorff. Ludendorff was acquitted while the others were found guilty, and Hitler was sentenced to five years' "fortress arrest," of which he served only nine months. The bloody confrontation between the party faithful and the police became enshrined in Nazi legend, and the victims among Hitler's followers were elevated to the status of martyrs; later there was an annual commemoration of the event under the Third Reich.

Cyprian Blamires

See Also: CALENDAR, THE FASCIST; FRICK, WILHELM; GERMANY; GOERING, HERMANN; HITLER, ADOLF; LUDENDORFF, ERICH; *MEIN KAMPF;* MYTH; NAZISM; ROEHM, ERNST; STREICHER, JULIUS; SWASTIKA, THE; THIRD REICH, THE

References
Dornberg, John. 1982. *The Putsch that Failed: Munich 1923, Hitler's Rehearsal for Power.* London: Weidenfeld and Nicholson.
Gordon, H. 1972. *Hitler and the Beer Hall Putsch.* Princeton: Princeton University Press.

MUSIC (Germany)

Music had an eminent position in the self-understanding of National Socialism, and Nazi ideologues considered it the most German of all the arts since the time of the Romantics. The National Socialist state understood music as the purest expression of the national character and subsidized musical life generously. On account of that high valuation of music, whose character-building powers it undoubtedly overestimated, it had the concert program controlled and "cleansed." Works that were regarded as "un-German" were excluded. Adolf Hitler saw musicality as the expression of a deep life of feeling. He attributed to music the status of a divine revelation of eternal validity and a generator of meaning. For him the appropriate response to music was not critical hearing but reverent and sensitive listening. Hitler expected of his own audiences a devoted attention similar to that accorded a Bruckner symphony. Aesthetic fascination was to lead through intimidation to assent.

This revived conception of the Romantic religion of art was at the opposite pole from all "cultural Bolshevism." Under this heading the National Socialist state fought against the atonality of Arnold Schoenberg, experimental forms and modern dance rhythms in Paul Hindemith, Ernst Krenek, Kurt Weill, and Igor Stravinsky as an expression of chaos and anarchy. Its "cleansing" was directed against known modernists, against supporters of the Weimar Republic, social democrats, communists, foreigners, and last but not least, Jews. From 1936 open racism displaced the hitherto mainly political and aesthetic foundation of the "cleansing." The concept of "cultural Bolshevism" gave way to the reproach of "degeneracy," which originally derived from medicine and biology. In imitation of the Munich exhibition of "Degenerate Art" of 1937, the Weimar artistic director Hans Severus Ziegler organized the propaganda show "Degenerate Music" on his own initiative. When he opened it in May 1938, during the Düsseldorf Reich Music Day, he attacked all mingling of races. He referred in this connection to Wagner's tract *Das Judentum in der Musik (Judaism in Music)* and to Hitler's *Mein Kampf.*

It now became obligatory to refer to Germanic racial roots and "Aryan instincts." Inspired by Wagner's musical dramas, musicologists studied Germanic culture. Among the chief characteristics of "Nordic man" they identified in particular "inwardness" and "joy in battle." Corresponding to the alleged constant of race, National Socialist musical life was now, over its whole spectrum, from symphony concert to Hitler Youth performance, directed to the heroic and the metaphysical, so as to strengthen through the performance of standard works the threatened instincts of the "national community." Composers such as Bach, Beethoven, Wagner, and Bruckner were considered classic representatives of the German national character and educators of the people. Their genius was held to support the legitimation of the German claim to domination. In 1944, Wolfgang Stumme, music adviser to the Reich youth leadership, explained musical policy goals thus: "Music policy means for us today: the deployment of music as a life-giving power to form the people and uphold the state; it means the protection and nurturing of German music as the form of expression of our blood and our soul, hence as a way to the attainment of higher knowledge and the higher development of our race."

Albrecht Dümling
(translated by Cyprian Blamires)

See Also: ANTI-SEMITISM; ART; ARYANISM; BAYREUTH; BLOOD; BOLSHEVISM; CHRISTIANITY; CIVILIZATION; CULTURE; DECADENCE; DEGENERACY; GERMANNESS (*DEUTSCHHEIT*); GERMANY; HERO, THE CULT OF THE; HITLER, ADOLF; LEISURE; MATERIALISM; *MEIN KAMPF;* MODERNISM; MUSIC (ITALY); NAZISM; NORDIC SOUL, THE; RACIAL DOCTRINE; RACISM; SOUL; *VOLKSGEMEINSCHAFT,* THE; WAGNER, (WILHELM) RICHARD; WARRIOR SPIRIT, THE; WEIMAR REPUBLIC, THE; YOUTH MOVEMENTS

References

Brinkmann, R., and C. Wolff, eds. 1999. *Driven into Paradise: The Musical Migration from Nazi Germany to the United States.* Berkeley: University of California Press.
Cobley, Evelyn. 2002. *Temptations of Faust: The Logic of Fascism and Postmodern Archaeologies of Modernity.* Toronto: University of Toronto Press.
Dümling, Albrecht. 2002. "The Target of Racial Purity: The 'Degenerate Music' Exhibition in Düsseldorf, 1938." In *Art, Culture and Media under the Third Reich,* edited by R. A. Eltin. Chicago: University of Chicago Press.
Musgrove, Jan. 2003. *Music and Nazism.* Laaber: Laaber.

MUSIC (Italy)

Italian Fascism was well aware of music's power as a tool of propaganda. Sung at rallies and other gatherings, its choral songs, or *inni* (hymns), had an integral place in party ritual. "Giovinezza" ("Youth"), the "Triumphal Hymn of the National Fascist Party," took on the status of joint national anthem alongside the official "Marcia reale" ("Royal March"). The authorities also encouraged the production of a more commercial, but no less propagandistic, variety of popular song: most famously, "Faccetta nera" ("Little Black Face"), from the time of the Ethiopian campaign. With its monopolistic control of the new medium of radio through the state broadcasting company, the Ente Italiano Audizione Radio (EIAR), Fascism was able to disseminate its music to every corner of the nation. This was also the period when gramophone records became available to a mass public. But Italian listeners were not restricted to blatantly politicized material. There was also operetta, light music, and American jazz, Italianized as *gez,* and increasingly performed by home-grown musicians.

Throughout Fascism's two decades in power, opera, traditionally the Italian musical form par excellence, was rapidly losing audiences to cinema, which, with the advent of sound, became another important source of popular music. The regime responded with state subsidies for opera houses and, from 1938 (by order of the General Administration for Theatre and Music, a department of the Ministry of Popular Culture), a drive to promote operas by contemporary composers. By contrast, the period was one of growth in the field of purely instrumental music. Permanent orchestras were founded in Florence, Turin, and Rome. Tensions among Italian Fascism's leading "serious" composers came to a head in the "Manifesto of Italian Musicians for the Tradition of Nineteenth-Century Romantic Art" (1932), a thinly veiled attack on the modernists Alfredo Casella (1883–1947) and Gian Francesco Malipiero (1882–1973). Signed by both Ottorino Respighi (1879–1936) and Ildebrando Pizzetti (1880–1968), among others, this was the work of Alceo Toni (1884–1969), music critic of the Fascist daily *Il popolo d'Italia* and an influential figure in the Fascist Union of Musicians (set up in 1924, and ever more powerful thereafter). But one should not draw too many conclusions from this episode. As in other areas of culture, the Fascist musical hierarchy gave support to modernists just as much as to conservatives. From the early 1930s, at prestigious festivals sponsored by the regime in Florence (the Maggio Musicale Fiorentino) and Venice, enfants terribles such as Luigi Dallapiccola (1904–1975) and Goffredo Petrassi (1904–2003) could attend premieres of their latest works alongside performances of music by leading international representatives of the compositional vanguard. Stravinsky, for one, was a frequent visitor. Later in the decade, however, after the imposition of anti-Semitic legislation and the beginning of the campaign for musical autarky, the possibilities for such cosmopolitan experiences were restricted.

Ben Earle

See Also: ANTI-SEMITISM; ART; COSMOPOLITANISM; FASCIST PARTY, THE; FILM; FUTURISM; ITALY; MODERNISM; MUSIC (GERMANY); PROPAGANDA; RADIO

References
Illiano, Roberto, ed. 2004. *Italian Music during the Fascist Period.* Turnhout: Brepols.
Mazzoletti, Adriano. 2004. *Il jazz in Italia. Dalle origine alle grandi orchestre.* Turin: EDT.
Sachs, Harvey. 1987. *Music in Fascist Italy.* London: Weidenfeld and Nicolson.

MUSIC (POPULAR): *See* ROCK MUSIC; SKREWDRIVER; WHITE NOISE

MUSLIM VOLUNTEERS IN THE WAFFEN-SS

Numerous Bosnian Muslim volunteers were incorporated into units of the Waffen-SS. The largest was the thirteenth Handschar ("scimitar") division, comprising more than 21,000 men, which was involved in operations against communist partisans in the Balkans. Muslim imams were attached to the division. An active participant in the encouragement of this volunteering was Palestinian grand mufti Amin al-Husseini. By November 1944, the division had disbanded.

Cyprian Blamires

See Also: MIDDLE EAST, THE; PALESTINE; WAFFEN-SS, THE; WORLD WAR II

Reference
Lepre, George. 1997. *Himmler's Bosnian Division: Waffen SS Handschar Division 1943–1945.* Lancaster, PA: Schiffer.

MUSSERT, ANTON ADRIAAN (1894–1946)

Dutch fascist leader and founder of the Nationaal Socialistische Beweging (NSB; National Socialist Movement). After completing secondary school, Mussert studied road construction and hydraulics at what is now called the Technical University of Delft. He developed a successful career at the Ministry of State Waterworks. Initially a liberal, Mussert soon became an ultranationalist. The immediate cause was a proposed treaty with Belgium that was seen by many in The Netherlands as contrary to Dutch territorial and economic interests. Mussert's public activities against the treaty were successful, and it was rejected by parliament in 1927. Mussert was impressed by the formation of a corporatist fascist state in Italy by Mussolini. In 1931, Mussert founded the Dutch NSB together with Cornelis van Geelkerken; the NSB party program was largely a copy of Hitler's NSDAP program. In 1935 the NSB obtained a remarkable success in the provincial elections. Mussert supported Mussolini's attack on

Ethiopia, and in 1936 he came out in open support of Hitler's policies. He met with Hitler on several occasions, for the first time on 16 November 1936. The ties with Nazi Germany became stronger. Mussert adopted the Nazi theory of races and its violent anti-Semitism. The radicalization of the NSB drove many voters away. From then on, the fortunes of the NSB began to wane quickly.

After the start of World War II, Mussert demanded strict neutrality for The Netherlands. But with the occupation of the country by the German armies he changed his view and started to promote a Germanic alliance of states under German leadership. During the war, members of the NSB were appointed to important positions within the occupation government. A large number of young NSB members joined the Waffen-SS. Mussert and the NSB largely supported the German occupation of The Netherlands. Hitler was impressed by Mussert, whom he mentions on more than one occasion in his *Table Talk*. After the liberation in 1945, Mussert was arrested and condemned to death on the grounds of treason, attacking constitutional rule, and collaboration with the enemy.

Philip van Meurs

See Also: ANTI-SEMITISM; BELGIUM; CORPORATISM; FASCIST PARTY, THE; HITLER, ADOLF; ITALY; MUSSOLINI, BENITO ANDREA; NATIONALISM; NAZISM; NETHERLANDS, THE; PANGERMANISM; RACIAL DOCTRINE; WAFFEN-SS, THE; WORLD WAR II

References

Jonge, A. A. de. "Mussert Anton Adriaan (1894–1946)." In *Het Biografische Woordenboek van Nederland*.
Littlejohn, D. 1973. *The Patriotic Traitors*. London: Heinemann.
Meyers, Jan. 2005. *Mussert, een politiek leven*. Soesterberg: Aspekt.
Warmbrunn, W. 1963. *The Dutch under German Occupation*. Stanford: Stanford University Press.

MUSSOLINI, ALESSANDRA (born 1962)

Granddaughter of Benito Mussolini and founder of Libertà d'Azione (Freedom of Action), which later became part of the Alternativa Sociale coalition. She was elected to the European Parliament on this ticket in 2004. Having started out as an actress and model,

Mussolini took a medical degree and then was elected to a Naples constituency on the MSI list. She left in 2003 after Gianfranco Fini, deputy prime minister and leader of the Alleanza Nazionale (into which the MSI had been merged in 1995), apologized on a visit to Israel for Italy's treatment of the Jews and described Fascism as "an absolute evil."

Cyprian Blamires

See Also: ANTI-SEMITISM; FASCIST PARTY, THE; ITALY; MOVIMENTO SOCIALE ITALIANO, THE; MUSSOLINI, BENITO ANDREA; POSTWAR FASCISM

MUSSOLINI, BENITO ANDREA AMILCARE (1883–1945)

Founder of Italian Fascism and head of the Italian government from October 1922 until July 1943. Mussolini was born at Predappio in Romagna on 29 July 1883; his father, Alessandro, was a blacksmith, and his mother, Rosa Maltoni, was an elementary school teacher. The social milieu into which he was born was marked by fervent political passions and powerful social and economic tensions. The father of the future dictator was a socialist agitator with anarchical sympathies, which explains the three names given to the son: Benito, in memory of the Mexican revolutionary Benito Jaurez; Andrea, as a homage to the anarchist thinker and leader Andrea Costa; and Amilcare, in honor of the internationalist and member of the Paris Commune Amilcare Cipriani. Mussolini's childhood and youth were marked by a great restlessness of spirit, by a total lack of discipline, and by aimless reading and erratic studies culminating in an elementary teacher's certificate. Under the influence of his father and of the environment he became a socialist early on, but with an attitude strongly marked by voluntarism and subversive in spirit—hence, with a polemical attitude toward the parliamentary legalitarian socialism that at this period dominated the leadership of the Italian Socialist Party.

The political culture of the young Mussolini—reinforced by his experience between 1902 and 1904 as an expatriate in Switzerland, where he came into contact with European revolutionary milieux (among others with the Ukrainian Angelica Balabanoff)—was a curious mixture of elements: republican radicalism, anticlericalism, Blanquism, utopian communism, internationalism, and Jacobin maximalism. He read the sacred texts of orthodox Marxism in abridged versions and second-hand, but for temperamental reasons his politico-ideological sympathies were above all with revolutionary syndicalism, with which he shared the cult of direct action, voluntarism, the rejection of the principle of representation, and the recognition of the crucial role of political avant-gardes. Along with political works he was also interested in the philosophical writings of Nietzsche and Stirner, from which he assimilated an irrationalistic conception of historical becoming, based on force, on subjectivism, and on the active role of violence.

On his return from Switzerland, Mussolini tried a teaching career, first at Tolmezzo and then at Oneglia, but he had to make do with temporary posts that were poorly remunerated. Dissatisfied with teaching, he threw himself headlong into journalism and writing. But his real vocation was for political militancy. Impulsive and generous, the young Mussolini was always at the head of political demonstrations: after 1908, when he went back to Predappio and abandoned teaching for good to become a "professional revolutionary," he frequently got involved in the street battles and factory workers' and agricultural laborers' protests that were common at that period of Italian history. He soon acquired a reputation as a hothead and a belligerent and intransigent militant. In January 1909 he moved to Trento, where he became secretary of the Chamber of Labor and editor of the weekly *l'Avvenire del lavoratore*. A few months later he was expelled by the Austrian authorities because of his subversive activities. In September 1911 his strong opposition to the Libyan war, pursued by the Giolitti government and bitterly attacked by the Left with strikes and demonstrations, led to his arrest and several months' imprisonment.

The career of Mussolini the socialist as journalist and leader was brilliant. In the space of a few years, thanks to his resolute character, to an undoubted political flair, and to a certain open-mindedness, he climbed the rungs of the Socialist Party till, with the National Congress of Reggio Emilia in July 1912, he became the recognized head of the "maximalist" revolutionary tendency. His consecration as national leader of the Italian Socialist Party took place at the next National Congress, in April 1914 in Ancona, when the "reformists" were routed and the definitive victory went to the revolutionary tendency. Mussolini was entrusted with the editorship of the party daily *Avanti!*, whose sales he pushed up to nearly 80,000 on the back of his political campaigning and his mordant journalistic style. To take

Benito Mussolini, who established the very first fascist regime anywhere in the world in Italy in 1922. World War I played a significant part in shaping his new ideology but it was his commitment to World War II that led to his downfall. (The Illustrated London News Picture Library)

up this new post he moved definitively to Milan, where he set up home with Rachele Guidi, a young girl from the Romagna with whom he had been living for years (he eventually married her in a civil ceremony in 1915) and by whom he already had a daughter named Edda. The marriage produced four further children: Bruno, Vittorio, Romano, and Anna Maria.

The outbreak of World War I in the summer of 1914 marked a crucial turn in Mussolini's political biography. The Italian socialists were outspokenly against the war, which they considered an internal matter for the international bourgeoisie and the imperialist powers. Mussolini, who officially took the party line, in reality nurtured many doubts as to this interpretation, which in his opinion denied all value to the patriotic and national feelings of the proletariat. Moreover he saw in the war a unique opportunity to revolutionize the domestic political order, putting an end to the political equilibrium guaranteed by the liberal system. On 18 October 1914 he therefore published an article entitled "From Absolute Neutrality to Active Neutrality," in which he argued for an Italian intervention in the war: it represented his decisive break with socialism, officially hallowed on 24 November following his expulsion from the party. In the meantime, on 15 November, he founded a new daily newspaper, *Il Popolo d'Italia,* which became the organ of the "interventionists" and which was eventually to be the official daily of the Fascist regime. Considered a traitor by his former associates, Mussolini soon placed himself at the head of an assorted politico-intellectual movement that included nationalists, Futurists, revolutionary socialists, anarchists, and radical democrats, all united in their desire to bring about a change in Italian politics through the regenerative instrument of war.

Even before the end of the war, in which Mussolini took part in the ranks, he grasped the important role that would be played in the postwar Italian political and social scene by war veterans and former servicemen once they had gone back into civilian life. In his newspaper he sang the praises of the "aristocracy of the trenches," prophesied the advent of an anti-Marxist national socialism, predicted the birth of a "new Italy," and preached a synthesis between "class" and "nation" and agreement between "fighters" and "producers." On that basis, a few months after the Armistice, he founded in Milan on 23 March 1919 the Fasci di combattimento, whose political program, clearly national-revolutionary in outlook and with a strong impress of the democratic Left, proposed, among other things, the abandonment of the monarchy, the reduction of the working day to eight hours, the confiscation of "war profits," the expropriation of uncultivated land, and participation by the workers in the organization of industry. The electoral beginnings of the Fascist movement in November 1919 were, however, disastrous from the point of view of support at the ballot box (scarcely more than 5,000 votes in the Milan district, the only one in which the Fascists managed to organize a list); Fascism seemed in danger of disappearing at birth, just like so many evanescent political grouplets that sprang up on the Italian political scene at this unsettled period.

The turning point—that is to say, the transformation of the movement into a reality with a growing political following—happened in the months that followed. In the autumn of 1920, a new Fascism began to emerge in the rural areas and provinces of the Po Valley in northern Italy, linked to the world of the farmers and the landowners and violently opposed to the trade unions, to the socialists, and to the workers' and peasant organizations (even to those with Catholic origins). The action of *squadrismo*—inspired by individuals like Italo Balbo and Roberto Farinacci, who went on to become leaders of the regime—transformed Fascism from a small, subversive revolutionary group without support or alliances into a real political force that was dynamic and innovative, attracting increasing interest above all from the world of the small and middle bourgeoisie, who had no party to represent their political claims, economic interests, and ideal aspirations. The initial "Fascism of the Left" gave way progressively to a Fascism inspired by nationalism and the cult of order. In a situation like this the great talent of Mussolini was to succeed in spreading on the table of national politics, and drawing from it the greatest advantage, this new image of Fascism as a force that was no longer subversive but restorative of civil and political order after the chaos resulting from the ending of the war, the economic crisis, and the political conflict between "reds" and "blacks" (which was developing into downright civil war, especially in Northern Italy.

The gravity of the institutional crisis; the tactical ability of the head of the "Black Shirts"; the political mistakes committed by the socialists and the Catholic Popular Party; the connivance of the monarchy and the liberal ruling class; the psychological and military pressure of *squadrismo*—these were the other basic elements in the success that Fascism gained in October 1922, when King Victor Emmanuel III entrusted the task of forming the new government to none other than Mussolini himself. In spite of the revolutionary choreography laid on with the March on Rome, Fascism in reality came to power by legal means and with due respect for constitutional rules. However, in accord with his own doctrinal formation, Mussolini very quickly showed that he did not have much time for parliament and the political forces of the opposition, preferring to concentrate all the power into his own hands. Fascism was in reality born out of the violence of war on an ideological basis that was antiliberal and antiparliamentary: the idea of "constitutionalizing" and "normalizing" Fascism was thus the great illusion of the political and institutional forces that allowed it to accede to power without having understood properly its profoundly subversive stance in respect to the rules of the game of the liberal constitutional system. However, it was not until the publication of the *leggi fascistissime* (from January 1925) that dictatorship pure and simple was born. In this phase, to put an end to the political crisis precipitated by the murder of the socialist deputy Giacomo Matteotti in the summer of 1924, Mussolini began in fact to launch a series of norms that provided for a limitation on civil liberties and the suppression of the freedom of the press and of political parties. The "Fascist regime" had begun.

Within a few years, fortified now by absolute power without either formal or substantial limits, the head of Fascism set to work on a profound political-institutional transformation, based on an ethical, absolute, and organic conception of the state. With the promulgation in 1927 of the *Carta del Lavoro* ("Charter of Labor") was begun the constitution of the corporative order, based on cooperation between providers of work and workers forcibly organized together into national syndicates. In its various articulations, society was progressively organized on military criteria within obligatory associative structures, according to the typical logic of all regimes of a totalitarian nature. Particular attention was paid to the world of work and to youth, with the constitution of bodies like the Opera Nazionale Dopolavoro, which was concerned with organizing the free time of Italian workers, or the Opera Nazionale Balilla (transformed in 1937 into the Gioventù italiana del Littorio), aimed at the politico-military and ideological formation of the young. Great attention was also paid to the world of culture and the school: in April 1925 the *Manifesto of Intellectuals of Fascism* was launched (and answered in May of the same year by Croce's *Manifesto of Antifascist Intellectuals*). In 1925 the program for the *Enciclopedia italiana* was launched under the direction of Giovanni Gentile; it was destined to become the most ambitious cultural production of Fascism. In 1926 the Accademia d'Italia was established.

In 1929, now solidly entrenched at the helm of his country, Mussolini won his most important political victory: he signed the Lateran Pacts with the Vatican, finally putting an end to the long-lasting conflict between the Catholic Church and the Italian state. By the late 1920s, Fascism was a political regime that recognized itself fully in its Duce, whose figure was now the object of a growing public political cult and of a massive propagandistic activity of indoctrination that involved the whole of Italian society.

Holding absolute power domestically, the dictator began to imagine himself increasingly as a historic figure of world significance, destined to play a crucial role on the international scene. In the early 1930s he therefore declared Fascism to be a universal doctrine, from which a new political civilization could emerge. Mus-

solini began to nurture dreams of imperial conquest, inspired culturally by the myth of Rome, but in reality aroused by the Hitlerian conquest of power and by the birth in Europe and the wider world of political movements inspired by the Italian prototype. In his vision, Fascist Italy, forgetting the humiliation of the past, was ready to aspire to a "place in the sun" and to play a role of hegemonic power in the Mediterranean and the Balkans. From the mid-1930s foreign policy became the heart of Mussolinian strategy. In October 1935 came the military conquest of Ethiopia, which marked the rupture of Italy with the Western powers, beginning with Great Britain. In July 1936, following the outbreak of the Spanish Civil War, he decided together with Germany to intervene in support of the nationalist forces led by General Franco. With Germany there were growing diplomatic contacts, cultural exchanges, and military collaboration: in May 1939 this developed into an organic alliance, the Pact of Steel.

The first steps in the war and the growing entente with Nazism took Italy toward totalitarianism pure and simple. In 1937 with the constitution of the Ministry of Popular Culture, all mass cultural activities came under the rigid control of a single political organ. Civil life was increasingly militarized. Measures and provisions were adopted to oppose the bourgeois spirit and to favor the diffusion among the people of martial virtues. In imitation of the German goosestep, the *passo romano* was introduced for parades and military march-pasts; all public employees were made to wear an obligatory uniform. But the gravest measure and the one with the most tragic consequences was the introduction in November 1938 of a systematic anti-Jewish legislation that at a stroke deprived thousands of Italians of Jewish origin (many of whom were in fact Fascists or sympathizers with the regime) of all political and civil rights.

The fatal result of this process was the involvement of Italy in World War II. After an initial neutrality (so-called nonbelligerence), in June 1940 Mussolini declared war on France and Great Britain. It was the beginning of an irremediable disaster, all the more irresponsible considering that the country did not have sufficient technical preparation to cope with a war on a continental scale (and soon to become a world scale). After a few successes on the French front, Mussolinian Italy showed all of its lack of preparation in the expedition for the conquest of Greece (beginning in October 1940). Then came the defeat in North Africa and the tragic Russian campaign. The poor outcomes of the conflict created in the country at large and also within the Fascist ruling class itself a state of growing unease and anxiety, which on 25 July 1943 led to a coup supported by the monarchy and the army. During a meeting of the Grand Council of Fascism Mussolini was disowned by his chiefs, a majority of whom voted for a motion proposed by Dino Grandi calling for the restoration to the monarchy of the "supreme decision-making initiative"—that is, of political power and the capacity to govern. A few hours later, in the morning of 26 July, Il Duce was arrested and taken to prison by a direct order of the king.

It was the end of the Fascist regime, but not yet of Fascism itself, which in fact rose again after 8 September 1943 (the date when the Armistice was signed between Italy and the Allies) through the establishment, in the area of northern Italy controlled by German troops, of the Salò Republic. Mussolini returned to the stage after a dramatic escape that saw him pass through Hitler's headquarters before returning to Italy. But the man now at the helm of the Salò Republic was no longer an idolized leader of the masses feared by his (few) enemies, as in the preceding decade, but the ghost of his former self—tired and ill and having lost his force and lucidity. Kept under surveillance by the Germans, surrounded by weird personages who showed him a tenacious and fanatical devotion, in the last months of his life, while the end of the war drew rapidly closer, Mussolini abandoned himself to dreams of a return to his old revolutionary socialist passions. In reality, he was obliged to watch impotently while the Italian nation fell slowly apart, more and more enmeshed in the spiral of a brutal civil war, of which he was to be the most illustrious victim (alongside the philosopher Giovanni Gentile, killed by partisans on 15 April 1944).

After he was captured in Dongo on 27 April 1945, in the course of a last attempt to escape in the direction of Switzerland, Mussolini was killed the next day at Giulino di Mezzegra, in the province of Como, together with his mistress Clara Petacci. The circumstances and modalities of this dual execution have never been fully explained. The body of Il Duce was taken to Milan and exposed to public view in the Piazzale Loreto, together with those of other chiefs shot by the partisans. After a day of macabre collective delirium the abuse of the corpses was interrupted at the wish of the resistance leaders themselves. Mussolini was then buried with great secrecy in the Milanese cemetery of the Musocco, but a group of young Fascists managed to pick out the coffin and make off with it. After having been recovered by the police, the body was hidden in a friary, where it remained until August 1957, when the Italian government decided to restore the mortal remains of the dictator to his family. Mussolini's body was eventually buried in the cemetery at Predappio, in the family mausoleum, where it is still today a focus for thousands of visitors every year. His granddaughter Alessandra Mussolini has taken up the torch of far-right politics in the modern era.

Alessandro Campi
(translated by Cyprian Blamires)

See Also: INTRODUCTION; ACERBO LAW, THE; ACTUALISM; ALBANIA; *ANSCHLUSS*, THE; "ANTI-" DIMENSION OF FASCISM, THE; ANTICLERICALISM; ANTI-SEMITISM; ARISTOCRACY; AUSTRIA; AVENTINE SECESSION, THE; AXIS, THE; BALBO, ITALO; BOLSHEVISM; BOURGEOISIE, THE; CAPORETTO; CATHOLIC CHURCH, THE; CIANO, COUNT GALEAZZO; CLASS; COLONIALISM; CORPORATISM; CROCE, BENEDETTO; D'ANNUNZIO, GABRIELE; DEMOCRACY; *ENCICLOPEDIA ITALIANA*, THE; ETHIOPIA; FARINACCI, ROBERTO; FARMERS; FASCIO, THE; FASCIST PARTY, THE; FILM; FIUME; FUTURISM; GENTILE, GIOVANNI; GERMANY; GOOSESTEP, THE; GRAND COUNCIL OF FASCISM, THE; GRANDI, DINO; GREECE; HITLER, ADOLF; IMPERIALISM; INTERNATIONAL FASCIST CONGRESSES, THE; INTERVENTIONISM; ITALY; LAW; LEADER CULT, THE; LEISURE; LIBERALISM; LIBYA; MANIFESTO OF FASCIST INTELLECTUALS, THE; MARCH ON ROME, THE; MARXISM; MATTEOTTI, GIACOMO; MILITARISM; MONARCHY; MOVIMENTO SOCIALE ITALIANO, THE; MUSSOLINI, ALESSANDRA; NATIONALISM; NAZISM; NIETZSCHE, FRIEDRICH; ORGANICISM; PALINGENETIC MYTH; PAPACY, THE; PARLIAMENTARISM; PIUS XI, POPE; PIUS XII, POPE; POLITICAL CATHOLICISM; POSTWAR FASCISM; PRODUCTIVISM; PROPAGANDA; RATIONALISM; RELIGION; REVOLUTION; ROME; SALÒ REPUBLIC, THE; SKORZENY, OTTO; SOCIALISM; SOREL, GEORGES; SPANISH CIVIL WAR, THE; SPANN, OTHMAR; SPENGLER, OSWALD; *SQUADRISMO;* SYNDICALISM; TOTALITARIANISM; TRADITION; UTOPIA, UTOPIANISM; VICTOR EMMANUEL/ VITTORIO EMANUELE III, KING; VIOLENCE; VOLUNTARISM; WAR; WAR VETERANS; WARRIOR ETHOS, THE; WORLD WAR I; WORLD WAR II; YOUTH MOVEMENTS; ZIONISM

References

Bosworth, R. J. B. 2002. *Mussolini.* London: Arnold.
Cannistraro, Philip V., and Brian R. Sullivan. 1993. *Il Duce's Other Woman: The Untold Story of Margherita Sarfatti, Benito Mussolini's Jewish Mistress, and How She Helped Him Come to Power.* New York: William Morrow.
Gregor, J. A. 1979. *Young Mussolini and the Intellectual Origins of Italian Fascism.* Berkeley: University of California Press.
Hibbert, C. 1972. *Mussolini.* London: Pan.
Kirkpatrick, I. 1964. *Mussolini: Study of a Demagogue.* London: Odhams.
Leads, C. 1972. *Italy under Mussolini.* London: Wayland.
Mack-Smith, D. 1981. *Mussolini.* London: Weidenfeld and Nicholson.

Ridley, J. G. 1999. *Mussolini*. London: Constable.
Williamson, D. G. 1997. *Mussolini: From Socialist to Fascist.* London: Hodder and Stoughton.

MVSN: *See MILIZIA VOLONTARIA PER LA SICUREZZA NAZIONALE (MVSN)*

MYSTICISM

The combination of Italian Fascism and German Nazism with mysticism has little bearing on historical notions of mysticism, but pertains to the process of secularization, in which modern ideologies of race, nationalism, and socialism have assumed the nature of pseudo-religions involving unswerving belief, radical commitment, and missionary zeal. In this form, ideologies imitate religion in the form of idolatry, inviting worship and sacrifice. Secular mysticism typically manifests as an acute form of identification with political references such as the leader, the party, the nation, or some other idealized focus of group identity such as territory, tribe, race, or blood. Mystical ideologies of group identity elevate one or more historical or cultural facets of political life into a sacred object of devotion. The elaboration of race into a mystical substrate of national identity was particularly evident in the work of Arthur de Gobineau, Richard Wagner, and Houston Stewart Chamberlain.

Alfred Rosenberg's major work, *The Myth of the Twentieth Century* (1930), was indebted to this tradition of racist nationalism. Rosenberg's own inspiration in Eastern religions, Arthur Schopenhauer, and the Gnostics, including the Manichaeans and the Cathars, indicate his aversion to received Roman Catholicism and his attempt to substitute for it a de-Judaized mystical religion rooted in the German nation. He credited the medieval German mystic Meister Eckhart with having rediscovered the German racial soul. He was also attracted to Eckhart because he had a (vastly exaggerated) reputation of being a Catholic in revolt against the Church. Secular mysticism was also directed against materialism and rationalism as the twin disorders of industrial modernity. Such writers as Paul Lagarde,

Guido von List (1848–1919), and Julius Langbehn articulated a mystical worldview that elevated the spiritual, natural, and artistic dimensions against the banal claims of social and economic life. Their outlook has a certain affinity with the "life-philosophy" of Friedrich Nietzsche and the vitalism of Henri Bergson.

In Italy, mystical notions of the state were elaborated by Julius Evola, who posited a mythical traditional order of Aryan society based on the four castes in a rigid hierarchy led by the warriors. He also conceived of rulership as divine and as a bridge to the higher metaphysical order of reality. Evola was not a biological racist, however, preferring a doctrine of spiritual hierarchy among the races. Some of his ideas were adopted by Mussolini as official Fascist racial theory in 1938, when Italy enacted its own racial laws distinct from those in Germany. The praxis of the interwar fascist regimes offers a rich field of study for these mystical identifications, systematically orchestrated by the authorities. The pageantry of the Nazi rallies and their quasi-liturgical nature encouraged religious identification with the regime. Huge congregations, banners, sacred flames, processions, and memorials were essential props for the cult of race and nation. The messianic figure of Adolf Hitler, the savior of Germany, towered over the entire project.

Nicholas Goodrick-Clarke

See Also: INTRODUCTION; ARYANISM; *BHAGAVADGITA*, THE; BUDDHISM; CATHOLIC CHURCH, THE; CHAMBERLAIN, HOUSTON STEWART; COMMUNITY; CULTS OF DEATH; ECKHART, "MEISTER" JOHANN; EVOLA, JULIUS; FASCIST PARTY, THE; GERMAN FAITH MOVEMENT, THE; GERMANIC RELIGION; GERMANNESS (*DEUTSCHHEIT*); GERMANY; GOBINEAU, COMTE ARTHUR DE; HERO, THE CULT OF THE; HIMMLER, HEINRICH; HITLER, ADOLF; ITALY; LAGARDE, PAUL DE; LANGBEHN, JULIUS; LEADER CULT, THE; LUDENDORFF, MATHILDE; MASSES, THE ROLE OF THE; MATERIALISM; MYTH; NATIONALISM; NORDIC SOUL, THE; NUREMBERG RALLIES, THE; OCCULTISM; PROPAGANDA; RACIAL DOCTRINE; RELIGION; ROSENBERG, ALFRED; SCHOPENHAUER, ARTHUR; SECULARIZATION; SOUL; SS, THE; SWASTIKA, THE; SYMBOLS; THEATER; TIBET; TOLKIEN, JOHN RONALD REUEL; VITALISM; *VOLKSGEMEINSCHAFT*, THE; WAGNER, (WILHELM) RICHARD; WAGNER AND GERMANNESS; WARRIOR ETHOS, THE

References
Felice, Renzo de. 1976. *Fascism: An Informal Introduction to Its Theory and Practice.* New Brunswick, NJ: Transaction.
Mosse, George L. 1964. *The Crisis of German Ideology: Intellectual Origins of the Third Reich.* New York: Grosset and Dunlap.
Noll, Richard. 1997. *The Aryan Christ: The Secret Life of Carl Jung.* New York: Random House.

Poewe, Karla. 2005. *New Religions and the Nazis.* London: Routledge.

Pois, Robert A. 1986. *National Socialism and the Religion of Nature.* Beckenham: Croom Helm.

MYTH

Every fascist ideology subsumes a number of unique myths that condition its particular policies and political liturgy. However, the core myth that drives all permutations of fascism has been widely identified as the rebirth of the organically conceived nation from an all-pervasive decadence—both of these components being themselves deeply mythic. It is this myth that can be shown to form the common denominator, for example, of Italian Fascism's vision of itself as completing the *Risorgimento* or fulfilling the revolutionary process inaugurated by World War I, the cult of *Romanità,* the imperialistic projects adopted after 1930, the creation of a Fascist calendar, the celebration of the Fascist "New Man," and the elaborate rituals and ceremonies designed to sacralize the state. In the Third Reich the myth of national rebirth subsumed such overtly mythic components as the belief in the "re-Aryanization" of the Germans, the war against cultural decadence in the name of an artistic renaissance, the myth that a new German had been born in the trenches of World War I, the vision of a regenerated *Volksgemeinschaft,* and the myth of Germans as a "master race" pitted against subhumans. Mythic thinking also pervaded the elaborate Fuehrer cult, as well as the intense ritual activity associated with such public events as the Nuremberg Rallies, the Berlin Olympics, the "Blood Flag" ceremony, and the annual commemoration in Munich of the martyrs of the failed Munich putsch. Other examples of the same phenomenon are to be found in the belief in a Dacian "root-race," in the coming of the *omul nou* ("new man"), and in an imminent national resurrection infused with Christian symbology as cultivated by the Romanian Iron Guard; the vision of Spain's sixteenth century as a *siglo d'oro* ("golden century") so important to the Falange; or the British Union of Fascists' invocation of the Tudor Age as a Golden Age in Britain's history to be emulated under Mosley, not to mention the myth of the natural genius of the race expressed in the British Empire and the Industrial Revolution.

One of the curiosities of interwar fascism is the way its defiant rejection of the Enlightenment tradition of rationalism and humanism could at times lead it not only to celebrate violence and war but also the power of myth itself in overtly Sorelian terms. Thus, on the eve of the March on Rome, Mussolini (who cited Sorel as one of his influences) declared: "We have created our myth. The myth is a faith, a passion. It is not necessary for it to be a reality. It is a reality in the sense that it is a stimulus, is hope, is faith, is courage. Our myth is the nation, our myth is the greatness of the nation! And to this myth, this greatness, which we want to translate into a total reality, that we subordinate everything else." In a similar vein, Alfred Rosenberg, one of the foremost ideologues of Nazism, called his famous (though little read) work on Germany's rebirth from decadence *The Myth of the Twentieth Century.*

Once the mythic ideological and liturgical component in all fascist thinking is recognized, it becomes possible to see even its most horrific acts of mass murder, such as the Nazis' euthanasia campaign, their calculated slaughter of millions of military and civilian "enemies," and the Holocaust itself as informed by a logic of ritual destruction in which the forces of decadence are purged to enable national rebirth to take place. However, in recognizing the central importance of myth in determining the style and policies of fascism, it is important not to overemphasize its role. Certainly, some individual fascist ideologues were deeply antirationalist and overtly mythopoeic in their worldview, notably Heinrich Himmler and Julius Evola. In many ways their overt appeal to occult notions of the forces shaping contemporary reality are atypical of fascism as a whole, however. Not only did elements of rational choice continue to have a significant impact on voting behavior in Weimar Germany until the Nazi "seizure of power," but important factions within both Italian Fascism and German Nazism incorporated significant components of technology, science, and bureaucratic and political pragmatism. Indeed, fascism is to be seen less as a regressive flight into unreason driven by a collective fear of the modern world, than a bid to create an alternative modernity through the fusion of modern science, technology, rationality, and the power of the modern state with the archetypal forces of spirituality and myth. The hallmark of fascist thought is thus antirationalism and scientism rather than irrationalism and hostility to science, which makes fascism very much a product of modernity rather than its rejection.

Roger Griffin

See Also: INTRODUCTION; ANTI-SEMITISM; ARYANISM; BAR-
BAROSSA, FREDERICK, HOLY ROMAN EMPEROR; BERLIN
OLYMPICS, THE; BLOOD; CALENDAR, THE FASCIST; DECA-
DENCE; ENLIGHTENMENT, THE; EUTHANASIA; EVOLA,
JULIUS; FALANGE; FASCIST PARTY, THE; FREDERICK II, THE
GREAT; GERMANY; GREAT BRITAIN; HERO, THE CULT OF
THE; HIMMLER, HEINRICH; HITLER, ADOLF; HOLOCAUST,
THE; HOLY ROMAN EMPIRE, THE; IMPERIALISM; IRON
GUARD, THE; ITALY; LEADER CULT, THE; MARCH ON
ROME, THE; MODERNISM; MODERNITY; MOSLEY, SIR OS-
WALD; MUNICH (BEER-HALL) PUTSCH, THE; MUSSOLINI,
BENITO ANDREA; MYSTICISM; NAZISM; NEW MAN, THE;
NUREMBERG RALLIES, THE; PALINGENETIC MYTH; PSY-
CHODYNAMICS OF PALINGENETIC MYTH, THE; RACIAL
DOCTRINE; RATIONALISM; *RISORGIMENTO*, THE; ROMA-
NIA; ROME; ROSENBERG, ALFRED; SCIENCE; SECULARIZA-
TION; SLAVS, THE (AND GERMANY); SOREL, GEORGES;
SPAIN; TECHNOLOGY; THIRD REICH, THE; TOLKIEN, JOHN
RONALD REUEL; *UNTERMENSCHEN* ("SUBHUMANS");
UTOPIA, UTOPIANISM; VIOLENCE; *VOLKSGEMEINSCHAFT,*
THE; WAR; WEIMAR REPUBLIC, THE; WORLD WAR I

References

Bauman, Z. 1989. *Modernity and the Holocaust.* Cambridge:
    Polity.
Brustein, W. 1996. *The Logic of Evil: The Social Origins of the
    Nazi Party, 1925–1933.* New Haven: Yale University Press.
Cassirer, E. 1974 [1946]. *The Myth of the State.* New Haven:
    Yale University Press.
Eliade, M. 1971 [1949]. *The Myth of Eternal Return.* Princeton:
    Princeton University Press.
Fenn, R. K. 1997. *The End of Time.* London: SPCK.
Flood, C. 1996. *Political Myth: A Theoretical Introduction.* New
    York: Routledge.
Gentile, Emilio. 2005. *Politics as Religion.* Princeton: Princeton
    University Press.
Roth, Jack. 1980. *The Cult of Violence: Sorel and the Sorelians.*
    Berkeley: California University Press.
Theweleit, K. 1989. *Male Fantasies.* 2 vols. Cambridge: Polity.
Tudor, H. 1972. *Political Myth.* London: Pall Mall.

NASJONAL SAMLING: See QUISLING, VIDKUN

NATIONAL BOLSHEVISM

Term employed in the study of Continental European ultranationalism that has been used by some fascists for self-description as well as by many researchers as an analytical category for a variety of inter- and postwar ideologies defying easy classification as right- or left-wing. Neither necessarily signifying a subtype of fascism, nor merely implying socialist independent-mindedness, "national Bolshevism" lies between the concepts of "national socialism" and "national communism." Its various notions with regard to Russia, the Soviet Union, and Germany include, among others the favorable reception, by anticommunist Russophiles, of the Bolsheviks' re-creation of the Russian Empire (for example, Nikolai Ustrialov); the blending of economic socialism with chauvinism in the thinking of important leaders of the international communist movement (for example, Stalin); the combination of radical anticapitalism with ethnocentrism in some ultranationalist ideologies (for example, Ernst Niekisch); the approval of etatist policies or a rapprochement with the Soviet Union by various extremely right-wing West European publicists (for exam-

ple, the Conservative Revolution); and a late-twentieth-century meta-ideology synthesizing anti-Western ideas of the Left and Right (for example, Eduard Limonov).

Andres Umland

See Also: BENOIST, ALAIN DE; BOLSHEVISM; CAPITALISM; EUROPEAN NEW RIGHT, THE; MARXISM; NATIONALISM; NAZISM; SOCIALISM; SOVIET UNION, THE; STALIN, IOSIF VISSARIONOVICH; THIRD WAY, THE

References

Mathyl, Markus. 2002. "Der 'unaufhaltsame Aufstieg' des Aleksandr Dugin: Neo-Nationalbolschewismus und Neue Rechte in Russland." *Osteuropa* 52, no. 7: 885–900.
Van Ree, Erik. 2001. "The Concept of 'National Bolshevism': An Interpretative Essay." *Journal of Political Ideologies* 6, no. 3: 289–307.

NATIONAL COMMUNITY, THE: *See* VOLKSGEMEINSCHAFT, THE

NATIONAL FRONT (FRANCE)/ (FRONT NATIONAL), THE

The emergence of the Front National (FN) as a significant force in French politics coincided with the rise of the radical Right in several West European countries during the 1980s and 1990s. The party's relative success and the distinctive features of its campaigning style, policy platform, and strategy of implantation made it an example for national-populist parties elsewhere—for example, the British National Party when it started to modernize itself from 1999 onward. Ideologically, the roots of the French extreme Right can be traced to the royalist counter-revolutionary theorists of the late eighteenth and early nineteenth centuries. The importance of reactionary monarchism later waned in favor of more modern forms of authoritarian nationalism or even fascism. Today, the FN claims to offer a new ideological synthesis, having discarded extremism, racism, and hostility to democracy. Thanks to the influx of activist-intellectuals from New Right think tanks in the late 1980s, the party developed an elaborate neonationalist policy platform. This centered on opposing and reversing immigration, but was not confined to that issue. It offered a full range of policy proposals purporting to restore national integrity and social cohesion under a strong but limited state; these combined authority with elements of direct democracy, an economy synthesizing neoliberalism with welfarism—though only for nonimmigrants—the revival of traditional education and culture, and a more independent and assertive foreign policy, including hardline Euro-skepticism (rejection of the whole European Community project, or at least extreme suspicion of it).

At the outset, the party's prospects were poor. The political high point of the French extreme Right in the twentieth century had been during the German Occupation in 1940–1944, which offered reactionary authoritarians a brief triumph under the leadership of Pétain, while fascists enjoyed their own short-lived apotheosis in active collaboration with Germany. Banished to the margins after the postwar purges, it briefly appeared threatening at the end of the 1950s through its links with dissident elements in the military during the Algerian crisis. Annihilated once again by de Gaulle, it had subsequently remained a fragmented, disputatious, ineffectual fringe. The FN was founded in 1972 from a group of neofascist and ultranationalist organizations seeking to offer a more united and more appealing face to the electorate. During its first ten years the party was prone to internal divisions, personal rivalries, expulsions, and occasional self-inflicted violence; it made no electoral impact, never receiving even 1 percent of the national vote. In 1981 its leader, Jean-Marie Le Pen, having scored a mere 0.74 percent in the 1974 election, failed even to gain the necessary 500 signatures of public office holders to qualify as a candidate. Yet, three years later, with the Left in power, the FN had started its breakthrough. Over the next fifteen years, notwithstanding setbacks, it established itself as a significant force with a small but active membership of about 40,000 and a sophisticated communications apparatus.

By the late 1990s the Front National had consolidated support at roughly 15 percent of the national vote, drawn from all classes and age groups, but particularly from the working classes and the unemployed. Geographically, its strongest support lay to the east of an arc running roughly from Le Havre to Valence, then Toulouse, with particular concentrations in the Paris region, the Lyons/Saint-Etienne/Grenoble region, Alsace, and across the south from Marseilles to Nice. There was often a correlation with areas of high immigrant population (especially North Africans), high crime rates, high unemployment, and problems of urban or suburban blight, but there was also a halo effect of insecurity in areas neighboring those with high concentrations. The FN's representation in the Assemblée Nationale stood at one or zero, except from 1986 to 1988, when it exceeded thirty, thanks to the proportional voting system used experimentally in 1986; it had not improved its very limited representation in the European Parliament since 1984, but the party had gained many seats on municipal and regional councils, allowing it to shape or influence local government policy in its areas of strongest support. Although it had not broken the mold of French politics, it was a significant player. The solidity of its support suggested that, beyond offering a repository for protest votes, it provided a real sense of affiliation for many people. However, when rivalry between Le Pen and his deputy, Bruno Mégret, split the party in the winter of 1998–1999, it caused profound disarray among supporters because the FN had claimed to be unique among French parties in its devotion to unity rather than factionalism and personal rivalries. This disillusionment was reflected in lower support for the FN and its rival offshoot, the MN (later, the MNR) in the European elections of 1999, with scores of 5.7 percent and 3.3 percent, respectively. Since that time, neither party has fully recovered. Nevertheless, while the MNR's leader, Bruno Mégret, scored only 2.3 percent in the 2002 presidential election, Le Pen's astonishing 16.9 percent caused national shockwaves, even though he was massively defeated in the second round with just under 18 percent against Jacques Chirac's 82 percent. In the parliamentary elections of 2002 the FN scored less well, with 11.3 percent in the first round, still trouncing the MNR's pitiful 1.1 percent. Neither received any seats.

The MNR effectively disappeared from national politics, and the FN's hopes of revival have so far proved unfounded.

Christopher Flood

See Also: ACTION FRANÇAISE; AUTHORITARIANISM; BRITISH NATIONAL PARTY, THE; DEMOCRACY; ECONOMICS; EUROPEAN NEW RIGHT, THE; FRANCE; GREAT BRITAIN; IMMIGRATION; INTEGRAL NATIONALISM; LE PEN, JEAN-MARIE; MAURRAS, CHARLES; MONARCHISM; NATIONALISM; NEOPOPULISM; PETAIN, MARSHAL HENRI PHILIPPE; POSTWAR FASCISM; POUJADE, PIERRE MARIE RAYMOND; REVOLUTION; VICHY; WELFARE

References

Arnold, E. J., ed. 2000. *The Development of the Radical Right in France: From Boulanger to Le Pen.* Basingstoke: Macmillan.

Atkin, N. 2003. *The Right in France: From Revolution to Le Pen.* London: I. B. Tauris.

Bastow, S. 1998. *The Ideological Mobility of Front National Discourse.* Colchester: Department of Government, University of Essex.

Davies, P. 1999. *The National Front in France: Ideology, Discourse and Power.* London: Routledge.

———. 2002. *The Extreme Right in France, 1789 to the Present: From de Maistre to Le Pen.* London: Routledge.

Rydgrens, J. 2002. *Political Protest and Ethno-Nationalist Mobilization: The Case of the French Front National.* Stockholm: Dept. of Sociology, Stockholm University.

NATIONAL FRONT (UK), THE

The National Front (NF) was formed in 1967 following the merger of several racist, anti-Semitic, and far-right groups. It grew rapidly in the wake of Enoch Powell's "Rivers of Blood" speech, peaking at 17,500 members in 1974, though thousands more passed through its ranks during its history. More responsible news media reporting, coordinated antifascist action, and a resurgent Conservative Party seen as "tough" on immigration meant that although the NF fielded 300 candidates in the 1979 general election, it was heavily defeated. Thereafter the NF declined and fragmented during a period of ideological ferment based on "third position" ideas. John Tyndall left to found the British National Party in 1982, while the remainder of the membership split into two ever-diminishing factions.

Graham Macklin

See Also: BRITISH NATIONAL PARTY, THE; CONSERVATISM; GREAT BRITAIN; IMMIGRATION; RACISM; THIRD POSITIONISM; TYNDALL, JOHN

References

Taylor, Stan. 1989. *The National Front in English Politics.* London: Macmillan.

Walker, Martin. 1977. *The National Front.* London: Fontana/Collins.

NATIONAL SOCIALISM: *See* NAZISM

NATIONALISM

As one of the most contested generic terms in the lexicon of the human sciences, the term *fascism* has generated scores of rival approaches, theories, and explanatory models over the years. The one constant that is common to all of them, however, is nationalism. Even the classic Comintern definition of fascism, which presented it as the product of capitalism at its most openly imperialistic and terroristic, saw "chauvinism" as a key component. Mussolini can thus be considered to have been speaking for fascists everywhere when he declared on the eve of the March on Rome in 1922: "Our myth is the nation, our myth is the greatness of the nation! And to this myth, this greatness, which we want to translate into a total reality, we subordinate everything else." Some scholars, while seeing Italian Fascism as a particular form of nationalism, do not consider that Nazism fits into this generic category because of the racial, "biological" concept of the nation that led it to embrace eugenics and commit the mass murder and genocide, on an unprecedented scale, of those who had no place in the national/racial community. Indeed, Gregor goes so far as to reject the widely held assumption that Nazism is a form of nationalism at all, seeing it as a form of racism that places it outside any generic concept of fascism.

One way out of this dilemma is to distinguish, for heuristic purposes, between nationalism and ultranationalism. The first refers to forms of nationalism that embrace individualism and accommodate a wide diversity of ways of life, cultural identities, and religious faiths on the basis of a common citizenship, a common humanity, and a commitment to liberal values of mutual tolerance that reject notions of the superiority of one nation or race over another. Ultranationalism, on the other hand, has a mystic and organic rather than a rational and functional concept of the nation, which fosters extreme forms of xenophobia that do not consider foreigners to be fully human. That leads to the equation of the rights of citizenship with ethnicity and extensive cultural assimilation, and subordinates the individual to the primacy of the nation, which is personified to the point that it is endowed with the capacity to decay, flourish, die, or be reborn. Sacrifice to the higher cause of the nation thus guarantees a form of this-worldly immortality. Once seen in these terms it is clear that ultranationalism is essentially racist, whether or not it legitimates itself through deeply mythicized narratives of past cultural or political periods of historical greatness or of old scores to settle against alleged enemies, or whether it draws on vulgarized forms of physical anthropology, genetics, and eugenics to rationalize ideas of national superiority and destiny, of degeneracy and subhumanness.

Building on the groundbreaking work of G. L. Mosse and Stanley Payne in the 1970s and 1980s, theoreticians of fascism have increasingly come to see the key definitional components of interwar fascism as the combination of ultranationalism with the myth of rebirth. It is a combination that has assumed extremely diverse forms according to the political and historical culture in which fascism emerged and the particular movement that developed an ideology of national reawakening. It has ranged from the deeply secular and technocratic form of ultranationalism encountered in the British Union of Fascists, focused on Britain's industrial might and its need to reconquer its imperial and commercial greatness, to the Iron Guard's campaign to bring about Romania's resurrection from decadence, which fused biological and cultural forms of extreme chauvinism and anti-Semitism with elements appropriated from Orthodox Christianity and pagan mysticism. Seen in this perspective the Nazi incorporation of eugenics, Social Darwinism, and anthropology into its myth of the regenerated national community makes it unmistakably another permutation of generic fascism and simultaneously a form of ultranationalism. Nazism certainly had no monopoly on "biological" concepts of racial purity, ethnic racial cleansing, or eliminationist anti-Semitism in interwar Europe, and, far from being somehow "antinationalist," its biological racism served to underpin its bid to integrate all ethnic Germans in a new nation-state.

Although narrowly chauvinistic forms of ultranationalism dominated fascism in the interwar period, there were several initiatives under Mussolini to create a universal Fascism, or Fascist International, before the war. There is also evidence that some Nazi forward planning envisaged the formation of a "New European Order" based on collaboration between fascistized nations; toward the end of the war soldiers recruited to International Brigades of the SS were being told that they were defending not just their own national homelands but also Europe as a whole from destruction at the hands of the United States and Russia. Since the defeat of the Axis Powers in April 1945, the tendency of fascists to see their struggle for a new order against the decadent materialism of liberalism, communism, and capitalism in supranational terms has become more pronounced, as has the tendency to dissociate the fate of the ethnic grouping (ethnie) from that of the existing nation-state (which many fascists now reject as hopelessly decadent in the age of rampant multiculturalism and globalized consumerism). Thus it is that neo-Nazis the world over see themselves as engaged in the fight for Aryan supremacy over degenerate races, while Europe's more intellectual fascists imagine themselves as fighting on the front line of an ideological battle for the soul of Europe. Nevertheless, these supranational dimensions do not transcend national consciousness and the need for cultural roots and identity, but rather locate them in a larger geopolitical entity and broader historical narrative. Swedish neo-Nazis still defend an organic concept of "Swedishness" as a component of their sense of belonging, while German New Rightists want to stimulate a renaissance based on a Germanic culture purged from the scourge of multiculturalism and globalization. Indeed, a significant development away from interwar role models of fascism pioneered by the European New Right is the lucidity with which they reject an ultranationalism based on the nation-state for the (utopian) notion of a "Europe of a thousand flags."

Another important development within fascist ultranationalism that stems from the New Right's radical revision of classic fascist discourse is that it has formally abandoned notions of biological or cultural racial superiority ("master races"), stressing instead the contemporary need, in the context of accelerating ethnic and cultural "miscegenation," to preserve the traditional differences between national cultures and to uphold the right of each individual to a distinctive "national identity." The effect of this "differentialist" nationalism is that liberal democracy and its commitment to multiculturalism and increasing globalization can be attacked not on the basis of biological racism but as a force that is creating "cultural genocide." That has the rhetorical effect of transforming antiracists into the enemies of all races because, by welcoming mass immigration culturalism, they in effect defend the processes by which cultural identities are being eroded and human diversity is being lost through the intermingling of cultures. In other words, differentialism can be seen as a new and highly sophisticated form of ultranationalism whose combination with the longing for the end of the current "interregnum" and for a total cultural transformation underlines the New Right's structural affinity with (and historical roots in) interwar fascism, despite its repeated rejection of fascism, totalitarianism, racism, and nationalism.

The protean quality of both nationalism and of the palingenetic myths that lie at the core of the fascist worldview helps to account for the bewildering variety of ideological forms that fascism can take. One illustration of the complexity of the topic is that some ideologues of one form of postwar fascism known as Third Positionism, which seeks to transcend the polarization of left and right and repudiate the term *fascism* altogether, claim that the mistake made by Italian Fascism and German Nazism was to attempt to carry out a program of renewal without radically transforming capitalism. Significantly, the name they do accept for themselves is "revolutionary nationalism," which underlines how they persist in seeing their own struggle in terms of a fusion of nationalism with the myth of renewal, despite being fully committed to the rebirth of Europe and despite their rejection of the existing nation-state as the source of identity and belonging. Another such illustration is the way in which a new form of political racism emerged in the last two decades of the twentieth century that embraced political pluralism and democracy yet operated a narrowly ethnocratic conception of the state that vehemently opposed multiculturalism. In spite of their affinities with interwar fascism, it is best to treat the "right-wing populism" or "neo-populism" of Jean-Marie Le Pen's Front National or Jörg Haider's Austrian Freedom Party as distinct from fascism, precisely because they reject the revolutionary scenario of founding a "new order." Whereas in the interwar period it was the crisis of liberalism and achievements of communism that incubated fully fledged fascist movements, the mainspring of ultranationalism now is the very success of liberal capitalism in encouraging the globalization, secularization, and homogenization of world society in a way that deeply alarms all of those for whom religious and nationalist roots define their sense of belonging and identity.

Roger Griffin

References
Bardèche, M. 1961. *Qu'est-ce que le fascisme?* Paris: Sept Couleurs.
Gregor, A. J. 1999. *Phoenix.* New Brunswick, NJ: Transaction.
Griffin, R. 2001. "Interregnum or Endgame? Radical Right Thought in the 'Post-fascist' Era." In *Reassessing Political Ideologies,* edited by M. Freeden. London: Routledge.
Herzstein, R. E. 1982. *When Nazi Dreams Come True.* London: Abacus.
Ledeen, M. 1972. *Universal Fascism.* New York: Howard Fertig.
Mosse, G. L. 1975. *The Nationalization of the Masses.* New York: Howard Fertig.
Ozkirimli, Umut. 2000. *Theories of Nationalism: A Critical Overview.* Basingstoke: Macmillan.
Sternhell, Z. 1986. *Neither Right nor Left: Fascist Ideology in France.* Berkeley: University of California Press.

NATIONALIZATION

Coming to power after the great wave of socialist advance from 1917 to 1921, Mussolini and Hitler had predicted that they alone would meet the economic and social demands of the people. One way that promise would be achieved would be through the partial integration of industry into the state. The "corporate" economy would plan the future without trade unions, employers' associations, or other selfish parties, but in the interests of the whole people. For contemporary critics of fascism, the evaluation of those promises marked a key test of whether fascism had actually been as revolutionary as it claimed.

At the level of ideas, fascists advocated an economy with some degree of collective ownership. What was important, however, was that this control should be managed by a state that had been "purified" of all nonfascist influences. Werner Daitz spoke of "soldierly socialism" (*Soldatensozialismus*), a system in which hierarchical military lines of command would be repeated in the administration of civilian economic life. The synthesis of limited nationalization with state authoritarianism was said to represent a "third way," standing somewhere between both communism and capitalism. In Spain, Primo de Rivera used the phrase "national syndicalism." "Faced by the individualist economy of the bourgeoisie," he wrote, "the socialist one arose, which handed over the fruits of production to the state, enslaving the individual." National syndicalism would transcend these false alternatives. "It will do away once and for all with political go-betweens and parasites. It will free production from the financial burdens with which financial capital overwhelms it. It will overcome the anarchy it causes by putting order in it. It will prevent speculation with commodities, guaranteeing a profitable price. And above all, it will pass on the surplus value not to the capitalist, not to the state, but to the producer as a member of his trade union" (Griffin 1995, 188–189). The rhetoric, at least, showed a certain continuity with the debates of 1910 to 1914.

Similar ideas were also taken up in Britain, where Alexander Raven Thomson was the most important intellectual advocate of corporatism. He wrote about the idea in the following terms: "There is no need for any conflict between the individual and the State as neither can exist without the other. An individual exiled from the civilized communion must inevitably lapse into savagery: a state deprived of loyal co-operation from its citizens must inevitably collapse into barbarism. It is only by a true balance between the needs of the individual and the state that progress can be achieved for both. The corporate state, with its functional organization of human effort in communal purpose, best achieves this essential balance" (Raven Thomson 1937, 47–48).

Under Mussolini, the most sustained attempt was made to turn this idea into reality. The economy was divided into twenty-two "corporations." Each industry was managed as a whole. The overarching corporate body was said to be the supreme location of decision-making. Workers and employers were supposed to meet as equals. Former revolutionary syndicalists were involved in the early planning of the corporate structure, as were other figures, including the jurist Alfred Rocco, often associated with the Fascist "Right." A series of laws refined the system. In July 1926, a Ministry of Corporations was established. From 1929 the Italian legislature was reorganized, so that candidates would be elected not on a geographical basis but by professional, social, and economic categories. In March 1930 the National Council of Corporations began work, ostensibly as a sort of economic parliament. Its work was run down, however, following the formation of the Institute for Industrial Reconstruction in 1933. There was a limited process of nationalization, in the sense that some businesses were taken under greater state supervision. But in the absence of any democratic control of the state, the result was only the bureaucratization of industry. Even the state's commitment to corporatism waned. The National Council of Corporations had no power to originate or veto policy. In the words of Gaetano Salvemini, "The mountain travailed and gave birth to a mouse" (Renton 2001, 9).

David Renton

See Also: BANKS, THE; BOLSHEVISM; BOURGEOISIE, THE; CAPITALISM; CORPORATISM; ECONOMICS; FASCIST PARTY, THE; GERMANY; GREAT BRITAIN; HITLER, ADOLF; INDIVIDUALISM; INDUSTRY; ITALY; LAW; MARXISM; MILITARISM; MUSSOLINI, BENITO ANDREA; NAZISM; PRIMO DE RIVERA, JOSÉ ANTONIO; PRODUCTIVISM; REVOLUTION; ROCCO, ALFREDO; SOCIALISM; STATE, THE; SYNDICALISM; THIRD WAY, THE; TRADE UNIONS

References

Griffin, R. 1995. *Fascism.* Oxford: Oxford University Press.
Raven Thomson, A. 1937. *The Coming Corporate State.* London: Action.
Renton, D. 2001. *This Rough Game: Fascism and Anti-Fascism.* Stroud: Sutton.

NATURE

Mussolini and his followers viewed the state as a supraindividual organism that was hierarchically organized and, to a large extent, embodied the natural world. The most tangible expression of his regime's concern for the natural world was the *Bonifica Integrale,* an ambitious program of land reclamation inaugurated in 1928 under the direction of Arrigo Serpiere (1877–1960) and designed to counter urban migration. It included a wide range of measures such as digging aqueducts, planting trees, and draining swamps. The program was initially intended to culminate in the distribution of land to impoverished peasants, a goal that was abandoned because of opposition from large landowners. Instead, the regime concentrated on the attempt to obtain more territory through conquest.

Germany had industrialized quickly but thoroughly in the latter nineteenth and early twentieth centuries. When the Nazis came to power in 1933, the country was still pervaded by a sentimental longing for a rustic past. The veneration of nature was an essential part of Nazi culture, but nature was conceived in ways that were exceptionally eclectic. The "Blood and Soil" movement led by Nazi minister of agriculture Walther Darré identified nature with idealized images of traditional rural life. Other intellectuals, such as the novelist and war veteran Ernst Jünger, saw nature in terms of elemental powers, harnessed by modern machinery and released in war. The biologist Konrad Lorenz saw nature as a realm of absolute order, which he contrasted with the chaos of urban life. These and other conceptions of nature were imperfectly fused in an ideology that viewed race as an integral part of the biotic community, irrevocably tied to the landscapes of a geographic area. The Nazis saw their adversaries, such as Jews, Gypsies, and Slavs, as enemies of the natural world, themselves as its defenders. In contrast with traditional notions of nature as feminine, the Nazis identified nature with their "fatherland." The Nazis rationalized the strictly hierarchical social order that they imposed on Germany and the conquered territories by analogies with the natural world—for example, with the perceived social organization of wolves and other animals.

The Nazi government passed several laws for the protection of nature and animals, including an extensive Law for the Protection of Nature enacted in 1935. This legislation gave Hermann Goering the title of forest master and the mandate to "protect all of nature including plants, animals that cannot be hunted, and birds" (Sax 2000, 116). He was also given the power to appropriate land without compensation for the purpose of protecting nature. The Nazi leaders drew up grandiose plans to reforest vast areas in the East, including virtually the entire Ukraine. Large botanical stations were established at Auschwitz and other areas in the conquered territories, where scientists would study plants that might be used to help replicate German landscapes.

Boria Sax

See Also: ABSTRACTION; ANIMALS; ANTI-SEMITISM; AUSCHWITZ (-BIRKENAU); BLOOD AND SOIL; DARRE, (RICHARD) WALTHER; ECOLOGY; FARMERS; GERMANY; GOERING, HERMANN; ITALY; JÜNGER, ERNST; *LEBEN-SRAUM*; LORENZ, KONRAD; MECHANISTIC THINKING; MUSSOLINI, BENITO ANDREA; NAZISM; ORGANICISM; RACIAL DOCTRINE; ROMA AND SINTI, THE; RURALISM; SLAVS, THE (AND GERMANY); STATE, THE; VITALISM

References

Dominick, R. 1992. *The Environmental Movement in Germany.* Bloomington: Indiana University Press.

Herf, J. 1984. *Reactionary Modernism: Technology, Culture, and Politics in Weimar and the Third Reich.* New York: Cambridge University Press.

Sax, B. 2000. *Animals in the Third Reich: Pets, Scapegoats and the Holocaust.* New York: Continuum.

NAZI PARTY, THE: *See* NAZISM
NAZIFICATION: *See* GLEICHSCHALTUNG
NAZIS: *See* NAZISM

NAZISM

The ideology, policies, and practices of the National Socialist German Workers Party (NSDAP, or Nationalsozialistische Deutsche Arbeiterpartei) in Germany between 1919 and 1945; sometimes also used to refer to postwar fascist groups with varying levels of adherence to Nazism. Permutations include National Socialism and occasionally Hitlerism; adherents are variously called National Socialists, Nazis, or Hitlerites. The latter designation refers to Adolf Hitler, undisputed leader, or Fuehrer, of the Nazi Party from 29 July 1921 until his suicide on 30 April 1945. Nazism produced a coherent worldview and exerted dictatorial rule in Germany for a dozen years—called the Third Reich in commemoration of the previous two "Germanic" empires (the thousand-year Holy Roman Empire and the Wilhelmine Empire of the nineteenth and early twentieth centuries)—while accumulating many millions of adherents and many millions of victims.

Along with the call *Deutschland Erwache!,* Nazism used a variety of slogans, symbols—such as the swastika and images of Hitler—and political rituals (from fixed oaths of allegiance to Hitler to the massively synchronized torch-lit Nuremberg Rallies) to attempt the rebirth, or "palingenesis," of Germany from perceived sociopolitical decay through an anthropological revolution amounting to nothing less than the creation of a "new man." Nazism's mythic construction of Aryanism, antiliberalism, anticommunism, biological racism, strict social paternalism—not to mention the NSDAP's totalitarian structure and genocidal assault on European Jewry—are all comprehensible as manifestations of a new political ideology arising after World War I. Yet the existence of ideological parallels with interwar European fascisms should not obscure the Nazi Party's particularly virulent racism and the specific Germanic traditions making up a number of Nazism's characteristic features.

Extreme-right-wing groups multiplied in the aftermath of World War I in Germany. The terms of the Treaty of Versailles mandated radical departures from the Wilhelmine "Second Reich" of 1870/1871–1918. In particular, the loss of all overseas colonies, some 12–13 percent of pre-1914 German territory and population (including centers of industrial production), a severely limited military, and the assumption of German "war guilt" at Versailles combined to light a fuse of radical nationalism running throughout the German Republic, and exploding with Hitler's appointment as chancellor in January 1933. That Nazism resonated with the German public in the years leading to the Nazi takeover of power, especially given the hardships following the 1929 Great Depression, is evidenced by the sharp rise in Nazi Party membership (389,000 at the end of 1930; 800,000 at the end of 1931; 1,435,000 at the end of January 1933) and electoral support, the latter peaking at 37.3 percent of the German electorate on 31 July 1932, representing 13.8 million votes and 237 Reichstag seats.

The NSDAP's first ten years or so, from Anton Drexler's and Karl Harrer's founding of the DAP (Deutsche Arbeiterpartei) in early 1919 to Nazism's eventual breakthrough in the 1930 Reichstag election (18.3 percent; 6,406,924 national votes), were called the "time of struggle" by Nazi "old fighters" (Alterkampfer). By 1920, the year that the DAP changed its name to the NSDAP (thus emphasizing the "national" and "socialist" aspects of the fledgling movement), the Nazi Party could boast of three features distinguishing it from many other extreme-right-wing groups in early interwar Germany. First, the party program announced on 24 February 1920 was declared to be unalterable, and only ever clarified with respect to Point 17 in 1928: this guaranteed no expropriation of the "Aryan" peasantry's land, appealing for rural support. From this twenty-five-point program derives much of the ideology and many of the policies of Nazism: revolutionary nationalism, anti-Semitism, militarism, and the demand for the creation of a Greater German "national community." Second, acquiring a party newspaper in December 1920 called

the *Völkischer Beobachter,* or *People's Observer,* the Nazis were able to propagate their ideas through the publication of speeches and editorials, while the paper was also used to help in organizing events, publicizing regional branches, and soliciting donations. Third, after his appearance on the scene in September 1919, the speaking talents, enthusiasm, and propaganda efforts of Adolf Hitler made him increasingly valuable to the Nazi Party; he wrested dictatorial control at a special leadership conference convened for that purpose on 29 July 1921.

None of these strengths were enough to raise the Nazi Party from a relatively marginal and localized German phenomenon in its first period of existence. Centered on Munich in Bavaria—briefly a Socialist Republic (1918/1919) and thereafter a haven for right-wing groups such as the Freikorps—the early Nazi Party was overwhelmingly middle class, generally elitist, and openly revolutionary, tactically focused on seizing power violently rather than attracting widespread support. This strategy led to regional banning orders throughout much of Germany by 1922, only very limited support beyond southern Germany (especially Bavaria), and a total of only 57,787 members (35,000 joining in 1923); the Nazis then staged an attempted coup on 9 November 1923, remembered as the "Munich Putsch." In the resulting 1924 trial, Hitler and the other failed conspirators received national attention, painting themselves as attempted saviors of an endangered and weakened Germany that was saddled with an unwanted liberalism, under threat from atheistic Bolshevism, and plagued by internal enemies (especially Jews) responsible for Germany's "stab in the back" in 1918. *Völkisch* circles rallied to Hitler's defense, as did conservatives in Bavaria, making sure that his crime of high treason was punished with only the minimum sentence. During his eleven months in Landsberg Prison, Hitler composed his political testament, *Mein Kampf,* and decided upon a new course of action for the Nazi movement.

Any possibility for Germany of fully escaping the legacies of World War I, the Treaty of Versailles, and the difficult conditions of interwar Europe was ended by the 1929 Great Depression, which resulted in the collapse of major banks, 4.5 million unemployed (21.9 percent of the working population), and the rise of right- and left-wing revolutionary groups. Foremost among these was the NSDAP, able to respond to a radicalized and dissatisfied electorate with massive propaganda campaigns containing promises of comprehensive change once German democracy had been overthrown. This was a consequence of Hitler's change in political tactics after his 1925 release from prison. Once the attempted violent revolution by a fascist elite had been shot down by state power in November 1923, Hitler's refounded Nazi Party turned toward creating a mass-based party able to transcend class barriers and challenge the legitimacy of the Weimar Republic on its own terms: in party membership, political funding, and at the ballot box. A number of organizational changes of long-standing importance thereafter took effect in this "second" period in Nazi history, comprising the eight years between the re-establishment of the Nazi Party on 27 February 1925 and the establishment of the Third Reich in 1933.

One change was the deliberate cultivation of the "Fuehrer Myth," promoting Hitler as a quasi-religious savior of a revitalized German *Volksgemeinschaft,* or "people's community." Exhaustive research has now demonstrated that Nazism's claim to represent all classes of Germans in a *Volkspartei* was more or less accurate: in both membership and elections, working-class support accounted for roughly 40 percent of Nazis' support; as a result, the middle class was only slightly over-represented in supporting Nazism (whether civil servants or tenant farmers, master artisans or white-collar professionals). This has overturned the long-held thesis that Nazism was the product of a crisis of middle-class values or economic prospects; in short, Germans of all types were susceptible to Nazi rhetoric. Whereas the first phase of the Nazi movement was generally middle class, southern German, overtly racist, and revolutionary, Hitler's decision to contest elections meant extending both propaganda and local party branches toward other groups: the working class, the peasantry, more conservative elements throughout Germany, and, especially, women. For these latter newly enfranchised German voters, Nazism diluted much of its chauvinistic rhetoric and frequently emphasized the importance attached to votes or to membership from "Aryan" women—a healthy majority of the electorate. Women voted in increasingly large numbers for the Nazi Party, while 7,625 women became members between 1925 and 1930, with another 56,386 women joining in the two years leading to Nazism's seizure of state power.

Another method of determining which groups were receptive to the Nazi message is offered by a study of yet another of Hitler's tactical changes from 1925: the incorporation of auxiliary organizations. Founded in late 1931, the NSF (National Socialists' Women's Movement), for example, boasted 110,000 members a year later, and fully 11 million members (out of 35 million German women) in 1935. Similarly affiliated or-

ganizations representing Nazi students, doctors, teachers, and civil servants proliferated as new party branches were founded throughout Germany (including northern Germany, in social-democratic strongholds such as Berlin, where Goebbels was regional leader, or *Gauleiter*). Alongside this, two additional Nazi organizations came to prominence as "protection squads": the SA and the SS. The membership of these two organizations swelled exponentially in the late 1920s and early 1930s: the SA had roughly 30,000 members by mid-1929 and 77,000 two years before Nazism's triumph; thereafter, membership rapidly rose to 450,000 in January 1933, and numbered nearly 2 million uniformed storm troopers on the eve of their political decapitation by the SS on 30 June 1934, the so-called Night of the Long Knives. Always a smaller and more elite organization, first charged with protecting Hitler in 1925, the SS numbered 1,000 men at the end of 1928, with some 14,000 around the time of Himmler's takeover of leadership in 1931, and more than 200,000 at the end of 1932. The SS were the most ideologically committed Nazis, responsible for running the apparatus of the Holocaust, and they represented a cross-section of German vocations, religious confessions, and places of residence (although not sex or age, as only German men between twenty and thirty-five could apply). By 1930, the mobilization of mass support for Nazism played no small role in the final chapter of Germany's first democratic experiment.

Thus despite slow initial popularity, over the late 1920s Nazism had developed political momentum and a sizable combat arm, effective propaganda and campaign techniques, a more or less demographically representative base of support, and a leadership composed around Hermann Goering and Heinrich Himmler, along with others such as the Strasser brothers, Alfred Rosenberg, Robert Ley, Walther Darré, and, of course, Adolf Hitler. The expected coming of the Third Reich was frequently heralded in party propaganda and campaigning as the Weimar Republic limped forward without parliamentary mandate or effective economic remedies for Germany. By dint of mobilizing new political supporters, taking (some) votes from other nationalist parties, increasing the role of localized violence against political opponents (such as members of the KPD, or German Communist Party), and exploiting the benefits of parliamentary representation to engineer its own takeover through constitutional mechanisms, the Nazi Party was appointed to national governance.

At first, the coalition cabinet of the new "thousand-year Reich" contained a minority of National Socialists, with Hitler as chancellor (appointed by Reich president Hindenburg following the failure of three successively appointed chancellors from 1930) and posts taken up by Goering, Goebbels, Wilhelm Frick, and Bernhard Rust. Over 1933/1934, the process of coordination with the Nazi state, or *Gleichschaltung,* resulted in the swelling of Nazi membership and specialist organizations, dictatorial rule over Germany by Hitler and Nazi Party functionaries (through passage of the 28 February 1933 "Enabling Act"), the establishment of concentration camps for persecuted groups (overwhelmingly political opponents during this period), and various other socioeconomic strategies to tighten Nazism's control in Germany: these always involved the careful manipulation of "legal" means framed by the Weimar Constitution.

Thereafter, Nazi Germany embarked on a host of initiatives aimed at socially including Aryan Germans and persecuting those outside of that tightly coordinated community. In the third period of the Nazi movement, during which it was the governing party in interwar Germany between 1933 and 1939, the consolidation of the Third Reich overran all attempts at internal resistance or constraint in the years leading up to World War II. Policies during this period include dismissals of noncompliant democrats or conservatives from the civil service (all leftist parties were abolished in the early months of 1933), promotion of "Aryan" marriages, and legal discrimination against Jews (as with the 1935 Nuremberg Laws) and others, such as Jehovah's Witnesses, Roma and Sinti travelers, homosexuals, pacifists, and dissenting intellectuals. But Nazism also owed much of its success to the conditional support and miscalculations of moderates; effective techniques of propaganda campaigning; piecemeal infiltration of traditionally independent institutions such as the foreign ministry, the presidency, the universities, and the military (now called the Wehrmacht); as well as to population politics; state terror; popular fears of Marxist revolution; and the collaboration and conformism of millions of German citizens. Whatever the interplay of complex factors contributing to the rise of Nazism, by the time of Goering's introduction of the Four Year Plan in 1936, capping an economic and military rearmament program while initiating a search for war production and autarky (via raw materials such as gasoline, rubber, and aluminum), the Nazis had achieved nearly full employment, the overthrow of the Versailles international "system" so constraining to German nationalism, and unprecedented control over the machinery of an industrialized bureaucratic state.

Counterbalancing all of the social gains for many citizens of Nazi Germany in the 1930s was the growing expectation of international warfare and the ever tighter chokehold exercised on nationally persecuted groups—instanced by public book burnings, Gestapo deportations (often via denunciation), the 9–10 November 1938 *Kristallnacht* pogroms against Germany Jewry, and the compulsory sterilization of some 200,000 "hereditarily unfit" German citizens (such as alcoholics, "habitual" criminals, the disabled, and the infirm) between 1933 and 1939. In that latter year, Nazism commenced the first systematic campaign of industrialized mass murder against "undesirables." Victims were, at first, disabled German children and asylum patients murdered in the months before World War II. Perhaps some 100,000 innocents perished through the selection and killing processes operating in German and (after September 1939) Polish children's wards, hospitals, and mental asylums. In terms of secrecy in arranging deportation and murder, increasingly radicalized and arbitrary killings (especially gassings), and pillaging of the dying and the dead, the T-4 "Euthanasia" Program may be seen as a prior blueprint for the Holocaust.

For any who had failed to grasp the nature of Nazism by 1939, the initiation and conduct of the second world conflagration of the twentieth century by the Nazi leadership soon provided shocking and irrefutable evidence of its character. The Blitzkrieg on Poland and the invasions of other European countries that followed demonstrated the modernity, technological sophistication, and killing power with which the German armed forces had been endowed and provided the main course for which Guernica had been just an appetizer. Nazi Germany's invasion of the Soviet Union on 22 June 1941 was unprecedented in the scale and savagery of the fighting, but also in regard to the "criminal orders" issued to German combat units before the war. These orders meant automatic execution or starvation for millions in Central-Eastern Europe over 1941, despite the inefficiency and psychological burden of close-proximity shooting of women, men, and children. Moreover, on 20 January 1942, the Nazi implementation of genocide was organized at the Wannsee Conference, establishing the logistical foundations, bureaucratic streamlining, and specific intent to systematically exterminate European Jewry. Over the course of the year, extermination centers—staffed with T-4 personnel—appeared in Sobibor, Treblinka, Belzec, and elsewhere, replete with SS executioners like Mengele or Barbie, and white-collar "technocrats" like Eichmann and Bormann, to centralize interagency relationships, ensure efficiency, and produce quantifiable results. Some 5.7 million Jews were murdered between the invasion of the USSR in 1941 and V-E Day in 1945 (Victory in Europe), constituting 90 percent of the prewar Jewish populations of Poland, Germany, Austria, Czechoslovakia, and the Baltic countries, as well as more than 1 million Russian Jews. These largely accurate figures were established in early assessment for the war crimes trials held by the Nuremberg Court. In addition to the attempted "Final Solution of the Jewish Question," millions more European noncombatants were similarly murdered by means of on-the-spot executions, slave labor, concentration camp conditions, death marches, poison gas, and so on. Popularly seen as the apogee of state-directed brutality, Nazism's direct responsibility for the mass murder of perhaps 10 million noncombatants remains at the forefront in the collective European psyche, and arguably, global consciousness, insofar as mechanisms are in place to prevent genocide at a national and international level.

Matt Feldman

See Also: INTRODUCTION; *ANSCHLUSS*, THE; "ANTI-" DIMENSION OF FASCISM, THE; ANTI-SEMITISM; APPEASEMENT; ARENDT, HANNAH; ARYANISM; ASOCIALS; AUSCHWITZ (-BIRKENAU); AUSTRIA; AUTARKY; AUTOBAHNS; BANKS, THE; BARBAROSSA, OPERATION; BARBIE, KLAUS; BLITZKRIEG; BOLSHEVISM; BOOKS, THE BURNING OF THE; BORMANN, MARTIN; BRÜNING, HEINRICH; COMMUNITY; CONCENTRATION CAMPS; DARRE, RICHARD WALTHER; DECADENCE; DEMOCRACY; DEMOGRAPHIC POLICY; *DEUTSCHLAND ERWACHE!* ("GERMANY AWAKE!"); DREXLER, ANTON; ECONOMICS; EICHMANN, OTTO ADOLF; ELITE THEORY; EMPLOYMENT; ENABLING ACT (*ERMÄCHTIGUNGSGESETZ*), THE; EUGENICS; EUTHANASIA; FARMERS; FASCIST PARTY, THE; FINANCE; FORCED LABOR; FREIKORPS, THE; FRICK, WILHELM; GERMANNESS (*DEUTSCHHEIT*); GERMANY; GESTAPO, THE; *GLEICHSCHALTUNG*; GOEBBELS, (PAUL) JOSEPH; GOERING, HERMANN; GUERNICA; HEALTH; HEIDEGGER, MARTIN; HIMMLER, HEINRICH; HINDENBURG, PAUL VON BENECKENDORFF UND VON; HITLER, ADOLF; HOLOCAUST, THE; HOLY ROMAN EMPIRE, THE; HOMOSEXUALITY; ITALY; JEHOVAH'S WITNESSES; *KRISTALLNACHT* (NIGHT OF BROKEN GLASS); LAW; LEADER CULT, THE; LEY, ROBERT; LIBERALISM; MARXISM; MASSES, THE ROLE OF THE; MEDICINE; *MEIN KAMPF;* MENGELE, JOSEF; MILITARISM; MUNICH AGREEMENT/PACT, THE; MUNICH (BEER-HALL) PUTSCH, THE; MYSTICISM; MYTH; NATIONALISM; NEO-NAZISM; NEW AGE, THE; NEW MAN, THE; NIGHT OF THE LONG KNIVES, THE; NOVEMBER CRIMINALS/*NOVEMBERBRECHER*, THE; NUREMBERG LAWS, THE; NUREMBERG RALLIES, THE; NUREMBERG TRIALS, THE; OCCULTISM; PACIFISM; PALINGENETIC MYTH; PAPACY, THE; PIUS XI, POPE; PIUS XII, POPE; POSTWAR FASCISM; PROPAGANDA; RACIAL DOCTRINE; RACISM; REICHSTAG FIRE, THE; REVOLUTION; ROMA AND SINTI, THE; ROSENBERG, ALFRED; SA, THE; SLAVS, THE (AND GERMANY); SOCIAL DARWINISM; SOCIALISM; SOVIET UNION, THE; SS, THE; STRASSER BROTHERS, THE; SWASTIKA, THE; SYMBOLS; TECHNOLOGY; THIRD REICH, THE; TOTALITARIANISM; UNIVERSITIES (GERMANY); *UNTERMENSCHEN* ("SUBHUMANS"); VERSAILLES, THE TREATY OF; *VOLK, VÖLKISCH; VÖLKISCHER BEOBACHTER,* THE; *VOLKSGEMEINSCHAFT,* THE; WALL STREET CRASH, THE; WANNSEE CONFERENCE, THE; WEHRMACHT, THE; WEIMAR REPUBLIC, THE; WORLD WAR I; WORLD WAR II

References

Burleigh, Michael. 2000. *The Third Reich: A New History.* London: Macmillan.

Cobley, Evelyn. 2002. *Temptations of Faust: The Logic of Fascism and Postmodern Archaeologies of Modernity.* Toronto: University of Toronto Press.

Fischer, Conan. 2002. *The Rise of the Nazis.* Manchester: Manchester University Press.

Griffin, Roger, with Matthew Feldman, eds. 2004. *Fascism: Critical Concepts.* 5 Vols. London: Routledge.

Hiden, John, and John Farquharson. 1983. *Explaining Hitler's Germany: Historians and the Third Reich.* London: Batsford.

Kershaw, Ian. 2000. *Hitler.* 2 Vols. London: Penguin.

Leitz, Christian, ed. 1999. *The Third Reich: The Essential Readings.* London: Blackwell.

Muhlberger, Detlef. 1991. *Hitler's Followers: Studies in the Sociology of the Nazi Movement.* London: Routledge.

Noakes, Jeremy, and Geoffrey Pridham, eds. *Nazism 1919–1945: A Documentary Reader.* 5 Vols. Exeter: University of Exeter Press.

Peukart, Detlev. 1989. *Inside Nazi Germany: Conformity, Opposition and Racism in Everyday Life.* London: Penguin.

Stakelberg, Roderick, and Sally A. Winkle, eds. 2002. *The Nazi Germany Sourcebook: An Anthology of Texts.* London: Routledge.

NEOFASCISM: *See* POSTWAR FASCISM

NEO-NAZISM

Neo-Nazism is an ideology or political movement in the tradition of historic National Socialism. *Tradition* in that context refers mostly to ideological aspects, such as racism or anti-Semitism, as well as to the use of well-known symbols such as the swastika. Neo-Nazism is often linked with the international movement of Holocaust denial. Its propaganda is aggressive. Neo-Nazistic activists tend to use violence against foreigners, colored people, Jews, or political opponents, as well as against the facilities used by such groups, such as cemeteries and religious buildings. The term *neo-Nazism* often gets mixed up with similar terms describing right-wing movements or phenomena. Political groups or persons in the tradition of historical Fascism, as in Italy, or of collaborationist fascist regimes, as in Slovakia or Romania, are more accurately to be labeled as neofascists. In political discussions, especially in the news media or on the Internet, the term *neo-Nazism* is sometimes further (incorrectly) employed for right-wing populist parties like the Austrian Freedom Party or the French Front National. Strictly speaking, the term *neo-Nazism* should be reserved for those persons or groups whose aims and ideology clearly refer to historical National Socialism.

Immediately after World War II, National Socialist aims and ideology were officially banned in Europe, and any activities in that field were made subject to harsh punitive measures. As early as the beginning of the 1950s, however, a political party was founded (the Sozialistische Reichspartei) in Western Germany that the authorities soon afterward rated as being neo-Nazi in tendency, and it was consequently dissolved in 1952. In Austria the first public demonstrations by neo-Nazistic-oriented youth organizations—which led to trials of the representatives and the dissolution of these groups by state authorities—took place in 1959. On the whole, it took neo-Nazistic movements in Europe and the United States until the late 1960s or 1970s to emerge. These groups were founded mostly by persons of the first postwar generation, though often they were in contact with prominent former National Socialists. Since then a growing radicalization has been evident. The next wave of neo-Nazi parties and groups involving younger people emerged in the late 1980s and early 1990s. The later a group came into existence, the more radical and violent it was. While the parties of the 1960s seemed fairly traditionalistic and in a way conservative, more recent and younger groups created their own uniformlike outfits, were more militant and more physically dangerous for their perceived enemies, and gave the impression of a degree of "modernity."

Neo-Nazi ideology consists of a few basic elements that most of the groups and persons share, in addition to a few additional elements related to the identity of the particular country, the social context, and the character of the group. First of all, neo-Nazism adheres to racist points of view that it uses to explain history as well as present social, economic, or political problems. Following Hitlerian Nazism, it holds that the "white or Aryan race" is destined to dominate the rest of mankind, but in the postwar world of mass immigration to Europe from her former colonies, it is blacks or Asians rather than Jews who are highlighted as having inferior status. The mixture of races is said to produce all the evil in society. Therefore neo-Nazis oppose any form of immigration of nonwhites into Europe. The

specific enemies vary from country to country: Neo-Nazis fight Turkish immigrants in Germany, immigrants from Northern Africa in France, and immigrants from Asia in Britain. On the whole, most neo-Nazis can be called ideologically white supremacists. Related to racism but not identical with it is anti-Semitism, which all neo-Nazis have in common, though the topics, arguments, and contents of anti-Semitic propaganda may differ depending on the leading ideological tendency of the different groups. Traditional anti-Semitic myths and legends are adapted to modern ends and are mostly interwoven with the phantasmagoria of a worldwide Jewish conspiracy dominating world politics and especially international financial markets. In this context anti-Semitism plays a major role in arguing against globalization—a position held in common with neo-Nazis by a wide variety of other groups including not a few on the Left. Very often anti-Semitism is strongly connected to anti-Zionism and propaganda against U.S. policies. The United States is presented as the protector of world Jewry and Israel—or the other way round, as dependent on the benevolence of "the Jews." Even neo-Nazis in the United States use these arguments against their own country.

Holocaust denial serves as an ideological bridge for neo-Nazis to other internationally active groups, such as certain parts of the Islamist movement. There are also neo-Nazis, such as Skinhead music groups, who praise the Nazi murder of Jews and other minorities such as the Roma and Sinti. This strategy of minimizing and denying National Socialist crimes can be explained by the need of neo-Nazis to shed a positive light on historical National Socialism. Some hope for a "Fourth Reich"; others engage in organizing memorial demonstrations (*Gedenkmärsche*) for leading National Socialists such as Rudolf Hess. Most neo-Nazis are nationalistic; in the German-speaking countries they generally preach German nationalism, in other European countries the nationalism of the relevant country. Certain ideological elements can be found only in particular neo-Nazi groups. Some of them espouse neopagan ideas and join with New Age and esoteric circles. Others are opposed to Christianity for the same reason that many Nazis were—because, from their point of view, the Christian religion is in reality a "Jewish" religion and therefore not fit for "Aryan" people.

For most neo-Nazis the only role appropriate for women is that of mother, giving birth to as many racially pure children as possible. In neo-Nazi ideology there is no room for women's rights and equality. An important feature of neo-Nazism is the tendency toward using physical and verbal violence against political enemies and people seen as racial enemies or scape-goats. Attacks range from the vocabulary of hatred to the use of fists, weapons, and explosives. Especially in Europe, neo-Nazi activists often desecrate Jewish cemeteries or inflict damage on synagogues or mosques. These ideological positions are spread by various means; since the 1990s the use of periodicals, books, or leaflets has diminished in importance and propaganda via the Internet has been developing rapidly. The Internet offers many advantages: it is inexpensive, it reaches huge numbers of people, and it is a space quite free from any legal persecution up to now. Rock music is an important means of the spread of ideology among young neo-Nazi skinheads. Some groups, such as international Blood and Honor or National Alliance in the United States, have specialized in the distribution of that kind of music.

In reaction to the ban on traditional neo-Nazi groups and parties, a new form of neo-Nazi youth movement has emerged in Germany and Austria, the so-called *Freie Kameradschaften* ("free comradeships"). These *Kameradschaften* lack any noticeable internal structure. Neo-Nazis tend to wear uniforms and use National Socialist symbols, or symbols that strongly resemble National Socialist ones. But not all groups march in black boots. Rightist youth culture in particular has quite a number of different dress codes. Neo-Nazis can be found in all of Europe, as far east as Russia, and in the Americas and Australia. Asia and the Arab world have different cultural, religious, and political traditions, though some ideological aspects of fundamentalist Islam and neo-Nazism are quite similar. From the legal viewpoint, there are significant differences between most European countries, the United States, and other countries. Germany and Austria have laws explicitly forbidding neo-Nazi activities and banning Holocaust denial. Most other countries have passed laws against the incitement of racial hatred in recent years, reacting especially to the growing propaganda efforts of Holocaust deniers and racist activists. The legal system of the United States knows no law restricting freedom of speech. Only individuals can sue if they feel offended or discriminated against.

Brigitte Bailer-Galanda

See Also: ANTI-SEMITISM; ARYANISM; AUSTRIA; CHRISTIANITY; COMBAT 18; CONSPIRACY THEORIES; CYBERFASCISM; GERMANY; GLOBALIZATION; GREAT BRITAIN; HAIDER, JÖRG; HESS, RUDOLF; HITLER, ADOLF; HOLOCAUST DENIAL; IMMIGRATION; IRVING, DAVID JOHN CAWDELL; ITALY; MODERNITY; NATIONAL FRONT, THE (FRANCE); NATIONALISM; NAZISM; POSTWAR FASCISM; RACIAL DOCTRINE; RACISM; REMER, OTTO-ERNST; ROCK MUSIC; ROMA AND SINTI, THE; ROMANIA; RUSSIA; SKINHEAD FASCISM; SKREWDRIVER; SLOVAKIA; SWASTIKA, THE; SYMBOLS; THULE SEMINAR, THE; UNITED STATES, THE (POSTWAR): WHITE NOISE; WHITE SUPREMACISM; WORLD WAR II; YOUTH MOVEMENTS

References

Anti-Semitism Worldwide. Series of biennial reports, edited by the University of Tel Aviv, Lester and Sally Entin Faculty of Humanities, the Stephen Roth Institute for the Study of Contemporary Anti-Semitism and Racism, Anti-Defamation League, World Jewish Congress.

Ferrarotti, Franco. 1994. *The Temptation to Forget: Racism, Anti-Semitism, Neo-Nazism.* Westport, CT: Greenwood.

Goodrick-Clarke, Nicholas. 2000. *Hitler's Priestess: Savitri Devi, the Hindu-Aryan Myth and Neo-Nazism.* New York: New York University Press.

Lee, Martin A. 1999. *The Beast Reawakens: Fascism's Resurgence from Hitler's Spymasters to Today's Neo-Nazi Groups and Right-wing Extremists.* London: Routledge.

Moore, William V. 1983. *Extremism in the United States: A Teaching Resource Focusing on Neo-Nazism.* Washington, DC: National Education Association.

Mudde, Cas. 2000. *The Ideology of the Extreme Right.* Manchester: Manchester University Press.

NEOPOPULISM

The majority of populist movements that started mobilizing in the 1970s have been on the far right of the political spectrum. By adopting a populist strategy, the new far Right has consciously distanced itself from the ideology of the traditional extreme Right, while at the same time promoting a political project that aims at fundamental social, cultural, and ultimately political change. Unlike the fascists and other extreme right groups, the contemporary radical populist Right explicitly espouses democracy. At the same time, however, it is vehemently antiliberal, marketing itself as a democratic alternative to the established system, denounced as corrupt, in the grip of special interests, and far removed from the concerns of ordinary people. Prominent radical right-wing populists such as Jean-Marie Le Pen in France, Jörg Haider in Austria, Umberto Bossi in Italy, Pia Kjaersgaard in Denmark, Christophe Blocher in Switzerland, and Winston Peters in New Zealand promote themselves as political outsiders who say out loud what ordinary citizens only dare to think, as courageous fighters against elite hypocrisy and the "new tyranny" of political correctness imposed from above.

It would be wrong, however, to characterize radical right-wing populism as nothing more than an opportunistic and cynical strategy to exploit genuine problems and grievances for political gain. Radical right-wing populism poses a serious challenge to the basic principles of liberal democracy. Radical right-wing populists defend a hard-line program that appeals to the "right" to identity and the defense of cultural distinctiveness and diversity to lend legitimacy to a comprehensive policy of "national preference" and exclusion. For the radical populist Right, one's "own people" (as a community rather than individuals), its interests and concerns, must come first. Radical right-wing populists have spent considerable energy on defining what they mean by "the people," who rightfully belongs to it, and who should be excluded. Radical right-wing populists do not exclude the possibility that foreigners can become a part of the people. Foreigners who integrate themselves into society by adopting the norms, values, customs, and way of life of the majority are generally accepted. The precondition for naturalization is assimilation. For the radical populist Right, assimilation assumes, however, a high level of cultural compatibility, which, it maintains, does not exist with certain cultures, above all Islam. Particularly after September 11, Islamophobia has become a central feature of radical right-wing populist ideology, which portrays the "Muslim invasion" (that is, immigrants from Muslim countries) as the most serious threat to the survival of Western culture and civilization. Islamophobia has allowed the radical populist Right to promote itself as the defender of Western liberal values (for example, Pim Fortuyn in The Netherlands and Filip Dewinter in Belgium) and of Europe's Christian heritage (for example, the FPÖ in Austria and the Lega Nord in Italy). At the same time, it has been used to bolster the radical populist Right's strict rejection of multiculturalism.

Hans-Georg Betz

See Also: AUSTRIA; BELGIUM; CHRISTIANITY; DENMARK; EUROPE; HAIDER, JÖRG; IMMIGRATION; ITALY; LE PEN, JEAN-MARIE; LIBERALISM; MULTICULTURALISM; NATIONAL FRONT (FRANCE), THE; NATIONALISM; NETHERLANDS, THE; POSTWAR FASCISM; SWITZERLAND; VLAAMS BLOK

References
Betz, Hans-Georg. 1994. *Radical Right-Wing Populism in Western Europe.* Basingstoke: Palgrave Macmillan.
———. 2004. *La droite populiste en Europe: Extrême et démocrate?* Paris: autrement.
———, ed. 1998. *The New Politics of the Right: Neo-Populist Parties and Movements in Established Democracies.* Basingstoke: Palgrave Macmillan.
Hermet, Guy. 2001. *Les populismes dans le monde.* Paris: Fayard.
Mény, Ives, and Yves Surel. 2000. *Par le people, pour le people: Le populisme et les démocraties.* Paris: Fayard.
Taggart, Paul. 2000. *Populism.* Buckingham: Open University Press.
Taguieff, Pierre-André. 2002. *L'illusion populiste.* Paris: Berg International.

NETHERLANDS, THE

In The Netherlands of the 1920s, there were a great number of rather sectarian groups and organizations inspired by the Italian Fascist example. These organizations and groups were not necessarily anti-Semitic. Most ultra-right-wing parties and groups did not have a great impact on Dutch society. The only party of any substance was the Nationaal Socialistische Beweging (NSB; National Socialist Movement), founded by Anton Mussert and Cornelis van Geelkerken in 1931. It even had Jewish members. Not until 1935 were Jews expelled from the party. The NSB party program was largely a copy of Hitler's NSDAP program. In 1935 the NSB obtained a remarkable success in the provincial elections. However, in parliamentary elections the NSB obtained only four seats. Resistance against the NSB was expressed at all levels in Dutch society. All major religions, the conservatives, socialists, and communists were hostile. Members of the NSB began to hide their membership even from their families. This situation changed when The Netherlands was occupied by Germany. On 10 May 1940, German troops entered the territory of The Netherlands. This was not entirely unexpected, in spite of Hitler's confirmation that Germany would never attack a "brother people." In the view of Hitler the Dutch were a Germanic people. That "fact" was vindicated, in his view, by the establishment of a large colonial empire in the seventeenth century. Dutch forces resisted the Wehrmacht for five days. The bombing of Rotterdam forced the Dutch to abandon armed struggle, however, and to surrender to the Germans. The government and the royal family escaped to London.

The view that the Dutch were Germanic had some consequences for The Netherlands. First of all, they did not get a military occupation but a civilian Nazi government headed by Austrian Nazi Arthur Seyss-Inquart. The first goal of this government was the nazification of the Dutch population. Another more long-term goal was the preparation of the Dutch for the annexation of The Netherlands by Germany. A further consequence was one of propaganda. Many people were led to believe that the intentions of the Nazis with regard to the Dutch were not so bad after all. Racial pride certainly played a role for about 23,000 young men who joined the Waffen-SS. Many of them were members of the NSB. Members of the NSB were appointed to important positions within the occupation government. Mussert and the NSB largely supported the German occupation of The Netherlands. Except for the outright collaboration of the NSB and its members, collaboration with the Nazis remained limited. Because of the level of industrialization of The Netherlands and its geographical situation, the Germans tried to integrate Dutch industries and port facilities into the war effort, and resistance to this was of course made very difficult.

Anti-Semitism had never played a big role in The Netherlands. Jewish citizens were seen as people of Jewish religion, and racial considerations did not play a role. With the emancipation of the Catholics had come the emancipation of the Jews, who obtained equal rights with the rest of the population. Many Jews entered public service. Jews could be found at all levels of the population. That also explains why the NSB in its early days permitted Jews to become members. But the German occupation cost a large number of Jews their lives. Many Dutch citizens tried to hide their Jewish fellow citizens from the Gestapo. Resistance against the deportation of the Jews also took the form of general strikes in February 1941 and in April and May of 1943. But at the same time, many Jews were also betrayed by their fellow citizens. Anne Frank is a notorious example of this. At the beginning of World War II, a total of 160,000 people of the Jewish religion lived in The Netherlands, 22,000 of whom were, like Anne Frank, refugees from Germany. The Nazis arrested 120,000 Jews and deported them to extermination camps such as Auschwitz, or to work camps where they were worked to death. Out of the total number of 120,000, 110,000 were killed.

Since the war, The Netherlands has not been entirely free from ultra-right-wing and xenophobic movements and organizations. In the 1980s, the Centrumpartij (Center Party, established 1980) and the Centrum Democraten (Democrats of the Center, established 1984) became notorious. In 2002 a new populist party emerged, the Lijst Pim Fortuyn (LPF; Pim Fortuyn List), led by the sociologist Pim Fortuyn, who was murdered on 6 May 2002. The ideas of Fortuyn had some similarity with those of Mussert. They were xenophobic and strongly nationalistic. The LPF scored some success in 2002, but today it has dwindled in significance. The impact of Fortuyn and his party has been to encourage a real limitation of immigration and a more restrictive approach toward non-European citizens, notably Moroccans and Turks. More stringent policies in the area of policing and the criminal justice system are also partly the result of the influence of the views of Fortuyn.

Philip van Meurs

See Also: ANTI-SEMITISM; AUSCHWITZ (-BIRKENAU); CONCENTRATION CAMPS; EXPANSIONISM; FASCIST PARTY, THE; FRANK, ANNE; GESTAPO, THE; HITLER, ADOLF; HOLOCAUST, THE; IMMIGRATION; ITALY; MUSSERT, ANTON ADRIAAN; NATIONALISM; NAZISM; PANGERMANISM; POSTWAR FASCISM; RACIAL DOCTRINE; SEYSS-INQUART, ARTHUR; WAFFEN-SS, THE; WEHRMACHT, THE; WORLD WAR II; XENOPHOBIA

References
Daalder, H. 1974. *Politisering en Lijdelijkheid in de Nederlandse Politiek.* Assen: Van Gorcum.
Eatwell, R. 1995. *Fascism: A History.* London: Chatto and Windus.
Griffin, R. 1993. *The Nature of Fascism.* London: Routledge.
Hirschfeld, Gerhard. 1988. *Nazi Rule and Dutch Collaboration: The Netherlands under German Occupation, 1940–45.* Trans. L. Wilmot. Oxford: Berg.
Jong, L. de. 1969–1985. *Het Koninkrijk der Nederlanden in de Tweede Wereldoorlog.* The Hague: Staatsuitgeverij.
Payne, S. 1995. *A History of Fascism 1914–1945.* London: University College London Press.
Warmbrunn, W. 1963. *The Dutch under German Occupation.* Stanford: Stanford University Press.

NEW AGE, THE

One of the key characteristics of all fascist ideologies is the manifestation of a relationship to the nation that views it as able to enter into a "new age" through fascist agency. In Fascist Italy, these tropes of national rebirth were highly prevalent in a number of major Fascist projects. For example, the "Philosopher of Fascism," Giovanni Gentile, developed his own idiosyncratic concept of "actualism"—a postliberal "ethical state" that was fused with a neo-Hegelian spirit in order to end the degeneration of the notion of the heroic—so that he could present Fascism as the completion of the *Risorgimento.* This allowed Gentile to tap into rhetorical tropes of the Mazzini legend, experiences of World War I, and a more general desire for national renewal in his own intellectual vision. Another example of an Italian variant of the "palingenetic myth" was a movement nurtured by Mussolini's son Vittorio called *Novismo* ("Newism"), a radical project among younger Fascists that rejected both Gentile's actualism and political Futurism in favor of its own youthful, renovating ideological thrust. This ethos of the renewal of national "health" was also found in propaganda that promoted a return to rural life; the chauvinism that crystallized women's gender roles into narrow stereotypes; the emulation of the Roman Empire by the creation of an Italian African empire after the defeat of Haile Selassie's Ethiopia; and the later attempts to form an empire in Europe in order to symbolize the nation's renewed power and influence. Ultimately, the instigator of this new age was Mussolini, and the presentation of Il Duce as the epitome of the Fascist New Man was critical to the continued success of his *ducismo* ("leader-cult"), at least until 1936.

The trope of the mythic inauguration of a "new age" was also characteristic of the thinking of many Nazi ideologues. The idea of the "Third Reich" was adopted by the Nazi movement before it took power, and Nazism drew considerable mythic force from references to World War I as the origin of a movement of national revival, which also made it possible for Nazi ideology to exploit the widespread *Los-von-Weimar* ("out of Weimar") mood. Following the economic crises after 1929, many "ordinary" Germans also began to believe in the subjective idea that the old order was crumbling to make way for the new movement and, therefore, a new nation. The idea of a new "thousand-year Reich"; the slogan "Germany Awake!"; and the swastika, symbolic of mystical regeneration, were all typical of Nazi semiotics, which emphasized this idea of the beginning of a new era. Furthermore, Hitler became convinced of his own destiny as the only German capable of not only reuniting but also expanding and regenerating Germany, all of which highlights a conviction in his own psychology that he was living at a unique turning point in history when a new age was truly beginning. This was typical of the dialectic of decadence and renewal in Nazi ideology. Further examples of this subtext can be found in Nazi racism, such as the *Aufnordung* project that sought to renew Germany's "racial purity" to its "unspoiled" Nordic condition. Often, for "ordinary Germans," the impression of entering a new age under Nazism consisted of a sense that the old, "corrupt" system had ended, that the Nazis emphasized the unifying tradition of a racial community, *Volksgemeinschaft,* and that Germany once again possessed a common destiny,

Schicksalsgemeinschaft. Like Mussolini, Hitler personified the utopian desires of both Nazi Party and nonparty members. For example, one hagiographic poem claimed that through Hitler's agency: "Springtime is here at last."

Similarly, other interwar fascisms developed highly idiosyncratic conceptions of entering a new age. Mosley's BUF synthesized a sophisticated economics that drew on Keynes and "social credit" with an intellectual concoction that included Lamarck, Spengler, Nietzsche, and Bergson, to create an ideology that could regenerate both Britain's economy and its "degenerate" morality. Vidkun Quisling saw "Nordic socialism" as the vehicle for "awakening" Norway and starting a new era in alliance with Germany. The Iron Guard based its ideas for the rebirth of the Romanian nation on a concoction of obsessive anti-Semitism and Orthodox Christianity, and viewed their ideology as part of a massive national "spiritual renewal." In Hungary, Ferenc Szálasi developed an ideology that viewed racially "pure" Hungarians as Turanians—a characteristic that they believed they shared with Jesus—and called for a new corporate racial state that would lead to a completion of the Hungarian renewal that had begun with its release from the grip of the Habsburgs.

Paul Jackson

See Also: INTRODUCTION; ACTUALISM; "ANTI-" DIMENSION OF FASCISM, THE; ANTI-SEMITISM; ARYANISM; AUSTRO-HUNGARIAN EMPIRE, THE; CORPORATISM; DECADENCE; DEGENERACY; *DEUTSCHLAND ERWACHE!* ("GERMANY AWAKE!"); ECONOMICS; ETHIOPIA; FASCIST PARTY, THE; FUTURISM; GENTILE, GIOVANNI; GREAT BRITAIN; HERO, THE CULT OF THE; HITLER, ADOLF; HUNGARY; IRON GUARD, THE; ITALY; LEADER CULT, THE; LEGION OF THE ARCHANGEL MICHAEL, THE; LIBERALISM; MOSLEY, SIR OSWALD; MUSSOLINI, BENITO ANDREA; NAZISM; NEW ORDER, THE; NEW MAN, THE; NIETZSCHE, FRIEDRICH; NIHILISM; NORDIC SOUL, THE; NORWAY; ORTHODOX CHURCHES, THE; PALINGENETIC MYTH; QUISLING, VIDKUN; RACIAL DOCTRINE; RACISM; *RISORGIMENTO*, THE; ROMANIA; ROME; RURALISM; SPENGLER, OSWALD; SWASTIKA, THE; SZÁLASI, FERENC; THIRD REICH; TURANISM; UTOPIA, UTOPIANISM; *VOLKSGEMEINSCHAFT,* THE; WALL STREET CRASH, THE; WEIMAR REPUBLIC, THE; WOMEN; WORLD WAR I

References

Griffin, Roger. 1991. *The Nature of Fascism.* London: Routledge.
Mussolini, Benito. 1939. *My Autobiography.* London: Hutchinson.
Payne, Stanley G. 1995. *A History of Fascism, 1914–1945.* London: University College Press.
Rauschning, H. 1939. *Hitler Speaks.* London: Thornton Butterworth.

NEW CONSENSUS, THE: *See*
INTRODUCTION, THE; "ANTI-"
DIMENSION OF FASCISM, THE;
NIHILISM

NEW EUROPEAN ORDER (NEO), THE

Describes the Nazi project to bring about the wholesale geopolitical, economic, and cultural transformation of the European continent during the period of German occupation. This vision of a reconstituted Europe purported to be more ideologically substantial than imperialism: it represented the defense of the Western cultural tradition against the threat from within of degenerate liberal democracy, and that from without of aggressive Soviet communism. Although dominated by German Nazism, the proposed New European Order would involve the active collaboration and alignment of indigenous national fascisms within the framework of a far-reaching political superstructure. Much debate has surrounded the question of the authenticity of the NEO as a vision of supranational fascism. There is compelling evidence (not least in statements made by Hitler and other high-ranking Nazis) to suggest that the program was little more than an elaborate facade, attempting to obscure a bold, imperialistic opportunism. By introducing the notion of systematic collaboration and ideological synthesis, it is argued, Nazi Germany provided the Occupied Territories with a validation of their ignominious defeat and the opportunity to participate in a regenerative pan-European movement, all the while plotting the enslavement of the continent under Nazi rule.

Taken at face value, however, the program for the creation of the New European Order was significant and persuasive. The strategic basis of the NEO rested upon the territorial integrity of the European continent, conceived essentially within the boundary created by the Occupied Territories and Axis partners, but with a view toward expansion in the East particularly. According to the vision of the NEO, though, such internal distinctions would become obsolete through a (benevolent) process of geopolitical synthesis. Econom-ically, it was proposed that a powerful and autarkic European market would be created, harnessing land and labor resources as a bulwark against Soviet communism and liberal capitalism: in that regard, the Reich economic minister, Walther Funk, was particularly creative and outspoken. In matters of culture, there was a clear expectation that within the New European Order, all peoples would submit to the general will of Nazi Germany in terms of indoctrination and socialization, though this position was never specifically established. The question of race within the scope of the NEO was also somewhat problematic, given the mixed composition of many areas of Occupied Europe. In particular, the racial question threw doubt upon the position of Latin and Eastern peoples who did not fit the orthodox Germanic view of biological community. Nonetheless, prominent Nazis such as Goebbels and Daitz, as well as Hitler himself, frequently emphasized the need for racial integrity within the NEO.

Stephen Goward

See Also: AUTARKY; AXIS, THE; BOLSHEVISM; CAPITALISM; DECADENCE; DEGENERACY; DEMOCRACY; *DRANG NACH OSTEN* ("DRIVE TO THE EAST"), THE; ECONOMICS; EUROPE; EXPANSIONISM; FUNK, WALTHER EMANUEL; GOEBBELS, (PAUL) JOSEPH; GERMANY; HAUSHOFER, KARL ERNST; HITLER, ADOLF; IMPERIALISM; INTERNATIONAL FASCISM; IRREDENTISM; *LEBENSRAUM;* LIBERALISM; MARXISM; NAZISM; PALINGENETIC MYTH; RACIAL DOCTRINE; SLAVS, THE (AND GERMANY); WORLD WAR II

References

Kallis, A. 2003. "To Expand or Not to Expand? Territory, Generic Fascism and the Quest for an "Ideal Fatherland." *Journal of Contemporary History* 38, no. 2, pp. 238–260.
Noakes, J., and G. Pridham. 1974. *Documents of Nazism 1919–1945*. London: Jonathan Cape.
Ready, J. L. 1987. *The Forgotten Axis*. Jefferson, NC: McFarland.

NEW MAN, THE

Interwar Italian Fascists and German Nazis and their imitators tended to view themselves as people existing at a point in history at which the old liberal order was decaying, and they felt that the counterpoint to this was for a new "breed" of man to emerge who would form a new governing elite and lead their national communities into a new age. The many permutations of fascism's chauvinistic rhetoric spawned in the interwar and postwar periods have built on notions of the need for a "heroic" male vanguard to gain self-consciousness and enact a political and cultural revolution, thereby embodying, quite literally, the process of cultural and moral rebirth, or "palingenesis," within a new political and social order. The concept of the New Man was not exclusive to fascist ideology. It is central to the Pauline doctrine of the Old and New Adam, and underlies both Enlightenment and Romantic concepts of progress—in particular the utopian education of Emile depicted by Jean-Jacques Rousseau. It is also a recurrent topos of communist policy and propaganda (for example, "the New Soviet Man"), and of all other bids to create a radically new moral order in the modern age, a totalitarian project that necessarily involves a moral and anthropological revolution as well as a political one. However, unlike the communist variants of the New Man, who had shed all traces of the reactionary past, fascist permutations synthesized past and future and blended national traditions with a revolutionary dimension.

Central to interwar fascism's variations on this new identity were tropes of the experiences of combat and camaraderie forged during World War I, highlighting the fact that fascists saw themselves as the true inheritors of the experiences and politics of the war. Broadly, the ideal blended perceptions of romanticism and realism, passion and seriousness as experienced in combat. For fascists the concept emphasized a soldierly comportment that conformed to an ascetic, strong-willed, dynamic, and emphatically masculine archetype. The fascist New Man was presented as the figure of action who had learned the lessons of facing death in war, something that distinguished him sharply from the bourgeoisie. Further, the archetype always privileged the role of the body over that of the mind. Fascist ideologies placed great stress on the role of sport in producing the New Man in peacetime, and they viewed the youth of their nation as particularly suitable for remolding into the fascist masculine ideal.

In Italian Fascist discourse the Futurists were highly influential in the Italian variant of the New Man. They proposed an individual who, paradoxically, was detached from traditions and acted as an autonomous individual, yet who also was duty-bound to the fatherland. Also influential was Giovanni Papini, who, drawing on Nietzsche, presented a new model for Italian masculinity in his collection of essays of 1915, *Maschilità*. This "male discourse written for men" argued that the new men must detach themselves from bourgeois institutions of family, school, and romantic love in order to encounter the spiritual revolution of the new Italy. The wartime experiences were crucial in generating an appreciation among "ordinary people" of this previously intellectual discourse. After the war, Italian Fascism emphasized the voluntary aspect of the New Man as expressive of his superior spirit and individual will to action. Further preoccupation with wartime experiences was highlighted by the sacrificial element of combat, promoted through the cult of the fallen soldier. For Mussolini, the New Man looked to past ideals of masculinity, such as classical Rome, as inspirational catalysts for future projects, highlighting a regenerative and open-ended conception of the New Man within Italian Fascism. The centrality of the concept in the Italian regime can be seen, for example, in 1939, when Achille Starace stated that the creation of the New Man was the constant focus of attention of the Fascist Party.

In Nazi discourse, the New Man was more historically and racially defined, the Aryan superman being the ideal. This ideal highlights the fact that, for the Nazis, not only was the true Germany an organic nation from which a racial state would grow, but also that their ideal of the Aryan man leading this process would be indicative of a "healthy" nation. As in Fascist Italy, the New Man as portrayed in Nazi propaganda was endowed with a heroic personality but shorn of a sense of individuality, reflecting the tendency of fascist ideology to conceive of people only in terms of disciplined masses. Nazi ideology also sought to synthesize the dialectic between family life on the one hand, and paramilitarized masculinity on the other. Nazism drew on Greek ideals of masculinity and often believed itself to be re-creating that ideal in the present. The Greek ideal of male beauty from the past was supplemented by an anthropological discourse centered on the idea of the Nordic race, which offered body measurements and descriptions of the ideal human form that the Nazis sought to forge for the future. The Nazis also developed a sophisticated semiotics of the fallen soldier, drawing on the myths romanticizing the youthful soldier from the Battle of Langemarck and a more depersonalized and mechanized memory of the German soldier from the Battle of Verdun.

Paul Jackson

See Also: INTRODUCTION; ANTHROPOLOGY; ARYANISM; BODY, THE CULT OF THE; ELITE THEORY; FAMILY, THE; FASCIST PARTY, THE; FUTURISM; GERMANY; HEALTH; HERO, THE CULT OF THE; ITALY; LIBERALISM; MILITARISM; MUSSOLINI, BENITO ANDREA; NAZISM; NEW AGE, THE; NIETZSCHE, FRIEDRICH; NORDIC SOUL, THE; ORGANICISM; PALINGENETIC MYTH; PAPINI, GIOVANNI; PARAMILITARISM; REVOLUTION; ROME; SALUTES; SPORT; STARACE, ACHILLE; TOTALITARIANISM; WAR VETERANS; WARRIOR ETHOS, THE; WORLD WAR I; YOUTH MOVEMENTS

References

Gentile, Emilio. 2000. "The Sacralisation of Politics: Definitions, Interpretations and Reflections on the Question of Secular Religion and Totalitarianism." *Totalitarian Movements and Political Religions* 1, no. 1 (summer); 18–55.

Haynes, John. 2003. *New Soviet Man, Gender and Masculinity in Stalinist Soviet Cinema.* Vancouver: British Columbia Press.

Hüppauf, Bernd. 2004. "The Birth of Fascist Man from the Spirit of the Front." Pp. 264–291, vol. 3, in *Fascism: Critical Concepts in Political Science,* edited by Roger Griffin with Matthew Feldman. 5 vols. Routledge: London.

Mosse, G. L. 1996. *The Image of Man: The Creation of Modern Masculinity.* Oxford: Oxford University Press.

Payne, Stanley G. 1995. *A History of Fascism, 1914–1945.* London: UCL.

See Also: INTRODUCTION; "ANTI-" DIMENSION OF FASCISM, THE; FASCIST PARTY, THE; GERMANY; *GLEICHSCHALTUNG;* HITLER, ADOLF; ITALY; JAPAN; LEADER CULT, THE; MUSSOLINI, BENITO ANDREA; NAZISM; NEW AGE, THE; NEW MAN, THE; PALINGENETIC MYTH; RELIGION; REVOLUTION; TOTALITARIANISM; UTOPIA, UTOPIANISM; *WELTANSCHAUUNG*

References

Griffin, R. 1991. *The Nature of Fascism.* London: Routledge.

Mosse, G. L. 1999. *The Fascist Revolution: Towards a General Theory of Fascism.* New York: H. Fertig.

Payne, S. 1995. *A History of Fascism 1914–1945.* London: University College London Press.

NEW RIGHT, THE: *See* EUROPEAN NEW RIGHT, THE

NEW ORDER, THE

Both Mussolini and Hitler envisaged their mission as very much more than a reformation of the existing political system or the institution of a repressive governmental regime; they were interested in establishing a completely new social and political order, with all that it implied in terms of the indoctrination of the people to make them think "fascistically," even down to the regeneration of the individuals composing the nation, which meant nothing less than the generation of a "new man." The Hitlerian expression for his proposed totalitarian and root-and-branch renewal of German society, life, and politics, to make it fit in with the Nazi vision of the world, was *Neuordnung* ("new order"). As far as Hitler was concerned, when he took power in 1933 this was just the beginning of a total transformation of Germany, the promised national revolution. In political terms it involved the replacement of parliamentary government by the establishment of a totalitarian police state under the sole dictatorship of the Fuehrer. The process of *Gleichschaltung* would restructure the whole social and political order so that it was geared to the fulfillment of the Nazi utopia. The result would be a future of unparalleled power and prosperity for Germany and the evolution of a Nazi "new man." The concept of a "new order" was picked up from European fascism by Japanese imitators, though the means they proposed to employ to attain it were different from those envisaged in Europe.

Cyprian Blamires

NIEMOELLER, MARTIN (1892–1984)

Outspoken German Protestant leader and opponent of Hitler. Because of his seven years in Nazi concentration camps, Niemoeller became a symbol of Christian opposition to fascism. His politics after 1945 were decisively leftist, and he became an advocate of East-West detente and a foe of nuclear weapons and the arms race. A German submarine commander during World War I, Niemoeller emerged from the war a fervent nationalist and an early supporter of the National Socialist movement. His support for Nazism dissipated quickly, however, in the face of the regime's pressures on the churches. Niemoeller was pastor from 1931 to 1938 of the Protestant parish in Berlin-Dahlem, a wealthy suburb populated by a number of prominent politicians and intellectuals. In 1933, Niemoeller was a leader in the German church struggle, the controversy within German Protestantism between the pro-Nazi German Christians, who sought a nationalized Reich Church that would conform to Nazi racial policies, and the Confessing Church movement, which fought to maintain church independence from Nazi ideology. Niemoeller co-founded the Pastors' Emergency League, which defended "non-Aryan" clergy from German Christian efforts to remove them on racial grounds. The church in Dahlem became a center of Confessing

Church activity, and Niemoeller used his pulpit to attack church moderates who tried to remain neutral. Increasingly he also preached against the regime and its policies, and he was arrested and tried in 1938 for anti-Nazi statements. Although acquitted, Niemoeller was immediately rearrested on Hitler's personal orders. He was imprisoned first in Sachsenhausen Concentration Camp and then, until 1945, in Dachau.

Victoria Barnett

See Also: ANTIFASCISM; ARYANISM; CONCENTRATION CAMPS; CONFESSING (OR CONFESSIONAL) CHURCH, THE; GERMAN CHRISTIANS, THE; GERMANY; HITLER, ADOLF; LUTHERAN CHURCHES, THE; NATIONALISM; NAZISM; PROTESTANTISM; RACIAL DOCTRINE; THEOLOGY; WORLD WAR I

References
Barnett, Victoria. 1992. *For the Soul of the People: Protestant Protest against Nazism.* New York: Oxford University Press.
Bentley, James. 1984. *Martin Niemoeller.* Oxford: Oxford University Press.

NIETZSCHE, FRIEDRICH (1844–1900)

One of the most influential and most frequently cited philosophers of the twentieth century, often associated with German Nazism and also with Italian Fascism. Indeed, Nietzsche has often been treated as having been fascism's spiritual forebear—for example, by the German press in the 1930s. He was the precocious son of a Protestant pastor and became a professor of classics at the University of Basle in his mid-twenties. He lived a life of retirement from 1879 but contracted a brain disease in 1889, and for the last few years of his life he was cared for by his sister Elisabeth Förster-Nietzsche. In his philosophical writings he moved away from the discursive style of argument traditional to almost all of Western philosophy since the Greeks and showed a preference for a new kind of Sibylline quasi-poetic utterance.

In 1934, Adolf Hitler paid a visit to the Nietzsche archives at Weimar. The picture of Hitler contemplating the bust of Nietzsche, which stood in the reception room, duly appeared in the German press with a caption that read: "The Fuehrer before the bust of the German philosopher whose ideas have fertilized two great popular movements: the National Socialism of Germany and the Fascist movement of Italy." Although Benito Mussolini was certainly familiar with Nietzsche's writings and was a longtime admirer of the philosopher, Hitler's own connection with Nietzsche remains uncertain. There is no reference to Nietzsche in *Mein Kampf,* and in Hitler's *Table Talk,* he refers only indirectly to the philosopher. Nonetheless, Nietzsche's "nazification" in the course of the Third Reich is a historical fact that cannot be denied.

Nietzsche was an elitist who sometimes wrote as if nations existed primarily for the sake of producing a few "great men" who could not be expected to show consideration for "normal humanity." Mussolini, for example, raised the Nietzschean formulation "live dangerously" (*vivi pericolosamente*) to the status of a fascist slogan. His reading of Nietzsche was one factor in converting him from Marxism to a philosophy of sacrifice and warlike deeds in defense of the fatherland. Equally, there were other representatives of the World War I generation, such as the German nationalist writer Ernst Jünger, who found in Nietzsche's writings a legitimization of the warrior ethos. The radical manner in which Nietzsche thrust himself against the boundaries of conventional (Judeo-Christian) morality, and dramatically proclaimed that God is dead, undoubtedly appealed to something in Nazism that wished to transcend all existing taboos. The totalitarianism of the twentieth century (of both the Right and Left) presupposed a breakdown of all authority and moral norms, of which Nietzsche was indeed a clear-sighted prophet—precisely because he had diagnosed nihilism as the central problem of his society.

Much of the confusion surrounding the issue of Nietzsche and National Socialism can be traced back to the role of his sister Elisabeth Förster-Nietzsche, who took control of his manuscripts in the 1890s, when he was mentally and physically incapacitated. She began to promote her brother as "the philosopher of fascism" in the 1920s, sending her warmest good wishes to Benito Mussolini as "the inspired re-awakener of aristocratic values in Nietzsche's sense"; similarly, she invited Hitler to the archive in Weimar. Nazi propaganda encouraged such (mis)appropriation—for example, by publishing popular anthologies and short collections of Nietzsche's sayings that were then misused in their truncated form to promote militarism, hardness, and Germanic values. Alfred Baeumler, who was professor of philosophy in Berlin after 1933, played a key role in the increasing appropriation of Nietzsche as a philosopher of the so-called Nordic race. Aware that Nietzsche had no theory of *Volk* or race, Baeumler nonetheless concocted a spurious link between the philosopher's in-

Friedrich Nietzsche, one of the most influential European philosophers of all time. His influence on both Italian Fascism and German Nazism is unquestionable, but its extent and degree remain a subject of intense debate. (Bettmann/Corbis)

dividual struggle for integrity and Nazi collectivism. With the same sleight of hand, he could explain away Nietzsche's break with Wagner merely as a product of envy, and dismiss Nietzsche's tirades against the Germans as expressing no more than his disapproval of certain "non-Germanic" elements in their character.

No less convoluted were the efforts of the Nazi commentator Heinrich Härtle in his 1937 book on Nietzsche and National Socialism to present the philosopher "as a great ally in the present spiritual warfare." Härtle realized that Nietzsche's advocacy of European unity, his individualism, his critique of the state, his approval of race-mixing, and his rejection of anti-Semitism were incompatible with Nazi ideology. By relativizing these shortcomings as minor issues and as reflections of a different political environment in the nineteenth century, Härtle could present Nietzsche as a precursor of Hitler. Such distortions were echoed in Allied war propaganda and in newspaper headlines in Britain and the United States that sometimes depicted the "insane philosopher" as the source of a ruthless German barbarism and as Hitler's favorite author. Phrases torn out of their context such as the "Superman" (*Übermensch*), the "blonde beast," "master morality," or the "will to power" were turned into slogans.

Opponents of Nazism, such as the German philosophers Karl Jaspers and Karl Löwith, also sought to invalidate the official Nazi appropriation of Nietzsche in the 1930s. Together with a number of French intellectuals, they contributed to a special issue of *Acéphale* published in January 1937 and entitled "Réparation à Nietzsche" ("Reparation Offered to Nietzsche"). The most prominent of the French antifascist Nietzscheans was the left-wing thinker Georges Bataille, who sought to rescue the German philosopher by demonstrating his abhorrence of racism as opposed to the rabid anti-Semitism of Hitler's followers.

In the United States, the most eminent postwar advocate of Nietzsche was Walter Kaufmann from Princeton, who provided many of the most authoritative translations into English of Nietzsche's writings. His *Nietzsche: Philosopher, Psychologist, Antichrist* (1950) became a standard work in the rehabilitation of Nietzsche in the postwar English-speaking world, seeking to dissociate him from any connection with Social Darwinism and the intellectual origins of National Socialism. One of Kaufmann's virtues was to document the scale of Nietzsche's contempt for the racist anti-Semites of his generation, such as the schoolteacher Bernhard Förster (his sister's husband), Theodor Fritsch, Paul de Lagarde, and Eugen Dühring. Nonetheless, particularly on the basis of Nietzsche's declared hostility to Christianity, liberal democracy, and socialism, it is possible to see him as a precursor of fascism. Some aspects of his admiration for ancient Greek culture were used by Nazis, while they thoroughly distorted his philosophical intent. Although he took the ancient Greeks as cultural models, he did not subscribe to that self-conception that prompted them as a "breed of masters" to brand non-Greek foreigners as "barbarians," fit only to be slaves. This explains his revulsion from the German nationalism that had come into vogue in the 1880s following the success of Bismarckian power politics. In many respects Nietzsche was the least patriotic and least German of his philosophical contemporaries in the Second Reich.

What Nietzsche prized above all was spiritual power (*Macht*), rather than brute political force (*Kraft*), which he denounced with all the sarcasm at his command. In his eyes, *Macht* is a sublimated *Kraft*. This spiritual power of the "free spirit" who is "master of a free will" involved a long and difficult process of sublimation that would eventually culminate in self-mastery. It was a vision that might be seen as fundamentally antithetical to totalitarian collectivism, whether of the Right or Left; however, it might also be seen as contributing to the fascist philosophy of the "new man." Nietzsche's indictment of the Christian and nationalist Right as well as of official *Machtpolitik* and its consequences for German culture was unequivocal. The break with Wagner is especially illuminating because the Wagnerian ideology and the cult that developed in Bayreuth was a much more real precursor of *völkisch* and Hitlerian ideas. Once Nietzsche had thrown off the romantic nationalism of his early days, his devastating critique of Wagner reveals with what penetrating insight he saw through its dangerous illusions. National Socialism could plausibly derive a comprehensive inspiration from Wagner, but its use of Nietzsche had to be selective.

Other, even more crucial questions hover over this issue. Was Nietzsche not trying to manipulate an entire culture and society to cultivate a new kind of man and mode of life (as the Nazis were trying to do)? Has not the fact that he had neither a systematic philosophy, nor a normative ethics, nor a normative politics facilitated his misappropriation? Should we not consider his attempt to overthrow the values of the Enlightenment and eradicate the foundations of Christian morality an extremely dangerous maneuver, especially when he could clearly hear the loud sounds of Wagnerian music and the nationalism of Bayreuth? Nietzsche abhorred the state only insofar as it became a goal in itself and ceased to function as a means for the advancement of autonomous and creative human beings. His preferred and most admired models to achieve the latter ideal were the Greek *polis,* ancient Rome, and the Italian Renaissance—cultural patterns that had never made national supremacy the cornerstone of their ideal or regarded the ethnic attributes of their citizens as a mark of creativity or superiority. Moreover, Nietzsche did not reject the state where it was conducive to life's aspirations. Once this legitimate creation changed its nature and became a manifestation of extreme nationalism that hindered free and spontaneous creativity, Nietzsche vehemently opposed it and wished to curb its destructive effects. Perhaps under the influence of Hobbes, Nietzsche called this kind of state, "the coldest of all cold monsters." However, where it encouraged individuals to shape and form their cultural identity in an authentic way, Nietzsche regarded the state as a "blessed means."

But what of Nietzsche's famous immoralism and rejection of traditional Judeo-Christian values? What of his thoughts about regeneration, which at times seemed to envisage the "breeding" of a new elite that would eliminate all the decadent elements within European culture? Did the Nazis not draw some inspiration from his shattering of all moral taboos, his radical, experimental style of thinking, and his apocalyptic visions of the future? Certainly, there were National Socialists who tried to integrate Nietzsche into the straitjacket of their ideology and who exploited his dangerous notion of degeneration. But stripped of its biological racism and anti-Semitism, the Nazi worldview would have been a rather different animal, and Nietzsche was as fierce a critic of these aberrations as one can imagine.

Certainly, Nietzsche was a disturbing thinker whose ideas will always remain open to a diversity of interpretations. He was no admirer of modernity or of the liberal vision of progress, nor was he a "humanist" in the conventional sense of that term. His work lacked a concrete social anchor, and his solution to the problem of nihilism led to a cul-de-sac. But to hold Nietzsche directly responsible for Auschwitz is to turn things on their head. No other thinker of his time saw as deeply into the pathologies of fin de siecle German and European culture or grasped so acutely from within the sickness at the heart of anti-Semitism in the Christian West. It would be more just to see in Nietzsche a tragic prophet of the spiritual vacuum that gave birth to the totalitarian abysses of the twentieth century.

Jacob Golomb

See Also: INTRODUCTION; ANTI-SEMITISM; ARISTOCRACY; ARYANISM; AUSCHWITZ (-BIRKENAU); BAEUMLER, ALFRED; BATAILLE, GEORGES; BAYREUTH; CHRISTIANITY; CULTURE (GERMANY); DECADENCE; DEMOCRACY; DÜHRING, (KARL) EUGEN; ELITE THEORY; ENLIGHTENMENT, THE; EUROPE; FASCIST PARTY, THE; FÖRSTER-NIETZSCHE, ELISABETH; GERMANNESS (*DEUTSCHHEIT*); GERMANY; HERO, THE CULT OF THE; HITLER, ADOLF; INDIVIDUALISM; JÜNGER, ERNST; LAGARDE, PAUL DE; LIBERALISM; MARXISM; *MEIN KAMPF*; MODERNITY; MUSSOLINI, BENITO ANDREA; NATIONALISM; NAZISM; NEW MAN, THE; NIHILISM; NORDIC SOUL, THE; PALINGENETIC MYTH; PROGRESS; RACIAL DOCTRINE; RACISM; SCHOPENHAUER, ARTHUR; SECULARIZATION; SOCIAL DARWINISM; SOCIALISM; SOUL; STATE, THE; THIRD REICH, THE; TOTALITARIANISM; *VOLK, VÖLKISCH;* WAGNER, (WILHELM) RICHARD; WARRIOR ETHOS, THE; WORLD WAR I

References

Appel, Frederick. 1999. *Nietzsche contra Democracy.* Ithaca: Cornell University Press.
Aschheim, Steven E. 1992. *The Nietzsche Legacy in Germany 1890–1990.* Berkeley: University of California Press.

Bataille, Georges. 1985. "Nietzsche and the Fascists." Pp. 182–196 in his *Visions of Excess: Selected Writings 1927–1939,* edited by A. Stockl. Manchester: Manchester University Press.

Brinton, Crane. 1940. "The National Socialists' Use of Nietzsche." *Journal of the History of Ideas* 1: 131–150.

Conway, Daniel. 1996. *Nietzsche and the Political.* London: Routledge.

Detwiler, Bruce. 1990. *Nietzsche and the Politics of Aristocratic Radicalism.* Chicago: University of Chicago Press.

Gentile, Emilio. 1996. *The Sacralization of Politics in Fascist Italy.* Trans. Keith Botsford. Cambridge: Harvard University Press.

Golomb, Jacob, ed. 1997. *Nietzsche and Jewish Culture.* London: Routledge.

Golomb, Jacob, and Robert S. Wistrich. 2002. *Nietzsche, Godfather of Fascism? On the Uses and Abuses of a Philosophy.* Princeton: Princeton University Press.

Harrison, Thomas, ed. 1988. *Nietzsche in Italy.* Saratoga, CA: Stanford University Press.

Kuenzli, Rudolf E. 1983. "The Nazi Appropriation of Nietzsche." *Nietzsche Studien* 12: 428–435.

Ludovici, A. 1937. "Hitler and Nietzsche." *English Review* 64 (January): 44–52 and (February): 192–202.

Nicolas, M. P. 1970 [1938]. *From Nietzsche down to Hitler.* Trans. E. G. Echlin. Port Washington, NY: Kennikat.

Santaniello, Weaver. 1994. *Nietzsche, God, and the Jews: His Critique of Judeo-Christianity in Relation to the Nazi Myth.* Albany: State University of New York Press.

Sluga, Hans. 1993. "Fichte, Nietzsche, and the Nazis." Pp. 29–52 in his *Heidegger's Crisis: Philosophy and Politics in Nazi Germany.* Cambridge: Harvard University Press.

Viereck, Peter. 1941. *Metapolitics: The Roots of the Nazi Mind.* New York: Capricorn.

Weinreich, M. 1995. *Hitler's Professors.* 2d ed. New Haven: Yale University Press.

NIGHT OF THE LONG KNIVES, THE

On the night of 30 June 1934, SS units acting at the behest of Hitler took action to neutralize the potential threat from a powerful SA organization by executing its leaders as well as other real or potential enemies. The action was executed with military precision by squads operating in different venues. These murders were justified retroactively by Hitler on 3 July 1934 as having been directed against "treason." The bloody massacre signified the ascendancy of the SS and the curtailing of the SA's power and ambitions. Ernst Roehm, longtime head of the SA, was murdered on 1 July 1934; the SS took over most of the SA's responsibilities, and the armed forces pledged direct allegiance to Hitler on 20 August 1934. Also among those murdered were former Chancellor Kurt von Schleicher, Gustav von Kahr, Gregor Strasser, Edgar Jung, and other notables. The motives for these murders included revenge, internal politics, elimination of anticapitalist or socialist factions within the NSDAP, and, paradoxically, regime stabilization.

Matt Feldman

See Also: CAPITALISM; GERMANY; HITLER, ADOLF; NAZISM; ROEHM, ERNST; SA, THE; SCHLEICHER, KURT VON; SOCIALISM; SS, THE; STRASSER BROTHERS, THE

References

Maracin, Paul. 2004. *Night of the Long Knives: Forty-eight Hours that Changed the History of the World.* Guilford, CT: Lyons.

Noakes, Jeffrey, and Geoffrey Pridham. 1983. *Nazism 1919–1945.* Vol. 1: *The Rise to Power 1919–1934: A Documentary Reader.* Exeter: University of Exeter Press.

NIHILISM

Until the 1960s interwar fascism was routinely explained in fundamentally negative terms of reaction against, or resistance to, a process considered positive, such as the rise of rationalism, socialism, liberalism, progress, or "civilization." The most extreme form of this negative characterization has been to identify it with nihilism, the product of a total moral collapse and tide of irrationalism that was expressed in the barbaric rejection of all higher values, the celebration of destructive power for its own sake, or, in popular theological terms, calculated acts of pure evil. That attitude to fascism is still sometimes applied by Christian authors such as Eugene Rose and neo-Marxists such as Gilles Deleuze and Félix Guattari, one of whose pronouncements is that "[t]here is in fascism a realized nihilism. Unlike the totalitarian State, which does its utmost to seal all possible lines of flight, fascism is constructed on an intense line of flight, which it transforms into a line of pure destruction and abolition." Popular films, books, and unsophisticated documentaries depicting the Third Reich and World War II have done much to popularize this view. Moreover, the mass atrocities committed by the Nazis popularized the view of fascists as ruthless, hate-filled sadists reveling in their power over the life and death of their victims, or simply obeying orders in a way that betrays an inner moral vacuum.

The first specific equation of fascism with nihilism of any note was made by Hermann Rauschning, part of the Nazi inner circle till he fled Germany in 1935 to warn the world of the danger that the Third Reich posed. His *Revolution of Nihilism,* first published in 1938, is a sustained portrayal of the regime as one dedicated to a program of totalitarian transformation in Germany and vast territorial expansion with terrible consequences for human life and Western values, but driven by no idealism other than the lust for violence and conquest for its own sake. However, this book provides the key to another way to approach fascism's relationship to nihilism when Rauschning reveals that he was originally drawn to the Nazi movement because it seemed to offer the prospect that it could *stop* the rising tide of nihilism that he saw all around him—unaware as he was at that point of the fact that Nazism was *itself* nihilism's most destructive product. Such an admission acquires great significance within the tradition of fascist studies embodied in G. L. Mosse, Juan Linz, Stanley Payne, Ze'ev Sternhell, and the "new consensus," which sees interwar fascists as engaged in a struggle to put an end to the nihilism that they see as threatening the West, as the creators of new values capable of saving their particular nation or race. In other words, like the Russian nihilists of the nineteenth century, their destructiveness was in their own mind directed at ridding society of institutions, values, and their human incarnations that they believed were the manifestations of decadence, perversion, and degeneracy, thereby making way for a new society based on healthy, life-asserting forces. The most powerful philosophical expression of this "antinihilistic nihilism" was to be found in the works of Friedrich Nietzsche, but it is implicit in the countless works of artistic and cultural "modernism" produced in the period from 1880 to 1939 that sought to overcome the process of moral crisis and decadence into which the European intelligentsia believed the world was sinking despite, or because of, its material and technological progress.

Once fascism is seen as the politicized attempt to overcome decadence and regenerate the national community, it is clear that its driving force was the urge to transcend nihilism, however catastrophic in practice were the actual effects of its attempt to establish a "healthy" new order. In this context a key work for understanding fascism as the political expression of a generalized revolt against nihilism is Oswald Spengler's *Decline of the West,* a major best-seller of the early 1920s. This book sees the rise of a society based on materialism, the power of money, and the forces both of atomized individualism and of the amorphous masses as symptoms of an inexorable process of decay and senescence that has brought about the West's present terminal phase of "civilization" that inevitably follows one of genuine "culture." Significantly, Spengler himself eventually abandoned his fatalistic pessimism and dedicated his energies to promoting his own fascist program to save Germany from further destruction as an alternative to Nazism. At the heart of all interwar fascisms can be detected the same impulse to destroy the present liberal world order, along with the humanist and Enlightenment traditions that underpin it, and crush the threat posed by communism as the ultimate nation-destroying and hence nihilistic creed, in order to make way for a new order based on a heroic, suprapersonal morality rooted in the nation.

Interwar fascists generally conceived their revolutionary mission in terms of the war against decadence rather than nihilism as such. However, whether the fascist project was predominantly pagan (as in Britain, Germany, Brazil, and Italy), or accommodated considerable elements of organized Christianity (as in Spain, Belgium, Hungary, Romania, Finland, and South Africa), it was always directed against the moral and spiritual "dissolution" allegedly fostered by secular liberal individualism. However, in the aftermath of the crushing defeat of German Nazism and Italian Fascism by the combined forces of liberal and communist "materialism" in 1945, one prominent extreme-right-wing ideologue, Armin Mohler, addressed the topic of nihilism specifically in his *Conservative Revolution in Germany: A Handbook* (1950), which went on to have a major impact on neofascist thinking, especially within the European New Right. It appealed to those convinced of the moral vacuum of the modern world to realize that they are living in an "interregnum" that will one day give way to a comprehensive rebirth of healthy values all but destroyed by the forces of modernity. In the book Mohler evokes the plight of "the lonely, adventurous heart which, now that traditional connections have broken down and become meaningless, must seek out the new way of connecting up with the world on the other side of isolation." This is to be achieved "by marching toward a *magic zero* which can only be passed beyond by someone who has access to other, invisible sources of energy." It is this point of utter spiritual void that takes us to the heart of what Mohler calls "German nihilism"—in other words "the belief in unconditional destruction which suddenly transforms into its opposite: unconditional creation."

The same attitude of antinihilistic nihilism was advocated by the most important influence on Italian neofascism, Julius Evola, in the detailed portrait of the decay of the contemporary *kali yuga,* or black age of dissolution, that he provides in *L'uomo e le rovine* (*Man and the Ruins,* 1953) and *Cavalcare la tigre* (*Riding the Tiger,* 1961). These works helped to inspire several devastating acts of "black" terrorism committed during the 1970s and 1980s for no other purpose than to display contempt for the utter decadence of the present and faith in a new world of higher spiritual values that will one day exist on the other side of modern nihilism. The publications of the European New Right, such as the periodical *Éléments* of the *Nouvelle Droite,* Michael Walker's *Scorpion,* or the articles published on the "Eurasianist" *Arctogaia* website provide illuminating samples of contemporary neofascist critiques of the alleged nihilism of the contemporary globalized, liberal democratic world order. They show how extensively traditional fascist defenses of organic nationalism against the forces of nihilism are now located by their ideological descendants within a concern for pre-Christian European values, and how they have been enriched by an appropriation of Green attacks on ecological malpractice, left-wing critiques of capitalism, and radical protests against the globalization of neoliberalism, U.S. imperialism, and an increasingly Americanized monoculture ("one-world" system, or *mondialisme*).

Roger Griffin

See Also: INTRODUCTION; AMERICANIZATION; "ANTI-" DIMENSION OF FASCISM, THE; ART; BELGIUM; BOLSHEVISM; BRAZIL; CHRISTIANITY; CIVILIZATION; CONSERVATISM; CULTURE; DECADENCE; DEGENERACY; ECOLOGY; ENLIGHTENMENT, THE; EUROPE; EUROPEAN NEW RIGHT, THE; EUROPEANIST FASCISM/RADICAL RIGHT, THE; EVOLA, JULIUS; FASCIST PARTY, THE; FINLAND; GERMANY; GLOBALIZATION; GREAT BRITAIN; GRECE; HUNGARY; ITALY; LIBERALISM; MARXISM; MATERIALISM; MODERNISM; MODERNITY; NATIONALISM; NAZISM; NEW ORDER, THE; NIETZSCHE, FRIEDRICH; ORGANICISM; PALINGENETIC MYTH; POSTWAR FASCISM; PROGRESS; RATIONALISM; RAUSCHNING, HERMANN; ROMANIA; SOCIALISM; SOUTH AFRICA; TENSION, THE STRATEGY OF; THIRD REICH, THE; TOTALITARIANISM; UNITED STATES (POSTWAR); VIOLENCE; WORLD WAR II

References

Deleuze, Gilles, and Félix Guattari. 1987. *A Thousand Plateaus: Capitalism and Schizophrenia.* Minneapolis: University of Minnesota Press.

Mohler, Armin. 1950. *Die Konservative Revolution in Deutschland 1918–1932.* Stuttgart: Friedrich Vorwerk

(extract reprinted in *Fascism,* pp. 351–354, edited by Roger Griffin. Oxford: Oxford University Press, 1995).

Rauschning, Hermann. 1938. *The Revolution of Nihilism: Warning to the West.* Trans. E. W. Dickes. New York: Alliance (extract reprinted in *Fascism, Critical Concepts in Political Science,* vol. 1, pp. 42–48, edited by R. Griffin and M. Feldman. London: Routledge, 2003,).

Rose, Eugene. 2001. *Nihilism: The Root of the Revolution of the Modern Age.* Platina, CA: Saint Herman of Alaska Brotherhood.

NOBILITY: *See* ARISTOCRACY
NOLTE, ERNST: *See HISTORIKERSTREIT,* THE
NORDHEIT: See NORDIC SOUL, THE

NORDIC SOUL, THE

Term used by German ideologues of the early twentieth century to refer to the spirit of the Northern European peoples, to whom they attributed a superior culture; part of the classic vocabulary of some Nazi circles. "Nordic" was sometimes simply another word for *Aryan.* The expression was not used simply of contemporary Germans but was also applied to a way of seeing the world that was reckoned to be innate both to Northern Europeans (including Scandinavians, but not Slavs) and to all Europeans by virtue of colonization in earlier centuries of Southern Europe by Vandals, Goths, Vikings, and other "Nordic" tribes (but see below). The argument was that as a result of the nineteenth-century drive to colonization by various European states, the whole world was becoming "Nordic" through a process of *Aufnordung,* or "nordification." In other words, these theorists considered that they were merely commenting on established facts. In some ways this was simply a rehash of the nineteenth-century theory of imperialism, according to which it was not merely the destiny of the white man to bring civilization to the world but that this was indeed a sacrifice that he was called to make in the interests of the world—"the white man's burden."

The superiority of the Nordic soul was believed to be reflected in physiognomy and physical appearance, and it was argued by some that it arose out of the nature of the Northern European (in fact often German) landscape in general, in conjunction with the quality of the light. Whereas many Northern European artists and poets had been attracted to the Mediterranean (for example, Provence or Greece) by the quality of its light, some propagandists claimed that the initially less appealing but subtler and gentler shades of Northern European light had greater "depth," while the seeming "purity" of the Mediterranean light was merely "imposing." This kind of thinking echoes the old suspicion of Catholic Southern Europe among Protestant Northern Europeans. There is a confusing tendency in its exponents sometimes to claim the Spanish and Italians and Greeks as "Nordic," by virtue of their past subjection to the inroads of Northern European invaders, and at other times to assume that theirs is a lesser civilization. A book entitled *die Nordische Seele* by L. F. Clauss includes photographs, for example, of a "truly Nordic Arab lady"; her face is supposed to show "Nordic blood." Another photograph shows an Italian lady who is said to have Nordic blood by virtue of her Lombard ancestry. But most of the photographs are of German faces.

"Nordic" thinking could be discerned in Nazi attitudes to the arts, literature, and philosophy, and was deeply bound up with the *völkisch* movement and with currents of scientized anthropology and racism. The foremost theoretician of the latter was Hans Günther, whose *Rassenkunde des deutschen Volkes,* first published in 1922, became a set text in high schools under the Third Reich, and who in 1935 was appointed professor of ethnography, ethnic biology, and regional sociology at the University of Berlin. Although Nordic thinking claimed to be essentially "German" and used the term *Deutschheit* ("Germanness") almost interchangeably with *Nordheit* ("Nordicness"), the truth was that it spoke almost exclusively for a Protestant or secularized Protestant Germany. In philosophy, for example, the canon of thinkers representative of this spirit comprised individuals such as Luther, Leibniz, Kant, Goethe, Schiller, Fichte, Hegel, and Nietzsche (though with reservations), while the presence of a German Catholic cultural tradition particularly strong in Bavaria and southern Germany was ignored. This does not seem to have troubled leading Nazis with a Catholic upbringing like Hitler himself, or Goebbels, or Himmler. Some light is thrown on this in the autobiography of a Prussian former Jesuit, Count Paul von Hoensbroech, who in his youth was a pupil at a school run by the Jesuits, at that time widely considered to be very gifted educators both within and without the Catholic Church. He records that as a consequence of their "international"

character the Jesuits held aloof from all "national" literature, but noted that the aversion of German Jesuits to the classics of German literature (such as the works of Goethe or Schiller) was especially fierce, describing it as "blind hatred."

Significantly, "Nordic" thinking had little time for the Slavs, and this seems to support the argument that there was a connection between Nordicism and Protestantism, since the Slavs were to a very large extent either Orthodox or Catholic. With the advent of Bolshevism and the creation of the Soviet Union, a further justification was created in Nazi eyes for despising the Slavs—now often identified with the Russians and the "Red Menace."

"Nordic" thinking ran directly counter to the historical perspective of the Enlightenment, which had worked on the assumption that two great Southern European cultures—those of Ancient Greece and Rome—had founded the greatness of Europe. For the Enlightenment it was the irruption of the barbarous Northern European and Scandinavian tribes that had all but destroyed the glorious Graeco-Roman heritage preserved in the Roman Empire: the Renaissance had restored the greatness of Europe by retrieving what had survived of the riches of that heritage of the ancient world from the East, where they had been preserved in the Byzantine and Muslim cultures. According to this account, it was the Gothic German/Northern cultures that needed to be civilized. So entrenched is this version of history in post-Enlightenment Western Europe that it is difficult for anyone brought up in it to grasp the message of "Nordic" theorists. Undoubtedly, these theorists were reacting against a "French" Enlightenment account of European history that treated the Northern Europeans as "Goths" who had to be civilized from the South.

Italian Fascists clearly did not have much to gain by espousing this "Nordic" thinking, and they took little interest in it. Their mission was to restore Italy to the greatness she had enjoyed in the days of the Roman Empire, and they were not very interested in what Germanic tribes might have contributed to their own culture. They had no need of such a hypothesis. It seems likely that Nordic theorists developed the story of an Aryan ancestry for the very reason that they had no obvious glorious past like that of the Italians to turn to for inspiration. Hypothesizing a descent from a noble Aryan race about which very little was known, the Nordicists could generate a myth to rival that of Ancient Greece and Rome—and even Egypt. Nordic thinking was not necessarily dependent on the theories of Aryanism, but one way or another, it serves as one of the most dramatic distinguishing marks that separate German Nazism from Italian Fascism.

"Nordic" thinking was picked up in other countries—for example, in Great Britain, where the Nordic League was founded in 1937 as a secret movement of "race-conscious" Britons. Supporters included William Joyce and Arnold Leese. That, however, had more to do with violent anti-Semitism than with a doctrine of "Nordic" superiority. Postwar Nordic thinking persists in fascism in the form of neo-Nazism or white supremacism—and therefore not as exclusively "Germanic."

Cyprian Blamires

See Also: INTRODUCTION; ANTHROPOLOGY; ANTI-SEMITISM; ARYANISM; BLOOD; BLOOD AND SOIL; BOLSHEVISM; CHAMBERLAIN, HOUSTON STEWART; CIVILIZATION; ENLIGHTENMENT, THE; FASCIST PARTY, THE; FÖRSTER-NIETZSCHE, ELISABETH; GERMAN FAITH MOVEMENT, THE; GERMANIC RELIGION; GERMANNESS (*DEUTSCHHEIT*); GERMANY; GOBINEAU, JOSEPH ARTHUR COMTE DE; GOEBBELS, (PAUL) JOSEPH; GREAT BRITAIN; GÜNTHER, HANS FRIEDRICH KARL; HIMMLER, HEINRICH; HITLER, ADOLF; IMPERIALISM; ITALY; JESUITS, THE; JOYCE, WILLIAM; LEESE, ARNOLD SPENCER; LUTHER, MARTIN; MARXISM; MUSIC (GERMANY); NAZISM; NEONAZISM; NIETZSCHE, FRIEDRICH; NUEVA GERMANIA; PROTESTANTISM; RACIAL DOCTRINE; RACISM; ROME; ROSENBERG, ALFRED; SLAVS, THE (AND GERMANY); SOUL; SOVIET UNION, THE; THEOLOGY; TRADITION; TRADITIONALISM; *VOLK, VÖLKISCH*; WHITE SUPREMACISM

References
Clauss, L. S. 1933. *Die Nordische Seele. Ein Einführung in die Rassenseelenkunde.* München: J. F. Lehmanns.
Glockmann, Hermann. 1942. *Vom Wesen des deutschen Philosophie.* Stuttgart: Kohlhammer.
Hermand, Jost. 1992. *Old Dreams of a New Reich: Volkish Utopias and National Socialism.* Trans. Paul Levesque and Stefan Soldovierei. Bloomington: Indiana University Press.
Hoensbroeck, Count Paul von. 1911. *Fourteen Years a Jesuit.* 2 vols. London: Cassell.
Linehan, Thomas. 2000. *British Fascism 1918–1939: Parties, Ideology, and Culture.* Manchester: Manchester University Press.
Mangan, J. A. 1999. *Shaping the Superman: Fascist Body as Political Icon.* London: Frank Cass.

NORDIC THINKING, NORDIFICATION, "NORDICISM": See NORDIC SOUL, THE
NORMANDY LANDINGS, THE: See D-DAY LANDINGS, THE

NORWAY

When the homecoming army officer and international relief agent Vidkun Quisling launched his fascist party NS—"National Unity"—in Norway in 1933 to a great fanfare of publicity, he gained support from certain impoverished farmers, especially from the debt-ridden Landfolks' Crisis Movement, and from the sympathy he was able to mobilize within sectors of the petty bourgeoisie. The established parties from Left to Right and their press, however, opposed him fiercely. The NS party polled so poorly, in 1933 and again in 1936, that by the end of the 1930s it seemed likely to collapse altogether. In the 1920s the Fatherland League, a broad, electoral organization promoting cooperation between the bourgeois parties so as to bar the socialists from government, had adopted certain views similar to Continental fascism, furthered by a general bourgeois sense of political tiredness, a democratic fatigue, brilliantly formulated by the league's president, the ambitious industrialist Hermann Lehmkuhl. Young conservatives were generally enthusiastic about both Mussolini and Hitler, as was the case in other Nordic countries as well, even if their mother party decided to stay away from electoral alliances with Quisling. Influential newspapers such as the Oslo paper *Tidens Tegn,* one of the most daring journalistic enterprises in Norway, actively promoted "new politics" with an unmistakable flair of fascist ideas. When these amorphous antidemocratic tendencies crystallized in the shape of a single fascist party, the NS, they found the party distasteful. It was as if it had lost its support in the moment it was created: some potential supporters found the NS distasteful and vulgar; others disliked its obvious imitation of the NSDAP style and political behavior. Quisling, who considered himself a man of national stature, soon became an extremely controversial figure, involved in street fighting and disturbances. Although the NS enjoyed a certain influx of new members in the months January to July 1934, when membership increased from 2,000 to some 8,000, membership soon dwindled again. In the general election in 1936 the NS polled no more votes than it had obtained in 1933—some 28,000 in all, insufficient to gain seats in the Storting. In the real world of campaigning and voting, the idea of "new politics" came to nothing. There was simply no political space for fascism in interwar Norway.

The German military occupation of April 1940 altered that situation fundamentally. Unlike occupied

Denmark, where the government surrendered and the established parties cooperated to maintain democratic rule until August 1943, Norway became a battlefield between German and Allied forces till the Allies withdrew and the king and his cabinet fled to London in June 1940. The Germans felt free to install a government to their own liking, and they allowed the NS to take power after all of the other parties had been abolished. With substantial German subsidies the NS was built into a proper mass organization, which by February 1942 was saddled with the responsibility of serving as the foundation for a proper "national government." German policy in Norway ran contrary to their approach in The Netherlands, where the NSB was denied the rank of a *staatsträgende Partei*, or Denmark, where the fascist party was deliberately kept away from power. It was, indeed, contrary to German rule anywhere in Europe. The establishment of a fully fledged fascist regime modeled after the constitution in Germany, with a Fuehrer and a monopolistic party at the head of the state, was indeed an experiment, and not a very successful one. Hitler soon repented his willingness to let Quisling in—or at least that is what he told the Dutch leader Anthon Mussert in March 1942.

From the German point of view, the fascist regime in Norway from 1942 to 1945 failed to contribute to uphold the civil peace and order that the Nazis required to maintain industrial production for war purposes and for the general exploitation of the country's resources (fisheries, forestry, and hydroelectric energy) for civilian German use. In addition, the NS government actively resisted German claims. At the same time it was so unpopular with the population that it provoked widespread civil disobedience, particularly in 1941 and 1942, with unrest among teachers, the clergy, and other professions. A long-term German absorption of a peaceful, racially pure Norway into the Greater Reich seemed highly improbable. From the NS point of view the regime failed miserably to teach the Norwegians to be proud of their *Germanentum* and to prefer German to British or U.S. cultural influence—not to mention its lack of success in implementing the institutions of the New Order, a corporative political system, and the introduction of the Fuehrer principle at all levels of decision-making. Apart from some viable reforms in local government, the only successful institution created by the regime was the NS party itself. German advisors from the NSDAP helped to build the organization, which recruited 55,000 members, plus youth and children's branches, dressed in full fascist style, all of which continued to operate throughout the war. But this well-functioning party was completely unable to implement its own policies. Quisling and the leadership bitterly blamed the German *Reichskommissar* in Norway, the Rhineland *Gauleiter* Josef Terboven, for his negative contribution in this respect. Indeed, the constant rivalry between Quisling and Terboven dominated the image of the regime, with the NS as the hopelessly weaker part. In the purges following the liberation of Norway in May 1945, Quisling and two of his cabinet ministers were shot, the party leadership jailed for an average of ten years, and every one of its members convicted of treason and punished with fines and loss of civic rights.

H. F. Dahl

See Also: BOURGEOISIE, THE; CORPORATISM; DEMOCRACY; EXPANSIONISM; FARMERS; GERMANNESS (*DEUTSCHHEIT*); GERMANY; HAMSUN, KNUT; HITLER, ADOLF; ITALY; LEADER CULT, THE; MUSSERT, ANTON ADRIAAN; MUSSOLINI, BENITO ANDREA; NAZISM; NETHERLANDS, THE; NEW ORDER, THE; PANGERMANISM; QUISLING, VIDKUN; SOCIALISM; STYLE; WORLD WAR II; YOUTH MOVEMENTS

References
Dahl, Hans F. 1995. *Quisling: A Study of Treachery.* London: Cambridge University Press.

Høidal, Oddvar. 1988. *Quisling: A Study of Treason.* Oslo: Universitetsforlaget.

Lindström, U. 1985. *Fascism in Scandinavia, 1920–1940.* Stockholm: Almqvist and Wiksell.

Loock, Hans-Dietrich. 1970. *Quisling, Rosenberg und Terboven.* Stuttgart: Deutsche Verlags-Anstalt.

Milward, Alan S. 1972. *The Fascist Economy of Norway.* Oxford: Oxford University Press

---

NOUVELLE DROITE: See EUROPEAN NEW RIGHT, THE

NOVEMBER CRIMINALS/ *NOVEMBERBRECHER,* THE

Term used by Nazi propagandists to discredit the political leaders who concluded the Armistice of 11 November 1918 that brought World War I to an end. It was part of a wider theory of the "stab in the back," according to which Germany had not actually been defeated militarily; the brave soldiers at the front had been betrayed by the politicians at home and more specifically by German Jews. This propaganda did in fact reflect a widespread belief in the German army that it had been "stabbed in the back" by the civilian population. After the war a report commissioned by the Reichstag on the collapse of the war effort actually stated it as certain that "a pacifistic, international, antimilitary, and revolutionary undermining of the army took place." This is clearly a reference to Marxism and the Left, but Hitler and the Nazis were more inclined to blame the Jews as allegedly archetypal "traitors" and internationalists who were alleged to be incapable of being loyal to any nation in which they lived.

Cyprian Blamires

See Also: ANTI-SEMITISM; ARYANISM; CONSPIRACY THEORIES; COSMOPOLITANISM; GERMANY; HITLER, ADOLF; MARXISM; *MEIN KAMPF;* NAZISM; PACIFISM; PROPAGANDA; SOCIALISM; VERSAILLES, THE TREATY OF; WAR VETERANS; WEIMAR REPUBLIC, THE; WORLD WAR I

References
Kleine Ahlbrandt, William Laird. 1995. *The Burden of Victory: France, Britain, and the Enforcement of the Versailles Treaty, 1919–1925.* Washington, DC: University Press of America.
Muhlberger, Detlef. 2005. *Hitler's Voice: The Völkischer Beobachter, 1920–1933: Organisation and Development of the Nazi Party/Nazi Propaganda.* 2 vols. Berne: Peter Lang.

NSDAP: *See* NAZISM

NUEVA GERMANIA ("NEW GERMANY")

Name given to a chillingly prophetic project to create a "purified" Aryan community in the 1880s in Paraguay that was to be free from Jewish "taint." It was the brainchild of Bernhard Förster-Nietzsche and his wife, Elisabeth, sister of the philosopher Friedrich Nietzsche—who did not approve of the plan. Paraguay was chosen partly because it had been savagely depopulated after a very bloody war. Following the suicide of Bernhard, his wife returned to Germany, and the colony was bought out in 1890 by a corporation of businessmen that included an Italian, a Spaniard, an Englishman, and a Dane. Although the colony was abandoned long ago, descendants of the original colonists still live in the neighborhood.

Cyprian Blamires

See Also: ANTI-SEMITISM; ARYANISM; BLOOD; FÖRSTER-NIETZSCHE, ELISABETH; NIETZSCHE, FRIEDRICH; PARAGUAY

Reference
Macintyre, Ben. 1992. *Forgotten Fatherland: The Search for Elisabeth Nietzsche.* New York: Farrar Strauss Giroux.

NUREMBERG

City chosen by Hitler, for several reasons, as the site of the huge symbolic annual Nazi rallies. In 1219, Emperor Frederick had conferred on the city the rights of a free imperial town; it was the first of the imperial towns to adopt Protestantism, so that it stood as a symbol of freedom from the power of the Catholic Church and the papacy. It had also been a very wealthy city in the Middle Ages, as well as being a center of artistry and industry. In Hitler's day the city retained a combination of medieval streets with fine artistic monuments, including a number of beautiful fountains. By choosing to make Nuremberg the symbolic heart of Nazism, Hitler was making a statement about Nazism's continuity with all that he believed to be best in Germany's past—artistic beauty, industrial excellence, historical independence, and prosperity.

Cyprian Blamires

See Also: ANTI-SEMITISM; ART; CATHOLIC CHURCH, THE; CHRISTIANITY; GERMANY; HITLER, ADOLF; NAZISM; NUREMBERG LAWS, THE; NUREMBERG RALLIES, THE; NUREMBERG TRIALS, THE; PAPACY, THE; TRADITION

References
Burden, Hamilton Twombly. 1967. *The Nuremberg Party Rallies.* London: Pall Mall.
Wuttke, Dieter. 1987. *Nuremberg, Focal Point of German Culture and History: A Lecture.* Munich: H. Kaiser.

NUREMBERG LAWS, THE

Decreed by Adolf Hitler and other leading Nazis at the annual party rally in Nuremberg, 9–15 September 1935, directed principally against Jews in Germany. Both the Reich Citizenship Law, distinguishing between German "citizens" and Jewish "subjects," and the

Law for the Defense of German Blood, forbidding intermarriage and certain forms of employment involving "Aryans" and Jews, formed the pivotal legislation in the more than 2,000 anti-Semitic decrees passed under the Third Reich. Supplementary guidelines to the Nuremberg Laws were later included on Nazi definitions of "Jewishness" by parental descent, and were employed at the Wannsee Conference as guidelines by which Jews would be murdered in the Holocaust.

Matt Feldman

See Also: ANTI-SEMITISM; ARYANISM; BLOOD; FAMILY, THE; GERMANY; HITLER, ADOLF; HOLOCAUST, THE; LAW; NAZISM; NUREMBERG; SEXUALITY; THIRD REICH, THE; WANNSEE CONFERENCE, THE

References
Friedländer, Saul. 1997. *Nazi Germany and the Jews.* Vol. 1: *The Years of Persecution 1933—1939.* London: Weidenfeld and Nicolson.
Newman, Amy. 1999. *The Nuremberg Laws: Institutionalized Anti-Semitism.* San Diego, CA: Lucent.

NUREMBERG RALLIES, THE

From 1927 to 1938, Nuremberg was the venue for the annual party congresses of the NSDAP, which combined internal party assemblies with great public rallies, concerts, sporting events, and military ceremonies. This resulted in a rapid growth of the Nazi movement in Nuremberg, with Julius Streicher as one of its most notorious anti-Semitic demagogues. In 1927 the NSDAP succeeded in organizing its third congress (*Reichsparteitag*) as an event that conveyed the impression of a tightly led and militarily disciplined party to the general public. The fourth *Reichsparteitag* (1929) gathered 25,000 members of the SA and SS, as well as up to 40,000 nonuniformed NSDAP followers. With guests of honor like Prince August Wilhelm von Preußen or industrialist Emil Kirdorf, the NSDAP began to become socially acceptable. At the same time violent clashes between NSDAP members, leftist opponents, and the police resulted in two people dying. After 1933 the NSDAP leadership intensified their program of exploiting the tradition of Nuremberg as a free city of the Holy Roman Empire and organized the party congresses as occasions designed to secure the loyalty of the German population, as well as to impress the diplomatic corps and convince its members that the Nazi

Typical scene from the annual Nuremberg Rallies—this one in 1935. These gigantic gatherings served both to fire up the zeal of supporters for the Nazi cause and to propagate to the wider world the image of Nazism as an unstoppable force. (National Archives)

government had broad public support. As part of a set of celebrations, public rallies, and events distributed all through the year, the party congresses, which had been partly combined with sittings of the Nazi-controlled Reichstag, were given a different political focus each year, ranging from Reich Party Congress of Victory (1933) and Reich Party Congress of Unity and Strength (1934) to themes such as Freedom (1935), Honor (1936), Work (1937), and Greater Germany (1938). Because of the war of aggression against Poland in 1939 the *Reichsparteitag*—originally having "Peace" as its motto—was canceled.

The NSDAP planned to make Nuremberg one of the "Fuehrer Cities," so that the layout, size, and architecture of the Reich Party rally grounds were to embody German supremacy over Europe. In 1934 architect Albert Speer was entrusted with the overall planning for the Reich Party rally grounds, to be built over an area of 11 square kilometers: Luitpoldhain Park was leveled off and prepared as a marching ground for the SA and SS with room for 150,000 participants plus a further 50,000 spectators on the surrounding stands. The Luitpold Hall held another 60,000 people. The Zeppelin Field—with its grandstand 23 meters high and its ramparts with stone turrets and pillars between which swastika flags were stretched—had a capacity of more than 200,000 persons. A parade ground for the Wehrmacht, called Marsfeld, a sports stadium where as many as 60,000 young persons lined up in front of Hitler, the German Stadium destined to hold a crowd of more than 400,000, and the Congress Hall completed the setting, to which a large boulevard led.

Coming on thousands of special trains or even marching, as many as 950,000 people took part in the annual party congresses of the NSDAP, which lasted about a week. The first day would see the arrival and welcome of Hitler, who was feted frenetically by the masses; successive days were dedicated to the Hitler Youth, the Reich Labor Service, the Wehrmacht, and the SA. The whole program—with its ceremonies to honor the dead, its choreography of vast numbers of participants, its vows of fidelity, its tens of thousands of banners and flags, and its antiaircraft searchlights creating a "vault of light" over the evening parades—followed a fixed set of strict rules. Its purpose was to produce a feeling of unity, agreement, and identification between the leadership and the followers, not least because Hitler used the Reichsparteitäge to announce important political decisions—for example, the racist and anti-Semitic Nuremberg Laws—and to get them acclaimed.

Finally, the arrangements and the experience of the Reichsparteitäge and their political message were disseminated widely in books, pamphlets, radio programs, and films, the best known being *The Triumph of the Will* by Leni Riefenstahl. After 1939 the completion of the construction work at the Reich Party rally grounds went on only slowly, because of the concentration of human and industrial resources for the purpose of war. When the U.S. Army held its parade of victory on 22 April 1945 at the Reich Party rally grounds, it blew up the huge gilded swastika that for some years had been atop the grandstand of the Zeppelin Field.

Fabian Virchow

See Also: ANTI-SEMITISM; ARCHITECTURE; CALENDAR, THE FASCIST; FILM; GERMANY; GOEBBELS, (PAUL) JOSEPH; HITLER, ADOLF; HOLY ROMAN EMPIRE, THE; LABOR SER-VICE, THE; NAZISM; NEW EUROPEAN ORDER, THE; NUREMBERG; NUREMBERG LAWS, THE; PROPAGANDA; RADIO; RIEFENSTAHL, LENI; SA, THE; SPEER, ALBERT; STREICHER, JULIUS; SWASTIKA, THE; THEATER; *TRIUMPH OF THE WILL;* WEHRMACHT, THE; WORLD WAR I; YOUTH MOVEMENTS

References
Burden, Hamilton Twombly. 1967. *The Nuremberg Party Rallies.* London: Pall Mall.
Dietzfelbinger, Eckart, and Gerhard Liedtke. 2004. *Nürnberg—Ort der Massen.* Berlin: Ch. Links.
Kershaw, Ian. 1981. "The Führer Image and Political Integration: The Popular Conception of Hitler in Bavaria during the Third Reich." Pp. 133–164 in *Der "Führerstaat." Mythos und Realität,* edited by Gerhard Hirschfeld, and Lothar Kettenacker. Stuttgart: Klett-Cotta.
Loiperdinger, Martin. 1987. *Rituale der Mobilmachung. Der Parteitagsfilm 'Triumph des Willens' von Leni Riefenstahl.* Opladen: Leske and Budrich.
Wykes, Alan. 1970. *Nuremberg Rallies.* London: Macdonald.
Zehnhefer, Siegfried. 2002. *Die Reichsparteitage der NSDAP. Geschichte, Struktur und Bedeutung der größten Propagandafeste im nationalsozialistischen Feierjahr.* Nuremberg: Nürnberger Presse.

NUREMBERG TRIALS, THE

In the Nuremberg war criminal trial of 1945/1946, twenty-four prominent members of the Nazi regime were accused before an Allied military court. Nineteen were condemned, twelve of them to death. Between 1946 and 1949, twelve subsequent proceedings took place before the American Military Tribunal in Nuremberg. In the middle of the war, the Soviet Union, Great Britain, and the United States had agreed upon the punishment of the main Nazi exponents and functionaries after the end of the war. In accordance with the Allied Moscow declaration of 1 November 1943, war criminals were to be sentenced by the courts of the states on whose territory they had committed their acts. The main war criminals, whose crimes had not been restricted to a geographically limitable area, were expressly excluded. They were to be punished according to a common decision of the governments of the Allied powers. This common decision was made on 8 August 1945 in the London Agreement, signed by twenty-three states. According to the London statute, twenty-four leading members of the Nazi regime were accused of preparation of a war of aggression, crimes against peace, war crimes, and crimes against humanity before

A view of some of the Nazi defendants during the Nuremberg war crimes trials in the aftermath of World War II. (National Archives)

the International Military Tribunal in Nuremberg. One of them, Robert Ley, had committed suicide before the trial began. The tribunal was composed of nominees from the governments of the four powers: the Americans sent Francis A. Biddle, the Soviet Union Iola T. Nikitschenko, France Henri de Vabres, and Great Britain Geoffrey Lawrence, who became the tribunals' chairman. In the prosecution authority, each of the four powers placed a main prosecutor: Robert H. Jackson (U.S.A.), R. A. Rudenko (Soviet Union), Sir Hartley Shawcross (Great Britain), and François de Menthon (France).

The trial proceedings lasted from 20 November 1945 to 1 October 1946, and ended with nineteen condemnations and three acquittals. Martin Bormann, Hans Frank, Wilhelm Frick, Hermann Goering, Alfred Jodl (chief of the operations staff of the armed forces, 1939–1945), Ernst Kaltenbrunner, Wilhelm Keitel, Joachim von Ribbentrop, Alfred Rosenberg, Fritz Sauckel (chief of forced labor recruitment), Arthur

Seyss-Inquart, and Julius Streicher were condemned to death. Terms of imprisonment were meted out to Walther Funk (life), Rudolf Hess (life), Erich Raeder (grand admiral, German navy—life), Baldur von Schirach (twenty years), Albert Speer (twenty years), Konstantin von Neurath (Hitler's adviser on foreign affairs—fifteen years), and Karl Doenitz (ten years). Hans Fritzsche, Franz von Papen, and Hjalmar Schacht were acquitted. The original plan to accuse further prominent Nazis before the International Military Tribunal was dropped. According to the Control Council Law No. 10 of 20 December 1945, proceedings were to be led in the occupation zones by the courts of the respective powers. Between 1946 and 1949, twelve large processes (subsequent proceedings) took place before the American Military Tribunal in Nuremberg: against physicians of the Wehrmacht and the SS; against general field marshal Erhard Milch because of cooperation with the armament program; against sixteen leading lawyers; against eighteen members of the Wirtschaftsverwaltungshauptamt of the SS, which administered the concentration camps; against the industrialist Friedrich Flick; against twenty-three leaders of the I.G.-Farben-Industrie-AG; against twelve high officers because of illegal shootings of hostages in the Balkans; against fourteen leading members of the Rasse- und Siedlungshauptamt of the SS, the agency Reichskommissar für die Festigung des deutschen Volkstums, and the Lebensborn association; against twenty-four leaders of the state police and the SD because of their participation in murder actions in the occupied areas in Eastern Europe; against Alfried Krupp von Bohlen und Halbach and eleven leading employees of the Krupp Company; against twenty-one ministers, undersecretaries of state, Gau leaders, higher SS leaders, and further leading persons of the Nazi regime; and against the fourteen highest officers of the Wehrmacht for war crimes and crimes against humanity. Some 142 out of the 184 accused persons were condemned (24 of them to death); 35 were acquitted, and 7 prosecutions failed on account of illnesses or deaths.

Although courts had been set up in the past for purposes of judging political crimes, this was the first one to win universal recognition. The crimes that the Nuremberg Court was set up to judge were crimes against peace, humanity, and defenseless minorities. The court has proved to be an important precedent for subsequent war crimes trials, and for the erection of a permanent European war crimes tribunal at The Hague.

Christian Koller

See Also: AXIS, THE; BORMANN, MARTIN; CONCENTRATION CAMPS; DOENITZ, KARL; FRANK, HANS; FRICK, WILHELM; FUNK, WALTHER EMANUEL; GERMANY; GOERING, HERMANN; HESS, RUDOLF; IG FARBEN; KALTENBRUNNER, ERNST; KEITEL, WILHELM; KRUPP VON BOHLEN UND HALBACH, ALFRIED; LAW; LEY, ROBERT; MEDICINE; NAZISM; NUREMBERG; PAPEN, FRANZ VON; RIBBENTROP, JOACHIM VON; ROSENBERG, ALFRED; SCHIRACH, BALDUR VON; SD, THE; SEYSS-INQUART, ARTHUR; SPEER, ALBERT; SS, THE; STREICHER, JULIUS; WEHRMACHT, THE; WORLD WAR II

References

Bloxham, Donald. 2001. *Genocide on Trial: War Crimes Trials and the Formation of Holocaust History and Memory.* Oxford: Oxford University Press.

Ginsburgs, George, and V. N. Kudriavtsev, eds. 1990. *The Nuremberg Trial and International Law.* Dordrecht: Martinus Nijhoff.

Heydecker, Joe J., and Johannes Leeb. 2003. *Der Nuernberger Prozess.* Koeln: Kiepenheuer and Witsch.

Robson, K. 1993. *Papers of the International Military Tribunal and the Nuremberg Military Tribunals 1945–9.* MS 200. Southampton: University of Southampton.

Sanchez, James Joseph, et al. 1995. *Nuremberg War Crimes Trials Online.* Seattle: Aristarchus Knowledge Industries.

OCCULTISM

A significant influence on certain currents of thought within Nazism, though not on Italian Fascism, where Julius Evola was the only significant figure to be attracted to it. In the late nineteenth century it gained considerable international notoriety, first through the activities of Madame Blavatsky (1831–1891), founder of the New York Theosophical Society and the alleged possessor of psychic powers, and Annie Besant (1847–1933), who was also celebrated for her advocacies of birth control and socialism. Theosophy popularized notions of lost continents, ancient wisdom rediscovered in texts of occult knowledge, and the idea of hidden masters or adepts guiding humanity from a remote fastness in Tibet. Racist nationalists in search of a prehistoric "Aryan" race and its cultural traditions combined *völkisch* notions of Germanic identity with the occult lore of Theosophy to create a hybrid Ariosophy of racial mysticism. Guido von List (1848–1919) elaborated a rich mythology of the ancient Ario-Germans, detecting Aryan traditions at archaeological sites, in heraldry, folksongs, and legal customs. His Viennese colleague Jörg Lanz von Liebenfels employed a similar occult reading of culture to attribute a racial significance to Holy Scripture and archaeological, anthropological, and contemporary scientific discoveries. In this sense, occultism operated as an epistemological reinterpretation of cultural information in order to le-

gitimate or even sacralize political values of hierarchy and racial superiority. In the 1920s, Lanz attracted a circle of racial occultists who practiced astrology, numerology, graphology, and divination as Aryan racial sciences.

The inference of a hidden, suppressed tradition logically posits the existence of a suppressing agent, which leads to conspiracy theory. Political occultists typically regard the current establishment as under the sway of hostile powers opposed to the unveiling and revival of the occult tradition. List and Lanz began by impugning the Catholic church as the instrument of this suppression but later identified the Jews as the architects of an age-old conspiracy against the Aryans. The combination of Germanic culture with notions of occult wisdom appealed to Heinrich Himmler, who employed Karl Maria Wiligut (1866–1946), an elderly Ariosophist in the Listian tradition, as a special advisor on matters of runes, ancestral clairvoyance, and German prehistory. References to an ancient lost Germanic world vindicated Himmler's vision of a prehistoric world opposed to the modern Christian West. Himmler also consulted an astrologer, Wilhelm Wulff, in the later stages of the war.

Nicholas Goodrick-Clarke

See Also: ANTHROPOLOGY; ANTI-SEMITISM; ARYANISM; CATHOLIC CHURCH, THE; CONSPIRACY THEORIES; DEMOGRAPHIC THEORY; EVOLA, JULIUS; FASCIST PARTY, THE; GERMANIC RELIGION; GERMANNESS (*DEUTSCHHEIT*);

GERMANY; HIMMLER, HEINRICH; ITALY; LIEBENFELS,
JÖRG ADOLF JOSEF LANZ VON; MYSTICISM; MYTH;
NAZISM; ORGANICISM; RACIAL DOCTRINE; RACISM; RA-
TIONALISM; RELIGION; SOCIALISM; TIBET; TOLKIEN,
JOHN RONALD REUEL; *VOLK, VÖLKISCH*

References
Goodrick-Clarke, Nicholas. 2002. *Black Sun: Aryan Cults,
Esoteric Nazism, and the Politics of Identity.* New York: New
York University Press.
———. 2004. *The Occult Roots of Nazism: Secret Aryan Cults
and Their Influence on Nazi Ideology.* New York: New York
University Press.
Mosse, George L. 1980. *Masses and Man: Nationalist and
Fascist Perceptions of Reality.* New York: Howard Fertig.
Treitel, Corinna. 2004. *A Science for the Soul: Occultism and the
Genesis of the German Modern.* Baltimore, MD: Johns
Hopkins University Press.

ODESSA

Acronym for one of several postwar underground networks allegedly formed to provide assistance to wanted Nazi fugitives who were seeking to elude Allied dragnets and escape to safe havens outside their own homeland. The Organisation der ehemaligen SS-Angehörigen (ODESSA; Organization of Former SS Members) has undoubtedly become the most notorious of these purported support networks, in large part because of Frederick Forsyth's 1972 fictional best-seller *The Odessa File.* However, much of the existing information about ODESSA and other clandestine Nazi networks remains difficult to corroborate, and there is as yet no consensus among historians about their precise role and significance.

Several observers, most of whom have been professional "Nazi hunters," former intelligence officers, and journalists seeking fame and fortune or pushing an "antifascist" political agenda, have claimed that ODESSA was an elaborate, highly efficient, and powerful clandestine organization that provided many dangerous wanted Nazis with false identity papers and thereafter carefully arranged for their escape from the ruins of the occupied Third Reich to safe havens in Spain, Latin America, or the Middle East. The single most influential account of the organization is that of Simon Wiesenthal, who described it as a secret SS escape network set up in 1947 that had established "ports of call"

every forty miles along the German-Austrian border, two principal escape routes for fugitives (one from Bremen to Rome and the other from Bremen to Geneva), "export-import" companies with representatives overseas and links with Catholic monastic orders, professional smugglers, and friendly foreign embassy personnel. ODESSA, one of whose main organizers was reportedly SS officer Franz Röstel, also supposedly had access to Nazi loot, including funds that had been secretly transferred abroad by Nazi officials prior to the end of the war.

In contrast to this sinister depiction, other investigators have insisted that ODESSA—assuming that it existed at all—never constituted a single coherent network but at most consisted of a loose collection of small cells of SS men who engaged in parallel and sometimes overlapping exfiltration activities. Indeed, intelligence reports in the U.S. National Archives suggest that much of the information gathered by U.S. Army Counter-Intelligence Corps (CIC) field agents about the supposed activities of ODESSA was based on unreliable hearsay that subsequent investigations were unable to verify. Nevertheless, these files are anything but comprehensive, and it remains possible that other reports on ODESSA are either stored elsewhere or still remain classified, so that the verdict is still out concerning the true scope of the organization.

The relationship between ODESSA and other purported Nazi underground networks is also far from clear. Michael Bar-Zohar described the Schleuse ("Lock-Gate") organization in terms identical to those used by Wiesenthal to describe ODESSA, but there are no references to this group in other sources. The available descriptions of the so-called Spinne ("Spider") network are so varied and irreconcilable as to be virtually useless. On the other hand, the Kameradenwerk ("Comrades' Alliance") was a "patriotic" support organization set up in South America by former Luftwaffe ace Hans Ulrich-Rudel, whose proclaimed purpose was to raise money from expatriate German communities to help fugitive or imprisoned comrades back home who were having financial or legal problems. It in turn employed a host of secretive far-right groups and veterans' or prisoners' "aid societies" inside Germany as intermediaries, including the Stille Hilfe für Kriegsgefangene und Internierte ("Silent Aid for Prisoners-of-War and Internees") organization, which developed friendly relations with both occupation authorities and German government ministers despite its many links to extreme-right groups. Finally, the Bruderschaft ("Brotherhood") and Naumann-Kreis ("Naumann Circle") were not escape and support networks at all, but rather covert cadre organizations operating inside West Germany that aimed to infiltrate their members into established political parties and the state apparatus.

It may well be that some of the more sensational reports about secret Nazi escape organizations were the products of disinformation campaigns designed to distract public attention away from two far more significant postwar phenomena: the covert exfiltration of wanted Nazi, Fascist, and Axis intelligence and counterinsurgency experts by much more powerful institutions, including (1) the Vatican's Refugee Bureau, and (2) various Allied security agencies, which subsequently recruited many of them. These latter sought to utilize former enemy assets, including Eastern Front intelligence expert Reinhard Gehlen, former Gestapo leader Klaus Barbie, and famous SS commando Otto Skorzeny, in the looming struggle against the Soviet Union. The Soviet intelligence services also recruited wanted Nazis to work against the West.

Jeffrey M. Bale

See Also: ANTIFASCISM; AXIS, THE; BARBIE, KLAUS; BOLIVIA; CATHOLIC CHURCH, THE; GERMANY; GESTAPO, THE; LUFTWAFFE, THE; MENGELE, JOSEF; MIDDLE EAST, THE; NAZISM; PARAGUAY; SKORZENY, OTTO; SOVIET UNION, THE; SPAIN; SS, THE; THIRD REICH, THE; WIESENTHAL, SIMON; WORLD WAR II

References
Brockdorff, Werner [pseudonym for Alfred Jarschel]. 1969. *Flucht vor Nürnberg: Pläne und Organisation der Fluchtwege der NS-Prominenz im "Römischer Weg."* Munich: Welsermühl.
Camarasa, Jorge. 1995. *ODESSA del sur: La Argentina como refugio de nazis y criminales de guerra.* Buenos Aires: Planeta.
Chairoff, Patrice [pseudonym for Dominique Calzi]. 1977. *Dossier néo-nazisme.* Paris: Ramsay.
Geifer, Rena, and Thomas Geifer. 1991. *Die Rattenlinie: Fluchtwege der Nazis: Eine Dokumentation.* Frankfurt: Hain.
Goni, Uki. 2003. *The Real Odessa: How Perón Brought the Nazi War Criminals to Argentina.* Cambridge: Granta.
Pomorin, Jürgen, et al. 1981. *Geheime Kanäle: Der Nazi-Mafia auf der Spur.* Dortmund: Weltkreis.
Rudel, Hans-Ulrich. N.d. *Zwischen Deutschland und Argentinien: Fünf Jahre in Übersee.* Göttingen: Plesse.
Schröm, Oliver, and Andrea Röpke. 2001. *Stille Hilfe für braune Kameraden: Das geheime Netzwerk der Alt- und Neonazis.* Berlin: C. H. Beck.
Simpson, Christopher. 1989. *Blowback: America's Recruitment of Nazis and Its Effects on the Cold War.* New York: Collier.
Wiesenthal, Simon. 1967. *The Murderers among Us: The Simon Wiesenthal Memoirs.* New York: McGraw Hill.

O'DUFFY, EOIN (1892–1944)

Irish fascist leader in the interwar years. After the foundation of independent Ireland in 1922, O'Duffy was appointed commander of the newly formed national police force, the Garda Siochana. O'Duffy was dismissed from this post in February 1933 and took over the leadership of the veterans' organization, the Army Comrades Association. He was instrumental in transforming that body into the fascist-style Blueshirts, and he acted as its head until he resigned in August 1934 because of the organization's adherence to legal means of protest. O'Duffy went on to form the openly fascist but short-lived National Corporate Party. In 1936 he led an Irish brigade to Spain in support of Franco; it returned to Ireland, having seen little action, in the summer of 1937.

Mike Cronin

See Also: INTERNATIONAL BRIGADES, THE; IRELAND; SPANISH CIVIL WAR, THE; WAR VETERANS

References
Cronin, M. 1997. *The Blueshirts and Irish Politics.* Dublin: Four Courts.
McGarry, F. 1999. *Irish Politics and the Spanish Civil War.* Cork: Cork University Press.
McMahon, C. 2002. "Eoin O'Duffy's Blueshirts and the Abyssinian Crisis." *History Ireland* 10, no. 2: 36–39.

OKLAHOMA BOMBING, THE

The 19 April 1995 bombing of a federal building in Oklahoma City and the resulting deaths of 168 people were connected with the extreme Right in a number of ways. The bomber, Timothy McVeigh, had long been an admirer of the *Turner Diaries,* the novel in which the veteran neo-Nazi William Pierce portrayed a future terrorist campaign including the bombing of a federal building. At one time a member of the Ku Klux Klan, McVeigh had sought to contact Pierce's organization, the National Alliance, shortly before the bombing. The Oklahoma bombing was intended as revenge for the burning to death two years earlier of seventy-six people during the FBI siege of the Branch Davidian sect in Waco, Texas. Claims that the deaths had been deliberately brought about by the government had a far-reaching effect on many on the far Right and were a central factor in the emergence of the militia movement in 1994. However, instead of supporting the Oklahoma bombing, many in the militias claimed that McVeigh had been a "patsy," and that the attack had been part of a conspiracy linked to the federal government. In particular, they were suspicious of a German, Andreas Strassmeier, whom McVeigh attempted to telephone shortly before the bombing at a Christian Identity compound in Oklahoma, Elohim City.

While contending that McVeigh had carried out the attack on his own, federal prosecutors believed that his plans had involved others. One man, Michael Fortier, subsequently became a key government witness against McVeigh, while another, Terry Nichols, was sentenced to life imprisonment. Convicted of murder, McVeigh was executed in June 2001. While he had pleaded not guilty, a journalist who had interviewed him in custody subsequently co-authored a book revealing that McVeigh had admitted his responsibility for the Oklahoma bombing. Militia activists, however, continued to believe in a broader conspiracy, as did his lawyer, Stephen Jones; in 2002 a professor at Indiana State University, Mark Hamm, published a book suggesting a link between McVeigh and a racist gang, the Aryan Republican Army, which had carried out a series of bank robberies in the early 1990s.

Martin Durham

See Also: ARYANISM; CHRISTIAN IDENTITY; KU KLUX KLAN, THE; MCVEIGH, TIMOTHY; NEO-NAZISM; PIERCE, WILLIAM; POSTWAR FASCISM; RACISM; UNITED STATES, THE (POSTWAR); WHITE SUPREMACISM; ZIONIST OCCUPATION GOVERNMENT, THE (ZOG)

References
Hamm, Mark S. 2001. *In Bad Company: America's Terrorist Underground.* Boston: Northeastern University Press.
Jones, Stephen, and Peter Israel. 1998. *Others Unknown: The Oklahoma City Bombing and Conspiracy.* Collingdale, PA: Diane Publishing.
Michel, Lee, and Dan Herbeck. 2001. *American Terrorist: Timothy McVeigh and the Oklahoma City Bombing.* New York: Regan.

OLYMPICS: *See* BERLIN OLYMPICS, THE; SPORT

OPERATION BARBAROSSA: *See* BARBAROSSA, OPERATION

ORGANICISM

GENERAL

The particular philosophy of state and society that Italian Fascist and German Nazi ideologues believed themselves to be implementing in preference to the "abstract," "mechanistic," liberal individualism that they held to be embodied in parliamentary regimes. The classic liberal tradition that seemed to be in the ascendancy in the aftermath of World War I (it was, of course, the ideology of the main victorious powers—Britain, France, and the United States) was based on an assumption that society and the state are, and must be, the product of the consent of the citizens. The symbols of this view of society and the state were the ballot box, in which individual citizens gave or withheld their consent, and the parliament, which was supposed to represent the individual citizens in arriving at decisions regarding society and state. This, in effect, made individuals prior to society and the state, both of which were created by their consent. The archetypal historical event embodying this philosophy was the French Revolution, and conservative thinkers throughout the nineteenth century had complained about the subordination of society and the state to the individual as a source of anarchy. They also pointed out that individuals are not "born free" as Rousseau had famously asserted at the beginning of the *Social Contract*—the bible of many liberals—but "born dependent," a helpless baby unable to survive without the care of both his immediate family and the wider society that sustains his family. At the same time, ideologues on the Left complained that the ballot box and the parliamentary system are a sham because they do not feed the poor or improve their lot but fob them off with useless paper "rights" designed to give them an illusion of being "free."

Organic theories, by contrast, start not from the individual and his rights but from society and the state as palpable realities that have priority over the individual. They argue or assume that individuals are not isolated atoms born independent of each other but creatures born into a state of mutual dependence and owing everything to the nurture of family, society, and state. In the theory of Italian Fascist philosopher Gentile, the individual's awareness of his existence is bound up with his sense of need of the other. Not only are the health of the family, society, and the state in this way of thinking to be prioritized over the welfare of the individual, but the individual is only a part of a pre-existing organic entity called society into which he is born. That being the natural way, liberal individualism is thus "against nature," and interwar fascists saw it as their mission to restore the natural order of things by re-ordering society and state so that they were in harmony with their properly organic nature. The institutions of the state must embody the principle of the priority of the state over everything, for the state was the corporate expression and embodiment of the life of the individuals within it. Individuals were willy-nilly part of the state, and just as they were not asked for their consent to be born or to be raised, so they were not asked for their consent to the state and its activities. And as "society" is an abstraction until it receives an embodiment, fascist ideologues theorized the state as the embodiment of society and sought ways of remolding society accordingly. What they established has been called an "occupation" of society by the state in which the state increasingly invaded every part of the life of individuals in a process whose goal has aptly been designated "totalitarianism." The state pushed or ingratiated itself into the lives of citizens by constructing compulsory monocultural and monolithic associations for them as places where they were obliged to express their sociability—most spectacularly in the case of young people who were enrolled in nationalistic and militaristic youth movements for leisure, sport, and indoctrinational activities. In the institutions of corporate society the workplace was also invaded by the state, as traditional trade unions were abolished and replaced by monolithic state-led organizations. Interwar fascism was in fact the "occupation" of society by the state in the name of the "natural" organic order.

Some of the elements of this thinking were commonplace in nineteenth-century conservative ideologies, but fascism drew the threads together and focused all the energies of a mass movement toward the realization of an organic state, harnessing the energies of modern science and technology to the cause. Arguably, it was the combination of traditionalist-style social and political thought on organic lines with the appeal to science that gave such a powerful edge to interwar fascist movements. There was an appeal to traditional conservative values contained in the fascist vision of an ordered state based on the readiness of the individual to sacrifice himself for the community; there was an appeal to "scientific" values in the exploitation of the elit-

ist conclusions implied by Darwinistic "survival of the fittest" theories and in the frank recognition and indeed downright adulation of the combative military type of role model which that theory seemed to necessitate.

Cyprian Blamires

References
Gentile, Emilio. 1996. *The Sacralisation of Politics in Fascist Italy.* London: Harvard University Press.
Gregor, A. James. 2001. *Giovanni Gentile: Philosopher of Fascism.* New Brunswick: Transaction.

ORGANICISM AND NAZISM

Although the organic view of society and the state was characteristic of fascism in general, the distinctive importance that biological racism had in German Nazism but not in Mussolinian Fascism gave another dimension to the "organic" concept in Nazi thinking, a concept with a long tradition in Germany and a key element in the Nazi worldview. In the wake of the disappointment occasioned by the excesses of the French Revolution, it was Romanticism, especially in Germany, which argued that an authentic community of people or a nation is an organic whole, reflecting some kind of inner identity or spirit; that society is neither simply a conglomerate of individuals bound together mechanically by an artificial social contract, nor the product of the enactment of legislation detached from the influence of historical traditions; moreover, it was asserted that society could not evolve from the mechanistic promulgation of abstract legal decisions which were blind to the authentic historical sentiments of a community that reflected a shared communal life experience. During the period of Romanticism in Germany, nationalist thinkers like Johann von Herder began to speak in organic terms of the prevalence of a *Volksgeist,* a spirit or soul particular to a national community. The *Volk,* as it came to be understood in Germany in the nineteenth century, implied a deep sense of national identity, and, as George Mosse has pointed out, it gave to the idea of the nation a "transcendental essence." The idea of the *Volk* was not necessarily racist, but over the course of time *völkisch* ideology acquired a clearly articulated racial dimension in Germany and in other countries as well.

In *völkisch* thinking, the Germans were linked to their natural environment and, it was assumed, were in contact with the deeper forces of nature. Nature

Nineteenth-century German zoologist Ernst Haeckel, advocate of a new synthesis of science and religious mysticism, was an undoubted influence on Nazism along with biologist Charles Darwin and the Social Darwinism which applied Darwin's ideas to human societies. (Library of Congress)

worship was encouraged and served to stimulate the birth of mystical movements that nurtured the powers of the occult and the cultivation of theosophical-type religious programs. Rather than believing in the viability of the *Rechtsstaat*—that is, the constitutional state—the *völkisch* ideology stressed the importance of biology and "blood," and it assumed the existence of a deep racial divide between the varied groups of people constituting mankind. The German *Volk,* by direct contact with the mystical force and organic unity of the cosmos, would experience a greater sense of belonging, a feeling of being able to overcome the isolation and the indignity of alienation that was engendered by conditions of modern urban and industrial life.

During the last three or four decades of the nineteenth century in Germany, *völkisch* ideas received a major impetus from the Monist science and secular religion of Ernst Haeckel (1834–1919), Germany's greatest zoologist. Haeckel advocated the creation of a Monist nature religion that would synthesize science and religious mysticism and serve as a replacement for Christianity and the Judeo-Christian faith in a transcendent God. In Monist religion, the Germans would be able to satisfy their yearning for a faith that was organically bound up with their national and racial identity.

Nature religion would also make possible the reawakening of many symbols of ancient German pagan religious rites and beliefs. These had been obscured, the *völkisch* thinkers insisted, by Jewish and Christian influences that had served to alienate the Germans from their natural roots. The Christian holidays had to be replaced by rituals that would worship nature—for example, sun worship, which became highly fashionable in Monist and *völkisch* circles. Wilhelm Ostwald, the famous chemist and Nobel Prize recipient and the first president of the German Monist League, said in famous words: "Waste no energy; turn it all to account." In other words, use the life-giving powers of the sun to aid in reconstituting the national life of Germany. Once Hitler came to power in the 1930s, the full force of these *völkisch* ideas came to realization. The Nazis defined their society in organic terms, a perspective that they believed derived from the findings of modern evolutionary science. Their racial anti-Semitism criticized the Jews for being materialistic, for lacking "soul," and for introducing Christianity, a harmful religion that protected the weak members of society. The Germans, on the other hand, were a sentient people organically attached to their natural surroundings. Nature mysticism, the belief in irrational spiritual forces, the biologically organic power of race—all served as active elements of National Socialist ideology.

Daniel Gasman

See Also: INTRODUCTION; ABSTRACTION; ACTUALISM; ANTI-SEMITISM; ARENDT, HANNAH; BLOOD; CALENDAR, THE FASCIST; CHRISTIANITY; CORPORATISM; CULTURE (GERMANY); ELITE THEORY; ENLIGHTENMENT, THE; FASCIST PARTY, THE; FREEDOM; FRENCH REVOLUTION, THE; GENTILE, GIOVANNI; GERMANNESS (*DEUTSCHHEIT*); GERMANY; HITLER, ADOLF; INDIVIDUALISM; LEISURE; LIBERALISM; MARXISM; MATERIALISM; MECHANISTIC THINKING; MILITARISM; MUSSOLINI, BENITO ANDREA; MYSTICISM; MYTH; NATURE; NAZISM; NORDIC SOUL, THE; OCCULTISM; ORGANICISM; PARLIAMENTARISM; RACIAL DOCTRINE; ROOTLESSNESS; SCIENCE; SOCIAL DARWINISM; SOCIALISM; SOUL; SPANN, OTHMAR; SPORT; TOTALITARIANISM; TRADES UNIONS; TRADITIONALISM; *VOLK, VÖLKISCH; VOLKSGEMEINSCHAFT,* THE; WARRIOR ETHOS, THE; WORLD WAR I; YOUTH

References

Gasman, Daniel. 2004 [1971]. *The Scientific Origins of National Socialism.* New Brunswick, NJ: Transaction.

Klemperer, Victor. 2002. *The Language of the Third Reich.* London: Continuum.

Mosse, George. 1981 [1964]. *The Crisis of German Ideology: Intellectual Origins of the Third Reich.* New York: Schocken.

Rosenberg, Alfred. 1982. *The Myth of the Twentieth Century: An Evaluation of the Spiritual-Intellectual Confrontations of Our Age.* Newport Beach, CA: Noontide.

ORJUNA: See YUGOSLAVIA

ORTHODOX CHURCHES, THE

THE RUSSIAN ORTHODOX

The response of the Orthodox Churches to interwar and wartime fascism, which they encountered mainly in the form of National Socialism, was far from uniform. Representatives and priests of Orthodoxy gave repeated assistance to those persecuted by the different regimes, but there was a persistent desire on the part of Orthodox Church leaders to come to an understanding with the holders of power of the day, no matter what policy they observed. The strongest tendency to adopt a positive attitude toward fascism was, however, shown by the Russian Orthodox Church in exile.

From the sixteenth century onward, Russian Orthodox bishops and priests had increasingly preached an extreme religious nationalism that attributed to Russia a very specific mission in salvation history as the "Third Rome" after ancient Rome and Byzantium. Around 1900, influential church leaders were closely associated with growing extreme-right and racially anti-Semitic groups like the "Black Hundred," founded in 1904–1905. This movement, in which Orthodox priests were in leading positions from the beginning, has frequently been compared by historians to the protofascist Action Française: it preached a close association of czar with church and militant nationalism and anti-Semitism, and it did not flinch from assaults on individuals in public life. It also agitated for the mobilization of the masses; at the high point of its influence, in 1906–1907, the Black Hundred was an association of about 3,000 extreme-right regional groupings, especially strong in Odessa, where it initiated the Jewish pogroms of 1905–1906.

In a sermon of 1906, the most influential Orthodox preacher of his time, the priest and adviser to the czar John of Kronstadt (Ioann Sergejew, 1829–1908) stated that the Jews themselves were responsible for the way in which they were persecuted, and that they had been punished for their sins against the state "by the hand of God." In right-wing conservative circles of Orthodoxy the anti-Semitic pamphlet *The Protocols of the Elders of Zion* fell on particularly fruitful terrain, with its talk of a worldwide conspiracy involving Jews and Freemasons. The monk Iliodor (Trufanow) prophesied a last battle between the armies of the Black Hundred and those of "alien races" under the leadership of the Jews (at this period, Orthodox preachers were particularly fascinated by end-of-the-world scenarios). In March 1908 the supreme synod of the Russian Church passed a resolution in which the bishops were called on to encourage their clergy to involve themselves with the Black Hundred.

During the October Revolution and the associated civil war between "Reds" and "Whites" (1917–1922), more than 2,000 priests and monks, but also bishops and metropolitans, were murdered, and many church leaders fled abroad, where they set up the Orthodox Church in exile. While the Orthodox leadership in Russia eventually made its peace with the communist regime, a very different development—ultimately leading to support for fascist regimes—was followed by the Russian Orthodox Church in exile. In February 1921, Metropolitan Antonij of Kiev (Aleksij Chrapovickij, 1863–1936) went to Sremski Karlowitz (near Belgrade in Serbia), where the majority of his faithful had fled, and one by one all of the senior exiled bishops followed him. In November 1921 the "Supreme Church leadership of the church in exile" was set up in Karlowitz with its own council under the presidency of Metropolitan Antonij. (This was also recognized by the Serbian Orthodox Church.) The monarchist council called on all Russians to liberate Russia from the Bolsheviks, since the revolution was "a work of Satan" and had destroyed the "hallowed order"; they also called for support to be given to the armies of the White Guard. Fallen fighters on the side of the Whites were acknowledged as "Christian martyrs," and on 1 March 1922 the council issued a challenge for volunteers to enter the armed struggle against the Bolsheviks. In 1927 the Karlowitz leadership broke off contact with a Moscow church leadership that was serving a "Godless Soviet power."

By 1937 the rigid monarchism of the Karlowitz leadership had provoked a split in the church in exile.

The Karlowitz Synod disowned the Moscow patriarchate's appointee as administrator of the Russian Orthodox Church in exile in Western Europe (Vasilij Georgiewskij, 1868–1946, known as Evlogij) in August 1928 and appointed Archbishop (after 1938, Metropolitan) Serafim (Aleksandr Lukjanow, 1879–1959) to the leadership of the Orthodox Church of West Germany, though he resided in Paris. After the death of the leader of the Karlowitz Synod, Metropolitan Antonij, in 1936, Metropolitan Anastasij (Aleksandr Grinabowskij, 1873–1965) was appointed his successor, and eighty-one Orthodox Church communities accepted him. He was the one who went furthest in identifying himself with National Socialism. In 1933 the Karlowitz leadership had welcomed Adolf Hitler as a potential liberator of Russia from Bolshevism. The Nazi leadership saw the potential of Orthodox support and recognized the Orthodox Church in exile on 14 March 1936 as "a corporate body in public law" in Germany. On the occasion of the dedication of a church in Berlin, Metropolitan Anastasij wrote on 12 June 1938 to Hitler: "[T]he best people of all nations, who want peace and righteousness, see in you the leader in the battle of the world for peace and right. May God . . . give to your armies in everything good success."

At the second general council under the presidency of Anastasij in 1938, the Karlowitz church leadership announced that world Jewry was organizing the international drug trade in order to undermine the Christian world. The synod attacked the Catholic Church bitterly for its alleged "closeness to Judaism" and accused the German bishops of protecting the Jews from the measures of the National Socialist authorities and protesting against divinely willed anti-Semitism. In Paris, Metropolitan Serafin (Lukjanow) welcomed Hitler's invasion of the USSR in 1941 as "a crusade against Jewish-Masonic Bolshevism" and called on the Russians to collaborate with the invading German troops. With a few representatives of the old Russia, he saw in the German domination of Russia a catalyst that would awaken Russia to new life. In 1945, however, he submitted to the patriarchate of Moscow. After German troops had to withdraw from Serbia in 1944, Metropolitan Anastasij and the supreme leadership of the church in exile fled through Switzerland to Munich in 1946, and in 1950, Anastasij went to the United States.

Since the Gorbachev era, some of the "free Orthodox Churches" (independent from the "state church") have gladly given their blessing to Russia's New Right and are making the old extreme nationalist and anti-Semitic movements acceptable again. They are equally opposed to socialism and to the "danger of a Western-ization" of "Holy Russia" and prefer a spiritual isolation of the Russian Church to ecumenical involvement. In 1991, the priest Konstantijn Wasslijew (under the name of Lasar) declared himself "archbishop" of Moscow and Kashira and supreme leader of the "true Russian Church." He not only directed bitter attacks on the official church leadership but also spoke in a pastoral letter of 1992 of the necessary battle against the "conspiracy" of Jews, Freemasons, and satanists against Russia, and he referred to *The Protocols of the Elders of Zion.*

THE UKRAINIAN ORTHODOX

In 1921 several national church movements in Ukraine broke away from the official Orthodox Church and called their own council, which was not, however, recognized by Moscow. The "autocephalous" church generally supported Ukrainian nationalistic and anti-Semitic projects against Soviet power and was later to rely on German support. The official national Orthodox Church of Soviet-occupied Ukraine submitted, however, to the patriarchate of Moscow. The Soviet law on religion of 1929 finally dissolved the Autocephalous Church, and Metropolitan Vasilij Lipkovskij was forced to resign and eventually to flee. On account of its nationalism, almost the whole Ukraine Church leadership was liquidated during the Great Stalinist Terror of 1937, and many priests were driven underground. It is hardly surprising, then, that the Ukrainian Church welcomed the invasion of German troops in 1941 and collaborated with the Germans. Under German leadership two Ukrainian churches formed again: the revived Autocephalous Church under Bishop Polycarp (Sikorskij) of Luzk (followed by fifteen Ukrainian bishops), who was considered particularly friendly to Germany; and the Autonomous Church under the Exarch Aleksij (Gromadskij) of Kremjanec, who had submitted to Moscow in 1940 and who was followed by sixteen Ukrainian bishops. Both church leaderships now sought to ingratiate themselves with the Germans and take over the vacant metropolitan see of Kiev.

Meanwhile, a power struggle had broken out among the German authorities over the position of the Ukrainian Church: the politically weak Reich minister for the occupied Eastern Territories, Alfred Rosenberg, had on 29 April 1941 written a memorandum on the significance for a successful German administration of a regulation of the church question in the Ukraine. On 19 June 1942 he issued a religious Tolerance Edict with which he intended to integrate the strengthened

Ukrainian National Church into his "Germanization Program" and break it completely free of Moscow. But that was opposed by the person with the real power, the brutal *Gauleiter* Erich Koch (1896–1986) as *Reichskommissar* for the Ukraine; he subjected the Ukrainian churches to harsh measures, since he considered all Ukrainians to be "subhumans," useful only as a supply of cheap labor for the German master race. In association with the rabidly church-hating and powerful *Reichsleiter* Martin Bormann, Koch gained the upper hand and pursued a policy of playing the church leaderships against each other. In Eastern Ukraine, Orthodox priests were put in as agents of the Gestapo against Soviet-friendly partisans. The Autocephalous Church maintained close relationships with the fascist national Ukrainian partisans, who terrorized alleged "friends of the Soviets" and in May 1943 murdered Exarch Aleksij, head of the Autonomous Church. With the reconquest of the Ukraine by the Red Army, Bishop Polycarp and the Autocephalous Church leadership fled in 1944 to Germany, and in April 1945, Polycarp was removed from the leadership of the Ukrainian Church in exile by a Ukrainian bishops' synod on account of his closeness to the Nazis.

THE ROMANIAN ORTHODOX

The Orthodox Church in Romania was also strongly nationalistic and identified itself with the Romanian royal house. After World War I, as a result of the extension of Romanian territory to the East and an influx of emigrants from Russia and the Ukraine, there was an increase in the Jewish population. The Orthodox Church now combined its nationalism with anti-Semitism; in March 1934 it was stated in a pastoral letter by Patriarch Miron that the Jews were increasingly forming the upper crust of society and monopolizing the economy. They were accused of being bringers of "corruption and other evils," and of conducting campaigns against the "Romanian soul"; Jews were said to represent a danger for Christian Romanian culture, and their removal was a "patriotic duty."

This anti-Semitism brought the church significantly closer to the leading fascist organization of Romania, the Iron Guard, which had emerged in 1930 from the nationalist and anti-Semitic Legion of the Archangel Michael, founded in 1927 by Corneliu Codreanu. Of all the fascist movements, the Iron Guard was the most strongly oriented in a Christian and mystical direction. Patriarch Miron and other higher clergy encouraged the guard but also tried to dampen their enthusiasm

Patriarch Miron Cristea (d.1939) of the Romanian Orthodox Church. The relationship between the Orthodox Churches and fascist ideologies—which they encountered mainly in the form of Nazism—was complex. As national churches, they could be vulnerable to extreme nationalistic propaganda. (Time Life Pictures/Getty Images)

for violence. The synod of bishops discreetly supported fascist legionaries who fought on the side of the Falangists in the Spanish Civil War. A pastoral letter by the Romanian bishops on 15 October 1936 welcomed General Franco's seizure of power in Spain in the summer of 1936 as a contribution to the "struggle between atheism and Christianity." Slain legionaries and guardists brought back home were carried to their graves by Orthodox priests with great pomp and splendor.

In the emerging power struggle between the royal house and the radical Right in Romania, the regime frequently had to call upon the representatives of the Orthodox Church to tame their enthusiasm for the guard. The Orthodox Church leadership eventually came out on the side of the royal house and supported the "putsch" of King Carol II on 10 February 1938: Patriarch Miron Cristea was the first minister president of the so-called king's dictatorship (up to the time of his death in March 1939). On 14 February 1938 he prohibited all political activity on the part of non-regime organizations, so that even the Iron Guard was driven underground until 1940. Under Miron's successor, Nicodim Munteanu (Patriarch 1939–1948), the church remained loyal to the monarchy but persisted in its anti-Semitism and also supported the dictatorship of General Ion Antonescu, who led Romania into the war as an ally of Nazi Germany.

Markus Hattstein
(translated by Cyprian Blamires)

See Also: ACTION FRANÇAISE; ANTI-SEMITISM; ANTONESCU, GENERAL ION; BARBAROSSA, OPERATION; BOLSHEVISM; CATHOLIC CHURCH, THE; CHRISTIANITY; CODREANU, CORNELIU ZELEA; CONSPIRACY THEORIES; CULTS OF DEATH; DICTATORSHIP; FALANGE; FRANCO Y BAHAMONDE, GENERAL FRANCISCO; FREEMASONRY, FREEMASONS; GERMANNESS (*DEUTSCHHEIT*); GERMANY; GESTAPO, THE; HITLER, ADOLF; LEGION OF THE ARCHANGEL MICHAEL, THE; MARXISM; MONARCHISM; MONARCHY; MYSTICISM; NATIONALISM; NAZISM; *PROTOCOLS OF THE ELDERS OF ZION, THE;* PROTOFASCISM; RACIAL DOCTRINE; ROMANIA; ROSENBERG, ALFRED; RUSSIA; SERBS, THE; SLAVS, THE (AND GERMANY); SOCIALISM; SOUL; SOVIET UNION, THE; SPAIN; SPANISH CIVIL WAR, THE; STALIN, IOSIF VISSARIONOVICH; *UNTERMENSCHEN* ("SUBHUMANS"); WORLD WAR II

References

Fireside, Harvey. 1971. *Icon and Swastika: The Russian Orthodox Church under Nazi and Soviet Control.* Cambridge: Harvard University Press.
Ioanid, R. 1990. *The Sword of the Archangel Michael: Fascist Ideology in Romania.* Boulder, CO: Eastern European Monographs.
Young, Alexey, Karl Pruter, and Paul David Seldis, eds. 1993. *The Russian Orthodox Church outside Russia: A History and Chronology.* San Bernardino, CA: Borgo.

THE SERBIAN ORTHODOX CHURCH

In the decades prior to World War II a number of religious thinkers and Christian associations in Serbia advocated a narrow and politicized view of Orthodox Christianity marked by anti-Westernism, ethnophiletism, and clerical nationalism. These ideas were espoused in journals such as *Svetosavlje* and *Hrišćanska Misao (Christian Thought)*, edited by Dimitrije Najdanović, Justin Popović, and other aspiring religious thinkers influenced by conservative Russian emigre theologians (such as Metropolitan Anthony Khrapovitsky) and by the right-wing Serbian bishop of Ohrid and Žiča Nikolaj Velimirović. Bishop Velimirović (1880–1956) was the patron of the Bogomoljci ("Devotionalists"), an Orthodox Christian evangelical movement that maintained strong links with the fascist movement Zbor, led by the pro-Nazi politician Dimitrije Ljotić. Bishop Velimirović is credited with helping to shape Zbor's political agenda. The clerical nationalism and anti-Western rhetoric in the writing of Bishop Nikolaj Velimirović is permeated with virulently anti-Semitic statements. On one occasion in 1935, the bishop expressed a favorable opinion of Hitler, although he subsequently recanted the statement and criticized Nazi policies. Shortly before his death in 1937, the head of the Serbian Church, Patriarch Varnava Rosić (1880–1937), also spoke of Hitler in an affirmative fashion. The most pro-Nazi among senior Serbian clergy was the bishop of Berlin and Germany, Seraphim Lade, an ethnic German who took an active part in the administration (and destruction) of Orthodox churches in Nazi-occupied Poland and Czechoslovakia.

The views of right-wing and pro-Nazi circles in Serbian Orthodoxy cannot be said to have been representative of the church as a whole. Varnava Rosic's successor, Patriarch Gavrilo Dožić (1881–1950), strongly objected to Yugoslavia's signing of the pact with the Axis forces in 1941 and took an active role in gathering public support for the putsch (25 March 1941) that annulled the agreement. For this he was arrested by the Nazis in April 1941 and held in captivity until December 1944. During the Nazi occupation, the Serbian Orthodox Church—undermined by the partitioning of Yugoslavia and under the temporary leadership of the metropolitan of Skoplje, Josif Cvijović—adopted an ambivalent stance toward the occupiers and the Serbian collaborationist administration. Between 1941 and 1944 it issued a number of public statements urging the population to collaborate with the authorities, but without unequivocally condemning the partisan and Chetnik insurgencies. Most priests in rural Serbia are believed to have been sympathetic toward the Chetniks of General Dragoljub Mihajlović. Because of Patriarch Gavrilo's anti-Nazi credentials and the pro-Chetnik sentiments among the clergy, the occupiers treated the Serbian Orthodox Church with suspicion. During the collaborationist government of Milan Nedić (September 1941–October 1944), the church was placed under the jurisdiction of the minister of education, Velibor Jonić, who endeavored to implicate the church in the collaborationist project, but without notable success.

Jovan Byford

See Also: ANTI-SEMITISM; AXIS, THE; CHRISTIANITY; CZECHOSLOVAKIA; GERMANY; HITLER, ADOLF; LJOTIĆ, DIMITRIJE; NAZISM; POLAND; SERBS, THE; WORLD WAR II; YUGOSLAVIA

References

Byford, J. T. 2004. "From 'Traitor' to 'Saint' in Public Memory: The Case of Serbian Bishop Nikolaj Velimirović." *Analysis of Current Trends in Anti-Semitism* 22. The Sassoon International Centre for the Study of Anti-Semitism, available online at http://sicsa.huji.ac.il/22byford.pdf.

Radic, R. 2002. *Država i verske zajednice 1945–1970* [*The State and Religious Communities between 1945 and 1970*]. Beograd: Institut za Noviju Istoriju Srbije.

ORWELL, GEORGE
(real name ERIC BLAIR, 1903–1950)

Political writer who by his parables—perhaps more than any other literary figure in the twentieth century—shaped popular attitudes toward totalitarianism. A revolutionary socialist and left-wing English patriot by conviction, Orwell fought on the Republican side during the Spanish Civil War because, he was alleged to have remarked, "someone had to kill fascists." His experiences, however, left him bitterly disillusioned with communism, which was seemingly more intent on persecuting its socialist rivals than in the successful prosecution of the war against fascism. From 1936 onward, through such powerful satires as *Animal Farm* (1944) and *Nineteen Eighty-Four* (1947), Orwell's very name became shorthand for the exposure of the follies of totalitarianism. Indeed the term *Orwellian* immediately conveys the dark dystopian terrors of state repression, the culture of betrayal, and the abasement of language for political ends, with the resulting "newspeak" or "doublethink." Pre-empting the Frankfurt school of Marxism, Orwell saw in the degradation of language and literacy a key mode of social control in totalitarian and, increasingly, democratic societies. During his own lifetime and since, many reviewers, particularly in the United States, have mistaken his denunciation of "Big Brother" as a renunciation of his own deep-seated socialist values, rather than understanding them as a savage critique of Soviet "state socialism" and fascism. Indeed, it is perhaps Orwell's rendering transparent of the murderous literary mechanics of totalitarianism of both Left and Right that has ensured his popularity as an author to this day.

Graham Macklin

See Also: ARENDT, HANNAH; BOLSHEVISM; INTERNATIONAL BRIGADES, THE; MARXISM; PROPAGANDA; RELIGION; SOCIALISM; SPANISH CIVIL WAR, THE; TOTALITARIANISM

References

Crick, Bernard. 1982. *George Orwell: A Life.* London: Penguin.

Hitchens, Christopher. 2002. *Orwell's Victory.* London: Verso.

Orwell, George. 1984. *Nineteen Eighty-Four.* London: Penguin.

OSSAWABRANDWEG, THE

Founded in 1938 by Colonel J. C. C. Lass, the Ossawabrandweg (OB), or "Ox Wagon Guard," was initially a *völkisch*-style cultural organization that promoted Afrikaner identity through a pseudo-military organization that at its height in 1940–1941 probably had around 200,000 members. In 1941, Johannes Frederik Janse van Rensburg, the former administrator of the Orange Free State, who was strongly influenced by German National Socialism, assumed the leadership of the OB. He prevented a major confrontation between more radical members and the South African government while promoting the need to create a South African republic freed from British influence. A bitter feud with both the Herenigde Nasionale Party (National Party) and the Afrikaner Broederbond meant that, with the defeat of Germany in World War II, the OB became marginalized and eventually dissolved in the early 1950s.

Irving Hexham

See Also: BROEDERBOND, THE; GERMANY; NAZISM; SOUTH AFRICA; *VOLK, VÖLKISCH*; WORLD WAR II

References

Furlong, Patrick, J. 1991. *Between Crown and Swastika: The Impact of the Radical Right on the Afrikaner Nationalist Movement in the Fascist Era.* Hanover: Wesleyan University Press.

Marx, Christoph. 1998. *Im Zeichen des Ochsenwagens: Der radikale Afrikaaner-Nationalismus in Südafrika und die Geschichte der Ossenwabrandwag.* Münster: LIT.

OSSIETZKY, CARL VON: *See* **PACIFISM**
OSTARA: *See* **LIEBENFELS, JÖRG ADOLF JOSEF LANZ VON**
OSTMARK: *See **ANSCHLUSS**,* **THE**

PACIFISM

Fascists in Italy and Germany disparaged pacifism as being opposed to their militarism and glorification of war, disbanded pacifist organizations after the seizure of power, and persecuted their members. Hitler, Goebbels, and other leading National Socialists frequently rejected the idea of pacifism in their speeches and writings. They used the term *pacifism* in connection with adjectives like "democratic," "internationalist," "Jewish," "Bolshevist"—that is, in a discourse in which pacifism did not signify particular political actions or projects to abolish war, but rather the total lack of a militant political style, of a readiness for nationalist self-determination and of unwavering support for militarization. This ideological antipacifism was more common than contemptuous remarks about individual pacifists, which occurred frequently only in articles by Alfred Rosenberg. Rare allusions to peacefulness in Hitler's speeches during the 1920s were only of a tactical and rhetorical nature. Mussolini began to turn pacifism into a target for his aggressive rhetoric in late 1914, when he advocated an Italian intervention in the war on the side of the Entente powers. He scorned socialist antiwar propaganda as a "propaganda of cowardice" and demanded to curb what he called *pacifondaismo astratto* ("abstract pacifundamentalism") (Mussolini 1934, 9, 53). Mussolini's attacks against pacifist politics were part of a political discourse that identified war and masculinity and rejected the search for peaceful solutions as effeminate.

After the Nazi seizure of power, pacifist journals like *Das Andere Deutschland* were banned in February 1933; pacifist organizations like the Deutsche Friedensgesellschaft (DFG; German Peace Society) and the Liga für Menschenrechte (Human Rights League) were disbanded in March 1933. Many of their leading members were put into custody without legal authorization or were confined in concentration camps. The majority of German high-profile pacifists went into exile. Important early destinations were Czechoslovakia (for example, Kurt Hiller and Friedrich Seger) and France (Hellmut von Gerlach and Kurt R. Grossmann). Other refugee countries included England, Norway, Sweden, and Switzerland. Many pacifists contributed frequently to newspapers and journals during their exile, criticizing the rearmament policies of Nazi Germany. Grossmann in Prague and Gerlach in Paris established refugee relief networks to help assuage the financial hardships of many emigrants, to foster emotional and intellectual cohesion among them, and to detect Nazi spies who often covered up as persecuted pacifists. The historian and prominent pacifist Ludwig Quidde (1858–1941), who had been awarded the Nobel Peace Prize in 1927 and who had been a chairman of the DFG, fled to Switzerland in 1933 and built up the Comité de secours aux pacifistes exilés (Committee for the Assistance of Exiled Pacifists). Together with Willy Brandt in Norway and Gerlach, Quidde was also involved in an attempt to rescue the pacifist Carl von Ossietzky, who had been the editor of the political journal *Weltbühne (World Stage)* from 1927 to 1933. Ossietzky had been arrested in February 1933 and imprisoned in the concentration camps at Sonnenburg and Papenburg-Esterwegen. Seriously ill, he was released to a hospital in Berlin in 1936. As a result of the initiative by Quidde and others, he was awarded the Nobel Peace Prize for 1935 but was kept in the hospital under police surveillance until his death in 1938.

Italian pacifism before 1922 was only loosely organized in small, mostly informal circles, and it had already suffered a severe blow after 1915 resulting from nationalistic war fervor among many pacifists. During the 1920s, the fascist police arrested several members of the Jehovah's Witnesses—the case of Remigio Cuminetti made the headlines in 1929—as well as members of Pentecostal groups who had refused to serve in the military.

Benjamin Ziemann

See Also: ABSTRACTION; ANTIFASCISM; ANTI-SEMITISM; ARISTOCRACY; BOLSHEVISM; CARLYLE, THOMAS; CHRISTIANITY; CONCENTRATION CAMPS; COSMOPOLITANISM; CZECHOSLOVAKIA; DEMOCRACY; ELITE THEORY; FASCIST PARTY, THE; FRANCE; GERMANNESS (*DEUTSCHHEIT*); GERMANY; GREAT BRITAIN; HITLER, ADOLF; ITALY; JEHOVAH'S WITNESSES; LAW; MILITARISM; MUSIC (GERMANY); MUSSOLINI, BENITO ANDREA; NATIONALISM; NAZISM; NIETZSCHE, FRIEDRICH; NORDIC SOUL, THE; NORWAY; PAPACY, THE; ROSENBERG, ALFRED; SOUL; SWEDEN; SWITZERLAND; WAR; WAR VETERANS; WARRIOR ETHOS, THE; WORLD WAR I; WORLD WAR II

References

Dülffer, Jost. 2003. "Der Pazifismus als Feind. Zur NS-Perzeption der Friedlichkeit." Pp. 167–180 in *Idem. Im Zeichen der Gewalt. Frieden und Krieg im 19. und 20. Jahrhundert.* Köln: Böhlau.

Giusepe, Massimo de, and Giorgio Vecchio. 2004. "Die Friedensbewegungen in Italien." *Mitteilungsblatt des Instituts für soziale Bewegungen* 32: 131–157.

Holl, Karl. 1988. "German Pacifists in Exile, 1933–1940. "Pp. 165–183 in *Peace Movements and Political Cultures,* edited by Charles Chatfield and Peter van den Dungen. Knoxville: University of Tennessee Press.

Mussolini, Benito. 1934. *Scritti e discorsi di Benito Mussolini.* Vol. 1: *Dall' intervento al fascismo (15 novembre 1914–23 marzo 1919).* Milano: Hoepli.

Siegel, Mona L. 2004. *The Moral Disarmament of France: Education, Pacifism and Patriotism, 1914–1940.* Cambridge: Cambridge University Press.

PACT OF STEEL, THE: See AXIS, THE

PAGANISM: *See* EUROPEAN NEW RIGHT, THE; GERMAN FAITH MOVEMENT, THE; GERMANIC RELIGION; GREECE; OCCULTISM; ORGANICISM

PALESTINE

The unresolved Palestine question allowed Italian Fascism and National Socialism to penetrate deep into the leadership of the Palestinian National Movement. The Arab Palestinians on the territory of the present-day state of Israel became increasingly disturbed by the great waves of immigration of Jews in the context of the Zionistic "Homeland Movement" from the end of the nineteenth century. In 1917 the Balfour Declaration by the British government gave the Zionists the promise of a "national homeland" for the Jews in Palestine. At an early stage, plans emerged for a separation of the territory into a Jewish and an Arab sector to be taken from Transjordania. After World War I, the Palestinians found an uncompromising leader who definitively and fully identified with the ideology of National Socialism: Hadjj Amin al-Husseini (1895–1974), mufti from 1920, and from 1926 to 1937 grand mufti of Jerusalem and chairman of the Supreme Islamic Council. He traversed the Arab states tirelessly and enlisted their leaders for a radically anti-Zionist policy. From 1923 he called for election boycotts and strikes against the British mandate authority, in 1928 demanded an independent Arab government for Palestine, and in 1929 organized a first uprising against the British, which they put down. In 1931 he organized a World Islamic Congress in Jerusalem that made known his position of strict anti-Zionism and pan-Arabism in the whole Islamic world. A general strike or "Great Uprising" of the Arabs in Palestine was organized by Husseini; it started on 19 April 1936, lasted 177 days, and led to more than three thousand deaths. In the face of the threat of punitive action by the British, the mufti fled in July 1936 to the holy environs of the Al-Aqsa Mosque and then escaped in October 1937 to Lebanon. In October 1939 he moved to Baghdad, where he was feted as a hero of Islam and supported Gailani's pro-German regime.

Al-Husseini was the first and most prominent Islamic leader to identify with fascism. On 31 March 1933 he sent a telegram to the Reich government to tell

Hadjj Amin al-Husseini, Grand Mufti of Palestine from 1926 to 1937 was one of the Muslim leaders most favorable to Nazism, calling on the Germans to wipe out the Jews completely. (Keystone/Getty Images)

Hitler that the Muslims in Palestine and the world welcomed his access to power "enthusiastically" and were hoping to see a fascist advance in the Middle East as well. The German government assured the mufti of its friendly disposition, but only after the establishment of the Pan-Arab Committee in Baghdad (spring 1934) did the Germans pay any sustained attention to the position of the Arabs. The NSDAP foreign affairs organization under *Gauleiter* Bohle dealt with the profascist powers in Palestine and increasingly recruited German residents there for the NSDAP. The party built its own organization in Palestine. On the occasion of the General Strike of 1936, German propagandists came out on the side of the Arabs, while Germany and Italy supplied Husseini and his fighters through Jordan and Saudi Arabia with weapons and enormous sums of money. Palestinian demonstrators cheered Hitler and Germany in the streets.

In July 1937, the Peel Report by the British government recommended a partition of Palestine and the foundation of a separate Jewish state. Germany and the mufti protested most strongly against this; the mufti was now openly representing the position of Germany politically and asking Hitler to put pressure on the governments of Poland and Romania not to allow any more East European Jews to travel to Palestine. His influence was also crucial in producing a fatal change in German policy toward Jews: between 1933 and 1937 the National Socialist government had supported the emigration of Jews from the Reich territory to Palestine, and even the SS had cooperated with an emigration office; from 1934 to 1937 they supervised a special "Transfer Camp" for all Zionists wanting to immigrate to Palestine (under the control of the SD-Section II/112–113). Up to 1935, Germany was concerned enough to get the agreement of Great Britain for its emigration plans. In 1938/1939, after the annexation of Austria, Germany increasingly encouraged the emigration of the Jews through the establishment of the Central Office for Jewish Emigration under Adolf Eichmann in Vienna. But now Palestine was no longer to be the exclusive destination, for plans were made to settle a "concentration of Jews" in Madagascar.

When Amin al-Husseini had to flee from the British occupation of Iraq at the end of May 1941, he moved even closer to the National Socialists. In June 1940 he had offered his services to the Reich government, and now he went to Berlin via Teheran, where he explained to the German ambassador, Ettel, his plan to bring all Arabs under the banner of Pan-Arabism over to the side of the Axis (25 June 1942). Here he came out unconditionally for the "final solution of the Jewish question," calling on the Germans to wipe out all the Jews, "not even sparing the children." He supported the establishment of Muslim Volunteer Divisions in the Waffen-SS and repeatedly called his people to an uprising. In 1945 the German government tried to get the mufti to neutral territory, but he was arrested and interned by the French. In 1946 he managed to escape, and he emerged in December of that year in Cairo, where he allied himself with the Islamic Muslim Brotherhood and formed the "Battalions of Allah" from among their ranks to fight against the Jews. In 1948 he decamped to Jerusalem and fought bitterly against the existence of the state of Israel and against King Abdullah of Jordan, who was ready to compromise, and who called al-Husseini "a devil straight from hell." In March 1949 a follower of the mufti made a first attempt on King Abdullah's life, and on 29 July 1951 the king was shot when visiting the Al-Aqsa Mosque by a follower of Husseini. With his pathological anti-Zionism, Al-Husseini, who went into exile in Beirut after the Israeli occupation of

East Jerusalem in 1967, eventually became completely isolated. He held firm to his positive opinion of National Socialism to the last.

Markus Hattstein
(translated by Cyprian Blamires)

See Also: ANSCHLUSS, THE; ANTI-SEMITISM; AUSTRIA; AXIS, THE; EICHMANN, OTTO ADOLF; FASCIST PARTY, THE; GERMANY; HITLER, ADOLF; HOLOCAUST, THE; IRAQ; ITALY; LEBANON; MIDDLE EAST, THE; MUSLIM VOLUNTEERS IN THE WAFFEN-SS; NAZISM; POLAND; ROMANIA; SS, THE; WAFFEN-SS, THE; WORLD WAR I; ZIONISM

References

Black, Edwin. 2001. *The Transfer Agreement: The Dramatic Story of the Pact between the Third Reich and Jewish Palestine.* New York: Carroll and Graf.
Brooman, J. 1989. *Conflict in Palestine: Jews, Arabs and the Middle East since 1900.* Harlow: Longman.
Khalaf, I. 1991. *Politics in Palestine: Arab Factionalism and Social Disintegration, 1939–1948.* Albany: State University of New York Press.
Nicosia, Francis R. 1986. *The Third Reich and the Palestine Question.* Austin: University of Texas Press.
Ofer, D. 1990. *Escaping the Holocaust: Illegal Immigration to the Land of Israel, 1939–1944.* New York: Oxford University Press.
Zweig, R. W. 1986. *Britain and Palestine during the Second World War.* Woodbridge, Suffolk: Boydell Press for the Royal Historical Society.

PALINGENETIC MYTH

Interwar fascism's mobilizing force as a political ideology is closely bound up with the way in which it synthesized two potent myths: that of the nation conceived as an organism that is "dying," "decadent," or "martyred," and the cyclical concept of historical time that imagines the possibility of total transformation and rebirth: "palingenesis." Within the context of individual national histories and political cultures, this mythic hybrid can subsume a wide variety of submyths, some of which may be extremely modern and scientific outside of their fascist context, such as the Futurist element within Italian Fascism and its cult of aviation, and the commitment to eugenics and scientific progress that were incorporated within the German Nazi commitment to racial hygiene and the development of rocket technology. It is a myth that clearly can exert widespread popular appeal only under conditions of protracted national humiliation and decline, or of acute sociopolitical crisis, both of which can give rise to widespread palingenetic longings for a new order and a new man. Italian Fascism, for example, though initially installed in power without the backing of a mass movement of public support, was eventually able to engender a considerable popular enthusiasm through its apparent success in creating a modern, efficient, powerful nation because it addressed in rhetoric, style, and deeds a deeply ingrained sense of national decline and inferiority. This process culminated in July 1935 with the conquest of Ethiopia, which was widely received as proof that contemporary Italy had witnessed the fulfillment of its Roman heritage, reversing centuries of national decay. Once the Wall Street Crash hit Weimar Germany in 1929, millions of ordinary Germans experienced a deep sense of national collapse that made the NSDAP's program of national reawakening and its promise to "resurrect" the nation from humiliation, decadence, and military impotence extraordinarily attractive, turning Hitler into a "charismatic leader."

Under both regimes the propaganda, the policies, the political religion, and the actions taken were imprinted with the palingenetic logic of removing anything associated with decadence to make way for national renewal, and adapting anything that was "recuperable" and incorporating it within the new order, stamped with new significance to embody the nation's regeneration. In that respect German Nazism was more radical than Italian Fascism. For example, whereas Italian Fascism tolerated many contrasting aesthetics and forms of cultural and social life, as long as they could be presented as signifiers of the nation's spiritual renewal and cultural renaissance, Nazism fought a dogged war against "degenerate art" that included the physical destruction of modernist paintings. While Italian Fascism merely attacked the degeneracy of some modern literature verbally, the Third Reich ritually burned books held to have "sinned" against the German spirit. While Italian Fascism stressed athleticism and physical health, Nazism actually carried out an extensive state campaign of "euthanasia" to rid Germany of those considered to have "life unworthy of life" and used sterilization on a vast scale to ensure that "degenerates" would not be born to compromise the health of the renewed *Volksgemeinschaft.* The mass murder of "racial enemies," including the genocide of Jews carried out in the Holocaust, is pervaded by the chilling palingenetic logic of ritual destruction needed to purge and regenerate the nation.

That logic is also the hallmark of the many abortive variants of fascism of the interwar period, all of which are demonstrably driven at their ideological core by palingenetic forms of ultranationalism. To take just two examples from among many thousands, the BUF's Black Shirts marched in the 1930s to an Anglicized version of the Nazi "Horst Wessel Lied," which opened with the words: "Britain awake! Arise from slumber! Soon comes the daybreak of Rebirth/We lift again thy trampled banners, Our marching legions shake the earth." Similarly, Rolão Preto, leader of the Portuguese Blue Shirts, was convinced in 1934 that the installation of fascism in Italy and Germany was the harbinger of a sea change in history, writing: "This reaction against the materialist and corrupting utilitarianism of a whole age is the beginning of the great Revolution whose spirit is going to burn and purify the earth. It is a singular aspect of the human condition that the onset of man's decadence and death always create the conditions of his salvation and deliverance."

Palingenetic myth plays a crucial role in determining two fundamental features of interwar fascism. The first is its tendency to behave both as movement and regime as a form of political religion that strives to imbue the party, the nation, the leader, and (once in power) the state itself with a sacral character demanding devotion and self-sacrifice on the part of the individual. The second is its "totalitarian" character, the bid (on the part of the most dedicated believers in the fascist cause) to bring about a revolution in all aspects of national life with a view to producing a transformation in the nation's political culture so profound that it brings forth a "new man." It is the anthropological thrust behind the fascist revolution driven by its core palingenetic myth that accounts for the vast experiment in social engineering undertaken by Italian Fascism and German Nazism, whose war against liberal forms of individualism, especially in the Third Reich, helped give the term "totalitarianism" connotations of oppression and terror. Within the fascist mindset, however, the logic of totalitarianism is not one of oppression and destruction, but of creative destruction, of destroying so as to build a new order.

Roger Griffin

See Also: INTRODUCTION; "ANTI-" DIMENSION OF FASCISM, THE; ANTI-SEMITISM; BODY, THE CULT OF THE; BOOKS, THE BURNING OF THE; CALENDAR, THE FASCIST; CONSERVATISM; DECADENCE; DEGENERACY; *DEUTSCHLAND ERWACHE!* ("GERMANY AWAKE!"); ETHIOPIA; EUGENICS; EUTHANASIA; FASCIST PARTY, THE; FUTURISM; GERMANY; GREAT BRITAIN; HEALTH; HITLER, ADOLF; HOLOCAUST, THE; INDIVIDUALISM; INFLATION; ITALY; LEADER CULT, THE; LEISURE; MARXISM; MATERIALISM; MODERNISM; MODERNITY; MOSLEY, SIR OSWALD; MUSSOLINI, BENITO ANDREA; MYTH; NATIONALISM; NAZISM; NEW AGE, THE; NEW MAN, THE; NEW ORDER, THE; NIHILISM; NOVEMBER CRIMINALS/*NOVEMBERBRECHER*, THE; PARAMILITARISM; PORTUGAL; PROGRESS; PROPAGANDA; PSYCHODYNAMICS OF PALINGENETIC MYTH, THE; RACIAL DOCTRINE; RELIGION; REVOLUTION; ROLÃO PRETO, FRANCISCO; ROME; SCIENCE; SOCIALISM; SPORT; TECHNOLOGY; THIRD REICH, THE; TOLKIEN, JOHN RONALD REUEL; TOTALITARIANISM; TRADITION; TRADITIONALISM; VERSAILLES, THE TREATY OF; *VOLKSGEMEINSCHAFT*, THE; WALL STREET CRASH, THE; WEIMAR REPUBLIC, THE; WESSEL, HORST; YOUTH MOVEMENTS

References

Ben-Ghiat, Ruth. 2001. *Fascist Modernities.* Berkeley: University of California Press.

Eliade, Mircea. 1971. *The Myth of the Eternal Return.* Princeton: Princeton University Press.

Gentile, Emilio. 2000. "The Sacralisation of Politics: Definitions, Interpretations and Reflections on the Question of Secular Religion and Totalitarianism." *Totalitarian Movements and Political Religions* 1, no. 1 (summer): 18–55.

Gottlieb, Julie, and Thomas Linehan, eds. 2004. *The Culture of Fascism: Visions of the Far Right in Britain.* London: I. B. Tauris.

Griffin, Roger. 1995. *Fascism.* Oxford: Oxford University Press.

Mosse, G. L. 1999. *The Fascist Revolution.* New York: Howard Fertig.

Vondung, Klaus. 1979. "Spiritual Revolution and Magic: Speculation and Political Action in National Socialism." *Modern Age* 23 (part 4): 391–402.

Williams, Howard. 2001. "Metamorphosis or Palingenesis? Political Change in Kant." *Review of Politics* 63, no. 4 (fall): 693–722.

"PAN-" MOVEMENTS, THE: *See* EXPANSIONISM

PANGERMANISM

Political movement that emerged in late-nineteenth-century Germany and anticipated National Socialism by its combination of an aggressive commitment to "Germanness" along with racial nationalist, anti-Slavist and anti-Semitic ideas, as well as with the promotion of war as a means of attaining imperialist objectives. Pangermanism contributed directly to the outbreak of the two world wars. Concerning the history of its focal idea, Pangermanism can be traced back to early-nineteenth-century Romantic nationalism. While until the end of the eighteenth century there existed only a rudimentary imaging of what was later grasped as "the German people," some poets and writers, as, for example,

Ernst Moritz Arndt and Johann Gottlieb Fichte, moved that idea into the center of their artistic and political statements. The wars of liberation against Napoleon made possible the imaging of a "German people," a process that was accompanied by dissociation from and hostility against the French and the Jews. The foundation of the Prussian Empire (1871) gave this aggressive nationalism a further boost and strengthened those views according to which Germany was also entitled to "a place in the sun."

Among the various political and ideological tendencies and organizations that promoted militant nationalism and the militarization of the German Reich, the Alldeutsche Verband (All-German Association or Pan-German League) became the symbol of Pangermanism. Under the leadership of Ernst Hasse (1846–1908) and Heinrich Claß (1908–1939), the Pan-German League propagated the whole range of "'national' issues," from the area of military, naval, colonial, and foreign policy, to the treatment of the outposts of "Germanness" abroad, the glorification of German "civilization," and the education of the German public to a strong sense of "national identity." The huge majority of the members of the Pan-German League belonged to the upper bourgeoisie, with some industrialists as financial supporters. Its total membership fluctuated between 21,000 (1891), 5,000 (1893), and 22,000 (1901). Including members of associated organizations, its membership reached well up to 130,000 in 1905. Local groups existed not only in Germany but also, for example, in Antwerp (Belgium), Cape Town (South Africa), and Austria, where Georg Ritter von Schoenerer became an active crusader for Pangermanism. Despite its not being a mass organization, the Pan-German League nevertheless had a rich and varied propaganda apparatus at its disposal, the *Alldeutsche Blätter* being its main publication. It could rely on more than thirty members of the Reichstag and was able to establish a well-coordinated cooperation with the German State Department in the years before World War I.

The idea of large German colonies was only part of a much broader concept of a Pan-German empire. Its core philosophy was the objective of a maximum expansion of German *Lebensraum,* if necessary by force of arms, and the consequent Germanization of territories in Europe and overseas. When colonial enthusiasm faded away, the Pan-German League intensified its racial nationalist minority politics on the European continent. For example, with regard to the Austro-Hungarian Empire, the Pan-German League painted the picture that the Magyar and Slav parts of the population would soon be in a majority over the Germans and struggled to prevent the assimilation of Germans living in Austro-Hungary. This agitation, complete with racist slurs on Magyars and Slavs, aimed at the protection of the racial nationalist status quo of the Germans and at the re-Germanization of Austro-Hungarian domestic policy, and favored the dominance of the Austrian Germans in the country in order to safeguard German imperialism on the European continent.

All of this was accompanied by intense rabble-rousing propaganda against those who were accused of being the "enemies within," especially the Social Democrats and the Jews. The Jews were attacked because they were associated with liberalism and cosmopolitanism. Accordingly, during the July crisis in 1914, General Gebsattel, the deputy president of the Pan-German League, demanded that, in order to secure the future of the German people, the "solution of the Jewish Problem" should be given the highest priority. In Ernst Hasse's racial nationalist ideology, which focused on the aim of breeding a "pure race," the Jews were also regarded as the main enemy.

World War I became the first attempt to carry out the imperialist concept of Pangermanism. The Pan-German League was strongly in favor of a resolute naval and colonial policy and, once again, stood up for an extreme annexationism policy that would enable "German *Lebensraum*" to be enlarged. The Baltic States, for instance, had been chosen for the settling of German farmers. The *Imperium Germanicum* that the Pangermanists hoped to achieve by means of war included an extended Germany dominating Continental Europe, a colonial empire on the African continent as well as a number of naval bases and, via Sudan and Suez, a link with the Middle East. The defeat of the imperialist German empire was a major setback for the Pan-German League, and after the 1918 democratic revolution the league set up a new program in August 1919, now demanding the restoration of the empire as well as the re-creation of a strong army and the recovery of former German territories. Instead of the democratic system of the Weimar Republic a dictatorship was favored, and the racist nationalist tendencies contained strong anti-Semitic currents. The Pan-German League thus paved the way for the National Socialists, and Hitler took up Pangerman ideas in *Mein Kampf.*

The National Socialist dictatorship not only radicalized some strands of Pangerman ideology but also started a second attempt to install an *Imperium Germanicum* by force of arms. Although the Pan-German League was dissolved by an order of Reinhard Heydrich in March 1939, its ideas of expansion and occupation, of expulsion and settlement, found its (radicalized) continuation in the Nazi wars of aggression and the activities of German administrative bodies such as the Reichskommissar für die Festigung des deutschen Volkstums (Reich Commissioner for the Strengthening of German Nationhood), founded in 1939. Part of the SS, this huge organization had far-reaching competence in Germany and inside the occupied territories to deport, expel, or resettle Jews and Poles and, as a countermove, to settle *Volksdeutsche* ("ethnic Germans") from the eastern parts of Europe in the now enlarged state territory of Nazi Germany. As many as 900,000 *Volksdeutsche* were resettled.

While the Pan-German League was not refounded after 1945, other organizations that have their historical roots and organizational precursors in the same set of ideas have been newly established—for example, the Verein für das Deutschtum im Ausland (VDA; Organization for Germans Abroad) in 1955. For decades the VDA supported Germans and Germanness all over the world by giving organizational and financial support to activities and institutions that encourage the use of the German language and foster (what is said to be) traditional German culture. In the 1990s the mainly statesponsored VDA came under criticism over the involvement of far-rightists in its activities.

Fabian Virchow

See Also: ANTI-SEMITISM; ARYANISM; AUSTRIA; AUSTRO-HUNGARIAN EMPIRE, THE; BELGIUM; BOURGEOISIE, THE; CIVILIZATION; COLONIALISM; COSMOPOLITANISM; DEMOCRACY; DICTATORSHIP; *DRANG NACH OSTEN* ("DRIVE TO THE EAST"), THE; EUGENICS; EXPANSIONISM; FARMERS; GERMANNESS (*DEUTSCHHEIT*); HEYDRICH, REINHARD; HITLER, ADOLF; IMPERIALISM; IRREDENTISM; *LEBENSRAUM; MEIN KAMPF;* NATIONALISM; NAZISM; NEO-NAZISM; NORDIC SOUL, THE; POLAND; POSTWAR FASCISM; RACIAL DOCTRINE; SCHÖNERER, GEORG RITTER VON; SLAVS, THE (AND GERMANY); SOUL; SS, THE; SOUTH AFRICA; WEIMAR REPUBLIC, THE; WORLD WAR I; WORLD WAR II

References
Chickering, Roger. 1984. *We Men who Feel Most German: A Cultural Study of the Pan-German League, 1886–1914.* Boston: Allen and Unwin.
Korinman, Michel. 1999. *Deutschland über alles. Le pangermanisme 1890–1945.* Paris: Fayard.
Oloukpona-Yinnon, Adaji Paulin. 1985. *". . . Notre place au soleil" ou l'afrique des pangermanistes (1878–1918).* Paris: L'Harmattan.
Peters, Michael. 1992. *Der Alldeutsche Verband am Vorabend des Ersten Weltkrieges (1908–1914).* Frankfurt: Lang.
Snyder, Louis L. 1984. *Macro-Nationalisms: A History of the Pan-Movements.* Westport, CT.: Greenwood.
Stern, Fritz. 1961. *The Politics of Cultural Despair.* Berkeley: University of California Press.

PANUNZIO, SERGIO (1886–1944)

Major theoretician of Italian Fascism in the 1920s. Born near Bari in southern Italy, he associated with syndicalist circles from a young age. He graduated in jurisprudence from Naples in 1908 and philosophy in 1911. In 1928 he was appointed head of the political sciences faculty at the University of Perugia. Panunzio believed that the traditional liberal state had outlived its usefulness, and he advocated replacing the Marxist "bourgeois/proletariat" polarity with a "conservative-reactionary/revolutionary" polarity. He claimed that the only genuine revolutionaries were militant syndicalists and anarchists. Clearly influenced by Sorel, he preached the "politics of energy," which would produce "the decisive act" of revolt. Panunzio considered that the revolutionary syndicalist elite had the vocation to mobilize the masses for revolution. The way to do that was to employ mass suggestion to inspire societywide sentiment through the exploitation of myths. As leftwing Fascism declined in the 1930s, Panunzio's influence also waned.

Cyprian Blamires

See Also: AUSTRIA; CONSERVATISM; FASCIST PARTY, THE; SOREL, GEORGES; ITALY; LIBERALISM; MARXISM; MUSSOLINI, BENITO ANDREA; MYTH; PROPAGANDA; REVOLUTION; SOCIALISM; STATE, THE; SYNDICALISM

References
Gregor, A. J.1978. *Sergio Panunzio: il sindacalismo ed il fondamento razionale del fascismo.* Roma: G. Volpe.
————. 1979. *Italian Fascism and Developmental Dictatorship.* Princeton: Princeton University Press.
————. 2005. *Mussolini's Intellectuals: Fascist Social and Political Thought.* Princeton: Princeton University Press.
Roth, J. J. 1980. *The Cult of Violence.* Berkeley: University of California Press.

PAPACY, THE

The attitudes and policies of interwar fascist and fascistic movements and regimes toward the papacy varied widely. Italian Fascism, German National Socialism, and the Spanish Falange viewed the papacy with a mixture of hostility and admiration, whereas various Austrian fascist movements, the Croatian Ustasha, and the semifascist Slovakian HSL'S movement were more positive. These movements, with their essentially Catholic, conservative outlook, were especially susceptible to papal teaching, in particular the form of Catholic corporatism set out in Pius XI's encyclical *Quadragesimo Anno* of 1931. But if Italian Fascism and German National Socialism shared a common suspicion of the power of the papacy, Italy's peculiar historical circumstances obliged Mussolini to follow a more circumspect and opportunistic policy in practice.

Early Italian Fascism was inevitably anticlerical in attitude, given the left-wing past of some of its leading members: Mussolini himself, Grandi, and Bianchi. Another founding member of the first *fascio*, Filippo Marinetti of the Futurists, once wrote that "the Papacy has always defecated on Italy throughout its history." On 18 November 1919, Mussolini wrote in his newspaper, *Il Popolo D'Italia,* "There is only one possible revision of the Law of Guarantees [regulating Italy's relations with the papacy] and that is its abolition, followed by a firm invitation to his Holiness to quit Rome." Mussolini's hostility toward the papacy had intensified during World War I because of the peace-making efforts of Pope Benedict XV. The latter's "Peace Note" of August 1917, which proposed to the warring powers the basis for peace negotiations, was blamed by Mussolini and others for spreading defeatism and pacifism and thus ultimately causing the catastrophic Italian defeat at Caporetto a few months later. Benedict followed the spread of Fascist violence with considerable concern.

Despite these inauspicious beginnings, Il Duce eventually saw the light, realizing that in a country that was 99 percent Catholic and that contained the seat of the papacy there was no future for an intransigently anticlerical policy. Just as he abandoned the initial anticapitalism and antimonarchism of early Fascism, so he abandoned its vocal anticlericalism, and in his maiden speech to parliament in May 1921 he declared: "The only universal values that radiate from Rome are those of the Vatican" (Pollard 1985, 6). By 1929, in the form of the Lateran Pacts, he had successfully negotiated a solution to the "Roman Question," the sixty-year church-state conflict in Italy. But the resulting "marriage of convenience" between Fascism and the papacy, though a useful prop to the regime, was by no means to the taste of all Fascists, and in the late 1930s, Mussolini himself became more and more impatient with the limitations that the relationship imposed on his totalitarian ambitions, not to mention

the rivalry it constituted to the "Cult of the Duce." After the dispute with Pius XI over the introduction of the Racial Laws of 1938, he confided to his son-in-law, Galeazzo Ciano, that sooner or later he would need to clip the papacy's wings.

Despite, or perhaps because of, the fact that several leading Nazis were former Catholics—Goebbels, Himmler, and even Hitler himself—German National Socialism was naturally hostile to the papacy and the influence it wielded over German Catholics, even if that was mingled with a grudging respect for the international organization's efficiency. Hostility to Catholicism and the papacy was pervasive among the Pangerman and *Völkisch* precursors of the National Socialist movement, as is evidenced by the *Los von Rom* ("Away from Rome") movement and Erich Ludendorff's tirades against "Jesuitical-Jewish-Roman" conspiracies. More important, it was a strong feeling among those leading members of the party who were committed Lutherans. To be German one had to be a Protestant; one could not be a Catholic, because then one's ultimate allegiance would lie beyond Germany. Although Hitler wisely stayed above the fray, the religious question was a divisive one inside the Nazi Party, where some, such as Dinter, campaigned strongly against the papacy: "The Roman Pope's church is just as terrible an enemy of a *völkisch* Germany as the Jew" (Steigmann-Gall 2003, 60).

In practice, National Socialism treated the Catholic Church as an enemy, both within Germany and without. In 1933, however, Hitler made the very opportunistic decision to negotiate a *Reichskonkordat* with the Vatican, something that papal diplomacy had long sought but that had been denied by the Weimar Republic. The Vatican's many demands for the legal guarantees of the rights of the German Church were conceded in return for an assurance that the Catholic Center Party would not be resurrected, and the new Nazi regime received what was widely (but mistakenly) seen as the blessing of the papacy. After the publication in 1937 of the encyclical *Mit Brennender Sorge,* which condemned Hitler's repeated violations of the *Reichskonkordat,* the Nazis feared further papal criticism of their policies. In consequence, as an international organization with the potential for undermining the total loyalty of the Germans to their *Volk,* Reich, and Fuhrer, the papacy was placed under close surveillance by German intelligence agencies during the course of World War II, and the Vatican was subjected to various, not very successful espionage campaigns by the SS-Gestapo. Pius XII's close relationship with Roosevelt and the presence of Allied ambassadors inside the Vatican after Italy's declaration of war on the

Western democracies in 1940 intensified Hitler's suspicions, and he seriously contemplated seizing the Vatican and deporting the pope during the German occupation of Rome between September 1943 and June 1944.

Two regimes with at least some fascist element to them, the Slovakian Republic of 1939–1945 and the Independent Croatian State of 1941–1945, also sought Vatican diplomatic recognition of their existence. The Vatican accorded this to the Slovak state on the grounds that it was not born out of a state of war, but the papacy's subsequent relations with Slovakia were clouded by a number of problems. The first was that the Slovaks refused to allow the papal nuncio to be doyen of the diplomatic corps, as was usual in Catholic countries, giving the German ambassador precedence instead. The second was closely linked to the first—that German influence increasingly predominated in Slovakia, leading to attempts to transform it in a national socialistic direction and, most important of all, leading to the deportation of Slovakia's Jewish community to the death camps, which the Vatican vigorously and repeatedly protested.

The Vatican's relationship with the self-proclaimed "Catholic" Croatian state was more ambiguous. Croatia clearly *was* a product of war, of the German invasion and destruction of Yugoslavia in the spring of 1941, from which the Croatian fascist Ustasha movement benefited by proclaiming independence. Thus the Vatican would not accord diplomatic recognition, though it did station an unofficial representative in Zagreb. But despite the fact that it must have known about the Ustasha regime's massacres of hundreds of thousands of Gypsies, Jews, and Serbs, the Vatican made no formal or informal protests, and after the war it turned a blind eye to efforts by Croatian clerics in Rome to smuggle the former Ustasha dictator, Ante Pavelić, and his lieutenants to South America.

John Pollard

See Also: ACTION FRANÇAISE; ANTICLERICALISM; ANTISEMITISM; AUSTRIA; CAPITALISM; CAPORETTO; CATHOLIC CHURCH, THE; CENTER PARTY, THE; CIANO, COUNT GALEAZZO; CLERICO-FASCISM; CONCENTRATION CAMPS; CONSPIRACY THEORIES; CORPORATISM; CROATIA; DINTER, ARTHUR; DOLLFUSS, ENGELBERT; FALANGE; FASCIST PARTY, THE; FRANCO Y BAHAMONDE, GENERAL FRANCISCO; FUTURISM; GERMANNESS (*DEUTSCHHEIT*); GERMANY; GESTAPO, THE; GOEBBELS, (PAUL) JOSEPH; GRANDI, DINO; HIMMLER, HEINRICH; HITLER, ADOLF; INTEGRAL NATIONALISM; IRELAND; ITALY; JESUITS, THE; LEADER CULT, THE; LUDENDORFF, ERICH; LUTHERAN CHURCHES, THE; MARINETTI, FILIPPO TOMMASO; MAURRAS, CHARLES; MONARCHISM; MONARCHY; MUSSOLINI, BENITO ANDREA; NAZISM; PACIFISM; PANGERMANISM; PAVELIĆ, DR. ANTE; PIUS XI, POPE; PIUS XII, POPE; PROTESTANTISM; RELIGION; ROMA AND SINTI, THE; ROOSEVELT, FRANKLIN DELANO; SCHUSCHNIGG, KURT VON; SERBIA; SLOVAKIA; SPAIN; SS, THE; TOTALITARIANISM; USTASHA; *VOLK, VÖLKISCH*; WEIMAR REPUBLIC, THE; WORLD WAR I; WORLD WAR II; YUGOSLAVIA

References
Alvarez, D., and R. Graham. 1997. *Nothing Sacred: Nazi Espionage against the Vatican, 1939–1945*. London: Frank Cass.
Kent, P. C., and J. F. Pollard. 1994. *Papal Diplomacy in the Modern Age*. Westport, CT: Praeger.
Muggeridge, M., ed., 1947. *Ciano's Diary, 1939–1943*. London: Methuen.
Pollard, J. F. 1985. *The Vatican and Italian Fascism: A Study in Conflict, 1929–1932*. Cambridge: Cambridge University Press.
Steigmann-Gall, R. 2003. *The Holy Reich: Nazi Conceptions of Christianity, 1919–1945*. Cambridge: Cambridge University Press.

PAPEN, FRANZ VON (1879–1969)

Right-wing German politician who smoothed the way for Hitler's rise to power. He served as regular officer until 1918. During most of the 1920s he was one of the most prominent politicians of the right wing of the Catholic Center Party in Prussia. Tolerated by the NSDAP, he chaired, as Reich chancellor, the "cabinet of the barons" in 1932, when he repealed the ban on the SA and the SS and played an important role in the dismissal of the Social Democrat government in Prussia (1932). He was a member of the first Hitler cabinet as the bourgeois figurehead and, in subsequent years, served as German ambassador in Austria and Turkey. In 1947 a German court gave him a work camp sentence of eight years, but he was released in 1949.

Fabian Virchow

See Also: CATHOLIC CHURCH, THE; CENTER PARTY, THE; GERMANY; HITLER, ADOLF; NAZISM; SA, THE; SS, THE

References
Adams, Henry Mason. 1987. *Rebel Patriot: A Biography of Franz von Papen*. Santa Barbara, CA: McNally and Loftin.
Hörster-Philipps, Ulrike. 1982. *Konservative Politik in der Endphase der Weimarer Republik: die Regierung Franz von Papen*. Köln: Pahl-Rugenstein.
Rolfs, Richard. 1996. *The Sorcerer's Apprentice: The Life of Franz von Papen*. Lanham, MD: University Press of America.

PAPINI, GIOVANNI (1881–1956)

Autodidact Italian philosopher and man of letters who helped to prepare the ground for the Fascist movement in the era before World War I. Papini was active in the early-twentieth-century artistic avant-garde, which had its capital in the city of Florence. Politically close to the nationalists of Enrico Corradini, he established the review *Il Leonardo* in 1903. In the following years he collaborated with *Il Regno, La Voce,* and *Lacerba.* He had a polemical and aggressive style and was a proponent of philosophical pragmatism and (for a short period) of the Futurist aesthetic. He was also one of the promoters of the cult of virility and the warrior ethos. After the Fascists came to power, he was initially an open supporter of the policies of the Mussolini regime, but by 1937 he had abandoned political involvement and aligned himself with the positions of dogmatic Catholicism. He did not support the Salò Republic.

Alessandro Campi
(translated by Cyprian Blamires)

See Also: CATHOLIC CHURCH, THE; CORRADINI, ENRICO; FASCIST PARTY, THE; FUTURISM; ITALY; MUSSOLINI, BENITO ANDREA; NEW MAN, THE; SALÒ REPUBLIC, THE; WARRIOR ETHOS, THE; WORLD WAR I

References

Adamson, W. L. 1993. *Avant-garde Florence: From Modernism to Fascism.* London: Harvard University Press.

De Grand, Alex. 1978. *The Italian Nationalist Association and the Rise of Fascism in Italy.* Lincoln: University of Nebraska Press.

Tannenbaum, Edward R. 1972. *The Fascist Experience.* New York: Basic.

PARAFASCISM

Building on Sternhell's alignment of interwar fascism with a type of "dissident" and distorted revolutionary nationalism, Griffin identified a number of interwar regimes (for example, Horthy's regime in Hungary, Metaxas's in Greece, and Salazar's in Portugal) as "parafascist" and therefore not directly comparable to Italian Fascism and National Socialism. The reason was that they appropriated only the "fascist style" but never subscribed to a genuine revolutionary transformation of politics and society that would set them apart from conventional authoritarianism, even one glossed over with some radical "loans" from Nazi Germany or Fascist Italy.

Predictably, the concept of "parafascism" created as many definitional and analytical problems as those that it aspired to resolve. While essentially intended to enhance the conceptual clarity of generic "fascism" as an autonomous category of political thought, it produced a dichotomy that was not (and could not be) negotiated in methodological terms. Many historians have questioned the validity of a definition of fascism that excludes from its remit a number of interwar and postwar regimes that had moved fairly close to the experience of the reference regimes in Italy and Germany. Others have upheld Ernst Nolte's view that fascism was a period-specific phenomenon to be located exclusively in the interwar European context, thus rejecting its application to postwar phenomena in Europe or indeed elsewhere. More alarmingly, so-called parafascism ran the risk of becoming the theoretical dumping-ground for all of those regimes that, while not easily dismissed as traditionally "authoritarian," could not be fitted into concrete definitions of "fascism." *Parafascism* has never been defined on its own terms; instead, it remains a shadowy limbo of qualified failure or insufficient success: neither "fascist" nor instantly rejected as nonfascist, neither revolutionary nor conventionally authoritarian.

At the heart of this complex definitional riddle lies a much wider issue of—at least partial—overlapping between "fascism" and particular traits of the conservative Right, particularly during the interwar period, that witnessed the emergence of fascism as a viable paradigmatic alternative to socialism, liberalism, and conservatism. As Martin Blinkhorn has demonstrated, it is problematic to assume two "ideal types" of "fascism" and "conservative Right," at least in the interwar period, when there was a highly permeable ideological and political barrier between them. It is true that the traditional Right proved amenable par excellence to the political message of fascism in its particular Italian or German form. In fact, as early as the late nineteenth century there were particular sectors in the conservative Right that sought to reconcile the idea of a national revolution with a more conservative framework of politics—such as the so-called conservative revolution thinking as articulated by Maurras before World War I and Spengler, Jung, and Jünger in the interwar period.

Conversely, the establishment of fascist regimes (even in the largely undisputed cases of National Socialist Germany and Fascist Italy) underlined the gap between radical revolutionary declarations and a generally more circumscribed political framework that did not involve a fundamental break with the past. Therefore, the historical experience of fascism as regime can be more accurately described as a process of approximating "fascism" from a more conservative starting point, be that as a result of initial compromises (as in Italy and Germany) or as a result of the (consciously or tactically) limited revolutionary agenda of the leaders themselves.

All these caveats point to a still unresolved relationship between "fascism" and "parafascism"—not on the level of ideology (since "parafascism," because of its hybrid nature, cannot be regarded as an intellectual doctrine)—but on that of political practice and historical experience. Methodologically, it is still possible (and potentially fruitful) to talk about "parafascism" within the broad analytical framework of fascist studies, not least because the linguistic designation of this category suggests a certain degree of affinity with fascism per se. However, rather than being treated as a (partly but not totally) failed experience of fascism, parafascism can be incorporated into the wider matrix of fascism as a specific pattern and chapter of its history as regime. Taking into account that even the German and Italian fascist regimes found themselves at odds with crucial aspects of their ideological origins and declarations, as well as the particular kind of "revolutionary" potential of interwar radical conservatism, parafascism becomes in many ways a process, a stage in the otherwise dynamic process of a regime's fascistization. This fascistization, indicating both an approximation of fascism and a qualitative departure from conventional notions of conservatism, points to a theory of fascist rule that may accommodate parafascism as a distinct model, phase, or avenue of the history of fascism.

Aristotle Kallis

See Also: INTRODUCTION; "ANTI-" DIMENSION OF FASCISM, THE; AUTHORITARIANISM; CONSERVATISM; DICTATORSHIP; FASCIST PARTY, THE; GERMANY; GREECE; HORTHY DE NAGYBÁNYA, MIKLÓS; HUNGARY; ITALY; JÜNGER, ERNST; LIBERALISM; MARXIST THEORIES OF FASCISM; MAURRAS, CHARLES; METAXAS, GENERAL IOANNIS; NATIONALISM; NAZISM; NEW ORDER, THE; NIHILISM; PALINGENETIC MYTH; PORTUGAL; POSTWAR FASCISM; REVOLUTION; SALAZAR, ANTÓNIO DE OLIVEIRA; SOCIALISM; SPENGLER, OSWALD; STYLE

References
Blinkhorn, Martin. 2000. *Fascism and the Right in Europe 1919–1945.* London: Longman.
Eatwell, Roger. 1993. "Fascism." Pp. 169–191 in *Contemporary Political Ideologies,* edited by Eatwell and A. Wright. London: Pinter.
———. 2001. "Universal Fascism: Approaches and Definitions." Pp. 15–45 in *Fascism outside Europe,* edited by Stein Larsen. Boulder, CO: Columbia University Press/ Social Science Monographs.
Griffin, Roger. 1994. *The Nature of Fascism.* London: Routledge.
Kallis, Aristotle. 2003. "'Fascism,' 'Para-fascism,' and 'Fascistization.'" *European History Quarterly* 33: 219–50.
Payne, Stanley G. 1997. *A History of Fascism, 1914–45.* London: UCL.
Sternhell, Zeev. 1994. *The Birth of Fascist Ideology.* Princeton: Princeton University Press.

PARAGUAY

As in the rest of South America, the German community in Paraguay tended to be extremely loyal to the homeland, living in isolated groups and assimilating slowly. In 1928, a small group of Nazi Party members in Paraguay formed an "organization center." Later, the Munich party chiefs designated the group as a foreign *Gruppenleitung* ("group leadership"). Then, in August 1931, the Auslands-Ableitung created a *Landesgruppe* (national party unit) in Asunción under the guidance of retired army officer Franz Reitzenstein. By 1933 there were sixty-two official Nazi Party members in Paraguay, the tenth largest group outside of Germany and the third largest in South America after Brazil and Argentina. However, in 1940, the group dissolved after the bombing of a Landesgruppe office in neighboring Uruguay.

In 1940, General Higinio Morínigo came to power in Paraguay on the death of President José Felix Estigarribia and ruled as a dictator with the support of the military. In particular, Morínigo had the backing of the Frente de Guerra, a group of three high-ranking, profascist military officers. Like many fascist leaders, Morínigo was also skilled at attracting the support of the masses. He brooked no opposition, either exiling his political rivals or sending them to concentration camps in the Chaco region. The Morínigo regime also practiced a great deal of censorship. However, after World War II, he was unable publicly to support fascism and sought to open Paraguay to a more democratic political system. He eliminated the profascist right-wing generals and briefly installed a coalition government. However, in 1947, he abandoned the attempt to make Paraguay more democratic. Instead, Morínigo set up a new government with the backing of the military and the Colorado Party, and that led to a period of civil war. This new regime survived until June 1948, when his opponents deposed Morínigo.

Some aspects of fascism appeared in the strongly anticommunist government of Alfredo Stroessner, who ruled Paraguay from 1954 to 1989. Born in 1912 to a German immigrant father and a Paraguayan mother, Stroessner fought in the Chaco War and was a decorated officer. After the 1947 civil war, he emerged as one of the leaders of Paraguay's purged armed forces. Then, in 1954, Stroessner seized power for himself. Early in his regime, Stroessner had the support of the *guionista* faction of the Colorado Party. The *guionista* movement was linked to fascist ideologies, and some of its leaders had even witnessed fascist developments first-hand in Europe. Like other fascist leaders, Stroessner utilized the Colorado Party as a mass organization that linked him to the "people." He never truly incorporated them into politics, but rather used the Colorado Party to gather intelligence on the population. While not a very charismatic leader, Stroessner did succeed at appealing to the general population through frequent public appearances. He emphasized his role as the "leader" and stressed that all acts of government derived from the work of Stroessner himself. He developed an almost cultlike following among many Paraguayans.

Like the interwar fascist leaders, Stroessner sought to dominate the population, as he believed that the great majority of Paraguayans were not prepared for participatory politics. He allowed a small group of elites to run the country while discrediting most of the traditional politicians. As in Nazi Germany, Stroessner practiced ethnic exclusion and even genocide. His government embarked on the removal, resettlement, forced labor, and killing of the Aché people in order to clear land for mining and cattle raising. Stroessner's fascist tendencies can also be seen in the fact that he provided protection for many former Nazis. Paraguay became a haven for Nazis who escaped war crimes trials in Europe. Many former SS members even gained Paraguayan citizenship. Some former Nazis reportedly trained Paraguayan prison guards. Perhaps the most famous former Nazi to seek refuge in Paraguay was Josef Mengele.

Ron Young

See Also: ARGENTINA; AUTHORITARIANISM; BOLSHEVISM; BRAZIL; DEMOCRACY; DICTATORSHIP; ELITE THEORY; FÖRSTER-NIETZSCHE, ELISABETH; GERMANY; HOLOCAUST, THE; LEADER CULT, THE; MARXISM; MASSES, THE

ROLE OF THE; MENGELE, JOSEF; MILITARY DICTATORSHIP; NAZISM; NUEVA GERMANIA; ODESSA; SS, THE; STYLE

References
Chomsky, Noam, and Edward Herman. 1979. *The Washington Connection and Third World Fascism.* Boston: South End.
Lewis, Paul H. 1980. *Paraguay under Stroessner.* Chapel Hill: University of North Carolina Press.
MacIntyre, Ben. 1992. *Forgotten Fatherland: The Search for Elisabeth Nietzsche.* New York: Farrar Straus Giroux.
McKale, Donald. 1977. *The Swastika outside Germany.* Kent, OH: Kent State University Press.
Miranda, Carlos R. 1990. *The Stroessner Era: Authoritarian Rule in Paraguay.* Boulder, CO: Westview.

PARAMILITARISM

Paramilitarism provided both the main value system and the key organizational form of the interwar fascist movements. Members of paramilitary organizations were always uniformed, marched in public, were armed and physically violent, made use of threatening and resolute symbols for their self-presentation, and aimed to destabilize the existing order. Three elements were important for paramilitarism: continuous violent propaganda, the image of the street fighter, and the presentation of paramilitary groups as mass organizations. An increase in popularity and the "bottom-up" quality of fascist paramilitarism made it attractive to traditional conservative elites who did not gain this mass support. Fascists always portrayed their violence against communists and socialists as a "defensive" method for winning the respect or support of state authorities. Paramilitarism was a new phenomenon of the early twentieth century whose emergence was facilitated by the economic, social, and cultural crises of the 1920s and 1930s. Paramilitary associations were attractive for persons who were affected by these crises because they offered a network that protected them from social isolation, and a diversion through its permanent activism and the possibility for its members to act out their frustrations in a violent manner. Members of fascist paramilitary organizations were characterized by their downward social mobility, although they had no coherent class background. Whereas storm troopers were mainly workers or members of the petty bourgeoisie, the Italian *squadristi* were members of the middle and upper classes. Fascist fighting corps were often made up of young, unmarried men who had little experience in the work force.

In contrast to the army, members of paramilitary organizations had political ambitions and defined themselves as political soldiers. Although they did not promote a clearly defined political program, they fought against the existing political system, communists, and socialists, and the alleged petty bourgeois mentality of security and respectability. The worldview of the paramilitarists was defined mainly by its destructive actions against socialists and ethnic minorities. Fascist paramilitaries marched in public (mainly in the streets), were equipped with weapons (if often very primitive ones), and made use of a hierarchy that was semidisciplined. Their organizational structure was characterized by a strong group mentality and the primacy of tiny groups. Paramilitary activities were time consuming, emotionally exhilarating, and tended to consume the life of each member. Discipline and obedience toward the leader was achieved through a form of comradeship that was generated by the commitment of its members on a horizontal level and through the voluntary recruitment of members. As a mass movement, fascist paramilitarism did not promote secret organizations.

Fascist paramilitary leaders claimed that violence could cleanse, purify, or regenerate the people and the national mentality. They promoted only vaguely defined political aims, but nevertheless viewed themselves as the idealistic avant-garde who fought for the moral regeneration of the nation. It was mainly the violence itself that functioned as a performative act and created meaning for the young street fighters. The experience of violence mobilized passions and resoluteness and was aestheticized by some fascist intellectuals as the beauty of surgical cleansing or the efficacy of will and strength. It was the emotional energy produced by acting violently that held the paramilitary groups together.

Fascist movements were dominated by their paramilitary arm. In Germany, 427,000 of the roughly 850,000 Nazis in 1933 were storm troopers, and nearly half of the 322,000 members of the Italian Fascist movement in May 1922 were *squadristi*. The same was true of the legionaries of the Romanian Legion of the Archangel Michael (sometimes called the Iron Guard), the Hungarian Arrow Cross, the assassination squads of the Croatian Ustasha, the guards of Degrelle's Rexist movement in Belgium, and the French Croix de Feu. The violent paramilitary corps of the fascists became increasingly dysfunctional when fascist movements gained power. The political activism and radicalism of paramilitary groups aggravated arrangements with traditional elites and threatened to disrupt political stability.

Sven Reichardt

See Also: INTRODUCTION; ARROW CROSS; BELGIUM; BOLSHEVISM; BOURGEOISIE, THE; CROATIA; DECADENCE; FASCIST PARTY, THE; FRANCE; GERMANY; HERO, THE CULT OF THE; HITLER, ADOLF; HUNGARY; ITALY; LEGION OF THE ARCHANGEL MICHAEL, THE; MARXISM; MASSES, THE ROLE OF THE; MILITARISM; MUSSOLINI, BENITO ANDREA; NAZISM; PALINGENETIC MYTH; PROPAGANDA; PSYCHODYNAMICS OF PALINGENETIC MYTH, THE; PSYCHOLOGY; REXISM; ROMANIA; SA, THE; SOCIALISM; *SQUADRISMO*; SS, THE; STYLE; SYMBOLS; USTASHA, THE; VALOIS, GEORGES; VIOLENCE; VOLUNTARISM; WAR; WAR VETERANS; WARRIOR ETHOS, THE

References

Diehl, James M. 1977. *Paramilitary Politics in Weimar Germany.* Bloomington: Indiana University Press.

Merkl, Peter H. 1980. "Comparing Fascist Movements." Pp. 752–783 in *Who Were the Fascists? Social Roots of European Fascism,* edited by Stein Ugelvik Larsen, Bernt Hagtvet, and Jan Petter Myklebust. Bergen: Universitetsforlaget.

Reichardt, Sven. 2002. *Faschistische Kampfbünde. Gewalt und Gemeinschaft im italienischen Squadrismus und in der deutschen SA.* Cologne: Boehlau.

Violence and Society after the First World War. Edited by Dirk Schumann and Andreas Wirsching. Munich: Beck, 2003.

Williams, Warren E. 1965. *Paramilitarism in Inter-State Relations.* London: Ph.D. dissertation.

PARETO, VILFREDO (1848–1923)

Celebrated economist and sociologist and important precursor of Italian Fascism. Pareto was born in Paris, where his father, Raffaele, a follower of Mazzini, had been exiled on political grounds. After completing a degree in engineering at Turin Polytechnic in 1870, he worked first as employee and subsequently as manager for some important companies in the railroad construction sector. An anarchical and polemical spirit and a polyglot cosmopolitan in background, Pareto soon began to make a name for himself with articles and writings in which he criticized all forms of economic protectionism and hotly defended free trade policies. In 1887 he began his collaboration with the prestigious *Journal des Economistes*. At the same period he tried his luck at a political career as deputy in the Italian parliament, but without success. At the suggestion of the economist Maffeo Pantaleone, he then devoted himself systematically to the study of pure economics and mathematics. However, a crucial encounter with Léon Walras convinced him to follow Walras in the chair of political economy at the University of Lausanne, to which he was appointed in 1893 (though for health reasons he was to abandon his university activity in 1911). In 1895 he edited with a substantial introduction extracts made by Paul Lafargue from Marx's *Das Kapital,* eliciting a very critical appraisal from Friedrich Engels. His fame as a scholar is linked to the publication in 1896–1897 of the *Cours d'économie politique,* which marked him out as one of the most original economists of his generation in the area of marginalist and neoclassical theory. Pareto's ambition at this point in his career was to make economics a formal science modeled on disciplines like physics and mechanics.

In 1901–1902 he published *Les systèmes socialistes,* a work in two volumes in which he maintained, in direct polemic with all the various forms of socialism, that the problem of social inequality can be resolved not by modifying the curve of distribution of wealth among the social classes (a curve that tends to remain constant in time whatever the socioeconomic regime of a country), but by increasing production and global wealth at a constant rate. Meanwhile he embarked on the redaction, destined to last about a decade, of his sociological magnum opus: the *Trattato di sociologia generale,* whose first edition appeared in Italy in 1916. It is an ambitious text that is difficult to read: in it, on the basis of a dichotomy between "logical actions" and "nonlogical actions" and of a distinction between "logico-experimental theories" and "non-logical-experimental theories," he developed a scientific classification of social systems in which a central role was played by the principle of social heterogeneity, by the theory of dominant groups, and by the idea of a circulation of elites. According to Pareto, society is not a homogeneous closed system but a dynamic conflictual reality, within which groups and social classes tend to assume a hegemonic role and to occupy the summit of the social hierarchy. The elites that form within each society are not, however, stable and rigid: they are subject in their turn to the inexorable law of social change. Hence Pareto's celebrated dictum: "History is a cemetery of aristocracies."

Like Gaetano Mosca (but unlike Roberto Michels), Pareto never ceased to be a convinced defender of economic liberalism and political liberty, so he cannot be considered an active, enthusiastic supporter of Italian Fascism, except in relation to the struggle that the latter led against socialism and in favor of the principle of authority. He was, however—though indirectly—a precursor of it on the intellectual level, through the emphasis in his writings on the criticism of the historical weakness of the bourgeoisie and the liberal state and through the importance that he attributed to force and

violence in the processes of social change. Nor should we forget his aversion to democratic ideology and humanitarian doctrines. As a social scientist, Pareto saw in Italian Fascism more a confirmation of his theses about the inevitable decline of political elites and about the role played by active minorities in the historical phases of transition than a real political solution. One of his last writings, the *Trasformazione della democrazia* of 1921, contains, alongside a harsh critique of the "demagogical plutocracy" that emerged victorious from World War I, a peroration in defense of elective parliamentary representation, administrative decentralization, and the independence of the magistracy; this certainly seems to confirm his substantial fidelity to liberal ideals. And yet in 1923, a few months before his death, he accepted first of all to represent Italy, and so the Fascist government, at the League of Nations, and subsequently to become a senator of the kingdom.

Alessandro Campi
(translated by Cyprian Blamires)

See Also: ABSTRACTION; ARISTOCRACY; BOURGEOISIE, THE; CLASS; DEMOCRACY; ECONOMICS; EGALITARIANISM; ELITE THEORY; FASCIST PARTY, THE; ITALY; LEAGUE OF NATIONS, THE; LIBERALISM; MICHELS, ROBERTO; MOSCA, GAETANO; PLUTOCRACY; PROGRESS; SOCIALISM; SOCIOLOGY; SOREL, GEORGES; STATE, THE; VIOLENCE

References

Ghiringhelli, R. 1992. *Elitism and Democracy: Mosca, Pareto and Michels.* Milan: Cisalpino.
Hughes, S. H. 1979. *Consciousness and Society: The Reorientation of European Social Thought, 1880–1930.* Brighton: Harvester.
Lyttelton, A., ed. 1973. *Italian Fascisms from Pareto to Gentile.* London: Jonathan Cape.
Nye, R. A. 1977. *The Anti-Democratic Sources of Elite Theory: Pareto, Mosca, Michels.* London: Sage.

PARLIAMENTARISM

Already in the last decades of the nineteenth century, the protofascist movement of "national syndicalism" had identified the syndicates as a powerful antidote to the ineffectiveness of parliaments as the main vehicle of societal representation. Around the turn of the century radical nationalists in Italy and France attacked the individualism and agnosticism of the liberal state, arguing instead in favor of a single powerful and holistic expression of collective national will. The Action

Française—for Ernst Nolte the most significant pre-1918 fascist movement—rejected parliamentary rule in favor of a return to monarchical authority and an emphasis on national (as opposed to class) political agendas.

But it was during the interwar period that parliamentarism (as a symbolic expression of liberalism) and fascism found themselves locked in binary opposition. Although the end of World War I and the spirit of the Versailles Treaty, with its emphasis on democratic reform and national self-determination, appeared at first to spell a new era of liberal vitality, such hopes were crushed under the shadow of both socialist revolution and fascist mobilization across the Continent. In Italy the liberal establishment that had ruled the country from unification onward was increasingly discredited by its ostensible inability to promote national goals—first with its failure to bring Italy into the war in 1914, and then with its inability to ensure territorial concessions on the Dalmatian coast as demanded by the radical nationalist opposition and the emerging Fascist movement. In Germany, the end of the war ushered in the first truly liberal political regime (the Weimar Republic) but deprived it of much-needed political legitimacy in the eyes of large sectors of the population, as it identified the system with national humiliation, political weakness, inefficiency, and social division. Liberal-parliamentary rule was established in all successor states of the deceased Austro-Hungarian empire, as well as in the Iberian peninsula, only to give way soon to a wave of antiliberal authoritarian regimes that gradually phased out interwar democracy and deepened the crisis of parliamentary politics.

Interwar fascism used the fear of socialism as a pivotal argument in favor of dictatorship and against the allegedly divisive nature of parliamentary politics. In the 1932 *Doctrine of Fascism,* Mussolini claimed that "the Fascist State is . . . a unique and original creation. It is not reactionary but revolutionary, for it anticipates the solution of certain universal problems which have been raised elsewhere, in the political field by the splitting up of parties, the usurpation of power by parliaments and the irresponsibility of assemblies." A few years earlier, Adolf Hitler had expressed his own views on parliamentary democracy in *Mein Kampf,* noting that "the starting point of [the national] plague in our country lies in large part in the parliamentary institution in which irresponsibility of the purest breed is cultivated. Unfortunately, this plague slowly spread to all other domains of life, most strongly to state life. Everywhere responsibility was evaded, and inadequate half-measures were preferred as a result."

In fact, fascist leaders like Hitler and Mussolini associated national humiliation and weakness with the very nature of the institution of parliament, not with its abuse under liberalism. Il Duce showed the way when in January 1925—after having headed a coalition government within a semiliberal political arrangement for more than two years—he boldly announced the introduction of dictatorial rule and embarked upon the construction of a "totalitarian" fascist state. But an authoritarian antiliberal reaction—already underway in Europe by the early 1920s (for example, the dictatorship of General Primo de Rivera in Spain in 1923; Admiral Horthy's regime in Hungary in the 1920s)—had turned into an avalanche by the end of the decade and continued unabated in the 1930s. One by one, European countries succumbed to a strong antiliberal/antiparliamentary trend: Portugal and Poland in 1926, Austria in 1932, Germany in 1933, Greece in 1936, Romania in 1938, Spain in 1939. By the outbreak of World War II the majority of central, southern, and eastern European countries had decidedly abandoned liberalism in favor of an authoritarian alternative that was becoming increasingly informed by the "fascist" innovations in Italy and Germany. At the same time, fascist movements—whether in power or in opposition—continued to attack parliamentarism vehemently as an allegedly fundamental hindrance to the promotion of genuine national interest.

Therefore, while interwar fascism emerged as a clearly and passionately antiparliamentary movement and contributed to the decline of liberalism across the Continent, it formed part of a wider disaffection with democracy and what appeared as divisive representation that engulfed Europe in the 1920s and 1930s. For many, the move to authoritarian rule and the adoption of "fascist" characteristics went together. In other words, the fascist political experiment emerged as the most popular and seemingly effective alternative to the—wider and more profound—crisis of liberalism and the impasses of parliamentary rule.

Aristotle Kallis

See Also: ABSTRACTION; ACERBO LAW, THE; ACTION FRANÇAISE; "ANTI-" DIMENSION OF FASCISM, THE; AUSTRIA; AUSTRO-HUNGARIAN EMPIRE/HABSBURG EMPIRE, THE; AVENTINE SECESSION, THE; COMMUNITY; CORPORATISM; DEMOCRACY; EGALITARIANISM; ELITE THEORY; ENABLING ACT, THE; FASCIST PARTY, THE; FREEDOM; GERMANY; GREECE; HITLER, ADOLF; HORTHY DE NAGYBÁNYA, MIKLÓS; HUNGARY; INDIVIDUALISM; INTEGRAL NATIONALISM; ITALY; LAW; LIBERALISM; MATTEOTTI, GIACOMO; MAURRAS, CHARLES; *MEIN KAMPF;* MUSSOLINI, BENITO ANDREA; NATIONALISM; NAZISM; NOVEMBER CRIMINALS/*NOVEMBERBRECHER,* THE; PARAMILITARISM;

POLAND; PORTUGAL; PRIMO DE RIVERA, JOSÉ ANTONIO; PROTOFASCISM; REICHSTAG FIRE, THE; REVOLUTION; ROMANIA; SOCIALISM; SPAIN; STATE, THE; SYNDICALISM; TOTALITARIANISM; VERSAILLES, THE TREATY OF; VIOLENCE; *VOLKSGEMEINSCHAFT,* THE; WARRIOR ETHOS, THE; WEIMAR REPUBLIC, THE; WORLD WAR I; WORLD WAR II

References

Cohen, Carl. 1996. *Communism, Fascism, and Democracy: The Theoretical Foundations.* Maidenhead, Berks: McGraw Hill Higher Education.

Dyzenhaus, David, et al., eds. 2000. *From Liberal Democracy to Fascism: Legal and Political Thought in the Weimar Republic.* Leiden: Brill.

Eliason, Leslie, and Lene Bogh Sorensen, eds. 2002. *Fascism, Liberalism and Social Democracy in Central Europe: Past and Present.* Aarhus: Aarhus University Press.

Fieschi, Catherine. 2004. *Fascism, Populism and the French Fifth Republic: In the Shadow of Democracy.* Manchester: Manchester University Press.

Ingersoll, David E. 1971. *Communism, Fascism, and Democracy: The Origins and Development of Three Ideologies.* New York: Merrill.

PARTITO NAZIONALE FASCISTA, THE: *See* FASCIST PARTY, THE

PÄTS, KONSTANTIN (1874–1956)

First prime minister of Estonia, who instituted an authoritarian regime in his country. As leader of the conservative Farmers' Union, he served as prime minister five times. On 12 March 1934, together with General Johan Laidoner, he declared martial law and arrested the leaders of the radical right Veterans' League. Although claiming that he was saving democracy from the threat of fascism, Päts in fact erected his own authoritarian regime. In 1937 he proclaimed a new constitution under which he was elected the first president in 1938. In 1940 the USSR annexed Estonia, and Päts was deported to Russia, where he died in captivity.

Andres Kasekamp

See Also: AUTHORITARIANISM; CONSERVATISM; ESTONIA; FARMERS; LATVIA; LITHUANIA; WAR VETERANS

Reference

Kasekamp, Andres. 2000. *The Radical Right in Interwar Estonia.* London: Macmillan.

PAVELIĆ, Dr. ANTE (1889–1959)

Lawyer, ultranationalist, and leader (or *Poglavnic*) of the Ustaši (or Ustasha). With Benito Mussolini's patronage, Pavelić developed a fascist ideology partly modeled on Italian Fascism but strongly emphasizing Croatian racial ascendancy in the Balkans, political Catholicism, and regenerative violence, ultimately leading to a radical campaign of ethnic cleansing in the then-Yugoslavia. Rivaled only by National Socialism in fascist violence, Pavelić's *Ustaši* orchestrated the assassination of Yugoslav king Alexsandar in France on 9 October 1934, formed the NDH (Independent State of Croatia) between 13 April 1941 and the conclusion of World War II, and was responsible for the mass murder, torture, and forced conversion of ethnic and religious groups in Yugoslavia, such as Serbs, Gypsies, Muslims, Orthodox Christians, Jews, and other "undesirable" groups. Following the war, Pavelić escaped to Argentina and eventually died in a Spanish monastery on 26 December 1959.

Matt Feldman

See Also: ANTI-SEMITISM; ARGENTINA; CATHOLIC CHURCH, THE; CLERICO-FASCISM; CROATIA; HOLOCAUST, THE; NATIONALISM; NAZISM; PALINGENETIC MYTH; PAPACY, THE; POLITICAL CATHOLICISM; RACIAL DOCTRINE; RACISM; ROMA AND SINTI, THE; SERBS, THE; USTASHA; WORLD WAR II; YUGOSLAVIA

References

Manhattan, Avro. 1986. *The Vatican's Holocaust.* Springfield, MO: Ozark.

Paris, Edmund. 1962. *Genocide in Satellite Croatia 1941–1945.* Chicago: American Institute for Balkan Affairs.

PEARL HARBOR

Location of the legendary Japanese airborne strike (without any formal declaration of war) on the U.S. fleet moored in Hawaii on 7 December 1941, which drew the United States into war with Japan and subsequently into World War II. Hitler's occupation of France and The Netherlands in 1940 had opened up the prospect of a Japanese takeover of their oil- and mineral-rich colonies in the East Indies and Southeast Asia. But Japan feared that strikes on those areas could lead to U.S. intervention, and the attack on the U.S. fleet was an attempt to make this difficult if not impossible. Five out of eight battleships were put out of action by Japanese air power in the raid, and the rest were damaged. For five months Japan was able to proceed with her planned imperialistic offensives unopposed. But the coup Japan had hoped to achieve in emasculating U.S. naval power was gravely weakened because the vital U.S. aircraft carriers were not in Hawaii, and in the long run the treacherous nature of the attack actually stiffened U.S. resolve to fight back. To this day argument rages over the possibility that prointerventionist U.S. president Roosevelt actually provoked the attack with the intention of inciting Japan's ally Germany to declare war on the United States (as it proceeded to do); for U.S. public opinion had been overwhelmingly hostile to any involvement in the war in Europe up to that point, whereas Roosevelt was in favor of it.

Cyprian Blamires

See Also: AXIS; FRANCE; GERMANY; HITLER, ADOLF; JAPAN; JAPAN AND WORLD WAR II; NETHERLANDS, THE; ROOSEVELT, PRESIDENT FRANKLIN DELANO; UNITED STATES, THE (PRE-1945); WORLD WAR II

References

Saki, D. ed. 1994. *From Pearl Harbour to Hiroshima: The Second World War in Asia and the Pacific, 1941–45.* London: Macmillan.
Schom, Alan. 2003. *The Eagle and the Rising Sun: The Japanese-American War, 1941–1943: Pearl Harbor through Guadalcanal.* New York: W. W. Norton.

PELLEY, WILLIAM DUDLEY (1890–1965)

U.S. interwar anti-Semitic propagandist and enthusiast for Hitler. Born in Lynn, Massachusetts, Pelley dropped out of high school to pursue successive careers as journalist, relief worker in Siberia, popular fiction writer, and author of Hollywood scripts. As a result of a mystical experience that supposedly took place in 1928, he saw himself as divinely chosen to lead a political movement. Moving to Asheville, North Carolina, in 1933 he founded the Silver Legion of America, usually known as the Silver Shirts. Membership peaked in 1934 with

15,000 adherents but tapered off to 5,000 by 1938. His vehicles included a number of journals, including *Liberation, Pelley's Weekly,* and *Roll-Call.* Pelley openly praised Hitler, cooperated with the German-American Bund, and espoused a vehement anti-Semitism. Although he disbanded the Silver Shirts in 1941, he was imprisoned from 1942 to 1950. After his release he went into semi-retirement.

Justus Doenecke

See Also: ANTI-SEMITISM; GERMAN-AMERICAN BUND, THE; HITLER, ADOLF; MYSTICISM; UNITED STATES, THE (PRE-1945)

References

Beckman, Scott M. 2003. "Silver Shirts and Golden Scripts: The Life of William Dudley Pelley." Ph.D. dissertation. Athens: Ohio University.
Ribuffo, Leo P. 1983. *The Old Christian Right: The Protestant Far Right from the Great Depression to the Cold War.* Philadelphia: Temple University Press.

PEOPLE'S COURT, THE: *See VOLKSGERICHT,* THE

PERÓN, JUAN DOMINGO (1895–1974)

Right-wing populist military dictator in Argentina; president of Argentina from 1946 to 1955 and from 1973 to 1974. The son of a farmer, he became a career soldier and spent a period in Italy as a military observer in the late 1930s. He entered the government as part of a military coup in 1943 but was forced out by enemies in the military in October 1945. He was then arrested, but such was his popularity that there were mass demonstrations organized by trade unions that brought about his quick release; in the elections of the following February he won the presidency. His political philosophy has been compared by many to fascism. Perón's popularity attained mythical proportions with his marriage to the legendary Eva Duarte (1919–1952), who, following her early death to cancer, spawned a posthumous legend of secular sanctity as "Evita." Perón was overthrown in a coup in 1955 and went into exile first in Paraguay and later in Madrid. His brief return to government in 1973 came about by popular acclaim, but he died in office.

Cyprian Blamires

See Also: ARGENTINA; AUTHORITARIANISM; ITALY; MILITARY DICTATORSHIP; PARAGUAY; PERONISM; POSTWAR FASCISM; TRADES UNIONS

References

Alexander, R. J. 1979. *Juan Domingo Perón: A History.* Boulder, CO: Westview.
Page, J. A. 1983. *Perón: A Biography.* New York: Random House.

PERONISM

The philosophy of Juan Domingo Perón, who had two spells as president of Argentina (1946–1955; 1973–1974): he admired European interwar fascism and especially accentuated fascists' success in putting economics at the service of the nation, which, according to Perón, was composed of its "living forces"—namely, its productive classes. Perón aspired to fulfill the type of productivist conception of fascism, although accompanied by social policies. That meant that, for him, the economic equilibrium which blended productivist policies based on "national interests" with populist social justice was biased toward the latter. At root, however, the idea of social justice was in his view far from being linked to any type of political autonomy for workers. The living forces of the nation were those that were identified with the Peronist syndicalist state, while social welfare was the basis for the transformation of Argentina from a dependent to an emancipated state. Indeed, Perón's labor policies continued the line promoted by his self-designed Syndical Statute, promulgated by the military government in 1943. It reflected the attempt to achieve corporatist authoritarian control of the workers' organizations. Housing rents were reduced and higher salaries were established for the most poorly paid workers in public administration. This trend of reforms gained momentum in November 1943, when the Departamento Nacional del Trabajo (National Department of Labor), until then an apparently minor branch of the interior ministry, became the Secretaria de Trabajo y Prevision (Secretariat for Labor and Planning), an autonomous department headed by Perón himself. Decree 156.074 of 27 November 1943

assigned to Perón the function of taking the necessary measures to increase harmony among the productive forces of the country. That role was the first step in Perón's meteoric rise to power. He had grasped the importance of the working class, and succeeded in disentangling pro-working-class ideology from communism. He was very clear on this point: "I am personally a syndicalist . . . and as such I am anti-communist, but I believe that labor must be organized on a syndicalist basis" (interview given by Perón to *El Mercurio* of Chile, republished in *La Prensa* (12 November 1943).

Perón made direct contact with union leaders through the good offices of Lieutenant-Colonel Mercante, the son of a railway worker. He met with syndicalists from the dissolved CGT, and in 1943 he intervened in favor of the workers in the Berisso "Frigorificos" strike in La Plata. With his support, the first collective agreement was reached between labor and government. However, that was not achieved by the representatives of the strong FOIC, but by an autonomous union led by Cipriano Reyes, the most important figure of the Partido Laborista (Labor Party), which later supported Perón's rise to power (although Reyes subsequently became Perón's enemy and was jailed). It was clear that Perón aimed to co-opt the workers' movement, and most of his military comrades agreed with his social and political agenda. His visit to Italy between 1939 and 1941 increased his admiration of Italian Fascism, especially the way it offered a solution to the problem of the working class. Perón's approach to industrial relations resembled Mussolini's. As labor secretary in the military junta, he brought most of the unions under his control through the 1945 Law of Professional Associations, whose provisions were almost identical with Mussolini's labor code. The bargaining between the government and the growing unions culminated in decree 23,852 of 2 October 1945. That decree established the unions' full legal rights by eliminating parallel unions. This provided the structures for elections of delegates and stewards and a network of bargaining with employers, with vague allusions to coparticipation in management decisions. It also attributed to unions' legal rights to participate in politics, giving workers the green light to form the political party that would eventually win the elections of February 1946. However, legal status required recognition from the Labor Secretariat (Article 43). Under this law, only government-recognized unions and employers' associations could sign labor contracts, and only one employers' association and one labor union were to be permitted in each economic field. Strikes and lockouts were forbidden. However, what at first sight seems a fascist type of antiworker authoritarianism was in reality a much more complex approach, because workers, in comparison with their previous situation, were the direct beneficiaries of a new authoritarian order, which they themselves negotiated with Perón.

The trade-off of concessions to labor in return for tentative support eventually paid off for both the working class and Perón himself. The decree of 2 October provided for the two largest unions, the commercial and the rail unions, to become the two first certified labor associations in Argentine history. The commercial union became the vanguard of the working-class resistance, which was to stand behind Perón when he was dismissed and then jailed by his army colleagues on 9 October 1945. The myth of 17 October 1945 was in reality a mass mobilization marking the definitive linking of labor's fate with that of the "worker colonel." On that day, which was to become an integral part of Peronist mythology, the workers of the capital, organized by Eva Duarte (the legendary "Evita"), Cipriano Reyes, and Colonel Mercante, invaded the streets. Perón was subsequently released, and on the same day he spoke to the people from the balcony of Casa Rosada of the "creation of an indestructible bond of brotherhood between the people and the army."

The military commanders realized that they had to yield to the pressure of the elections. Perón ran for office in 1946, together with two parties that symbolized the political synthesis between military populist nationalism, syndicalism, and the traditional intransigent wing of the Radical Party. Perón, together with Cipriano Reyes and the Union Civica Radical (Junta Renovadora), made up the nationalist coalition. They were opposed by a coalition of the parties—socialist, communist, "Alvearist" radicals, and conservatives that represented liberal democracy and socialist reformist political philosophy. This antinationalist coalition received the blessings of U.S. ambassador Braden, but U.S. intervention in Argentine politics undoubtedly contributed to Perón's success. Perón himself defined the political confrontation with a simple motto, "Braden or Perón," which transformed the confrontation between two different political conceptions into a confrontation between the nation and "American" imperialism. The determination of the United States to prove Perón's complicity with the Nazis actually guaranteed his success. Such complicity could never be proven. Nonetheless, Perón's corporatist intentions and his admiration for fascist labor policies were known to all.

After Perón had assumed the presidency, his government announced its intention of achieving a "just equilibrium among all the factors that take part in produc-

tion, . . . collaboration between labor and employer organizations, humanization of the function of capital . . . and improvement in workers' living conditions" (*Vicepresidencia de la Nacion,* 55–56, 68). This program was based on the conviction that, although Argentina was not a country with territorial ambitions, world politics demanded the development of a strong, autarkic nation. Perón wanted to develop heavy industry while promoting social justice. Indeed, mixed industrial complexes were created with the goal of exploiting national resources, and long-term loans were offered to national industry. All the instruments created by the state during Peron's administration were intended to further those ends. The symbol of the state regulatory economic power was the IAPI ("Argentine Institute of Production and Trade"), created to promote the *Plan Quinquenal,* an industrialization plan initiated in October 1946. Perón forced farmers to sell to the IAPI at low, fixed prices and then made profits for the government by selling those goods on the free market. The law that most frightened the rural oligarchy, however, was the *Estatuto del Peon,* which recognized agricultural laborers as workers with labor rights.

In a decidedly militaristic vein, the first Five Year Plan (1947–1951) was devised to transform a "civic and peaceful country into a country in arms," and the second Five Year Plan confirmed the tendency to "strengthen the armed forces in order to back the . . . decision to be a sovereign, just and free nation" (Perón 1954, 441).

The economic trend of combining corporatization and industrialization with social-welfare goals that faithfully reflected the integralist-populist formula could function only until 1949, the watershed year for labor in Argentina. From 1949 on, it was the principle of productivity rather than social justice that guided Peron's policies. Wages declined by more than 20 percent, while greater discipline was imposed upon the unions. In fact, from 1949 until 1955, Perón's populist policies resembled fascist corporatist practices more than they did under his pre-1949 social reformism. Perón promoted the organization of the working class, although only under state control, because "it suits the state to have organic forces it can control and lead rather than inorganic forces that escape its leadership. . . . We do not want unions divided into political factions, because what is dangerous is, precisely, the political unions." In other words, worker welfare could be guaranteed only under the tutelage of the state.

From an ideological perspective, welfare policy was clearly an issue that most Argentine nationalists of both the Right and the Left believed could be resolved only in a national-syndicalist state that represented the popular classes. The entire Peronist ideology was tailored to the concept of *Justicialismo*. In contrast to fascism and to the pure materialism of liberal and Marxist ideologies, the "third position" of *Justicialismo* sought a unifying point between idealism, materialism, collectivism, and individualism. Rhetorically, however, *Justicialismo* was reminiscent of Italian Fascism in that it emphasized nationalism, authoritarianism, and leadership. In the final analysis, the rights of citizens were rated lower than their national responsibilities. The basic idea was that of an organized community in which the individual would reach personal happiness. However, the concept of personal happiness was disassociated from bourgeois egoism; for the ethical state, however, both the Peronist and the fascist definition of bourgeois egoism included the expression of independent ideas. "Some say that we must capture the independent opinion [holders]. Great mistake. . . . We must marginalize them. . . . They cannot be led" (Perón 1952, 55). In other words, the concept of community was opposed to that of civil society.

The fourth section of the first Five Year Plan covered the cultural sphere and raised the issue of creating cultural uniformity. It noted that Argentina's various cultural institutions lacked both spirituality and a unifying framework, as well as the appropriate orientation needed to guide national culture. The program published in 1947 expressed the early tendencies of Peronism in shaping and molding a new national consciousness to be expressed particularly in the educational system. The second Five Year Plan, published in 1951, consolidated that plan under the concept of a national doctrine—namely, that national consciousness would be *Justicialista* doctrine. Indeed, from 1952 *Justicialismo* was legally charted as "National Doctrine." It expressed the spirit of the Organic Statute of the Peronist Party. Its second article emphasized that the Peronist Party was a doctrinaire unity in which any position conspiring against that unity would be rejected. Article 74 affirmed that the best way to learn to command was to learn to obey, while article 77 stated that there were two top figures in Peronism, Juan Perón and Eva Perón. The resemblance to fascism is more than clear.

Peronism, the most baffling and least understood of all Latin American populist movements, owes its fame to the leader Juan Domingo Perón and his legendary wife, Evita. Long after Perón's death and after the movement's political and ideological transformation, Peronism as a political party still holds sway in Argentina's political processes, to the extent that it is im-

possible to conceive of Argentina's politics without Peronism. It is clear, however, that any interpretation of present-day Peronism as fascism is far from the truth. On the question of whether the original Peronism was fascist or not, scholarly opinions differ widely. Thamer and Wippermann argue that Peronism can be explained only with the aid of the concept of fascism, albeit a very broadly defined fascism. Stanley Payne claims that Peronism had most, but not all, of the characteristics of European fascism. Probably the most important scholar of Argentina's political history, Tulio Halperin Donghi, asserts that Peronism shared some of the features of fascism, but, together with Cristian Buchrucker and Daniel James, he would not consider it a fully fascist phenomenon.

Alberto Spektorowski

See Also: INTRODUCTION; ARGENTINA; AUTARKY; AUTHORITARIANISM; BOLSHEVISM; BOURGEOISIE, THE; COMMUNITY; CORPORATISM; DEMOCRACY; ECONOMICS; EDUCATION; EMPLOYMENT; FASCIST PARTY, THE; ITALY; LABOR FRONT, THE; LEADER CULT, THE; LIBERALISM; MARXISM; MATERIALISM; MUSSOLINI, BENITO ANDREA; NATIONALISM; ORGANICISM; PERÓN, JUAN DOMINGO; PRODUCTIVISM; SOCIALISM; STATE, THE; SYNDICALISM; THIRD WAY, THE; TRADE UNIONS; WELFARE

References

Buchrucker, Cristian. 1987. *Nacionalismo y Peronismo. La Argentina en la crisis ideologica mundial (1927–1955).* Buenos Aires: Ed. sudamericana.

Deutsch, Sandra McGee, and R. H. Dolkart. 1993. *The Argentine Right: Its History and Intellectual Origins.* Wilmington, DE: Scholarly Resources.

Fayt, Carlos. 1973. *La naturaleza del peronismo.* Buenos Aires: Viracocha.

Halperin Donghi, Tulio. 1994. *La larga agonia de la Argentina Peronista.* Buenos Aires: Ariel.

Hayes, Paul M. 1973. *Fascism.* New York: Free Press.

Hernandez Arregui, J. J. 1960. *La formacion de la conciencia nacional.* Buenos Aires: Hachea.

James, Daniel. 1988. *Resistance and Integration: Peronism and the Argentine Working Class, 1946–1976.* Cambridge: Cambridge University press.

Munck, Ronaldo, et al. 1987. *Argentina from Anarchism to Peronism: Workers, Unions, and Politics 1855–1985.* London: Zed.

Perón, Juan. 1952. *Conduccion politica.* Buenos Aires: Ediciones Mundo Peronista.

———. 1954. *2o.Plan Quinquenal de la Nacion Argentina. Texto completo de la ley 14.184.* Buenos Aires: *Hechos e Ideas.*

Sebrelli, Juan José. 1983. *Los deseos imaginarios del Peronismo.* Buenos Aires: Legasa.

Thamer, Hans-Ulrich, and Wolfgang Wippermann. 1977. *Faschistische und neofaschistische Bewegungen.* Darmstadt: Wissenschaftliche Buchgesellschaft.

Vicepresidencia de la Nacion, Consejo Nacional de Postguerra, "Ordenamiento economico-social." Buenos Aires: Kraft.

PERU

Fascism appeared in several forms in Peru during the 1930s. There was an "aristocratic" fascism that sought to restore traditional values. José de la Riva Agüero led this movement of Peruvians who were unhappy with the political and social instability of their country. Riva Agüero was the voice of the Catholic Right in Peru, supported Mussolini, and viewed fascism as a needed counterweight to the influence of communism. He and his supporters saw fascism as a return to medieval, Catholic, and Hispanic traditions in response to the rise of socialism, populism, and bourgeois capitalism. A second form of fascism took root among middle-class professionals and intellectuals. That movement was linked to Peru's Catholic University and was inspired by Italian Fascism, the Nazis, and Spanish falangism. These middle groups sought to champion the process of *mestizaje,* which would reconcile the Native American and Western components of Peru. Furthermore, they disliked both the traditional elite and communists. The third and largest form was the "popular" fascism of the Unión Revolucionaria (UR) political party. The UR began as a vehicle to support Luis Sánchez Cerro in the 1931 presidential campaign. The party was nationalistic and strongly anticommunist. After Sánchez Cerro's assassination in 1933, Luis Flores took over the leadership of the UR and adopted a more openly fascistic stance.

The small but wealthy Italian community helped to finance a pro-Italian propaganda campaign in Peru during the 1930s. Many in Peru and abroad feared that fascism was spreading in the country. On the surface, this concern seemed merited, as Peru's main newspapers took on a pro-Italian stance and supported Italy's invasion of Ethiopia, fascist organizations grew, and the Peruvian government sought closer political and military ties with Italy. This propaganda campaign began in 1935 at the behest of Vittorio Bianchi, the Italian minister in Peru. The Peruvian Italian community helped to finance the Nucleo di Propaganda in order to shape public opinion. That organization was active during Italy's Ethiopian campaign, but wound down in 1937 after the Ethiopian crisis ended. There were also some attempts to indoctrinate young people in Italian schools in Peru. However, while the Italian community in Peru was certainly pro-Italian, it was generally not profascist. Furthermore, the Italian government provided little financial support. By 1939, it was clear that the campaign had failed.

Fascism was an important issue in the annulled 1936 presidential elections in Peru. Two right-wing candidates had clear links to fascism. Luis M. Flores ran as the leader of the UR. A former interior minister, Flores openly admired fascist ideology, going so far as to organize a 6,000-member paramilitary force complete with black shirts to attack the Peruvian Left. Another candidate was Manuel Vicente Villarán, who enjoyed the support of many conservative intellectuals, including Riva Agüero. Neither candidate had a chance to implement his policies, however, as President Oscar Benavides suspended the elections. He then pressured the congress to extend his own term until December 1939. Fascism continued to be a key issue in the subsequent 1939 election. Benavides supported the candidacy of Manuel Prado, the strongly antifascist leader of the Concentración Nacional. Prado faced the fascist-influenced ticket of José Quesada Larrea and Luis Flores. Prado won the election easily, and his antifascist tendencies led him to a closer relationship with the United States during and after World War II.

During the 1930s, fascism also influenced Peru as the issues of the Spanish Civil War affected the country. Many elite Peruvians feared the Spanish Republic, claiming that it "proved" the damaging effects of partisan politics. Thus, most wealthy and powerful Peruvians supported the profascist uprising and subsequent regime of Francisco Franco. The Peruvian press was also generally pro-Franco. Furthermore, Peruvian president Benavides was a strong Franco supporter. Indeed, Peru was one of the most pro-Nationalist countries in Latin America. As early as August 1936, Peru considered recognizing Franco's Burgos government. Peruvian authorities also tacitly recognized the Nationalist government when it allowed the Spanish minister plenipotentiary to remain at his post after defecting from the Republican government and declaring his support for the Nationalists. Peruvian support for Franco could also be seen in Madrid itself. Spanish refugees fleeing the Republican government sought asylum in the Peruvian legation. Leftist death squads operated in Madrid, and many opponents of the Republic received protection from Peruvian diplomats, who sometimes even aided the refugees in leaving the country. The issue came to a head in May 1937, when Spanish authorities attacked the Peruvian consulate in Madrid, claiming that Peru was aiding the rebel faction. The Republicans arrested more than 400 refugees and the honorary consul from Peru. The incident led to a formal break in relations between the two countries in March 1938. In May 1938, Peru recognized Franco's Nationalist regime.

Ron Young

See Also: ARISTOCRACY; AUTHORITARIANISM; BOLSHEVISM; BOURGEOISIE, THE; CAPITALISM; CATHOLIC CHURCH, THE; CONSERVATISM; ETHIOPIA; FALANGE; FRANCO Y BAHAMONDE, GENERAL FRANCISCO; ITALY; MARXISM; MUSSOLINI, BENITO ANDREA; SPAIN; SPANISH CIVIL WAR, THE; UNITED STATES THE (PRE-1945); WORLD WAR II

References
Ciccarelli, Orazio A. 1988. "Fascist Propaganda and the Italian Community in Peru during the Benavides Regime, 1933–39." *Journal of Latin American Studies* 20, no. 2 (November): 361–388.
———. 1990. "Fascism and Politics in Peru during the Benavides Regime, 1933–1939: The Italian Perspective." *Hispanic American Historical Review* 70, no. 3 (August): 405–432.
Falcoff, Mark, and Frederick Pike. 1982. *The Spanish Civil War: American Hemispheric Perspectives.* Lincoln: University of Nebraska Press.
Klarén, Peter Flindell. 2000. *Peru: Society and Nationhood in the Andes.* New York: Oxford University Press.
Marett, Sir Robert. 1969. *Peru.* New York: Praeger.

PETAIN, MARSHAL HENRI PHILIPPE (1856–1951)

Commander-in-chief of French armies in 1917 and head of the Vichy government in German-occupied France (1940–1944), Pétain advocated peace with Germany in June 1940. Prime minister from 17 June 1940, he accepted the armistice on 25 June. Voted full powers by parliament at Vichy (10 July), he decreed himself head of state on 11 July. Blaming the Third Republic's democracy for defeat, he instituted an authoritarian, corporatist, anti-Semitic, pro-Catholic "National Revolution." He met Hitler on 24 October 1940 and advocated "collaboration." Pétain was sentenced to death in 1945, but the sentence was commuted to life imprisonment.

Robert O. Paxton

See Also: ABSTRACTION; ANTI-SEMITISM; AUTHORITARIANISM; CATHOLIC CHURCH, THE; CORPORATISM; DEMOCRACY; FRANCE; GERMANY; INTEGRAL NATIONALISM; MAURRAS, CHARLES; NATIONALISM; POLITICAL CATHOLICISM; VICHY; WORLD WAR II

Reference
Atkin, Nicholas. 1998. *Pétain.* London: Longman.

PHALANGE (Lebanon)

Established in 1936 as a Maronite paramilitary youth organization by Pierre Jumayyil, who was consciously imitating the fascist organizations he had come across while taking part in the Berlin Olympics of that year. Phalange (the Arabic name was *Kataib*) was an authoritarian, highly centralized organization whose leader was all-powerful, and it soon developed into a significant political force in Mount Lebanon. As a political party Phalange has been closely associated with France and the West, although in the early 1940s it was temporarily dissolved by the French Mandate authorities because it had been calling for independence. Its motto is "God, the Fatherland and the family." At the core of Phalangist ideology is a notion of a special "Phoenician" identity of the Lebanese nation that sets it apart from the neighboring Muslim countries. The party has followed a consistently anticommunist and anti-Palestinian line, rejecting pan-Arabism. By 1958 membership of the Phalange Party had reached almost 40,000, and it was getting more than 60 percent of its candidates into the Chamber of Deputies. Although the party and its militia played a prominent part in the 1975 civil war, its influence waned through the 1980s, a process that was accelerated with the death of its founder in 1984. In 1987, George Saadah was appointed to the leadership and attempted to revitalize the party, but it was weakened by internal divisions.

Cyprian Blamires

See Also: BERLIN OLYMPICS; FAMILY, THE; GERMANY; LEADER CULT, THE; MIDDLE EAST, THE; NATIONALISM; NAZISM; PALESTINE; YOUTH MOVEMENTS

References
Fisk, R. 2001. *Pity the Nation: Lebanon at War.* Oxford: Oxford University Press.
Winslow, C. 1996. *Lebanon: War & Politics in a Fragmented Society.* London: Routledge.

PHILOSOPHY: See ACTUALISM; BAEUMLER, ALFRED; GENTILE, GIOVANNI; HEIDEGGER, MARTIN; NIETZSCHE, FRIEDRICH;

ORGANICISM; POSITIVISM;
RATIONALISM; ROSENBERG, ALFRED;
VITALISM; WELTANSCHAUUNG

PIASECKI, BOLESLAW (1915–1979)

Polish ideologue and leader of the National-Radical Movement (Ruch Narodowo-Radykalny; RNR), also known as the National-Radical Camp Falanga (Oboz Narodowo Radykalny "Falanga"; ONR "Falanga"), which emerged as a radical breakaway faction of the nationalist movement in 1935. Openly emulating Italian and German fascisms, the RNR was responsible for terrorist attacks against Jews and left-wing activists. It enjoyed some support among university youth. During World War II, Piasecki led his own resistance organization, the Confederation of the Nation (Konfederacja Narodu; KN). After 1945, he became the leader of the procommunist Catholic association "Pax."

Rafal Pankowski

See Also: ANTI-SEMITISM; CATHOLIC CHURCH, THE; DMOWSKI, ROMAN; NATIONALISM; PILSUDSKI, MARSHAL JOZEF; POLAND; POLAND AND NAZI GERMANY; WORLD WAR II

References
Blit, L. 1965. *The Eastern Pretender: The Story of Boleslaw Piasecki.* London: Hutchinson.
Polonsky, Antony. 1972. *Politics in Independent Poland, 1921–1939.* Oxford: Clarendon.

PIERCE, WILLIAM (1933–2002)

Globally renowned far-right U.S. author and broadcaster. A native of Atlanta, Georgia, Pierce acquired a Ph.D. in physics and taught for three years at Oregon State University from 1962. In 1966 he moved to Washington, D.C., where he became acquainted with George Lincoln Rockwell and took up the editorship of *The National Socialist World,* the theoretical journal of the American Nazi Party. Pierce subsequently broke with the party and became leader of the racist National Youth Alliance. In 1974, the organization became the National Alliance. Pierce is best known for his authorship of *The Turner Diaries,* a novel that since it was first published in 1978 has reportedly sold more than 350,000 copies. *The Turner Diaries* depicts a terrorist campaign that eventually leads to a racist seizure of power. Following Pierce's death in 2002, the National Alliance has continued under new leadership.

Martin Durham

See Also: MCVEIGH, TIMOTHY; NEO-NAZISM; OKLAHOMA BOMBING, THE; POSTWAR FASCISM; RACISM; ROCKWELL, GEORGE LINCOLN; *TURNER DIARIES, THE;* UNITED STATES, THE (POSTWAR); WHITE SUPREMACISM

References
Durham, M. 2004. "The Upward Path: Palingenesis, Political Religion and the National Alliance." *Totalitarian Movements and Political Religions* 5, no. 3, pp. 454–468.
Griffin, Robert S. 2001. *The Fame of a Dead Man's Deeds: An Up-close Portrait of White Nationalist William Pierce.* Bloomington, IN: AuthorHouse.

PILSUDSKI, MARSHAL JOZEF (1867–1935)

Right-wing dictator of Poland, 1926–1935. Pilsudski started his political activity as a leader of the underground Polish Socialist Party (Polska Partia Socjalistyczna; PPS) in the 1890s and became the commander of a Polish legion during World War I. From 1918 till 1922, Pilsudski was the head of the Polish state and commander-in-chief during the war against the Bolsheviks in 1920. Disillusioned with parliamentary democracy, he staged a military coup d'etat with the support of the Left in 1926 and established an authoritarian regime. A lifelong opponent of Roman Dmowski and his *endecja* movement, Pilsudski denounced fascism.

Rafal Pankowski

See Also: AUTHORITARIANISM; DEMOCRACY; DICTATORSHIP; DMOWSKI, ROMAN; PARLIAMENTARISM; PIASECKI, BOLESLAW; POLAND; POLAND AND NAZI GERMANY; SOCIALISM; WORLD WAR I

Reference
Garlicki, Andrzej. 1995. *Jozef Pilsudski: 1867–1935.* London: Scolar.

PINOCHET UGARTE, GENERAL AUGUSTO (born 1915)

Military dictator of Chile from 1973 to 2000, often branded "fascist" but fits the mold of a classic military dictator rather than that of a fascist. He participated in the military coup that overthrew the elected government of socialist Salvador Allende, and more than 3,000 supporters of the Allende government were disappeared or murdered during his regime; many thousands more were imprisoned, tortured, or forced into exile. In October 1998, Pinochet was arrested on charges of genocide, torture, and murder, and proceedings against him are ongoing.

Margaret Power

See Also: INTRODUCTION; AUTHORITARIANISM; CHILE; MILITARY DICTATORSHIP

Reference
Arriagada, G. 1998. *Pinochet: The Politics of Power.* London: Unwin Hyman.

PIUS XI, POPE (1857–1939)

Leader of the Catholic Church for most of the interwar period, during which he was obliged to contend with the threat to the Church from the two powerful new ideologies of Bolshevism and fascism. He was born Ambrose Damian Achille Ratti in Desio, Italy, on 31 May 1857, and elected pope in 1921, only five months after having been appointed archbishop of Milan. Popes at this time considered themselves prisoners in the Vatican. The problem extended back to the time when Italy had seized the remnants of the once-powerful Vatican States. With the capture of Rome on 20 September 1870, the papacy was left without a home. Italy gave certain concessions to the Holy See, but since they were not part of a negotiated agreement, the popes refused to recognize them. This difficulty between Italy and the Holy See was known as the Roman Question.

Benito Mussolini came to power in Italy only a few months after Pius XI's election. Il Duce had previously expressed a very hostile attitude toward the Catholic Church, but now it was to his political advantage to reach agreement with the Holy See. Negotiations began early in the fall of 1926 and continued over the next few years. An agreement, known as the Lateran Treaty was signed on 11 February 1929. Under its terms, the Church was granted an independent state (although it amounted to only about 100 acres); Italy recognized Catholicism as its official state religion; anticlerical laws that had been in effect since 1870 were declared null and void; and the Holy See received a cash settlement for the lands that had been confiscated in 1870. Despite this new relationship, Mussolini's government did not treat the Church well. Pius XI, who did not favor Catholic political parties (disbanding them in France, Italy, and Germany during his papacy), strove to energize the laity through the organization Catholic Action. In the spring of 1931, Mussolini's blackshirts physically harassed members of Catholic Action. By the early summer, the pope had issued an encyclical on the subject, *Non Abbiamo Bisogno.* In it, Pius speculated that the regime's apparent mildness toward the Church had in fact been a cloak for more hostile purposes.

Adolf Hitler was appointed chancellor, the head of the German government, on 30 January 1933. By April of that year, Pope Pius XI had sent a message to his representative in Berlin, telling him to intervene with the new government on behalf of Jewish people who were being persecuted. Despite mounting tensions, on 20 July of that year, Germany and the Holy See signed a concordat. It has been incorrectly reported that this was Nazi Germany's first international treaty. In fact, the Four Powers Pact between Germany, France, Italy, and Great Britain was signed on 7 June 1933. The Soviet Union on 5 May 1933 renewed a trade and friendship agreement with Germany, and on that same day the British parliament voted to accept an Anglo-German trade agreement. Moreover, Hitler's representatives were fully accredited and recognized by the League of Nations and took part in the disarmament discussions in Geneva, which also came before the signing of the concordat. Nevertheless, the concordat has caused some to speculate that Pius XI was too friendly toward the Nazi regime. Pius XI used concordats to ensure the Church's ability to hold services and carry out its functions; it had nothing to do with expressing approval of a regime. Under his leadership the Church reached agreement with twenty-one countries, and Pius XI was known as "the pope of the concordats." He had been trying to secure such an agreement with Germany for the better part of the 1920s. Officials from the Weimar Republic, however, had refused to meet the Vatican's demands. When Hitler rose to power, things changed. He never intended to keep his promises, so he was happy to agree to all of the Church's long-standing demands. Moreover, Hitler made it quite clear that if the Church were to reject his offer, he would simply publish his own terms and blame the pope for having rejected a favorable treaty that the Holy See itself had proposed. In a private conversation with Ivone Kirkpatrick, British ambassador to the Vatican, Cardinal Secretary of State Pacelli made clear that the concordat was not to be seen as an approval of Nazism. In fact, he expressed "disgust and abhorrence" of Hitler's reign of terror. The Vatican signed only because of pressure put on it by the Nazi regime.

Before the ink had dried on the concordat, Nazi troopers began rounding up suspected "traitors," and Catholic presses were shut down, as were Catholic labor unions. Catholic youth groups were decimated as children were required to join Hitler Youth groups. Bishops were denied access to their congregations and the right to travel to Rome. Finally, on 14 March 1937, Pope Pius XI issued an encyclical on the status of the Church and her relations with the German Reich. It was entitled *Mit Brennender Sorge.* Unlike most encyclicals, which are printed in Latin, this one was printed in German. It was smuggled into Germany and read on Palm Sunday in every Catholic church. In the encyclical, the pope called the Nazi leaders "superficial minds" who "could stumble into concepts of a national God, of a national religion; or attempt to lock within the frontiers of a single people, within the narrow limits of a single race, God, the creator of the universe, King and Legislator of all nations before whose immensity they are as a drop of a bucket." Pius went on to equate Nazi racial beliefs with a false god, and he criticized any suggestion of racism and racial hatred. The encyclical angered Hitler, and Nazis responded with physical retaliation against German Catholics. In 1938, Pius condemned anti-Semitic laws in Italy and Germany, and in September of that year, in a statement that soon made its way around the world, he declared: "Mark well that in the Catholic Mass, Abraham is our Patriarch and forefather. Anti-Semitism is incompatible with the lofty thought which that fact expresses. It is a movement with which we Christians can have nothing to do. No, no, I say to you it is impossible for a Christian to take part in anti-Semitism. . . . Spiritually, we are all Semites." Nonetheless, controversy has arisen in the post-

war era regarding the adequacy of his dealings as head of the Catholic Church with the fascist powers and of his response to the plight of the Jews.

Ronald Rychlak

See Also: ANTIFASCISM; ANTI-SEMITISM; ARYANISM; BOLSHEVISM; CATHOLIC CHURCH, THE; CENTER PARTY, THE; CATHOLIC CHURCH, THE; CLERICO-FASCISM; EDUCATION; GERMANY; HITLER, ADOLF; ITALY; LEAGUE OF NATIONS, THE; MUSSOLINI, BENITO ANDREA; ORTHODOX CHURCHES, THE; PACIFISM; PAPACY, THE; PIUS XII, POPE; POLITICAL CATHOLICISM; PROTESTANTISM; RACIAL DOCTRINE; WEIMAR REPUBLIC, THE; YOUTH MOVEMENTS

References
Anderson, Robin. 1981. *Between Two Wars: The Story of Pope Pius XI, 1922–1939.* Chicago: Franciscan Herald.
Aradi, Zsolt. 1958. *Pius XI: The Pope and the Man.* Garden City, NY: Hanover House.
Buchanan, Tom, and Martin Conway. 1996. *Political Catholicism in Europe, 1918–1965.* Oxford: Clarendon.
Passelecq, Georges, Bernard Wills, and Gary Suchecky. 1997. *The Hidden Encyclical of Pius XI.* Collingdale, PA: Diane.
Rychlak, Ronald J. 2000. *Hitler, the War, and the Pope.* Columbus, MS: Genesis.

PIUS XII, POPE (1876–1958)

Leader of the Catholic Church during World War II and the object of fierce critical scrutiny since the 1960s in respect to his dealings with fascist regimes and his response to the persecution of the Jews. He was born Eugenio Maria Giuseppe Giovanni Pacelli; he proved an exceptional student and was accepted into a prestigious seminary in Rome, the Capranica. Pope Leo XIII had set up a program for training promising young clerics to serve in the Vatican diplomatic service, and two years after Pacelli was ordained, Cardinal Gasparri invited him into this program. In the summer of 1917, Pacelli was consecrated bishop and sent to Munich to replace the papal nuncio to Bavaria, Archbishop Giuseppe Aversa, who had died. Munich in the 1920s was also the home of Adolf Hitler. Pacelli watched with rising alarm the spread of nationalist ideas. In 1921 a German newspaper quoted him warning people about the rise of this new ideology. In 1923 he wrote to Rome that "followers of Hitler" were persecuting Catholics and Jews. In fact, of the forty-four public speeches that

Nuncio Pacelli made on German soil between 1917 and 1929, at least forty contained attacks on nationalism, racism, or other values that were central to Hitler and his followers.

In 1929, Pacelli was recalled to Rome and elevated to the cardinalate. Early the next year he was made cardinal secretary of state. In 1933, after the Nazis had eliminated the Catholic Center Party in Germany, they approached the Holy See, through Pacelli, to obtain a concordat. Pacelli eventually negotiated on behalf of the Vatican for an agreement that protected Catholic rights in Germany. The terms also kept priests and bishops out of the Nazi Party and ended up helping the Church protect Jewish refugees. As secretary of state, Pacelli made trips on behalf of the pope to France, the United States, Hungary, and Buenos Aires. In the United States he met with Jewish leaders and reaffirmed the Vatican's 1916 condemnation of anti-Semitism. In two trips to France, Pacelli protested against the "superstitions of race and blood," spoke of "that noble and powerful nation whom bad shepherds would lead astray into an idolatry of race," and denounced the "pagan cult of race." The Reich and Prussian minister for ecclesiastical affairs wrote to the German foreign ministry that Pacelli's "unmistakable allusion to Germany . . . was very well understood in the France of the Popular Front and the anti-German world."

On 2 March 1939, Pacelli became pope. The Nazi invasion of Poland came on 1 September 1939. On 14 September, addressing the new Belgian ambassador, Pius described the Nazi invasion as "an immeasurable catastrophe" and declared that "this new war, which already shakes the soil of Europe, and particularly that of a Catholic nation, no human prevision can calculate the frightful carnage which it bears within itself, nor what its extension and its successive complications will be." On 26 September, addressing a group of German pilgrims, Pius called the war "a terrible scourge of God" and directly warned the German clergy not to celebrate German militarism. On 30 September, while addressing Cardinal Hlond and a group of Polish pilgrims, Pius made an unmistakable reference to the Nazis as "the enemies of God." Pius followed these statements with a strong statement of antitotalitarianism, *Summi Pontificatus*. This profound encyclical made reference to "the ever-increasing host of Christ's enemies" and noted that these enemies of Christ "deny or in practice neglect the vivifying truths and the values inherent in belief in God and in Christ." The encyclical also dealt with racial matters and expressed the pope's conviction that through the Church "there is neither Gentile nor Jew, circumcision nor uncircumcision, barbarian nor Scythian, bond nor free. But Christ is all and in all." The equating of Gentiles and Jews was a clear rejection of Hitler's fundamental ideology. Allied forces dropped thousands of copies of it behind enemy lines for propaganda purposes.

Pius followed his first encyclical with a Christmas address in which he spoke of "a series of deeds, irreconcilable either with natural law or with the most elementary human feelings. . . . In this category falls the premeditated aggression against a small, hardworking and peaceful people, under the pretext of a 'threat' nonexistent, not thought of, not even possible." His 1942 Christmas statement, coming at the end of the year in which the Nazis had decided on the "Final Solution," spoke of "the hundreds of thousands who, through no fault of their own, and solely because of their nation or race, have been condemned to death or progressive extinction." Pius also supported priests and bishops around the world who stood against the Nazis. His opposition to the Nazis was well recorded in the press, particularly in Christmas day editorials in the *New York Times* in 1941 and 1942.

When Hitler occupied Rome in September 1943, Pius opened Vatican City to Jewish and non-Jewish refugees. He offered gold to pay ransom to protect Jews; he opened St. Peter's, Castelgandolfo (the papal summer home), seminaries, convents, and other Church properties to shelter refugees; and he operated a relief program to help people across Europe. With his encouragement, a vast underground of priests, religious, and laity served as a covert organization dedicated to protecting Jewish and non-Jewish refugees from the Nazis. It is commonly estimated that the Church under Pius aided more than half a million Jewish refugees during the war. This work so infuriated Hitler that at least twice he planned to invade the Vatican and kill or kidnap the pope. He was dissuaded only because his military leaders convinced him that such a course of action would make continued occupation of Italy too difficult. One of the Jewish people sheltered by the Vatican was the chief rabbi of Rome, Israel Zolli. Shortly after the war, he converted to Catholicism. In tribute to the pope for all he had done to protect Jews and others, Zolli chose the name Eugenio for his Christian name, and Pius XII served as his godfather. Zolli lived long enough to see the Israeli Philharmonic Orchestra play a concert of thanks to Pius XII and the Catholic Church in Vatican City in 1955.

Upon the liberation of Rome in 1944, Pius made one of his most fervent pleas for tolerance. "For centuries," he said, referring to the Jews, "they have been most unjustly treated and despised. It is time they were treated with justice and humanity. God wills it and the Church wills it. St. Paul tells us that the Jews are our brothers. Instead of being treated as strangers they should be welcomed as friends." The end of the war saw Pius XII hailed as "the inspired moral prophet of victory." He enjoyed near-universal acclaim for aiding European Jews through diplomatic initiatives, thinly veiled public pronouncements, and the unprecedented continentwide network of sanctuary. When he died at Castelgandolfo on 9 October 1958, the messages of condolence included tributes from Jewish leaders Golda Meir, Nahum Goldmann, and Rabbi Elio Toaff, as well as from the Anti-Defamation League, the World Jewish Congress, and the Rabbinical Council of America.

One of the things Pius had feared in his lifetime was that the spread of Soviet influence would bring persecution to the Church (which in fact it did). He had used his enhanced postwar status to try to offset communist influence in Western Europe, especially in Italy, where communism almost took over in the late 1940s. It seems significant that it was precisely during this political campaign that communists first voiced the allegations that were later used by papal critics to argue that Pius XII was "silent" in the face of Nazi persecution of Jews. These allegations were picked up and given global publicity in 1963, when East German playwright Rolf Hochhuth wrote a play entitled *The Deputy (Der Stellvertreter)*. It was a scathing indictment of Pius XII's alleged indifference to Jewish suffering in the Holocaust. Although the play was fictional, Hochhuth wrote an appendix in which he drew on communist propaganda from the late 1940s to justify his work. The play spawned a great deal of academic writing about the role of the Church and the papacy during World War II. Several works, critical and supportive, appeared in the 1960s and up through 1980.

In 1964, Pope Paul VI, who knew and strongly defended Pius XII, asked a team of three Jesuit historians (later joined by a fourth) to conduct research in closed Vatican archives and publish relevant documents from the war years. The project was completed in 1981 with the publication of the eleventh volume of the *Actes et Documents du Saint Siège relatifs à la seconde guerre mondiale*. These volumes seemed to quell the controversy. The diplomatic correspondence contained therein, as well as notes and memoranda from meetings with diplomats and Church leaders, clearly showed that the pope and the Catholic Church were heavily involved in many efforts to rescue Jewish and other victims from the Nazis. They also showed that Pius XII was opposed to Hitler and that he was concerned about Jewish victims. Very little was written about this controversy from 1981 until the release of John Cornwell's book *Hitler's Pope* in 1999. Cornwell changed the terms of the debate. Rather than arguing that Pius XII was anti-Semitic or that he sympathized with Nazi ideals, Cornwell argued that the wartime pope was concerned primarily about establishing a strong papacy and that he lacked moral courage. Therefore, Cornwell argued, he was a perfect pope for Hitler. Much of his evidence was quickly discredited, and serious scholars—even those critical of Pius XII—largely rejected his claims, but Cornwell had reignited the argument about the role that the pope had played during World War II. Since 1999 there have been numerous books and articles critical of Pope Pius XII and the Catholic Church for their role in the war. Hochhuth's play *The Deputy* was even filmed and released as a motion picture entitled *Amen*. There have also been some more nuanced books and many that praise Pius XII and Catholic efforts during that era. This flurry of attention has resulted in several new allegations, many of which are inconsistent with the charges raised by other critics. The controversy seems likely to continue.

Ronald Rychlak

See Also: ANTI-SEMITISM; ARYANISM; BLOOD; BOLSHEVISM; CATHOLIC CHURCH, THE; CENTER PARTY, THE; CHRISTIANITY; CLERICO-FASCISM; COLD WAR, THE; COSMOPOLITANISM; FASCIST PARTY, THE; GERMANY; HITLER, ADOLF; HOLOCAUST, THE; ITALY; JESUITS, THE; MARXISM; MILITARISM; MUSSOLINI, BENITO ANDREA; NATIONALISM; NAZISM; ORTHODOX CHURCHES, THE; PAPACY, THE; PIUS XI, POPE; POLAND AND NAZI GERMANY; POLITICAL CATHOLICISM; PROTESTANTISM; RACIAL DOCTRINE; RACISM; RELIGION; SLOVAKIA; TOTALITARIANISM; TRADITION; WORLD WAR II

References

Blet, Pierre. 1999. *Pius XII and the Second World War*. Trans. Lawrence J. Johnson. New York: Paulist.

Cornwell, John. 1999. *Hitler's Pope: The Secret History of Pius XII*. London: Penguin.

Dalin, David G. 2005. *The Myth of Hitler's Pope*. Washington, DC: Regnery.

Friedländer, Saul. 1966. *Pius XII and the Third Reich*. London: Chatto and Windus.

Halecki, Oscar, and James F. Murray, Jr. 1954. *Pius XII: Eugenio Pacelli, Pope of Peace*. New York: Farrar, Straus and Young.

Rychlak, Ronald J. 2000. *Hitler, the War, and the Pope*. Columbus, MS: Genesis.

PLUTOCRACY

Term of abuse in the lexicon of interwar fascists. Their underlying argument was that "privileged minorities"—small numbers of extremely wealthy individuals ("plutocrats")—were pulling the strings and holding countries to ransom. The fact that many Jews were wealthy, and in positions of power and influence, added to the poignancy of "plutocracy" as an issue for fascists. Key fascist leaders employed the term liberally. Mussolini declared that the "old plutocracies" denied Italy wealth and power. Goebbels used the word four times in quick succession with reference to Britain in a speech to celebrate Hitler's birthday in 1940. For the Nazis, the term was often simply a code word for "the Jews."

P. J. Davies

See Also: ANTI-SEMITISM; BANKS, THE; CAPITALISM; CONSPIRACY THEORIES; COSMOPOLITANISM; GOEBBELS, (PAUL) JOSEPH; GREAT BRITAIN; HITLER, ADOLF; ITALY; MATERIALISM; MUSSOLINI, BENITO ANDREA

PNF: *See* FASCIST PARTY, THE
POETRY: *See* ART; D'ANNUNZIO, GABRIELE; ECKART, JOHANN DIETRICH; GEORGE, STEFAN; JÜNGER, ERNST; MODERNISM; POUND, EZRA; SARFATTI-GRASSINI, MARGHERITA; SOUTH AFRICA; YEATS, WILLIAM BUTLER

POL POT
(1925–1998)

Nom de guerre for Saloth Sar, prime minister of Kampuchea (1976–1979), who advocated an extreme form of communism reminiscent of fascism by its combination with extreme nationalism and terror. He joined the French Communist Party in 1952. By 1963, he

headed what would become the Communist Party of Kampuchea (Khmer Rouge). When the Khmer Rouge took power in 1975, he unleashed a radical communist revolution with nationalist tendencies. When Vietnam invaded Cambodia in 1979, he fled to the Thai-Cambodian border and remained there until his death.

Susan Ear and Sophal Ear

See Also: BOLSHEVISM; KAMPUCHEA; KHMER ROUGE, THE; MARXISM; NATIONALISM

References
Chandler, David. 1999. *Brother Number One*. Boulder, CO: Westview.
Kiernan, Ben. 1984. *How Pol Pot Came to Power*. New Haven: Yale University Press.

POLAND

Because of its fate during World War II, Poland has traditionally been seen as a victim of fascism rather than as a homeland of indigenous fascist movements, but a number of Polish fascist or parafascist groups existed throughout the twentieth century. Nevertheless, despite their relative strength they never came close to seizing power. Boleslaw Piasecki's fully fledged fascist National-Radical Movement was popular among university youth in the late 1930s, but its wider influence remained limited. After the re-emergence of Poland in 1918, this Central European country could be seen as a potentially fertile soil for fascism. The new state included some 35 percent of national minorities, and ethnic tensions were a constant feature of the country's political life right until 1939. Popular anti-Semitism in particular was growing, directed against the country's sizable (10 percent) Jewish community. The parliamentary system disappointed many in the early 1920s, appearing unstable and corrupt. Moreover, the economic situation remained difficult for the greater part of the interwar period, and the results of the global Great Depression for Polish industry were particularly devastating. The right-wing nationalist movement *endecja* (National Democracy) was clearly impressed by the success of Mussolini, and the slogan "Long Live Polish Fascism!" was popular among its supporters, not least during the mass demonstrations that preceded the assassination of the liberal president Gabriel Narutowicz in December 1922. Nevertheless, despite the gradual radi-

Poland 523

calization of *endecja* in terms of its antidemocratic and, especially, anti-Semitic ideology, it never transformed itself into a truly fascist movement. One reason was the internal division within *endecja*: its "old" leadership remained committed to economic liberalism and the parliamentary road to power, while the "young" generation, supported by the main ideologue of *endecja*, Roman Dmowski, pressed for a more militant political policy.

After the 1926 coup d'etat by Pilsudski, which was perceived as a preventative move from the Left, the frustration at the inability of *endecja* to seize power grew. Dmowski tried to emulate Italian Fascism by setting up the extraparliamentary Greater Poland Camp (Oboz Wielkiej Polski; OWP). The OWP was banned by the authorities in 1932–1933, which contributed to the further alienation of "young" activists who were disappointed by the allegedly passive reaction of *endecja* leaders. In 1934 a breakaway organization was formed under the name of the National-Radical Camp (Oboz Narodowo-Radykalny; ONR). It consisted of some 4,000 former *endecja* activists, mostly university students. The ONR called for the stripping of the Jews of Polish citizenship and criticized the capitalist system. The ONR saw itself as the vanguard in the struggle against the Pilsudski regime. After the ONR was banned in 1934, two rival factions emerged as its successors: the so-called ONR "ABC" and the National-Radical Movement (Ruch Narodowo-Radykalny; RNR), also known as the ONR Falanga (*ABC* and *Falanga* were the titles of rival nationalist publications). Both "national-radical" groups remained active semilegally until 1939. The RNR, led by Boleslaw Piasecki, espoused an overtly totalitarian program, calling for a "National Revolution." In 1937 the RNR came close to being incorporated as part of the ruling National Unity Camp (Oboz Zjednoczenia Narodowego; OZN), a new mass organization set up by former followers of Pilsudski, which itself gravitated to the nationalist Right. This move, however, was met with a counteraction from the left-liberal wing of the ruling elite. Both ONR factions were responsible for terrorist attacks against Jews and left-wing activists in the late 1930s. They succeeded in forcing some universities to introduce the physical segregation of Jewish and non-Jewish students at university lectures. They gradually radicalized their demands for removing Jewish students from Polish universities altogether. *Endecja* and its splinter groups pledged their strong allegiance to the Catholic faith, and they were supported by a significant part of the clergy. Nevertheless, a neopagan fascist group with a limited appeal also appeared in the late 1930s: the Zadruga group, led by Jan Stachniuk.

There was no political collaboration with Nazi occupiers in Poland during World War II on a scale comparable to France or Norway. Apart from the traditional anti-Germanism of *endecja*, this can also be explained in terms of a lack of interest on the German side: the founder of the short-lived collaborationist National Radical Organization (Narodowa Organizacja Radykalna; NOR), Andrzej Swietlicki (pre-1939 member of the RNR), was eventually killed by the Nazis in 1940. Nevertheless, the level of the involvement of some Poles in the Holocaust has been the subject of a lively debate since the publication of Jan Gross's book *Neighbors* about a 1941 pogrom in Jedwabne. Piasecki himself was arrested by the Gestapo in 1939 and released after intervention by his friends in the Italian Fascist establishment. With a group of followers he continued his activity in the framework of his own resistance organization, the Confederation of the Nation (Konfederacja Narodu; KN). Imprisoned by the Soviet security service, NKVD, in 1945, he agreed to form a procommunist Catholic group that became known as "Pax." Its ideology blended elements of Catholicism, Marxism, and nationalism.

In the 1990s, extreme nationalist and fascist groups reappeared on the Polish political landscape, most notably the Polish National Community (Polska Wspolnota Narodowa; PWN), led by Boleslaw Tejkowski, and Adam Gmurczyk's National Rebirth of Poland (Narodowe Odrodzenie Polski; NOP), which is a part of the London-based International Third Position (ITP). Neo-Nazi skinhead networks such as "Blood and Honour" appeared in Poland in the late 1990s, too, and found themselves a niche in youth popular culture. A number of skinhead activists joined larger political parties—such as the post-*endecja* League of Polish Families (Liga Polskich Rodzin; LPR) and the populist Self-Defense (Samoobrona)—that received a combined 18 percent of the vote in the 2001 parliamentary election.

Rafal Pankowski

See Also: ANTIFASCISM; ANTI-SEMITISM; BOLSHEVISM; CAPITALISM; CATHOLIC CHURCH, THE; CONCENTRATION CAMPS; DEMOCRACY; DMOWSKI, ROMAN; FRANCE; GERMANY; HITLER, ADOLF; HOLOCAUST, THE; ITALY; LIBERALISM; MARXISM; MILITARY DICTATORSHIP; MUSSOLINI, BENITO ANDREA; NATIONALISM; NAZISM; NEO-NAZISM; NORWAY; PARAFASCISM; PARLIAMENTARISM; PIASECKI, BOLESLAW; PILSUDSKI, MARSHAL JOZEF; POLAND AND NAZI GERMANY; POSTWAR FASCISM; PROGRESS; SKINHEAD FASCISM; THIRD POSITIONISM; TOTALITARIANISM; WALL STREET CRASH, THE; WORLD WAR II

References

Blit, L. 1965. *The Eastern Pretender: The Story of Boleslaw Piasecki.* London: Hutchinson.

Gross, Jan T. 2001. *Neighbors: The Destruction of the Jewish Community in Jedwabne, Poland.* Princeton: Princeton University Press.

Lipski, Jan Jozef. 1994. *Katolickie Panstwo Narodu Polskiego.* London: Aneks.

Polonsky, A. 1972. *Politics in Independent Poland, 1922–1939.* Oxford: Clarendon.

Rudnicki, Szymon. 1985. *Oboz Narodowo-Radykalny: Geneza i dzialalnosc.* Warszawa: Czytelnik.

POLAND AND NAZI GERMANY

The Polish republic founded in 1918 was composed of Polish-speaking territories in Russia, Austria, and Germany. These areas contained significant sectors that were not, however, Polish by culture or language, and there were significant German elements. The Treaty of Versailles established a "Polish Corridor" of land that gave access to the sea, and this was a particular focus of conflict. The ancient port of Danzig (modern Gdansk) at the mouth of the river Vistula had traditionally been one of the Germanic Free Ports of the Hanseatic League, but at the same time it had been subject to the old Kingdom of Poland. The Versailles Treaty enacted its demilitarization as a "Free City." That and the creation of the "Polish Corridor" caused huge offense to German nationalists.

France viewed the new Polish state as a valuable buffer against any future German expansion. In 1934, Hitler attempted to weaken Polish ties to France by signing a ten-year nonaggression pact with Poland. But in March 1939 the German dictator demanded an end to the Versailles status of Danzig and the Polish Corridor, and made the "liberation" of the German part of the population a pretext for his invasion and conquest of Poland in September 1939. German-speakers in Poland were treated as citizens of the Reich, but the rest were subjected to brutal treatment as racial inferiors. In western Poland, German settlers were encouraged to take over land belonging to Poles. Poland was the location for many of the concentration camps in which the Holocaust was implemented.

Cyprian Blamires

See Also: ARYANISM; AUSCHWITZ (-BIRKENAU); CONCENTRATION CAMPS; EXPANSIONISM; FRANCE; *GENERALGOUVERNEMENT*/GENERAL GOVERNMENT, THE; GERMANY; GHETTOS, THE; HITLER, ADOLF; NATIONALISM; NAZISM; PANGERMANISM; POLAND; RACIAL DOCTRINE; SLAVS, THE (AND GERMANY); VERSAILLES, THE TREATY OF; WORLD WAR II

References

Bernhard, Michael M. 2005. *Institutions and the Fate of Democracy: Germany and Poland in the Twentieth Century.* Pittsburgh, PA: University of Pittsburgh Press.

Citino, Robert M. 1987. *The Evolution of Blitzkrieg Tactics: Germany Defends Itself against Poland, 1918–1933.* Westport, CT: Greenwood.

Cordell, Karl, and Stephan Wolff. 2005. *Germany's Foreign Policy and the Czech Republic: Geopolitik Revisited.* London: Routledge.

Diemut, Majer. 2003. *"Non-Germans" under the Third Reich: The Nazi Judicial and Administrative System in Germany and Occupied Eastern Europe with Special Regard to Occupied Poland, 1939–1945.* Baltimore: Johns Hopkins University Press.

Tec, Nechama. 1986. *When the Light Pierced the Darkness: Christian Rescue of Jews in Nazi-occupied Poland.* New York: OUP.

POLITICAL CATHOLICISM

The response of Italian Catholic parties to the rise of Mussolinian Fascism was generally hostile: led by Luigi Sturzo, the Popolari opposed Mussolini's new movement and consequently became one of the chief targets of squadrist violence. Very unwillingly, Sturzo agreed to his party's participation in Mussolini's first government, formed in November 1922. A not dissimilar situation was to be found in Germany: there the Center Party and its Bavarian sister party, the BVP, suffered little from Nazi electoral inroads. In both cases, however, the Catholic parties' internal divisions were successfully exploited to defeat them. In Italy, Mussolini managed to attract supporters from among the right-wing Popolari and leading Catholic businessmen and financiers: these "clerico-fascists," as they were called, played an important role in Mussolini's consolidation of the Fascist dictatorship and in his early contacts with the Vatican. In Germany, a major defector from the right of the Center Party, Franz Von Papen, helped to prepare the way for Hitler's installation as chancellor in 1933.

The greatest problem for the Catholic parties in their efforts to resist the rise of Fascism was the attitude of Pope Pius XI, who did not like Catholic political parties in and of themselves. In addition, Pius was averse to priests having a political role: Sturzo of the Popolari, Kaas of the Center Party, Seipel of the Austrian Christian Socials, and Hlinka and Tiso of the Slovak People's Party were all both clerics and leaders of their respective parties. Thus Pius was happy to oblige Mussolini by forcing Sturzo to resign in 1923, and he sent Sturzo into exile the following year. Mussolini was equally happy when the PPI (Popolari) was dissolved in 1926 and the Center Party brought about its own dissolution in 1933.

Catholic politicians and groups played an important part in the resistance to Nazism in Belgium, Holland, and France. In the latter case, Catholic participation brought about a renewal of French Catholic political activity, culminating in the formation of the Christian democratic Mouvement Républicain Populaire at the end of the war. In Italy, though the majority of former Popolari did not actively resist the Fascist regime, a small nucleus of them went into exile, and Alcide De Gasperi, the future Christian Democratic prime minister, was put on trial and imprisoned. During the period of the Salò Republic, from 1943 to 1945, several Catholic groups organized partisan brigades to fight Mussolini, and with the former Popolari they would form the nucleus of the postwar Christian Democratic Party. Similarly, though on a very much smaller scale, Catholics in Germany participated in the resistance to Hitler, and some paid with their lives for their role. It can be argued, in the longer term, that Catholic opposition to Fascism and Nazism provided the springboard for the post-1945 "triumph" of Christian Democratic parties in the countries of Western Europe.

In Slovakia, however, the involvement of the Slovak People's Party regime in alliance with Nazi Germany, its secession from the Czechoslovak state, and its complicity in the deportation of Slovakian Jews to the death camps led to the executions of its leaders, Tiso and Tuka.

John Pollard

See Also: ANTIFASCISM; CATHOLIC CHURCH, THE; CENTER PARTY, THE; CLERICO-FASCISM; CONCENTRATION CAMPS; CROATIA; CZECHOSLOVAKIA; DEMOCRACY; FASCIST PARTY, THE; GERMANY; HITLER, ADOLF; HOLOCAUST, THE; ITALY; MUSSOLINI, BENITO ANDREA; NAZISM; PAPACY, THE; PAPEN, FRANZ VON; PIUS XI, POPE; PIUS XII, POPE; SALÒ REPUBLIC, THE; SCHMITT, CARL; SLOVAKIA; TISO, MGR. JOSEF; TUKA, DR. VOJTECH; USTASHA

References
Blinkhorn, M., ed. 1997. *Fascists and Conservatives: The Radical Right and the Establishment in Twentieth Century Europe.* London: Unwin Hyman.

Conway, M. 1997. *Catholic Parties in Europe, 1918–1945.* London: Routledge.
Pollard, J. 1994. "Fascism." In *The New Dictionary of Catholic Social Thought,* edited by Judith A. Dwyer. Collegeville, MN: Liturgical Press.
Wolff, R. J., and J. K. Hoensch, eds. 1987. *Catholics, the State and the European Radical Right.* Boulder: University of Colorado Press.

POLITICAL RELIGION: *See* RELIGION
POPULISM: *See* NEOPOPULISM

PORTUGAL

Despite the fact that it was governed by an authoritarian right-wing regime for almost half of the twentieth century, there is remarkably little evidence of active fascist movements in interwar Portugal. Some political movements did adopt some of the radical fascistic-type programs popular in early-twentieth-century Europe, but they enjoyed limited popular support. Having said this, there were exceptions. As an organized movement, the radical integralist group Integralismo Lusitano, which was formed by students at the University of Coimbra in 1914, adopted and adapted many of the ideals being espoused in France by Charles Maurras's Action Française. Yet while the Integralists were only too willing to push a vision of a corporatist, integralist, and authoritarian state, they did not advocate any of the more radical policies associated with fascism, nor indeed the racial doctrines of German Nazism. Created as a radical monarchist response to the recently created republic, the Integralists were basically nationalists whose main goal was the regeneration of the Portuguese nation through the re-establishment of traditional forms of societal control. While their views were unquestionably elitist, insofar as they advocated the top-down reform of Portuguese society, they did not create any violent heroic myths of their own.

The continuing failure of the First Republic to legitimate itself created a set of social, economic, financial, and political factors that were conducive to endemic instability within civil society. The decision of the Republic's leaders to engineer Portugal's entry into World War I on the side of the Allies was crucial in providing the

The Portuguese National Syndicalist Movement salute their leader, Francisco Rolão Preto, in typical fascist style. The Portuguese regime under Salazar is sometimes referred to as a 'fascist' dictatorship, but Salazar showed his true colors by banning this fascistic movement and exiling its leader. (Hulton-Deutsch Collection/Corbis)

catalyst that would tear Portuguese society apart in unforeseen ways. The decision to enter the war was, above all, a party political one, and it was taken against the wishes of both the Portuguese armed forces and the governments of Britain and France. The fact that it was common knowledge that Portugal's entry into the war was not desired provided a fillip for antirepublican and anti–Republican Party forces. Far from uniting Portuguese society under the Republic against a common external enemy, entry into the war created new divisions within Portuguese society and exacerbated existing ones. One of the major consequences, however, was the politicization of the armed forces. With the partial exception of the navy, the Portuguese military had studiously avoided taking a position with respect to the nature of the political regime. From being neutral onlookers during the republicans' overthrow of the monarchy in 1910, the military now became a major

player. In effect, the politicians had somehow overlooked the fact that the Portuguese military was a top-heavy and elitist institution, with an officer corps that was drawn largely from the old aristocracy. While they may not have been willing to risk their positions to save a corrupt and generally disliked monarchy, they were similarly unwilling to risk their lives to fight in a war against an enemy they admired, on the side of the "great democracies" that they so distrusted.

Matters came to a head when the majority of the officer corps simply refused their orders to fight. The government backed down and allowed them to remain in Portugal, while hastily training a new republican officer corps to fight in their stead. This was to create new problems. In the meantime, however, the antirepublican officer corps was able to remain in Portugal, where they were to become a major problem for the republican government, which had now lost that part of the army upon whom it could depend to defend it. Political agitation within the army was not slow to spread, culminating in the attempted uprising led by Machado Santos in October 1916. Nevertheless, while the ideals that were gaining some popularity within the armed forces were undoubtedly authoritarian and right-wing, they were much more reactionary than radical; rather than promoting the ideals that were to become associated with twentieth-century Italian Fascism or Nazism, they tended to advocate the overthrow of the Republic and the re-establishment of Portugal's monarchy.

In December 1917, Major Sidonio Pais took advantage of the Republican Party's unpopularity and the absence of any forces capable of defending the government, to launch a coup against it. Pais's coup was supported by a heterogeneous collection of groups that were discontented with the existing republican regime, ranging from Integralists to traditional monarchists, socialists, trade unionists, and many more. Their common enemy was the Republican Party, but there was no agreement on what type of regime should follow. While Pais adopted many of the characteristics that were to become associated with fascist leaders in the future (for example, the creation of a personality cult around him as the national savior), these characteristics were developed as a reaction to his failure to create a unified movement that would be capable of promoting a new vision. Basically, he used his charismatic appeal to compensate for the lack of any real ideological movement. His attempt at creating a single party in his image, his adoption of populist policies (such as the program of government-supported soup kitchens), the creation of a unicameral chamber, and his advocacy of corporatist and presidentialist solutions to the regime question—all failed to unite the Portuguese people. His continued advocacy of republicanism and his failure to take Portugal out of the war cost him his monarchist allies, who refused to join his single party. His failure to address any of the real social problems affecting the Portuguese working classes lost him the support of the working-class organizations that had manned the barricades with him. The disrespect he displayed to his party's leader, Brito Camacho, lost him the sympathy of many republicans. In the end, devoid of any real ideas as to how to resolve the regime question, Sidonio stuttered from one crisis to the next until, in the course of an attempt to assuage a promonarchist military movement in the north of the country, he was assassinated by a prorepublican World War I veteran. Within one month of his death the republicans were back in power in Lisbon and the south, while the monarchists controlled Oporto and the north. Sidonio's legacy was civil war.

Obviously, the civil war of 1919 hardened opinions on all sides of the political spectrum. The Integralists, who had become one of the most precocious political groups of the time, had been damaged as a result of their collaboration with Sidonio. Their program, which was still largely that of Action Française, advocated the creation of an absolute monarchy and the establishment of local corporatist-style representation. While this may have had something in common with the ideals being espoused by Mussolini in Italy, it is not sufficient grounds to claim that Integralism was fascistic. Nevertheless, there were elements within Integralism that did express their admiration for Italian Fascism. One leading Integralist, Francisco Rolão Preto, wrote a series of articles in 1922 in which he openly praised the political ideals espoused by Mussolini. As the decade progressed, and as the political, financial, social, and economic instability of the Republic grew worse, more and more radical and reactionary grouplets of varying size and importance appeared. Some of these groups, such as the Cruzada Nuno Alvarez, were openly sympathetic to fascist ideology, and some, such as Homens Livre, even had important political supporters. Nevertheless, these groups had very little—if any—influence at the political level, and even at the grass roots they were little more than small gangs of thugs, never amounting to a serious political force. Consequently, all of the attempts to overthrow the Republic were made by conservative groups within the armed forces, and not by the fascistic groups. Following the successful coup of May 1926, the small radical movements were very quickly trampled underfoot by the successful military.

One slight exception to this general survey was the National Syndicalist Movement that was formed by Rolão Preto in 1929. Rolão Preto had left the Integralists because he believed that they had undermined their own position by supporting factions within the post–May 1926 military leadership, a leadership that very early on had shown itself to be republican. He had then become increasingly alarmed at the path that the recently installed military dictatorship was taking. He believed that it was far too conservative, and that the appointment of the former Catholic Party deputy and university economics professor António Salazar as minister of finance, with veto authority over all aspects of government policy, meant that there would be little chance of any movement toward his preferred option of an absolute monarchy. The National Syndicalist Movement brought together radical students, disillusioned republicans, absolutist monarchists, nationalists, and some trade unionists in a loose ideological movement. While its declared aim was to overthrow the regime and establish a corporate state, and while it did establish a blue-shirted militia organization and institute a cult of personality around Preto, the real motivation driving the National Syndicalists was, undoubtedly, their common desire to rid Portugal of Salazar. He was the obstacle preventing the attainment of all of their privately disparate goals. Salazar, however, was far too astute for them, and he simply banned the movement, while offering its members positions within his regime and its party, the National Union. More than half of the movement accepted Salazar's offer and moved into positions within the party and the many party and regime organizations. Rolão Preto and his deputy, Alberto de Monsaraz, were exiled to Spain. The National Syndicalist movement ceased to exist.

After banning the only overtly fascist movement that Portugal had known, Salazar set about creating his own institutions, which were to adopt fascist-style rituals, rites, and symbols, such as the Roman salute and the leadership principle. At the outbreak of the Spanish Civil War, the Portuguese regime introduced the Portuguese Legion, a volunteer corps that would fight alongside Franco's insurgents, and also the Portuguese Youth, which was loosely modeled on the Italian Balilla. Nevertheless, such organizations were kept at arm's length from the regime: they were little more than window-dressing, with no political power or influence whatsoever. As soon as the Spanish Civil War was over, the use of fascist-style symbol and ritual was officially discouraged by the regime, which was increasingly protective of its pro-British orientation. By the time that World War II broke out, Portugal was quite clearly within the British sphere of influence. While Portugal remained neutral during the war, and while it did trade with Germany, Salazar's intervention was crucial in securing Spanish neutrality and the protection of shipping lanes. In an act that bordered on belligerent, Portugal offered first Britain, then the United States, use of the Azores Islands for refueling and resupply.

In the few tumultuous months immediately following the military overthrow of the dictatorship of Salazar's successor, Marcello Caetano, in 1974, there was a sudden appearance of extremist political groups, each with its own agenda and goals. While the vast majority of these groups were on the left of the political spectrum, there were one or two that continued to espouse ideals that bordered on the fascistic. These groups, however, were very rarely more than one- or two-man enterprises, and they disappeared almost as quickly as they appeared. The restoration of democracy and the country's promised accession to the European Union very quickly undermined the extremists, depriving them of a receptive audience.

Stewart Lloyd-Jones

See Also: INTRODUCTION; ACTION FRANÇAISE; AUTHORITARIANISM; BOLSHEVISM; CATHOLIC CHURCH, THE; CLERICO-FASCISM; CONSERVATISM; CORPORATISM; DEMOCRACY; DICTATORSHIP; ELITE THEORY; FASCIST PARTY, THE; FRANCO Y BAHAMONDE, GENERAL FRANCISCO; GERMANY; INTEGRAL NATIONALISM; ITALY; LEADER CULT, THE; LEISURE; MARXISM; MAURRAS, CHARLES; MONARCHISM; MONARCHY; MUSSOLINI, BENITO ANDREA; MYTH; NAZISM; PALINGENETIC MYTH; PAPACY, THE; PARAFASCISM; POLITICAL CATHOLICISM; REVOLUTION; ROLÃO PRETO, FRANCISCO; SALAZAR, ANTÓNIO DE OLIVEIRA; SALUTES; SOCIALISM; SPAIN; SPANISH CIVIL WAR, THE; STYLE; SYMBOLS; SYNDICALISM; WORLD WAR I; WORLD WAR II; YOUTH MOVEMENTS

References

Lloyd-Jones, J. S. 1999. *Integralismo Lusitano and Action Francaise.* Dundee, Scotland: University of Dundee Occasional Papers.

———. 2003. "*Integralismo Lusitano:* 'Made in France.'" *Penelope* 28: 93–104.

Maxwell, K., ed. 1986. *Portugal in the 1980s: Dilemmas of Democratic Consolidation.* Westport, CT: Greenwood.

Pinto, A. C. 1991. "The Radical Right in Contemporary Portugal." Pp. 167–190 in *Neo-fascism in Europe,* edited by L. Cheles, R. Ferguson, and M. Vaughan. London: Longman.

———. 2000. *The Blueshirts: Portuguese Fascists and the New State.* Boulder, CO: Social Science Monographs.

———, ed. 2003. *Contemporary Portugal: Politics, Society and Culture.* Boulder, CO: Social Science Monographs.

POSITIVISM

A theory that had a special significance in the vocabulary of fascist propagandists. Revolutionary Syndicalists like Georges Sorel and early fascist theoreticians in general often regarded their program as conceived directly in opposition to what they regarded as the materialistic superficialities of a positivistic approach to solving intellectual problems; their ire was especially aroused by positivism's naive optimism and superficial faith in social progress and equality. (In its original meaning, as defined by Claude-Henri Saint-Simon and adopted by his disciple Auguste Comte, positivism denoted the factual analysis of phenomena based on science, apart from any form of metaphysics.) The idea that Italian Fascism emerged as a direct response to positivism has been stressed in the writings of prominent historians such as Norberto Bobbio and Zeev Sternhell, especially in the latter's *Birth of Fascist Ideology* (1994). This analysis is undermined by the fact that the term *positivism* became a virtual misnomer in Italy during the final decades of the nineteenth century, because by that time its content had departed substantially from its original nonmetaphysical Comtian framework of ideas and intentions. Rejection of the ideas of Auguste Comte was explicit among a number of Italian "positivist" leaders. Thus, what is generally taken to be "positivism" in Italy, and generally considered as a system of ideas against which nascent Fascist ideology rebelled, was actually an inspiration behind some of the key concepts of Fascist ideology. Sternhell's argument that fascism arose as a concerted reaction against positivism therefore requires some fine tuning.

The main branch of Italian positivism under the leadership of Enrico Morselli (1852–1929), Roberto Ardigò (1828–1920), and Giuseppe Sergi (1841–1936), writers and scientists under the direct tutelage of the monism of the German zoologist Ernst Haeckel, contributed to Fascism a basic antipathy toward the values of traditional Western civilization, a support for policies of extreme Social Darwinism, and a commitment to the spread of a new faith based on secular mysticism. Above all, Fascism derived from positivism a belief that science constituted the foundation of its understanding of the nature of man and society. After Fascism attained political power in Italy in the 1920s, many statements of its basic principles appearing in official Fascist publications clearly reflected the influence of the Italian positivist tradition. Fascism's assumption that it was proceeding along the paths marked out by the tradition of the scientific revolution and the findings of modern evolutionary science bore the imprint of the positivist tradition. In addition, a good number of former positivist writers, such as the anthropologist Giuseppe Sergi and the criminologist Enrico Ferri (1856–1929), warmly embraced Fascism.

Daniel Gasman

See Also: ANTHROPOLOGY; FASCIST PARTY, THE; ITALY; MATERIALISM; MECHANISTIC THINKING; MOSCA, GAETANO; ORGANICISM; SCIENCE; SOCIAL DARWINISM; SPIRITO, UGO

References

Gasman, Daniel. 1998. *Haeckel's Monism and the Birth of Fascist Ideology*. New York: Lang.
Sternhell, Zeev. 1994. *The Birth of Fascist Ideology*. Princeton: Princeton University Press.

POSTWAR FASCISM

The political and social climate that prevailed after World War II condemned all attempts to create mass-based parties with a paramilitary wing to failure, but the tenacity of fascism as an ideological force led some of its most ardent activists to adopt three basic tactics to survive in a climate now hostile to all forms of revolutionary nationalism: internationalization, whereby concern with reversing decadence of the nation (increasingly often conceived as a homogenous ethnic group or culture rather than as a nation-state) was located within anxieties over the fate of Europe, the white race, or the West as a whole; groupuscularization, whereby fascism assumed the form of small units or cells of ideological or violent activism with no aspiration to be a mass party, and often with no ambition even to become an electoral presence; and metapoliticization, whereby resources were concentrated not on winning power in political space but on achieving cultural hegemony in civic (or what has been described as "uncivic") space as the precondition for radical sociopolitical change. These tactics, adopted more out of necessity than choice, mean that postwar fascism typically no longer manifests itself in the type of visible political formation familiar from the party rallies and theatrical events of the 1930s, with a conspicuous leader and uniformed followers. Instead, much of it increasingly operates "rhizomically," spawning new groupuscules that together operate not as a movement but as a network, analogous to the World Wide Web, which has come to play such an important role in disseminating (or attempting to disseminate) fascist ideas of inaugurating a new era.

Those historians who hold that postwar fascism is an irrelevancy can point to the fact that, in marked contrast with interwar Europe, hardly any fascist parties have made inroads into the sphere of democratic politics since 1945. The partial exceptions are the Nationaldemokratische Partei Deutschlands and the Movimento Sociale Italiano, both of which once gained some notoriety in their attempts to perpetuate German Nazism and Italian Fascism, respectively. They could do so only by drastically watering down the revolutionary programs of their interwar forebears, despite which they remained utterly marginalized by mainstream politics. It was only when in 1994 the MSI transformed itself into the democratic right-wing and "postfascist" Alleanza Nazionale under Gianfranco Fini that it

managed to become sufficiently electable to form part
of the government coalition, having publicly jettisoned
its Fascist baggage. Other fascist parties, such as the
United Kingdom's National Front in the 1970s, have
been able to ride high on occasional waves of national
anxiety about mass immigration and have attracted
considerable news media attention, but they have never
seriously threatened the status quo. As for high-profile
parties that espouse overt forms of xenophobia or make
covert appeals to fascist sentiments, such as France's
National Front, Germany's Republicans, the Austrian
Freedom Party, or the Belgian Vlaams Blok, non-Marxist political scientists generally classify these not as fascist but as forms of right-wing populism, or "neopopulism," that pursue policies aimed to put the
(ethnically conceived) nation first without calling for a
radically "new order." It is a sign of the times that the
British National Party, which was originally neo-Nazi
in its core values, was by the early 2000s presenting itself as a populist party in order to gain more votes,
thereby underlining the basic impotence of fascism as
an electoral force. This trend is conformed by the utter
political failure of Italy's Fiamma Tricolore, the party
formed by intransigent Fascists who refused to participate in Fini's "sell-out" in 1994, and the rapid rise and
fall of the extreme xenophobe Vladimir Zhirinovsky,
whose party program mixed fascist and neopopulist elements, as a possible presidential candidate in the new
Russia.

The internationalized and metapoliticized subculture of extremism created by fascist groupuscules forms
the backcloth to more high-profile political and cultural pressure groups at work in particular countries; it
can easily generate the illusion of a vast virtual community of believers working for the fascist cause all over
the world, either trying to create the spark that will ignite the final conflict or keeping the faith for the duration of the protracted "interregnum" that must precede
the transformation as long as liberal materialism holds
sway. Fascism may have largely evacuated conventional
party-political space and hierarchical organizations for
civic and rhizomic ones, but it now constitutes an ag-
gregate antisystemic force greater than the sum of its
component parts, one that cannot be analyzed adequately using the historiographical techniques and assumptions appropriate to interwar Europe.

This organizational transformation has been accompanied by some significant changes in ideology.
Not only have some groups renounced the prospect of
the imminent rebirth of the nation and abandoned
the nation-state as the primary unit of regeneration,
but many "modern" fascists now campaign on such is-

*Alessandra Mussolini, who has become a torch bearer of the
Far Right in modern Italy; her grandfather was the Fascist
Dictator Benito Mussolini. (Alessandra Benedetti/Corbis)*

sues as the need to transcend capitalism—sometimes
advocating a new synthesis of Left and Right known
as Third Positionism—to combat globalization and
the One-World system, to stem the tide of multiculturalism and mass migration that is eroding cultural
difference (producing a form of racism known as "differentialism"), and to resolve the crisis of the ecosys-
tem, often arguing in terms that bring them close to
revolutionary left-wing critiques of international capitalism. Much fascist ideological energy and pseudo-
scholarship has also been channeled into Historical
Revisionism and Holocaust Denial in the attempt to
remove the psychological blocks that prevent people
from being drawn to policies that they still subliminally associate with the horrors of Nazism. There is
also a flourishing subculture that has spawned occult

and neopagan forms of Nazism in Germany, created new blends of Bolshevism with fascism in Russia, and fused Christianity with racism in the United States in ways that in practice bring it very close to fascism (post-Soviet Russia and the contemporary United States are now the most important laboratories for new variants of fascism). At the same time, heavy metal music and ballads have been used as vehicles for spreading the fascist hatred of modern multiculturalism, internationalism, and materialism, thereby creating a "white noise" music industry that has come to be a major source of revenue for revolutionary nationalism. The most creative forms of fascism's ideological adaptation are associated with the European New Right, which has deliberately abandoned party politics, paramilitary violence, and any overt links with interwar fascism, especially Nazism, in its quest to destroy the hegemony of liberal democratic values whose globalization it regards as a form of totalitarianism that is largely responsible for a profound crisis in human history.

Roger Griffin

See Also: INTRODUCTION; AMERICANIZATION; AUSTRIA; BELGIUM; BOLSHEVISM; BRITISH NATIONAL PARTY, THE; CAPITALISM; CHRISTIANITY; COLD WAR, THE; COSMOPOLITANISM; CYBERFASCISM; DEMOCRACY; ECOLOGY; EUROPEAN NEW RIGHT, THE; EUROPEANIST FASCISM/RADICAL RIGHT, THE; EVOLA, JULIUS; FASCIST PARTY, THE; FRANCE; FREY, DR. GERHARD; GERMANY; GLOBALIZATION; GRAMSCI, ANTONIO; GRECE; GROUPUSCULES; HAIDER, JÖRG; HOLOCAUST, THE; HOLOCAUST DENIAL; IMMIGRATION; ITALY; KÜHNEN, MICHAEL; LE PEN, JEAN-MARIE; LIBERALISM; MARXIST THEORIES OF FASCISM; MATERIALISM; MOVIMENTO SOCIALE ITALIANO, THE; NATIONAL BOLSHEVISM; NATIONAL FRONT (FRANCE), THE; NATIONAL FRONT, (UK) THE; NAZISM; NEO-NAZISM; NEOPOPULISM; NEW ORDER, THE; NIHILISM; PALINGENETIC MYTH; PARAMILITARISM; RACISM; REVOLUTION; ROCK MUSIC; RUSSIA; SKINHEAD FASCISM; TENSION, THE STRATEGY OF; THIRD POSITIONISM; TOLKIEN, JOHN RONALD REUEL; TOTALITARIANISM; UNITED STATES, THE (POST-1945); VLAAMS BLOK; WHITE NOISE; WHITE SUPREMACISM; XENOPHOBIA; ZHIRINOVSKII, VLADIMIR VOL'FOVICH

References

Coogan, Kevin. 1999. *Dreamer of the Day: Francis Parker Yockey and the Postwar Fascist International.* New York: Autonomedia.

Eatwell, Roger. 1995. *Fascism: A History.* London: Chatto and Windus.

Griffin, Roger. 2001. "Interregnum or Endgame? Radical Right Thought in the 'Post-fascist' Era." In *Reassessing Political Ideologies,* edited by Michael Freeden. London: Routledge.

Griffin, Roger, with Matt Feldman, eds. 2003. *Critical Concepts in Political Science: Fascism.* Vol. 5. London: Routledge.

Kaplan, Jeffrey. 1997. *Radical Religion in America: Millenarian Movements from the Far Right to the Children of Noah.* Syracuse, NY: Syracuse University Press.

Laqueur, Walter. 1996. *Fascism: Past, Present, Future.* New York: Oxford University Press.

Lee, Martin. 1998. *The Beast Reawakens.* London: Warner.

Lipstadt, Deborah. 1994. *Denying the Holocaust.* New York: Plume.

Payne, Stanley. 1996. *A History of Fascism 1914–1918.* Madison: University of Wisconsin Press.

Shenfield, Stephen. 2001. *Russian Fascism.* Armonk, NY: M. E. Sharp.

POUJADE, PIERRE MARIE RAYMOND (1920–2003)

French right-wing populist politician whose Union de Défense des Commerçants et Artisans (UDCA) briefly enjoyed electoral success in the 1956 elections; he gave his name to the Poujadiste movement of small shopkeepers and businessmen who felt that he articulated their grievances. Poujade portrayed himself as an "ordinary guy" fed up with an unjust and corrupt political system, but in fact he had been involved in his teens with Doriot's PPF and for a while had associated himself with the Vichy government. After organizing a movement of resistance against a visit by tax inspectors to his region in 1953, he traveled throughout France calling for lower taxes and a new corporatist constitution and vilifying other politicians and the news media. As time passed, his movement grew increasingly nationalistic, xenophobic, and hostile to parliamentary institutions. *Poujadisme* passed into French political vocabulary as a term suggestive of support for protest, dislike of taxation, and defense of the small man. This is in spite of the fact that Poujade enjoyed prominence for only two years, from 1954 to 1956. He found himself quarreling with the deputies elected in his name and showed signs of megalomania, acquiring the nickname Poujadolf. He gradually retired from public life, and when he re-emerged to put forward candidates in the 1979 European elections, they were a dismal failure at the hustings. However, National Front leader Jean-Marie Le Pen won his first election victory on the Poujadiste ticket in 1956.

Cyprian Blamires

See Also: CORPORATISM; DORIOT, JACQUES; FRANCE;
LE PEN, JEAN-MARIE; NATIONAL FRONT (FRANCE), THE;
NATIONALISM; PARLIAMENTARISM; VICHY; XENOPHOBIA

References

Borne, D. 1977. *Petits bourgeois en révolte? Le mouvement
    Poujade.* Paris: Flammarion.
Davies, Peter. 2002. *The Extreme Right in France, 1789 to the
    Present.* London: Routledge.
Hanley, D. L., A. P. Kerr, and N. H. Waites. 1991.
    Contemporary France: Politics and Society since 1945. London:
    Routledge.

POUJADISME: See POUJADE, PIERRE MARIE RAYMOND

POUND, EZRA (1885–1972)

One of the major modernist poets of the twentieth century, notorious for his enthusiasm for Italian Fascism and for his broadcasts from Radio Rome during World War II. The son of a U.S. government employee, Pound was born on 30 October 1885 in Hailey, Idaho. From early on he started traveling to Europe, first as a child and then as a student, eventually spending most of his adult life in Europe and particularly in Italy. He studied languages at Hamilton College, Connecticut, and later embarked on postgraduate studies at the University of Pennsylvania that he eventually abandoned in 1907. Having crossed the Atlantic the following year, he fell in with the modernist avant-garde in Venice. In London in 1914 he married Dorothy Shakespeare and became a close friend and admirer of W. B. Yeats. He first began work on his (unfinished) poetic magnum opus the *Cantos* in 1915. With Wyndham Lewis he had launched the magazine *Blast* in 1914 and coined the word *Vorticism* as a name for an artistic movement analogous to Italian Futurism, similarly hailing the dynamic volitional element of forward-moving modernism. Pound settled in Paris after World War I and befriended James Joyce (whose work he helped see through the press), Hemingway, and T. S. Eliot. In 1924 he moved on to the Italian coastal town of Rapallo, near Genoa.

In the mid-1920s, Pound espoused a Fascist and anti-Semitic political ideology and in 1925 wrote a letter in favor of Mussolini. He also began to use a letterhead bearing Mussolini's motto: "Liberty Is a Duty not a Right"; he met Il Duce for the first and only time in 1933 and immediately fell under his spell. Pound bombarded Mussolini and the Fascist government—as well as politicians all over the world, bankers, the U.S. president, and virtually everyone in power—with his theories on political economy, monetary matters, and whimsical financial reforms. He developed a lifelong hatred of usury, which he saw as the major evil behind modern political, economic, and moral decadence. He made some strange ideological connections, comparing Mussolini and Hitler to Confucius (whom he was translating), though later he complained that the two European dictators did not follow the Chinese master faithfully. He was convinced that Mussolini was working for peace and that Il Duce and Hitler (whom he began to praise after Mussolini's fortunes became increasingly bound up with Hitler's) would "free us from international capital." His fanatical anti-Semitism and lifelong anticommunism grew steadily in tandem with his admiration for Italian Fascist policy and his loathing for British politicians and the British press—which he labeled "Judo-cratic"—and the League of Nations. He even wrote an article praising the Nazis in Oswald Mosley's magazine *Action.*

On 23 January 1941, as a seven-minute part of the "American Hour" program on Radio Rome, Pound embarked on his wartime propaganda broadcasts on behalf of Fascism. Initially he was thought to be a double agent, and his texts were checked by radio censors prior to the broadcasts. These continued at the rate of roughly ten per month until Pearl Harbor and America's official involvement in the war early in 1942. Increasingly erratic and incomprehensible, most of the later programs ended with Pound being carried away and seeing Jews everywhere—including in the U.S. presidency. Following his broadcast of 25 July 1943, an indictment for (radio) treason (the first of its kind) was formally issued against him by the D.C. District Court in the United States. On the same day in Italy a coup ousted Mussolini, and on hearing of this Pound exclaimed: "Our culture lies shattered in fragments." He fled in fear of his life but eventually came back to serve the Salò Republic, working as a speechwriter for Radio Milan.

On 28 April 1945, Pound was arrested by Italian partisans and handed over to U.S. troops. In an American newspaper interview he declared that "Hitler was a Joan of Arc, a martyr." There followed a six-month military internment near Pisa, where he wrote the famous *Pisan Cantos,* and then on 18 November 1945 he was flown to the United States to face a court of law and a new grand jury indictment. His counsel advised him to plead insanity, and he was committed to St. Elisabeth's Hospital Asylum in Washington, D.C., following an examination by psychiatrists who pronounced him mentally unstable. He was officially released on 7 May 1958 after the treason indictment had been dismissed. He left almost immediately for Italy. Toward the end of his life he claimed that his worst mistake was that "stupid, suburban prejudice of anti-Semitism." Some modern scholars have tried to demonstrate an influence of fascism in his poetry, criticism, and wider literary work.

Byron Kaldis

See Also: ANTI-SEMITISM; BOLSHEVISM; CAPITALISM; DECADENCE; FASCIST PARTY, THE; FUTURISM; GERMANY; HITLER, ADOLF; ITALY; LEAGUE OF NATIONS, THE; MARXISM; MODERNISM; MOSLEY, SIR OSWALD; MUSSOLINI, BENITO ANDREA; NAZISM; PEARL HARBOR; PROPAGANDA; RADIO; SALÒ REPUBLIC, THE; UNITED STATES, THE (PRE-1945); WORLD WAR II; YEATS, WILLIAM BUTLER

References

Heymann, C. G. 1976. *Ezra Pound: The Last Rower: A Political Profile.* London: Faber and Faber.
Morrison, P. 1996. *The Poetics of Fascism: Ezra Pound, T.S. Eliot, Paul de Man.* Oxford: Oxford University Press.
Redman, T. 1991. *Ezra Pound and Italian Fascism.* Cambridge: Cambridge University Press.

PRECURSORS OF FASCISM: *See* PROTOFASCISM

PRESS, THE

Like their Soviet counterparts, the regimes of Mussolini and Hitler regarded the press as a means of disseminating propaganda, contemptuously rejecting the liberal notion of the press popularized in the nineteenth century by thinkers such as J. S. Mill, according to which it was (in addition to a source of news) a useful arena for public debate over issues of importance to society. Such issues had for the fascist mindset largely been resolved by their doctrine or else were to be decided by the leadership without reference to the masses. When Mussolini (himself an experienced and successful journalist) came to power in 1922, the press was still the only significant means of propaganda available, but by the 1930s radio broadcasting and cinema newsreels had grown in importance and were exploited with particular success by Hitler's regime. A year after the inauguration of Mussolini's rule, the government took wide powers to confiscate or close publications regarded as constituting a threat to national interests, and that measure was reinforced in 1926, when the Communist and Socialist party newspapers were closed down. From that time on, editors were kept on a tight leash by Mussolini's press office, and after 1930 regular written announcements informed them of how they were to propagate the image of the renewed and revitalized Italy that Fascism believed itself to have achieved. The chief uncensored source for foreign news was the Osservatore Romano, which was published by the Vatican; its circulation had increased massively by the late 1930s, by which time it was selling 250,000 copies daily. It reprinted stories from other European papers whose sale was forbidden in Italy.

The Nazi regime in Germany also took measures to convert the press into a propaganda arm. In Nazi propaganda prior to their assumption of power in 1933 and before they were able to control it, the press was regularly associated with "Jewishness"; "the Jewish press" was an expression they were fond of. Branding the press in this way came naturally to a mentality steeped in conspiracy theories, and it offered a means of explaining why the press might be critical of themselves. In 1933, Communist and Socialist papers were closed down, and thereafter all papers were required to conform to the Nazi worldview, with rebellious journalists suffering persecution by the regime. Even an illustrious paper like the *Frankfurter Zeitung* was unceremoniously closed down when it caused offense by criticizing Hitler's favorite architect. The paper that acted as a direct mouthpiece for the regime was the *Völkischer Beobachter,* which broke new ground in becoming something close to a national daily (with a circulation of more than a million by 1941) in a country that had previously had only a regional press. The task of bringing the German press to heel was carried out by the press chief of the Reich, Otto Dietrich (1897–1952), a highly qualified graduate in economics, philosophy, and political science who worked for a newspaper in a management capacity and who was also married to the daughter of an influential newspaper owner.

Cyprian Blamires

See Also: BOLSHEVISM; BOOKS, THE BURNING OF THE; COMMUNITY; CONSPIRACY THEORIES; FASCIST PARTY, THE; FILM; GERMANY; HITLER, ADOLF; ITALY; MARXISM; MUSSOLINI, BENITO ANDREA; NAZISM; PAPACY, THE; PROPAGANDA; RELIGION; SOCIALISM; STREICHER, JULIUS; *STÜRMER, DER;* TOTALITARIANISM; *VÖLKISCHER BEOBACHTER,* THE

References

Broszat, M. 1981. *The Hitler State.* London: Longman.

Bytwerk, Randall L. 2001. *Julius Streicher: Nazi Editor of the Notorious Anti-Semitic Newspaper "Der Stürmer."* New York: Cooper Square.

Cannistraro, Philip V. 1982. *Historical Dictionary of Fascist Italy.* Westport, CT: Greenwood.

Dobroszycki, Lucjan. 1995. *Reptile Journalism: Official Polish-Language Press under the Nazis, 1939–1945.* New Haven: Yale University Press.

Germino, D. L. 1971. *The Italian Fascist Party in Power: A Study in Totalitarian Rule.* Minneapolis: University of Minnesota Press.

Muhlberger, Detlef. 2003. *Hitler's Voice: The Völkischer Beobachter, 1920–1933.* Oxford: Peter Lang.

Thompson, D. 1991. *State Control in Fascist Italy: Culture and Conformity.* Manchester: Manchester University Press.

Welch, D. 2002. *The Third Reich: Politics and Propaganda.* London: Routledge.

PRETO: *See* ROLÃO PRETO, FRANCISCO

PREZZOLINI, GIUSEPPE (1882–1982)

Italian nationalist critic of democracy who helped create the environment that nurtured Fascism. In 1908, Prezzolini founded *La Voce,* the most important Italian review in the years preceding the outbreak of World War I, among whose collaborators were to be found historian Gaetano Salvemini, philosopher of idealism Giovanni Gentile, theoretician of Marxism Antonio Gramsci, and Benito Mussolini himself. Although he was a nationalist and critic of the liberal political class and of democracy, as well as a collaborator in the *Popolo d'Italia,* Prezzolini moved abroad after the victory of Fascism.

Alessandro Campi
(translated by Cyprian Blamires)

See Also: FASCIST PARTY, THE; GENTILE, GIOVANNI; GRAMSCI, ANTONIO; ITALY; MUSSOLINI, BENITO ANDREA; NATIONALISM; WORLD WAR I

References

Adamson, W. L. 1993. *Avant-garde Florence: From Modernism to Fascism.* London: Harvard University Press.

Diggins, J. P. 1972. *Mussolini and Fascism.* Princeton: Princeton University Press.

PRIMO DE RIVERA, JOSÉ ANTONIO (1903–1936)

The son of the Spanish dictator General Miguel Primo de Rivera, José Antonio was a charismatic, aristocratic, eloquent, and handsome lawyer, fascinated by Fascist Italy. His first political steps came as vice secretary of the Unión Monárquica Nacional, and as an "independent" at the 1931 Madrid by-elections; he then went on to edit *El Fascio,* before founding the fascistic *Falange Española* in October 1933. He preached national syndicalism and the "dialectic of the fists," and actively conspired against the Republic. José Antonio was imprisoned in Alicante on 6 July 1936 and was executed by a Republican firing squad on 20 November. The nascent regime made a martyr of him, elaborating a powerful cult of the "absent one" *el ausente* and his body lies at the Valley of the Fallen, alongside that of General Franco.

Sid Lowe

See Also: FALANGE; FASCIST PARTY THE; FRANCO Y BAHAMONDE, GENERAL FRANCISCO; FRANCOISM; ITALY; MUSSOLINI, BENITO ANDREA; SPAIN; SPANISH CIVIL WAR, THE

References

Ellwood, S. M. 1987. *Spanish Fascism in the Franco Era: Falange Española de las Jons, 1936–76.* Basingstoke: Macmillan.

Payne, S. G. 1962. *Falange: A History of Spanish Fascism.* London: Oxford University Press.

———. 1999. *Fascism in Spain, 1923–1977.* Madison: University of Wisconsin Press.

PRODUCERS: *See* PRODUCTIVISM

PRODUCTIVISM

In the columns of his newspaper *Popolo d'Italia,* the young Mussolini called for the creation of a new post–World War I Italy of "fighters and producers": this was to replace the existing domination of the parasitic financial speculators. They had profited from wartime speculation and in the aftermath of the war were comfortably enjoying the fruits of that speculation and dominating the regime while the war veterans found themselves excluded. The term *producers* was also intended to distinguish those who worked for a living from the hereditary aristocracy. Mussolini clearly imported the idea from his socialist days, for socialism is, of course, a crusade against those like financial speculators whose profits are deemed to derive from unproductive activities, as well as against the "capitalist class" whose income is considered to be essentially based on theft from the workers of the results of their labor. In preferring the word *producers* over that of *workers,* Mussolini was harking back to an early-nineteenth-century pre-Marxian kind of socialistic thinking that called not for a war of all workers against bosses, but for a war of "the productive" against the "drones"—by which term was mainly intended the hereditary aristocracy. Thus Mussolini was able to tap into the proletariat's resentment of the "idle rich" while retaining the possibility of a national solidarity that could include the bosses insofar as they were themselves involved in productive activity as employers and as entrepreneurs. This was the "utopian socialism" of the Frenchman Henri Saint-Simon (1760–1825), and it allowed for the promotion of the philosophy of corporatism—with its stress on solidarity rather than class war—by the Italian Fascist regime. Saint-Simon himself had combined ideas taken from the Traditionalist (that is, right-wing) critique of the revolution with a (left-wing) belief in the need for association or collaboration of the productive in society (by which he meant workers and bosses) with the representatives of science to counterbalance the influence of the aristocracy and the speculators. This might qualify him to be a distant precursor of Italian Fascism.

Cyprian Blamires

See Also: ARISTOCRACY; BANKS, THE; BOLSHEVISM; CORPORATISM; ECONOMICS; FASCIST PARTY, THE; FRENCH REVOLUTION, THE; ITALY; MARXISM; MUSSOLINI, BENITO ANDREA; PERONISM; PLUTOCRACY; SOCIALISM; TRADITIONALISM; UTOPIA, UTOPIANISM; WAR VETERANS; WORLD WAR I

References
De Grand, A. 1982. *Italian Fascism: Its Origins and Development.* London: University of Nebraska Press.
Knight, P. 2003. *Mussolini and Fascism.* London: Routledge.
Taylor, Keith. 1975. *Henri Saint-Simon 1760–1825: Selected Writings on Science, Industry, and Social Organization.* New York: Holmes and Meier.

PROGRESS

Interwar fascism believed itself to be at the forefront of social progress, defining itself aggressively over against bourgeois society, which it called reactionary; it believed that bourgeois society had bankrupted itself with World War I and was standing on the edge of collapse. As an agent of progress, fascism set itself up as a rival to organized socialism and Marxism—especially Bolshevistic-style Marxism—which portrayed itself as "spearhead of the Proletariat" at the head of "the progressive forces in society." Bolshevism and fascism alike set themselves up at the start of the 1920s to step into the place of "dying" bourgeois society. Italian Fascism entered into an alliance with the "progressive" forces of society—not merely the technological forces but also the artistic and literary avant-garde. By contrast, National Socialism, while equally enthusiastic for technological progress, condemned all modernism in art as "cultural Bolshevism." There was a rapprochement between early Italian Fascism and Futurism, both of them combining an aggressive hostility to the bourgeois as it had been formulated by Marinetti, the leading spirit of Futurism, with the cult of speed, movement, dynamism, technology, and revolution.

Interwar fascism in general combined an aggressive taste for modernity with a call for a return to national traditions and "soldierly values," which won it the cooperation of right conservative and anti-Marxist circles. Italian Fascism and later also National Socialism made a point of selling themselves to the young; they saw themselves as "young" organizations, as the Nazi propaganda minister Joseph Goebbels emphasized in a speech of 15 November 1933: "The revolution that we have accomplished is a total revolution. It has embraced all areas of public life and transformed them from the bottom up. It has completely changed and reformed the relations between man and the state and indeed the whole question of existence itself. It is nothing less than a breakthrough to a young worldview."

Like organized socialism and Marxism, Italian Fascism and National Socialism favored their own form of group solidarity, known by them in the soldierly tradition as "comradeship," and gave their supporters the consciousness of belonging to a social (or racial) elite called to be at the forefront of social progress. Italian Fascism and National Socialism made extensive use of the then most modern means of communication, such as radio, amplification, and film, for purposes of propaganda and the manipulation of the masses. They also made extensive use of cars and airplanes in order to keep on the move and appear "omnipresent." Both Italian Fascism and National Socialism liked to talk about "marching together into the future" in order to stress the progress that the "young world view" brought. Thus Adolf Hitler in a speech of 10 April 1933: "Today we have conquered power. . . . [O]ur highest duty is to think of those to whose sacrifice we owe this power. . . . [We] march with them into a great future."

In Italian Fascism and National Socialism, the concepts of "mastery, conquest, domination" of the future were used for progress; both celebrated the "mastery and conquest" of machines and technologies in the production process, which was seen as the sign of a decisively future-oriented "will to power" of the new man marked by fascism. Even the use of free time was subjected to a "total mobilization" by Italian Fascist and National Socialist Youth and Sports Organizations with marches, parades, military and gymnastic exercises, or hikes. All these served the Italian Fascist and National Socialist philosophy of the "steeling and hardening" of bodies and spirits, in order to make modern men fit for the "new era about to dawn." Both movements aimed to control and channel the general activism and forward movement of modernity in paths of their choice, while associating it with an unashamedly conservative ideal of order and discipline.

Markus Hattstein
(translated by Cyprian Blamires)

See Also: INTRODUCTION; "ANTI-" DIMENSION OF FASCISM, THE; AUTOBAHNS, THE; BERLIN OLYMPICS, THE; BODY, THE CULT OF THE; BOLSHEVISM; BOURGEOISIE, THE; ELITE THEORY; FILM; FUTURISM; GERMANY; GOEBBELS, (PAUL) JOSEPH; HITLER, ADOLF; ITALY; LEISURE; MARINETTI, FILIPPO TOMMASO; MARXISM; MARXIST THEORIES OF FASCISM; MODERNISM; MODERNITY; MUSSOLINI, BENITO ANDREA; NEW AGE, THE; NEW MAN, THE; NEW ORDER, THE; NUREMBERG RALLIES, THE; PALINGENETIC MYTH; PROPAGANDA; PROTOFASCISM; REVOLUTION; SCIENCE; SOCIALISM; SPORT; STATE; TECHNOLOGY; WARRIOR ETHOS, THE; YOUTH MOVEMENTS

References

Arvidsson, Adam. 2003. *Marketing Modernity: Italian Advertising from Fascism to Postmodernity.* London: Routledge.

Carlston, Erin G. *Thinking Fascism: Sapphic Modernism and Fascist Modernity.* Stanford: Stanford University Press.

Gentile, Emilio. 2003. *The Struggle for Modernity: Nationalism, Futurism, and Fascism.* Westport, CT: Praeger.

Gispen, Kees. 2002. *Poems in Steel: National Socialism and the Politics of Inventing from Weimar to Bonn.* New York: Bergbahn.

Herff, Jeffrey. 1986. *Reactionary Modernism: Technology, Culture, and Politics in Weimar and the Third Reich.* Cambridge: Cambridge University Press.

PROPAGANDA

The Italian Fascist and German Nazi leadership were among the first in the political arena to grasp the opportunities offered by new media and communications technologies for the rapid dissemination of ideas and by the development of techniques of persuasion on a mass level. They not only realized that the new mass media were there to be used but they also understood how to use them. They saw that a symbolic event like the nationwide burning of books in Germany, communicated at a mass level through the medium of newspaper and magazine pictures and newsreel clips, had more impact than a hundred printed explanations of the Nazi philosophy. In other words, they understood that propaganda is all about the communication of images and symbols and the exploitation of emotions. Events like the carefully orchestrated and choreographed Nuremberg Rallies had an immediate emotional impact on those who took part, generating a sense of huge excitement in participants, a dramatic sense of being involved in an unprecedented national adventure with limitless potential under the magic leadership of the Fuehrer. The extent of their propagandist impact and converting power even on foreigners can be measured in accounts like that to be found in Anne de Courcy's life of the wife of British fascist leader Sir Oswald Mosley. But these were also events designed to be photographed and communicated across the nation and worldwide, to convey an impression to a global audience of the awesome greatness and power of Germany, her military might, and the huge enthusiasm of her people for the Nazi regime. If the German people believed in Nazism, it was in no small part because of the skillful manipulation to which they were subjected through newsreel, newspaper, and radio. In addition to their exploitation of the image and the appeal to the visual imagination, the Nazis invested very substantially in the new medium of radio. At the same time, they had at their disposal the *Völkischer Beobachter* newspaper. But their propagandistic drive penetrated much further into the psyche of their citizens by the enforcement of gestures used daily, such as the *Heil Hitler!* greeting, which meant that the Fuehrer's name was on everybody's lips many times each day. Equally, the Nazis saw the nation's leisure time as an opportunity for propagandization, which they exploited through control of mass leisure organizations that inculcated the desired ethos.

All of this went according to plan, and the plans were those of Dr. Joseph Goebbels, Hitler's minister for public enlightenment and propaganda. Goebbels was a man with a Ph.D. and a very powerful mind, a keen student of U.S. advertising methods; indeed, he made a particular study of the psychology of propaganda. Goebbels was, in fact, a master of what we would now call "hype." He took the idea of a mass rally, which of course was nothing new in itself, and "hyped it" into an enormously more powerful instrument for intensifying the convictions and the purpose of the participants. He did this by transforming the rally into a gigantic spectacle involving thousands of persons and forests of flags, all to the accompaniment of inspirational music and, in the evenings, a background of searchlights throwing their beams dramatically into the night sky. The intoxication of being a participant in such events is hard to imagine. Their power is shown by the fact that, even today, when newspapers or publishers desire to provide a symbolic pictorial representation of what the Hitler regime was all about, they often reproduce a picture of one of the Nuremberg Rallies. Moreover, even today the celebrated rally film made by Leni Riefenstahl has the power to move. A similar kind of propaganda effort was the revival of an old Teutonic tribal assembly known as the *Thing*. In huge open-air locations with an appropriate backdrop, shows were mounted that involved military tattoos, pagan oratorios, circus acts, and displays of prowess on horseback. Mock battles were put on by large numbers of Hitler Youth members, and there were special ceremonies in honor of Nazi "martyrs."

But the mass rallies, powerful though they were, represented only a part of Goebbels's propaganda expertise. He had also grasped the power of the slogan. His slogans appeared on banners, on newspaper mastheads, in pamphlets, and in graffiti all over Germany. One of the most widely propagated was the slogan *Die Juden sind unser Unglück!*—"The Jews are our misfortune." Goebbels understood that a phrase repeated incessantly by agents considered authoritative easily takes on the status of a statement of fact. Another of his favorite slogans was *Volk ohne Raum* ("A people without space")— suggesting as a fact that Germany was somehow straitjacketed in her territory and was therefore justified in adopting a belligerent policy of expansionism. And always the slogans were accompanied by the omnipresent swastika. Goebbels did not invent the swastika or choose it as the symbol of Nazism, but in plastering it everywhere he fulfilled the advertisement manager's dream—he turned the regime's symbol into a universally recognizable logo: essentially, Goebbels "branded" Nazism. So devoted to his task was Goebbels that he had literally hundreds of staff working shifts on propaganda teams twenty-four hours a day. He also appointed propaganda attaches for German embassies around the world.

To enter on the subject of fascism and propaganda with Nazism is not to imply that Italian Fascism was not also adept at propaganda. Mussolini's regime was equally well attuned to propaganda opportunities, in which it was to some extent perhaps influenced by D'Annunzio's tactics at Fiume. But the historical fact is that Nazi propaganda has made a much more profound historical impact than has Mussolini's. Goebbels's skills as a propagandist have lasted the test of time, in that even many decades after his death, the images and slogans that he promoted continue to resonate in the German imagination and undoubtedly constitute one of the reasons for the continuing appeal of neo-Nazism. To focus on the images of the Nuremberg Rallies today is to feel that somehow the regime was "successful" in generating national pride and in heightening Germany's prestige.

Mussolini too used the mass media to promote the images of Fascism that he wanted to implant in the imaginations of his people and the wider world. He disseminated pictures of himself to encourage a leader cult. But perhaps the most effective means of indoctrination that he shared with the Nazis was the mass movement for youth. He and Hitler both grasped the simple, fundamental truth that the battle for the mind must focus on the rising generation, and he devised the method of enrolling young people—forcibly if necessary—in youth movements, where they could be made the target of propaganda during their leisure time; the pill could, of course, be sweetened by the provision of pleasurable activities like sport and hiking. In Germany the "propagandization" of leisure accompanied the Nazification of education, which of course offered the main means of reaching young minds. From early years, anti-Semitic themes were introduced into the imagery and the texts of school textbooks. The great events of the Nazi calendar, such as the Munich Putsch, were introduced into the teaching of history. Biology lessons and textbooks offered endless scope for indoctrination with Nazi ideas about race. Religious instruction was downgraded. Likewise, Mussolini went to great lengths to inculcate the identification of his regime with the greatness of Ancient Rome, ordering newspaper editors to devote space to it and organizing the release of Gallone's film *Scipione l'Africano* after the conclusion of the war in Ethiopia. His adoption of the Roman salute and the *passo romano* were all part of the same propaganda strategy, which was reinforced by the performance of Latin dramas at night in specially illuminated ancient amphitheaters.

Along with all the exploitation of modern communications technologies went the exploitation of architecture and the arts. The architecture of the Nuremberg Rally Grounds was designed to create the maximum impression of size and greatness. Albert Speer was commissioned by Hitler—for whom architecture was a passion—to plan a new Berlin whose dramatic boulevards and massively imposing buildings adorned with Nazi symbols would carry a message about the greatness of Nazi Germany. The project was never completed because of the war. Mussolini wanted his capital to become the new Rome, and he undertook archaeological excavations at the expense of dwellings, isolating and rehabilitating ancient monuments so that they looked more impressive to the eye. After five years of planning, a massive exhibition opened in the city, designed to celebrate the two-thousandth anniversary of the death of the emperor Augustus. The exhibition was devoted not simply to Ancient Rome but also to making the connection with twentieth-century Italian Fascism. Every attempt (including the classic incentive of reduced rail fares) was made to encourage tours by school children and youth groups and students to visit this propagandistic phenomenon. The presentation of a live eagle to Mussolini at the closing ceremonies suggested that he had taken on the mantle of Ancient Rome.

The technique of the exhibition was also employed by the Nazis, but in a very different way; they used their Exhibition of Degenerate Art to send out a powerful message to the nation and the world about how they saw the purpose of art and the role of the artists—namely, to propagate the values of the regime. Again, this means of propaganda was infinitely more powerful in its impact than a mere pamphlet or pronouncement would have been. Events like this, and the burning of the books, sent out powerful signals whose meaning was unmistakable; as communications of intent and warning, they were outstanding in their efficacy. Another arena where Mussolini and Hitler both exploited propaganda opportunities to the full was that of sport. As "young" movements they had a natural affinity for the sporting world, with its emphasis on physical prowess and perfection. Realizing that the eyes of the world were increasingly focusing on great international sporting occasions, Mussolini exploited the opportunities provided by Italy's hosting of the soccer World Cup as Hitler did those provided by the Berlin Olympics.

There was nothing new about propaganda in the 1920s and 1930s; what was new was the sheer scale, ambitiousness, and systematic organization of the barrage of influences to which the citizens of Italy and Germany were subjected under Mussolini and Hitler. The same techniques were of course employed by the Soviet communists and were later imitated by many others. But it is arguable that fascist propaganda was particularly successful because the fascist perceptions about human nature and the importance of emotional and imaginative responses were substantially accurate; at any rate, they certainly play a fundamental role in modern Western advertising techniques, where visual impact and the role of repetition are fundamental. The Nazis made great efforts to propagandize the British during the war with radio broadcasts by William Joyce, the celebrated "Lord Haw-Haw." This classic technique of using an enemy "national" (though, in fact, Joyce was not a British citizen) to demoralize the enemy apparently backfired, for the popularity of the nickname suggests that the broadcasts were regarded primarily with amusement in Britain. The Mussolini regime exploited the talents of the much more celebrated Ezra Pound on Radio Rome, but his attitudes were too eccentric and extreme to be convincing. Both regimes made use of the lesser-known British profascist agitator John Amery (1912–1945), who was hanged as a traitor at the end of the war.

Since the 1990s the growth of the Internet has opened up a whole array of new propaganda opportunities for fascists, as for other political movements. Holocaust deniers and white supremacists and others have availed themselves freely of the opportunities opened up to them by a means of mass communication that is difficult if not impossible to police effectively.

Cyprian Blamires

See Also: ANTI-SEMITISM; ARCHITECTURE; ART; BERLIN OLYMPICS, THE; BOOKS, THE BURNING OF THE; CALENDAR, THE FASCIST; D'ANNUNZIO, GABRIELE; EDUCATION; ETHIOPIA; FASCIST PARTY, THE; FILM; FIUME; GERMANY; GOEBBELS, (PAUL) JOSEPH; GOOSESTEP, THE; *HEIL HITLER!;* HITLER, ADOLF; HOLOCAUST DENIAL; ITALY; JOYCE, WILLIAM; LEADER CULT, THE; *LEBENSRAUM;* LEISURE; MUNICH (BEER-HALL) PUTSCH, THE; MUSSOLINI, BENITO ANDREA; NAZISM; MYSTICISM; NEO-NAZISM; NUREMBERG RALLIES, THE; POSTWAR FASCISM; POUND, EZRA; PRESS, THE; PROGRESS; RACIAL DOCTRINE; RADIO; RELIGION; RIEFENSTAHL, LENI; ROME; SALUTES; SPEER, ALBERT; SPORT; *STÜRMER, DER;* SWASTIKA, THE; SYMBOLS; TECHNOLOGY; THEATER; TOTALITARIANISM; *TRIUMPH OF THE WILL; VÖLKISCHER BEOBACHTER,* THE; WHITE SUPREMACISM; YOUTH MOVEMENTS

References

Bramstead, E. K. 1965. *Goebbels and National Socialist Propaganda, 1925–1945.* London: Cresset.

Courcy, Anne de. 2003. *Diana Mosley.* London: Chatto and Windus.

Doherty, Martin. 2000. *Nazi Wireless Propaganda: Lord Haw-Haw and British Public Opinion in the Second World War.* Edinburgh: Edinburgh University Press.

Gentile, E. 1996. *The Sacralization of Politics in Fascist Italy.* London: Harvard University Press.

Giesen, Rolf. *Nazi Propaganda Films: A History and Filmography.* Jefferson, NC: McFarland.

Herzstein, R. E. 1979. *The War that Hitler Won: The Most Infamous Propaganda Campaign in History.* London: Hamish Hamilton.

Hurndall, Christopher. 1996. *The Weimar Insanity: Photographs and Propaganda from the Nazi Era.* Lewes: Book Guild.

Kallis, Aristotle. 2005. *Nazi Propaganda and the Second World War.* Basingstoke: Palgrave Macmillan.

Taylor, Richard. 1998. *Film Propaganda: Soviet Russia and Nazi Germany.* London: I. B. Tauris.

Vincent, Arnold W. 1998. *The Illusion of Victory: Fascist Propaganda and the Second World War.* Berne: Peter Lang.

Welch, D. 2002. *The Third Reich: Politics and Propaganda.* London: Routledge.

Williams, Manuela. 2005. *Mussolini's Propaganda Abroad.* London: Frank Cass.

Zeman, Zbynek. 1973. *Nazi Propaganda.* Oxford: Oxford University Press.

PROSTITUTION: See SEXUALITY

PROTESTANTISM AND NAZISM

National Socialist writers like Alfred Rosenberg, Dietrich Klagges (1891–1971), Graf Ernst zu Reventlow (1869–1943), Jakob Wilhelm Hauer, and many others all saw Martin Luther, the founder of German Protestantism, as a folk hero who inspired their work. Some historians have attributed blame to German Protestantism as at least partially responsible for the disaster of National Socialism—for example, a recent work by Steigmann-Gall. But the claim that Martin Luther's theology led directly to National Socialism has little scholarly support. Uwe Siemon-Netto (1995) discusses this issue at length, refuting the claims of William Shirer and various other writers who promoted the viewpoint. There is, however, considerable evidence that nineteenth-century German liberal theology indirectly contributed to the growth of National Socialism. For example, the works of authors like Adolf von Harnack were very popular among National Socialists. Reading his *What Is Christianity?* (1901) appears to have led to a widespread loss of faith among many young intellectuals who later embraced National Socialism as a political religion. This relationship was recognized in the 1930s by authors like the Swiss theologians Karl Barth (1886–1968) and Arthur Frey (born 1897) in the *Cross and Swastika: The Ordeal of the German Church* (1938) and E. O. Lorimer in her *What Hitler Wants* (1939). Similarly, in *Germany's New Religion: The German Faith Movement* (1937), Jakob Wilhelm Hauer, Karl Heim (1874–1958), and Karl Adam (1876–1966) all agreed that the theological roots of National Socialist ideology were to be found in the emergence of liberal Bible criticism and the development out of Protestant liberalism of increasingly heterodox versions of traditional Christianity. More recently, Alan Davies (1988) confirmed this argument, as did James Biser Whisker (1990), demonstrating the connections between German Protestant Liberalism and Nationalist thinking.

Further evidence of the degeneration of Liberal Protestant theology leading to a complete rejection of Christianity that paved the way for conversions to National Socialism is found in numerous archival documents, particularly private letters. These documents show that many intellectuals understood their personal involvement with National Socialism in terms of a process of conversion in which Protestant Liberal Theology led them to view orthodox Christian teaching as "unscientific" and unsuited for the modern world. Instead of embracing Protestant liberalism, they realized that it failed to answer the very questions that it raised against traditional theology. The classic spiritual journey was from orthodox childhood Christian belief, often in the form of Pietism, through Liberal Theology, which they embraced during their early years at university, to agnosticism. As agnostics, particularly following their experiences in the army during World War I, they began to read Nietzsche, and through his works they saw what they perceived to be the logic of National Socialism, often experiencing intense emotional conversion experiences that caused them to repudiate the teachings of Christ in favor of a new Germanic identity. Apart from people and movements that sought to create a new personal and national identity based on a spiritualized version of National Socialism, there were others that claimed to be discovering a new form of German Christianity. The most famous of these groups was the Glaubensbewegung "Deutsche Christen," or Faith Movement of the German Christians, which attracted large numbers of Protestant clergy and laity during the 1930s. While some sincere Christians were initially misled by this movement, the truth was that its leaders embraced religious beliefs that clearly placed them well beyond the fold of historical Christianity.

Irving Hexham

See Also: ANTI-SEMITISM; ARYANISM; BONHOEFFER, DIETRICH; CHRISTIANITY; CONFESSING CHURCH, THE; DINTER, ARTHUR; GERMAN CHRISTIANS, THE; GERMAN FAITH MOVEMENT, THE; GERMANNESS (*DEUTSCHHEIT*); GERMANY; HAUER, JAKOB WILHELM; HITLER, ADOLF; LIBERALISM; LIBERALISM (IN THEOLOGY); LUTHER, MARTIN; LUTHERAN CHURCHES, THE; NAZISM; NIEMOELLER, MARTIN; NIETZSCHE, FRIEDRICH; RELIGION; ROSENBERG, ALFRED; THEOLOGY

References
Bergen, Doris L. 1996. *Twisted Cross: The German Christian Movement in the Third Reich.* Chapel Hill: University of North Carolina Press.
Conway, John. 1968. *The Nazi Persecution of the Churches.* Toronto: Ryerson.
Davies, Alan. 1988. *Infected Christianity: A Study of Modern Racism.* Montreal: McGill-Queens University Press.
Goebbels, Michael Joseph. 1989. *Michael.* Los Angeles: Amok.
Poewe, Karla. 2005. *New Religions and National Socialism.* London: Routledge.
Siemon-Netto, Uwe. 1995. *The Fabricated Luther.* St. Louis: Concordia.
Steigmann-Gall, Richard. 2003. *The Holy Reich: Nazi Conceptions of Christianity, 1919–1945.* Cambridge: Cambridge University Press.
Whisker, James Biser. 1990. *The Social, Political, and Religious Thought of Alfred Rosenberg: An Interpretive Essay.* Washington, DC: University Press of America.
Zabel, James A. 1976. *Nazism and the Pastors: A Study of the Ideas of Three Deutsche Christen Groups.* Missoula, MT: Scholars Press.

PROTOCOLS OF THE ELDERS OF ZION, THE

Anti-Semitic Russian literary invention dating from the end of the nineteenth century, describing an international Jewish elite plotting to subvert and control society. This myth of Jewish world conspiracy with demonological and millenarian motifs was an early element of Nazi ideology in the 1920s. Addressing perennial concerns about Jewish separation and success, such conspiracy theory invariably projects believers' fears, hopes, and intentions onto a demonized "other," who may be then legitimately persecuted or exterminated. Described as a "warrant for genocide," the *Protocols* encouraged pogroms in czarist Russia and contributed to the atmosphere of opinion in which the Holocaust became possible. The tract sets out the Elders' secret plans for a Jewish world government. The first nine protocols criticize liberalism and outline methods for achieving global power, while the remaining fifteen outline the nature of the final world state. The first protocol indicates that a plot has been in operation over many centuries to place political power firmly in the hands of the Elders of Zion (that is, the Jewish elite). All traditional order and authority are supposedly being dissolved by liberalism and democracy, thus identified as the best means to destabilize the traditional Gentile world and render it more amenable to Jewish despotism. The Elders have destroyed religion, especially the Christian faith, through the intellectual fashions of Darwinism and Marxism. The Elders' final goal is the Messianic Age, when the world will be ruled by a Jewish sovereign of the House of David. Such dominion will be divinely ordained, since the Jews are God's chosen people.

The origins of the *Protocols* lie in medieval anti-Judaism in the Christian world. Jews were then supposed to worship the Devil, and a corresponding political myth described a secret Jewish government in Muslim Spain, directing a war against Christendom with the aid of sorcery. The myth of Jewish world conspiracy represents a modern adaptation of this old demonology. During the French Revolution conspiracy theories involving philosophes, liberals, and Freemasons circulated among those disturbed by the profound revolutionary challenges to traditional authority of the Church and monarchy. By the early nineteenth century, Jews had become fellow suspects in this political mythology of subversive and secret elites. By the mid-nineteenth century, democracy, liberalism, secularism, and socialism had become significant political factors abhorrent to many conservatives. Their fears and anxieties about the future of the old order led to a rearguard action against the proponents of the new, mobile society. As this political transformation offered manifold new opportunities to Europe's Jews, they in turn became the target of this powerful reaction.

Norman Cohn has traced the origin, motivation, and development of the *Protocols* through French, German, and Russian anti-Semitic texts of the nineteenth century up to their actual composition sometime around 1897 by the Russian secret police or other reactionaries wishing to defend the autocratic czarist regime. At the same time, these conspiracy texts were used by agitators to incite pogroms against ordinary Jews living in the Pale of Settlement. Mythical accounts of the *Protocols'* origins vary. The earlier editions, published by Russian anti-Semitic agitators between 1903 and 1906, claimed that the translation was made from a document taken from the "Central Chancellery of Zion, in France"; White Russian emigres believed that they originated among late-nineteenth-century French occultists and Theosophists. A mystical-apocalyptic edition of the *Protocols* was first included in the second edition of *The Great in the Small* (1905) by Sergei Nilus (1861–1930). A fanatical defender of the czarist autocracy, Nilus hated secular modernity, seeing in democracy and technological progress the omens of Antichrist. A later edition of 1917, *He Is Near, Hard by the Door,* was read by Alfred Rosenberg in Russia. Nilus described the *Protocols* as a strategic plan for the conquest of the world, worked out by Jewish leaders during the many centuries of dispersion, and finally presented to the Council of Elders by Theodor Herzl at the first Zionist Congress, held at Basle in August 1897.

Following the Russian Revolution and the Civil War (1917–1921), many White Russian refugees brought the *Protocols* to Germany, and a German edition appeared in 1919. The myth of a secret Jewish plot in Russia was then transformed by Nazi ideology into powerful political propaganda, implicating all Jews in the subversion of nations, cultural Bolshevism, and international finance, and thereby legitimizing the Holocaust. The *Protocols* appealed to international readerships dislocated by war, defeat, and economic loss in the 1920s, and they were translated into English, Swedish, Danish, Norwegian, Finnish, Romanian, Hungarian, Lithuanian, Polish, Bulgarian, Spanish, Italian, Greek, Japanese, and Chinese. Arabic and South American editions have continued to be published since the defeat of Nazi Germany, while reprints of older European editions circulate among small neo-Nazi parties and groupuscules in Europe, Russia, and the United States up to the present.

Nicholas Goodrick-Clarke

See Also: ANTI-SEMITISM; ARYANISM; BOLSHEVISM; CONSPIRACY THEORIES; COSMOPOLITANISM; DEMOCRACY; FREEMASONRY/FREEMASONS, THE; FRENCH REVOLUTION, THE; GROUPUSCULES; HOLOCAUST, THE; LIBERALISM; MARXISM; MIDDLE EAST, THE; MYSTICISM; MYTH; NAZISM; NEO-NAZISM; OCCULTISM; ORTHODOX CHURCHES, THE; RACIAL DOCTRINE; ROSENBERG, ALFRED; RUSSIA; SECULARIZATION; SOCIAL DARWINISM; SOCIALISM; TRADITIONALISM; UNITED STATES, THE (POST-1945); ZIONISM

References

Cohn, Norman. 1967. *Warrant for Genocide: The Myth of the Jewish World-conspiracy and the Protocols of the Elders of Zion.* London: Eyre and Spottiswode.

Eisner, Will. 2005. *The Plot: The Secret Story of the Protocols of the Elders of Zion.* New York: W. W. Norton.

Leo Baeck Institute Year Book. 1987. *Leo Baeck Institute Year Book: Nineteenth-Century Antisemitism and Nazi Rule.* Vol. 32. London: Secker and Warburg.

Marsden, Victor E., ed. 1921. *The Protocols of the Learned Elders of Zion.* London: Britons.

PROTOFASCISM

Term used to categorize what is seen as an earlier or primitive, rather than fully fledged, form of generic fascism. Applied to individual personalities, political thinkers, and intellectuals, as well as to intellectual and cultural currents and political and cultural movements, it indicates their partial ideological kinship to interwar fascism and usually, though not necessarily, identifies them as precursors of it. The term *protofascism* can be applied to the ideas and practices of a wide range of ideologues and movements. It may be applied to individual figures such as Maurice Barrès, the French novelist and militant "integral" nationalist who fought an election campaign in 1898 on a platform of what he called "socialist nationalism," and was an acknowledged ideological inspiration to interwar French and other European fascists; Giovanni Papini, a major Italian nationalist intellectual whose writings both before, during, and after World War I influenced the Italian Fascist leader Benito Mussolini and gave a general cultural credibility to the Fascist regime; Gabriele D'Annunzio; Pierre Drieu La Rochelle, the French poet, novelist, and essayist who in the late 1930s joined and then left Jacques Doriot's fascist movement, the PPF, and who was a collaborationist writer during the Nazi wartime occupation of France; Julius Evola, the artist and maverick philosopher who, while never holding any official political or cultural position in the Italian Fascist regime, was one of the voices behind the emergence of "totalitarian" and racist extremism of the late 1930s, continuing to publicize his views after 1945.

Barrès, D'Annunzio, and Papini were themselves contributors to and participants in the development of a general European protofascist cultural climate in the decades immediately before the outbreak of World War I that affected a significant minority of Europe's intellectual and cultural elites and its educated classes, especially in France, Italy, Germany, and the Austrian Empire. New ideas challenged what was and remained the dominant mode of thinking, that human "progress" would ensue from the application of reason and the scientific method to the management of society as well as to material production. The "revolt against reason" drew on the sometimes misapplied works of the English naturalist Charles Darwin and the German philosopher Friedrich Nietzsche, and on the findings of the new social sciences, which in the rational pursuit of knowledge about human society and mentality were exposing the irrationality of much of human behavior. The French thinker Georges Sorel's revision of a materialist Marxism, which made violence and "myth" the inspiration of mass revolutionary action, greatly influenced the outlook of the prewar syndicalist movements of Italy and France, and of other unconventional socialists like Mussolini, a revolutionary socialist leader in Italy before the war.

Some of the carriers and proponents of the "counter-culture of unreason" straddled the worlds of culture and politics. The Italian Futurists, later among the earliest members of the Italian Fascist movement in the 1920s, were cultural iconoclasts who promoted politics-as-art, celebrating the dynamism, speed, and excitement of the modern machine age and vandalizing everything that was old, established, and traditional. A prewar Florentine cultural journal, *La Voce,* which also influenced Mussolini, anticipated a new national spiritual consciousness among Italians to be realized by imperialist war. These ideas were also given a more obviously political shape by extreme nationalist movements—for example, the Action Française and various prewar patriotic and anti-Semitic leagues in France—and in Italy, the Nationalist Association formed in 1910.

In other areas of the prewar European radical Right touched by the late-nineteenth-century counterculture, particularly in Germany and the Austrian empire, there developed a *völkisch* nationalism that—in place of what was seen as the soulless materialism and rootless individualism and anonymity of secularized mass urban industrial society—offered a "superior" and distinctive ethnic German "folk" culture and way of life. *Völkisch* nationalism was often racist, with "Germanic" blood regarded by Julius Langbehn, one of its most widely read exponents, as literally the carrier and transmitter of the German people's moral virtues and qualities. Politically, *völkisch* nationalism marked the various anti-Semitic movements and parties in the German-speaking parts of the Austro-Hungarian Empire, and in Germany itself, the Pan-German League, an umbrella organization for a collection of racist and middle-class special interest and pressure groups.

After, and as a result of, Germany's traumatic defeat in World War I in 1918 and transition to the democratic Weimar Republic, the country's protofascist counterculture was broadened by new streams of radical nationalist ideas. These were expressed, as before the war, in cultural circles, the press, books, and pamphlets, wherein the main authors of the denunciation of Weimar as national cultural humiliation and decline were the "conservative revolutionaries" Arthur Moeller van den Bruck and Edgar Jung, and "national revolutionaries" such as the soldier-writer Ernst Jünger, who, like the war veterans' paramilitary leagues, made a myth of the experience of wartime combat and of the frontline soldier as the basis of national regeneration.

Philip Morgan

See Also: INTRODUCTION; ACTION FRANÇAISE; ANTI-SEMITISM; ART; AUSTRO-HUNGARIAN EMPIRE/HABSBURG EMPIRE, THE; BARRES, AUGUSTE MAURICE; BLOOD; BOULANGISM; CAESARISM; CONSPIRACY THEORIES;

D'ANNUNZIO, GABRIELE; DECADENCE; DORIOT, JACQUES; DRIEU LA ROCHELLE, PIERRE; EVOLA, JULIUS; FASCIST PARTY, THE; FIUME; FRANCE; FUTURISM; GERMANNESS (*DEUTSCHHEIT*); GERMANY; GOBINEAU, COMTE ARTHUR DE; IMPERIALISM; INTEGRAL NATIONALISM; ITALY; JÜNGER, ERNST; LAGARDE, PAUL DE; LANGBEHN, JULIUS; MARXISM; MATERIALISM; MAURRAS, CHARLES; MOELLER VAN DEN BRUCK, ARTHUR; MOSCA, GAETANO; MUSSOLINI, BENITO ANDREA; MYTH; NATIONALISM; NAZISM; NIETZSCHE, FRIEDRICH; PALINGENETIC MYTH; PANGERMANISM; PAPINI, GIOVANNI; PARAMILITARISM; PARETO, VILFREDO; PROGRESS; *PROTOCOLS OF THE ELDERS OF ZION, THE;* RACISM; ROOTLESSNESS; SCHÖNERER, GEORG RITTER VON; SOCIAL DARWINISM; SOREL, GEORGES; SPENGLER, OSWALD; SYNDICALISM; TECHNOLOGY; TOTALITARIANISM; TRADITIONALISM; VIOLENCE; *VOLK, VÖLKISCH;* WAR VETERANS; WEIMAR REPUBLIC, THE; WORLD WAR I

References

Griffin, Roger. 1993. *The Nature of Fascism.* London: Routledge.

———. 1995. *Fascism.* Oxford: Oxford University Press.

Hermand, Jost. 1992. *Old Dreams of a New Reich: Volkish Utopias and National Socialism.* Bloomington: Indiana University Press.

Pulzer, P. G. 1988 [1964]. *The Rise of Political Anti-Semitism in Germany and Austria.* London: Peter Halban.

Sternhell, Zeev. 1978. *La droite révolutionnaire, 1885–1914. Les origines françaises du fascisme.* Paris: Seuil.

———. 1986. *Neither Left nor Right: Fascist Ideology in France.* London: University of California Press.

PSYCHIATRY: *See* EUGENICS

PSYCHOANALYSIS

Both the ideals of this movement—antiauthoritarian, individualist, secular, and egalitarian—and the ethnic composition of its leadership and its membership could lead only to a head-on collision with the interwar fascist regimes in Europe. Psychoanalysis was officially condemned and eliminated by the Nazis wherever they went. However, following the departure for exile of all Jewish psychoanalysts in Germany, there were psychotherapists, those considered of pure Aryan race, who continued to work in Nazi Germany, using psychoanalytic techniques, under the aegis of the German Institute for Psychological Research and Psychotherapy, led by M. H. Goering.

Most of those identifying with psychoanalysis who had regarded themselves as German-speaking intellectuals in the new modern Europe found themselves after 1933 (or even before) threatened with annihilation. Not only their ideals but also their physical survival was at stake. The encounter with Nazism meant becoming exiles and refugees. The great human tragedy was not only a shock and a trauma. For intellectuals committed to Enlightenment ideals, this was also a challenge. From their places of exile, mostly the United States, early generations of psychoanalysts offered their contributions in an attempt to account for the massive failure of modernity in the form of fascist mass movements. To do that, what was needed was a combination of political (Marxist, or Marxian) and psychological (psychoanalytic) analysis. Attempts to combine Marxism and psychoanalysis were common during the twentieth century. Freud himself, however, had been an elitist, almost a reactionary, and a combination of psychoanalysis and Marxism was not something he could fathom. What Wilhelm Reich, Herbert Marcuse, Erich Fromm, Theodor Adorno, Max Horkheimer, and others claimed was that vulgar Marxism, which views culture as a mere appendix to the relations of production, had failed. Marxism had to be combined with cultural-psychological analysis in order to explain historical processes. The challenge was to uncover the psychological mechanism underlying political domination. With the help of psychoanalytic concepts, focusing on unconscious learning in early childhood, new questions were being posed and then answered. Is conformity a matter of realistic adaptation, or is it internalized? Could domination become a permanently assimilated part of one's personality structure? The unanimous opinion was, following Wilhelm Reich, that the suppression of all spontaneity in the authoritarian family is the prototype for all oppressive social structures. Because it is tied to the character structure of all individuals, it gains the support of the masses. This led to the authoritarian personality concept, and to the legacy of the idea of authoritarianism in the social sciences. Authoritarianism, despite its limitations, still plays a role in social science research on fascism all over the world.

There have been other approaches inspired by psychoanalysis. Erik H. Erikson, another exile who grew up in Germany and wrote about Germans with real empathy and identification, initially offered an interpretation of Adolf Hitler as an individual and of the Nazi movement that was quite classical in its emphasis on Oedipal elements. Hitler presented as a glorified older brother, rebelling against a harsh father and attached to an idealized mother. Subsequently, however, Erikson preferred using his own formulation, focusing on adolescence and identity. He described a "traumatic identity loss" that overtook Germany following the 1918 defeat and the Treaty of Versailles and that resulted in a widespread "historical identity confusion," leading to a takeover by a gang of overgrown criminal adolescents. During World War II, Walter C. Langer produced a secret personality analysis of Hitler that focused on his attachment to his mother, expressed in his always using the term *Motherland* for Germany, and on his hostility toward his father, projected on the Austro-Hungarian Empire. Bruno Bettelheim, who spent time in the Dachau Concentration Camp in 1938, offered an original and controversial analysis of prisoners' behavior in the camp situation, using psychoanalytic terms, that has been a classic since its publication in 1943.

Benjamin Beit-Hallahmi

See Also: INTRODUCTION; ANTI-SEMITISM; AUSTRO-HUN-GARIAN EMPIRE/HABSBURG EMPIRE, THE; AUTHORITARI-ANISM; CONCENTRATION CAMPS; ELIADE, MIRCEA; ELITE THEORY; ENLIGHTENMENT, THE; FAMILY, THE; FREUD, SIGMUND; FROMM, ERICH; GERMANY; HITLER, ADOLF; INDIVIDUALISM; NAZISM; NOVEMBER CRIMINALS/ *NOVEMBERBRECHER*, THE; PSYCHODYNAMICS OF PALIN-GENETIC MYTH, THE; PSYCHOLOGY; REICH, WILHELM; VERSAILLES, THE TREATY OF; WAR VETERANS; WORLD WAR I

References

Beit-Hallahmi, B. 2004. "Authoritarianism and Personality: Some Historical Reflections." In *History and Psychoanalysis: Tel-Aviv Yearbook for German History 2004*, edited by M. Zuckerman. Tel-Aviv: Tel-Aviv University.

Bettelheim, Bruno. 1943. *Individual and Mass Behavior in Extreme Situations.* New York: Ardent Media.

Cocks, G. 1985. *Psychotherapy in the Third Reich.* New York: Oxford University Press.

Goggin, James E., and Eileen Brockman Goggin. 2000. *The Death of Jewish Science: Psychoanalysis in the Third Reich.* West Lafayette, IN: Purdue University Press.

Langer, Walter C. 1973 [1943]. *The Mind of Adolf Hitler.* London: Secker and Warburg.

Reich, W. 1970. *The Mass Psychology of Fascism.* Trans. Mary Higgins. Edited by Mary Higgins and Chester M. Raphael. New York: Farrar, Straus and Giroux.

PSYCHODYNAMICS OF PALINGENETIC MYTH, THE

The psychodynamics of the palingenetic myth, which has been identified as the core of generic fascism, are irreducibly complex. However, aspects have been illumi-nated by Klaus Theweleit's theory that some of the more fanatical Nazis were plagued by deep-seated fears of dissolution and disintegration and the drive to be reborn in a highly regimented and structured new order devoted to destroying external enemies that were at bottom projections of inner "demons." Another fruitful approach, pioneered by Richard Fenn, attributes the conspicuous role played by fascist mythopoeia and liturgy in interwar Europe to the recourse to ritualistic emotions and behavior provoked by the apparent collapse of society and Western civilization as a whole that unleashed fears that the "world" is literally running out of time. This reflex can be seen as driven by a profound urge to escape from what Mircea Eliade has called the "terror of history," the deep-seated fears unleashed at a time of social breakdown of falling into the well of meaningless linear time that is devoid of transcendence and denies the prospect of even a secular redemption and immortality. Clearly, all these notions are deeply imbued with archetypal mythic elements that underline how much the contents of "political myth" are still shaped by the patterns of sacred myth.

Roger Griffin

See Also: INTRODUCTION; ARENDT, HANNAH; CALENDAR, THE FASCIST; CIVILIZATION; DECADENCE; DEGENERACY; FASCIST PARTY, THE; GERMANY; ITALY; MYTH; NAZISM; NEW ORDER, THE; PALINGENETIC MYTH; PSYCHOANALY-SIS; PSYCHOLOGY; RELIGION; REVOLUTION; SECULARIZA-TION; SPENGLER, OSWALD; TOTALITARIANISM

References

Griffin, Roger. 1991. *The Nature of Fascism.* London: Routledge.

Theweleit, Klaus. 1987–1989. *Male Fantasies: Women, Floods, Bodies, History.* 2 vols. Minneapolis: University of Minnesota Press.

PSYCHOLOGY

First, psychology contributed to the development of some key ideas in Nazi racial ideology. There were notable psychologists who claimed that there are inherent differences in the capacities and temperaments of the different "races." Eugenics, or the so-called science of racial improvement, was established by Francis Galton, the founder of British psychology. Racial and eugenic psychology has declined since the end of World War II, but it survives in the work of several psychologists who continue to assert racial differences in intelligence. The second connection between psychology and Nazism is that many psychologists, especially those who emphasize the role of learning rather than biology in human behavior, have sought to understand the psychological roots of racist beliefs. It has been claimed that one personality type—the authoritarian personality—is particularly susceptible to the message of generic fascism.

Much early psychology developed as a form of Social Darwinism. Francis Galton, who was Darwin's cousin, attempted to construct a psychology based on the principles of the new evolutionary theory. He sought to show that there were inherent differences in ability between individuals and between groups. Accordingly, humanity could be divided into separate biological "races" that could be graded as "superior" or "inferior" on the basis of their inherited characteristics. According to Galton, European "races" possessed the highest, most evolved qualities, while African races had the lowest, least evolved ones. In keeping with later theorists of race, Galton worried that the racial strength of the "superior races" was under threat, because their biologically inferior members were breeding at a higher rate than their superior members. Galton devised the concept of "eugenics" as an applied psychology that would recommend measures for improving the racial quality of the nation. Eugenics, in the Galtonian version, sought to implement a "scientific" politics that would discourage, or even forbid, the "inferior" members of society from breeding—and also prevent members of "superior races" from breeding with members of "inferior" ones. Societies for the promotion of eugenic ideas were set up in Britain, the United States, and other European countries. Many of the eugenicists, including Galton, believed that democracy imperiled the biological health of "the superior" race because the "inferiors" outnumbered the "superiors." Eugenic policies, therefore, would be possible only in a society governed by an elite oligarchy, for the masses would not willingly restrict their own right to breed.

In the early years of the twentieth century, the biological and eugenic aspects of psychology were particularly influential. Galton's successor at London University was Karl Pearson, who is known within psychology for having developed complex statistical techniques for differentiating clusters of characteristics. Pearson, even more than Galton, was concerned about the deleterious effects of breeding between races. William McDougall, whose *Introduction to Social Psychology* (1908) was the first textbook of social psychology, was another eugenicist desperately worried by the racial state of the Northern Europeans. When he immigrated to the United

States, McDougall joined a growing band of psychologists who believed that immigration policy should be determined by strict racial and eugenic considerations. McDougall was cautiously hopeful that the rise of fascism would enable eugenic politics to be put fully into operation.

The ideologues of Nazi Germany took over the key ideas of eugenic philosophy, as they claimed that their policies were based on "race-science." There were a number of psychologists in Germany who explicitly supported the Nazi regime, most notably E. R. Jaensch, whose book *Der Gegentypus* (1938) contrasted the healthy Aryan personality with the biologically degenerate personalities of liberals, communists, and Jews. Despite this, Nazi race science tended to draw more upon the work of physical anthropologists, biologists, and anatomists than psychologists. However, the assumptions of Galtonian eugenics can be detected within the Nazi policy of "euthanasia," designed to eliminate so-called unhealthy racial characteristics within the "superior race" and to weaken or destroy "weaker" races.

After 1945, when the full horror of eugenic politics was revealed, the racist elements of psychology went into decline. Not only was the very notion of "race" questioned by social anthropologists, but behaviorists and social psychologists disputed the extent to which human characteristics are fixed by genetic inheritance. However, the eugenic tradition was given a boost in the late 1960s and the 1970s, when Arthur Jensen in the United States and Hans Eysenck in Britain claimed that blacks are genetically less intelligent than whites. These findings were greeted with enthusiasm by neofascist groups. A network of conservative and racist foundations has continued to fund such work. Jensen and Eysenck based their arguments on the results of IQ studies reporting that African-Americans tended on average to have lower scores than white Americans. They argued that individual differences in intelligence can be largely explained in terms of genetic factors. Accordingly, group differences, such as the average IQ scores of whites and blacks in the United States, could also be assumed to be genetically determined. Critics claimed that the argument was flawed because it is illegitimate to generalize from findings about individuals to those about groups. The genetic determination of individual differences within a group does not mean that differences between groups must be explained genetically. For instance, one might suppose that individual differences in height are determined to a large extent by heredity. However, the fact that one generation might be taller on average than their parents does not mean that these group differences should be explained genetically. Therefore, the mean differences in IQ scores between blacks and whites can be explained in terms of social factors, such as poverty and social discrimination.

Within the history of psychology, the emphasis on biological factors has always been contested by those psychologists who stress the importance of learning and culture. In the 1930s, many psychologists, especially Jewish psychologists in Germany, transformed the psychological issue of race. For them, the key issue was not the racial determination of psychological characteristics but the unwarranted belief in race differences. Thus the problem of race became recast as the problem of race prejudice. This transformation was to be seen clearly in the work of experimental psychologists who fled from Nazi Germany to settle in the United States. For example, Kurt Lewin explored the social conditions in which groups were likely to develop antidemocratic and prejudiced attitudes. Lewin was particularly influential in inspiring a younger generation of U.S. social psychologists to study group relations and prejudice. This work provided the foundations for much modern experimental social psychology.

Another trend to emerge from opponents to Nazism was the incorporation of insights from psychoanalysis to understand the psychological basis of fascism. This was particularly marked in the work of the Frankfurt School, which combined unorthodox Marxist social theory with Freudian insights. Max Horkheimer and Theodor Adorno argued that the irrational appeal of fascism was based in the conditions of advanced capitalism. Wilhelm Reich suggested that sexual frustration lay at the core of fascism's appeal. Erich Fromm claimed that modern society produces existential insecurity; consequently, many people sought to find psychological security in the certainty of authoritarian beliefs and racist prejudices.

The most systematic attempt to study the psychological basis of fascism came after World War II in the United States. Adorno, in collaboration with psychologists Frenkel-Brunswick, Levitt, and Sanford, constructed a series of opinion and personality scales, as well as conducting in-depth psychoanalytic interviews. They claimed that there is a "fascist personality" that displays an "authoritarian syndrome." Authoritarians need firm, hierarchical beliefs as a reaction against their own inner psychological insecurities. Race prejudice was one component within this attitudinal and emotional syndrome. The theory of authoritarianism provoked a huge amount of empirical research, not to mention methodological critique. Although there is some evidence that contemporary fascist and right-wing groups may recruit proportionally more authoritarians, the support for fascism is not necessarily confined to one particular personality type. Moreover, it is now recognized that not only authoritarians will obey orders to commit cruel, even genocidal actions. Fascism, as a complex social phenomenon, cannot be explained in terms of a single personality dimension.

Michael Billig

See Also: ANTHROPOLOGY; ANTI-SEMITISM; ARYANISM; AUTHORITARIANISM; BOLSHEVISM; CAPITALISM; ELITE THEORY; EUGENICS; EUTHANASIA; EYSENCK, HANS JÜRGEN; FREUD, SIGMUND; FROMM, ERICH; GERMANY; HEALTH; HITLER, ADOLF; HOLOCAUST, THE; LIBERALISM; LORENZ, KONRAD; MARXISM; NATIONALISM; NAZISM; PSYCHOANALYSIS; PSYCHODYNAMICS OF PALINGENETIC MYTH, THE; RACIAL DOCTRINE; REICH, WILHELM; SCIENCE; SOCIAL DARWINISM; SOCIOLOGY; *SONDERWEG*, THE; UNITED STATES, THE (PRE-1945); WAR VETERANS; WORLD WAR I; WORLD WAR II

References

Duckitt, John. 2003. "Prejudice and Intergroup Hostility." Pp. 559–600 in *Oxford Handbook of Political Psychology*, edited by David Sears et al. Oxford: Oxford University Press.

Kühl, Stefan. 1994. *The Nazi Connection: Eugenics, American Racism and German National Socialism*. Oxford: Oxford University Press.

Richards, Graham. 1997. *"Race": Racism and Psychology*. London: Routledge.

Staub, Ervin, and Daniel Bar-Tal. 2003. "Genocide, Mass Killing and Intractable Conflict." Pp. 710–751 in *Oxford Handbook of Political Psychology*, edited by David Sears et al. Oxford: Oxford University Press.

Tucker, William H. 1994. *The Science and Politics of Racial Research*. Urbana: University of Illinois Press.

QADHAFI (GADDHAFI), MU'AMMAR (born 1942)

Effective sole ruler of Libya since 1969 and practitioner of a political philosophy with echoes of classic fascism. Mu'ammar al-Qadhafi was born in 1942 in a desert location some 30 kilometers from Sirta. He distinguished himself in his schooldays by being punished for his antimonarchist political activities. His studies culminated in a course of higher military education in Benghazi that he completed in 1965. He also attended a course at the British military academy at Sandhurst. After World War II, with the termination of Italian occupation and later British administration of Tripolitania and Cyrenaica, and French administration of Fezzan, king Idris al-Sanusi returned in late 1950 to reign over Libya as the grandson of the founder of the Sanusi dynasty. Libya joined the League of Arab States (1953) and UNO (1956). From the mid-1960s the rich oil and natural gas reserves of the country were exploited, transforming a hitherto poor land into a rich country. Arab nationalist and socialist agitation, in line with the ideas of Egyptian president Gamal Abdel Nasser, suppressed in Libya by the royal authorities, resulted nonetheless in the formation of a clandestine Central Committee of Unionist Free Officers, with Mu'ammar al-Qadhafi as its leader. On 1 September 1969 the monarchy was toppled by a twelve-member Revolutionary Command Council headed by Qadhafi. From then onward he became the effective sole ruler of the country, called initially the Arab Libyan Jamhiriyya (Republic)—to which a list of other adjectives was progressively added: "Socialist," "Popular," and "Great."

In general terms, Qadhafi's ideas have elements of puritan Islam, a sense of mission, and a radical populism. He has not limited his agitation to Arab or Islamic countries, extending it to Africa and even the entire world, as openly declared in his booklet *Al-Kitab al-Akhdhar (The Green Book)*, widely disseminated and translated into many languages. His consolidation of absolute power started in the early 1970s (Zuwara speech of 15 April 1973) with a number of measures, including the abrogation of all existing legislation, "freeing" Libya (the country of the "Revolution"), eliminating the "nation's enemies," an administrative revolution, a cultural revolution in the direction of the desired consciousness (that is, state-imposed mode of thinking), and the introduction of paramilitary organizations (branded as the "armed nation"). In early 1973, so-called people's committees were introduced with the aim of promoting direct participation by the masses in public life, as opposed to the parliamentary form of government, which was rejected. Arab, African, and Islamic elements of the ideology were emphasized, Qadhafi's vanguard rule in all these spheres being promoted. *The Green Book* treated Libyan practices as the final solution to the problem of democracy. According to it, only the Libyan option is truly democratic, all others being distorted, false versions of democracy.

Next, Qadhafi claims that he has solved the economic problems of humanity by the introduction of socialism. Finally, he deals with the "solution" of the social problem by introducing the concepts of the individual, family, tribe, nation, state, and community—defining all of these terms and claiming to have found the final solution to humanity's major problems.

Qadhafi has subjected all state institutions and virtually every citizen to the will of an authoritarian-type hierarchical rule, with himself at the top. The range of discretionary powers includes the persecution of Libyan opposition both inside the country and abroad, assassination of opponents abroad, support for extremists in the Arab world (especially extremist Palestinians), interference in African affairs, and organization of terrorist acts (openly admitted in the case of the 1987 Lockerbie bombing).

Hassan Jamsheer

See Also: AUTHORITARIANISM; COMMUNITY; CORPORATISM; DEMOCRACY; DICTATORSHIP; ECONOMICS; FAMILY, THE; LIBYA; MASSES, THE ROLE OF THE; MIDDLE EAST, THE; PALESTINE; PARAMILITARISM; PARLIAMENTARISM; REVOLUTION; SOCIALISM; STATE, THE; TOTALITARIANISM; *VOLKSGEMEINSCHAFT*, THE; WORLD WAR II

References
Arnold, Guy. 1996. *The Maverick State: Gaddafi and the New World Order.* London: Continuum International.
Calvocoressi, Peter. 1996. *World Politics since 1945.* London: Longman.
Haley, P. Edward. 1984. *Gaddafi and the United States.* Westport, CT: Greenwood.
Qadhafi, Mu'ammar. 1980. *Al-Kitab al-Akhdhar (The Green Book).* Tripoli: International of Studies upon "The Green Book."
The Middle East and North Africa. 2000. London: Europa.

QUADRUMVIRS, THE

The four Fascist leaders (*Quadrumviri*) appointed by Mussolini to plan and lead the March on Rome: Michele Bianchi, Emilio de Bono, Cesare M. De Vecchi, and Italo Balbo. The title recalled that of the four magistrates who governed a *municipium* in Ancient Rome.

Cyprian Blamires

See Also: BALBO, ITALO; BONO, EMILIO DE; FASCIST PARTY, THE; ITALY; MARCH ON ROME, THE; MUSSOLINI, BENITO ANDREA

Reference
Lyttelton, Adrian. 2004. *The Seizure of Power: Fascism in Italy 1919–1929.* London: Routledge.

QUISLING, VIDKUN (real name Abraham Laurits 1887–1945)

Fuehrer of Norway's fascist party, NS, and (unlike some of his colleagues in European fascism) a man of considerable moral reputation when he entered politics in 1933. Quisling's early military education had won him awards as a most gifted army officer, but in 1922 he abandoned his career in the general staff to devote himself to international relief and refugee work, acting as the Red Cross representative in Ukraine in 1922–1923, later as a League of Nations envoy in the Balkans, and ending up in Moscow from 1925 to 1929, working for Dr. Nansen's Armenian repatriation project. During these years he also was employed by the Norwegian legation to take care of the then empty British legation, 1927–1929, which earned him an MBE. Originally left-leaning and somewhat of an amateur philosopher, Quisling was by the 1920s seduced by racist and rightist ideas. In 1931 he founded an unsuccessful clandestine "Nordic" movement that he had to leave when serving as minister of defense in the agrarian cabinet from 1931 to 1933. Thereafter, the movement was transformed into a political party, Nasjonal Samling (NS; National Unity), but even though its ranks seemed to be swelling with enthusiastic young fascists, the NS polled so unsuccessfully in the elections of 1933 and 1936 that it subsequently almost disintegrated. Quisling, however, trusted that his time would come; indeed, after the September 1939 outbreak of World War II, when his minuscule party acted as one of the very few organizations in Norway sympathizing with Germany, he managed to make his way to Berlin and to Hitler himself, with whom he conducted two long secret talks in the Reich chancellery on 14 and 18 December 1939. Through these talks Hitler became convinced that German control over Scandinavia would be vital in the war with Britain, and Quisling in return received generous subsidies for his party. When the Wehrmacht struck on 9 April 1940, Quisling, confident of Hitler's backing, proclaimed himself prime minister, but he had to step down as his coup proved counterproductive for the German army's campaign. Later he was summoned to Hitler, who promised to re-install him as soon as his party, bolstered with new German grants and enjoying the position of the only legal movement in Norway, had gained sufficient strength. Thus, by January 1942, Quisling became prime minister for the second time.

The Quisling regime in Norway, from 1942 to 1945, was a failure, squeezed as it was between Germany's steadily more repressive occupation measures and the growing hostility of the Norwegian population. Quisling's stubborn attempts to implement Nazi principles in public life and to encourage young Norwegians to enroll in the Waffen-SS increased his unpopularity further. When he was arrested after the liberation and put on trial in Oslo, the verdict quite naturally was that of capital punishment. Ever since, the word *quisling* has served as a synonym for *traitor* in the world's major languages.

H. F. Dahl

See Also: ARYANISM; EXPANSIONISM; GERMANY; HITLER, ADOLF; NAZISM; NORDIC SOUL, THE; NORWAY; WAFFEN-SS, THE; WEHRMACHT, THE; WORLD WAR II

References
Dahl, Hans F. 1999. *Quisling: A Study in Treachery.* London: Cambridge University Press.
Høidal, Oddvar. 1989. *Quisling: A Study in Treason.* Oslo: Universitetsforlaget.

RACIAL DOCTRINE

A crucial element in the ideology of German Nazism but not in that of Italian Fascism; consequently, not a part of the core of generic fascism. The origins of allegedly "scientific" classifications of mankind on the basis of "race" are to be found at the end of the eighteenth century (for example, Christian Meiners, Johann Friedrich Blumenbach). These classifications were results both of Enlightenment efforts to reconstruct a complete world order based on logical criteria and of the urge of a Protestant religious revival movement known as pietism to define the position of man in nature. They set up a hierarchy of the races based on the criterion of aesthetics. There was considerable debate as to whether the development of the races was affected up to a certain degree by the environment (for example, J. B. Antoine de Lamarck) or whether racial characteristics were completely determined by heredity.

In the nineteenth century, different thinkers interpreted history and society as a function of human "races" and their rivalry for supremacy. There were several attempts to assess "races" and their mixtures statistically. In close relationship with these theories, which were frequently subject to fears about the "decline" of the "white race," was the development of eugenics or racial hygiene, established by Francis Galton (1822–1911). Eugenics was aimed not simply against hereditary diseases but also against the mixture of races.

In the second half of the nineteenth century, politicians picked up on racial doctrine. It played a substantial role as a legitimizing ideology for imperialist expansion. Two variations are to be differentiated: Darwinist racism postulated a right of the "higher races" to subjugate and exterminate the "lower" ones. The ideology of the civilizing mission legitimized imperialist expansion with the obligation to transfer the achievements of civilization to the "lower races." In the remaining slave-owner states (the United States and Brazil), the racial doctrine played an important political role. In addition to racism directed against people of color, there emerged also a new form of racist anti-Semitism. In contrast to traditional anti-Judaism, it did not reject the Jews because of their religion but regarded them as an "alien" and essentially hostile nation or hostile race (for example, Wilhelm Marr). This ideology, which was a reaction to the gradual emancipation of the Jews, did, however, partly merge with religious anti-Judaism (for example, Adolf Stoecker). Anti-Semitism culminated in theories of a Jewish world conspiracy. Richard Wagner's "Germanism" had a great impact, as did the racial theories of Joerg Lanz von Liebenfels, whose magazine *Ostara*—"newspaper for blond people" (founded in 1905)—was eagerly read by the young Adolf Hitler. The shock of World War I was favorable to the further proliferation of racial doctrine. The collapse of apparently eternal institutions made plausible race theories with their inherently apocalyptic visions. Race theories experienced a boom in politics, journalism, and science during the interwar period, especially in the states on the losing side at the end of World War I. The *Rassenkunde* ("race lore") of Hans F. K. Guenther, for example, sold several hundred thousands of copies in Germany between 1922 and the end of the Nazi period. Within the ideology of National Socialism, racism, which postulated an antagonism between Aryans and Jews, was always in competition with Pangermanist nationalism in the categories of traditional power politics. Racial doctrine was transferred into law soon after Hitler's seizure of power: The *Gesetz zur Wiederherstellung des Berufsbeamtentums* (Act for the Re-establishment of the Civil Service with Tenure) of 7 April 1933 excluded "non-Aryan" people from public office. The Nuremberg Laws of September 1935 excluded Jews from the citizenry and prohibited marriage as well as sexual intercourse (considered as "race dishonor") between non-Jews and Jews. Racial doctrine culminated in the millionfold murder of "non-Aryan" people in the course of World War II.

In other fascist movements, racial doctrine played a less important role. For instance, in Italy it did not become part of the official state ideology until 1938. However, the borders between nationalism and the racial doctrine had already become fluid. After World War II, racial doctrine had lost its legitimacy. States that based their constitutions on it were internationally outlawed (South Africa, Rhodesia). Nevertheless, neofascist organizations like the NSDAP Aufbau- und Ausland organisation, White Aryan Resistance, or Blood and Honour continued to espouse a racial ideology.

Christian Koller

See Also: ANTHROPOLOGY; ANTI-SEMITISM; ARYANISM; CHRISTIANITY; COSMOPOLITANISM; EUGENICS; FAMILY, THE; FASCIST PARTY, THE; GERMANNESS (*DEUTSCHHEIT*); GERMANY; GÜNTHER, HANS FRIEDRICH KARL; HEALTH; HITLER, ADOLF; HOLOCAUST, THE; ITALY; KU KLUX KLAN, THE; LIEBENFELS, JÖRG ADOLF JOSEF LANZ VON; MEDICINE; NATIONALISM; NAZISM; NEO-NAZISM; NORDIC SOUL, THE; NUREMBERG LAWS, THE; PANGERMANISM; POSTWAR FASCISM; PROTESTANTISM AND NAZISM; *PROTOCOLS OF THE ELDERS OF ZION, THE*; RACISM; ROOTLESSNESS; SCIENCE; SEXUALITY; SOCIAL DARWINISM; SOUTH AFRICA; SS, THE; STOECKER, ADOLF; UNITED STATES, THE (POST-1945); WAGNER, (WILHELM) RICHARD; WHITE SUPREMACISM; WORLD WAR I; WORLD WAR II; ZIMBABWE

References

Balibar, Etienne, and Immanuel Wallerstein. 1992. *Race, Nation, Class: Ambiguous Identities.* New York: Verso.
Fredrickson, George M. 2002. *Racism: A Short History.* Princeton: Princeton University Press.
Gillette, Aaron. 2001. *Racial Theories in Fascist Italy.* London: Routledge.
Memmi, Albert. 1999. *Racism.* Minneapolis: University of Minnesota Press.
Miles, Robert. 1989. *Racism.* London: Routledge and Kegan Paul.
Mosse, George L. 1978. *Towards the Final Solution: A History of European Racism.* New York: Howard Fertig.
Taguieff, Pierre-André. 2001. *The Force of Prejudice: On Racism and Its Doubles.* Minneapolis: University of Minnesota Press.

RACIAL HYGIENE: *See* EUGENICS; MEDICINE; RACIAL DOCTRINE

RACISM

A distinctive feature of German Nazism—though not of Italian Fascism—that it proclaimed enthusiastically and unapologetically as based on "scientific" findings. This new layer of "scientific" racism was superimposed on a pre-existing tradition of racial, cultural, and religious prejudice that had taken various forms in previous centuries. Perhaps its most dominant—and definitely its most widely shared—form was anti-Semitism. A number of historians have invoked the Nazi regime's unique emphasis on "eliminationist anti-Semitism" and its distinct obsession with an extreme form of "racial revolution" as evidence of its departure from the generic mold of fascist ideology as established by Mussolini. It is true that, on the level of both ideological fanaticism and political determination, National Socialist Germany went far beyond any comparable form of racialism sponsored by fascist movements or regimes in the rest of interwar Europe. If, however, one accepts that fascism's itinerary to racism passes through specific indigenous traditions (which, in turn, signified particular notions of "rebirth") and an overriding focus on national elitism, then neither anti-Semitism nor any other form (or intensity) of racism should be considered as either a sine qua non or a qualitative *differentia specifica*. Fascist ideology remained flexible enough to endorse or reject particular strands of racialism, to prioritize, mitigate, or abandon racist intentions.

It is, indeed, more accurate to speak about fascism's propensity for some form of racism as an integral aspect of its self-legitimation as an elite force. Italian Fascist ideology—which had shown little inclination to subscribe to either biological theories or cliche anti-

Semitism prior to the late 1930s—used the experience of imperialism after the victory in Ethiopia (1936) to promulgate a racist doctrine of segregation between "white" (Italian) and "coloured" (Ethiopian) people. At the same time, anti-Semitism (biological or not) became a point of ideological convergence between a host of interwar fascist movements—from Hungary's Arrow Cross (whose leader, Szálasi, propagated his vision of an "a-Semitic" country) to the BUF's conversion to an anti-Jewish platform to combat what was seen as the principal "threat" to the supremacy of the British Empire. The experience of National Socialist policy in the direction of actively persecuting and, later, murdering Jews and other forms of "life unworthy of living" acted as a political catalyst, moral instigation, and psychological legitimation for the launching of similar projects of racism (though not comparable in intensity) across the continent.

While the pseudo-scientific model of interwar racism was brought into overwhelming disrepute in the shadow of the revelations concerning the "Final Solution," racism's relevance to ethnocentric models of nationalism has not worn off. Generic economic shifts—first with the wave of immigration during the boom years of the 1950s and 1960s, and subsequently through the "unwanted" influx of immigrants desperate to escape from the poverty of the Third World—have kept a reservoir of racially motivated resentment alive in some sectors of postwar European societies. Extreme-right-wing movements or parties—from the violent neo-Nazi groups in Germany to "systemic" parties in many European countries (National Front in France, British National Party in the United Kingdom, the Swiss People's Party)—have championed (though by no means monopolized) the case for recapturing a nationally homogeneous society and impeding further alleged "erosion" of the national and wider European population pool. For different reasons, verbal and sometimes physical assaults on immigrants barely conceal the persistence of a racist discourse that remains the preferential terrain of extreme-right-wing movements but that has also made substantial inroads into more mainstream contemporary political discourse. The primary emphasis may have shifted—from the biological to the economic and social field—but patterns of continuity between interwar and postwar arguments (as well as of their primary sponsors) are unmistakable.

Aristotle Kallis

See Also: INTRODUCTION; ANTI-SEMITISM; ARROW CROSS; ARYANISM; CROATIA; DECADENCE; DEGENERACY; ELITE THEORY; ETHIOPIA; EUGENICS; EXPANSIONISM; FÖRSTER-NIETZSCHE, ELISABETH; GERMANNESS (*DEUTSCHHEIT*); GERMANY; GREAT BRITAIN; HITLER, ADOLF; HOLOCAUST, THE; HUNGARY; IMMIGRATION; IMPERIALISM; ITALY; KU KLUX KLAN, THE; MEDICINE; MOSLEY, SIR OSWALD; MUSSOLINI, BENITO ANDREA; NATIONAL FRONT (FRANCE), THE; NATIONAL FRONT (UK), THE; NATIONALISM; NEO-NAZISM; PALINGENETIC MYTH; PANGERMANISM; POSTWAR FASCISM; PSYCHOLOGY; RACIAL DOCTRINE; ROCK MUSIC; SCIENCE; SKINHEAD FASCISM; SOUTH AFRICA; SWITZERLAND; SZÁLASI, FERENC; UNITED STATES, THE; USTASHA; WHITE SUPREMACISM; XENOPHOBIA; ZIMBABWE

References

Burleigh, M., and W. Wippermann. 1991. *The Racial State, Germany 1933–1945.* Cambridge: Cambridge University Press.

Cheles, L., R. Ferguson, and M. Vaughan, eds. 1995. *The Far Right in Western and Eastern Europe.* New York: Longman.

Macmaster, N. 2001. *Racism in Europe, 1870–2000.* New York: Palgrave.

Weindling, P. 1989. *Health, Race and German Politics between National Unification and Nazism.* Cambridge: Cambridge University Press.

RADIO

The rise of Italian Fascism and Nazism in the early twentieth century coincided with a golden age of radio. As the tool of choice for propagandists, radio also dominated mass communications in the domestic sphere. Totalitarian movements generally valued mass participation in politics. Traditional autocracies had distrusted the masses and sought to exclude them as much as possible, but communists and fascists wanted to mobilize the masses—albeit under conditions in which they could be easily manipulated. The marriage of totalitarianism and radio broadcasting was an important marker of the shift from elite to mass society.

Lenin's description of radio as a paperless newspaper that could reach the masses would have had particular appeal to the Nazis. For Hitler and Mussolini, radio was an extension of the mass rally, although it lacked the feedback provided by the roar of the crowd. Ultimately, the Nazis aimed to systematize the propaganda process as an integral part of a new political system. They drew on early communications research into the relationship between the communicator and the audience. Propaganda effects were to be more important than debates about the message. Truth, half-truth, or downright falsehood could be used to mobilize the

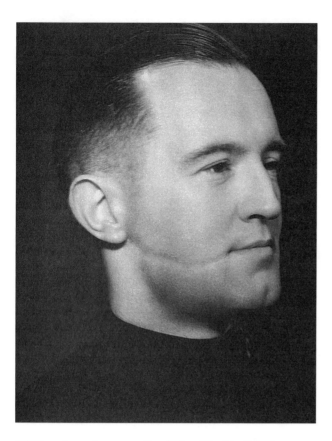

William Joyce, known as 'Lord Haw Haw' in Britain, was a leading figure in Oswald Mosley's British Union of Fascists in the 1930s who later broadcast Nazi propaganda from Germany to the UK during World War II. (Corbis)

frowned upon. All things "Aryan" or German were glorified. Political mobilization of the masses was facilitated by their mobilization behind the new medium. State radio was to have a monopoly of audience time and attention. There were severe penalties for unauthorized listening to foreign broadcasts, access to short-wave radios was restricted, and many foreign stations were jammed. The Reich mass-produced inexpensive receivers, the *Volksempfänger*, optimized for easy tuning to *Deutschlandsender* frequencies. These were found in homes and workplaces alike. The drama of Nazi rallies was conveyed through live broadcasts. In the absence of the satellite feeds of today, short-wave radio links were used to relay coverage of events over great distances. There were direct radio links with Italy and even with Japan. Radio thus contributed to the globalization of the Axis system.

Guglielmo Marconi, the radio pioneer, helped Radio Rome in its early years. Italy also hired Ezra Pound, the poet, to broadcast in English to North America. Radio was obviously more than a domestic propaganda tool: radio signals ignore political boundaries. There was a fear of their potential power, especially among the democracies. Symptomatic of the desire to control aggressive nationalist broadcasts was a 1936 League of Nations declaration outlawing war propaganda altogether. As in other things, German and Italian broadcasters merely ignored these League pronouncements. Ironically, fascist international broadcasting was a spur to the development of BBC external services. The British initially believed that propaganda was essentially a wartime activity. The vitriol of Italian broadcasts to Arab countries, exploiting British human rights violations in Palestine, convinced them, however, to begin regular peacetime transmissions in Arabic and to see international broadcasting as more than a home service for the empire.

Radio played a crucial role in the prelude to war in Central Europe during the late 1930s. Initial Nazi efforts focused on German-speaking populations across European frontiers where Hitler had irredentist claims. Germany's medium-wave transmitters were ideal for broadcasting over short distances. Moreover, the message frequently fell on receptive ears. Because of their chauvinist tone, fascist external services were more successful in reaching German or Italian cultural communities abroad than at persuading foreigners. Germany therefore directed concerted broadcast campaigns at the Saar region, which was disputed with France, at Austria, at Sudeten Germans in Czechoslovakia, and at Germans in Poland. Alleged discrimination against those populations was a common theme. In the case of

population once the technique was properly mastered. As soon as they came to power, the Nazis quickly dismantled the Weimar Republic's fledgling public service broadcasting network, and radio became the responsibility of the Ministry of Public Enlightenment and Propaganda, rather than of the state telecommunications apparatus. This ministry was headed by Joseph Goebbels, propaganda chief of both party and state. Goebbels's closeness to the Fuehrer at the end testified to his commitment to Nazism, as well as to the value that Hitler attached to propaganda. Radio was undoubtedly the primary instrument in his arsenal.

The national domestic service, *Deutschlandsender* ("German Transmitter/Station"), accompanied by regional stations, was soon subject to tight control. Censorship not only prevented criticism, as in traditional autocracies, but also prescribed "correct" opinion. Although light entertainment or classical music softened the pill, even low culture was politicized. Supposedly "Jewish" musical forms and African-American jazz were the Saar and Austria, expectations were raised that they would eventually be rejoining the Reich. The barrage was not entirely unexpected. Yet, as the Nazis matched their broadcasts with other provocative acts, ranging from coup plots in Austria to troop movements on several frontiers, international broadcasting became even more controversial and elicited diplomatic protests. As with risky military maneuvers, the Germans were capable of toning down broadcasts when realpolitik demanded it.

The outbreak of fighting posed a new and exciting challenge for Goebbels. Despite efforts to soften some of his overseas output, the bombastic tone of domestic propaganda came through. Victories were announced with a loud, sometimes trumpeted announcement, the *Sondermeldung*. While propaganda broadcast into Russia emphasized liberation from Bolshevism, Hitler sometimes hinted at future coexistence with a weakened Britain. This led the Germans to vary the hostility of messages beamed to the United Kingdom, depending on the prevailing mood. Prefiguring later communist transmissions in esoteric languages during the Cold War, they tried to broadcast in West European minority languages, including Breton and Irish, though with derisory results. There were also black propaganda stations like the New British Broadcasting Station, purporting to represent fascist supporters in Britain. The programs actually came from German-occupied territory. Such tactics, of course, occur in all propaganda wars. Yet their use by the fascists was particularly ironic, because it was doubtful if ethnic groups cultivated by Hitler would really have thrived in a future German-dominated world order.

The seminal figure in Germany's broadcasts to Britain was William Joyce, nicknamed "Lord Haw Haw" by the British press. He was born in the United States of Irish parents but had a British passport. He had been a supporter of Mosley's fascists when he lived in London. As war approached, Joyce went to Berlin to work for Germany's overseas radio service, the Rundfunk Ausland. His broadcasts, featuring much sarcasm and anti-Semitic content, aroused as much amusement as support for the Nazis. He was captured, tried for treason, and hanged by the British at the end of the war. Japan's star broadcaster was Ikoku Toguri, dubbed "Tokyo Rose" or "Orphan Ann." Her "Zero Hour" programs targeted U.S. troops in the Pacific, though there were also broadcasts to North America itself. Many were relatively professional—certainly more so than those of postwar Asian totalitarian states like North Korea. The Japanese interspersed jazz request shows with the seductive tones of Tokyo Rose. She

sounded caring and easy-going. Newscasts were blatantly biased but framed to sound factual rather than emotional. The overall tone was lighter than that of Germany's broadcasts. (For audio excerpts, see Kaelin 2002). However, the shriller Japanese domestic radio censored U.S. cultural fare, including much of its popular music, as "decadent." In both domestic and foreign output, the Japanese could not bridge the gap between the reality of heavy losses and the theme of struggle until victory. Because the war was supposedly fought for a near-divine emperor, many simply believed the propaganda from the national radio, Nippon Hoso Kyokai (NHK). The decision to put the emperor on air to announce surrender, albeit without using the word, finally rendered him human and compelled the Japanese people to reassess their fate.

The Italian Fascist and Nazi regimes invested heavily in technology as a symbol of power. Germany built a state-of-the-art radio-transmitting complex to compete with the facilities of the BBC. The Zeesen transmitter site near Berlin had only two weak short-wave transmitters in 1933. Up to seven 50-kilowatt transmitters were added in 1936, to provide coverage of the Olympic Games. More were added in 1939 and during the war. Some could operate at 100 kilowatts. In addition, there were numerous medium-wave transmitters on Germany's borders with most European states. Since medium wave was used for national broadcasting in Europe, this increased the prospects of accidental reception by potentially new listeners. Transmitters seized in captured territories were also used. These included the powerful Luxembourg station that was later recaptured by advancing Allied armies. It was particularly well sited for broadcasting to Britain.

Italy also had well-designed short-wave transmitters, though fewer than the Germans. In addition, Italy used a medium-wave facility at Bari to reach Greece and the Arab countries. In the Far East, Japan established a chain of medium and short-wave relays, the *Toa Hoso*, incorporating stations in Korea, China, Singapore, and the Philippines. Yet despite much preparation for war, NHK had no relay stations in the Americas. Short-wave broadcasts had to cross polar regions to reach eastern North America and Europe, mostly by means of 50-kilowatt transmitters. This was relatively low power for transpacific broadcasting, and the polar route left signals vulnerable to atmospheric disturbance.

A spectacular but short-lived use of radio by extremists of the Right occurred in the early 1990s under the auspices of the Japanese Aum Shinrikyo cult. Although ostensibly religious, they engaged in quasi-military preparations and had a clear political agenda. Their focus on tradition located them on the Right rather than the Left, although that is a relatively loose classification. Aum exploited the chaos in Russia as communism unraveled. The cult rented much of Radio Moscow's vast array of powerful transmitters to beam a daily half-hour short-wave broadcast across Eurasia. It was also broadcast locally in Japan. The programs were largely incoherent and inaccessible, and, as such, were more attractive to cult followers than to newcomers. Like Goebbels's transborder broadcasts to Central Europe, they reinforced the loyalty of the base. The Russian contract was terminated after Aum's sarin gas attack on the Tokyo subway system in 1995.

A fringe outgrowth of U.S. right-wing talk radio in the 1990s provided the next opportunity for far-right access to radio power. The AM broadcast band emerged as a home for mainstream conservative opinion in the Clinton years. However, the far Right were also quick to jump on this bandwagon. Armed groups holed up in shacks or on ranches pronounced themselves in revolt against Washington. Some declared sovereignty; others prepared for violence. Falling foul of the law, the militia Right was forced to regroup and redirect its message at core supporters to avoid further hostile attention. This underground movement required a new medium: short-wave radio, targeting a domestic audience. Private short-wave stations now carried programming by figures associated with neo-Nazism, or that backed far-right militia causes, such as those associated with the Waco and Ruby Ridge controversies. Militia programs and the more extreme neo-fascist output seemed to operate alongside a broader strand of "patriot" broadcasting. The patriots labored on survivalist themes, including advice on food storage under adverse environmental conditions, and preparations for biochemical or even nuclear warfare. They encouraged amateur and short-wave radio hobbies as alternative media outlets in a time of danger. Stations that carried patriot programming, such as WWCR in Nashville, were nominally evangelical services broadcasting to countries outside the United States. Yet their actual signal coverage area, program themes, and contact phone numbers pointed to a U.S. target audience. Short-wave was being used as a means of narrowcasting, consolidating a niche following rather than chasing the mass listenership sought by the 1930s fascist propagandists.

Derek Lynch

See Also: ANTI-SEMITISM; ARYANISM; AUSTRIA; AXIS, THE; BERLIN OLYMPICS, THE; BOLSHEVISM; CHRISTIANITY; COLD WAR, THE; COUGHLIN, FR. CHARLES EDWARD; CZECHOSLOVAKIA; EXPANSIONISM; FASCIST PARTY, THE; GERMANNESS (*DEUTSCHHEIT*); GERMANY; GREAT BRITAIN; HITLER, ADOLF; IRREDENTISM; ITALY; JAPAN; JAPAN AND WORLD WAR II; JOYCE, WILLIAM; LEAGUE OF NATIONS, THE; LEISURE; MARCONI, GUGLIELMO; MARXISM; MASSES, THE ROLE OF THE; MIDDLE EAST, THE; MOSLEY, SIR OSWALD; MUSIC (GERMANY); MUSIC (ITALY); MUSSOLINI, BENITO ANDREA; NATIONALISM; NAZISM; NEO-NAZISM; NUREMBERG RALLIES, THE; PALESTINE; POLAND AND NAZI GERMANY; POSTWAR FASCISM; POUND, EZRA; PROGRESS; PROPAGANDA; SOVIET UNION, THE; SUDETENLAND, THE; SURVIVALISM; TECHNOLOGY; TOTALITARIANISM; UNITED STATES, THE (POSTWAR); WEIMAR REPUBLIC, THE; WHITE SUPREMACISM; WORLD WAR II

References

Herzstein, Robert. 1980. *The War that Hitler Won: The Most Infamous Propaganda War in History.* London: Abacus.

Kaelin, J. C. 2002. "EarthStation1.com's Radio Propaganda Page: Orphan Ann/Tokyo Rose." http://www.earthstation1.com/Tokyo_Rose.html (accessed 1 October 2004).

Kenny, Mary. 2003. *Germany Calling: A Personal Biography.* New York: New Island.

Maes, Ludo. 2004. "Shortwave Radio Transmitters in Germany." *Transmitter Documentation Project.* http://www.tdp.info/d.html (accessed 1 December 2004).

O'Donoghue, David. 1998. *Hitler's Irish Voices: The Story of German Radio's Wartime Irish Service.* Belfast: Beyond the Pale.

Owen, Ursula. 1998. "Hate Speech: The Speech that Kills." *Index on Censorship* (online edition) no. 1 (January). http://www.oneworld.org/index_oc/issue198/hate-speech.html (accessed 1 January 1999).

Robbins, Jane. 2001. "Presenting Japan: The Role of Overseas Broadcasting by Japan during the Manchurian Incident, 193–37." *Japan Forum* 13, no. 1: 41–54.

Ryo, Namikaya. 1983. "Japanese Overseas Broadcasting: A Personal View." Pp. 319–333 in *Film and Radio Propaganda in World War II,* edited by K. R. M. Short. London: Croom Helm.

Zeman, Z. A. B. 1964. *Nazi Propaganda.* Oxford: Oxford University Press.

RASSENHYGIENE: See EUGENICS

RATIONALISM

National Socialism rejected "rationalism" as "one-sided intellectualism," the attitude of a "spiritually rootless modern man," or denounced it as "Jewish rationalism," although "irrationalism" was not presented as a positive counterconcept. Italian Fascism spoke of the dissolution of everything firm in "pure movement" and made a cult out of the permanent, restless mobilization of the masses on the basis of a diffuse vitalistic feeling of life. Mussolini followed an innate sense of mission when he portrayed himself in the tradition of Augustus and the Roman emperors, while Hitler too spoke frequently of his and Germany's "destiny."

In National Socialism the formula "blood and soil" was one of the most blatantly irrationalist slogans of the movement. It implied an antirationalistic emotionalism of "rootedness, earthedness, love of home, connectedness to earth and blood." In 1934 an official *Pocket Book of the National Socialist State* stated: "These two words [that is, blood and soil] comprise the whole National Socialist program." But the Nazi leadership did not speak with one voice in this area. In the Nazi leadership there were terrifyingly "rational" political technocrats like Fritz Todt, Albert Speer, and a great number in the ministerial and administrative bureaucracy, as well as cold power politicians like Joseph Goebbels and Martin Bormann. Alongside them there were mystical-irrationalist dreamers like Himmler, with his mystique of a Blood Order and a racial elite, Julius Streicher with his pathological and pornographic race hatred, or the "Chief Ideologist," Alfred Rosenberg, with his confused Germanic religion and his fantasies of colonizing the East. In general, irrational motifs in National Socialism resulted from a specific hostility to modernity combined with *völkisch*-reactionary race utopias and sentimental, antirational Romanticism. But there was also a contrasting embrace of "modernity," with technocratic-rational features such as the mobilization and militarization of all areas of life and the politicization of the whole of existence, powerful and speedy industrialization of the economy, and bureaucratic efficiency—culminating in the "murderously efficient" registration and elimination of whole population groups.

Markus Hattstein
(translated by Cyprian Blamires)

See Also: INTRODUCTION; ABSTRACTION; ANTI-SEMITISM; BLOOD; BLOOD AND SOIL; BORMANN, MARTIN; ELITE THEORY; ENLIGHTENMENT, THE; FASCIST PARTY, THE; FUTURISM; GERMANIC RELIGION; GERMANNESS (*DEUTSCHHEIT*); GERMANY; GOEBBELS, (PAUL) JOSEPH; HIMMLER, HEINRICH; HITLER, ADOLF; ITALY; LIBERALISM; MATERIALISM; MODERNITY; MUSSOLINI, BENITO ANDREA; MYSTICISM; MYTH; NATURE; NAZISM; NORDIC SOUL, THE; PALINGENETIC MYTH; PARLIAMENTARISM; POSITIVISM; PSYCHOLOGY; RELIGION; ROOTLESSNESS; ROSENBERG, ALFRED; SCIENCE; SOUL; SPEER, ALBERT; STREICHER, JULIUS; SYMBOLS; TECHNOLOGY; TOTALITARIANISM; UTOPIA, UTOPIANISM; VITALISM; *VOLK, VÖLKISCH*; WARRIOR ETHOS, THE; *WELTANSCHAUUNG*

References
Aschheim, S. 1992. *The Nietzsche Legacy in Germany, 1890–1990.* Berkeley: University of California Press.
Cobley, Evelyn. 2002. *Temptations of Faust: The Logic of Fascism and Postmodern Archaeologies of Modernity.* Toronto: University of Toronto Press.
Golomb, Jacob, and Robert S. Wistrich, eds. 2002. *Nietzsche, Godfather of Fascism? On the Uses and Abuses of a Philosophy.* Princeton: Princeton University Press.
Gregor, A. J. 1969. *The Ideology of Fascism: The Rationale of Totalitarianism.* New York: Free Press.
Griffin, R. D. 1991. *The Nature of Fascism.* London: Routledge.
Lukács, George. 1981. *The Destruction of Reason.* Trans. P. Palmer. Atlantic Heights, NJ: Humanities.
Mosse, George L. 1964. *The Crisis of German Ideology: Intellectual Origins of the Third Reich.* London: Weidenfeld and Nicholson.
Wolin, Richard. 2004. *The Seduction of Unreason: The Intellectual Romance with Fascism from Nietzsche to Postmodernism.* Princeton: Princeton University Press.

RAUSCHNING, HERMANN (1887–1982)

Nazi politician who turned into one of the most celebrated contemporary "insider" critics of Hitler. His book *The Revolution of Nihilism* and later books bore testimony to the ruthlessness of Nazism. Rauschning spent his early years in Danzig as a farmer and acted as a conservative publicist. When the NSDAP won broad support, he joined its ranks (1931) and became president of the Senate of Danzig (1933). He was forced by Hitler to retire after he had some differences with Gauleiter Forster on questions relating to the economy. Rauschning immigrated to Switzerland in 1936, and in 1948 to the United States.

Fabian Virchow

See Also: ANTIFASCISM; "ANTI-" DIMENSION OF FASCISM, THE; GERMANY; HITLER, ADOLF; NAZISM; NIHILISM

References
Conway, John. 1983. "Hermann Rauschning as Historian and Opponent of Nazism." *Canadian Journal of History* 8: 67–78.
Rauschning, Hermann. 2004. *Voice of Destruction: Conversations with Hitler.* Whitefish, MT: Kessinger.
———. 2005. *Revolution of Nihilism: Warning to the West.* Whitefish, MT: Kessinger.

RAUTI, GIUSEPPE ("PINO") (born 1926)

Important figure in Italian Neo-Fascism and disciple of Julius Evola. Rauti fought for the Salò Republic, and after the war he joined the Movimento Sociale Italiano. Initially he found its policies too moderate for him, and he left to form Ordine Nuovo. In 1969 he returned to the MSI and went on to be elected to both the Italian and European parliaments.

Cyprian Blamires

See Also: EVOLA, JULIUS; ITALY; MOVIMENTO SOCIALE ITALIANO, THE; POSTWAR FASCISM; SALÒ REPUBLIC, THE

Reference
Ferraresi, Franco. 1996. *Threats to Democracy: The Radical Right in Italy after the War.* Princeton: Princeton University Press.

REBATET, LUCIEN (1903–1972)

Novelist and journalist on *L'Action Française* from 1929, anti-Semite, antidemocratic advocate of dictatorship, and admirer of Hitler who was regarded by his fellow fascist Brasillach as "the most stubborn and the most violent among us all." His work *Les Décombres* (1942, later re-edited and enlarged as *Mémoires d'un Fasciste*) demonstrated that he had moved from being a supporter of the integral nationalism of Action Française to being an enthusiast for Nazi Germany: it contains a virulent attack on French "decadence." During the Vichy regime Rebatet worked as drama and film columnist. After the war he was condemned to death in 1946, but the sentence was commuted; he emerged from imprisonment in 1952. He later wrote further novels that attracted high praise in some quarters.

Cyprian Blamires

See Also: ACTION FRANÇAISE; ANTI-SEMITISM; DEMOCRACY; DICTATORSHIP; FRANCE; GERMANY; INTEGRAL NATIONALISM; NAZISM; VICHY

References
Carroll, David. 1995. *French Literary Fascism: Nationalism, Anti-Semitism and the Ideology of Culture.* Princeton: Princeton University Press.
Pryce-Jones, David. 1981. *Paris in the Third Reich.* London: Collins.

REBIRTH: *See* PALINGENETIC MYTH
REDESDALE, LORD: *See* MITFORD FAMILY, THE
REGENERATION: *See* PALINGENETIC MYTH

REICH, WILHELM (1897–1957)

Psychoanalyst and student of fascism who popularized the idea that the prevalence of the pattern of the traditional family made the masses receptive to the appeal of authoritarian regimes. On account of his independent and unconventional opinions, Reich was expelled in 1933 from the German Communist Party and in 1934 from all psychoanalytical organizations. In 1933 he immigrated to Scandinavia and in 1939 to the United States, where he died in prison in 1957. He was the first to apply psychoanalytical methods to the phenomenon of fascism. The first edition of his *Mass Psychology of Fascism,* published in 1933, was an attempt at a psychoanalytical explanation of fascist movements and tried to answer the question of why the crisis situations of the 1920s and 1930s had not led—as Marxist ideologues had prophesied—to the dictatorship of the proletariat. In the third edition, in 1942, Reich replaced all of the Marxist conceptions with general ones.

For Reich, fascism was the "expression of the irrational structure of mass man." In his view, the mediator of this irrational structure and the receptivity for mystique is the authoritarian family. The mediation takes place through moral inhibition of the natural sexuality of the child. The inhibition is accomplished with the help of religious angst. The result is an anxious child, timid, fearful of authority, and obedient. Sexual repression makes a person passive and apolitical and leads to a quest for satisfaction through substitutes, such as sadism, a mass psychological foundation of war. It also makes people receptive to uniforms, military parades, and marching. The association of the masses with National Socialism took place, according to Reich, because of their identification with the Fuehrer, a father figure promising to be an authoritarian protector. On the grounds of their identification with the Fuehrer and the authoritarian state, Hitler's supporters could look upon themselves as defenders of "the people" and "the nation." Reich attributed particular importance to race theory. He pointed to its irrational character and posited a connection between sexual repression and class domination.

The concept put forward by Reich and others to explain the success of fascism with the help of a particular socialization, the authoritarian personality, has provoked a great deal of criticism. The main objection is that the relationship between the authoritarian personality and authoritarian behavior is not unambiguously defined. We cannot either deduce or prognosticate the behavior of a man out of a knowledge of the features of an authoritarian personality. Moreover, critics have questioned the close connection between social behavior in relation to psychic structures and the early childhood socialization process.

Michael Schäbitz (translated by Cyprian Blamires)

See Also: ARENDT, HANNAH; AUTHORITARIANISM; DICTATORSHIP; FROMM, ERICH; FAMILY, THE; GERMANY; HITLER, ADOLF; ITALY; LE BON, GUSTAVE; LEADER CULT, THE; MARXIST THEORIES OF FASCISM; MASSES, THE ROLE OF THE; MILITARISM; MUSSOLINI, BENITO ANDREA; NATIONALISM; NAZISM; PROPAGANDA; PSYCHOANALYSIS; PSYCHODYNAMICS OF PALINGENETIC MYTH, THE; PSYCHOLOGY; RACIAL DOCTRINE; RACISM; RATIONALISM; RELIGION; SEXUALITY; TOTALITARIANISM

References

Boadella, David. 1973. *Wilhelm Reich: The Evolution of his Work.* London: Vision.

Sharaf, Myron. 1983. *Fury on Earth: A Biography of Wilhelm Reich.* New York: St. Martin's/Marek.

REICHSTAG FIRE, THE

On 27 February 1933, a few weeks after Hitler's assumption of power, the German Reichstag (parliament building) in Berlin was destroyed by fire. Dutch anarchist Marinus van der Lubbe was arrested on the spot, and the Nazi leadership, soon on the scene, spoke im-

The fire in the Reichstag (parliament building) in Berlin in February 1933; although a Dutch anarchist admitted to having caused it, the finger of suspicion has always been pointed at the Nazis themselves, well known for their hatred of parliamentarism. However, no proof of their involvement has ever been found. (National Archives)

mediately of a "communist torch" for an uprising against Hitler's regime. The following day the "Reichstag Fire Decree" annulled the personal freedoms guaranteed under the Weimar Constitution (freedom of opinion, of assembly, of the press, invulnerability of the home, property, letters, and postal secrecy) and increased the penalties for many crimes, while about 4,000 Communist Party and Socialist Party officials on a prepared list were arrested and held in "protective custody." The swift, prepared reaction of the Nazi leadership gave rise to the suspicion that the fire might have been started by the Nazis themselves, in order to push through their measures. However, no clear proof has ever been found of direct Nazi involvement, and the question has remained a matter of controversy among historians down to the present. The "Reichstag fire trial" ran before the Leipzig Reich court from 21 September to 23 December 1933; the accused were van der Lubbe, Communist Party chairman Ernst Torgler, and Comintern officials Georgi Dimitrov (later president of Bulgaria), Popov, and Tanev. Van der Lubbe, who claimed to have been acting alone, was condemned to death—in accordance with a law introduced for the purpose—and executed; the other accused were acquitted. The Nazi leadership had to abandon their intention of mounting a show trial against the communists after Dimitroff had managed to make president of the Reichstag Hermann Goering, who was appearing as a witness, look ridiculous in public.

Markus Hattstein
(translated by Cyprian Blamires)

See Also: BOLSHEVISM; GERMANY; GOERING, HERMANN; LAW; MARXISM; NAZISM; PARLIAMENTARISM; SOCIALISM; WEIMAR REPUBLIC, THE

Reference
Fritz, T. 1963. *The Reichstag Fire: Legend and Truth.* London: Secker and Warburg.

REICHSWEHR, THE: See WEHRMACHT, THE

RELIGION

The attitude of Italian Fascism and German Nazism and other leading fascist movements to religion was neither univocal nor consistent, but often marked by tensions, conflicts, and antagonisms. However much they may have purported to support and defend Christianity as the religion of the nation, Italian Fascism and National Socialism did not propose to model politics, society, and the state in accord with Christian doctrine. Therefore they cannot be defined as Christian political movements or as Christian in inspiration. Moreover, the only activity that the two regimes allowed the churches to undertake was their pastoral practice; no church criticism was permitted of their totalitarian policies, which subordinated traditional religion to the ideology of the totalitarian regime. The Fascist state, warned Mussolini in 1929, a few weeks after having signed the Concordat with the Holy See, "is Catholic, but it is Fascist, in fact above all, exclusively, essentially Fascist"; for that reason it claimed the monopoly of the education of the new generations for itself and did not hesitate on two occasions—1931

and 1938—to launch aggressive campaigns against Catholic Action to force the Church to remain confined within pastoral practice. The Nazi regime harshly persecuted practicing Protestants, and even more Catholics, who dared to criticize National Socialist ideology and politics. When, in 1937, Pius XI condemned the persecution of Catholics in Germany with the encyclical *Mit brennender Sorge,* though without mentioning Nazism, Hitler warned that the churches "have no title to criticize the morals of a state. . . . [F]or the morals of the German state and of the German people the leaders of the German state will be responsible."

The truth is that as an integralist conception of politics that claimed uniquely for itself the prerogative of independently defining the significance and the ultimate end of human existence on this earth, fascism took on the essential features of a political religion. This interpretation of fascism as a political religion does not, however, derive from fascism's own self-representation. Apart from Italian Fascism, which did officially define itself as "a religious conception," no fascist movement presented explicitly as a new secular religion. The interpretation of fascism as a political religion was developed by antifascists of various stripes like Luigi Sturzo, Waldemar Gurian, Eric Voegelin, and Raymond Aron. These antifascists were motivated to define fascism as a political religion by a consideration of the concrete aspects of the fascist movements—that is: the claim of the fascists to be the sole and exclusive interpreters of the nation; the practice of violence to regenerate the nation by eliminating all of its internal enemies; the political style, which laid great emphasis on the symbolism of banners, uniforms, and collective rituals; the cult of the leader; and the collective enthusiasm, irrational and fanatical, that fascism inspired with its propaganda and its organizations.

All fascist movements had in common the sacralization of politics—that is, the tendency to confer on a secular entity the attributes of a sacred reality—supreme, unarguable, and intangible—placing it at the center of a system of beliefs, myths, rituals, symbols, and commandments that defined the significance and the ultimate end of terrestrial existence for the individual and the masses. Fascist movements shared a political mysticism that sacralized the nation, the state, and the race, as well as the movement itself. In all fascist movements, support, organization, and militancy were based not on knowledge, motivation, and rational choices but on an irrational adherence summed up in Mussolini's commandment "Believe, Obey, Fight," which can be considered the emblem of fascism. All fascist movements exalted faith as the foundation of political militancy.

Even devotion and obedience to the leader was conceived by fascism in terms of mystical communion.

Fascist political mysticism imposed dedication to the primacy of the national community, divinized as a supreme absolute reality, a transcendent totality, which is perpetuated in time, acting through the consciousness and will of an elect minority. "The totality of the nation," claimed Ferenc Szálasi, leader of the Hungarian National Socialist Movement Arrow Cross, "is the perfect totality." The fatherland, proclaimed José Antonio Primo de Rivera, founder of the Spanish Falange, "is a total unity . . . a transcendent synthesis, an invisible synthesis, with its own goals to fulfill; and we want this movement of today, and the state it creates, to be an efficient, authoritarian instrument at the service of an indisputable unity, of that permanent unity, of that irrevocable unity that is the Fatherland." For fascist movements, the mystical totality of the nation was realized in the unity of the new state, created and governed by a spiritual aristocracy of "New Men" that exercised absolute power to realize a homogenous, integral, national community, eliminating by any means possible persons and groups considered harmful to the existence of the national collectivity. "The new state," affirmed Corneliu Zelea Codreanu, founder in Romania of the Legion of the Archangel Michael, "cannot be founded on the theoretical concepts of constitutional law. The new state presupposes in the first place and as an essential a new type of man. . . . The New Man or the renewed nation presupposes a great spiritual renewal, a great spiritual revolution of the whole people." The political struggle was conceived by fascists as an apocalyptic war between Good and Evil. All fascist movements could have echoed—with due allowances for their particular version of the ideology—the statement of the leader of Norwegian fascism, Vidkun Quisling, that the Nordic Principle "is allied to the Divine," while its enemies, Jewish liberalism and Marxism, were allies of the devil.

Syncretism between political religion and traditional religion was another classic feature peculiar to fascist political mysticism. This occurred especially in fascist movements that professed a nationalist, racist, and anti-Semitic ideology that they considered wholly coherent with Christian doctrine. "God is Fascist," claimed a legionary of the Iron Guard. The version of the Christian religion actually professed by many chiefs and militants of National Socialism was in reality a hybrid racist ideologization of Christianity that "Aryanized" and "Germanized" Christ and God. The National Socialist revolution, said the Fuehrer in 1934, was a manifestation of the divine protection of the German people.

As to the legitimacy of the concept of political religion to define fascism, it should be noted that among the most important interpreters of fascism as a secular religion were Catholic and Protestant theologians such as Jacques Maritain, Paul Tillich, and Karl Barth; for them the use of the concept of religion with reference to a political phenomenon was not wholly metaphorical but aimed at defining an effective religious dimension of politics, which they identified with a modern manifestation of idolatry and paganism. For this reason they condemned every form of compromise and collaboration by the churches with fascism, considering it by its very nature incompatible with Christian doctrine. This, moreover, was also the conviction of Pope Pius XI. In 1931 the pontiff condemned the statolatrous religion of the Fascist regime with the encyclical *Non abbiamo bisogno,* and shortly before his death in 1939 he was preparing to publish a solemn condemnation of totalitarian doctrines that sacralized the nation, race, or class in an encyclical entitled *Humani Generis Unitas.* This remained unpublished after his death at the desire of his successor, Pius XII.

Emilio Gentile
(translated by Cyprian Blamires)

See Also: INTRODUCTION; ANTICLERICALISM; ANTIFASCISM; ANTI-SEMITISM; ARYANISM; ARISTOCRACY; ARROW CROSS; BOLSHEVISM; CATHOLIC CHURCH, THE; CHRISTIANITY; CLERICO-FASCISM; CODREANU, CORNELIU ZELEA; CONFESSING CHURCH, THE; COSMOPOLITANISM; CULTS OF DEATH; EDUCATION; ELITE THEORY; FALANGE; FASCIST PARTY, THE; GERMAN CHRISTIANS, THE; GERMANNESS (*DEUTSCHHEIT*); GERMANY; HITLER, ADOLF; ITALY; LEADER CULT, THE; LEGION OF THE ARCHANGEL MICHAEL, THE; LIBERALISM; LIBERALISM·(IN THEOLOGY); LUTHERAN CHURCHES, THE; MARXISM; MATERIALISM; MUSSOLINI, BENITO ANDREA; MYSTICISM; MYTH; NATIONALISM; NAZISM; NEW MAN, THE; NIHILISM; NORDIC SOUL, THE; NORWAY; PALINGENETIC MYTH; PIUS XI, POPE; PIUS XII, POPE; PRIMO DE RIVERA, JOSÉ ANTONIO; PROTESTANTISM; QUISLING, VIDKUN; RACIAL DOCTRINE; RACISM; RATIONALISM; REVOLUTION; ROMANIA; SCHIRACH, BALDUR VON; SECULARIZATION; SPAIN; STYLE; SYMBOLS; SZÁLAZI, FERENC; THEOLOGY; TOTALITARIANISM; VIOLENCE; *VOLKSGEMEINSCHAFT,* THE

References

Bergen, Doris. 1996. *Twisted Cross: The German Christian Movement in the Third Reich.* Chapel Hill: University of North Carolina Press.
Blinkhorn, Martin. 1990. *Fascists and Conservatives.* London: Unwin Hyman.
Cheles, Luciano, Ronnie Ferguson, and Michalina Vaughan. 1995. *The Far Right in Western and Eastern Europe.* London: Longman.
Cornwell, J. 2000. *Hitler's Pope: The Secret History of Pius XII.* London: Penguin.

Evans, E. L. 1981. *The German Center Party 1870–1933: A Study in Political Catholicism.* Carbondale: Southern Illinois University Press.

Gentile, E. 1996. *The Sacralization of Politics in Fascist Italy.* London: Harvard University Press.

———. 2000. "The Sacralization of Politics: Definitions, Interpretations and Reflections on the Question of Secular Religion and Totalitarianism." *Totalitarian Movements and Political Religions* 1, no. 1.

Griffin, R. 1991. *The Nature of Fascism.* London: Routledge.

Halls, W. D. 1995. *Politics, Society and Christianity in Vichy France.* Oxford: Berg.

Helmreich, Ernst Christian. 1979. *The German Churches under Hitler: Background, Struggle, and Epilogue.* Detroit, MI: Wayne State University Press.

Ioanid, R. 1990. *The Sword of the Archangel Michael: Fascist Ideology in Romania.* Boulder, CO: Eastern European Monographs.

Maier, Hans, ed. 2004. *Totalitarianism and Political Religions: Concepts for the Comparison of Dictatorships.* Vol.1. London: Routledge.

Mallett, Robert. 2002. *International Fascism 1919–1945.* London: Frank Cass.

Pollard, J. 1985. *The Vatican and Italian Fascism.* London: Macmillan.

Rychlak, R. J. 2000. *Hitler, the War, and the Pope.* Huntington, IN: Our Sunday Visitor.

Tal, Uriel. 2004. *Religion, Politics and Ideology in the Third Reich.* London: Frank Cass.

Wolff, R. J., and J. R. Hoensch, eds. 1987. *Catholics, the State and the European Radical Right.* Boulder, CO: Social Science Monographs.

REMER, OTTO-ERNST (1912–1997)

German army officer who played a crucial role in frustrating the July Plot against Hitler and who remained an unrepentant supporter of the Hitler regime till the end of his life. As commander of the Grossdeutschland guard regiment in Berlin, he moved quickly to suppress the revolt after the assassination attempt had failed and was promoted to major-general for his efforts. After the war, Remer was imprisoned by the Americans until 1947. In 1950 he founded the neo-Nazi Socialist Reich Party, but the party was dissolved in 1952. In 1992 he was sentenced by a German court for publication of Holocaust denial articles in a newsletter. He fled to Spain, and the Spanish authorities refused a request for extradition.

Cyprian Blamires

See Also: GERMANY; HITLER, ADOLF; JULY PLOT, THE; HOLOCAUST DENIAL; KREISAU CIRCLE, THE; NATIONALISM; NEO-NAZISM; SKORZENY, OTTO

Reference
Galante, Pierre. 2002. *Operation Valkyrie: The German Generals' Plot against Hitler.* New York: Cooper Square.

REPARATIONS

One of the many festering grievances on which Nazism fed in Germany was that of the reparations demanded of her as a result of the Versailles Treaty. Eventually, the sum of 132,000 million gold marks was settled on in 1921. By 1923, with the German mark collapsing, French troops entered the Rhineland to enforce payment of outstanding reparations. It was in November of that year, when 1 billion marks were the equivalent of one dollar, that Hitler launched the abortive Munich Putsch. The following year a new repayment scheme was fixed, known as the Dawes Plan after Charles Dawes, director of the U.S. Bureau of the Budget. It proposed repayment at a rate of 2,000 million gold marks per year. In 1929 the Young Plan (after Owen D. Young, successor to Dawes as chairman of the Allied Committee) scaled down the debt to 37,000 million gold marks, which were to be repaid over fifty-nine years. Two years later a conference in Lausanne resulted in the abandonment of reparations claims.

Cyprian Blamires

See Also: ECONOMICS; GERMANY; HITLER, ADOLF; INFLATION; MUNICH (BEER-HALL) PUTSCH, THE; NOVEMBER CRIMINALS/*NOVEMBERBRECHER*, THE; VERSAILLES, THE TREATY OF; WALL STREET CRASH, THE; WORLD WAR I

Reference
Kent, B. 1989. *The Spoils of War: The Politics, Economics and Diplomacy of Reparations 1918–1932.* Oxford: Clarendon.

REPRESENTATION: *See* DEMOCRACY; PARLIAMENTARISM
RESISTANCE RECORDS: *See* ROCK MUSIC; SKINHEAD FASCISM; UNITED STATES, THE (postwar)

REVISIONISM: *See HISTORIKERSTREIT,*
THE; HOLOCAUST DENIAL; IRVING,
DAVID JOHN CAWDELL

REVOLUTION

Fascism's ideologues have always claimed their movement to be revolutionary, and, though traditionally that
claim has been routinely repudiated by most academics
and antifascist activists, by the 1990s there was evidence
of an increasing willingness on the part of serious scholars not to reject it out of hand. Ever since the violent attacks on socialists by Italian Fascist Action Squads in the
"red biennium" (1920–1921), it has been axiomatic for
Marxists that fascism was by its very nature a counterrevolutionary bid by capitalism to crush revolutionary
socialism and the power of organized labor. Even those
"sophisticated" Marxists prepared to accept that fascism
may have been used by reactionary forces as an instrument of class repression have generally been reluctant to
consider the ideology and ultimate goals of the instrument itself. They thus denied themselves the possibility
of realizing that in the interwar period conservative interests (big business, the monarchy, the Church, the
bourgeoisie) attempted in several countries to highjack
fascism and deflect it from fulfilling its deeply anticonservative objectives as it saw them, in the case of Italy
and Germany unsuccessfully but in Spain and Romania
successfully, at least for a time.

Meanwhile in the liberal camp the untested (and erroneous) assumption that fascism's core social basis was
the middle classes, plus the deep confusion that prevailed in the liberal camp about what constituted fascism, a confusion compounded by the deep sense of
horror that pervaded the human sciences after 1945 at
the atrocities committed by Nazism in the name of the
"New Order," meant that fascism was widely treated as
a phenomenon that could have been described only in
negative terms (antisocialist, antihumanist, antiliberal,
antimodern, anticulture, irrational, barbaric, pathological, nihilistic, and so forth). A further obstacle to recognizing any authentic revolutionary dimension within
fascism has been the assumption that a "true" revolution involves first and foremost the transformation of
the socioeconomic basis of society, the emancipation of
all oppressed sectors of humanity from oppression, or a
vision of the future that makes a definitive break with

the past—preconceptions that naturally dominate socialist thinking but that have had a deep impact on liberal theory as well. However, a close study of the archetypal European revolution, the French Revolution,
confirms that at the heart of the attempted socioeconomic transformation lay the vision of inaugurating a
new worldview, a new set of values, a new historical era,
and a new type of man.

Once the semantic emphasis in the discussion of revolution shifts to highlight ideological, temporal, and anthropological transformation, then it is soon clear that
fascism in all of its permutations seeks to revolutionize
society and not merely to restore some lost Golden
Age—even if one of its outstanding features is the way
in which it tends to use the myth of some epic high
point of cultural homogeneity and vitality as the inspiration for the future. The Ancient Romans, the Aryans,
the Dacians, the Magyars, the Elizabethans, the Indo-
Europeans, and especially the Ancient Greeks, the white
settlers in the United States and South Africa, the
Spaniards, the Brazilians, and the Russians that allegedly
first created that nation in a heroic act of will—all have
been used by fascists as mythic sources of inspiration for
a new, postliberal future. At bottom this is no different
from the way in which Republican Rome served as a
role model for French revolutionaries, and utopian visions of primitive communism helped to inspire French
revolutionaries, anarchists, Marxist-Leninists, and Hippies alike.

The pioneers of the recognition of fascism's revolutionary dynamic were G. L. Mosse, Stanley Payne
(U.S.), and Zeev Sternhell (Israel), who by 1980 had all
published insightful analyses of fascism's attempted regeneration of national culture, politics, morals, and art,
to produce a "New Man." More recently the Italian
scholar Emilio Gentile has added an important theoretical dimension to this analysis by revealing the nexus
between a movement's aspiration to bring about an anthropological revolution, its totalitarian drive to gain
political, economic, and cultural control of society, and
its tendency to create a political religion that sacralizes
the new state, a syndrome manifested in both fascist
and communist societies. Once approached in this way
it becomes obvious that fascism, far from being antimodern, is an attempt to create an alternative modernity that harnesses the power of modern technology,
science, and the state while intensifying the sense of national identity and cultural roots by creating a ritual,
liturgical style of politics and appealing to a mythicized
national or racial history. The reason for its rejection of
so many aspects of modernity (individualism, rationalism, and the like) can then be understood, not as

reaction, but as a bid to reverse the process of decay and create a new order based on the national community. At this point the collaboration in the fascist project of technocrats, scientists, engineers, artistic modernists such as the Futurists, and modern architects, not to mention millions of "modern," well-educated, and socialized individuals, no longer seems paradoxical: even apparently reactionary elements like antiurbanism, collusion with organized religion, celebration of a mythicized past, and antifeminism, so prominent in some spheres of fascist ideology, can be seen as integral to the creation of a new sense of spiritual belonging, of nationhood, and collective purpose.

The revolutionary aspect of fascism is also central to an understanding of its most nefarious crimes against humanity—namely, the genocides committed by the Third Reich against such alleged racial enemies as Slavs, Jews, Sinti, and Roma. Although it is tempting to explain such highly organized and industrialized mass murder in terms of hatred and nihilism, there is deeper explanatory value in seeing them as concomitants of the attempt to realize the utopia of a racially and ideologically homogeneous national community (*Volksgemeinschaft*), and hence as "dialectically" related to the emphasis on the spiritual and physical health of the nation ("racial hygiene") that manifested itself in the cult of art, music, nature, sport, and physical fitness. From that perspective the extermination camps are to be seen as products of the same logic of "creative destruction" that caused "decadent" books and paintings to be burned so as to make way for Germany's intellectual and artistic renaissance, imbued with the spirit of Aryan values. The slaughter committed in the name of the reborn German *Volk* thus acquires deeply mythic connotations of the ritual cleansing, purging, and "sacrifice" through which a new cycle in historical time is inaugurated.

Even in its most purely metapolitical reincarnations, postwar fascism continues to have a revolutionary thrust, albeit a highly utopian one. The self-professed aim of the more politicized contributors to the European New Right is to "take over the laboratories of culture" and so achieve cultural hegemony for ideas that reject multiculturalism, materialism, and the globalization of Western/U.S. values, and to reinject a decadent European civilization with "Indo-European" cultural values and a new sense of identity and belonging. For modern intellectual fascists (a term they bitterly reject), we are very far from "the end of history" in a time that can expect no more major ideological upheavals, as the last pockets of resistance to the secular humanist and capitalist system of values are eroded or capitulate. On the contrary, we are in a protracted "interregnum" that will one day be terminated in a dramatic reversion "back to the future," when archetypal values are rediscovered in a new synthesis of old and new, a scenario that, were it ever to be actualized, would have to sacrifice yet more categories of human beings to the Moloch of the new order.

Roger Griffin

See Also: INTRODUCTION; AMERICANIZATION; "ANTI-" DIMENSION OF FASCISM, THE; ANTI-SEMITISM; ARCHITECTURE; ART; ARYANISM; BODY, THE CULT OF THE; BOOKS, THE BURNING OF THE; BOURGEOISIE, THE; BRAZIL; CALENDAR, THE FASCIST; CAPITALISM; COMMUNITY; CONCENTRATION CAMPS; CONSERVATISM; COUNTER-REVOLUTION; DECADENCE; EUROPEAN NEW RIGHT, THE; FASCIST PARTY, THE; FEMINISM; FRANCOISM; FRENCH REVOLUTION, THE; FUTURISM; GERMANY; GLOBALIZATION; HITLER, ADOLF; HOLOCAUST, THE; HUNGARY; INDIVIDUALISM; ITALY; MARXISM; MARXIST THEORIES OF FASCISM; MATERIALISM; MODERNITY; MONARCHY; MULTICULTURALISM; MUSIC; MUSSOLINI, BENITO ANDREA; NATIONALISM; NATURE; NAZISM; NEW MAN, THE; NEW ORDER, THE; NIHILISM; PALINGENETIC MYTH; POSTWAR FASCISM; RATIONALISM; RELIGION; ROMA AND SINTI, THE; ROMANIA; ROME; RURALISM; RUSSIA; SCIENCE; SLAVS, THE (AND GERMANY); SOCIALISM; SOUTH AFRICA; SPAIN; SPORT; *SQUADRISMO;* STATE, THE; TECHNOLOGY; THIRD REICH, THE; TRADITION; UTOPIA, UTOPIANISM ; *VOLK, VÖLKISCH; VOLKSGEMEINSCHAFT,* THE

References

Bauman, Z. 1989. *Modernity and the Holocaust.* Cambridge: Polity.

Gentile, E. 2000. "The Sacralisation of Politics: Definitions, Interpretations and Reflections on the Question of Secular Religion and Totalitarianism." *Totalitarian Movements and Political Religions* 1, no. 1.

Griffin, R. 2000. "Revolution from the Right: Fascism." In *Revolutions and the Revolutionary Tradition in the West 1560–1991,* edited by David Parker. London: Routledge.

Mosse, G. L. 1999. *The Fascist Revolution.* New York: Howard Fertig.

Payne, S. 1995. *A History of Fascism, 1914–45.* London: UCL.

Weber, E. 1976. "Revolution? Counter-revolution? What Revolution?" In *Fascism: A Reader's Guide,* edited by Walter Laqueur. Harmondsworth: Penguin.

REVOLUTIONARY NATIONALISM

A term adopted by some contemporary neofascist groups (especially in France) who reject the term *fascist* because of its persistent connotations of Nazism and genocide. However, from an outsider perspective it is to be seen as a militant postwar form of palingenetic ultra-nationalism, and hence of fascism.

Roger Griffin

See Also: FRANCE; HOLOCAUST, THE; NATIONALISM; NAZISM; PALINGENETIC MYTH; POSTWAR FASCISM

Reference
www://rosenoire.org/articles/bloodandsoil.php.

REXISM

In the 1936 Belgian legislative elections, fascistic parties (Rexists and Flemish nationalists) stunned the Belgian electorate by winning 37 out of 202 parliamentary seats. This feat was remarkable, since the newly founded Rexist movement (which won 31 parliamentary seats) had no party organization or prior legislative experience. Belgium had seemed so unsuitable for fascism. Linz has noted that fascism is usually seen as a novel response to crises brought on by such postwar dislocations as defeat, ambivalence about a nation's entry into war, disappointment with peace terms, or unsuccessful revolution. But Belgium emerged as one of the victors in World War I and escaped the deprivation and humiliation associated with the postwar period. Moreover, Belgium had a stable and well-established parliamentary system, no tradition of indigenous right-wing groups, and minerally rich central African colonies.

The relative stability of Belgium's tripartite political landscape was severely shaken in 1936 with the unprecedented electoral success of the Rexist Party. The Rexists (from *Christus Rex,* "Christ the King") emerged from the ranks of the conservative Catholic Union. Accusing the Catholic Union of weakness and inactivity in the face of a corruption-ridden society, Rexist founder Leon Degrelle and his followers promised bold measures to restore order. At the heart of the Rexist program was a call for a corporate state modeled on Fascist Italy. According to Degrelle, corporatism was the best means to overcome the chaos of class struggle. The Rexist corporate state would be authoritarian and fully imbued with Christian values. As its first political act, the Rexist state would carry out a physical and moral reform of the Belgian nation. The Rexists opposed the parliamentary system and called for the complete elimination of political parties. Rexists felt that political parties had sown national discord and that their leaders were to blame for the numerous politico-financial scandals that had riddled the country during the 1930s. On economic issues, the Rexists were decidedly anticommunist, seeing communism as the chief destructive force in the world. They were equally opposed to big business; they blamed the major financial institutions for the worldwide economic depression and the impoverishment of small- and medium-scale family-run businesses. But they were not opposed to private property or to capitalism, and they demanded that the state aid small- and medium-size businesses and farms. In particular, they called for more accessible agricultural credit and restrictions on large agrobusinesses. Among the competing political parties, the Rexists most strongly favored the family-owned farm.

One key Rexist concern was the well-being of the family. For them, the family was the core of society, and they felt that the state should do everything possible to protect, favor, and strengthen the family. The Rexists believed that the state should protect the family from such evils as pornography and prostitution, guarantee inheritance based on direct descendancy, and replace universal suffrage by the "integral family vote," which would have given a second vote to families with at least four children. By 1939 the electoral strength of the Rexists had waned. In 1939, the Rexist Party obtained only 4.4 percent of the national vote. The fascist character of the party, which might not have been totally apparent in 1936, had become quite clear by 1939, and many Rexists would go on to support the Nazi occupation of Belgium.

William I. Brustein

See Also: BELGIUM; BOLSHEVISM; CATHOLIC CHURCH, THE; CLASS; CONSERVATISM; CORPORATISM; DEGRELLE, LEON; ECONOMICS; FAMILY, THE; FARMERS; FASCIST PARTY, THE; HEALTH; ITALY; MAN, HENDRIK/HENRI DE; MARXISM; NAZISM; PARLIAMENTARISM; POLITICAL CATHOLICISM; RELIGION; SEXUALITY; WALL STREET CRASH, THE; WAR; WORLD WAR I; WORLD WAR II

References
Brustein, William I. 1988. "The Political Geography of Belgian Fascism: The Case of Rexism." *American Sociological Review* 53: 69–80.
Bruyne, Eddy, and Marc Rikmenspoel. 2004. *For Rex and Belgium: Léon Degrelle and the Walloon Political and Military Collaboration.* Solihull: Helion.

Conway, Martin. 1993. *Collaboration in Belgium: Léon Degrelle and the Rexist Movement, 1940–44*. New Haven: Yale University Press.

Chertok, R. H. 1975. "Belgian Fascism." Ph.D. diss. St. Louis, MO: Washington University.

Etienne, J. M. 1968. *Le Mouvement Rexiste jusqu'en 1940*. Paris: Colin.

Linz, Juan. 1976. "Some Notes toward a Comparative Study of Fascism in Sociological Historical Perspective." Pp. 3–121 in *Fascism: A Reader's Guide*, edited by W. Laqueur. Berkeley: University of California Press.

Littlejohn, D. 1972. *The Patriotic Traitors*. London: Heinemann.

Schepens, Luc. 1980. "Fascists and Nationalists in Belgium 1919–1940." Pp. 501–516 in *Who Were the Fascists*, edited by Stein Ugelvik Larsen, Bernt Hagtvet, and Jan Petter Myklebust. Bergen: Universitetsforlaget.

tion forced the Smith regime into conversations with the moderate Black Freedom Organizations from 1974. In April 1979, the Smith regime reluctantly handed power over after international negotiations; the moderate black bishop Abel Muzorewa became prime minister. In 1980, Rhodesia's first free elections saw Robert Mugabe's ZANU take power in the country, which was officially renamed "Zimbabwe."

Markus Hattstein
(translated by Cyprian Blamires)

See Also: PARAMILITARISM; RACISM; SOUTH AFRICA

Reference
Godwin, P. 1993. *"Rhodesians Never Die": The Impact of War and Political Change on White Rhodesia, c. 1970–1980*. Oxford: Oxford University Press.

RHINELAND, THE: *See* FREEDOM; REPARATIONS; VERSAILLES, THE TREATY OF

RHODESIA/ ZIMBABWE

Between the Unilateral Declaration of Independence (from Great Britain, whose colony the country had been) by Ian Smith in 1965 and 1979, a bloody race war raged in Rhodesia, in the course of which nearly 40,000 men, most of them blacks, were killed. The white settlers formed their own militias and paramilitary associations that to some extent had openly fascistic forms of organization and ideologies, and they carried out massacres of black civilians not only in Rhodesia but also in neighboring countries, to which 10,000 had fled. They were supported by units of the regular Rhodesian army; the borderlines between "vigilante groups," militias, and army were often blurred, and racist and fascist ideas came with radical white soldier bands from South Africa and Namibia into Rhodesia. On the other hand, black guerrilla forces in some areas fell on the poorly protected farms of the whites and slaughtered the occupants. The escalation of violence and increasing isola-

RIBBENTROP, JOACHIM VON (1893–1946)

Diplomat, close associate of Hitler, and fanatical anti-Semite who urged the extermination of Jews in the Occupied Territories. The son of an army officer, Ribbentrop went to Montreal in Canada, where he trained as a bank clerk (1911), worked for the railways (1912), and became a member of the national Canadian ice hockey team (1914). When World War I began he immediately returned to Germany to become a cavalry officer. At the end of the war he was a member of the German military mission in Constantinople, where he came into contact with Franz von Papen. In 1920 he married the heiress of the champagne producer Henkell and subsequently became a successful businessman, importing and exporting spirits. Having been editor of a nationalist political publication in the 1920s, he first met Hitler in 1930. Ribbentrop joined the NSDAP in 1932 and later became an SS officer. He played an important role as mediator between sectors of the conservative elite and the Nazi movement. After the Nazi seizure of power, he became Hitler's advisor in foreign affairs and was head of the "Ribbentrop Department," a rival to the state department led by Konstantin von Neurath between 1932 and 1938.

During the disarmament conference in Geneva (1934), Ribbentrop spoke up for the arming of Germany. In 1936 he became ambassador in London, where his main task was to forge an anti-Soviet alliance between Great Britain and Germany. The failure of this attempt made him fiercely anti-British and later led him to serious political misjudgments—for example, about the likely British response in the event of a Nazi attack on Poland. Ribbentrop was appointed secretary of state in early February 1938; the Munich Agreement and the nonaggression pact between Nazi Germany and the Soviet Union in August 1939 marked the climax of his career. In the following years he focused on the consolidation of the alliance between Nazi Germany, Fascist Italy, and Imperial Japan (Axis pact, 1940; convention on military affairs, 1942). Ribbentrop used the diplomatic apparatus to support the Holocaust; again and again the German diplomatic missions in the vassal states of Vichy (France), Slovakia, and Hungary, as well as in formally independent Denmark, were ordered to intensify their efforts to deport Jews to the extermination camps. In 1943, Hitler gave Ribbentrop gifts worth a million reichs marks, but in Hitler's will of late April 1945, Ribbentrop's name was replaced by that of Seyß-Inquart. At the end of the war, he went into hiding but was captured in mid-June 1945 in Hamburg. Sentenced to death in the Nuremberg Trials, he was executed on 16 October 1946. His memoirs appeared posthumously under the title *Between London and Moscow.*

Fabian Virchow

See Also: ANTI-SEMITISM; AXIS, THE; CONCENTRATION CAMPS; DENMARK; FASCIST PARTY, THE; FRANCE; GERMANY; HITLER, ADOLF; HITLER-STALIN PACT, THE; HOLOCAUST, THE; HUNGARY; ITALY; JAPAN; JAPAN AND WORLD WAR II; MUNICH AGREEMENT/PACT, THE; NATIONALISM; NAZISM; NUREMBERG TRIALS, THE; PAPEN, FRANZ VON; SEYSS-INQUART, ARTHUR; SLOVAKIA; SS, THE; VICHY; WORLD WAR I; WORLD WAR II

References
Bloch, Michael. 1994. *Ribbentrop.* New York: Bantam.
Browning, Christopher R. 1978. *The Final Solution and the German Foreign Office: A Study of Referat D III of Abteilung Deutschland 1940–1943.* New York: Holmes and Meier.
Douglas-Hamilton, James. 1970. "Ribbentrop and War." *Journal of Contemporary History* 5, no 4: 45–63.
Kley, Stefan. 1996. *Hitler, Ribbentrop und die Entfesselung des Zweiten Weltkrieges.* Paderborn: Schöningh.
Watt, Donald C. 1955. "The German Diplomats and the Nazi Leaders." *Journal of Central European Affairs* 15: 148–160.
Weinberg, Gerhard L. 1980. *The Foreign Policy of Hitler's Germany: Starting World War II 1937–1939.* Chicago: University of Chicago Press.
Weitz, John. 1992. *Hitler's Diplomat: The Life and Times of Joachim von Ribbentrop.* New York: Houghton Mifflin.

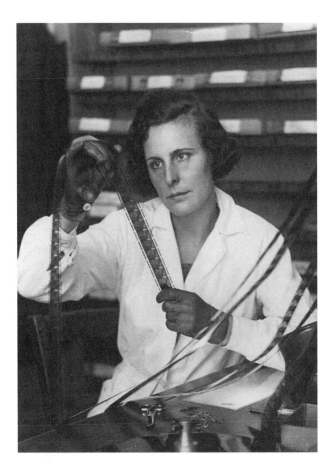

Leni Riefenstahl, whose famous documentary of the 1934 Nuremberg Rally ('Triumph of the Will'*) was a propaganda triumph for the Nazis. (Austrian Archives/Corbis)*

RIEFENSTAHL, LENI (1902–2003)

Controversial German film maker whose brilliant cinematographic techniques were applied to the glorification of the Nazi regime. Helene Bertha Amalie "Leni" Riefenstahl had already made her name as an actress and movie director during the Weimar Republic when Hitler personally chose her to direct two now infamous propaganda movies about the 1933 and 1934 Nuremberg Rallies. *Der Sieg des Glaubens* ("Victory of Faith") was released in 1933, while the better known successor, *Triumph des Willens (Triumph of the Will),* was shown nationally and internationally from March 1935 onward to promote the ideas of National Socialism. Ever since, Riefenstahl has been seen as one of the main propagandists of the Nazi regime. It took her until 2002, the year of her one hundredth birthday, to see her first postwar film released, the deep-sea diving documentary *Impressions under Water.*

The mountaineer and film maker Arnold Fanck discovered the dancer Riefenstahl and made her the star of a movie in 1925. In 1932 she released her first feature film, the Alpine story *Das blaue Licht* (*The Blue Light*). She starred in and directed that film, which she had also co-written with Hungarian scriptwriter Bela Balazs. In 1933, she was approached by Nazi propaganda experts to direct a documentary film about the first Nuremberg Rally. While *Der Sieg des Glaubens* was far more conventional in its technique and imagery than her previous movie, *Triumph of the Will* is still hailed as a milestone in cinematography. Although it is crudely propagandistic, Riefenstahl has always maintained that she was interested in art, not politics, when shooting in Nuremberg. In many interviews, even late in life, she argued that she had partly choreographed the rally to suit her work, rather than just depicting what had happened. Innovative camera angles and the clever montage of images are among the modernist features of that film. Nevertheless, *Triumph of the Will* was by no means subversive of the Nazi regime. Hitler is always the center of attention, even when he is not in the picture: when the various Nazi organizations and paramilitary associations march by, all their eyes are turned toward the Fuehrer in unison. German military traditions were celebrated at a time when military activity was still severely curtailed by the Versailles Treaty, and the emblems of National Socialism, like the eagle and the swastika, were central to many shots.

A year after the release of *Triumph of the Will,* Riefenstahl was chosen to film a documentary about the 1936 Berlin Olympic Games. Generally known as *Olympia,* the two-part opus was released in Germany in 1938 as *Fest der Völker* (*Celebration of the Peoples*) and *Fest der Schönheit* (*Celebration of Beauty*). The language of images focused on masculinity and the body. Riefenstahl was the first cinematographer to use moving cameras to follow the athletes in action. It has been argued that it is mainly because of Riefenstahl's imagery that the 1936 Olympics are now remembered solely as the Nazi Games, whereas they should also have been remembered as the very last manifestation of tolerance and internationalism within Nazi Germany.

Riefenstahl started filming her second and last feature film, *Tiefland* (*Lowland*), in 1940, but it was not completed until 1953 and released only in 1954. Less than a year before her death in September 2003, con-troversy flared up about Riefenstahl's use of more than 100 so-called Gypsies taken from concentration camps in Austria and Germany to participate in the filming of *Tiefland* as extras. Victims' organizations claimed that the Gypsies were returned to the camps afterward, where many of them were murdered. Riefenstahl, however, maintained that nothing happened to her extras, and that she saw many of them again after the war. In the postwar era Riefenstahl became a pariah in the film-making world because of her involvement with Nazi Germany. Disillusioned, she turned toward traveling and photography. Her photographs of the Nuba tribe in Sudan won awards, but also brought accusations of racism. As a septuagenarian, Riefenstahl discovered deep-sea diving. Her final documentary, *Impressions under Water,* was released in 2002 and was the product of more than 200 dives with a camera. In the last decade of her life, Riefenstahl's work experienced a renaissance: her role as a pioneer of cinematography was reassessed, her photographs were exhibited in major galleries, and internationally successful pop bands like Rammstein and U2 used images from her earlier films for their stage shows.

Christoph H. Müller

See Also: ART; AUSTRIA; BERLIN OLYMPICS, THE; BODY, THE CULT OF THE; CONCENTRATION CAMPS; FILM; GERMANY; HITLER, ADOLF; HOLOCAUST, THE; LEADER CULT, THE; LEISURE; MODERNISM; NAZISM; NUREMBERG RALLIES, THE; PARAMILITARISM; PROPAGANDA; ROMA AND SINTI, THE; SPORT; SWASTIKA, THE; *TRIUMPH OF THE WILL;* VERSAILLES, THE TREATY OF; WARRIOR ETHOS, THE; WEIMAR REPUBLIC, THE

References

Hinton, David B. 2000. *The Films of Leni Riefenstahl.* 3d ed. Lanham: Scarecrow.
Rother, Rainer. 2002. *Leni Riefenstahl: The Seduction of Genius.* New York: Continuum-Academi.

RISORGIMENTO, THE

The period during which Italian unification was achieved in the first half of the nineteenth century; literal meaning, "renewal." It had mixed connotations in Italian Fascist eyes, since on the positive side it had laid the foundation for a renewal of Italian national pride, but on the negative it had promoted a liberal ethos.

Cyprian Blamires

See Also: FASCIST PARTY, THE; ITALY; LIBERALISM; MUS-SOLINI, BENITO ANDREA; NATIONALISM; SECULARIZATION

Reference

Salomone, A. William, ed. 1971. *Italy from the Risorgimento to Fascism: An Inquiry into the Origins of the Totalitarian State.* Plymouth: David and Charles.

ROCCO, ALFREDO (1875 –1935)

One of the most important conservative legal theorists of the twentieth century, legal architect of the Fascist state, and Mussolini's justice minister from 1925 to 1932. Before World War I, Rocco was a law professor and a prominent member of the Italian Nationalist Association. In 1919 he coedited with Francesco Coppola the periodical *Politica,* which proposed an imperialist foreign policy and a totalitarian conception of the state. Rocco drafted the syndical law of 1926, which formed the basis of the Fascist corporative state, and in 1931 completed a substantial revision of the Italian penal code.

Alex de Grand

See Also: CORPORATISM; FASCIST PARTY, THE; ITALY; LAW; MUSSOLINI, BENITO ANDREA; NATIONALISM; STATE, THE; SYNDICALISM; TOTALITARIANISM; WORLD WAR I

References

Gregor, A. James. 2005. *Mussolini's Intellectuals: Fascist Social and Political Thought.* Princeton: Princeton University Press.
Roberts, David D. 1979. *The Syndicalist Tradition and Italian Fascism.* Chapel Hill: University of North Carolina Press.
Ungari, P. 1963. *Alfredo Rocco e l'ideologia giuridica del fascismo.* Brescia: Morcelliana.

ROCK MUSIC

White power rock 'n' roll, or "white noise," with its burgeoning network of concerts, fanzines, and merchandise represents a particularly potent recruitment tool for the "hearts and minds" of white youth. As Ian Stuart Donaldson, singer with the seminal "skinhead" band Skrewdriver noted, a pamphlet is read only once, but a song is sung a thousand times. The lyrics of white power music both reflect and reproduce the violent racist subculture in which band and listeners alike are immersed. Nowhere is this more evident than in the lyrics of the English band No Remorse, which celebrated the murderous attack on an asylum center in Rostock, East Germany, in 1992 with the song "Barbecue in Rostock." As well as vicious racist invective at their core, the lyrics of white power music also convey the "palingenetic" themes of fascist ideology, indoctrinating listeners who may not have realized the wider implications of the music.

White power rock 'n' roll emerged from the English "skinhead" culture during the 1970s before migrating to the United States in the 1980s. Today there are more than 540 white power bands, based mainly in Europe and the United States, though the reach is global. In the U.S., white power music is dominated by Resistance Records, formed in 1993 by George Eric Hawthorne, formerly a leading figure in the World Church of the Creator and singer in the band RA-HOWA (Racial Holy War). A lucrative undertaking, Resistance Records reportedly turned an annual profit of $50,000 before falling foul of both tax and racial hate laws in 1997. The following year the concern was sold to Willis Carto, leader of the Liberty Lobby, though barely a year later it changed hands again, when Carto was declared bankrupt as a result of his feud with the Institute for Historical Review. Its new owner was William Pierce, leader of the violent National Alliance (NA).

White power music represents a small fortune to any groups able to control it, providing a welcome source of funding for impecunious neo-Nazi movements which can raise revenue through sales of CDs that are cheaply produced before being sold for several times their cost. The NA claimed that Resistance Records receives fifty orders per day, each totaling approximately $70 worth of merchandise, leading Pierce to predict gross annual sales totaling $1 million in 2001. Increasingly, white power music is being marketed, as is commercial music, through the Internet. Resistance Records, for instance, maintains a sleek, professional-looking website complete with on-line "radio station" and downloadable MP3s from its inventory to enable curious listeners to sample its music. The Internet enables white power concerts to be promoted to a far wider audience than a humble flyer could hope to reach. Its bulletin boards and fan sites also help to bring disparate white power music fans together with the aim of forging them into a palpable racial community while also harnessing their purchasing power to fund the movements themselves.

Graham Macklin

See Also: CANADA; CARTO, WILLIS; CYBERFASCISM; INSTITUTE FOR HISTORICAL REVIEW, THE; MUSIC; NEO-NAZISM; PALINGENETIC MYTH; PIERCE, WILLIAM; POSTWAR FASCISM; RACISM; RADIO; SKINHEAD FASCISM; SKREWDRIVER; UNITED STATES, THE (POSTWAR); WHITE NOISE; WHITE SUPREMACISM

References
Burghart, Devin, ed. 1999. *Soundtracks to the White Revolution: White Supremacist Assaults on Youth Music Subcultures.* Chicago: Center for New Community.
Cotter, John M. 1999. "Sounds of Hate: White Power Rock and Roll and the Neo-Nazi Skinhead Subculture." *Terrorism and Political Violence* 11, no. 2 (summer): 111–140.
Lowles, Nick, and Steve Silver, eds. 1998. *White Noise: Inside the International Nazi Skinhead Scene.* London: Searchlight.

ROCKWELL, GEORGE LINCOLN (1918–1967)

Founder of the American Nazi Party in 1959. Rockwell, who was born in central Illinois, served in World War II and in the Korean War as a U.S. Navy pilot. Later he concluded that "Jewish propaganda" had deceived the American people as to the heroic nature of German National Socialism and its struggle against the Jews. He was assassinated in 1967 in Arlington, Virginia. His supporters like to present him as the "quintessential American folk-hero": tall, handsome, athletic, reminiscent of a John Wayne or a Clark Gable. In the American Nazi Party program issued by Rockwell in 1960, he proposed to protect workers from "political exploitation" and to offer free medicine, free health care, and free legal services. Speculation was to be abolished and monopolies were to be owned by the whole people, while "honest enterprises" were to be left alone. Rockwell had a strong leadership doctrine and had absorbed Gustave Le Bon's theories about how the "feminine" crowd responds to "masculine" leadership. Rockwell alleged that Americans had become feminized and believed that he could help to reverse this. He also espoused Social Darwinism, arguing that humans are territorial, aggressive, tribal, and patriarchal. Every tribe seeks "biological in-

tegrity" as well as territory. Thus, white Christian America inevitably fought for the preservation of the white race. The theories of liberalism simply ignore these basic facts of nature; liberalism is a "sin against nature." Ultimately, Rockwell's "Nazism" was a very American phenomenon.

Cyprian Blamires

See Also: ABSTRACTION; ANTI-SEMITISM; CONSPIRACY THEORIES; GERMANY; HEALTH; LE BON, GUSTAVE; LIBERALISM; MEDICINE; NATURE; NAZISM; NEO-NAZISM; PIERCE, WILLIAM; POSTWAR FASCISM; RATIONALISM; SOCIAL DARWINISM; UNITED STATES, THE (POSTWAR); WARRIOR ETHOS, THE; WHITE SUPREMACISM; WORLD WAR II

Reference
Simonelli, F. J. 1999. *American Fuehrer: George Lincoln Rockwell and the American Nazi Party.* Urbana: University of Illinois Press.

ROEHM, ERNST (1887–1934)

Fought as an officer in World War I and later joined the counter-revolutionary Free Corps Epp, a group that was a precursor of Nazism. As a good friend of Hitler, he took part in the attempted coup in 1923. On his return from Bolivia, where he had served as military adviser, Roehm was made chief of staff of the SA by Hitler in 1930. Differences in opinion about questions of strategy and the power that Roehm had as the commander of the million-strong SA led Hitler to the decision to eliminate him and others, arguing that Roehm had been preparing a coup. Roehm was shot dead on 1 July 1934 by SS officers.

Fabian Virchow

See Also: BOLIVIA; GERMANY; FREIKORPS, THE; HITLER, ADOLF; HOMOSEXUALITY; MUNICH (BEER-HALL) PUTSCH, THE; NAZISM; NIGHT OF THE LONG KNIVES, THE; PARAMILITARISM; SA, THE; SS, THE

References
Campbell, Bruce. 1998. *The SA Generals and the Rise of Nazism.* Lexington: University Press of Kentucky.
Grant, Thomas D. 2004. *Stormtroopers and Crisis in the Nazi Movement: Activism, Ideology and Dissolution.* London: Routledge.
Smelser, Ronald, and Rainer Zitelmann, eds. 1989. *The Nazi Elite.* Basingstoke: Macmillan.

ROLÃO PRETO, FRANCISCO (1894–1977)

Portuguese politician and admirer of Italian Fascism during the 1920s. In 1932 he founded the short-lived and overtly fascist National Syndicalism movement. Divisions within the movement resulted in a substantial number of its leaders integrating into the authoritarian regime one year later, however, and Preto became increasingly disillusioned with fascism. His gradual move away from fascism was completed when he published critiques of his own earlier writings on Mussolini and became involved with the Democratic Opposition Movement during the 1940s.

Stewart Lloyd-Jones

See Also: AUTHORITARIANISM; FASCIST PARTY, THE; ITALY; MUSSOLINI, BENITO ANDREA; PORTUGAL; SALAZAR, ANTÓNIO DE OLIVEIRA; SYNDICALISM

Reference
Pinto, A. C. 2000. *The Blue Shirts: Portuguese Fascists and the New State.* Boulder, NY: University of Columbia Press Social Science Monographs.

ROMA AND SINTI, THE ("GYPSIES," THE)

Targeted by the Nazis for destruction along with Jews and others in the Holocaust. Traditionally, there were never large numbers of Roma in the German states or in post-1871 Germany. However, the 30,000 to 33,000 Roma who lived there prior to Adolf Hitler's accession to power in 1933 were accustomed to harsh legal restrictions on their movements and activities. In fact, early Nazi officials considered such restrictions initially adequate to deal with what they regarded as the "Gypsy menace." But Nazi officials then began to use various immigration and racial laws to force foreign Roma out of the country or restrict the movements of German Roma. In 1935, the Criminal Police (Kripo) began to force Roma into special camps known as *Zigeunerlager.* Prior to the opening of the 1936 Berlin Olympics, police throughout Prussia raided Roma camps and homes and force-marched them to the Marzahn Concentration Camp in the capital's suburbs. The 1935 anti-Jewish Nuremberg Laws were later applied to Roma, whom the Nazis regarded as a people, like the Jews, infected with *artfremdes Blut* ("alien blood"). In 1936, Dr. Robert Ritter was appointed head of the Eugenic and Populations Biological Research Station of the Reich Health Office, which would be the principal German research institute on the Roma. Ritter and his assistant, Eva Justin, did extensive genealogical surveys of 30,000 German and Austrian Roma, ranking them in five categories from *Vollzigeuner* ("full Gypsy") to *Nicht-Ziguener* ("non-Gypsy").

Nazi racial laws, when combined with Ritter's later work with Kripo, gave German authorities the leverage they needed to initiate a massive campaign against the Roma, first in the Greater Reich and later throughout Europe. By the time that World War II broke out, the Roma of the Third Reich had been deprived of most of their civil and socioeconomic rights. A new wave of Roma deportations followed, usually in conjunction with *Aktionen* against Jews. In the fall of 1939, Kripo circulated a secret order that prevented Roma from moving, in preparation for the shipment of Roma with Jews to Nisko in the newly established General Government in German-occupied Poland. After that plan failed, the Nazis sent more than 5,000 Roma to the Lodz ghetto in Poland. Yet in 1941 there were still Roma registered for the draft, married to non-Roma, or even attending public school in the Reich. That quickly changed. In 1941–1942, new anti-Roma regulations removed many of these remaining rights. On 16 December 1942, Heinrich Himmler, head of the SS and the RSHA (Reichssicherheitshauptamt, Reich Main Security Office), Nazi Germany's super police, ordered all Reich Roma deported to Auschwitz.

Himmler's decree was not all-inclusive, and it provided temporary exemptions for pure Sinti and Lalleri Roma. (The Sinti were the "pure-blooded" German Roma who had lived in the German lands for four to five centuries. The Lalleri were part of the larger subgroup of East European Roma who had migrated into the German states in the eighteenth and nineteenth centuries.) He later appointed a number of Sinti and Lalleri leaders to identify those who were "pure-blooded," with the idea of allowing those selected to live within specially confined areas. Martin Bormann strongly objected to Himmler's efforts to save this handful of Roma, and protested to Hitler. Himmler countered Bormann's arguments in a personal conversation with the Fuehrer, and the Sinti-Lalleri exemp-

Entrance to the gypsy camp in Lodz ghetto in Poland after their deportation to Chlemno concentration camp in 1942. The Nazi war on the gypsies was part and parcel of their endeavor to 'cleanse' the German people of 'alien' elements who would be a 'taint' in the racial stock. (United States Holocaust Memorial Museum)

tions remained. In reality, though, Kripo paid little attention to this special list of Roma. In early 1943, the RSHA decreed that there were no pure Roma in the Third Reich. Most had been sent to the Gypsy Family Camp at Auschwitz II-Birkenau, where some suffered from the inhumane medical experiments conducted by the Gypsy camp's physician, Dr. Josef Mengele, who was particularly interested in Roma twins. About 21,000 Roma would die at Auschwitz.

There were also widespread murders of Roma during the early stages of the German invasion of the Soviet Union in the summer of 1941. Specially trained killing squads, the Einsatzgruppen, systematically murdered Jews, Roma, and the handicapped as the units moved into various parts of Russia. The Roma in other parts of Central and Eastern Europe were more fortunate, though they did suffer persecution because of the application of Nuremberg-style racial laws in countries that were active Nazi allies during much of World War II. Estimates are that 5,000 Bulgarian Roma died dur-

ing the Holocaust (out of a prewar population of 150,000). Most of the 6,540 prewar Czech Roma were murdered in the Holocaust, while most of Slovakia's 100,000 Roma, some of them wartime refugees, survived. About a quarter to a third of Hungary's 72,000 to 100,000 Roma were murdered, while some 12 to 14 percent of Romania's 262,000 to 300,000 Roma perished. About half of Yugoslavia's 80,000 Roma died during the Holocaust.

David Crowe

See Also: ANTI-SEMITISM; ARYANISM; AUSCHWITZ (-BIRKENAU); BARBAROSSA, OPERATION; BERLIN OLYMPICS, THE; BLOOD; BORMANN, MARTIN; BULGARIA; CONCENTRATION CAMPS; CZECHOSLOVAKIA; EUGENICS; *GENERAL GOUVERNEMENT*/GENERAL GOVERNMENT, THE; GERMANY; GHETTOS; HIMMLER, HEINRICH; HITLER, ADOLF; HOLOCAUST, THE; HUNGARY; MENGELE, JOSEF; NAZISM; NUREMBERG LAWS, THE; POLAND; RACIAL DOCTRINE; RACISM; ROMANIA; SLOVAKIA; SOCIAL DARWINISM; SOVIET UNION, THE; SS, THE; THIRD REICH, THE; WORLD WAR II; YUGOSLAVIA

References

Crowe, David M. 1994. *A History of the Gypsies of Eastern Europe and Russia.* New York: St. Martin's.

———. 2000. "The Roma Holocaust." Pp. 179–202 in *The Holocaust as Ghost: Writings on Art, Politics, Law and Education,* edited by F. C. Decoste and Bernard Schwartz. Edmonton: University of Alberta Press.

Lewy, Guenther. 2000. *The Nazi Persecution of the Gypsies.* Oxford: Oxford University Press.

Zimmermann, Michael. 1996. *Rassenutopie und Genozid: die nationalsozialistische Lösung der Zigeunerfrage.* Hamburg: Hans Christian.

ROMANIA

Fascism in Romania was the result of the artificial creation of the modern Romanian state after World War I and of the abrupt introduction of democracy into a predominantly rural and patriarchal Romanian society. In 1919, Romania was rewarded for its role in the war with a doubling of its territory and population (including many non-Romanian minorities). Within Romania, World War I led to land for the peasants and to the introduction of universal suffrage. The bankruptcy of the democratic system in Romania in the 1930s was the result of the discrepancy between the programs of the political parties and their continuing role as traditional vehicles of power.

After a short period of populism in the first years after the war and nine governments in four years, the old prewar Liberal Party returned to power under Ion I. C. Bratianu. Bratianu's government lasted four years, and attempted to implement the reforms needed to lift the young state to a Western level. One important concern of the liberals was higher education. Romania lacked a middle class. It was believed that the best way to create such a class was through education. In the first years after the war, education for the children of peasants had become a tool for political parties to build a strong clientele in rural milieus. The liberals continued this policy. When the first of these students from the countryside entered the university, they began to realize that they would have to compete with their Jewish colleagues. Jewish students generally came from urban milieus, were intellectually better prepared, and were proportionally more strongly represented at the university than their Romanian colleagues. The wave of anti-Semitism this caused was concentrated at the second most important university of the country, the University of Iasi, near the Russian border. In 1922, the students called for a *numerus clausus* for Jewish students. In 1923, A. C. Cuza—a law professor in Iasi—founded the "League of National-Christian Defense" (LNCD). Cuza campaigned against the abolition of the article in the constitution that denied Jews any rights in the new Romanian state.

In 1926, the liberal government of Bratianu ended its four years in office. Meanwhile, an important new party had appeared on the political scene, the National Peasants Party. This party was the result of a merger between the Transylvanian Nationalist Party and the Peasant Party. The National Peasant Party was the first true alternative to the authoritarian Liberal Party. It addressed itself to broad layers of the population, and led to a temporary moderation of the extremism prevalent among the students. The elections of 1928 meant the end of the power of the Liberal Party, and the end of an era. The National Peasants Party was elected with an overwhelming majority (77.76 percent). The country had been making great economic progress under the Liberal Party, and the expectation was that the National Peasants Party would now also bring true democracy. Cuza's party participated in the elections but did not get elected. His anti-Semitic line, however, was continued by one of his students, Corneliu Zelea Codreanu. Codreanu represented the hard core of Cuza's LNCD. In 1924 he killed the police prefect of Iasi, a crime for which he was acquitted. Codreanu's acquittal by the court strengthened him in his belief in violence as the basis of political struggle. On 24 June 1927, Codreanu gathered his former fellow inmates to found the Legion of the Archangel Michael, with himself as its leader. Initially, the legion was a modest society of students, with "no other program than the life of struggle" of Codreanu and his friends. Its ultimate goal, however, was the creation of a "New Man" through certain world-renouncing practices. Later, Codreanu organized the legion as a nationwide movement on the basis of "nests," groups of three to thirteen members. In the first months of its existence, however, the public impact of the legion was limited. The Romanians had put all of their hopes in the National Peasants Party and were still optimistic about the outcome of the democratic experiment.

The year 1929, the year of the Great Depression, brought this period of optimism abruptly to an end. The year 1929 was also the year of the legion's turn to the masses. On 3–4 January, Codreanu convoked in Iasi a meeting of all nest leaders. In December the legion held its first public rally. In the following months, Codreanu and the legionnaires marched singing from village to village. Mounted on a white horse, Codreanu was hailed by the peasants as a messiah. In 1930, Bessarabia called. This was a former Russian territory, and only recently added to Romania. Codreanu planned a large anti-Jewish and anticommunist march through Bessara. To avoid the problems with the authorities that he had encountered on his previous marches, Codreanu founded a new group, the "Iron Guard." Codreanu received the authorization for his march from the minister of internal affairs, but under great pressure the decision was revoked and the minister replaced. The new minister, Mihalache, seized the first occasion to deal with the legion. In December 1930, after an attempted murder by a young supporter of the legion, Mihalache prohibited the organization. Codreanu was arrested and brought to Bucharest to stand trial. Once again, he was acquitted by the court.

Codreanu's second acquittal did not lift the ban on the legion. Encouraged by increasing popular support for the legion and strengthened by the knowledge that he had the law on his side, Codreanu ran for the elections under the pseudonym "Group Corneliu Z. Codreanu." His first attempt to get elected failed. Three weeks later, however, fresh elections were held in a county in which one seat had fallen vacant. Codreanu summoned all of his supporters to the county, and—after an intensive campaign—finally obtained his first seat in the parliament. In March 1932 the legion was banned for the second time, but its ascent proved to be irreversible. In elections four months later, the legion doubled its number of votes, which entitled it to five seats in parliament. In 1933, two new propaganda tools were adopted by the legion. The "death team" was a group of legionnaires who had solemnly pledged to accept death with perfect equanimity. In May, a first team was sent to tour around the country. A more lasting and efficient innovation were the "labor camps." The first large-scale labor camp was set up in response to an appeal by legionnaires in the countryside for help in the construction of a dam. On 10 July, more than 200 legionnaires turned up in what became the first of a series of labor camps.

The return of the Liberal Party to power (14 November 1933) presaged little good for the legion. In December 1933 the new prime minister (Ion Duca) ordered its complete elimination. Hundreds of people who were even slightly suspected of links with the legion were arrested and imprisoned. Public opinion was shocked, and the government was forced to release all detainees. On 29 December, the legionnaires took revenge and killed Duca. Codreanu was again acquitted and could continue with his propaganda. In 1936 the legion lost its most important channel of recruitment, when the authorities prohibited all public works undertaken by private organizations. The legion now decided to set up a network of shops and restaurants. These would be run by legionnaires, and had the additional advantage that they would challenge the Jews in a sector that traditionally used to be theirs. The strongest display of the legion's presence in Romania, however, was the glorious return to Romania (in January 1937) of the bodies of two legionnaires who had fallen in the Spanish Civil War: Ion I. Moţa and Vasile Marin. Hundreds of thousands of people turned out to greet the bodies, and in Bucharest legionnaires took an oath to follow in Moţa's and Marin's footsteps. King Carol II was deeply impressed by the public support for Codreanu displayed at these events, and he offered him a share in power. Codreanu declined.

In 1938, the two decades of the democratic experiment came to an end. King Carol II abrogated the constitution and established an authoritarian monarchy. The new constitution made legionary propaganda virtually impossible: it significantly raised the minimum age for voting and prohibited political propaganda by priests or in churches, as well as all oaths other than those approved by the state. The pretext to deal with Codreanu himself came when Codreanu was sued for slander by one of the king's ministers. Codreanu was sentenced to six months in prison and then executed by secret agents of the king. King Carol's persecution of the legionnaires in 1939, and the fact that, in 1940, he ceded Transylvania to the Germans, led to his forced abdication on 5 September 1940. On 14 September 1940, General Antonescu invited the legionnaires to form a government. Antonescu was an important ally of the Germans in their plans to attack Russia. This assured him of their full support when in January 1941 he suppressed a rebellion of the legionnaires. The legionnaires and their leader, Horia Sima, were sent into exile, and on 14 February, Antonescu abrogated the National-Legionary State. The role of the legion was over.

Philip Vanhaelemeersch

See Also: INTRODUCTION; ANTI-SEMITISM; ANTONESCU, GENERAL ION; AUSTRO-HUNGARIAN EMPIRE/HABSBURG EMPIRE, THE; AUTHORITARIANISM; BOLSHEVISM; BOURGEOISIE, THE; CLERICO-FASCISM; CODREANU, CORNELIU ZELEA; CULTS OF DEATH; FALANGE; FARMERS; GERMANY; LEGION OF THE ARCHANGEL MICHAEL, THE; LIBERALISM; MARXISM; MILITARISM; MONARCHISM; MONARCHY; MOŢA, ION I.; NEW MAN, THE; ORTHODOX CHURCHES, THE; PARAMILITARISM; RURALISM; SIMA, HORIA; SPANISH CIVIL WAR, THE; VIOLENCE; WALL STREET CRASH, THE; WARRIOR ETHOS, THE; WORLD WAR I; WORLD WAR II

References

Heinen, A. 1986. *Die Legion "Erzengel Michael" in Rumänien. Soziale Bewegung und Politische Organisation. Ein Beitrag zum Problem des Internationalen Faschismus,* (Südosteuropäische Arbeiten, 83). München: R. Oldenbourg.

Livezeanu, I. 1995. *Cultural Politics in Greater Romania: Regionalism, Nation Building and Ethnic Struggle, 1918–1930.* Ithaca: Cornell University Press.

Nagy-Talevera, N. M. 2001 [1970]. *The Green Shirts and the Others: A History of Fascism in Hungary and Romania.* Iasi: Center for Romanian Studies.

Ornea, Z. 1999. *The Romanian Extreme Right: The Nineteen Thirties,* Boulder, CO: East European Monographs.

Tismaneanu, V., and D. Pavel. 1994. "Romania's Mystical Revolutionaries: The Generation of Angst and Adventure Revisited." *East European Politics and Societies* 8, no. 3 (fall): 402–438.

Volovici, L. 1991. *Nationalist Ideology and Antisemitism: The Case of Romanian Intellectuals in the 1930s.* Oxford: Pergamon.

Weber, E. 1965. "Romania." Pp. 501–574 in *The European Right: A Historical Profile,* edited by H. Rogger. London: Weidenfeld and Nicholson,.

ROMANITÀ: See ROME

ROME

Whereas Rome, the historical Roman Empire, constituted the mythological core of Italian Fascist ideology, it evoked rather less enthusiastic responses from German National Socialists and their Pangerman and *Völkisch* precursors. Italian Fascism claimed to be inspired by *Romanità,* Roman values of order, discipline, and hierarchy. The 1932 statement of Fascist ideology, "The Doctrine of Fascism," proclaimed: "The Fascist state is the will to power and empire. The Roman tradition is also an idea of power" (*Enciclopedia Italiana,* vol. 14, p. 85); Fascism in its propaganda promoted the idea of Fascist Italy's creating a "Second Roman Empire" in the Mediterranean, North Africa, and the Middle East. In May 1936, after the conquest of Ethiopia by Italy, Mussolini proudly announced, "The Empire has returned to the hills of Rome." All of the items on Mussolini's list of territorial claims in the Mediterranean—Malta, Nice, Corsica, Tunisia, Palestine, Albania, the Adriatic coast of Yugoslavia, Greece, a large

Ancient Roman lictors (bodyguards to the magistrates) carrying fasces ('bundles') as the symbol of Roman authority. The term fascist *as used by Mussolini's movement and regime in Italy was derived from the Latin 'fascio' ('bundle') and was a deliberate reference to an ambition to restore Italy to her ancient greatness. (Ridpath, John Clark,* Ridpath's History of the World, *1901)*

chunk of Anatolia and Egypt—had been part of the Roman Empire. From 1939 onward, mosaic maps of both the Roman Empire at the time of Augustus and of "Mussolini's Roman Empire" began to appear side by side on the walls of Italy's municipal buildings.

Fascist rhetoric was saturated with Roman imagery and Latin words. Even Mussolini's own title, Duce, was a translation of the Latin *dux* ("leader"), and the very symbol of Fascism, the *fasces,* was taken from the bundle of rods borne before the Roman lictors. As another visual prop to his Roman imperial ambitions, Mussolini proceeded to demolish parts of medieval Rome in order to excavate its classical past, thus revealing more of the Forum area; a new triumphal way, the present-day Via dei Fori Imperiali, was constructed from

Piazza Venezia (site of Mussolini's office) to the Coliseum. Fascist military parades and other public ceremonies were choreographed against a genuine classical Roman backdrop. And in the new suburb south of Rome constructed to house the Universal Exhibition of Rome planned for 1942, a magnificent Museum of Roman Civilization was set up.

Until the introduction of the Racial Laws in 1938, Italian Fascism also operated by the Roman concept of citizenship as an acceptance of superior cultural values by subject peoples, with the result that the Italian concept of race remained officially an essentially cultural one, defined by language, history, and even geography, rather than by blood. Thus the Jews of Italy were thoroughly assimilated and until 1938 were not subject to discrimination or persecution. The principle of *Civis Romanus Sum* ("I am a Roman citizen") may not in practice have been applied to the inhabitants of either Libya or Ethiopia in the Fascist period, but the Fascists did not seek to expel or exterminate the German and Slav minorities in the territories that Italy acquired in the Versailles Peace Settlement but rather to forcibly "Italianize" them. It was precisely Roman universalism, however, which was usually equated by its enemies with pernicious Catholic and Jewish influences, that some precursors of National Socialism rejected. The Austrian Pangermanist Guido von List, for example, exulted in the defeat of two Roman legions by Arminius at the battle of the Teutoberg Forest in A.D. 9 and a later defeat of the Romans at Carnuntum in A.D. 375. List and other *völkisch* writers in the decades before World War I rejected Roman civilization (including Roman law) in favor of the Aryan pagan values of "Germandom," arguing that they had produced a great civilization which the Germans needed to reclaim. But the Nazis between 1919 and 1945 do not appear to have been overly influenced by such thinking, though many would also have equated Rome with Catholicism and the power of the papacy. Despite that, Hitler's admiration for Roman art and architecture was unabated, as his state visit to Italy in 1938, with the tours of the art galleries and architectural sites of Florence and Rome, demonstrates.

Neofascist and neo-Nazi groups in the post-1945 period have demonstrated a rather less ambivalent attitude to Rome than their predecessors. The Italian neo-Fascist ideologue Julius Evola deplored the subversion and destruction of Roman ideas of duty and honor, as well as Rome's accession to Judaism and Christianity, a feeling shared by the more recent U.S. neo-Nazi organization the Church of the Creator; David Lane and another North American group, the racial Odinists, accuse the Jews of destroying the Roman Empire through the "invention" and propagation of Christianity. Rome is thus for them an achievement of the Aryan race.

John Pollard

See Also: ALBANIA; ANTI-SEMITISM; ARCHITECTURE; ART; ARYANISM; BARBAROSSA, FREDERICK, HOLY ROMAN EMPEROR; BLOOD; CATHOLIC CHURCH, THE; CHRISTIANITY; CORFU; DALMATIA; D'ANNUNZIO, GABRIELE; *EHRE* ("HONOR"); ETHIOPIA; EVOLA, JULIUS; EXPANSIONISM; FASCIO, THE; FASCIST PARTY, THE; FIUME; GERMANNESS (*DEUTSCHHEIT*); GERMANY; HITLER, ADOLF; HOLY ROMAN EMPIRE, THE; IRREDENTISM; ITALY; LIBYA; MIDDLE EAST, THE; MUSSOLINI, BENITO ANDREA; NAZISM; NEO-NAZISM; NORDIC SOUL, THE; PANGERMANISM; PAPACY, THE; POSTWAR FASCISM; PROPAGANDA; RACIAL DOCTRINE; SLAVS, THE (AND ITALY); TRADITION; UNITED STATES, THE (POSTWAR); VERSAILLES, THE TREATY OF; *VOLK, VÖLKISCH;* WHITE SUPREMACISM; WORLD WAR I

References

Gentile, G. ed. 1951. "Rome." In *Enciclopedia Italiana,* vol. 14. Rome: Istituto Treccani.

Goodrick-Clarke, N. 2002. *Black Sun: Aryan Cults, Esoteric Nazism and the Politics of Identity.* New York: New York University Press.

———. 2004. *The Occult Roots of Nazism.* London: Tauris.

Painter, Borden. 2005. *Mussolini's Rome: The Fascist Transformation of the Eternal City.* Basingstoke: Palgrave Macmillan.

Pollard, J. F. 1998. *The Fascist Experience in Italy.* London: Routledge.

ROOSEVELT, FRANKLIN DELANO (1882–1945)

President of the United States and longtime opponent of the totalitarian ideologies of the Axis powers. Roosevelt was born into a wealthy background in New York and studied in Europe and at Harvard and Columbia Law schools. He embarked on a career first as a lawyer and then as a politician, becoming assistant secretary of the navy from 1913 to 1920. Despite being paralyzed by polio in the early 1920s, he was able to become governor of New York in 1928. He became U.S. president in 1932 and was subsequently to be re-elected on a record three occasions for a total of four terms. His success was partly the result of his celebrated "New Deal" strategy of combating the Depression; the main planks of his program were the abandonment of the gold standard, the devaluation of the dollar, state intervention in the credit market, agricultural price supports, and the enablement of provision for unemployment and old age insurance. Roosevelt was not happy with the isolationist attitude of many of his compatriots in the face of the war that broke out in 1939, and in August 1941 he met with Churchill to frame the Atlantic Charter, which clearly signified the anti-Axis tendency of U.S. foreign policy. A few months later, after the Japanese assault on Pearl Harbor, he brought his country into the war. He was involved in further meetings with Churchill in 1943 and subsequently met with Stalin as well, in Teheran in December of that year, to coordinate the conduct of the war effort against Germany. Although again present at a meeting with Churchill and Stalin at Yalta in 1945, Roosevelt was already dying.

Cyprian Blamires

See Also: AXIS, THE; CHURCHILL, SIR WINSTON LEONARD SPENCER; ECONOMICS; INFLATION; JAPAN; JAPAN AND WORLD WAR II; LEAGUE OF NATIONS, THE; PEARL HARBOR; STALIN, IOSIF VISSARIONOVICH; TOTALITARIANISM; UNITED STATES, THE (PRE-1945); WALL STREET CRASH, THE; WORLD WAR II

References
Casey, Steven. 2004. *Cautious Crusade: Franklin D. Roosevelt, American Public Opinion, and the War against Nazi Germany.* New York: OUP.
Dallek, Robert. 1995. *Franklin D. Roosevelt and American Foreign Policy, 1932–45.* New York: OUP.
Doenecke, Justus D., and Mark A. Stoler. 2005. *Debating Franklin D. Roosevelt's Foreign Policies, 1933–1945.* New York: Rowman and Littlefield.
Heinrichs, W. H. 1988. *Threshold of War: Franklin D. Roosevelt and American Entry into World War II.* Oxford: Oxford University Press.
Simson, M. 1989. *Franklin D. Roosevelt.* Oxford: Basil Blackwell.

ROOTLESSNESS

One of the "enemies" that interwar fascists saw themselves as called to oppose. "Rootless" persons were those regarded as lacking in connectedness to a specific nation. The classic models of rootlessness in the Nazi understanding were the Jews; they were a people who were present everywhere but who seemed to belong nowhere. Anti-Semitic propagandists denounced them as owing loyalty only to their own people and none to the states in which they resided. Ironically, the Jews were sometimes denounced as "rootless" in the same breath as the Jesuits, who were directly answerable to the Holy See and therefore regarded as without any national loyalties. There was moreover a centuries-old tradition of "international conspiracy" theorizing about the Jesuits, and this made them well suited to be hooked up with the alleged "international conspiracies" of the Jews that became fashionable in nineteenth-century Europe. However, the main class of persons envisaged along with the Jews as being "rootless" were the socialist or communist Left, with their advocacy of internationalism, often denounced by interwar fascists as "cosmopolitanism." Whereas for Italian Fascists "rootlessness" had a fairly straightforward reference to the classes of person mentioned above, for Nazis it could relate to a particular philosophy of "Germanness" according to which there was an intrinsically "rooted" quality that was characteristic of racially pure Germans. Their conception of the "rootedness" of the Germans in the soil of their country had a uniquely mystical quality and was expressed in a vague notion that German "blood" had a special relationship to German soil.

Cyprian Blamires

See Also: INTRODUCTION; ABSTRACTION; "ANTI-" DIMENSION OF FASCISM, THE; ANTI-SEMITISM; ARYANISM; BARRES, AUGUSTE MAURICE; BLOOD; BLOOD AND SOIL; CATHOLIC CHURCH, THE; COMMUNITY; CONSPIRACY THEORIES; COSMOPOLITANISM; EUROPE; FASCIST PARTY, THE; GERMANIC RELIGION; GERMANNESS (*DEUTSCHHEIT*); GERMANY; GLOBALIZATION; INDIVIDUALISM; ITALY; JESUITS, THE; LEAGUE OF NATIONS, THE; LIBERALISM; MYSTICISM; NATIONALISM; NAZISM; NIHILISM; NORDIC SOUL, THE; ORGANICISM AND NAZISM; PACIFISM; PALINGENETIC MYTH; PAPACY, THE; RACIAL DOCTRINE; SOUL; UNITED NATIONS, THE; *VOLKSGEMEINSCHAFT,* THE

References
Bauman, Z. 1991. *Modernity and Ambivalence.* Cambridge: Polity.
Bramwell, Anna. 1985. *Blood and Soil: Richard Walther Darré and Hitler's "Green Party."* Bourne End: Kensal.
Durkheim, E. 1964. *The Division of Labor in Society.* New York: Free Press.
Griffin, R. 1993. "Identification and Integration: Conflicting Aspects of the Human Need for Self-transcendence within Ideological Communities." *Journal for the Study of European Ideas* 18, no. 1.
Mosse, George L. 1964. *The Crisis of German Ideology: Intellectual Origins of the Third Reich.* London: Weidenfeld and Nicholson.
Toennies, F. 2002. *Community and Society.* New York: Dover.

ROSENBERG, ALFRED
(1893–1946)

Chief Nazi philosopher and ideologue, editor of the *Völkischer Beobachter*, publisher, and promoter of *The Protocols of the Elders of Zion*. Rosenberg was born into a lower-middle-class family of German origin. His father was director of a local subsidiary of a German merchant company in the Baltic. As a member of the small German minority in Estonia and Latvia, young Rosenberg embraced German nationalism, devouring the works of Houston Stewart Chamberlain and Gobineau, as well as books on German mysticism, Indian philosophy, and history. While he was studying in Moscow in 1917, the Russian Revolution swept across the country. Rosenberg then discovered *The Protocols of the Elders of Zion*, a notorious anti-Semitic forgery, and he became convinced that the Jews were the architects of the revolution. In November 1918, Rosenberg left the fledgling Soviet Union and immigrated to Germany, traveling to Munich. While socialist politicians discussed Bavarian separatism and spoke of German war guilt, conservative, Catholic, and monarchist forces began to rally in the rancorous atmosphere of a lost war and a bewildered population. From February 1919, Rosenberg was employed by Dietrich Eckart as special correspondent on communism and Jewry for his magazine *Auf Gut Deutsch*. Rosenberg found a receptive audience for his eyewitness experience of the Russian Revolution and its interpretation as a nefarious Jewish world plot.

When revolution came to Bavaria in April 1919, Eckart and Rosenberg played an active part in the resistance against the Soviet regime in Munich. Rosenberg next linked up with the German Workers' Party (DAP), founded on 5 January 1919 out of the political workers' circle within the Thule Society. The leader of the DAP, Anton Drexler, was an admirer of *Auf Gut Deutsch* and introduced himself to Eckart and Rosenberg in May 1919, when they accepted his invitation to address the party on Bolshevism and the Jewish question on 15 August. Eckart's link with the party may well have been the reason that the army sent Hitler as an informant to the next meeting on 12 September 1919. Eckart and Hitler first met at the former's home during the drafting of the DAP program in November

and December 1919, and Rosenberg also met Hitler on such an occasion. Rosenberg joined the DAP in late 1919 and then settled down as the party writer and researcher. Between 1920 and 1923, Rosenberg published six books on Jewish conspiracy topics. *Die Spur des Juden im Wandel der Zeiten* (1920) identified the Jew as the source of both anarchism and communism. A list of leading Jews in England identified London as the center of world Jewry. *Das Verbrechen der Freimauererei* (1921) added in the Freemasons, a nineteenth-century conspiracy favorite.

Now the official philosopher of the Nazi party, Rosenberg published *Die Protokolle der Weisen von Zion und die jüdische Weltpolitik* (1923). With extended commentaries on brief excerpts, Rosenberg attempted to prove the validity of the *Protocols* by showing the persistence of the Jewish world conspiracy in current events and among leading political figures, including Herbert Louis Samuel; Edwin-Samuel Montague; Lord Reading, notorious as a speculator in the Marconi scandal, lord chief justice, and ambassador in New York, as well as viceroy of India; Sir Alfred Mond, world industrialist, newspaper magnate, and minister for public works, and an active Zionist. The list continues with French and Italian Jews in high places, before expanding into U.S. Jewry. Rosenberg concluded that New York had by 1920 succeeded London as the center of the Jewish world conspiracy. He and Dietrich Eckart together forged the radical anti-Semitic ideology of Nazism before Hitler appeared on the scene and were a powerful influence on the latter's ideological development. Rosenberg succeeded Eckart as editor of the *Völkischer Beobachter*, the Nazi Party newspaper, in 1921.

Rosenberg marched with Hitler as one of his closest comrades in the Munich Putsch of November 1923. When Hitler was jailed in 1924, he appointed Rosenberg head of the Nazi Party during his absence. In 1927 Rosenberg became head of the Nazi cultural and educational society, renamed the Kampfbund für deutsche Kultur (Combat League for German Culture) in 1929. This Munich-based organization codified and enforced Nazi racial notions in the arts and literature. Rosenberg next published his major work, *Der Mythus des 20. Jahrhunderts* (*The Myth of the Twentieth Century*, 1930), which gave a comprehensive Nazi view on Aryan racial origins, religion, philosophy, aesthetics, and the racial interpretation of history. Second only to Hitler's *Mein Kampf*, the book enjoyed massive sales with a million copies sold by 1942. Coupled with Rosenberg's several offices in ideological education during the 1930s, this book was a major force in promoting ideas of German racial superiority and anti-Semitism throughout the Third Reich. After the 1941 German invasion of the Soviet Union, Rosenberg was appointed Reich minister for the Eastern Occupied Territories in recognition of his special expertise on international Jewry, Marxism, and Russia. All orders for deportations and expropriations were routed through his office, yet his advice about the ethnic complexity of the Soviet Union was typically ignored, as were his protests against the excesses of the SS in the Ukraine. After the fall of the Third Reich, Rosenberg was tried at Nuremberg. Convicted of war crimes and crimes against humanity, he was hanged on 16 October 1946.

Nicholas Goodrick-Clarke

See Also: ANTI-SEMITISM; ARYANISM; BARBAROSSA, OPERATION; BOLSHEVISM; CHAMBERLAIN, HOUSTON STEWART; CONSPIRACY THEORIES; DREXLER, ANTON; ECKART, JOHANN DIETRICH; ECKHART, "MEISTER" JOHANN; ESTONIA; FREEMASONRY/FREEMASONS, THE; GERMANNESS (*DEUTSCHHEIT*); GERMANY; GOBINEAU, JOSEPH ARTHUR COMTE DE; HITLER, ADOLF; LATVIA; LIBERALISM (IN THEOLOGY); LUTHER, MARTIN; MARXISM; MATERIALISM; *MEIN KAMPF;* MYSTICISM; NATIONALISM; NAZISM; NORDIC SOUL, THE; NUREMBERG TRIALS, THE; ORTHODOX CHURCHES, THE; *PROTOCOLS OF THE ELDERS OF ZION, THE;* RACIAL DOCTRINE; RELIGION; RUSSIA; SOVIET UNION, THE; SPANN, OTHMAR; SS, THE; THIRD REICH, THE; THULE SOCIETY, THE; *VÖLKISCHER BEOBACHTER,* THE; WORLD WAR II; ZIONISM

References

Cecil, Robert. 1972. *The Myth of the Master Race: Alfred Rosenberg and Nazi Ideology.* London: Batsford.
Lane, Barbara Miller, and Leila J. Rupp. 1978. *Nazi Ideology before 1933: A Documentation.* Manchester: Manchester University Press.
Rosenberg, Alfred. 1971. *Selected Writings.* Edited by Robert Pois. London: Jonathan Cape.
———. 1982. *The Myth of the Twentieth Century: An Evaluation of the Spiritual-Intellectual Confrontations of Our Age.* Newport Beach, CA: Noontide.
Whisker, James B. 1990. *The Philosophy of Alfred Rosenberg: Origins of the National Socialist Myth.* Costa Mesa, CA: Noontide.

ROYAL FAMILY, THE BRITISH: *See* WINDSOR, EDWARD DUKE OF
RSI: *See* SALÒ REPUBLIC, THE

RURALISM/RURALIZATION (Italy)

Mussolini's intention to "ruralize" Italy, announced in his Ascension Day speech in May 1927, took as its premise the belief that Italy faced demographic decline that could be reversed only by stopping the population drift to the towns and transferring resources to the countryside. In Mussolini's logic, the towns were centers of bourgeois materialism, hedonism, and corruption, and thus low birth rates. Rural society, on the other hand, encouraged hard work, frugality, and fecundity, and the ideal peasant type would provide both Italy's food and its manpower in the next war. As an alternative to politically unpalatable land reform, Fascism promoted land improvement and reclamation schemes. Ruralism was also a not very successfully camouflaged way of discouraging migration to the cities, which, in Fascist minds, threatened to undermine the rural agrarian social structure and render the cities more politically anti-Fascist than they already were: unemployment in the countryside was easier to deal with than unemployment in the towns. Such a policy made little sense in a country in which, culturally speaking, the city was everything and the countryside a backwater, and where agriculture, especially in the south, was technologically backward and there was serious rural overpopulation and landless poverty. Ruralism ultimately failed. Despite 1930s Fascist equivalents of the South African "pass laws," Italian country people persisted in migrating to the cities throughout the period of the Fascist regime, the birth rate continued to decline, and Fascist Italy never did become self-sufficient in grain production.

John Pollard

See Also: AUTARKY; BOURGEOISIE, THE; COSMOPOLITANISM; DEMOGRAPHIC POLICY; FARMERS; FASCIST PARTY, THE; ITALY; MATERIALISM; MODERNITY; MUSSOLINI, BENITO ANDREA; NATURE; PROGRESS; RURALISM (GERMANY); TECHNOLOGY

References

Cannistraro, P. V. 1982. *Historical Dictionary of Fascist Italy.* Westport, CT: Greenwood.
Clark, M. 1996. *Italy—A Modern History, 1971–1995.* London: Longman.

RURALISM (Germany)

In the context of interwar Germany, ruralism refers to the belief of certain movements like the Artamans in the decadence of urban societies and the need for a return to the land. This kind of thinking, chiefly associated in Nazism with the *Blut und Boden* (Blood and Soil) ideology, had a particular attraction for Heinrich Himmler and Walther Darré, both of whom were members of the Artamans. Although Darré was successful in spreading the Nazi message in the countryside with *Blut and Boden* propaganda, in terms of Nazi government policy and practice it was in fact sidelined. It remained largely a matter of theory because the main thrust of Nazism was toward a technologically and scientifically advanced society, for Nazism was essentially a party of progress and modernity.

Cyprian Blamires

See Also: INTRODUCTION; ARTAMAN LEAGUE, THE; BLOOD AND SOIL; COSMOPOLITANISM; DARRE, RICHARD WALTHER; DECADENCE; FARMERS; HIMMLER, HEINRICH; LEISURE; MATERIALISM; MODERNITY; NATURE; PROGRESS; RURALISM (ITALY); SCIENCE; TECHNOLOGY; *WANDERVÖGEL,* THE; YOUTH MOVEMENTS

References

Bramwell, Anna. 1985. *Blood and Soil: Walther Darré and Hitler's "Green Party."* Bourne End: Kensal Press.

Farquharson, J. 1976. *The Plough and the Swastika: The NSDAP and Agriculture in Germany 1928–45.* London: Sage.

RUSSIA

Extreme right-wing ideas were prominent in late czarist political discourse and found a variety of expressions in the writings of, among others, the novelist Fëdor Dostoevskii (1821–1881), biologist Nikolai Danilevskii (1822–1885), and philosopher Konstantin Leont'ev (1831–1891). Prefascist trends have been detected in the activities of the secret police officer Sergei Zubatov (1864–1917) and various organizations known collectively as the "Black Hundreds," including the Union of the Russian People, founded in 1905 by Vladimir Pur-

ishkevich (1870–1920) and Aleksandr Dubrovin (1855–1918). However, no significant prerevolutionary Russian political thinker or group developed an ideology consistently combining integral nationalism with revolutionary aspirations. During the Soviet period, a number of proto-, crypto-, and fully fascist trends appeared in various sectors of society, including the Russian emigre community, but they had little impact on society at large. Since the gradual introduction of political pluralism in the Soviet Union in 1985, a broad spectrum of extremely right-wing groups have appeared in Russia, comprising several fascist political parties, intellectual circles, and groupuscules.

The first significant post-Soviet organization with affinities to fascism, merging ideas of prerevolutionary Black Hundred anti-Semitism, official Soviet "anti-Zionism," and Orthodox monarchism was the National-Patriotic Front Pamiat' (Memory), which emerged in the mid-1980s. Extensively described in Western press reports of the late 1980s, Pamiat' was a small circle of activists that broke up into minuscule splinter groups in 1990. Although a marginal political phenomenon, the Moscow section of the initial Pamiat' emerged as significant by providing, around 1990, a training ground for the subsequent founders of numerous ultranationalist, fundamentalist, and neo-Nazi groupings that populated the lunatic fringe of Russia's nationalist spectrum throughout the 1990s. Fascists who began their political careers in Pamiat' included: Aleksandr Barkashov (born 1953), leader of Russkoe Natsional'noe Edinstvo (RNE; Russian National Unity); Nikolai Lysenko (born 1961), founder of the Natsional-respublikanskaia partiia Rossii (National-Republican Party of Russia) and state duma deputy, 1993–1995; Aleksandr Dugin, co-founder and chief ideologue, from 1994 to 1998, of the Natsional-bol'shevistskaia partiia (NBP; National-Bolshevik Party); and Viktor Iakushev (born 1963), founder of the groupuscule Natsional-sotsial'nyi soiuz (NSS; National-Social Union).

Until its split in late 2000, the RNE represented Russia's most important organization imitating interwar fascism. It was founded in 1990 as a paramilitary, hierarchical organization of young men dressed in black overalls and greeting each other with the Roman salute and cry *Slava Rossii!* ("Glory to Russia!"). Its symbol is a stylized left-handed swastika embedded in an eight-pointed star. Its ideology, too, contains Russian adaptations of German Nazi ideology, especially of the Aryan myth. The RNE's official program's major themes include national rebirth, antifederalism, imperi-

Russian National Unity Party member makes a Hitler salute at a conference in 1999. The aftermath of the breakup of the Soviet Union has seen a revival of Russian nationalism, though some scholars argue that much Soviet-era 'internionalist' rhetoric was in reality merely a cloak for this. (Yuri_Kochetkov/EPA/epa/Corbis)

alism, protectionism, autarky, militarism, eugenics, discouragement of interethnic sexual relations, a mixed economy, special appreciation of the peasantry, limitation of religious freedom to pro-Russian faiths, and creation of a new national elite. According to some sources, RNE documents spoke of plans to kill all Jews and Gypsies in Russia.

In spite of the RNE's imitation of Nazism, its founder, Barkashov, has rejected the labels *fashist* and *natsist*—though he admitted to be a *natsional-sotsialist*. Notwithstanding a high fluctuation of members, the RNE was of substantial organizational strength before its breakup in late 2000 and was estimated to have had, on the eve of its fracture, approximately 20,000 to 25,000 members. It constituted the most visible, obviously fascist Russian organization of the 1990s, and published the high-circulation newspaper *Russkii pori-*

adok (Russian Order). It participated prominently in the armed confrontation in Moscow in October 1993 and was involved in numerous homicides, robberies, and beatings as well as other crimes.

Russian neo-Nazism has drawn considerable attention and been often seen as the main manifestation of, or even been identified with, post-Soviet fascism. Although claiming to be preparing for the assumption of power and, until its split in 2000, to comprise a countrywide network of self-sufficient local cells, the RNE in fact represented only partly a properly political phenomenon. Using the symbols and ideas of a regime that caused a major catastrophe in recent Russian national history, this (until 2000) comparatively large organization represented as much a countercultural youth movement as a political party. The RNE's main bearing on post-Soviet Russian fascism has been indoctrination with racist ideas and the provision of skills in organization, combat, rhetoric, and legal matters to thousands of young Russian men who went through its ranks, its training, and its brainwashing during the 1990s.

The NBP, led by the notorious novelist Eduard Limonov (born 1943), is the second relevant extraparliamentary fascist party of post-Soviet Russia. Limonov, once a little-known avant-garde poet in the USSR, emigrated in 1974 and lived in New York and Paris, where, in the 1980s, he became a well-known prose writer acquainted with French far-right figures Jean-Marie Le Pen and Alain de Benoist. During glasnost, Limonov started to publish literary works and political articles in Russia. By the mid-1990s, he had become a widely read author known for his radical political opinions and frank autobiographical novels. Having returned to Russia, Limonov made, in 1992–1994, several unsuccessful attempts to enter political organizations and enjoyed temporary membership in the "shadow cabinet" of Zhirinovskii's so-called Liberal-Democratic Party of the Soviet Union in 1992. In November 1994, Limonov, Dugin, and Egor Letov (born 1966), lead singer of the popular Russian punk band Grazhdanskaia oborona ("Civil Defense"), founded the NBP and its organ, the biweekly *Limonka* (literally: "little lemon"; also: "hand-grenade"). The NBP's ideology is highly eclectic and merges elements of traditionalism, Leninism, classic Russian nationalism, anarchism, spiritualism, nonconformism, Stalinism, Satanism, situationism, and so forth. NBP publications have made reference to the Nazi SA, Romanian Iron Guard, and West German Rote Armee Fraktion, and shown affinities to the Konservative Revolution and European New Right. The NBP's aim is a total, unitary, one-party Russian empire with an etatist autarkic economy. Demanding a radically anti-U.S. foreign policy, the NBP's immediate focus is reannexation of the former Soviet republics; its long-term aim is a "gigantic continental Empire" from Vladivostok to Gibraltar. National membership is defined by loyalty to Russia. The party became widely known in the late 1990s in connection with extravagant actions across the former Soviet Union and had, in 1999, approximately 6,000 to 7,000 active members. However, as Limonov was imprisoned for illegal possession of weapons from 2001 to 2003, the survival of the party as a noteworthy political force is under question.

Whereas the fascist character of the RNE and NBP is rarely questioned, adequate classification of the ideology of Zhirinovskii's LDPR—since 1993 an important player in the state duma, the lower house of the Russian parliament—has been a matter of dispute. While Zhirinovskii's publications have become relatively less revolutionary and more populist since the mid-1990s, the early history of the LDPR was marked by its inclusion, in its higher echelons, of, among other extremists, the neo-Nazi Iakushev (NSS) as well as Andrei Arkhipov (born 1954) and Sergei Zharikov (born 1956 or 1958), editors of the expressly fascist journals *Sokol Zhirinovskogo* (nos. 1–3), *K toporu*, and *Ataka*. Zhirinovskii's major idea, in 1993, of the need for Russia to complete her "last dash to the South"—that is, the annexation of Iran, Turkey, and Afghanistan, reveals a fascist mindset: it implies Russia's national rebirth—her ultimate "soothing"—through a radical redrawing of her borders and redefinition of her international status. Official membership numbers given by the LDPR going into the hundreds of thousands are inflated, but the party may have had several thousand more or less active members in the late 1990s. Notwithstanding Zhirinovskii's and his party's weak performance in Russia's parliamentary elections of 1999 (6.1 percent), and presidential poll of 2000 (2.7 percent), the LDPR faction remains an important actor in the duma. In December 2003 state duma elections, Zhirinovskii's party achieved 11.45 percent, its second best result in a federal-level poll.

As the relative importance of parties within Russian fascism declined in the late 1990s, a vocal "uncivil society" has become important in the new century. It includes, among others: dozens of ultranationalist periodicals and websites, a racist skinhead movement, a fascistic countercultural youth scene, and various extremely anti-Western trends in intellectual life. Within the latter, Dugin's "neo-Eurasianism" especially has made inroads into mainstream political thinking, public discourse, mass media, and scholarly debate.

Andreas Umland

See Also: INTRODUCTION; ANTI-SEMITISM; ARYANISM; AUTARKY; BENOIST, ALAIN DE; BOLSHEVISM; DEMOCRACY; DUGIN, ALEKSANDR GEL'EVICH; ECONOMICS; ELITE THEORY; EUGENICS; EUROPEAN NEW RIGHT, THE; EXPANSIONISM; GROUPUSCULES; IMPERIALISM; INTEGRAL NATIONALISM; IRON GUARD, THE; IRREDENTISM; LE PEN, JEAN-MARIE; LIBERALISM; MARXISM; MILITARISM; NATIONAL BOLSHEVISM; NATIONALISM; NEO-NAZISM; OCCULTISM; ORTHODOX CHURCHES, THE; PALINGENETIC MYTH; PARAMILITARISM; PROGRESS; PROPAGANDA; RACIAL DOCTRINE; RACISM; REVOLUTION; ROCK MUSIC; ROMANIA; RURALISM; SA, THE; SALUTES; SEXUALITY; SKINHEAD FASCISM; SLAVS, THE (AND GERMANY); SOVIET UNION, THE; STALIN, IOSIF VISSARIONOVICH; SYMBOLS; TRADITION; TRADITIONALISM; YOUTH MOVEMENTS; ZHIRINOVSKII, VLADIMIR VOL'FOVICH

References

Laqueur, Walter. 1993. *Black Hundred: The Rise of the Extreme Right in Russia.* New York: HarperCollins.

Likhachëv, Viacheslav. 2002. *Natsizm v Rossii.* Moskva: Panorama.

Mathyl, Markus. 2002. "The National-Bolshevik Party and Arctogaia: Two Neo-Fascist Groupuscules in the Post-Soviet Political Space." *Patterns of Prejudice* 36, no. 3: 62–76.

Rogger, Hans. 1968. "Was There a Russian Fascism? The Union of the Russian People." *Journal of Modern History* 36, no. 4: 398–415.

Rossman, Vadim. 2002. *Russian Intellectual Antisemitism in the Post-Communist Era.* Jerusalem: Vidal Sassoon International Center for the Study of Antisemitism.

Shenfield, Stephen D. 2001. *Russian Fascism: Traditions, Tendencies, Movements.* Armonk, NY: M. E. Sharpe.

Umland, Andreas. 2002. *Toward an Uncivil Society? Contextualizing the Recent Decline of Extremely Right-Wing Parties in Russia.* Weatherhead Center for International Affairs Working Paper 02–03. http://www.wcfia.harvard.edu/papers/555_ Toward_An_Uncivil_Society.pdf.

Yanov, Alexander. 1995. *Weimar Russia? And What We Can Do About It.* New York: Slovo-Word.

SA, THE

Founded in 1920 as the paramilitary wing of the NS-DAP, the SA (Sturmabteilung), also known as the "storm troopers," was the NSDAP's most numerous subdivision until the early 1930s (1931: 77,000; January 1933: 700,000) after the world economic crisis had supplied many unemployed or socially marginalized recruits to its ranks. Its members were uniformed, armed, and, after 1926, subordinate to the supreme SA leadership. When Ernst Roehm took over the SA leadership in 1931, he introduced a brown uniform for the membership and this gave rise to their common nickname of "Brownshirts." The SA provoked bloody clashes with the leftist worker parties and, after 1933, established the first concentration camps in which political opponents were tortured and murdered. SA members were mainly responsible for the boycott of shops owned by Jews (April 1933) and the murder and destruction on *Kristallnacht* (November 1938). After Hitler came to power in 1933 he began to fear the power of the SA and to doubt its loyalty, and he had its chief of staff, Ernst Roehm, killed in 1934, along with other potential rivals in the notorious Night of the Long Knives. From that time on, the SS, Hitler's personal bodyguard, were in the ascendancy.

Fabian Virchow

See Also: ANTI-SEMITISM; CONCENTRATION CAMPS; GERMANY; HITLER, ADOLF; KRISTALLNACHT (NIGHT OF BRO-KEN GLASS); NAZISM; NIGHT OF THE LONG KNIVES, THE; PARAMILITARISM; ROEHM, ERNST; SS, THE; WALL STREET CRASH, THE

References
Bessel, Richard. 1984. *Political Violence and the Rise of Nazism: The Storm Troopers in Eastern Germany 1925–1934*. New Haven: Yale University Press.
Diehl, James. 1977. *Paramilitary Politics in Weimar Germany*. Bloomington: Indiana University Press.
Fischer, Conan. 1983. *Stormtroopers: A Social, Economic and Ideological Analysis, 1929–35*. London: Allen and Unwin.
Merkl, Peter M. 1980. *The Making of a Stormtrooper*. Princeton: Princeton University Press.

SALAZAR, ANTÓNIO DE OLIVEIRA (1889–1970)

Portuguese prime minister and dictator from 1932 until 1968 whose regime has often misleadingly been regarded as fascist. After completing his doctorate at the University of Coimbra, Salazar went on to become one of Portugal's most respected political economists. A devout Catholic, he was opposed to the liberal First Republic—not so much because of the nature of the regime as because of its anticlericalism. He was one of the founders of the Christian Democratic Academic Center, a Catholic political party, in 1912 and went on to become one of its most capable promoters. It was in this capacity that he proposed and defended the thesis that Catholics should oppose the Republican regime's anticlerical policies, but not the regime itself. He was elected to the Portuguese parliament at the 1921 elections, although he never officially took his seat in Lisbon. He served as finance minister for five days in the short-lived cabinet led by Mendes Cabeçadas following the May 1926 coup that overthrew the liberal republic, returning to Coimbra as soon as he realized that the military dictatorship was itself internally divided. He came to popular attention in the winter of 1927, when he published in the Catholic newspaper *Novidades* a series of articles critical of the military dictatorship's economic and financial policies. The response to these articles was such that the president, General Carmona, came to believe that he was the only man capable of saving the country from bankruptcy. Thus the myth of Salazar the financial wizard (*mago financeiro*) was born. In April 1928, the newly appointed prime minister, Vicente de Freitas, asked Salazar to accept the post of finance minister in the new government, which he agreed to do only on condition that he was given complete, sole, and unquestioned control over all government spending. His conditions being accepted, Salazar succeeded in transforming Portugal's finances, and within a year of his appointment he had guided the country to its first budget surplus since 1913. He soon became indispensable and built up a network of adherents. Between 1928 and 1930 he effectively vetoed any government appointments and directed government policy. By 1930 it was apparent that he was the de facto leader of the Portuguese government, although he did not become prime minister until July 1932, a position that he retained until September 1968. He was responsible for the abolition of the liberal state through the promulgation in April 1933 of a new corporatist-inspired constitution that gave birth to the New State (Estado Novo). Although his regime has been described as fascist, Salazar in fact opposed fascism and successfully eradicated fascist movements in Portugal during the 1930s. While the Salazarist regime did adopt some of the trappings of fascism during the Spanish Civil War, these were little more than symbolic gestures, quickly abandoned or allowed to wither away. Portugal remained neutral during World War II, but Salazar's policies were motivated more by the need to protect Portugal's African possessions than by any other reason. At the height of the war, Salazar allowed the Allies to use the Azores as a refueling base, paving the way toward Portugal's entry into NATO as a founding member.

In the postwar era, following the Indian occupation of the Portuguese colony of Goa and the outbreak of liberation wars in Portuguese Africa, Salazar adopted a policy of armed resistance, committing thousands of troops and almost half of the national product to maintaining Portuguese control over these territories in the face of world opinion. In 1968 he suffered a stroke after a domestic accident and remained bedridden until his death in 1970. He was replaced as prime minister by Marcello Caetano in 1968, although no one told him; he died believing he remained in charge.

Stewart Lloyd Jones

See Also: INTRODUCTION; "ANTI-" DIMENSION OF FASCISM, THE; ANTICLERICALISM; CATHOLIC CHURCH, THE; CLERICO-FASCISM; COLONIALISM; CORPORATISM; ECONOMICS; *ESTADO NOVO* ("NEW STATE"); POLITICAL CATHOLICISM; PORTUGAL; ROLÃO PRETO, FRANCISCO; SPANISH CIVIL WAR, THE; VARGAS, GETULIO DORNELLES; WORLD WAR II

References
Ferro, A. 1939. *Salazar: Portugal and Her Leader.* London: Faber and Faber.
Kay, H. 1970. *Salazar and Modern Portugal.* New York: Hawthorne.
Leonard, Y. 1998. *Salazarismo e fascismo,* Mem-Martins: Inquerito.

SALGADO, PLÍNIO (1895–1975)

Leader of Acão Integralista Brasileira, a Brazilian fascistic organization. Salgado became enthusiastic for fascism after meeting Mussolini in Italy. He ran for president, but was not elected. Salgado was very Catholic and represented the less radical wing of Acão Integralista Brasileira. After a failed conspiracy against President Vargas, he was exiled to Portugal from 1938 to 1945. He remained politically active after his return; in 1964 he spoke at a conservative rally against President Goulart and supported the military coup against him. Also known for his literary skills, Salgado wrote several novels in the 1920s and early 1930s that reveal his anti-Jewish and antifeminist feelings.

Margaret Power

See Also: ANTI-SEMITISM; BRAZIL; CATHOLIC CHURCH, THE; CLERICO-FASCISM; FEMINISM; MUSSOLINI, BENITO ANDREA; PORTUGAL

Reference
Deutsch, Sandra McGee. 1999. *Las Derechas: The Extreme Right in Argentina, Brazil, and Chile, 1890–1939.* Stanford: Stanford University Press.

SALÒ REPUBLIC, THE

The Italian Social Republic (RSI), or Salò Republic (named after the seat of the regime on Lake Garda in northern Italy), arose as a consequence of the Italian withdrawal from World War II on 8 September 1943 and the occupation of northern and central Italy by the Wehrmacht. Mussolini had been dismissed by King Victor Emmanuel III on 25 July 1943 after the Grand Council of Fascism voted to unseat him; he was transferred from one detention place to another but liberated from imprisonment on the Gran Sasso by German paratroopers on 12 September 1943. Following a radio address by Il Duce from Munich on 18 September, a new republican-fascist government was formed in northern and central Italy, and the Fascist Party was revived along with the militia, which was later brought over with the Carabinieri into the Republican National Guard. The Salò regime continued the battle against the Allies on the side of the Germans in competition with the royal government under Badoglio in the south. But relations with the Germans and their governor, Ambassador Rahn, and with the army commanders Rommel, Kesselring, and Vietinghoff, as well as the SS under Wolff, were always difficult. Mussolini was unable to reassert his authority successfully, for not only the south, freed by the advancing Allies, but also a part of Italy controlled by the Germans remained wholly or more or less completely beyond his grasp. The *Alpenvorland* and "Adriatic Coast" zones were to all intents and purposes annexed by Germany and subjected to the Reich governors of the neighboring regions (Friedrich Rainer in Karinthia, Franz Hofer in Tirol-Vorarlberg). Mussolini retained what autonomy he could in the remaining area, and a new republican army under Marshal Graziani was established, whose four divisions were initially sent to Germany for training and from the summer of 1944 were used chiefly for the battle against the anti-Fascist partisans.

The RSI began by dealing with those members of the Grand Council who in the night of 24/25 July 1943 had voted against Mussolini and who had thereby made possible his fall, and with all who were classified in the widest sense as "traitors" to Fascism. In January 1944 the trial of the chief conspirators was held in Verona, concluding with eleven death sentences *in contumaciam,* of which five were carried out immediately (on 11 January 1944). Victims included Mussolini's own son-in-law Galeazzo Ciano and the quadrumvir Emilio De Bono. At least 1,500 death penalties were also handed down and implemented by specially established provincial special tribunals. The Salò Republic manifested an intensification of violence and pursued a race policy that was deeply anti-Semitic, declaring all Jews to belong to a hostile nation and requiring them to be herded into camps and ordering that their property and investments be confiscated. The deportations organized subsequently by the Germans could never have been implemented without these preparations and without the collaboration of the organs of the Salò Republic. Altogether, more than 6,800 Jews were deported in forty-three transports to the East (for the most part to Auschwitz), of whom only 837 survived.

Salò had to engage in an increasingly brutal struggle with the developing resistance, and that struggle became the main job of the forces of order (police, national guard, black brigades) and the armed forces of the RSI. Assessment of this has remained a matter of controversy down to the present day, but it is increasingly interpreted as a real civil war. At the same time, relations with the German occupiers/allies worsened: agreement could not be reached as to the problem of the Italian military internees sent to Germany as forced labor, while the increasingly heavy-handed German reprisals—which degenerated into downright massacres in such cases as that of the Fosse Ardeatine on 24 March 1944—led to catastrophic consequences for the standing of Fascism in the country. Mussolini's last public appearance in Milan, on 16 December 1944, was astonishingly successful, but four months later he was killed by partisans on 28 April 1945 as he attempted to escape to Switzerland in the face of the advancing Allied forces. The war in northern Italy ended with the capitulation of the German troops on 29 April, which came into force on 2 May, about a week before the complete capitulation of the Wehrmacht.

Carlo Moos
(translated by Cyprian Blamires)

See Also: ANTI-SEMITISM; AUSCHWITZ (-BIRKENAU); AXIS, THE; BONO, EMILIO DE; CIANO, COUNT GALEAZZO;

FASCIST PARTY, THE; FORCED LABOR; GERMANY; GRAND COUNCIL OF FASCISM, THE; HOLOCAUST, THE; ITALY; MILIZIA VOLONTARIA PER LA SICUREZZA NAZIONALE (MVSN); MUSSOLINI, BENITO ANDREA; SKORZENY, OTTO; SS, THE; VICTOR EMMANUEL/VITTORIO EMANUELE III, KING; WEHRMACHT, THE; WORLD WAR II

References

Mack Smith, Denis. 1981. *Mussolini.* London: Weidenfeld and Nicholson.

Quartermaine, L. 2000. *Mussolini's Last Republic: Propaganda and Politics in the Italian Social Republic (R.S.I.) 1943–45.* Exeter: Elm Bank.

SALUTES

The Roman salute, in which the right arm is raised in a straight and perpendicular manner, was adopted by both Fascist Italy and Nazi Germany. It had been previously used by the Italian poet Gabriele D'Annunzio during his occupation of Fiume from September 1919 to December 1920. Like other rituals that were instituted by D'Annunzio in Fiume, the salute later became part of the rising Fascist movement's symbolic arsenal. In 1925, during Mussolini's work of fascistization of the state, the salute officially became part of the Fascist regime. In the fashion of imperial Rome, the salute was supposed to reflect a sense of discipline and respect. In 1932, the Fascist regime adopted the Roman salute as a substitute for the "bourgeois" handshake. The improper execution of the salute, or worse the continuation of the old habit of shaking hands, became a sign of a lesser Fascist spirit. The Fascist Party secretary, Achille Starace, issued daily injunctions during the 1930s reminding party members of the Roman salute's importance. The salute was believed to represent the physical, external sign of a truly transformed Italian man, whose gestures reflected his authentic Fascist nature. Like other rituals adopted by Mussolini's regime, the salute showed the enormous importance the Italian Fascists assigned to symbols and myths.

As part of its panoply of rituals and symbols that were supposed to identify and unify the members of the movement, Nazi Germany also adopted a version of the salute. Evidence of the first use of the salute by Hitler is found in photographs taken during a rally in Munich in late January 1923. By 1926, the straight-arm greeting had become standard in the Nazi movement and was prominently featured by party members

at the 1927 Nuremberg Rally. After Hitler took power, citizens showed their loyalty to the regime by greeting each other with the salute and a *Heil Hitler* cry. Failure to do so evidenced lack of allegiance. Together with the swastika, the salute became a most important symbol of the Nazi movement and testified to the great power that rituals and myths held for Hitler and his regime.

Simonetta Falasca-Zamponi

See Also: BOURGEOISIE, THE; D'ANNUNZIO, GABRIELE; FASCIST PARTY, THE; FIUME; GERMANY; GOOSESTEP, THE; *HEIL HITLER!;* HITLER, ADOLF; ITALY; MUSSOLINI, BENITO ANDREA; MYTH; NAZISM; NEW MAN, THE; NUREMBERG RALLIES, THE; PROPAGANDA; RELIGION; REVOLUTION; ROME; STARACE, ACHILLE; SWASTIKA, THE; SYMBOLS; TOTALITARIANISM

Reference

Falasca-Zamponi, Simonetta. 1997. *Fascist Spectacle: The Aesthetics of Power in Mussolini's Italy.* Berkeley: University of California Press.

SARFATTI-GRASSINI, MARGHERITA (1880–1961)

Journalist, art critic and patron, poet, novelist, and speechwriter for Mussolini, and his first biographer as well as his mistress and his muse—whose importance for the rise of Italian Fascism has only recently been fully revealed. She has been described as "the most powerful woman in Italy" or "the uncrowned queen of Italy" (Cannistraro and Sullivan, 1993) during the three years from 1927 to 1930 because of her influence over Il Duce. In 1923 she was appointed lady-in-waiting to Queen Elena, and the two women became firm friends. King Vittorio Emanuele was even hopeful of assuaging Mussolini's hatred of the monarchy through her.

Sarfatti-Grassini was born into the wealthy Jewish Grassini family in Venice and became an activist both in Italian socialism and in feminism while still a teenager, writing articles for numerous periodicals. She married a socialist lawyer named Cesare Sarfatti before World War I. She met Mussolini at the 1911 Socialist Party Congress, and by 1913 they had become very close. It was a relationship "across the tracks," for he came out of a background of rural poverty whereas she was accustomed to the sophisticated metropolitan

Margherita Sarfatti-Grassini, wealthy Italian Jewish writer, journalist, art critic and patron, and for many years mistress of Benito Mussolini; her salons were a social focus for leading fascists. (Bettmann/Corbis)

Nazi Germany). She was crucially involved in promoting both Futurism and the Novecento movement. By the late 1920s she was known as the "dictator of culture." Her salons were attended by the likes of the young (and later legendary) writer Alberto Moravia. She was a prominent participant in the Bologna Congress of Fascist Intellectuals that produced the *Manifesto of Fascist Intellectuals.* In fact, she played a very significant role in endowing Italian Fascism with a cultural aura that counterbalanced the general impression of philistinism which clung to a movement that was addicted to violence and brutality. Fascist leaders like Balbo, Grandi, and Bottai frequented her salons, but she opened her doors to visitors of all persuasions, and some thought that she was acting as a spy for Il Duce. Many eminent foreign visitors were also invited. Sarfatti was unable, however, to sustain her earlier feminist viewpoint, which cut very little ice with the Fascist movement and which had very little appeal to Mussolini. Her semiautobiographical novel *il Palazzone* (1929) reflected the images and the thinking of the classic "romance."

For six years Sarfatti penned articles that appeared under Mussolini's name for William Randolph Hearst publications in the United States. *Dux,* her biography of Mussolini published in 1926 (and with a preface by its subject), was a huge best-seller, running to seventeen editions at home and being translated into eighteen languages. Some 300,000 copies were sold in Japan alone. It was a sanitized account that omitted all mention of the violent means by which its subject had contrived to attain power, and it played a massive role in creating a global myth of Mussolini as a man of heroic stature and a new Caesar.

By 1936, Sarfatti had become alienated from Il Duce, and in 1938 she fled to Argentina. One reason for the split between her and Mussolini may have been his turn to anti-Semitism in the late 1930s. In 1947 she returned to Italy and took up her writing again.

Cyprian Blamires

See Also: ANTI-SEMITISM; ARCHITECTURE; ART; BALBO, ITALO; BOTTAI, GIUSEPPE; FASCIST PARTY, THE; FEMINISM; FUTURISM; GERMANY; GRANDI, DINO; HEARST, WILLIAM RANDOLPH; HERO, THE CULT OF THE; ITALY; JAPAN; MANIFESTO OF FASCIST INTELLECTUALS, THE; MODERNISM; MUSSOLINI, BENITO ANDREA; NATIONALISM; NAZISM; ROME; SOCIALISM; *SQUADRISMO;* TRADITION; VIOLENCE

References

Cannistraro, Philip V., and Brian R. Sullivan. 1993. *Il Duce's Other Woman: The Untold Story of Margherita Sarfatti, Mussolini's Jewish Mistress.* New York: William Morrow.

world of culture and the arts. While his socialist colleagues and friends dropped away with his turn to nationalism, Sarfatti remained a faithful supporter and embraced nationalism with him. She became art editor for his paper *Popolo d'Italia.* For the first few months of its existence, she coedited Mussolini's magazine *Gerarchia* (founded in 1922), which became widely known as the semiofficial organ of the regime. After Mussolini's departure for Rome in October of that year, Sarfatti effectively became editor of *Gerarchia,* though she ran the articles by Mussolini each month over the phone. In 1924 she assumed sole editorial responsibility when Mussolini decided that as prime minister he was not in a position to take legal responsibility with regard to the journal.

For many years Sarfatti hosted salons in Milan and later in Rome that were a haunt of artists and intellectuals sympathetic to Fascism, and she played an important role in fostering modernism, helping to make that movement palatable to the regime (by contrast with

Marzorati, Sergio. 1990. *Margherita Sarfatti: Saggio biografico.* Como: Nodolibri.

Michaelis, Meir. 1978. *Mussolini and the Jews: German-Italian Relations and the Jewish Question in Italy, 1922–1945.* Oxford: Oxford University Press.

SCHINDLER, OSKAR: *See* ANTIFASCISM

SCHIRACH, BALDUR VON (1907–1974)

From 1931, Reich youth leader of the National Socialist Party; in the late 1930s his pictures were used more widely throughout Germany than those of any other Nazi leader save Hitler himself. He was born in Berlin, his father being an army officer who later became a theatrical director, while his mother was an American lady who claimed descent from two signatories of the American Declaration of Independence. Schirach studied art history and German folklore in Munich, where he first joined the Nazi Party. He wrote flattering poems about Hitler: "His soul touches the stars/And yet he remains a man like you and me." Schirach was a fierce opponent of Christianity and considered that his altar was the steps of the Munich Feldherrn Halle, spattered with blood during the 1923 Munich putsch. In 1929 he was appointed to the leadership of the German Students' League, his brief stint being to bring the university system under the control of the Nazis. In 1931 he became Reich youth leader of the National Socialist Party, and in 1932 he gathered more than 100,000 young people in a massive parade in front of Hitler at Potsdam. In 1933 he had the title of youth leader of the German Reich conferred upon him by Hitler. As honors were showered upon him, Schirach was presented more and more as embodying all that was noble in German youth. But success also aroused jealousy around him and made him many enemies; in 1941, Hitler demoted him to *Gauleiter* of Vienna. At the Nuremberg Trials Schirach was condemned to twenty years' imprisonment as a participant in the deportation of Jews from Vienna.

Cyprian Blamires

See Also: ANTI-SEMITISM; CALENDAR, THE FASCIST; CHRISTIANITY; GERMANY; HITLER, ADOLF; HOLOCAUST, THE; IRAN; MUNICH (BEER-HALL) PUTSCH, THE; NAZISM; PROPAGANDA; RELIGION; UNIVERSITIES, THE (GERMANY); YOUTH MOVEMENTS

References
Smelser, Ronald, and Rainer Zitelmann, eds. 1989. *The Nazi Elite.* Basingstoke: Macmillan.

Stachura, P. D. 1976. *Nazi Youth in the Weimar Republic.* Santa Barbara, CA: ABC-CLIO.

Wortmann, M. 1982. *Baldur von Schirach, Hitlers Jugendführer.* Köln: Böhlau.

SCHLEICHER, KURT VON (1882–1934)

Hitler's predecessor as chancellor. He was from an old Prussian military family and had a career in the army, rising to the rank of colonel and becoming head of the Armed Forces division of the Reichswehr Ministry in 1926. A born political intriguer, he succeeded Von Papen as chancellor on 3 December 1932. He offered to support a National Socialist government on condition that Hitler gave him a seat in the cabinet and leadership of the Reichswehr. But Von Papen intrigued with Hitler, who became Von Schleicher's successor himself on 30 January 1933, with Von Papen as his vice chancellor. Von Schleicher was one of those murdered on Hitler's orders in the Night of the Long Knives.

Cyprian Blamires

See Also: GERMANY; HITLER, ADOLF; NAZISM; NIGHT OF THE LONG KNIVES, THE; PAPEN, FRANZ VON; WEHRMACHT, THE; WEIMAR REPUBLIC, THE

References
Feuchtwanger, E. J. 1995. *From Weimar to Hitler, 1918–1933.* Basingstoke: Macmillan.

Plehwe, Friedrich-Karl von. 1983. *Reichskanzler Kurt von Schleicher: Weimars letzte Chance gegen Hitler.* Munich: Bechtle.

SCHMITT, CARL (1888–1985)

Legendary "crown jurist" of the Third Reich whose reputation has undergone a renaissance over the last decades of the twentieth century. Schmitt, a political theorist as well as a jurist, was born at Plettemberg, a small town in the Sauerland. After a Catholic schooling he studied at the universities of Berlin, Munich, and Strasbourg and was subjected to the influence of philosophical neo-Kantianism. Germany's defeat in World War I had a crucial impact on his intellectual development: in the advent of the parliamentary republic and the multiparty system following the collapse of the Wilhelmine authoritarian state, he saw a victory for liberal individualism of Romantic origin, a tendency that he strongly opposed, following in the footsteps of reactionary Catholic conservative writers like Joseph de Maistre and Donoso Cortés. Basing himself on the conceptual distinction between "democracy" and "liberalism," he became a radical critic of parliamentarism, the multiparty state, and the liberal constitutional state, to which he contrasted—in works like *Die Diktatur* (1921), *Politische Theologie* (1922), and *Römischer Katholizismus und Politische Form* (1923)—a conception of political order based on the decision of the sovereign, on charismatic authority, and on presidential power. From the juridical point of view, he contrasted with liberal constitutionalism a doctrine taken from the French Revolutionary tradition and based on the constituent power of the people: the constitution, as Schmitt wrote in his *Verfassungslehre* (1928), is not a document or a formal act, but a "fundamental decision" and a collective act of political will, on which depends the historical legitimacy of the political order.

The first edition of the essay "Der Begriff des Politischen" dates from 1928, and this is the work that mainly created his posthumous fame. Substantially revised in 1932 and 1933, it developed a competitive, conflictual idea of politics: Schmitt argued that it is a form of human activity based on the friend/enemy distinction, and his thinking reflected a pessimistic conception of human nature typical of the tradition of realism from Machiavelli up to modern times. Schmitt convinced himself, as shown in his book of 1931, *Der Huter der Verfassung,* that the only way to save the weak Weimar Constitution from the combined attacks of communists and Nazis was that of entrusting extraordinary powers to the president of the republic, thus giving life to an "authoritarian democracy" supported by the military class and the bureaucrats. But the crisis of the German state had become unstoppable: in January 1933, Hitler was appointed chancellor, the first step toward the single-party dictatorship and the suppression of political liberties. Out of an excessive respect for the legalities and not without opportunism, Schmitt supported the new regime, within which he held various official posts over a period of several years: among oth-

ers, those of Prussian councilor of state, member of the Akademie für Deutsches Recht, and editor of the law review *Deutsche Juristen-Zeitung.* But it was sensed that his was not an authentic ideological conversion, and repeated violent attacks were made on him by individuals in the ambit of National Socialist radicalism, who accused him of having remained an authoritarian Catholic and a neo-Hegelian, and of being a conservative supporter of the "total state" but not a defender of the authentic "national community." Troubled by these attacks, which made him fearful for his physical safety in spite of the protection guaranteed him directly by Nazi chiefs like Hermann Goering and Hans Frank, Schmitt withdrew from public life. In the late 1930s his studies were directed almost exclusively toward international law. Central in this phase of his intellectual production was the concept of *Grossraum,* through which he sought to explain the transformations in the world political order.

After the end of World War II, Schmitt was imprisoned and tried for his collaboration with National Socialism, and was subsequently relieved of his university teaching work. He withdrew to his hometown, but although isolated and deprived of academic employment, he continued to exercise a vast influence on the German intellectual world through his numerous pupils. From the 1970s, his work became the object of an important critical debate that soon spread to a great number of countries and involved scholars of a variety of cultural orientations. His works were translated into numerous languages and became the subject of many commentaries. The *Kronjurist* of the Third Reich, for a long time marginalized by the global academic community, eventually came to be regarded as one of the most original and brilliant political thinkers of the modern era.

Alessandro Campi
(translated by Cyprian Blamires)

See Also: INTRODUCTION; ABSTRACTION; AUTHORITARIANISM; BOLSHEVISM; CATHOLIC CHURCH, THE; CONSERVATISM; DEMOCRACY; DENAZIFICATION; DICTATORSHIP; ELITE THEORY; FRANK, HANS; FRENCH REVOLUTION, THE; GOERING, HERMANN; INDIVIDUALISM; LAW; LEADER CULT, THE; LIBERALISM; MACHIAVELLI, NICCOLÒ; MARXISM; NAZISM; PARLIAMENTARISM; POLITICAL CATHOLICISM; THIRD REICH, THE; TRADITIONALISM; *VOLKSGEMEINSCHAFT,* THE; WEIMAR REPUBLIC, THE; WORLD WAR I; WORLD WAR II

References
Balakrishnan, Gopal. 2002. *The Enemy: An Intellectual Portrait of Carl Schmitt.* London: Verso.
Bendersky, J. W. 1983. *Carl Schmitt, Theorist for the Reich.* Princeton: Princeton University Press.

Kennedy, Ellen. 2004. *Constitutional Failure: Carl Schmitt in Weimar.* Durham, NC: Duke University Press.

Müller, Jan-Werner. 2003. *A Dangerous Mind: Carl Schmitt in Postwar European Thought.* New Haven: Yale University Press.

Scheuerman, William E. 1999. *Carl Schmitt: The End of Law.* New York: Rowman and Littlefield.

SCHOLTZ-KLINK, GERTRUD (1902–1999)

Appointed by Hitler as Reich women's leader and head of the Nazi Women's League. She was born Gertrud Treusch, the daughter of a civil servant in Adelsheim. She worked as a teacher and journalist before marrying in 1920. Her first husband was Friedrich Klink, a teacher and later office-holder in the NSDAP, and she had six children by him, two of whom died. She herself joined the NSDAP in 1929. Klink died in 1930, and that year she became *Gauleiterin* of the Deutschen Frauenordens (DFO; German Women's Order), which was attached to the NSDAP. In 1931 she took over the leadership in Baden of the Nationalsozialistische Frauenschaft (NSF; National Socialist Women's Association), which Gregor Strasser had set up as a single replacement for several like-minded women's organizations. She was then asked to take over running the work in Hesse, and she devoted herself to mobilizing women for the Nazi cause. In 1932 she married Günther Scholtz, a doctor. In 1934, in addition to the positions mentioned above, she became head of the Women's Bureau in the Labor Front and was regarded as the leader of all National Socialist women (*Reichsfrauenfuehrerin*)—and as such the most influential woman in the Reich. She stated that the role of women in the Third Reich was the care of men. She was not expected to take leadership initiatives herself but officially acted as the representative of Erich Hilgenfeldt, head of the National Socialist People's Welfare Organization (Nationalsozialistische Volkswohlfart; NSV); this was an organization affiliated to the Nazi Party that was concerned with the welfare of party members and their families, especially mothers and children. In 1939, Scholtz-Klink visited Britain and was hailed in the British press as "the perfect Nazi woman." The previous year she had divorced Günther Scholtz, and in 1940 she married SS officer August Heissmeyer. After the war ended, Scholtz-Klink was interned briefly in a So-

viet camp but managed to escape; she hid for three years, and after her capture in 1948 she was imprisoned for a time. In 1950 she was given a further sentence of thirty months in a work camp and banned from political activities for life; she was also banned from journalism and teaching for ten years and fined. In her autobiography, published in 1978, she indicated that she remained an unrepentant Nazi.

Cyprian Blamires

See Also: FAMILY, THE; GERMANY; HITLER, ADOLF; LABOR FRONT, THE; NAZISM; SEXUALITY; SS, THE; STRASSER BROTHERS, THE; THIRD REICH, THE; WELFARE; WOMEN

References

Böltken, A. 1995. *Führerinnen im "Führerstaat": Gertrud Scholtz-Klink, Trude Mohr, Jutta Rüdiger und Inge Viermetz.* Pfaffenweiler: Centaurus.

Koonz, C. 1988. *Mothers in the Fatherland: Women, the Family, and Nazi Politics.* New York: St Martin's Griffin.

Stephenson, Jill. 1980. *Nazi Organisation of Women.* New York: Barnes and Noble.

———. 2002. *Women in Nazi Germany.* London: Longman.

SCHÖNERER, GEORG RITTER VON (1842–1921)

An early advocate of Pangermanism, Germanic religion, and anti-Semitism, and an important influence on the young Hitler. In 1869 and again from 1873 to 1888 and from 1897 to 1907, he was a member of the Austrian House of Delegates; in 1888, as a result of his involvement in an act of violence against political opponents, he was condemned to four months' imprisonment and loss of his parliamentary mandate. After 1907 he became politically very isolated in Catholic Austria on account of his Los-von-Rom movement, in which he called for people to leave the Catholic Church (on the grounds of her alleged "friendliness to Slavs") and to become Protestants. In 1879, Schönerer was involved in the foundation of the Pan-German Nationalist Party. In the *Linzer Programme* of 1882 he demanded the annexation of Austria to Germany under the leadership of the Hohenzollerns as a "fulfillment" of the German Reich, and the abandonment of the "Slavic territories." As leader of the Alldeutsche Bewegung he established a hero cult of Richard Wagner—whom he saw as liberator of German art from "Judaization"—and Bismarck, who remained reserved toward him. Schönerer pursued an aggressively anti-Semitic campaign in his newspapers (*Unverfalschte Worte, Alldeutsches Tagblatt*). He claimed that a "Greater German Reich" was the "desire of all Germans" and pointed to the Jews as "an unproductive and alien element" (speech of 11 May 1882), undermining the "moral and material foundations" of the German *Volk*.

Schönerer regarded anti-Semitism as "the central pillar of the national idea" (28 April 1887), called for a battle for the "purity of German blood," and attacked the "Jewish press." Many of his demands anticipated later Nazi measures, such as his demand for special laws even for baptized Jews ("the swinishness is in the race") to establish a limitation of freedom of domicile, exclusion of Jews from the civil service, from the teaching profession and the press, and the creation of special "Jewish registers." From February 1884 his gatherings took place under a banner that read: "Entry forbidden to Jews!" In his newspapers Schönerer introduced the greeting "Heil to the Fuehrer!" (addressed to himself). His German nationalism took on more and more strongly religious overtones; in 1883, he had described "German *Volkstum* (national character)" as "the perfect replacement for religion." With his cult for old Germanic symbols like runes and midsummer, midwinter, and Yuletide festivals, and his introduction of old Germanic names of the months and ways of living among his followers, he influenced the later Germanic cult of Heinrich Himmler and the SS. Schönerer also argued that his followers should marry only "Aryan partners" and must be investigated for the "healthiness of their line." Hitler referred to Schönerer admiringly many times in *Mein Kampf* but criticized him for his failure to win mass support and his faith in the parliamentary system.

Markus Hattstein (translated by Cyprian Blamires)

See Also: *ANSCHLUSS*, THE; ANTI-SEMITISM; ARYANISM; AUSTRIA; AUSTRO-HUNGARIAN EMPIRE/HABSBURG EMPIRE, THE; BLOOD; CATHOLIC CHURCH, THE; COMMUNITY; EUGENICS; EXPANSIONISM; FAMILY, THE; GERMANIC RELIGION; GERMANNESS (*DEUTSCHHEIT*); GERMANY; HERO, THE CULT OF THE; *HEIL HITLER!*; HIMMLER, HEINRICH; HITLER, ADOLF; MASSES, THE ROLE OF THE; *MEIN KAMPF*; NATIONALISM; OCCULTISM; PANGERMANISM; PARLIAMENTARISM; PROTESTANTISM; RACIAL DOCTRINE; SEXUALITY; SLAVS, THE (AND GERMANY); SS, THE; *VOLK, VÖLKISCH; VOLKSGEMEINSCHAFT*, THE; WAGNER, (WILHELM) RICHARD

References

Pulzer, Peter. 1988. *The Rise of Political Anti-Semitism in Germany and Austria.* London: Peter Halban.

Whiteside, A. G. 1975. *The Socialism of Fools: Georg Ritter von Schönerer and Austrian Pan-Germanism.* Berkeley: University of California Press.

SCHÖNHUBER, FRANZ (1923–2005)

Well-known journalist before becoming the chairman of the far-right Republikaner Party from 1985 to 1994. Under his leadership the party entered the state parliament of West Berlin and the European Parliament (both 1989), where Schönhuber led his faction. Known for his fiery xenophobic rhetoric, he was ousted by his own party for cooperating too closely with other well-known right-wing extremists—notably Gerhard Frey. A highly talented figure but a hugely controversial one, as when he publicly defended his time with the Waffen-SS, Schönhuber remained active to the end as an author and publicist in right-wing circles with his own weekly column in Frey's *National-Zeitung*.

Thomas Grumke

See Also: FREY, DR. GERHARD; GERMANY; NAZISM; POSTWAR FASCISM; WAFFEN-SS, THE; XENOPHOBIA

Reference

Hirsch, K. 1989. *Schönhuber: der Politiker und seine Kreise: mit einem Beitrag von Thomas Assheuer über die "Ideologischen Brücken nach rechts."* Frankfurt: Eichborn.

SCHOOLS: See EDUCATION

SCHOPENHAUER, ARTHUR (1788–1860)

German philosopher who was one of most influential figures in the late-nineteenth-century revolt against positivism of which Nazism (and according to some accounts, Italian Fascism) was one of the inheritors: Hitler carried a volume of Schopenhauer around with him during his war service. The starting point of his philosophy was idealism, but he developed on that basis a philosophy in which a unique place is occupied by the human will, as indicated by the title of his celebrated book *The World as Will and Representation* (1818). Schopenhauer observes that as well as being aware of things existing in space and time, we are also aware of ourselves, both in the act of perceiving and as will, and more specifically, as will to live. We are aware of ourselves and our behavior as the phases of a will. It is reasonable, then, to assume that the same is true of the external world, whose inner being must likewise be constituted by will. This idea of the primacy of the will was mediated through Nietzsche to the interwar fascists, for whom it constituted something of a revelation, meeting up with the current of Social Darwinism to produce a strong emphasis on our calling to act to shape our world. Schopenhauer also exercised an immense influence through his interest in Oriental thinking. One of his main inspirations was the Hindu *Upanishads*. He was the first Western philosopher to relate his thought to Hindu and Buddhist ideas. He thus gave a powerful impetus to a trend that was very important in Nazism. The whole Aryan myth so central to the Nazi worldview was a product of Orientalism, and many Nazi ideologues found inspiration in Buddhism or Hinduism.

Cyprian Blamires

See Also: ABSTRACTION; ACTUALISM; ANTHROPOLOGY; ARYANISM; *BHAGAVADGITA,* THE; BUDDHISM; FASCIST PARTY, THE; GENTILE, GIOVANNI; GERMANY; HAUER, JAKOB WILHELM; HITLER, ADOLF; ITALY; NAZISM; NIETZSCHE, FRIEDRICH; POSITIVISM; SOCIAL DARWINISM; VOLUNTARISM; WAR; WARRIOR ETHOS, THE; WORLD WAR I

SCHUSCHNIGG, KURT VON (1897–1977)

Chancellor of Austria, 1934–1938. He served as minister of justice, then education, in the cabinet of Engelbert Dollfuss and became chancellor after Dollfuss was assassinated in a failed Nazi putsch. Schuschnigg followed Dollfuss's authoritarian course while facing growing threats to Austrian independence from Germany. He capitulated to Hitler's demands for *Anschluss* on 11 March 1938. He was interned in concentration camps until 1945. Barred from the practice of law in postwar Austria, he taught history and politics at St. Louis University from 1948 to 1967, returning in that year to his native Tyrol, where he died in 1977 in Mutters bei Innsbruck.

Laura Gellott

See Also: *ANSCHLUSS,* THE; AUSTRIA; CATHOLIC CHURCH, THE; CLERICO-FASCISM; CONCENTRATION CAMPS; DOLLFUSS, ENGELBERT; GERMANY; HITLER, ADOLF; NAZISM

Reference
Bischof, G., A. Anton Pelinka, and A. Lassner, eds. 2003. *The Dollfuss/Schuschnigg Era in Austria: A Reassessment.* New Brunswick, NJ: Transaction.

SCHUTZSTAFFEL, THE: *See* SS, THE

SCIENCE

With varying stringency, the interwar fascist states imposed racial or political criteria resulting in purges of scientific personnel; there were also ideological pressures, which again met with variable success, on the content and direction of research. On the other hand, many varieties of fascism claimed that they were, at some level, rooted in the findings of science—most notably, a supposedly "scientific" racism. Fascist states were also eager to promote modern science when it supported goals of national prestige, economic autarky, or militaristic expansion. This analysis applies particularly to National Socialist Germany. In the early twentieth century, Germany was, by most measures, one of the leading scientific powers in the world; hence, the fate of science under Nazism has been analyzed in considerable detail. Similar comments, though with some variations, also apply to Fascist Italy.

Science was strongly affected by Nazi purges directed against racially or politically undesirable individuals. The German Law for the Restoration of the Career Civil Service of April 1933 ordered the dismissal from government service—with a few exceptions, for seniority and war service—of "non-Aryans" and persons whose loyalty was suspect. The law applied to universities as well as to many nonuniversity laboratories, such as most institutes of the prestigious Kaiser Wilhelm Society. Jewish and politically dissident scholars also faced other pressures; for example, after 1933, a political evaluation by the National Socialist Teachers' League became a standard part of the dossier for any academic appointment.

The quantitative scope of the purges is hard to measure, in part because many scientists resigned rather

Werner Heisenberg, one of the greatest physicists of the twentieth century; although the object of hostility on the part of some Nazis who wished to promote 'an Aryan physics', he was given a university post after intervention from Heinrich Himmler. (Library of Congress)

than being officially fired. Examples included Albert Einstein, who was traveling abroad and who resigned in protest against Nazi policies, and Fritz Haber, director of the Kaiser Wilhelm Institute (KWI) for Physical Chemistry, who declined to make use of his war service exemption. The extent of the purges also varied widely from one institution to another; some universities had virtually no dismissals, but some departments lost the majority of their members. In any event, the number of dismissals was significant: as many as 25 percent of scientists in some fields, with an overall average probably between 10 and 15 percent. The qualitative effects were also considerable. The dismissals and resignations included twenty researchers who had won or who would later win Nobel prizes. Many dismissed scientists emigrated and pursued their careers elsewhere, making significant contributions to the scientific life of countries such as the United States and Great Britain, and playing major roles in fields such as nuclear energy and mo-

lecular biology. However, many other purged scientists were unable to find positions abroad or were unable to re-establish their careers once they did. Also difficult to assess quantitatively is the effect racial and political scrutiny had on the recruitment of a new generation of scientists.

The reaction of most scientific institutions toward these mandates was general compliance, along with selective noncooperation. Some "non-Aryan" or politically suspect scientists were sheltered through astute manipulation of the Nazi bureaucracy, but in the large majority of cases the relevant institutions implemented the purges as a matter of bureaucratic routine. This "self-coordination" preserved the semblance of professional autonomy, but at the cost of many individuals' careers. It should also be noted that although the purges had a dramatic effect on German science, they were by no means directed at science in and of itself: many professional and academic fields saw similar events.

In some fields the Nazi era saw attempts to transform the content of science along ideological lines. The most conspicuous controversy occurred in physics. A vocal minority, including the Nobel Prize winners Philipp Lenard and Johannes Stark, promoted the idea of an "Aryan physics," which rejected a number of recent theoretical developments, above all Albert Einstein's theory of relativity, as too abstract, mathematically formalistic, and unconnected to an intuitive understanding of nature. These supposedly undesirable traits were ascribed to Jewish influence in the field. But in many respects, this stance was a politicization of intraprofessional rivalries and nostalgia for the classical physics of the previous century.

The Aryan physicists sought to redirect physics through changes in the science curriculum and through influence on faculty appointments. A notorious case occurred when the Munich theorist Arnold Sommerfeld sought the appointment of his most famous student, Werner Heisenberg, as his successor. Heisenberg was attacked rhetorically in Nazi Party publications, and the post eventually went in 1939 to an obscure applied mathematician, Wilhelm Müller. Although this appeared to be a victory for Aryan physics, actually by this time the influence of its advocates was waning, and internal dissensions had divided the group. The public attacks on Heisenberg were stopped by order of Heinrich Himmler, and Heisenberg was appointed to a dual post at the University of Berlin and the KWI for Physics. An agreement was reached that relativity theory could be openly taught again—as long as Einstein remained unnamed. By this time, military authorities, the SS, and the Reich Education Ministry were concerned about the state of defense research, and it was apparent that Aryan physics had little to offer in that regard. Analogous efforts to promote a distinctly "German" science in opposition to allegedly "Jewish" influences also occurred in chemistry and mathematics, but none of these campaigns had the impact of the *arische Physik* controversy.

The purges and the Aryan physics controversy, considered by themselves, might give the impression of an innately "antiscience" Nazi regime. But that would be an incomplete picture. There were also many examples of continuity in the German scientific tradition during the Third Reich. In fields such as oncology, biochemistry, biophysics, and nuclear physics, Germany remained at the forefront of world science throughout the 1930s. Moreover, there were also examples of a symbiosis between science and the state: racial, autarkic, and militaristic ambitions presented opportunities for scientists. Nazi race ideology purported to be an application of evolutionary biology, physical anthropology, and genetics. More than a few researchers in genetics, physical anthropology, and related fields offered their expertise toward the implementation of these policies and in turn garnered government support for their research. "Racial courts," staffed by eugenics experts, were established to scrutinize marriage licenses. Ernst Rüdin, codirector of the KWI for Psychology and an authority on neurological diseases, helped to craft the 1933 eugenical sterilization law. Eugen Fischer, director of the KWI for Anthropology, even despite some political disagreements with Nazism, promoted the work of his institute as contributing to the national revival. Ultimately, the shift toward "medical killing" and genocide provided the context, in some cases, for a science without moral boundaries that included experimentation on human subjects.

The Nazi focus on autarky also bolstered government support of organic chemistry (especially geared toward production of synthetic fuels and rubber), silicates research (ceramics, concrete, and other construction materials), metallurgy (specialized alloys), and plant and animal genetics (the production of oils, fats, and fibers). Beyond alignment with perceived interests of their government patrons—a pervasive pattern throughout the history of science—some German scientists collaborated with the state in ways that were unique to the Nazi regime. For example, horticultural research stations were established in occupied territories to study indigenous plant material, and laborato-

ries in occupied regions of the Soviet Union, a country that in the 1920s and 1930s had developed a rich tradition in plant genetics, had their specimen collections appropriated by German researchers.

German rearmament also called to the attention of both scientists and government officials the importance of modern science to the Nazi state. Rocketry and aerodynamics provide two of the most obvious examples of generous state support of military-related research, but other fields ranging from applied mathematics to metallurgy to psychology benefited from governmental support in the form of funding, establishment of new research laboratories, and so forth. Scientists in fields deemed "necessary to the war effort" were also exempt from military service. Research on nuclear weapons was an exception that proves the general rule of scientific participation in rearmament and the war effort. Despite interest among both scientists and military officials, in view of perceived technical difficulties and shortages of materials it was decided to continue research but prioritize other projects during the war. Although evidence of deliberate sabotage of the project is debatable at best, there is little doubt that individual hesitations, as well as institutional rivalries, also hampered German nuclear weapons research.

Italy's reputation in science, though venerable, had by the early 1900s fallen relative to that of other European countries. Fascism, though partly harking back to the supposed glories of Italy's past, also presented itself as a forward-looking, modernist movement. The regime sought to reinvigorate Italian science, both for economic and strategic advantages and for reasons of national prestige. A National Research Council was founded in 1923 to channel government support to deserving projects; conversely, the main Italian professional organization for Italian scientists (the Italian Society for the Progress of Science), in its meetings in the 1920s, stressed the potential contributions of science to national defense. The most successful effort to bolster national prestige through science was Enrico Fermi's laboratory for atomic research, established at the University of Rome in 1926 under the patronage of Orso Corbino, himself a physicist but also a senator and erstwhile cabinet member. During the 1930s, Fermi's laboratory became perhaps the leading center of neutron research in the world, and certainly fulfilled Corbino's aim of putting Italian science back on the map.

Alongside the promotion of science, the Fascists also became concerned about the ideological commitments of scientists. An Academy of Italy was established in parallel, and essentially in rivalry, to the traditional Academy of the Lynx; appointments to the former clearly favored those who were sympathetic to the regime. In 1925, scientists were among the signatories of both the manifesto of profascist intellectuals organized by Giovanni Gentile, and also of Benedetto Croce's countermanifesto, but in 1931, when a loyalty oath was required of all university professors, only a few refused to sign and were consequently dismissed. Racism in general and anti-Semitism in particular played a less central role in Italian Fascism than in German National Socialism, and this was also reflected in science policy. Jewish scientists were not purged, although they faced considerable informal prejudice. Eugenics was also a popular theme in 1920s Italy, but more in the mode of pronatalist measures rather than efforts to screen out the genetically "unfit." That changed, however, with the formation of the Rome-Berlin Axis. In 1938, Italy also promulgated racial laws that led to the dismissal of Jewish academics. Among the emigrants was Fermi; his political indifference had been largely shielded under Corbino's powerful patronage, but inasmuch as his wife, Laura, was Jewish, he decided to move to the United States following his receipt of the 1938 Nobel Prize. There, among other accomplishments, he headed the creation of the first successful nuclear reactor in association with the Manhattan Project.

Richard Beyler

See Also: INTRODUCTION; ABSTRACTION; ANTHROPOLOGY; ANTI-SEMITISM; ARYANISM; AUTARKY; AXIS, THE; CROCE, BENEDETTO; EDUCATION; EUGENICS; EUTHANASIA; FASCIST PARTY, THE; GENTILE, GIOVANNI; GERMANNESS/ (*DEUTSCHHEIT*); GERMANY; HEALTH; HIMMLER, HEINRICH; HOLOCAUST, THE; ITALY; MANIFESTO OF FASCIST INTELLECTUALS, THE; MEDICINE; MILITARISM; MODERNITY; NATURE; NAZISM; NORDIC SOUL, THE; PROGRESS; RACIAL DOCTRINE; RACISM; SOCIAL DARWINISM; SS, THE; TECHNOLOGY; THIRD REICH, THE; UNIVERSITIES; WAR

References
Goodstein, Judith R. 1984. "The Rise and Fall of Vito Volterra's World." *Journal of the History of Ideas* 45: 607–617.
Holton, Gerald. 1978. "Fermi's Group and the Recapture of Italy's Place in Physics." Pp. 155–198 in Holton, *The Scientific Imagination.* Cambridge: Cambridge University Press.
Renneberg, Monika, and Mark Walker, eds. 1994. *Science, Technology, and National Socialism.* Cambridge: Cambridge University Press.
Szöllösi-Janze, Margit, ed. 2001. *Science in the Third Reich.* New York: Berg.

SD, THE

Created in 1932 as the intelligence service of the SS, the SD (Sicherheitsdienst) eventually became the primary such agency of the Third Reich. By 1936 it was wedded to the national detective police force (Sicherheitspolizei) that included the Gestapo and the Kriminalpolizei, through which it shaped social control, crime fighting, and national security policies. Under the leadership of young Nazi intellectuals, it also sought to monitor and shape all aspects of the public mind through influence in education, social and political research and publication, cultural life, and the shaping and dissemination of "population policy." Thus it played a key role in the planning and execution of Nazi programs of genocide and ethnic cleansing.

George Browder

See Also: DEMOGRAPHIC POLICY; EDUCATION; EUGENICS; EUTHANASIA; GERMANY; GESTAPO, THE; HOLOCAUST, THE; NAZISM; SS, THE; THIRD REICH, THE; TOTALITARIANISM

References
Browder, George C. 1996. *Hitler's Elite: The Gestapo and the SS Security Service in the Nazi Revolution.* New York: Oxford University press.
Wildt, Michael, ed. 2003. *Nachrichtendienst, politische Elite und Mordeinheit. Der Sicherheitsdienst des Reichsfuehrers SS.* Hamburg: Hamburger Edition.

SEARCHLIGHT

International antifascist magazine that has been published monthly since 1975. Its origins can be traced back to the early 1960s and the antifascist operations of the direct-action 62 Group. *Searchlight* actively investigates fascist and racist activities, scoring particular successes with its "shut down the peddlers of hate" campaign, which exposed the white music scene to name but one. It is the premier antifascist source of today, gathering and disseminating up-to-date information on fascism to media outlets, trades unions, and the government. It was described by Nazi-hunter Simon Wiesenthal as the best English-language publication of its kind anywhere in the world.

Graham Macklin

See Also: ANTIFASCISM; RACISM; ROCK MUSIC; WHITE NOISE; WIESENTHAL, SIMON

Reference
http://www.searchlightmagazine.com.

SECULARIZATION

Interwar fascism had a complex relationship with the process of secularization. Unlike most right-wing ideologies, fascism was, in the main, a secular political system, though one that flirted with concepts of the sacred. To act as a resacralizing counterpoint to the materialism, rationalism, egalitarianism, and determinism manifest in liberal and Marxist political and economic systems, fascists turned to appeals to higher concepts, especially "the nation," which they enriched through concepts such as the New Man and a renewed heroic mentality; philosophical tropes of vitalism, idealism, and the will to power; and an aesthetic that inspired awe toward the idea of the nation. Broadly, this was in order to generate an ideology that would transcend the sense of individualism manifest in secular and bourgeois culture by developing a new, "liturgical" form of politics and the generation of nationalized "civic religions." Fascisms were, therefore, ideological systems that generated structures of nationalized myths that held the power to inculcate within the individual a level of faith and transcendence in the wider movement. Consequently, they synthesized a messianic aspect of "mission" and a sense of nationalized redemption with a "this-worldly" ideology. In this process they can be seen as conforming to a far wider trend for modern ideologies that sacralize politics in response to secularization and modernity—traditions which, for example, can also be seen in the rituals of the French Revolution and the public displays and leadership cults of Soviet communism. In order to achieve this, fascists sought to destroy, to subvert, or to reduce to a secondary aspect other religions—in the main Christianity, though also aspects of pre-Christian religious structures—in these projects, and often incorporated traditional religious rituals and narratives into their own

public semiotics. This co-option of a Christian semiotic was especially visible in the Falangist movement, the Romanian Iron Guard, the Croatian Ustasha, and the Afrikaner Ossawabrandweg.

In addition to this, the nationalized sense of the suffering and sacrifice of World War I formed a reservoir of mythopoeic resources for the interwar fascist movements. In Fascist Italy, the regime sought to build on a historicism from Mazzini and the *Risorgimento* in order to generate a new sense of an Italian civic religion, augmented especially through memories of the Battle of Caporetto. That event literally became the "Italian Golgotha" for some Italians, typical of resacralization through the suffering of war experiences. In the period 1923–1926, when Italian Fascism was consolidating its power, the use of sacralized politics was especially prevalent. One key ideologue of this period was Giovanni Gentile, who synthesized the ideal of a moral revolution from the Mazzini era with the Fascist project, and who provided an intellectual backdrop for the resacralization of politics in Fascist Italy. The various "civic religions" of fascism were little more than simulacra of religious faith, yet, no matter how hideous to our sensibilities, they should be understood as attempts by their protagonists to generate a new sense of moral consciousness—albeit one predicated on deeply flawed moral precepts. Consequently, fascisms should not be viewed as "genuine" religious systems but rather as modern political religions that emerge from and maintain a sense of collective sociopolitical crisis, necessarily eschew political and cultural senses of stability, and are the antithesis to thought systems that develop states of community open to all.

Paul Jackson

See Also: INTRODUCTION; "ANTI-" DIMENSION OF FASCISM, THE; ARYANISM; BOLSHEVISM; BOURGEOISIE, THE; CAPORETTO; CHRISTIANITY; COMMUNITY; CROATIA; EGALITARIANISM; FALANGE; FASCIST PARTY, THE; FRENCH REVOLUTION, THE; GENTILE, GIOVANNI; GERMANY; INDIVIDUALISM; IRON GUARD, THE; ITALY; LIBERALISM; MARXISM; MATERIALISM; MYTH; NATIONALISM; NAZISM; NEW MAN, THE; NEW ORDER, THE; NIHILISM; NORDIC SOUL, THE; OSSAWABRANDWEG, THE; PALINGENETIC MYTH; RATIONALISM; RELIGION; *RISORGIMENTO*, THE; ROMANIA; SOUL; SOUTH AFRICA; SOVIET UNION, THE; TOTALITARIANISM; USTASHA; UTOPIA, UTOPIANISM; *VOLKSGEMEINSCHAFT*, THE; VOLUNTARISM; WARRIOR ETHOS, THE

References
Gentile, Emilio. 1996. *The Sacralization of Politics in Fascist Italy.* Cambridge: Harvard University Press.
Griffin, Roger. 1991. *The Nature of Fascism.* London: Routledge.

Steigmann-Gall, Richard. 2003. *The Holy Reich: Nazi Conceptions of Christianity, 1919–1945*. Cambridge: Cambridge University Press.

SERBS, THE

Serbian fascism is epitomized by the right-wing movement Zbor (Rally), founded in 1935 by Dimitrije Ljotić. Zbor was the outcome of the unification of a number of profascist Yugoslav organizations, including Jugoslovenska Akcija (Yugoslav Action), which operated mainly in Croatia; Boj (Battle), based in Slovenia; and a group of Serbian journalists and writers assembled around the Belgrade-based right-wing publications *Zbor, Otadžbina (Fatherland)*, and *Buđenje (Awakening)*. In 1937 the movement was formally joined by the local German fascist organization Kulturbund, which operated among Serbia's *Volksdeutsche* (ethnic German) community in the northern Serbian province of Vojvodina. Although Zbor started out as a Yugoslav movement (its full title was the Yugoslav Popular Movement Zbor), its sphere of influence soon became confined to Serbia, especially in the aftermath of the election debacle in the winter of 1935. Zbor's political program consisted of a blend of Italian Fascism, German Nazism, and Orthodox Christian fundamentalism. Ljotić spoke of "the people" as an "organic being" that must abandon individualism, parliamentary democracy, communism, and other legacies of the Enlightenment and modernity. He argued that the nation must rally round a charismatic leader (preferably the king from the Karađorđević dynasty) and return to its religious and cultural traditions. Leaders of Zbor advocated a strong state based on the categories of "God, King and *domaćin* [that is, *pater familias*]," in which the teaching of Orthodox Christianity and Serbian peasant traditions would provide the main organizing principles. Zbor's uncompromising antimodernist stance was justified and rationalized by reference to a global international Jewish-Masonic-communist conspiracy against Serbs and other Orthodox Christians.

In the 1930s, Zbor's base was confined to students of the University of Belgrade (where the organization even had its own restaurant), the urban middle classes, and the Orthodox clergy. Zbor was also popular among the Devotionalists, a conservative Orthodox Christian evangelical movement that operated in the 1920s and 1930s under the patronage of a controversial Serbian

nationalist theologian, Bishop Nikolaj Velimirović (1880–1956). The clerical nationalist teachings of Bishop Velimirović strongly influenced the religious component of Zbor's fascist ideology. Zbor was for the most part an unpopular political movement. In the parliamentary elections of 1935 and 1938, Ljotić's organization, whose membership never exceeded a couple of thousand, attracted less than 1 percent of the vote and failed to win a single parliamentary seat. Most Serbs rejected Zbor because its ideology was considered to be too close to Italian Fascism and German Nazism. The late 1930s were a time of widespread support for Western powers among the Serbs, accompanied by an intense distrust of Germany and its supporters.

Before World War II, Zbor's modus operandi consisted mainly of public rallies and the publication of overtly fascist and anti-Semitic newspapers and magazines such as *Otadžbina (Fatherland)*, *Naš Put (Our Path)*, *Novi Put (The New Path)*, *Bilten JNP Zbor (Bulletin of the Yugoslav Popular Movement Zbor)*, and a German-language publication, *Die Erwache (The Awakening)*, aimed at Serbia's *Volksdeutsche* community. As a profoundly antidemocratic movement, Zbor was subjected to regular police intimidation in the prewar years. Its assets were frequently confiscated, rallies interrupted, and prominent members arrested, especially after 1940, when the movement was officially outlawed by the authorities. During the German occupation of Serbia (1941–1945), Zbor and its military wing, the Srpski Dobrovoljački Korpus (SDK; Serbian Volunteer Force), were Serbia's most ardent collaborationist organizations. Members of the SDK fought alongside the Germans against partisan insurgents and were even involved in the organization of retaliatory executions of civilians. Ljotić founded the Serbian equivalent of the Hitler Youth and opened a prison camp in the town of Sremska Palanka, the aim of which was to reindoctrinate Serbia's communist youth. Also, a number of prominent members of Zbor obtained high positions in the Serbian collaborationist government of General Milan Nedić.

Zbor ceased to exist after 1945. Many of its members were executed by Tito's partisans, while others fled abroad. Strongly pro-Ljotić movements continued to operate among the Serbian expatriate communities in Germany, the United States, the United Kingdom, and Australia. In the early 1990s, the publishing house Nova Iskra (New Spark), devoted to the promotion of the works of Dimitrije Ljotić, was established in Belgrade. Since 2000, political ideas similar to those once propounded by Zbor have been promoted by a number of relatively marginal Christian right-wing youth organizations, most notably by Otacastveni Pokret Obraz (Patriotic Movement Dignity) and Srpski Sabor "Dveri" (Serbian Assembly "Dveri").

Jovan Byford

SEE ALSO ANTI-SEMITISM; BOLSHEVISM; CONSPIRACY THEORIES; CROATIA; DEMOCRACY; FASCIST PARTY, THE; GERMANY; ITALY; LIBERALISM; LJOTIĆ, DIMITRIJE; MARXISM; MODERNITY; NATIONALISM; NAZISM; ORGANICISM; ORTHODOX CHURCHES, THE; PARLIAMENTARISM; POSTWAR FASCISM; PROGRESS; STATE, THE; STOJADINOVIC, MILAN; YOUTH MOVEMENTS; YUGOSLAVIA

References

Burgwyn, H. James. 2005. *Empire on the Adriatic: Mussolini's Conquest of Yugoslavia, 1941–1943.* New York: Enigma.

Judah, Tim. 2000. *The Serbs: History, Myth, and the Destruction of Yugoslavia.* New Haven: Yale University Press.

Martić, Miloš. 1980. "Dimitrije Ljotić and the Yugoslav National Movement Zbor, 1935–1945." *East European Quarterly* 16, no. 2: 219–239.

Stefanović, Mladen. 1984. *Zbor Dimitrija Ljotića, 1934–1945.* Beograd: Narodna Knjiga.

SERRANO SÚÑER, RAMÓN (1901–2003)

Franco's brother-in-law, nicknamed the Cuñadísimo (Supreme Brother-in-law), Serrano Súñer was the architect of the Francoist New State and simultaneously interior minister and foreign secretary (October 1940 to September 1942)—Spain's most powerful man between 1938 and 1942. Having escaped Madrid early in the Civil War, he reached Franco's Salamanca headquarters in February 1937, where he masterminded the fusion of the nationalist coalition into a single party, FET y de las JONS, and laid the foundations of the regime. Pro-Axis, he was portrayed as a Nazi enthusiast who pushed an unwilling Franco toward Hitler during World War II—a depiction successfully debunked by recent historiography. After 1942 he withdrew from politics, dying in September 2003 at the age of 101.

Sid Lowe

See Also: AXIS, THE; FALANGE; FRANCO Y BAHAMONDE, GENERAL FRANCISCO; FRANCOISM; GERMANY; HITLER, ADOLF; NAZISM; SPAIN; SPANISH CIVIL WAR, THE; WORLD WAR II

References

Merino, I. 1996. *Serrano Suñer, historia de una conducta.* Barcelona: Planeta.

Payne, S. 1987. *The Franco Regime.* Madison: Wisconsin University Press.

Preston, P. 1995. *Franco: A Biography.* London: Fontana.

SEVEREN, GEORGES ("JORIS") VAN (1894–1940)

Belgian far-right politician, leader of the Verbond van Dietse Nationaal Solidaristen (Verdinaso; League of Pan-Netherlandic Solidarists), a fascistic party. From 1921 until 1929 he was elected to the Belgian parliament as a member of an anti-Belgian Flemish nationalist party. In 1931 he took the lead of the *Verdinaso,* which initially agitated for the dismantling of the Belgium state and the annexation of Flanders to The Netherlands, and which subsequently worked toward a link-up of Belgium (including the French-speaking part, Wallonia) with The Netherlands, Luxembourg, and parts of northern France. On the day of the German invasion of Belgium he was arrested by Belgian state security agents and deported to France, where he was executed by the French military (in Abbeville). One part of Verdinaso collaborated with the German occupation; the other part joined the resistance movement.

Bruno de Wever

See Also: BELGIUM; DEGRELLE, LÉON; FRANCE; GERMANY; HOORNAERT, PAUL; NATIONALISM; NETHERLANDS, THE; REXISM; WORLD WAR II

Reference

Van Landschoot, R. 1998. "Severen, Joris van." Pp. 2.739–2.745 in *Nieuwe Encyclopedie van de Vlaamse Beweging.* Tielt: Lannoo.

SEXISM: *See:* EMPLOYMENT; FAMILY, THE; FEMINISM; SEXUALITY; WOMEN

SEXUALITY

The Italian Fascist approach to sexual matters was characterized by a double morality that allowed men to have the extramarital sexual experiences that were precluded to women while hiding nonconformist behavior under the mask of a formal adherence to traditional morality. For this reason the Fascists neither opposed regulated prostitution—as prewar reformers had done—nor openly exalted it, preferring to stick to the traditional interpretation of prostitution as a necessary evil. They certainly did not subscribe to the definition of some Futurists who claimed that prostitution was a form of female sexual liberation. Instead, the 1923 "Mussolini regulation" reinstated an authoritarian approach to the problem, offering male clients an illusion of safety by forcing prostitutes to undergo medical checks for venereal disease.

After the seizure of power in 1922, and especially with the onset of the process of "normalization" after 1926, the Fascists gradually eliminated dissenting opinions either by using censorship and prohibitions or by taking control of existing activities and modifying their objectives. Thus the *Rassegna di studi sessuali* (*Journal of Sexual Studies*), founded by Aldo Mieli in 1921 with the aim of disseminating in Italy the results of German sexology and providing serious information about sexual matters, gradually lost its original character. It stopped publishing articles about controversial topics and was turned into an instrument of the Fascist pronatalist propaganda. With the Lateran Treaty of 1929 between the Catholic Church and the Fascist state, the regime formally adopted Catholic doctrine as the basis of its legislation regarding the family, sexuality, and other moral issues. Church and state joined forces in promoting large families and opposing any form of birth control. Contraceptives were outlawed and abortion became the object of an important—albeit not very successful—repressive campaign. The increase of the population had been the major aim of Italian Fascist population policies since Mussolini's 1927 Ascension Day speech. Convinced that "number means power," the regime invested much of its prestige and resources in this campaign, and both the carrot and the stick were employed to promote early marriages and big families: bachelors paid a surplus tax, fathers of big families were preferred over others for employment and career opportunities, and workers received financial awards if they had large families. The propaganda directed at women was quite effective: it convinced many women that by giving birth to children they were fulfilling their duty as loyal female citizens of the new Fascist state. Most of the measures, however, were directed at men, thus confirming the Fascist belief that the male initiative was decisive in sexual matters, where women supposedly had only a passive role.

Compared with Italy, where the Roaring Twenties lasted only briefly, in the German Weimar Republic the public debate about sexuality reached more radical conclusions, and, generally speaking, the dominant ideology was liberal. Women received the vote in 1919, information about birth control and contraceptives was readily available, laws against abortion were made less severe, and sexual dissidents gained an important role in public debate. Moreover, a highly visible network of bars, publications, and organizations developed in the major German cities and allowed homosexual men and women to express their sexual preferences. Already in 1897, Magnus Hirschfeld (1868–1935) had founded the Wissenschaftlich-Humanitäres Komitee (Scientific Humanitarian Committee) with the intention of promoting homosexual emancipation and combating discrimination. The Institut für Sexualwissenschaft (Sexology Institute) founded in Berlin in 1919 continued this tradition by expanding scientific knowledge of human sexuality and endorsing sexual reform.

This rapid and radical process of modernization, however, generated a conservative backlash as a large part of public opinion became more and more worried about declining birth rates, increasing divorce rates, and rampant homosexuality, and complained that the decline of family values was contributing to the more general crisis of the German nation. One of the major targets of criticism was the 1927 law that abolished state-regulated prostitution, granting more rights to prostitutes and severely limiting the powers of the morals police. According to conservative Catholics and Protestants, the law showed the republic's unwillingness to combat immorality and would result in a rapid increase of venereal disease. In its early phases the Nazi movement tried to exploit these fears by presenting itself as the defender of traditional notions of sexual morality, but soon after Hitler's seizure of power, plans for the reintroduction of licensed brothels emerged, and streetwalkers became the target of ever more vicious repression. Completely disregarding traditional moral objections, by September 1939 the regime was openly promoting the creation of brothels under police control in an attempt to stop the spread of venereal diseases among the military and to provide the large groups of foreign workers with a sexual outlet.

The racist context of these decisions emerges clearly in the creation of special brothels for foreign workers and in the severe punishments handed down for sexual relations between foreign workers and German women. The basis for similar legislation had been laid in the 1935 Nuremberg *Blutschutzgsetz,* the legislation that forbade "mixed marriages" and extramarital sexual relations between Jews and persons of "German or related blood," incriminating formally only the male partners but often also subjecting women to harsh disciplinary measures, especially if they were adulterous. In comparison, Italian racism had a different approach: in the colonies after 1937 the law punished the cohabitation of Italians and indigenous women—which was considered a threat to the superiority of the Italian colonialists—but did not criminalize occasional sexual relations. Racial and gender stereotypes contributed to the creation of an image of African women as willing victims of the sexual lust of the Italian colonialists.

The sexual policies of the French Vichy regime expressed a reaction to the feminist and unruly *femme moderne* who had emerged during the Third Republic. Strongly influenced by pronatalist and profamily pressure groups, to whom a 1942 law attributed a formal role in deciding about family issues, the Vichy regime tried to stop the decline of the birth rate and to convince women that their patriotic duty was to give birth to children. Abortion was punished more severely than before, and in 1943 a woman convicted of having carried out abortions was even guillotined. In France, as in Italy, regulated prostitution was deemed necessary to control the sexual behavior of men and women.

Like many other countries in the interwar period, including democratic France, Belgium, and The Netherlands, Nazi Germany introduced measures aimed at promoting an increase in the birthrate. The Nazi regime gave a specific role in profamilist propaganda to the Reichsbund der Kinderreichen (National League of Large Families), which had been created shortly after World War I in an attempt to counterbalance the influence of the many birth-control organizations active in the Weimar Republic. Its major objectives were to subvert demographic decline and to uphold traditional family values. The provision of material assistance to families and of practical advice to mothers and children was the task of the organizations falling under the NS-Volkwohlfahrt. In addition, the state created a system of child allowances and grants and helped big families in finding housing, raising the necessary resources by taxing unmarried persons and

childless couples. All of these measures were aimed exclusively at those who were considered racially and socially "fit." "Asocials" and "racial aliens" were instead subjected to an array of discriminatory measures by the Nazis, who were intent on creating a perfect and racially pure *Volksgemeinschaft,* a community in which there was no place for those who were defined as "inferior" human beings. In defining the categories of "asocial" and "racially alien," the Nazis depended heavily on theories of racial hygiene elaborated by members of the eugenics movement since before 1933, when scientists like Alfred Ploetz and Fritz Lenz had promoted notions of "Aryan" superiority and proposed the elimination of "unfit" elements. The 1933 *Gesetz zur Verhütung erbkranken Nachwuchses*—Law for the Prevention of Hereditarily Diseased Offspring—put these ideas into practice, leading to the compulsory sterilization of some 320,000 persons between 1934 and September 1939.

In Italy, the rules imposed on young women were much more severe than those applying to young men: it was considered normal and even necessary for young men to have premarital sexual relations, and their violation of Catholic morality was therefore easily excused. Women, on the other hand, were often blamed if they surrendered to male insistence. Unwed mothers and their children were often treated as social outcasts, while it was relatively easy for their male partners to escape all responsibility. Especially in small villages, unwed mothers were treated with mistrust, and they were accused of having offended the honor of their family and of their community. A 1927 law obliging the Italian Opera Nazionale per la Protezione della Maternità e dell'Infanzia (ONMI; National Foundation for the Protection of Motherhood and Infancy) to assist unwed mothers with the aim of combating child abandonment was therefore severely criticized and scarcely implemented. In the countryside of central and northern Italy, however, premarital sexual relations were often tolerated, and pregnancies did not necessarily cause major problems: pregnancy was sometimes simply considered proof of the fertility of a woman and served to convince a couple to anticipate the date of their marriage. In large cities like Milan and Turin, a more secular attitude often annulled at least in part the effects of moral condemnation.

Notwithstanding all the measures taken in the context of the "battle for births," the Italian Fascists failed in reversing the trend of a declining birthrate. Unforeseen consequences of the laws against birth control in Italy were the increase in the number of children born out of wedlock and a generalized recourse to abortion as a method of birth control. Female networks of support helped women to find physicians, midwives, or others who would carry out abortions; even though abortion was considered a crime against the health of the Italian nation and as such was severely punished, persecution was not frequent.

In spite of the prevalence of public support for a return of women to a more passive and dependent role, which also inspired opposition to the presence of women in the labor force, both in Italy and in Germany fascist ideas regarding women's role in society were ambiguous. In Italy, attempts to mobilize women (and especially young girls) in the Fascist mass movements met with opposition from the Catholic Church and from conservative parents who considered the participation of their daughters in public events inappropriate and a potential danger to their honor. In Germany participation in the Bund Deutscher Mädel—the Fascist youth organization for girls—allowed girls to escape from parental surveillance and gave them the impression that they could make their own contribution to the national cause. Opposition to the strict norms proposed by the Fascist regime and the Catholic Church came also from other sources and was especially strong among young Italians. Jazz music, modern dances, and American movies and literature all contributed to create an alternative to the more austere way of life propagated by the regime, but did not become the object of the same level of repression as in Nazi Germany, where young people belonging to dissident groups like the Edelweißpiraten (Edelweiss Pirates) even risked their lives. The Gestapo and the Hitler Youth were, in fact, well aware of the challenge that these groups posed to the regime's aspirations for totalitarian control over youth by promoting cultural, political alternatives. At the same time, the Hitler Youth contributed to the spread of sexual experimentation among young people by undermining the authority of parents. Thus Nazi efforts to impose on youth a more severe morality failed, and court records show an increase of teenage promiscuity, sexual offenses, and venereal disease from the mid-1930s onward. The inability of the regime to channel teenage sexuality became even more clear with the outbreak of the war, which offered young people more opportunities to escape public control and parental surveillance.

A comparison between Italian Fascist and German Nazi sexual policies shows that while in Italy the regime never even attempted to elaborate an autonomous sexual ideology, in Germany, after the initial period in which the regime sided with the conservative backlash against the "moral corruption" of the Weimar Republic, the Nazis did develop their own views, increasingly moving away from the mere repression of sexuality. Nazi leaders like Heinrich Himmler in fact proposed a more positive vision of sex, but reserved it for the exclusive enjoyment of the "racially fit" and gave it the political objective of strengthening the German nation. Moreover, Nazi repression of sexuality was founded first and foremost on racial and political considerations rather than on moral or religious values. Both in Italy and in Germany, racism and sexism played a role in sexual discourse, but only in Germany did racist ideology become the decisive element.

Bruno Wanrooij

See Also: AMERICANIZATION; ANTI-SEMITISM; ARYANISM; ASOCIALS; BODY, THE CULT OF THE; CATHOLIC CHURCH, THE; COMMUNITY; DECADENCE; DEGENERACY; DEMO-GRAPHIC POLICY; EDELWEISS PIRATES, THE; EUGENICS; FAMILY, THE; FEMINISM; FASCIST PARTY, THE; FRANCE; FUTURISM; GERMANY; GESTAPO, THE; HEALTH; HIMMLER, HEINRICH; HITLER, ADOLF; HOMOSEXUALITY; ITALY; MEDICINE; MUSSOLINI, BENITO ANDREA; NAZISM; NEW MAN, THE; NUREMBERG LAWS, THE; RACIAL DOCTRINE; RACISM; RELIGION; TOTALITARIANISM; VICHY; *VOLKSGE-MEINSCHAFT*, THE; WARRIOR ETHOS, THE; WEIMAR RE-PUBLIC, THE; WELFARE; WOMEN; WORLD WAR I; WORLD WAR II; YOUTH MOVEMENTS

References
Eder, Franz X., et al., eds. 1999. *Sexual Cultures in Europe*. Vol. 1: *National Histories;* Vol. 2: *Themes in Sexuality.* Manchester: Manchester University Press.
Herzog, D., ed. 2005. *Sexuality and German Fascism*. New York: Berghahn.
Pine, L. 1997. *Nazi Family Policy 1933–1945*. Oxford: Berg.
Spackman, B. 1996. *Fascist Virilities: Rhetoric, Ideology and Social Fantasy in Italy*. Minneapolis: Minnesota University Press.
Wanrooij, Bruno P. F. 1990. *Storia del pudore. La questione sessuale in Italia 1860–1940*. Venezia: Marsilio.
Weindling, P. 1989. *Health, Race and German Politics between National Unification and Nazism 1870–1945*. Cambridge: Cambridge University Press.
Willson, P., ed. *Gender, Family and Sexuality: The Private Sphere in Italy 1860–1945*. New York: Palgrave.

SEYSS-INQUART, ARTHUR (1892–1946)

Leading Austrian Nazi who held positions of power in Austria and The Netherlands. After taking part in World War I, the attorney Seyss-Inquart joined nationalist groups (Deutsch-Österreichischer Volks-bund, Steirischer Heimatschutz) in Austria in the mid-1920s and the NSDAP in 1931. He played a prominent role with the annexation of Austria in 1938 and became Reich governor in the Ostmark in 1938. A year later he was second most senior leader in occupied Poland and became Reich commissioner in The Netherlands, where he was responsible for the deportation of the Jews, for the plundering of the country, and for the persecution of the resistance. Sentenced to death in the Nuremberg Trials, he was executed on 16 October 1946.

Fabian Virchow

See Also: *ANSCHLUSS, THE;* ANTI-SEMITISM; AUSTRIA; GERMANY; HOLOCAUST, THE; NAZISM; NETHERLANDS, THE; NUREMBERG TRIALS, THE; WAR VETERANS; WORLD WAR I

References
Hirschfeld, Gerhard. 1992. *Nazi Rule and Dutch Collaboration: Netherlands under German Occupation, 1940–1945.* Trans. L Wilmot. Oxford: Berg.
Paetzold, Kurt, and Manfred Weißbecker, eds. 1999. *Stufen zum Galgen: Lebenswege vor den Nürnberger Urteilen.* Leipzig: Militzke.
Rosar, Wolfgang. 1971. *Deutsche Gemeinschaft. Seyss-Inquart und der Anschluss.* Wien: Europa.
Warmbrunn, W. 1963. *The Dutch under German Occupation, 1940–1945.* Stanford: Stanford University Press.

SHOAH: See HOLOCAUST, THE
SICHERHEITSDIENST of the *Reichsführer*
SS: See SD, THE

SIEG HEIL!

Rallying cry meaning "Hail to victory!" used at Nazi meetings and mass rallies. After Hitler had completed a speech, it was a common practice for Rudolf Hess to lead the crowd in chanting the words rapturously over and over again.

Cyprian Blamires

See Also: HESS, RUDOLF; HITLER, ADOLF; NAZISM; NUREMBERG RALLIES, THE; PROPAGANDA; SALUTES

SIMA, HORIA (1907–1993)

Successor to C. Z. Codreanu, first leader of the Romanian Iron Guard. Sima organized the guard after it had been banned under King Charles II (1938). The execution of Codreanu on 29–30 November 1938 forced Sima to flee to Germany. From there he continued to coordinate the struggle against the king in Romania. On 6 September 1940, Sima was officially appointed as Codreanu's successor. He served as the vice president of the Council of Ministers under the short-lived Legionary (that is, Guardist) State in Romania (1940–1941), organized German resistance against the Russians in Romania (1944), and died in exile in Spain in 1993.

Philip Vanhaelemeersch

See Also: CODREANU, CORNELIU ZELEA; GERMANY; LEGION OF THE ARCHANGEL MICHAEL, THE; ROMANIA; SOVIET UNION, THE; WORLD WAR II

References
Ioanid, R. 1990. *The Sword of the Archangel Michael: Fascist Ideology in Romania.* Boulder, CO: Eastern European Monographs.
Nagy-Talavera, N. 1970. *The Green Shirts and Others.* Stanford: Stanford University Press.

SINTI: See ROMA

SKINHEAD FASCISM

The diverse currents of fascism espoused by minoritarian elements within the international skinhead youth subculture. Since the 1980s, skinheads have been a highly visible component of the broader neofascist milieu and have been responsible for a significant portion of the opportunistic street violence—as opposed to the well-planned terrorist violence—associated with the radical Right in recent years. The original skinheads evolved out of one of the subgroups within the British "Mod" subculture, specifically the "hard Mods," who had gradually adopted a more masculine sartorial style

Far-right skinheads protesting in Prague against a meeting of the G-8 finance ministers. Neofascist and neo-Nazi ideas and music have met with some receptiveness in a particular skinhead subculture. (Reuters/Corbis)

than the foppish Mod majority. The first skinheads appeared in late 1966 or 1967 and carried the rough working-class style of the hard Mods to even greater lengths. The quintessential skinhead "look" consisted of closely cropped hair, Fred Perry shirts, suspenders (braces), shortened and sometimes bleached jeans, and Doc Martens work boots, though this uniform has since undergone a variety of subtle modifications, including complete head-shaving and the addition of "bomber jackets." The early "skins" preferred ska music and sometimes hung out in Jamaican clubs, but they generally disliked blacks, South Asians, homosexuals, and "middle-class" hippies and students, were often uncritically patriotic, and were periodically involved in "Paki-bashing" (physical assaults on Asian immigrants) and violence against other despised out-groups. By the

turn of the 1970s, however, only a few remnants of these original skins still survived.

Paradoxically, the skinhead subculture re-emerged in the wake of the mid-1970s rise of the punk counterculture, an avant-garde, taboo-breaking youth movement that was intrinsically ironic and antiauthoritarian and, to the extent that it was consciously political, tended toward libertinism, libertarianism, left liberalism, or anarchism. Although punk was largely a middle-class youth movement, punks adopted a "tough" and menacing image, played very aggressive and primitive rock 'n' roll, engaged in rowdy behavior at gigs, and affected the sort of antibourgeois, working-class "street" ethos that inadvertently appealed to some genuinely violent blue collar thugs. So it was that the gigs of certain "street punk" bands, notably Sham 69, soon attracted contingents of soccer "hooligans" who adopted traditional skinhead garb, gave Nazi salutes, and attacked punk rockers. Later, a musical subcategory of punk rock with gruff vocals and soccer-style choruses, known as "Oi!" ("hey!" in Cockney slang), was embraced by these neoskinheads, who increasingly separated themselves from the mainstream of the punk scene.

Among the chief reasons for this subcultural separation was the overt politicization of the punk scene itself. In response to the appearance of violent working-class youths at some punk gigs, the Socialist Worker's Party and other sectarian left-wing groups created front organizations like Rock Against Racism (RAR) to rally left-leaning and antiracist punks against the new "fascist" danger. Far-right organizations (especially the British Movement) then responded by making increasing efforts to mobilize and recruit neoskinheads, in part by creating front organizations of their own, such as the Young National Front's Rock Against Communism (RAC). Although most punks and skins ignored self-styled political organizers, the activist elements within the punk scene became increasingly associated with the Left, whereas the activist elements within the new skinhead scene increasingly adhered to the far Right. It would be wrong to conclude, however, that the majority of skinheads have since adopted overtly fascist ideologies or become affiliated with fascist or far-right political movements and parties. The most that can be said is that the skinhead subculture tends to be a "macho" milieu whose members are prone to violence, whatever their political ideology, and that many skinheads have unreflective nationalistic and conservative social values.

In the course of the 1980s and 1990s, a significant minority of skinheads did in fact become associated with fascist or far-right organizations. In Britain, a decisive step in the creation of an organized fascist skinhead scene was the establishment of the White Noise record label in the early 1980s, whose initial release was the re-formed band Skrewdriver's "White Power" EP. This label was perhaps the first to enable openly neo-Nazi, neofascist, racist, and ultranationalist skinhead bands to circumvent censorship, release records, and attract a larger national and international following; it served as an inspiration to fascist sympathizers in other countries. Soon after, Herbert Egoldt's Rock-O-Rama label in Germany began releasing right-wing skinhead bands along with diverse punk bands, and in France, Gaël Bodilis of the left-leaning fascist group Troisième Voie (Third Way) founded the Rebelles Européennes "Oi!" label in Brest. Meanwhile, shifts in the British National Front's leadership and ideology, away from barely disguised neo-Nazism and toward a radical left-fascist Third Position doctrine, caused Skrewdriver's vocalist Ian Stuart Donaldson and other Nazi skins to break away and form their own organization, label, and publication, called Blood and Honour.

Since that time, neo-Nazi and neofascist labels have cropped up all over the industrialized and industrializing world, wherever the skinhead subculture has been transplanted, including in Eastern Europe, Russia, Japan, and parts of Latin America. In 1994 the Canadian George Burdi co-founded Resistance Records, a North American label that released skinhead "Oi!" records along with "white power," hard rock, metal, and metallic hardcore bands; it was then purchased by the late William Pierce's National Alliance. Certain types of underground music have therefore served as an effective mechanism for recruiting alienated youth into radical right politics, and during the past two decades individuals and organizations associated with the fascist skinhead milieu have committed numerous acts of violence against immigrants and "undesirables." Perhaps the most notorious of these actions involved setting fire to various buildings housing Turkish immigrants in Germany, which resulted in several deaths.

In response, groups of so-called traditional (1960s-inspired), nonracist (such as the Skinheads Against Racial Prejudice, or SHARP skins), and left-wing skinheads (known as Redskins) have arisen to contest the subcultural influence of fascist skins, whom they refer to as "boneheads." Yet most skinheads continue to eschew organized politics of all types, in part because they tend to be much too unruly to follow orders or to engage in sustained political activism. Skinhead fascism thus remains a minority phenomenon, both within the neofascist and the skinhead subcultural milieux. Nevertheless, in recent years various types of music with far-right themes have become more mainstream, having spread far beyond the skinhead subculture and other so-called *Rechtsrock* genres.

Jeffrey M. Bale

See Also: ANTIFASCISM; ARYANISM; BLACK METAL; BOLSHEVISM; BOURGEOISIE, THE; CARTO, WILLIS; CLASS; FOOTBALL/SOCCER; GERMANY; HOMOSEXUALITY; IMMIGRATION; MARXISM; NATIONAL FRONT, THE (UK); NATIONALISM; NAZISM; NEO-NAZISM; PIERCE, WILLIAM; POSTWAR FASCISM; RACIAL DOCTRINE; RACISM; ROCK MUSIC; RUSSIA; SALUTES; SKREWDRIVER; THIRD POSITIONISM; UNITED STATES, THE (POSTWAR); WHITE NOISE; WHITE SUPREMACISM; XENOPHOBIA

References

Anti-Defamation League. 1995. *The Skinhead International: A Worldwide Survey of Neo-Nazi Skinheads.* New York: ADL.

Cotter, John M. 1999. "Sounds of Hate: White Power Rock and Roll and the Neo-Nazi Skinhead Subculture." *Terrorism and Political Violence* 11, no. 2: 111–140.

Dornbusch, Christian, and Jan Raube, eds. 2002. *RechtsRock: Bestandsaufnahme und Gegenstrategien.* Hamburg: Unrast.

Farin, Klaus, and Eberhard Seidel. 2002. *Skinheads.* Munich: C. H. Beck.

Knight, Nick. 1982. *Skinhead.* London: Omnibus.

Lowles, Nick, and Steve Silver. 1998. *White Noise: Inside the International Nazi Skinhead Scene.* London: Searchlight.

SKORZENY, OTTO (1908–1975)

Hitler's personal bodyguard and world-famous Nazi adventurer. Skorzeny was born in Vienna and joined the Freikorps when studying engineering. He was later a member of the Heimwehr before becoming a Nazi in 1930. In the 1930s he worked in business management but was appointed Hitler's bodyguard in 1939. He went on to serve with the Waffen-SS in France and Russia. In April 1943 he was appointed a colonel in the security services. In September of that year he won worldwide fame for leading an airborne raid by glider to release and take to freedom Mussolini, who had been imprisoned high in the Apennines after being forced out of office by the Grand Council of Fascism. The rescue involved a takeoff from a rocky field. Skorzeny was also involved in the aftermath of the abortive July Plot, organizing the reassertion of Hitler's authority. In October 1944 he kidnapped the Hungarian Regent Horthy to prevent him carrying out his intention of surrendering his country to the advancing Russians. Skorzeny was arrested by U.S. troops in May 1945 and put on trial but acquitted. He was subsequently arrested by the German authorities but escaped in July 1948. Using an assumed name he set up a secret organization (Die Spinne; "The Spider") that is said to have been formed to help his former SS colleagues escape from Germany. Eventually he settled in Spain and set up in business.

Cyprian Blamires

See Also: FREIKORPS, THE; GERMANY; GRAND COUNCIL OF FASCISM, THE; HEIMWEHR; HITLER, ADOLF; HORTHY DE NAGYBÁNYA, MIKLÓS; HUNGARY; ITALY; JULY PLOT, THE; MUSSOLINI, BENITO ANDREA; NAZISM; ODESSA; REMER, OTTO-ERNST; SALÒ REPUBLIC, THE; SS, THE; WAFFEN-SS, THE; WORLD WAR II

References
Foley, C. 1998. *Commando Extraordinary: Otto Skorzeny.* London: Cassell.

Skorzeny, Otto. 1997. *Skorzeny's Special Missions: The Memoirs of the Most Dangerous Man in Europe.* London: Greenhill.

SKREWDRIVER

Formed in 1977 by Ian Stuart Donaldson, Skrewdriver was the seminal Nazi rock band and the driving force behind the burgeoning "white noise" music scene in the 1980s. Donaldson was killed in a car crash in 1993. His influence on the white power music scene continues to be widely felt.

Graham Macklin

See Also: NEO-NAZISM; POSTWAR FASCISM; ROCK MUSIC; SKINHEAD FASCISM; WHITE NOISE; WHITE SUPREMACISM

Reference
Pearce, Joe. 1987. *Skrewdriver: The First Ten Years. The Way It's Got To Be.* London: Skrewdriver Services.

SLAVE LABOR: *See* FORCED LABOR

SLAVS, THE (and Germany)

Denotes a variety of ethnicities and nations in Central, Eastern, and South-East Europe whose tongues belong to the Slavic language group: "the Slavs" were seen by the Nazis as inferior peoples. In comparison to the Jews however, they occupied an indeterminate position in the Nazi racial hierarchy. They were collectively or separately characterized as *fremdvölkische* ("nationally alien"), *Untermenschen,* or "Asiatic," and constituted the majority of victims of Nazi annihilation, deportation, and exploitation policies from 1938 to 1945. Nevertheless, representatives of all three Slavic subgroups—Western, Southern, and Eastern—were, at one point or another, accepted as German allies. A number of Nazi publications considered parts (and some all) of the Slavs as belonging to the original "Nordic" or "Indogermanic" peoples. The Third Reich's attack on Eastern Europe may have been primarily determined by motives other than anti-Slavism, such as anti-Bolshevism and the quest for new *Lebensraum*. Yet implementation of the latter aims accounts only partly for the deaths of the millions of Russians, Ukrainians, Poles, and other Slavs who perished not only in combat against, but primarily under the occupation of, the Wehrmacht and the SS during World War II.

Nineteenth-century German public opinion and research on Eastern Europe and Russia showed, along with certain russophile tendencies, strong currents of anti-Slavism that continued earlier negative stereotypes about Poles and Russians. Views of Slavs as "unhistorical," "cultureless," or "barbaric" were voiced by representatives of both Right and Left—including Karl Marx and Friedrich Engels. In the *völkisch* discourse of late Imperial Germany, Slavs were described as "racially mixed" or "mongolized." A significant minority of nationalist and racist publicists with influence on the Nazi movement, including Houston Stuart Chamberlain, did, however, write positively about the Slavs. The Slavs played a relatively minor role in interwar German racist discourse in general and Nazi racial thinking in particular. Both official statements and unofficial procedures of the Third Reich regarding Slavic people continued to be marked by contradictions and shifts right down to 1945. Although the Czechs were viewed by Hitler in the 1920s more negatively than the Poles, German occupation policies in the *Reichsprotektorat* of Czechoslovakia were more permissive and less violent than those in the *Generalgouvernement* and other annexed Polish territories. Whereas "only" 40,000 or so Czechs perished during Nazi occupation, the overwhelming majority of the 1.8 to 1.9 million Polish civilian victims of World War II were killed by Germans. In spite of manifest SS anti-Polonism, Himmler's *Generalplan Ost* of 1942 made a distinction between *eindeutschungsfähige* Poles ("those who can be Germanized") and Poles who were to be deported to Siberia within the next decades. Earlier, the greater part of the Czech population had become regarded as assimilable by the Nazis, while the Slovaks had been allowed to form their own satellite state.

Whereas in the Balkans Orthodox Serbs were among the nations least respected by Hitler, Orthodox Bulgarians (seen as being of Turkic origin) occupied a relatively high position in the Nazi racial hierarchy and were referred to by Joseph Goebbels as "friends." Bulgaria was permitted to abstain from participation in the attack on the Soviet Union and to pursue an independent policy

with regard to its Jews. The Soviet people were labeled "beasts," "animals," "half-monkeys," "hordes," and the like. Among the approximately 10 million Soviet civilians who perished under the Nazis, there were 3.3 million POWs, most of them Eastern Slavs. Yet, as the German advance into Russia halted, the Waffen-SS recruited, among other soldiers from the USSR, a specifically Ukrainian division ("Galicia") and a Byelorussian unit. Impressed by the phenotype of the Ukrainians, Hitler, in August 1942, proposed the assimilation of Ukrainian women. Toward the end of the war, German troops were assisted by General Andrei Vlasov's Russian Popular Army of Liberation, consisting of tens of thousands of Russian POWs and emigres. The Cossacks—though being Eastern Slavs—were even seen as "Germanic." Shortly before his suicide, Hitler described the "Slavic race" as stronger than the Germanic one—whose destiny it was to succumb.

Andreas Umland

See Also: ANTI-SEMITISM; ARYANISM; AUSTRO-HUNGARIAN EMPIRE/HABSBURG EMPIRE, THE; BARBAROSSA, OPERATION; BOLSHEVISM; BULGARIA; CHAMBERLAIN, HOUSTON STEWART; CULTURE; CZECHOSLOVAKIA; *DRANG NACH OSTEN* ("DRIVE TO THE EAST"); EXPANSIONISM; *GENERALGOUVERNEMENT*/GENERAL GOVERNMENT, THE; GERMANNESS (*DEUTSCHHEIT*); GERMANY; HITLER, ADOLF; *LEBENSRAUM*; MARXISM; *MEIN KAMPF*; NAZISM; POLAND AND NAZI GERMANY; RACIAL DOCTRINE; RACISM; SERBS, THE; SLOVAKIA; SOVIET UNION, THE; SS, THE; THIRD REICH, THE; TURANISM; *UNTERMENSCHEN*; *VOLK, VÖLKISCH*; WAFFEN-SS, THE; WEHRMACHT, THE; WORLD WAR II; YUGOSLAVIA

References

Connelly, John. 1999. "Nazis and Slavs: From Racial Theory to Racist Practice." *Central European History* 32, no. 1: 1–33.

Laffin, John. 1995. *Hitler Warned Us: The Nazis' Master Plan for a Master Race*. Dulles, VA: Brassey's.

Schaller, Helmut. 2002. *Der Nationalsozialismus und die slawische Welt*. Regensburg: Friedrich Pustet.

Volkmann, Hans-Erich, ed. 1994. *Das Russlandbild im Dritten Reich*. Köln: Böhlau.

Wippermann, Wolfgang. 1996. "Antislavismus." Pp. 512–524 in *Handbuch zur "Völkischen Bewegung" 1871–1918*, edited by Uwe Puschner. München: Saur.

SLAVS, THE (and Italy)

Under the interwar Fascist regime, Italy's Slavic minorities suffered discrimination as a result of the state's Italianization campaign. Although unification incorporated autochthonous populations of Slovenes (in the

Veneto) and Croats (mainly in the Molise) into the new Italian state, after World War I the size of these populations expanded as a result of Italy's acquisition of former Habsburg lands in Friuli, Venezia Giulia, Istria, and Fiume. Estimates by Slovene scholars put the number of ethnic Slavs in these new Italian provinces at 350,000 Slovenes and 200,000 Croats.

Anti-South Slav feeling under Fascism drew on deep-rooted prejudices that contrasted a "superior" Italian *civiltà* ("civilization") to the "barbaric" and backward culture of the Slavs. These attitudes became particularly pronounced in the context of the Italian irredentist movement, which claimed eastern Adriatic territories on the grounds that they bore a historical Italian cultural imprint. Many Italians in the new ("redeemed") eastern provinces expressed sympathy for the Fascist movement well before 1922, in part because local Fascist squads targeted the associations of the ethnic minorities, together with those of leftists. Fascist squads in Trieste burned down the Narodni Dom, or National House, of the Slovene minority in 1920, for example, in an action emblematic of this "frontier Fascism." In 1923, the Gentile Reform eliminated the minority language schools that had existed under the Habsburgs for Slovenes and Croats. Minority language newspapers and associations were shut down, and the regime went as far as to forcibly Italianize personal names.

The suppression of the political and cultural life of Italy's Slovene and Croat populations prompted some of the earliest forms of armed resistance to Fascism in the 1920s by the groups Borba and TIGR (standing for Trieste-Istria-Gorizia-Rijeka). When Italy attacked Yugoslavia in April 1941, there thus already existed an underground network of Slavic resistance that would be joined by the Yugoslav communists in fighting against Fascism. The Italian military occupation of what became known as the Province of Lubiana (Ljubljana) and of Dalmatia led to widespread rebellion on the part of local populations. That, in turn, prompted Italian forces to intern and often mistreat Slavic civilians in camps on the grounds of antiguerrilla measures. The only Nazi extermination camp within Italy was established after 1943, with the complicity of local Italian Fascist authorities, at the Risiera di San Sabba (a former rice-processing plant) in Trieste. Of the estimated 3,000 persons executed at San Sabba, the majority were anti-Fascist Slavs.

At the end of World War II, both Italy and Yugoslavia claimed large parts of Venezia Giulia on ethnic grounds. Yugoslavia also cited the brutal policies that South Slavs had suffered under Fascism and the "blood sacrifice" made by Slovenes and Croats to "liberate" the territory. After a bitter nine-year territorial dispute, the region was partitioned, with Slovenes remaining a minority in Italy and Italians a minority in Yugoslavia; the mass migration of Italians from Istria between 1945 and 1955 significantly diminished the Italian population in Yugoslavia.

Pamela Balling

See Also: AUSTRO-HUNGARIAN EMPIRE/HABSBURG EMPIRE, THE; CIVILIZATION; CROATIA; DALMATIA; D'ANNUNZIO, GABRIELE; EXPANSIONISM; FASCIST PARTY, THE; FIUME; GENTILE, GIOVANNI; IRREDENTISM; ITALY; ROME; TRADITION; WORLD WAR I; WORLD WAR II; YUGOSLAVIA

References

Becker, Jared M. 1995. *Nationalism and Culture: Gabriele d'Annunzio and Italy after the Risorgimento.* Berne: Peter Lang.

Bon Gherardi, Silva. 1972. *La persecuzione antiebraica a Trieste (1938–1945).* Udine: Del Bianco.

Burgwyn, H. James. *Empire on the Adriatic: Mussolini's Conquest of Yugoslavia, 1941–1943.* New York: Enigma.

Stranj, Pavel. 1992. *La comunità sommersa.* Trieste: Editoriale Stampa Triestina [SLORI].

Walston, James. 1997. "History and Memory of the Italian Concentration Camps." *Historical Journal* 40, no. 1: 169–183.

Wolff, Larry. 2001. *Venice and the Slavs: The Discovery of Dalmatia in the Age of Enlightenment.* Stanford: Stanford University Press.

Zivojinovic, Dragan R. *Italy, America and the Birth of Yugoslavia, 1917–19.* New York: Columbia University Press.

SLOGANS: *See* PROPAGANDA

SLOVAKIA

The first Slovak Republic existed as a nominally independent nation from 14 March 1939 until 8 May 1945, and in that time, as a clericalist authoritarian state with residues of democracy, it came under strong pressure to adopt National Socialist policies. The Slovak Republic was born essentially as a result of Hitler's decision, in March 1939, to occupy the territory left to the Czechoslovak state by the terms of the Munich agreement of September 1938. The prime minister of the autonomous region established in the wake of the Munich agreement, Msgr. Tiso, was summoned to Munich and offered independence by Hitler on 13 March. The following day the regional assembly declared Slovakia independent, and Tiso became president of the new state. This move was very welcome to those Slovaks who had felt overruled by a hitherto fairly centralized Czechoslovak state system. Arguably the two parts of post–World War I Czechoslovakia were very different, which caused tensions between them. Bohemia and Moravia were more urbanized, industrialized, and secularized than strongly rural, agrarian, and Catholic Slovakia. The Slovak People's Party of Msgr. Andrej Hlinka, renamed the Hlinka Slovak People's Party (HSL'S) after his death, was an essentially conservative Catholic party (25 percent of its MPs, as well as its two successive leaders, were priests), with a more radical and anti-Semitic wing led by Vojtech Tuka that campaigned in the Prague parliament for Slovak autonomy. Although by no means a majority party, from 1939 onward the HSL'S, with its paramilitary Hlinka Guard and Hlinka Youth movement, was the core of what was in effect a one-party state.

The six-year history of "independent" Slovakia was a difficult one. Within a few months of its foundation, the state had to fight wars against Poland and Hungary over lost territory, and, surrounded as it was by the Axis powers, it became effectively a client state of the Greater German Reich. The Germans insisted that Tuka, prime minister after October 1939, replace Durcansky as foreign minister, and Mach, one of Tuka's leading supporters, was made minister of the interior. This had two effects: it put Tuka and the radical faction of his HSL'S, supported by the paramilitary Hlinka Guard, in a stronger position in the state. Consequently, Tuka sought to give the party and the state a strongly National Socialist policy. It also obliged Slovakia to accept German dictates in both foreign and domestic policy, most notably the establishment of German bases in the country, adherence to the Anti-Comintern Pact and involvement in the war against the Soviet Union, and agreement to deport the country's Jewish population to concentration camps in Poland.

Tiso, who belonged to the more moderate wing of the HSL'S, resisted both of these trends, seeking to preserve genuine Slovak independence under difficult circumstances, though with less and less success as time went by. He had opposed the anti-Jewish law, Codex Judaicus, of September 1941, which assigned a 51 percent shareholding of Jewish businesses to Christians and imposed other disabilities on Jews, including loss of citizenship rights, and he stopped the deportation of Jews to Poland when he discovered their destination, Auschwitz. In the end, the bulk of Slovakia's Jewish population perished, despite the repeated protests of the Vatican and its nuncio, Burzio: of approximately 130,000 Jews who had lived in Slovakia before World War II, some 60,000 died. In August 1944, following the unsuccessful uprising of the Slovak resistance led by the Slovak National Council, which included both communists and social/liberal democrats, German forces occupied Slovakia, and the deportations of the Jews resumed. By this time Russian troops had invaded the east of Slovakia, Ruthenia. In May 1945, Slovakia was liberated by the Red Army. Following the end of the war, Tiso was executed; Tuka died in prison.

Despite some discernible resemblance between the HSL'S and the Croatian Ustasha movement—that is, in that they were both fundamentally Catholic and seeking independent statehood for their people—and despite the presence of pro-Nazi elements in the HSL'S and the role played by the party's paramilitary wing, the Hlinka Guard, in the rounding up of Jews, the complex set of circumstances explained above demonstrates that the first Slovak Republic, unlike the Independent State of Croatia, was not fascist.

John Pollard

See Also: INTRODUCTION; ANTI-COMINTERN PACT, THE; ANTI-SEMITISM; APPEASEMENT; AUSCHWITZ (-BIRKENAU); AXIS, THE; CATHOLIC CHURCH, THE; CLERICO-FASCISM; CONCENTRATION CAMPS; CROATIA; CZECHOSLOVAKIA; GERMANY; HITLER, ADOLF; HOLOCAUST, THE; MUNICH AGREEMENT/PACT, THE; NAZISM; PAPACY, THE; PARAMILITARISM; POLITICAL CATHOLICISM; SOVIET UNION, THE; TISO, MGR. JÓSEF; TUKA, DR. VOJTECH; USTASHA; WORLD WAR I; WORLD WAR II; YOUTH MOVEMENTS

References
Innes, A. 2001. *Czechoslovakia: The Short Goodbye.* New Haven: Yale University Press.
Kirschbaum, S. J., ed. 1983. *Slovak Politics: Essays on Slovak History in Honour of Joseph Kirschbaum:* Cleveland, OH: Slovak Institute.
———. 1999. *Historical Dictionary of Slovakia.* London: Scarecrow.

SLUMP, THE: *See* **WALL STREET CRASH, THE**

SMETONA, ANTANAS (1874–1944)

Leading figure in the Lithuanian national movement and first president of Lithuania (1919–1920). In the 1920s, Smetona worked as a newspaper editor and university lecturer and led a small opposition party, the Nationalist Union (Tautininkai). After a military putsch cut short parliamentary democracy in 1926, Smetona became president. Smetona altered the constitution to strengthen the presidency. He believed that democracy was alien to Lithuania, and he built an authoritarian nationalist regime claiming to have uniquely Lithuanian characteristics. Smetona was referred to as *Tautas Vados,* or "leader of the nation." In 1940, when the Soviet Union occupied Lithuania, Smetona fled the country. He died in a house fire in Cleveland, Ohio.

Andres Kasekamp

See Also: AUTHORITARIANISM; DEMOCRACY; DICTATORSHIP; ESTONIA; LATVIA; LEADER CULT, THE; LITHUANIA; NATIONALISM

Reference
Sabaliunas, L. 1972. *Lithuania in Crisis: Nationalism to Communism, 1939–1940.* Bloomington: Indiana University Press.

SOCCER: *See* FOOTBALL

SOCIAL DARWINISM

A social theory developed in the second half of the nineteenth century that applied Darwinistic evolutionary ideas to human society, a significant element in Nazi ideology. Natural selection became a central concept in social and political thought soon after the first popularization of Darwin's evolutionary theory, both in Europe and in North America. Socialist thinkers emphasized the inevitability of social evolution, at the end of which the classless society would arise. Others used Darwin's thesis to justify the bourgeoisie's claim to power and social distinctions. Conflicts within societies were now interpreted as much on the premise of the struggle for existence and the survival of the fittest as on the premise of conflicts between peoples and nations. The oppression of colonial peoples and imperialistic expansion projects now acquired a significant natural scientific justification. But within Europe, too, representatives of certain nations such as Britain, France, and Germany thought of themselves as superior to each other and with the help of Darwinistic ideas argued the necessity of conflict. War and soldierly virtues were glorified as necessary and beneficial for men and progress.

With the popularization of racist ideas in the second half of the nineteenth century through Gobineau and others, a synthesis of racism and Social Darwinism was quickly made. In order to be able to survive the necessary struggle between the nations, one's own "race" must be strengthened. At the end of the nineteenth century many in Europe and North America thought that they could perceive massive signs of degeneration. The mass misery of the workers caused all kinds of rapid physical and mental decline, violent criminality, and alcoholism. Civilization was interpreted as a disturbance of natural selection, allowing a greater number of the allegedly biologically unfit to survive. Prophets of cultural pessimism prophesied unstoppable decline, unless and until the reproduction of "unworthy" life was blocked and the reproduction of the fittest furthered by massive state intervention.

Social Darwinism and racism were well entrenched both in North America and in Europe by the beginning of World War I. They entered even more into mainstream thinking, a store of ideas that well-known politicians and scientists and many racist, *völkisch,* nationalistic, and fascist movements (but also reformist groups and splinter groups) could make use of. From the beginning of the twentieth century, population policy concepts developed both in Europe and in North America that were intended to assist natural selection through sterilization and control. Some of these concepts were implemented in a few of the U.S. states and in Sweden. Although the U.S. laws on sterilization of the seriously handicapped passed before World War I were applied only in a few cases, they were put forward as a model in Germany. In Sweden a law was passed on 1 January 1935 that made possible the sterilization of persons with mental and physical illnesses, and it was applied as late as the 1970s.

Social Darwinism served National Socialist ideology as a justification for eugenics, euthanasia, the persecution of the Jews, and war. The radicalization of popular Social Darwinism took place during World War I and during the economic crises of the 1920s and 1930s. With Hitler and the NSDAP, a man and a party came to power that implemented Social Darwinistic ideas bound in with racism and anti-Semitism in a regime of terror. The law on the prevention of reproduction by those with inherited disorders, which came into force on 1 January 1934, belongs in this context, like the Nuremberg Race Laws of 18 October 1935 and the

Marriage Health Law of 18 October 1935. After the beginning of World War II all of the remaining barriers fell, and millions—including thousands of persons with mental and physical handicaps—were murdered in the "race war" in which the main targets were Jews and Slavs.

Michael Schäbitz
(translated by Cyprian Blamires)

See Also: ANTI-SEMITISM; ARYANISM; CIVILIZATION; COLONIALISM; CULTURE; DECADENCE; DEGENERACY; ELITE THEORY; EUGENICS; EUTHANASIA; GERMANY; GOBINEAU, COMTE ARTHUR DE; HEALTH; HITLER, ADOLF; HOLOCAUST, THE; IMPERIALISM; *MEIN KAMPF;* MOSCA, GAETANO; MICHELS, ROBERTO; NAZISM; NUREMBERG LAWS, THE; PARETO, VILFREDO; RACIAL DOCTRINE; SCIENCE; SLAVS, THE (AND GERMANY); SOCIOLOGY; TERROR; *VOLK, VÖLKISCH;* WALL STREET CRASH, THE; WARRIOR ETHOS, THE; WORLD WAR I

References

Gasman, D. 1971. *The Scientific Origins of National Socialism: Social Darwinism in Ernst Haeckel and the German Monist League.* London: Macdonald.
Hawkins, M. 1997. *Social Darwinism in European and American Thought, 1860–1945: Nature as Model and Nature as Threat.* Cambridge: Cambridge University Press.
Weindling, P. 1991. *Darwinism and Social Darwinism in Imperial Germany: The Contribution of the Cell Biologist Oscar Hertwig (1849–1922).* Stuttgart: Gustav Fischer.

SOCIALISM

FASCISM AS SOCIALISM

Discussion of the relationship of socialism with interwar fascism is complicated by a number of factors. On the face of it, fascism should seemingly be regarded as a variety of socialism. The Nazi Party in Germany was unabashedly, openly, and proudly the National *Socialist* Party. In Italy, Mussolini was reared in a socialist family and the Christian names he was given were in honor of socialist leaders; he himself was moreover for a while actually leader of the Italian Socialist Party. In calling for Italy to enter World War I, he did not abandon socialism as such but internationalism, to which he preferred nationalism. In theory he represented a strong policy of state interventionism, something much more favored by socialism than by conservatism. However, the Left has almost from the beginning universally regarded itself as being at the opposite extreme from fas-

cism of any stripe. Classic histories of European socialism do not pay any attention to the possibility that there could have been any socialism in National Socialism. This seems paradoxical, but the key to the enigma lies in the word *national.* "Mainstream" socialism has always regarded itself as a universal doctrine transcending national boundaries and proclaiming the shared interests of workers in every part of the world. It can no more be tied to national borders than can the Christian religion, which equally proclaims itself a universal dogma. There have been many internal disputes within socialism, and some, such as the followers of Marx, have excommunicated other brands that did not espouse such doctrines as dialectical materialism. But one thing they all have in common is a belief that they represent (at least in theory) a global belief system with some kind of priority being given to the worldwide proletariat or working class, irrespective of the nation to which they belong. This goes hand in hand with a proclaimed pursuit of the ideal of equality. Elites, aristocracies, and hierarchies are, generally speaking, objects of denigration in socialist thinking.

In combining the ideal of unashamedly elitist nationalism with that of socialism, Mussolini and Hitler caught the Left on the hop and popularized a kind of thinking that was not in essence new but that had not previously been successful. (A group of British socialists had, in fact, created a "National Socialist Party" in 1916 to emphasize their patriotism at the height of World War I, though only four years later they renamed themselves the Social Democratic Federation.) But the origins of National Socialism as a German creed go back to the end of the nineteenth century. The celebrated sociologist Max Weber was preaching an "economic nationalism," and he and Hans Delbrück sowed the idea of political nationalism in the mind of the Christian Socialist Friedrich Naumann and his followers. In July of 1895, Naumann observed that the best of social policies would be useless should Germany be invaded by the Russians. All good domestic policy required being built on the foundation of securing the fatherland and its boundaries, so as to provide for national power. Naumann argued that this was the Achilles heel of Social Democracy, which needed to be superseded by a nationalistic socialism. This was a potent mix indeed. What Hitler and Mussolini realized, and what the Left failed to realize, was that for many people the cosmopolitan ideal pursued by traditional socialism remained an abstraction. The ideal of universal "fraternity" as proclaimed by the French Revolution may have been attractive as a theory, but ties of family and nation always tended to prove the stronger in times of crisis. The tendency of "socialists" to catch "war fever" in 1914 was symptomatic of this; in theory they regarded the war as an affair for international capitalism and nothing to do with the workers, but in practice the feverish chauvinism that swept through the belligerent nations from the start infected them, too.

Another confusing aspect of fascism for its opponents was its claim to be a revolutionary movement. The term *revolution* had always been a bugbear for conservatives, and it was traditionally considered part of the panoply of socialism, although by the early years of the nineteenth century a trend had developed among some socialists that was evolutionary rather than revolutionary. The frank affirmation of revolutionary credentials by both Italian Fascists and National Socialists was another feature of their ideology that connected them to socialism. In reality, of course, the difference lay in the notion of what the "revolution" aspired to be. For socialists, it was to be an egalitarian revolution with a transformation of property ownership in favor of the workers; for fascists, it was a totalitarian revolution concerned with the regeneration of the nation from a prevalent state of decadence and the creation of a "new man" whose value system would privilege qualities like pride in the nation, honor, the virile and manly virtues of the soldier, and self-sacrifice for the sake of the collectivity.

Logically, it seems hard to deny that *national* socialism should simply be regarded as a variety of "socialism" tout court. After all, there have been so many varieties in the Broad Church of Socialism. The problem is, who is to define "socialism"? If Engels is to be believed, nobody can be a socialist who does not believe in dialectical materialism. Who can gainsay him? Stalin too called himself a socialist and was responsible for even more murders than the Nazis. In a country like the United Kingdom, "socialism" can even be regarded as an ideal in the twenty-first century by a Labour Party that believes in privatization of nationalized industries. If state interventionism is regarded as one of the hallmarks of socialism, then the Italian Fascist and German Nazi regimes do look socialist in some degree, although their proclaimed policies were often not matched on the ground. If adherence to class over nation is considered one of the hallmarks of socialism, then both regimes fail totally. Further complication is added by the fact that there were "left" and "right" variations within fascism itself: for example, in Germany the Strasser brothers represented a more left-wing and anticapitalist current that lost out when they were murdered in 1934.

Cyprian Blamires

See Also: INTRODUCTION; ABSTRACTION; AUTARKY; BOLSHEVISM; CAPITALISM; CHRISTIANITY; CLASS; CONSERVATISM; CORPORATISM; COSMOPOLITANISM; COUNTERREVOLUTION; DECADENCE; ECONOMICS; *EHRE* ("HONOR"); FASCIST PARTY, THE; GERMANY; HITLER, ADOLF; INDIVIDUALISM; ITALY; MARXISM; MARXIST THEORIES OF FASCISM; *MEIN KAMPF;* MUSSOLINI, BENITO ANDREA; NATIONALISM; NAZISM; NEW MAN, THE; NIGHT OF THE LONG KNIVES, THE; PALINGENETIC MYTH; REVOLUTION; SOVIET UNION, THE; SPANN, OTHMAR; STALIN, IOSIF VISSARIONOVICH; STATE, THE; STRASSER BROTHERS, THE; TOTALITARIANISM; WARRIOR ETHOS, THE

References

Adamson, W. L. 1993. *Avant-garde Florence: From Modernism to Fascism.* London: Harvard University Press.

Griffin, R. 1991. *The Nature of Fascism.* London: Routledge.

Lindemann, Albert S. 1983. *A History of European Socialism.* New Haven: Yale University Press.

Sternhell, Z. 1986. *Neither Right, nor Left.* Princeton: Princeton University Press.

Weber, Marianne. 1988 [1975]. *Max Weber: A Biography.* Trans. and ed. Harry Zohn. New Brunswick: Transaction.

FASCISM AGAINST SOCIALISM

Where fascism came to power, the prohibition of the labor movement and the persecution of its representatives were among its first measures. At the beginning was the murder of the socialist deputy Giacomo Matteotti in Italy in 1924. In November 1926, the Socialist Party of Italy (together with all other nonfascist parties) was forbidden. German socialists and communists hardly offered any resistance against Hitler's seizure of power in 1933. Although the left parties had their own militias—the communist Roter Frontkaempferbund and the socialist and republican Reichsbanner Schwarz-Rot-Gold, which united with the Social Democratic Party, the free trades unions, and the workers' sports organizations into the antifascist Eiserne Front (Iron Front) in December 1931—there was no serious attempt to prevent Hitler's seizure of power by military means. However, the Social Democratic Party was the only one to vote against the *Ermaechtigungsgesetz,* which transferred all legislative power to Hitler's government, in the Reichstag in March 1933 (the Communist Party having already been suppressed). On 2 May 1933—one day after their pompous Day of National Labor—the Nazis destroyed the socialist-oriented free trades unions, replacing them with the Deutsche Arbeitsfront. In June 1933, the Social Democratic Party was forbidden. Up to the end of the Third Reich, thousands of Social Democrats and communists continued to be deported to the concentration camps.

In February 1934, the Austrian Social Democrats tried to resist Engelbert Dollfuss's Austro-fascists with an armed uprising of the party militia Republikanischer Schutzbund, after the failure of which the Socialist Democratic Labor Party and all its affiliated organizations were forbidden. Thereupon, a part of its membership went underground as "Revolutionary Socialists." The proliferation of fascism made the Comintern change its politics in 1935. It now pleaded for creating antifascist people's front alliances between Social Democrats, democratic bourgeois parties, and communists. The French government of the Front Populaire, elected in 1936, accomplished several social reforms and was able to prevent a fascist seizure of power. And in Spain, the Frente Popular won the elections in 1936. The civil war that followed there, in which numerous foreign volunteers took part on both sides, was generally regarded as a decisive battle between socialism and fascism.

In World War II, socialists and communists took a prominent part in antifascist resistance movements in several fascist and occupied countries. Fascists considered socialists and communists as their main political opponents. They rejected socialism in particular because of its stress on the idea of equality and international solidarity, as well as its alleged "Jewishness." Benito Mussolini, a former socialist himself, thought that the "leftist" era that had started in 1848, an important element of which had been the socialist labor movement, had come to an end after World War I. In his article "The Doctrine of Fascism," published in the *Enciclopedia Italiana* in June 1932, he stated that man was nothing outside history. Fascism had picked out of the socialist (as of the liberal) doctrine all those elements that had preserved their vitality. He praised Italian Fascism for having integrated syndicalism into a corporatist system that served the state, whereas the socialists had misused it as a means of class warfare that had weakened the state.

In Germany, conservatives and Nazis accused the socialists of having deliberately caused the German defeat in World War I. The 1918 revolution had been a "stab in the back" for an undefeated German army. Speaking of the Social Democrats and their democratic allies, the Nazis and other right-wing extremists normally used the term "November criminals." Adolf Hitler was convinced that Marxism—which he carefully separated from his own "socialism"—was an ideology invented by the Jews in order to transfer the whole world to Jewish power. In *Mein Kampf,* he stated that Marxism was the Jewish attempt to eliminate in all fields of human life the outstanding importance of personality and to replace it by the quantity of the masses. The parliamentary system corresponded politically and economically to the system of a trade union movement that did not serve the real interests of the workers, but the destructive intentions of the international "World-Jew."

Christian Koller

See Also: ANTI-FASCISM; ANTI-SEMITISM; AUSTRIA; AUSTROFASCISM; BOLSHEVISM; COMINTERN, THE; CONCENTRATION CAMPS; CONSERVATISM; CONSPIRACY THEORIES; CORPORATISM; COSMOPOLITANISM; DOLLFUSS, ENGELBERT; FASCIST PARTY, THE; GERMANY; GRAMSCI, ANTONIO; HERO, THE CULT OF THE; HITLER, ADOLF; ITALY; LABOR FRONT, THE; MARXISM; MARXIST THEORIES OF FASCISM; MASSES, THE ROLE OF THE; MATERIALISM; MATTEOTTI, GIACOMO; *MEIN KAMPF;* NOVEMBER CRIMINALS/*NOVEMBERBRECHER*, THE; PARAMILITARISM; PARLIAMENTARISM; SPAIN; SPANISH CIVIL WAR, THE; STATE, THE; SYNDICALISM; THIRD REICH, THE; TRADES UNIONS; WORLD WAR II

References

Di Scala, Spencer M., ed. 1996. *Italian Socialism: Between Politics and History.* Amherst: University of Massachusetts Press.

Graham, Helen. 1991. *Socialism and War: The Spanish Socialist Party in Power and Crisis, 1936–1939.* Cambridge: Cambridge University Press.

Horn, Gerd-Rainer. 1996. *European Socialists Respond to Fascism: Ideology, Activism, and Contingency in the 1930s.* New York: Oxford University Press.

Lewis, Jill. 1991. *Fascism and the Working Class in Austria, 1918–1934: The Failure of Labour in the First Republic.* Oxford: Berg.

Sassoon, Donald. 1996. *One Hundred Years of Socialism: The West European Left in the Twentieth Century.* London: I. B. Tauris.

Winkler, Heinrich August. 1984–1987. *Arbeiter und Arbeiterbewegung in der Weimarer Republik.* 3 vols. Berlin: Dietz.

SOCIOLOGY

The relationship between sociology and interwar fascism has three related aspects. The first involves respects in which sociology as a social doctrine was a scholarly forerunner to fascism. The second concerns the complicity of sociologists with fascism. The third concerns sociologists as critics and analysts of fascism, both before and after 1945.

SCHOLARLY FORERUNNERS OF FASCISM

Because sociology was denounced by some Nazis as a "Jewish" science, it had the reputation of being an "oppositional science" hostile to Nazism. The reality is more complex. Sociology emerged as a discipline in the nineteenth century as a response to individualism and liberalism, and shared with fascism a concern for "community" and "solidarity." Emile Durkheim, the founder of academic French sociology, was a French "spiritual" socialist who regarded the capitalist division of labor as pathological because it lacked the organic, morally integrative character of the medieval guild system. The preface to the second edition of his *Division of Labor in Society* (1893), in which he argued for a kind of syndicalism in which collective obligation would have a large role, is similar to Italian Fascist syndicalism. The German sociologist Ferdinand Tönnies was famous for his ideologically freighted distinction between *Gemeinschaft* ("community") and *Gesellschaft* ("society"). His ideas were appropriated by the Nazis, whose similar critique of modern society pointed to the racialized notion of *Genossenschaft*. The prominent Austrian Catholic sociologist Othmar Spann argued for a society of ranks in which the classes would accept the responsibilities ordained by their hierarchical relations.

Another strand of early sociology concerned elites and leadership. In Germany, Max Weber, who introduced the nonreligious use of the term *charismatic* to apply to leaders, proposed a constitutional regime that retained parliamentary powers but that maximized the possibility of charismatic leaders rising to power and a presidency sufficiently powerful to overcome the constraints of interest politics. Robert Michels, Max Weber's friend and follower, became an enthusiastic supporter of Mussolini, to whom he applied Weber's concept of charisma, calling him the *capo carismatico*. Michels was also famous for the so-called Iron Law of Oligarchy, and in Italy such elitist antiliberal thinkers as Gaetano Mosca and Vilfredo Pareto were used in justification of the Fascist notion of elites and the idea of the necessary replacement of corrupt elites by new, more vigorous elites.

SOCIOLOGISTS IN THE FASCIST AND NAZI PERIODS

The overt involvement of sociologists with the Nazi regime and its "restructurings" was considerable, but the relationships were complex, and events, such as the forcible retirement of sociologists—for example, Alfred Weber (brother of Max)—often occurred behind the scenes. Nazism was a generational movement, it had a predominant attraction to the young, so the sociologists who were party members were generally obscure. Generational conflicts between older compromisers with the regime and ardent young Nazis who wanted to make sociology a practical science in service to the state, were central to the demise of the German Sociological Society in the early Nazi period. Sociologists had roles throughout the Nazi polyarchy, but they played a particularly large role in various planning exercises that related to the future of Nazi-occupied lands in the East. The Nazis were subject to internal ideological quarrels and sensitive to ideological competitors, and they did not welcome attempts to legitimate the regime by non-Nazis. Spann, for example, though a Nazi enthusiast, was rebuffed when he attempted to join the party; others were discovered to have Jewish blood, and still others, such as Hans Freyer, were pushed out of influence after being used.

"Empirical" sociologists both within fascist countries and elsewhere tended to treat the regimes as normal. In the United States, for example, William Fielding Ogburn noted the commonalities between the centralizing ideology and practices of the Roosevelt, Stalin, Italian Fascist, and Nazi regimes, and accepted these trends as inevitable. Similar arguments about centralization were put forward by the Italian statistician and sociologist Corrado Gini. Sociological criticism of fascism tended to be politically or morally motivated. Prominent sociologist Charles Ellwood, who spent time in Italy in 1927 and subsequently became an ardent antifascist, gave public lectures on the fascist danger and communicated with Italian anti-Fascists on his return. Ellwood's criticism, however, assimilated Italian Fascism to the spiritual failures of modernity and reflected his Christian viewpoint. Criticism from the Left took a different, ambiguous approach. The Frankfurt professor Henri de Man, a Belgian, was led to embrace the idea of fascism as a necessary step toward socialism, with the thought that the socialist revolution needed to inherit a strong state to bring about its goals, and that fascism would establish precisely that strong state. The early writings of the Frankfurt School tended to portray fascism not as an aberration but as the final stage of capitalism, characteristic of what it took to be the most advanced capitalist regime, Germany.

An important practical concern of sociologists in the United States prior to the war was to protect citizens against propaganda of the kind characteristic of World

War I, which had emphasized atrocities. Ironically, skepticism about propaganda may have been one of the factors in the reluctance of Americans to believe reports of the systematic extermination of the Jews.

POSTWAR SOCIOLOGICAL ANALYSIS OF FASCISM

The Frankfurt School eventually developed a sociological analysis of fascism, combining the concepts of false consciousness and Freudian ideas, leading to *The Authoritarian Personality* (1950), with contributions from Adorno and others. This work, which assimilated Frankfurt School methods to the emerging interdisciplinary behavioral science paradigm, became the standard "sociological" account of Nazism after the war. There were a few scholarly studies of fascism that were not ideologically motivated. The Polish American sociologist Theodore Abel contributed a significant study of Nazism based on biographies of party members that he had collected in the 1930s in Germany. Both before and after the war a significant amount of effort was spent on the question of who had voted for Hitler, primarily oriented to the hypothesis promoted by such figures as Hans Speier and associated with the Left, that the source of Hitler's support was the "New Middle Class" of office workers. More recently, rational choice analyses of Hitler's electoral successes has stressed the details of the tariff politics of the Nazi program.

Steve Turner

See Also: ANTI-FASCISM; ANTI-SEMITISM; AUTHORITARIAN-ISM; BELGIUM; BOURGEOISIE, THE; CAPITALISM; CLASS; COMMUNITY; ECONOMICS; ELITE THEORY; FARMERS; FASCIST PARTY, THE; GERMANY; HITLER, ADOLF; INDI-VIDUALISM; INDUSTRY; ITALY; LEADER CULT, THE; LIBER-ALISM; MAN, HENDRIK/HENRI DE; MARXIST THEORIES OF FASCISM; MICHELS, ROBERTO; MOSCA, GAETANO; NAZISM; PARETO, VILFREDO; PROGRESS; PROPAGANDA; PSYCHOANALYSIS; PSYCHOLOGY; RACIAL DOCTRINE; ROOSEVELT, FRANKLIN DELANO; SCIENCE; SOCIALISM; SPANN, OTHMAR; STALIN, IOSIF VISSARIONOVICH; STATE, THE; SYNDICALISM; *VOLKSGEMEINSCHAFT*, THE; YOUTH

References
Muller, Jerry Z. 1987. *The Other God that Failed: Hans Freyer and the Deradicalization of German Conservatism.* Princeton: Princeton University Press.
Pels, Dick. 1993. "Hendrik de Man and the Dark Side of Fascism." *History of the Human Sciences* 6, no. 2: 75–95.
Ranulf, Svend. 1939. "Scholarly Forerunners of Fascism." *Ethics* 50: 16–34.
Turner, Stephen P., and Dirk Kaesler, eds. 1992. *Sociology Responds to Fascism.* London: Routledge.

SOLDIERLY VALUES: *See* WARRIOR ETHOS, THE

SONDERKOMMANDOS ("SPECIAL DETACHMENTS")

I

Squads of male Jews entrusted with the disposal of bodies and other tasks in the concentration camps. In Auschwitz they were bribed to work in the gas chambers and crematoria, escorting groups of prisoners to their deaths. Given preferential treatment during their four-month duty periods, they were themselves killed when their period was over.

See Also: AUSCHWITZ (-BIRKENAU); CONCENTRATION CAMPS; GERMANY; HOLOCAUST, THE; SS, THE

Reference
Sofsky, Wolfgang. 1999. *The Order of Terror: The Concentration Camp.* Trans. William Templer. Princeton: Princeton University Press.

II

SS units assigned to policing and political roles in the Eastern occupied territories during World War I.

Reference
Knopp, Guido. 2004. *Hitler's Holocaust.* Stroud: Sutton.

Cyprian Blamires

SONDERWEG ("SPECIAL PATH"), THE

Term used by historians of Germany to label a German tradition and way of thinking that was considered to have deviated for many centuries from the trend of the rest of Europe. The horrors of Hitlerism and the Holocaust are regarded by these historians (for example, Peter Viereck, A. J. P. Taylor, William Shirer, and Daniel Goldhagen) as the inevitable result of a "pattern of aggression" and an ingrained Jew-hatred that long predated them. Far from being an aberration, the Third Reich was, in the eyes of these scholars, simply the logical continuation of what had gone before.

Cyprian Blamires

See Also: ANTI-SEMITISM; ARYANISM; GERMANNESS (*DEUTSCHHEIT*); GERMANY; *HISTORIKERSTREIT*, THE; HITLER, ADOLF; HOLOCAUST, THE; LAGARDE, PAUL DE; LANGBEHN, JULIUS; NAZISM; NORDIC SOUL, THE; PANGERMANISM; WAGNER, (WILHELM) RICHARD; WORLD WAR I

References

Elsässer, J. 2003. *Der Deutsche Sonderweg: historische Last und politische Herausforderung.* Kreuzlingen: Diederichs.

Müller, Jan-Werner. 2000. *Another Country: German Intellectuals, Unification, and National Identity.* New Haven: Yale University Press.

SOREL, GEORGES (1847–1922)

Former engineer turned social theorist whose doctrine of revolutionary syndicalism is claimed to have influenced Italian Fascism and notably the thought of Mussolini. Born into a bourgeois family in Normandy, Sorel was an engineer for the Department of Public Works until the age of forty-five, when he resigned and devoted himself to personal studies. Central to the trajectory of Sorel's subsequent studies and publications was a search for a moral grounding to a society that had seen "the dissolution of traditional morals into rationalistic individualism and hedonism." This could be achieved only by a "heroic effort" to regalvanize a culture that was always under threat of returning to barbarism, a vision that was clearly influenced by the work of the philosophers Bergson and Nietzsche.

Initially supportive of orthodox Marxism, Sorel gradually moved in the direction of revolutionary syndicalism as the vehicle for achieving his ethical ideal. He proposed a form of socialism aimed at the placing of the means of production in the hands of the workers who made up the Republic of Producers. Such ideas led Sorel to become increasingly antiparliamentary and antidemocratic, believing in the syndicate as the only means for change. In a key text of his revolutionary syndicalism, *Reflections on Violence* (1908), he called on workers to express their will through the myth of the general strike, described by Sorel as "a body of images capable of evoking instinctively all the sentiments which correspond to different manifestations of the war undertaken by socialism against modern society" (Sorel 1972, 127). Through the violence of the general strike, the masses would turn away from those who would like to move them in the direction of compromise. The emphasis here on myth as opposed to reason in historical development meant that there was no necessary inner logic directing the course of history toward socialism, nor was the proletariat to be regarded as the privileged vehicle of social transformation. This explains to some extent the subsequent variety of foci for his political action, ranging from a sympathy for the monarchist nationalism of the Action Française as a potential antibourgeois ally against the republic, to support for Lenin via his prediction in 1912 of a great future for Mussolini. This latter prediction, together with Sorel's dalliance with monarchists and support for violence, has led some to suggest that Sorel and his work were a great influence on Italian Fascism. Commentators such as Roth, however, give a more nuanced picture of that influence; Roth has described Mussolinian Fascism as "an organized and vulgarized transformation of the pre-War Sorelian movement" (Roth 1980, 211). Contemporary extreme-right groups—generally those propagating some form of "left" fascism—continue to claim Sorel as an intellectual progenitor.

Steve Bastow

See Also: ACTION FRANÇAISE; BOURGEOISIE, THE; DECADENCE; DEMOCRACY; ELITE THEORY; FASCIST PARTY, THE; FRANCE; INDIVIDUALISM; INTEGRAL NATIONALISM; ITALY; MARXISM; MICHELS, ROBERTO; MONARCHISM; MOSCA, GAETANO; MUSSOLINI, BENITO ANDREA; MYTH; NATIONALISM; NIETZSCHE, FRIEDRICH; PARETO, VILFREDO; PARLIAMENTARISM; POSTWAR FASCISM; PROTOFASCISM; REVOLUTION; SOCIALISM; SYNDICALISM; VIOLENCE

References

Bastow, S. 2002. "A Neo-Fascist Third Way: The Discourse of Ethno-Differentialist Revolutionary Nationalism." *Journal of Political Ideologies* 7, no. 3: 351—368.

Camus, Jean-Yves. 1998. *L'extrême droite aujourd'hui.* Toulouse: Editions Milan.

Horowitz, I. L. 1968. *Radicalism and the Revolt Against Reason.* Carbondale Ill: Southern Illinois University Press.

Hughes, S. H. 1979. *Consciousness and Society: The Reorientation of European Social Thought, 1880–1930.* Brighton: Harvester.

Roth, J. J. 1980. *The Cult of Violence: Sorel and the Sorelians.* Berkeley: University of California Press.

Sorel, G. 1972. *Reflections on Violence.* New York: Collier.

Sternhell, Z. 1994. *The Birth of Fascist Ideology: From Cultural Rebellion to Political Revolution.* Princeton: Princeton University Press.

SOUL (*die Seele*)

Extremely important concept in the vocabulary of Nazism. "Soul" was considered synonymous both with an inward depth of feeling and with a mystical kind of relationship to the outside world, both of which were held to be a particular strength of the German character. It was held to be the antithesis of terms such as *materialism, individualism, abstraction,* and *rationalism,* as well as of "mechanistic" philosophies. These were frequently regarded as characteristic of the Jews, who could have no pretension to possess "soul" and its noble, spiritual qualities, since they were alleged to be entirely bound up with materialism. On the positive side, "soul" was associated with vitalism and intuitionism and with the uniquely "German" way of perception, involving looking at/contemplating/seeing the world, as opposed to thinking rationally about it in the "Western" tradition of Descartes and the rationalists.

Cyprian Blamires

See Also: ABSTRACTION; ANTI-SEMITISM; ARYANISM; *EHRE* ("HONOR"); GERMANNESS (*DEUTSCHHEIT*); GERMANY; INDIVIDUALISM; MATERIALISM; MECHANISTIC THINKING; MYSTICISM; MYTH; NAZISM; NORDIC SOUL, THE; ORGANICISM; RATIONALISM; VITALISM; *WELTANSCHAUUNG*/WORLDVIEW

References
Clauss, L. S. 1932. *Die Nordische Seele: ein Einführung in die Rassenseelekunde.* München. Berlin: J. S. Lehmannn.
Hermand, Jost. 1992. *Old Dreams of a New Reich: Volkish Utopias and National Socialism.* Bloomington: Indiana University Press.

SOUTH AFRICA

A number of pro-Nazi organizations developed during the 1930s in South Africa, the most important being Oswald Pirow's (1890–1959) Neue Orde, the Ossawabrandweg (OB) of J. F. J. van Rensburg (1897–1966), and various "shirt movements," such as the Brownshirts and the Greyshirts. Although at its height the OB had around 100,000 members, its pro-Nazi influence and anti-Semitism need to be treated with caution. The Christian wife of Ferdinand Postma (1879–1950), the chairman of the powerful Broederbond, was Jewish in terms of the Nuremberg Laws, and many leading Afrikaner Nationalists had strong pro-Jewish feelings and ties based on personal relationships and their Calvinism. Afrikaner Nationalism, which its supporters usually called "Christian Nationalism," cannot be equated with National Socialism or with Italian Fascism. Nevertheless, it may be viewed as a form of generic fascism that represented a uniquely nationalist response to perceived decadence, requiring national regeneration. Its origins lie in the First Language Movement of the 1870s, the Genootskap van Regte Afrikaners (Fellowship of True Afrikaners), founded in 1875 by a Dutch immigrant, Arnoldus Pannevis (1838–1884), who was influenced by the founder of the Dutch Anti-Revolutionary Movement, Guillaume Groen van Prinsterer (1801–1876); his work was taken up and turned into a powerful political party by Abraham Kuyper (1837–1920), whose ideas were popularized in South Africa by S. J. du Toit (1847–1911). Du Toit's 1877 book *Di geskiedenis van ons land in di taal van ons volk* (*The History of Our Land in the Language of Our People*) led to the founding of South Africa's first political party—the Afrikaner Bond—in 1880. The ideas expressed by du Toit and a small group of enthusiastic supporters, like the converted Dutch Jew Jan Lion Cachet, (1838–1912), were spread through magazines like *Di Patriot* and later *Jong Suid Afrika*. Here the idea of an antirevolutionary worldview (by which was meant a rejection of the ideas of the French Revolution) was articulated as the basis for a "Christian Nationalism" that was said to express the true nature of the Afrikaner.

Following the defeat of the Boer Republics in the Second Anglo-Boer War (1899–1902), the newly developing Afrikaans language, which separated from Dutch between 1875 and 1925, gave expression to a highly nationalistic poetry and literary movement. This artistic renaissance depicted Afrikaners as an aristocratic people destined to create a new civilization in Africa. A focal point of the movement was the Women and Children's Monument in Bloemfontein, commemorating the more than 30,000 noncombatants who died in British concentration camps during the war. Books like those of Willem Postma (1874–1920) and Dr. O'Kulis—*Die Eselskakebeen (The Jawbone of the Ass,* 1909*)* and *Die Boervrouw (Boer Women,* 1919*)*—lamented the victimization of the *Volk* by the British and evoked a longing for national regeneration. The poetry of his brother-in-law, J. D. du Toit (1877–1953), Totius, expressed the same themes in powerful images that provided catharsis for those still suffering from the effects of the war. These and other works created a cultural foundation upon which General Hertzog (1866–1942) could build his political movement centered on the National Party. They also provided a mythic vision for the growth of the Broederbond.

Intellectually, the ideology of Afrikaner Nationalism was articulated in the three-volume *Koers in die Krisis* (1935, 1940, and 1941), while at a popular level it was promoted through *Die Tweede Trek-Reeks* (*The Second Trek Series*) published in 1940. Neither set of books espoused National Socialism. Volume 2 of *Koers*, published in 1940, contained an insightful critique of National Socialism that identified it as a state-inspired form of totalitarianism originating with the ideas of Machiavelli that promoted racism on the basis of a neo-pagan ideology. The works of Nazi writers such as Ernst Bergman (1881–1945) and Alfred Rosenberg were analyzed and rejected as anti-Christian, while opposition leaders like Martin Niemöller were praised. Afrikaner thinking about race—found in books like the *Tweede Trek* volumes *Die Afrikaner* (1940) and *Rasse en Rassevermenging* (1942) and Professor G. Conjé's *Regverdige Rasse-Apartheid* (1947)—clearly acknowledge the influence of German race theorists like Hans Günther, yet they cite U.S. writers like E. T. Thompson (born 1900) and the Swede Gunnar Myrdal (1898–1987) more than German authors. The possibility that at least some sections of Afrikaner Nationalism were influenced by ideas and movements that helped create National Socialism cannot be ruled out. For example, General Hertzog (1866–1942) was an admirer of Houston Stewart Chamberlain, whose works influenced National Socialism.

After the Afrikaner Nationalists won the 1948 election using the slogan *swartgevaar* ("the Black danger"), they were accused of being fascists in the tradition of German National Socialism. Probably the earliest writer to link Afrikaner Nationalism with fascism in general and National Socialism in particular was Arthur Keppel-Jones, in his *South Africa: A Short History* (1949). The idea became enshrined in popular consciousness through Brian Bunting's *The Rise of the South African Reich* (1964) and continued to be promoted until at least 1983 through books like Sipo E. Mzimela's *Apartheid: South African Nazism* (1983). Essentially, the identification between Afrikaner Nationalism and National Socialism seemed fairly simple. National Socialists were racists; so too were Afrikaner Nationalists. National Socialists segregated Jews; Afrikaner Nationalists segregated Blacks. National Socialists built heroic monuments and promoted folk dancing; so too did Afrikaner Nationalists. Both move-

ments used terms like *Volk* and *National* in their self-definition. Both looked to a history of suffering to justify their actions. Both saw themselves as victims. Many Afrikaner Nationalist leaders, such as Nico Diederichs (1903–1978) and Henrik Verwoerd (1901–1966), studied in Germany in the 1920s and 1930s. Most were interned during World War II, and some, like Oswald Pirow (1890–1959) and B. J. Vorster (1915–1983), appeared to identify with Nazism. Therefore, it seemed clear that the two movements were virtually identical This facile identification was challenged, however, in *South Africa: A Study in Conflict* (1965) by Pierre L. van den Berghe, who argued that the roots of Afrikaner Nationalism should be sought in nineteenth-century colonialism rather than twentieth-century fascism. This judgment was supported by Heribert Adam in *Modernizing Racial Domination* (1971), arguing that National Socialism was essentially expansionist, while Afrikaner Nationalism was defensive. Furthermore, while acknowledging superficial similarities, Adam argued that Afrikaner nationalism was structurally different from fascism because it rejected the *Führerprinzip* and control by terror in favor of a racially based democracy.

Dunbar Moodie (1975) and Irving Hexham (1981) further undermined the simplistic link between Afrikaner Nationalism, apartheid, and National Socialism through their historical studies of the origins and growth of the early Afrikaner Nationalist movement in South Africa. Both writers emphasized the role of Dutch neo-Calvinist thought, particularly the work of the Calvinist theologian-prime minister Abraham Kuyper (1837–1920) in shaping Afrikaner thought from the 1870s until the Nationalist victory in 1948. Their essential arguments were confirmed by revisionist Afrikaner writers who rejected Nationalist ideology, such as André du Toit and Herman Giliomee. Some neo-Marxist writers, such as Dan O'Meara in *Volkskapitalisme* (1983), have disputed these arguments, but none have suggested resurrecting the idea of a South African Nazism at the core of Afrikaner Nationalism.

Albrecht Hagemann (1989) explored historical links between Afrikaner Nationalism and National Socialism, as did Patrick J. Furlong (1991). Although links did exist between those movements, neither writer found evidence that Afrikaner Nationalism drew its primary inspiration from German National Socialism. Along similar lines, Milton Shain explored *The Roots of Anti-Semitism in South Africa* (1994), drawing attention to rising opposition to the acceptance of Jewish refugees and the impact of National Socialist propaganda among South Africans. Furthermore, the Voortreker Monument in Pretoria bears an uncanny visual resemblance to the Völkerschlachtdenkmal ("Battle of the Nations Monument") in Leipzig. Perhaps behind both movements and other manifestations of fascism there is a common intellectual, social, and cultural ethos—but until the intellectual and cultural influences on a number of key figures such as Hertzog, Diedrichs, and Verwoerd are investigated, the question will remain unclear.

Irving Hexham

See Also: INTRODUCTION; ANTI-SEMITISM; BROEDERBOND, THE; CHAMBERLAIN, HOUSTON STEWART; CHRISTIANITY; DECADENCE; EXPANSIONISM; FASCIST PARTY, THE; FRENCH REVOLUTION, THE; GERMANY; ITALY; LEADER CULT, THE; MACHIAVELLI, NICCOLÒ; MARXIST THEORIES OF FASCISM; NATIONALISM; NAZISM; NIEMOELLER, MARTIN; NUREMBERG LAWS, THE; OSSAWABRANDWEG, THE; PALINGENETIC MYTH; PROTESTANTISM; RACIAL DOCTRINE; RACISM; ROSENBERG, ALFRED; TERRA'BLANCHE, EUGÈNE; TOTALITARIANISM; *VOLK, VÖLKISCH;* WHITE SUPREMACISM; WORLD WAR II

References

Davenport, T. R. H. 1966. *The Afrikaner Bond.* Oxford: Oxford University Press.

Furlong, Patrick J. 1991. *Between Crown and Swastika.* Hanover, NH: Wesleyan University Press.

Hagemann, Albrecht. 1989. *Südafrika und das Dritte Reich.* Frankfurt: Campus.

Hexham, Irving. 1981. *The Irony of Apartheid.* Toronto: Edwin Mellen.

Moodie, Dunbar. 1975. *The Rise of Afrikanerdom.* Berkeley: University of California Press.

van Jaaarsveld, F. A. 1961. *The Awakening of Afrikaner Nationalism.* Cape Town: Human and Rousseau.

SOVIET UNION, THE

The Soviet Union's victory over Nazi Germany in the "Great Patriotic War" of 1941 to 1945 was one of the founding myths of the Soviet Union; until its breakup in December 1991, the Soviet Union played an important role in the history and interpretation of European fascism. Already in the 1920s, it had become an object of allusion in the first journalistic and scholarly comments on Mussolini's emerging dictatorship. Until 1945, the development of the Soviet Union was closely linked to the emergence, rise, and fall of the interwar European fascist movements. The Soviet Union–sponsored Comintern definition for *fascism,* voiced, in its fi-

nal version, by the Bulgarian communist Georgi Dimitrov (1882–1949) in 1935—"the open terrorist dictatorship of the most reactionary, most chauvinistic, and most imperialistic elements of finance capital"—remained obligatory for the Moscow-controlled world communist movement for decades. The Soviet Union's successful defeat of Nazi Germany's attack on its European territories constituted the foremost reason for the Allies' victory over the Axis powers in World War II.

On the other hand, Soviet ideas and institutions were, during Stalin's rule in particular, characterized by a number of features and tendencies that bore similarities not only to the structure but also to certain ideological elements and further attributes of the Italian Fascist and German Nazi states. Since the start of the gradual erosion of the Soviet political system in 1987, moreover, the Stalinist legacy has heavily informed the rise of post-Soviet Russian ultranationalism. The USSR represented the first one-party state with the ambition to create a new society and new human being by means of radical social engineering, rapid economic development, cultural and anthropological revolution, thorough re-education, and mass terror. It thus became a major reference point in the conceptualization of, and important object of comparison with, policies and institutions implemented by fascists in power. There are further remarkable similarities between the fascist and, particularly, Stalin's rule: (1) absolute rule by a charismatic leader; (2) militarization of society; (3) the dualism of their governments, composed of ministerial cabinets operating in parallel and, often, in conflict with party apparatuses; (4) treatment of real and imagined political enemies within the GULag (Glavnoe upravlenie ispravitel'no-trudovykh lagerei: Chief Directorate of Corrective Labor Camps) in the case of the Soviets, and KZ (Konzentrationslager: concentration camps) in the case of the Nazis; (5) aggressive foreign policies; (6) aggressiveness of their various security organs, including the Soviet NKVD (Narodnyi kommissariat vnutrennykh del: People's Commissariat for Domestic Affairs) and the Nazi RSHA (Reichssicherheitshauptamt: Imperial Security Chief Directorate); and (7) the two states' indoctrination instruments, such as their youth organizations—the Soviet Komsomol (Communist Youth League) and the Nazi Hitlerjugend (Hitler Youth), as well as their exploitation of the mass media. The similarities between the two states are generally reckoned to have outweighed the differences. The Third Reich during World War II, and the Soviet Union under Stalin, became, therefore, both paradigmatic cases for "totalitarianism"—a state-typological concept connoting institutional structures designed to secure the government's maximal control of, and influence over, all of its subjects.

While it is generally acknowledged that the USSR and Third Reich showed, in the late 1930s and, especially, in the 1940s, striking resemblances, the issue of how such similarities had become possible, in view of the fundamental incompatibility of the two states' official ideologies, remains a source of confusion. Researchers within the extremism-theoretical paradigm emphasize the uniformly revolutionary ambition, similar moral relativism, and comparable teleological utopianism of left- and right-wing radicals, of Marxists and fascists. Characteristics such as these are taken to account sufficiently for the correspondence of Hitler's policies with those of Stalin, as well as of other leaders of officially communist regimes. A related attempt to capture certain analogies in the social radicalism and political style of communist and fascist movements, including their eschatology, rituals, totalizing ambitions, and Manichean world views, has been to see them as permutations of a generic "political religion." Other interpretations go further, and highlight, apart from structural and stylistic similarities, also substantive parallels between official Nazi doctrine and the unofficial ideology of Stalin's government. These included nationalism, anti-Semitism, bigotry, sexism, as well as xeno- and homophobia, which, in encoded forms, became increasingly manifest in the Soviet Union from the mid-1930s until the early 1950s. In theories emphasizing the political and social importance of the latter developments, the relative likeness of Stalinist and Nazi political institutions and actions is explained not simply by a similar transformational drive but also as resulting from partly hidden yet nevertheless far-reaching resemblances in the social visions and political aims of the major decision-makers of both regimes.

A different version of this approach has been developed by A. James Gregor. Gregor has proposed a major reconceptualization of fascism that excludes Nazism and, instead, uses *fascist* to signify a generic nationalist ideology common to many contemporary mass-mobilizing developmental dictatorships, including not only Mussolini's Italy, but also Stalin's Russia, Mao's China, and a number of other nominally left-wing modernizing regimes, particularly in Asia and Africa, of the postwar period. Since the breakup of the Soviet Union and the partial opening of its archives, new studies have confirmed earlier hypotheses concerning the close linkage between unofficial non-Marxist ideas held within Stalin's ruling elite and official Soviet policies in the 1930s to 1950s. In particular, recent research has corroborated earlier suggestions on the relevance of Rus-

sian nationalism (disguised as "Soviet patriotism") and anti-Semitism (disguised as the battle against "cosmopolitanism" and an idiosyncratically defined "Zionism") to Stalin's outlook and policies. Whether such conclusions—as well as further findings showing the continued relevance of Russian nationalism to the Soviet regime after Stalin's death—justify as fundamental a reconstruction of the concept of generic fascism as suggested by Gregor remains, however, debatable.

The ferment of ideas in Russian exile circles in the 1920s to 1930s saw the rise of a number of trends that, after the breakup of the USSR, were to provide ideological ammunition for the formation of post-Soviet Russian fascism. They included such neonationalist movements as Eurasianism, represented, among others, by Nikolai Trubetskoi (1890–1938) or Petr Savitskii (1895–1965) and the Smena vekh (Change of Signposts) group led by Nikolai Ustrialov (1890–1938). Some members of these right-wing intellectual circles, consisting partly of serious scholars, welcomed, with qualifications, the Bolsheviks' restoration of the Russian Empire. More radical Russian emigre nationalists developed, at about the same time, a number of explicitly anti-Bolshevik political projects that later also became reference points for Russian nationalists inside Russia. They included, in Munich and Paris, the Union of Young Russians led by Aleksandr Kazem-Bek (1902–1977) and a Russian solidarist organization that became known under its short title of People's Labor Union and which was led, in the 1930s to 1940s, by Viktor Baidalakov (1900–1967).

The varieties of explicit imitations of Italian and other forms of interwar fascism within the Russian emigre scene included the Russian Fascist Party (later renamed the Russian Fascist Union), founded by Konstantin Rodzaevskii (1907–1946) in Manchuria in 1931, and the All-Russian Fascist Organization (later renamed the All-Russian National-Revolutionary Labor and Worker-Peasant Party of Fascists), founded by Anastasii Vonsiatskii (1898–1964) in the United States in 1932. During the period of Bolshevik rule in Russia, tendencies such as these were located not only outside the Soviet Union and its political establishment but also inside them. Russian ultranationalist and fascistic views continued to be permitted, encouraged, and in part represented by branches of the Soviet ruling elite throughout the Cold War. This trend became particularly pronounced after Nikita Khrushchev's (1894–1971) replacement in 1964 by a neo-Stalinist group of party apparatchiks under the leadership of Leonid Brezhnev (1906–1982), the first—and later general—secretary of the CPSU Central Committee until his death. The so-called era of stagnation included, apart from Brezhnev's rule, also the short reigns of Iurii Andropov (1914–1984) and Konstantin Chernenko (1911–1985), and lasted until the start of perestroika in 1985, when Mikhail Gorbachev (born 1931) became general secretary of the CPSU Central Committee. During the stagnation period, anti-Semitic nationalists infiltrated, and at times dominated, the central apparatuses of the Komsomol, official cultural syndicates (above all the Union of Writers), and certain public organizations such as the All-Russian Society for the Protection of Historical and Cultural Monuments. Although not much firsthand information is available on the political thinking of the officers of the Soviet secret services, a majority of the staff of the higher echelons in the KGB (Komitet gosudarstvennoi bezopasnosti: Committee on State Security) is believed to have been heavily anti-Semitic throughout the postwar period.

By the early 1970s, the editorial boards of some semiofficial, high-circulation literary-publicistic journals, including *Molodaia gvardiia (Young Guard)* and *Nash sovremennik (Our Contemporary),* had come under the permanent control of ultranationalist writers and literary critics including Sergei Vikulov (born 1922), Anatolii Ivanov (1928–1999), Vadim Kozhinov (1930–2001), and Sergei Kuniaev (born 1932). Although contributions to these so-called thick journals had to be written in Aesopian language, they provided an important medium of communications among Russian right-wing intellectuals. While some prominent crypto-nationalist intellectuals and cultural workers—such as the novelist Mikhail Sholokhov (1905–1984), the poet Sergei Mikhalkov (born 1913), and the painter Ilia Glazunov (born 1930)—became full members of the Soviet establishment, others were kept on the margins of Soviet society, put in prison, or driven into emigration by the Soviet authorities. They included the famous mathematician Igor' Shafarevich (born 1923) as well as the ethnologist Lev Gumilev (1912–1992). Gumilev's pseudoscholarly works have, since the breakup of the Soviet Union, been published in several editions; they are widely used as textbooks among the social science, humanities, and geography faculties of post-Soviet Russian and Central Asian higher education institutions. Whereas Shafarevich became notorious for blaming the presence of a "small people" (that is, the Jews) inside the Russian nation for Russia's misfortunes, Gumilev is known for his theory of ethnogenesis: this conceptualizes nations as biological units influenced by cosmic emissions and threatened with decline when mixing with other ethnic groups.

The "era of stagnation" also saw the rise of a new nativist-preservationist literary movement that became known as the "village prose" school; it included such prominent writers as Valentin Rasputin (born 1937) and Vasilii Belov (born 1932). More often than not, the representatives of this school were radically anti-Western and had affinities to other brands of Russian ultranationalism and anti-Semitism. Also during the 1960s, Stalinist "anti-Zionism" reappeared in Soviet propaganda and pseudo-academic writing. It matured, in the 1970s, into a full-blown school of "Zionology"—a term introduced by the Russian-Jewish emigre analyst of Russian anti-Semitism Semyon Reznik. This circle of notorious social activists and political publicists included Vladimir Begun (1929–1989), Valerii Emelianov (1929–1999), Iurii Ivanov (1930–1980), Evgenii Evseev (1932–1990), and Valerii Skurlatov (born 1938). Books and articles by some of the "Zionologists" were printed in large numbers and to some extent constituted assigned reading in Soviet study programs. They mixed anticapitalist, anti-American, anti-Judaic, and anti-Israeli agitation into a relatively new—if particularly primitive—anti-Semitic theory that, among others, saw Zionism as a variety of fascism, and, in some instances, made Jews coresponsible for the rise of the Nazi movement and the Holocaust. In the post-Soviet period, some of the "Zionologists"—such as the late Emelianov or political adventurer Skurlatov—became founders of small fascist parties.

In distinction from official Soviet Zionological literature, or the crypto-nationalist novels and short stories of the "village prose" of the 1960s to 1980s, the circulation of openly fascist texts remained, under Soviet rule, limited to illegal *samizdat* ("self-printed") and *tamizdat* ("printed abroad") literature, which had little impact on society at large. The nationalist dissident scene inside and outside Russia included different, often conflicting, tendencies that are difficult to classify adequately. Many of the dissidents, such as Vladimir Osipov, had—as anti-Soviet revolutionaries—ideas of a radically nationalist-palingenetic kind; they were aptly labeled by John Dunlop as *vozrozhdentsy*—"those aspiring to rebirth." They formed a peculiar kind of national liberation movement, and to call all of them "fascist" would thus be misleading. Instead, some of the most extremely anti-Western and anti-Semitic among the dissidents had considerable sympathy for the Soviet order as constituting Russia's shield against Westernization. Such putatively fascist activists of the nationalist spectrum of the Russian dissident movement included, among others, A. Fetisov

(1912–1990), Mikhail Antonov (born 1927), and Gennadii Shimanov.

Andreas Umland

References

Brandenberger, David. 2002. *National Bolshevism: Stalinist Mass Culture and the Formation of Modern Russian National Identity, 1931–1956.* Cambridge: Harvard University Press.

Brudny, Yitzhak. 1998. *Reinventing Russia: Russian Nationalism and the Soviet State, 1953–1991.* Cambridge: Harvard University Press.

Dunlop, John B. 1984. *The Faces of Contemporary Russian Nationalism.* Princeton: Princeton University Press.

Gregor, A. James. 1974. *The Fascist Persuasion in Radical Politics.* Princeton: Princeton University Press.

Kostyrchenko, Gennadi. 1995. *Out of the Red Shadows: Antisemitism in Stalin's Russia.* Amherst, NY: Prometheus.

Lewin, Moshe, and Ian Kershaw, eds. 1997. *Stalinism and Nazism: Dictatorships in Comparison.* Cambridge: Cambridge University Press.

Mitrokhin, Nikolai. 2003. *Russkaya partiya: Dvizhenie russkikh natsionalistov v SSSR, 1953–1985 gody.* Moskva: Novoe literaturnoe obozrenie.

Stephan, John J. 1978. *The Russian Fascists: Tragedy and Farce in Exile, 1925–1945.* New York: HarperCollins.

Yanov, Alexander. 1987. *The Russian Challenge and the Year 2000.* New York: Basil Blackwell.

SPAIN

Despite its identification with the Franco regime (1939–1975), and although Alfonso XIII described the military dictator General Miguel Primo de Rivera

Poster for Falange Espanola, the Spanish nationalist political party associated with General Francisco Franco's regime in Spain. Although Franco himself cannot be called a fascist, the ultranationalist Falangist creed did have some strong resemblances to Italian Fascism. (Library of Congress)

(1923–1930) as "my Mussolini," Spanish fascism's appearance was belated and, most historians have agreed, unsuccessful—certainly on its own terms. Spanish fascism (generally, if narrowly, seen as synonymous with Falange Española) remained minuscule until 1936, but within a year it had become the single state party of a regime that survived four decades. Its origins are found in February 1931, when Ramiro Ledesma Ramos set up La Conquista del Estado (The Conquest of the State), a radical national socialist movement that in October merged with the Juntas Castellanas de Actuación Hispánica (Castilian Juntas of Hispanic Action), led by the Catholic nationalist Ónesimo Redondo. The new party was called Juntas de Ofensiva Nacional-Socialista (JONS; Juntas of the National-Syndicalist Offensive). In early 1933, Ledesma Ramos met with the charismatic son of the late dictator, José Antonio Primo de Rivera, and together they launched the journal *El Fascio.*

José Antonio maintained conversations with Mussolini and called a meeting at a Madrid theater on 29 October 1933—the "first fascist meeting in Spain," according to contemporaries. Fours days later Falange Española was officially founded, an amalgam of rhetorical leftism (yet underlying conservatism), antiliberalism, and extreme nationalism. On 3 February 1934, Falange and JONS merged, becoming Falange Española y de las JONS, under the triumvirate of José Antonio, Ledesma Ramos, and Julio Ruíz de Alda. By October, though, José Antonio was sole national chief. Ledesma Ramos then departed in January 1935, irritated at José Antonio's social conservatism and aristocratic outlook. José Antonio continued to court monarchists, as well as visiting Mussolini and Hitler, but the party remained minuscule. At the February 1936 general election, it received 40,000 votes nationally, nowhere topping 4.1 percent. Existing right-wing options—especially the Catholic CEDA's radical youth movement, the JAP—closed political space. But the electoral defeat, inertia, and collapse of the Right changed everything: within six months Falange had doubled its membership, conspiring against the Republic and providing radicalized foot soldiers as well as the ideological machinery to drive a war effort (although Catholicism proved even more important). José Antonio's execution, however, left the party vulnerable, and in March 1937, Ramón Serrano Suñer fused it with Comunión Tradicionalista, making a single state party in the Nationalist zone the basis of the Franco regime—Falange Española Tradicionalista y de las JONS. A wide umbrella, it provided the regime with the litany, theater, and rhetoric of fascism. Some "old shirt," prewar Falangists complained of lost identity; the payoff was preferment.

When the World War II tide turned, Franco downplayed the regime's, and the party's, fascist characteristics. Falange was domesticated, and, with the return to the United Nations in 1950 and economic liberalization thereafter, Spain came increasingly under the influence of "apolitical" technocrats. Falangists still manned the state machinery, though, even as "old shirts" tentatively mobilized in opposition. Franco's death and the dismantling of his regime spawned Fuerza Nueva under Blas Piñar and a wealth of "Falanges," none of which enjoyed success—such as FE [not FET] y de las JONS, Falange auténtica, and Falange independente. The majority of the politically active from within the regime joined Alianza Popular, forerunner of the center-right Partido Popular. Some fascist groups, including Falange Española, still exist, alongside groupuscules of radical rightists and neo-Nazis, but fascism in Spain is now a minor force.

Sid Lowe

See Also: INTRODUCTION; CATHOLIC CHURCH, THE; CONSERVATISM; FALANGE; FRANCO Y BAHAMONDE, GENERAL FRANCISCO; GROUPUSCULES; GUERNICA; HITLER, ADOLF; LIBERALISM; MILITARY DICTATORSHIP; MUSSOLINI, BENITO ANDREA; NATIONALISM; NEO-NAZISM; PERU; POSTWAR FASCISM; PRIMO DE RIVERA, JOSÉ ANTONIO; SERRANO SÚÑER, RAMÓN; SPANISH CIVIL WAR, THE; WORLD WAR II

References
Carr, R. 2001. *Modern Spain, 1875–1980.* Oxford: Oxford University Press.
Ellwood, S. M. 1987. *Spanish Fascism in the Franco Era: Falange Española de las Jons, 1936–76.* Basingstoke: Macmillan.
Payne, S. G. 1999. *Fascism in Spain, 1923–1977.* Madison: University of Wisconsin Press.
Preston, Paul. 1995. *The Politics of Revenge: Fascism and the Military in Twentieth-century Spain.* London: Routledge.
Richmond, K. 1990. *Women and Spanish Fascism: The Women's Section of the Falange, 1934–1959.* London: Routledge.
Salas, A. 2003. *Diario de Un Skin: un topo en el movimiento neonazi español.* Madrid: Temas de hoy.

SPANDAU PRISON

The prison in the Berlin suburb of Spandau was constructed by the four Allied Powers to hold National Socialists sentenced at the Nuremberg Trials. In 1947, seven prisoners were interned: Karl Doenitz, Walther Funk, Rudolf Hess, Konstantin von Neurath, Erich Raeder, Baldur von Schirach, and Albert Speer. The Allies took monthly turns in guarding the prison. Hess was the only prisoner from 1966 until the time of his suicide on 17 August 1981. In order to prevent the site from becoming an attraction for neo-Nazis, the building was then knocked down, the rubble dispersed in the North Sea, and the area turned into a parking lot.

Christoph H. Müller

See Also: DOENITZ, ADMIRAL KARL; FUNK, WALTHER EMANUEL; GERMANY; HESS, RUDOLF; NAZISM; NEO-NAZISM; NUREMBERG TRIALS, THE; SCHIRACH, BALDUR VON; SPEER, ALBERT; WORLD WAR II

Reference
Bird, Eugene K. 1974. *The Loneliest Man in the World: The Inside Story of the Thirty-year Imprisonment of Rudolf Hess.* London: Secker and Warburg.

A soldier in General Franco's nationalist forces during the Spanish Civil War in 1938. This was widely seen as a conflict between fascism and the left, and as such it attracted volunteers from abroad on both sides of the political spectrum. However, the regime that Franco established after his victory cannot unambiguously be called fascist. (The Illustrated London News Picture Library)

SPANISH CIVIL WAR, THE

Hugely symbolic three-year conflict in which the Second Spanish Republic, governed by a center-right coalition including both conservative Catholics and liberals, was overthrown by right-wing nationalist forces led by General Franco, who went on to establish a dictatorship that lasted until his death. The impact of the war was felt far beyond Spain, and it aroused a huge emotional response across the world on both sides of the

political divide. Franco's cause was widely identified with the cause of fascism, and many volunteers made their way to Spain to help support or oppose him. Franco was, however, a devout Catholic, and his real ethos had more to do with authoritarian conservatism than with fascism. His true sympathies were obscured for a long time because he accepted military assistance from Mussolini and from Hitler. Moreover, in the public mind his cause was indelibly bonded to that of Nazism as a result of the horrific bombing of Guernica by the Condor Legion, an event that foreshadowed the mass bombings of World War II.

The uprising followed a period of considerable political and social unrest with general strikes, street fighting, and in 1934 a miners' uprising in Asturias. Its immediate cause lay in a lurch to the left in Spanish politics in 1936. The elections of 16 February brought to power a popular front government backed by the Left and the Center and opposed by the Right. This regime did not manage to stabilize the situation, and on 7 April the president was deposed by the parliament and replaced by Prime Minister Manuel Azaña. Whereas the fascistic Falange movement founded in 1933 had obtained only 0.07 percent of the vote in the February elections, membership had grown rapidly to 40,000 by July. Tensions continued to rise, and on 17 July a conservative uprising was initiated. In principle, the uprising—whose main leaders were Sanjurjo and Mola—had been agreed for 18 July 1936, but at 5:00 P.M. on the evening of the day before in Melilla, a group of military men jumped the gun with a coup; in a few hours the rebellion had spread to Morocco, where the high commissioner was imprisoned. On 18 July, Franco left Las Palmas de Gran Canaria for Tetuan, where he took command of the Moroccan troops on 19 July. However, at this point the scenario on the mainland was not very encouraging for the insurgents. The uprising collapsed disastrously in the majority of the industrial areas and in places like Valencia and the Basque Country, which fought to defend the Republican regime in exchange for the promise of obtaining the longed-for Statute of Autonomy, which in the end was promulgated by the Cortes on 1 October 1936, the same day that Franco took over as head of the Spanish state. However, the rebellion did triumph in Zaragoza, Valladolid, Burgos, Pamplona, and Galicia. In Seville, General Queipo de Llano managed to take control of the city in the space of a few hours. There were different scenarios in Madrid and Barcelona, where militants of the parties of the Left and the unions in collaboration with the Guardia de Asalto and the Guardia Civil held firm against the uprising. General Goded had reached Barcelona on 19 July to put himself at the head of the insurgents, but he was taken prisoner by Republican loyalists.

The government of the Republic acted with extreme pusillanimity. Casares Quiroga resigned, unable to cope with the situation; his successor, Martínez Barrio, held the position for only the 18th and 19th and tried to negotiate with the rebel general Mola, offering him the war portfolio, which he rejected. Finally, under the leadership of Barrio's successor, José Giral, between 19 July and 4 September the government decided to arm the voluntary popular militias. The vacuum of power grew, with committees and patrols everywhere corresponding to each party and union. A part of the army and the Civil Guard remained loyal to the Republic, and the rebels failed in their objective of taking Madrid; hence the rising turned into a civil war that lasted for about three years.

José Primera de Rivera, founder of Falange, threw in his lot with the nationalists, and Falange became the dominant political movement on that side. The Falange manifesto of November 1934 was highly nationalistic and spoke of Spain as entitled to a position "of pre-eminence in world affairs" as "the spiritual axis of the Spanish-speaking world." Its tone was jingoistic, and it played on nostalgia for Spain's great seaborne empire, which had been lost for more than a hundred years. It spoke unashamedly of the need for the Spanish state to be totalitarian and advocated the establishment of a corporatist system. It promised to abolish the parliamentary system and do away with divisive parties—the unity of the nation was to be paramount. It specifically rejected both capitalism and Marxism but spoke of nationalizing the banks while promising to preserve private property. The mission of the state in education was to "produce a strong, united, national spirit and fill the souls of future generations with joy and pride in their Fatherland." The role of "the Catholic spirit" was accepted, and it was indeed described as "glorious," although the Catholic Church was told not to do anything to "undermine the dignity of the state." The implied or expressed contempt for the Christian religion to be found in Italian Fascism and in German Nazism was absent here. The program was certainly ultranationalist, and it clearly proposed a "third way" between capitalism and socialism. But a number of powerful ingredients of classic fascism were missing, or at least muted—the glorification of violence, the warrior ethos, the elevation of a political creed to a new political religion that excluded the Catholic Church.

One of the declared aims of the rebellion was to combat the anticlericalism of the Republican government, and the war was a painful experience for the Catholic Church: a dozen bishops, nearly 300 nuns, well over 2,000 monks, and more than 4,000 priests were murdered by the progovernment forces, and that did little to endear the Republican cause to Catholics. Many churches and religious properties were torched. (The situation was different in the Basque region, because of the issue of Basque nationalism.) There were, however, a range of political ideologies on the two sides. Generally speaking, though, it is fair to say that the progovernment Republican side held leftist/liberal principles, while the Nationalists were rightists.

From the beginning, the Spanish Civil War acquired an international character. The government of the Republic had to draw on the gold reserves of the Banco de España to obtain arms abroad ("Moscow gold"); Hitler's Germany and Mussolini's Italy sent aid to the rebels in the form of every type of military equipment, men, and money. However, the France of Leon Blum—although favorable to the Republic—with the energetic support of Great Britain proposed the formula of "nonintervention" between 4 and 5 August 1936; on 6 August the USSR adhered to this accord, although with reservations. In practice the measure did not work, and the Germans and the Italians continued to send help to the rebel side, while the Communist Party was acquiring an increasingly influential role with the resolute support of the USSR for the Republican side. Meanwhile the International Brigades were being established to bring help to the Republic and for the cause of liberty in the battle against a cause widely identified as "fascist"; they comprised volunteers (intellectuals, workers, journalists, writers) of different nationalities.

In addition to the support they received through the German and Italian (and also Portuguese) governments (amounting to more than 100,000 professional soldiers), the Nationalist insurgents also attracted volunteers. Their numbers were modest, at around 12,000, compared with the 35,000 to 40,000 who flocked from all quarters to join the International Brigades, but still symbolic. Their motivations for rallying to the nationalist flag were diverse. They came from France, White Russia (mainly from Parisian emigre circles), Romania, Ireland, and the United Kingdom, among other places. For the Russians the battle seemed like the first step toward overturning the 1917 Revolution. There were romantic Catholic intellectuals like Roy Campbell and true fascist sympathizers like Eoin O'Duffy, who brought with him an Irish brigade 670 strong. The French integral nationalist Charles Maurras made many visits and reported what he had witnessed on his return home. The English Catholic convert Sir Arnold Lunn made two trips to the Peninsula that were orchestrated by Franco's propaganda agents and produced *Spanish Rehearsal,* which has been described as "a handbook for Franco's supporters in the English-speaking world."

Between April and October 1937 the last redoubts of the Cantabrian coast—Vizcaya, Santander and Asturias—fell into the hands of Franco with the help of the Carlist forces and the German air force, which on 26 April literally destroyed the city of Guernica with phosphorus bombs. On 7 May, General Moral died in a plane crash and was replaced by General Davila. On 19 June the rebels succeeded in occupying Bilbao, and the *gudaris*—Basque nationalist battalions—surrendered to Italian troops in Santoña. In July the Spanish episcopate, favorable to the Nationalists from the start, signed a collective letter—though without the signatures of the archbishops of Tarragona and Vitoria—giving support to the insurrection and recognizing its legitimacy. From May 1937 the military situation worsened for the Republican side; Largo Caballero resigned and was replaced by Negrin, until then minister of finance; the anarchists left the executive, and the government moved from Valencia to Barcelona on 30 October 1937. In December 1937 the battle raged around Teruel. The army of the Republic had taken the city on 7 January 1938 but lost it again on 22 February. Franco's troops razed government positions in Aragon, occupied the slopes of the Ebro, the zone of Maestrazgo, and reached Vinaroz on 15 April. Catalonia was isolated. Then they divided, one part headed East to Lerida, and the other south to attack Valencia. In May the Negrin government drew up a document—the "Three Points"—in which they proposed ending foreign interference and guaranteeing the continuity of democracy and the exclusion of all political persecution after the conclusion of hostilities; others proposed a peace treaty to avoid an anticipated cruel repression. By the end of 1938, Catalonia had fallen into the power of the rebels, who on 26 January 1939 took Barcelona to get to the Pyrenaean front on 10 February. The Negrin government favored continuing the war at all cost, hoping that a world war would break out and that Spain would become an integral part of the international war scenario. However, on 27 February, one month after the fall of Barcelona, the United Kingdom and France recognized the Franco government. On the following day Azaña—from his exile in France—resigned his position as president of the Republic.

On 28 March 1939, Franco made his entrance into Madrid, and the members of the Defense Council—with the exception of Julián Besteiro, who was taken prisoner, judged by a military tribunal, and condemned to thirty years' imprisonment—fled Spain. Meanwhile, Italian troops entered Alicante on 30 March and blockaded the port, and surrender soon followed. On 1 April 1939, Franco signed the last communique of the war: "The war is over." The Republic had been crushed.

Marta Ruiz Jiménez
and Cyprian Blamires

See Also: INTRODUCTION; ANTICLERICALISM; ANTIFASCISM; AUTHORITARIANISM; BLITZKRIEG; CAPITALISM; CATHOLIC CHURCH, THE; CHRISTIANITY; CLERICO-FASCISM; CONSERVATISM; CORPORATISM; EXPANSIONISM; FALANGE; FASCIST PARTY, THE; FRANCE; FRANCO Y BAHAMONDE, GENERAL FRANCISCO; FRANCOISM; GERMANY; GREAT BRITAIN; GUERNICA; HITLER, ADOLF; INTEGRAL NATIONALISM; INTERNATIONAL BRIGADES, THE; INTERNATIONAL FASCISM; IMPERIALISM; IRELAND; IRREDENTISM; ITALY; LUFTWAFFE, THE; MARXISM; MARXIST THEORIES OF FASCISM; MAURRAS, CHARLES; MUSSOLINI, BENITO ANDREA; NATIONALISM; NAZISM; O'DUFFY, EOIN; ORWELL, GEORGE; PARLIAMENTARISM; PERU; PORTUGAL; PRIMO DE RIVERA, JOSÉ ANTONIO; RELIGION; ROMANIA; SOCIALISM; SOVIET UNION, THE; SPAIN; TOTALITARIANISM; TRADITION; VIOLENCE; WARRIOR ETHOS, THE; WORLD WAR II

References

Alpert, M. 2004. *A New International History of the Spanish Civil War.* Basingstoke: Palgrave Macmillan.

Carr, R. 2001. *Modern Spain, 1875–1980.* Oxford: Oxford University Press.

Coverdale, John F. 1976. *Italian Intervention in the Spanish Civil War.* Princeton: Princeton University Press.

Ellwood, S. M. 1987. *Spanish Fascism in the Franco era: Falange Española de las Jons, 1936–76.* Basingstoke: Macmillan.

Keene, Judith. 2001. *Fighting for Franco: International Volunteers in Nationalist Spain during the Spanish Civil War, 1936–1939.* London: Leicester University Press.

Payne, S. G. 1999. *Fascism in Spain, 1923–1977.* Madison: University of Wisconsin Press.

Preston, Paul. 1995. *The Politics of Revenge: Fascism and the Military in Twentieth-century Spain.* London: Routledge.

Richmond, K. 1990. *Women and Spanish Fascism: The Women's Section of the Falange, 1934–1959.* London: Routledge.

Romero Salvadó, F. J. 2005. *The Spanish Civil War: Origins, Course, and Outcomes.* Basingstoke: Palgrave Macmillan.

Sánchez, José M. 1987. *The Spanish Civil War as a Religious Tragedy.* Notre Dame, IN: University of Notre Dame.

SPANN, OTHMAR
(1878–1950)

Austrian national conservative sociologist and philosopher who exercised a notable influence on early Italian Fascism and German National Socialism with his book *Der Wahre Staat—Vorlesungen über Abbruch und Neubau der Gesellschaft* (1921). In 1908, and from 1911 to 1919, Spann was professor of sociology at Brunn Technical College; from 1919 until his expulsion from his post by the Nazis in 1938, he was professor of political economy and social teaching at the University of Vienna. As a nationalist he opposed the *Anschluss* and was for that reason briefly interned in Dachau and banned from publishing. Spann founded a "universalistic sociology" that opposed all individualism and emphasized the priority of the "whole," of the state, over its "members," individuals: the individual must understand himself in terms of his "belongingness" to a corporative and hierarchically structured state. All individualism and egalitarian democracy destroy culture, while universalism furthers the life of the spirit and "righteousness." For Spann the individual does not derive his "spiritual being and essence" from himself, for it emerges first in society. He compares the state to an "organism" that first of all builds up the individual "cells" (individuals) in itself. As an Idealist, Spann understood society first of all as "spiritual community"; he stressed the "national community" resting on the shared knowledge and feeling of a people. He understood "the nation" as a cultural community, which meant that the term could never be used of the Slavs, whom he branded an uneducated passive mass. The original power of Germans, by contrast, lay in the "*völkisch* community, which is the pure community of our spirituality."

For Spann—following here a great tradition from Plato to Hegel—the state was the "expression of the community/*Gemeinschaft*" to be compared with human society/*Gesellschaft*. The state was the "most general and highest institution . . . , i.e., appearance of unity, bearer of unity." The model for this identity of society and state was for Spann the corporative order from antiquity up to the Middle Ages, and in *der Wahre Staat,* Spann sketched out a corporative order taken from Plato's *Politeia,* with "the wise" (the teaching class) at its head; he depicted a layered hierarchical order with gradations down from state and economic leaders to the "higher workers" (spiritual and artistic workers) and manual laborers. Spann spoke of democracy as an unstable constructed individualism; he argued that the "true state" does not reside in the struggle between individual groups but in a "general labor contract" and a "general order of labor" (collective wage agreements) of all social groups, which were all represented in the assembly of orders. The influence of Spann on early Italian Fascism, which borrowed this theory, cannot be overemphasized. Spann argued for the establishment of "guilds," in which all working people, especially industry and the unions, must be brought together. Their joint committee was to be an independent political body: the "council of orders" or the "house of orders." Spann strove—as did the young Mussolini later—not to exclude the workers but to associate them organizationally in a "higher whole," the "people's community." Unlike Italian Fascism, Spann argued, however, not for a strong unified state but for the decentralization and independence of organizations, though in the context of a common labor of all for the same whole.

Spann's influence went beyond the circle of his disciples, who began to meet regularly after 1919 (the Spann Circle), and who occupied the most important teaching positions in Austria. His greatest influence was on the syndicalist early phase of Italian Fascism, especially on the agreements between industry leaders and Fascist corporations (October 1925) and the Italian "trade union law" of 3 April 1926, milestones on the way to the social unification of Italy. According to Spann's conception of the state as "overall leader of economic associations" that were to put an end to economic competition within the people's community, Mussolini brought together all the employers' and workers' syndicates into central "corporations," retaining the capitalist way of production. The Spann Circle welcomed the Fascist order of syndicates unanimously but was split over the question of the strong authoritarian state. In 1933 and 1934, Mussolini made a change in the economic constitution that subjected the corporations to massive state control and viewed them more and more strongly as "compulsory associations."

After 1929/1930 the Spann Circle in Austria increasingly favored the emerging "clerico-fascist movement," especially with the regime of Dollfuss of 1932–1934 and its support by the Heimwehren. In September 1933, Dollfuss defended the introduction of a corporative state with a Catholic stamp, as Pope Pius XI had recommended in his encyclical *Quadragesima anno* of 1931 with the formula "Unity in well-organized multiplicity." The Spann Circle saw itself in agreement with the Church and the "Fatherland Front" of Dollfuss. The Catholic Church took over the social model of Spann in its political teachings, but proposed the concept "solidarism" (orientation to the common weal without prejudice to the property order) in preference to the more romantic "universalism." Spann criticized the idea of a free association of the orders in "solidarism" and called for a break with democracy and party rule in favor of a corporative order put in place from above. On 1 May 1934, Dollfuss proclaimed a corporative order for Austria ("Austrofascism"), which Spann rejected on account of the strong role of the authoritarian state; for him the state was to be only "overall leader of the orders" and so itself an "order."

The Spann Circle was ambivalent toward National Socialism. It welcomed the early NSDAP formula ("the common good goes before the individual good"), German national imperialism, and also the struggle of the Nazis for the annexation of Austria to Germany. Many also favored the idea of an exclusion of the Jews as "alien people"; Spann's call for the Jews on German territory to be placed in their own great ghetto had a significant influence on the early Nazi propagandists Rosenberg and Feder. In 1929, Spann became personally connected with Rosenberg, whom he at first supported. Several friends of Spann were active in the (illegal) NSDAP of Austria, which Spann secretly joined in 1933. Spann influenced the corporative state ideas of early National Socialism as they were represented before 1933 by the Strasser wing, the so-called Party Left of the NSDAP.

Spann abandoned the Romantic Pangerman ideas that he associated with National Socialism after the bloody putsch attempt of the National Socialists in Austria in 1934. The National Socialist "Reich orders" took on the ideas of the Spann Circle after the destruction of the German trades unions in May 1933, especially the "institute for orders," an association of interests of heavy industry around the Hitler financier Fritz Thyssen in Düsseldorf. Spann himself, however, explicitly rejected the National Socialist planned economy (in the form of the Four-Year Plans) and called for the self-regulation of the economy. With the annexation of Austria the Nazi leaders forcibly ended the political activities of the Spann Circle, after some members had already incurred speaking and publication bans in 1934.

Markus Hattstein
(translated by Cyprian Blamires)

See Also: ACTUALISM; *ANSCHLUSS,* THE; ANTI-SEMITISM; AUSTRIA; AUSTROFASCISM; CATHOLIC CHURCH, THE; CLERICO-FASCISM; CORPORATISM; DEMOCRACY; DOLL-

FUSS, ENGELBERT; ECONOMICS; EGALITARIANISM; FASCIST PARTY, THE; FEDER, GOTTFRIED; GERMANY; GHETTOS; *HEIMWEHR;* HITLER, ADOLF; INDIVIDUALISM; INDUSTRY; ITALY; LABOR FRONT, THE; MUSSOLINI, BENITO ANDREA; NATIONALISM; NAZISM; ORGANICISM; PANGERMANISM; PARLIAMENTARISM; PIUS XI, POPE; POLITICAL CATHOLICISM; ROSENBERG, ALFRED; SCHUSCHNIGG, KURT VON; SLAVS, THE (AND GERMANY); SOCIALISM; SOCIOLOGY; STATE, THE; STRASSER BROTHERS, THE; SYNDICALISM; THYSSEN, FRITZ; TOTALITARIANISM; TRADES UNIONS; *VOLK, VÖLKISCH; VOLKSGEMEINSCHAFT,* THE

References

Barkai, Avraham. 1990. *Nazi Economics: Ideology, Theory, and Policy.* New Haven: Yale University Press.

Bowen, Ralph Henry. 1971. *German Theories of the Corporative State, with Special Reference to the Period 1870–1919.* London, Russell and Russell.

Johnson, W. M. 1972. *The Austrian Mind.* Berkeley: University of California Press.

Lebovics, H. 1969. *Social Conservatism and the Middle Classes in Germany, 1914–1933.* Princeton: Princeton University Press.

Pichler, H. J. 1988. *Othmar Spann, oder: die Welt als Ganzes.* Wien: Böhlau.

SPEER, ALBERT (1905–1981)

Impressed by a Hitler speech, Speer joined the NSDAP and SA in 1931, later becoming Hitler's architect, carrying on gigantic building schemes like the New Reich Chancellery or the Reich Party rally venue in Nuremberg. He played a particularly important part in the creation of the special effects—such as the massive use of flags and banners and the special lighting effects—that made the Nuremberg Rallies so powerful as propaganda exercises. Hitler had had aspirations to be an architect himself, and that endeared Speer to him. He appointed Speer general architectural inspector of the Reich in 1937, and one of his tasks was to turn Berlin into the kind of magnificent city that Hitler considered appropriate to be the capital of his planned Third Reich. Hitler was full of admiration for the designs that Speer produced. As the Reich secretary for armament and war production, Speer successfully organized industrial production for "total war" after 1942 by using forced labor extensively; his skills in this role were undoubtedly a factor in enabling Germany to sustain the war effort. Speer was also given many other tasks, including being put in charge of the party's chief technology office. For a time he was one of the most important figures in the German leadership and played a very powerful role in the sphere of the economy. Sentenced to twenty years in the Nuremberg trials, he was released in 1966. His *Spandauer Tagebücher,* published in 1969, shows a strong apologetic tendency.

Fabian Virchow
and Cyprian Blamires

See Also: ARCHITECTURE; ECONOMICS; FORCED LABOR; GERMANY; HITLER, ADOLF; NAZISM; NUREMBERG RALLIES, THE; NUREMBERG TRIALS, THE; PROPAGANDA; SA, THE; SPANDAU PRISON; SYMBOLS; TECHNOLOGY; THIRD REICH, THE; WORLD WAR II

References

Fest, Joachim. 2002. *Speer: The Final Verdict.* London: Weidenfeld and Nicholson.

Helmer, Stephen. 1985. *Hitler's Berlin: The Speer Plans for Reshaping the Central City.* Ann Arbor, MI: UMI Research.

Paulhans, Peter. 1997. *Albert Speer & Partner: Architecture and Urbanism.* Basle: Birkhauser.

Zilbert, Edward. 1981. *Albert Speer and the Nazi Ministry of Arms.* Rutherford, NJ: Farleigh Dickinson University Press.

SPENGLER, OSWALD (1880–1936)

German cultural philosopher whose "Morphology of World History" prophesied not only the decline and the end of European civilization but also a future domination of the world by the German Reich with a new "Caesar" at its head. The one-time grammar school teacher lived from 1912 until his death as a freelance author in Munich. Spengler regarded the immensely successful first volume of his major work, *Der Untergang des Abendlandes* (*The Decline of the West*), which was published in April 1918, as his personal contribution to World War I—when he still firmly believed in the establishment of a German protectorate over the continent as far as the Urals. It was not until after Germany's defeat that his reputed cultural pessimism became central to the public perception of him.

Spengler's major thesis was that there was a law of the historical development of all past and present cultures. According to him, all cultures are subject to the organic rhythm of birth, maturity, aging, and death. Any culture will reach a turning point in its development in civilization whereby the loss of further creative development is accompanied by an irreversible general decadence, until the emergence of "barbarians" heralds a new historical epoch. It is the duty of "late" peoples to accept this "destiny" in the sense of Nietzsche's *amor fati.* Looking at the civilized European nations, Spengler associated with decadence the dominion of intellect and money, the concentration of all life in the cosmopolitan cities, home to irreligious atomized individuals, and the extinction of biological fertility as a counterpart to the "spiritual" infertility and moral decay of modern mass man. These phenomena were accompanied politically by the emergence of imperialism. Without being aware of it, the "young" nation of Germans would be the main player in the dawning imperialist era; they would take up the torch of Ancient Rome. "Blood" and instinct would regain their rights, while the erroneous belief in our ability to attain rational mastery of the world would finally and forcefully be shown up as absurd.

In 1919, Spengler wrote *Preußentum und Sozialismus* in the anti-English "Ideas of 1914" style of Johann Plenge and Werner Sombart. In this book he preached against English liberalism and parliamentarism and for a national socialism freed from Marx, for which a complete subordination of the individual to the state within a corporative organization would be necessary.

Having been a member of the board of the Nietzsche Archive since 1923, Spengler maintained numerous political contacts with the National Right between 1919 and 1924, mixing with people in big business and paramilitary circles. The expression of his ultimately unsuccessful political ambitions was a kind of agenda for government that he drew up in his *Neubau des Deutschen Reiches* of 1924. *Der Mensch und die Technik* (1931) was Spengler's swan-song on Enlightenment ideals and an apology for the "will to power" potentiated by technology. For Spengler man is not "good," but rather survives as a "predator" solely through attack and destruction. With *Jahre der Entscheidung* (1933), this admirer of Mussolini tried to offer his services to the politically powerful one final time, sending Hitler a copy and requesting a meeting with him. Like many conservative revolutionaries, Spengler welcomed the destruction of democratic institutions, parties, and trades unions following Hitler's seizure of power.

The extraordinary success of this last work—which within a few months overtook the entire edition of the *Decline of the West*—forced the NSDAP into a public debate with Spengler. A National Socialist press campaign launched by Alfred Baeumler against *Jahre der Entscheidung* focused on Spengler's reservations about

Hitler, his anti-working-class ethos, and his assumed fatalism. It accelerated after Spengler had turned down Goebbels's offers of participation in representative events organized by the new regime. Following this, Baeumler, in a lecture at the end of 1933 that was much discussed in the press and in three radio talks at the beginning of 1934, discredited Spengler the despiser of the masses as "Enemy of the people (*Volk*)." At about the same time the press was forbidden by the Reich Propaganda Ministry to promote any further discussion of the works of Spengler.

While the National Socialist Left saw in Spengler's *Jahre der Entscheidung* counter-revolution and a capitalist restoration at work, those critics who represented the party line could not deny the fundamental agreement of the political ideas of Spengler with those of National Socialism. Not least for this reason Spengler was—for example, in the Hitler Youth Organ *Wille und Macht*—rehabilitated in the middle of 1935 as a prophet of national revolution. Beyond a direct influencing of National Socialist ideology by Spengler there is unquestionably a spiritual kinship—to which Alfred Rosenberg referred in his *Mythus des 20. Jahrhunderts* (1930). This is reflected in the circumstance that *Jahre der Entscheidung* was never publicly banned. Even in times of paper shortage at the beginning of the 1940s there continued to be new editions of Spengler's complete works. He did not break with the Nietzsche Archive, which was loyal to National Socialism, or with Elisabeth Förster-Nietzsche, who admired Hitler, until 1935.

In Fascist Italy the ideas of Spengler were spread particularly through the translation of *Der Mensch und die Technik* and *Jahre der Entscheidung,* as well as through essays and debates about his writings. While Spengler was reproached by Benedetto Croce for dilettantism and an unscientific approach, Mussolini was impressed above all by the fanatical anti-Marxism of Spengler's critique of civilization, as well as by his theses on the development of population. Mussolini wrote an introduction to the Italian translation of a study by Richard Korherr, *Über den Geburtenrückgang* (1927), for which Spengler had already provided an "introduction" to the German edition. Spengler's *Jahre der Entscheidung* was reviewed by Mussolini at the end of 1933 for the newspaper *Popolo d'Italia,* and in an interview after 1933 he lamented the lack of impact of Spengler's writings in Italy. Mussolini's relationship to Spengler was positive, but in this Il Duce clearly had ulterior motives; it was not least a response to the unconcealed veneration for himself expressed by the German writer and to his description of Italy under Mus-

solini as "a great power." The critique of Spengler's determinism, his cultural pessimism, and his Pangermanism was left by Mussolini to other authors—like Julius Evola or the author of the Spengler entry in the *Dizionario di politica* produced by the Fascist Party in 1940.

Susanne Pocai

See Also: INTRODUCTION; ABSTRACTION; ARISTOCRACY; BAEUMLER, ALFRED; BLOOD; CIVILIZATION; CORPORATISM; COSMOPOLITANISM; CROCE, BENEDETTO; CULTURE; DECADENCE; DEMOGRAPHIC POLICY; EGALITARIANISM; ELITE THEORY; ENLIGHTENMENT, THE; EVOLA, JULIUS; FASCIST PARTY, THE; FÖRSTER-NIETZSCHE, ELISABETH; GERMANY; GOEBBELS, (PAUL) JOSEPH; HITLER, ADOLF; ITALY; LIBERALISM; MARXISM; MASSES, THE ROLE OF THE; MATERIALISM; MECHANISTIC THINKING; MODERNISM; MODERNITY; MUSSOLINI, BENITO ANDREA; NAZISM; NIETZSCHE, FRIEDRICH; NIHILISM; PALINGENETIC MYTH; PARLIAMENTARISM; PROPAGANDA; RATIONALISM; RELIGION; REVOLUTION; ROME; ROSENBERG, ALFRED; SCIENCE; SOCIAL DARWINISM; SOCIALISM; SOUL; STATE, THE; TECHNOLOGY; TRADITION; *VOLK, VÖLKISCH;* WORLD WAR I; YOUTH

References

Farrenkopf, John. 2001. *Prophet of Decline: Spengler on World History and Politics.* Baton Rouge: Louisiana State University Press.
Fischer, Klaus P. 1989. *History and Prophecy: Oswald Spengler and the Decline of the West.* New York: Lang.
Hughes, H. Stuart. 1952. *Oswald Spengler.* New York: Scribner.
Merlio, Gilbert. 1982. *Oswald Spengler: Témoin de son temps.* Stuttgart: Heinz.

SPIRITO, UGO (1896–1979)

Leading supporter of Fascism in Italian intellectual circles. At the University of Rome in 1918 he was drawn from an initial enthusiasm for positivism to the idealism of Gentile and others. By 1922 he had adopted Fascism under the influence of Gentile, whose doctrine of actualism he also espoused. In 1927, Spirito took on the editorship of the journal *Nuovi studi di diritto, economica e politica* together with fellow actualist Arnaldo Volpicelli. By now Spirito was applying actualist principles to the sphere of economics, and in particular to the advocacy of corporatism, and this found expression in a number of works between 1927 and 1932. Spirito held professorships at Pisa, Messina, Genoa, and Rome. He eventually fell out of favor with Mussolini.

Cyprian Blamires

See Also: ACTUALISM; CORPORATISM; FASCIST PARTY, THE; GENTILE, GIOVANNI; ITALY; MANIFESTO OF FASCIST INTELLECTUALS, THE; MUSSOLINI, BENITO ANDREA; POSITIVISM

References

Florinsky, Michael T. 1984. *Fascism and National Socialism: A Study of the Economic and Social Policies of the Totalitarian State.* Brooklyn, NY: AMS.

Gregor, A. James. 2005. *Mussolini's Intellectuals: Fascist Social and Political Thought.* Princeton: Princeton University Press.

Tannenbaum, Edward R. 1972. *The Fascist Experience.* New York: Basic.

SPORT

Sport has been used as a propaganda, recruiting, and militaristic tool by all the major ideologies of the twentieth century. Fascism, in its various forms, has been no exception. The apparent allure of the strong, aesthetically pleasing body, which could be turned into a military tool, has been a common feature of fascism. Whether publicly at the 1936 Berlin Olympics, through the resultant film spectacle of Leni Riefenstahl's *Olympia,* or in the local sports events hosted by a variety of fascist movements, organized physical games have appeared to go hand in hand with the ideology of fascism. Given the natural fit between the healthy body, the spectacle of sport, and the ideology of fascism, it is perhaps surprising to record that neither Hitler, Mussolini, nor Franco were sports enthusiasts. Their rise to power in the interwar years coincided however, with an upsurge in public interest in international sporting competition that was aided by a rapidly expanding mass media. Most fascist regimes or movements recognized the power of sport as a part of their propaganda mission and embraced it. The great value of sport, especially at the international level, was the public spectacle of winning. In an era when fascist governments and parties promoted nationalist and racist ideologies that spoke of their supremacy over other countries, sport allowed them to measure their superiority in a direct fashion. Sport was a natural agent with which to demonstrate, both domestically and to the wider world, the values of society as imagined by fascism.

Of the fascist leaders in Europe it was Mussolini who was first to recognize the power of sport. In 1934, Italy staged the World Cup finals, and the event was used as a way of showcasing the rebirth of Italy by transposing the athletic imagery of Ancient Rome with the modernism of contemporary Italy. Mussolini dictated which referee would officiate at the Italian games, and some questionable decisions during the tournament ensured that an average Italian team won the trophy. It was a great propaganda coup for Mussolini, and encouraged fascists across Europe to embrace sport more fully. As well as promoting team sports, both Mussolini and Hitler were keen to promote the individual sport of motor racing. This sport not only allowed fascism to chase the morale-boosting victory but also provided a natural synergy between brave, fearless manhood and the skills of modern fascist technology and engineering. Hitler promoted and funded Mercedes on the grand prix circuit, while Mussolini did the same for Alfa Romeo; they duly dominated the sport.

The Nazis harnessed the biggest international sporting event, the Olympic Games, in 1936 as a way of displaying German skill and superiority to the world. Both the winter and summer games were awarded to Germany, to be held at Garmisch-Partenkirchen and Berlin, with twenty-eight and forty-nine nations in attendance, respectively. Both events were used to promote the Nazi regime and ideas of Aryan racial superiority. In terms of spectacle, the Nazis were innovative. The Berlin games were the first to include a torch relay across Europe from Olympia; broadcast images of the events to theater screens across the city attracted a record-breaking 4.5 million spectators; and Leni Riefenstahl's documentary treatment of the games (*Olympia*) forever changed conceptions of how sports events should be filmed. Hitler officially opened both the winter and summer games, events that were fully funded by the state (at an estimated cost of $8 million) and ruthlessly promoted by the local organizers: Carl Diem for the German Olympic Committee and Joseph Goebbels as head of the Popular Enlightenment and Propaganda Ministry. To assist in the planning of the games, the Reich Sports Office, headed by Hans von Tschammer, which had overseen all German sports bodies and clubs and pursued an Aryans-only policy since 1933, was mobilized to make the event truly national.

Despite threats of a boycott, all competing nations (with the exception of the Soviet Union) did attend Berlin, although some individual Jewish athletes chose to stay away. The stage was set for a showdown between the cream of the Nazi athletes and representatives from

American black boxing champion Joe Louis (back to camera) and the German fighter Max Schmeling in a bout in 1938 which was widely seen as a symbolic struggle between totalitarianism and freedom. (Library of Congress)

supposedly "lesser" races. Germany topped the medal table at the close of the games, winning thirty-three medals more than their nearest rival. On those terms, and as a spectacle, the games were a tremendous success for the Nazi regime. However, high-profile victories by African Americans, most notably the four medals won by Jesse Owens, undermined Nazi claims of race supremacy.

The changing geography of Europe during the Nazi expansion period transformed the sporting map of Europe. To ensure that Germany became the best possible football team in the world, the Austrian team was abolished after the annexation in 1938, and its best players were drafted into the German squad. The only Austrian player to refuse to play for Germany, Matthias Sindelar, was killed by the Nazis within a year. In 1938 the English football team traveled to Berlin to meet their Ger-

man counterparts. On the direct orders of the foreign office, and in line with Chamberlain's policy of appeasement, the English team famously gave the Nazi salute during the prematch ceremonies. Although England won the game 6–3, the players were widely criticized in the British press for their salute.

The final pre–World War II clash between emblematic fascist sportsmen and their democratic counterparts came in June 1938, when Germany's Max Schmeling met America's Joe Louis in New York for the world heavyweight boxing title. When Schmeling had beaten Louis two years earlier, he had been heralded by the Nazis as the great Aryan sportsman and was used as an emissary to convince the Americans not to boycott the 1936 Olympics. In 1938 the Schmeling-Louis bout was touted by the press as a battle between Nazi Germany and free America. Interest was intense, and the bout was broadcast around the world, with a huge audience listening in Germany. In the match, Louis won in the first round: as Schmeling hit the canvas for the first time, the Nazi authorities stopped broadcasting the commentary.

The use of sport as a vehicle for the promotion of strength, order, and readiness for battle, as well as an important component of public display, was well understood by fascist movements in general. For example, Oswald Mosley, a keen sportsman, ensured that the British Union of Fascists had sports facilities installed at their London headquarters, and he encouraged boxing, football, and other sports across the country. Likewise in Ireland, the Blueshirts formed tennis and cycling clubs and started Gaelic football teams.

Mike Cronin

See Also: *ANSCHLUSS*, THE; ANTI-SEMITISM; APPEASEMENT; ART; ARYANISM; BERLIN OLYMPICS, THE; BODY, THE CULT OF THE; FASCIST PARTY, THE; FOOTBALL; FRANCO Y BAHAMONDE, GENERAL FRANCISCO; GERMANY; GOEBBELS, (PAUL) JOSEPH; GREAT BRITAIN; HITLER, ADOLF; IRELAND; ITALY; LEISURE; MODERNITY; MOSLEY, SIR OSWALD; MUSSOLINI, BENITO ANDREA; NATIONALISM; NAZISM; PROPAGANDA; RACIAL DOCTRINE; RACISM; RIEFENSTAHL, LENI; ROME; SALUTES; SOVIET UNION, THE; TECHNOLOGY; WARRIOR ETHOS, THE; YOUTH

References

Gori, Gigliola. 2004. *Female Bodies, Sport, Italian Fascism.* London: Frank Cass.

Krüger, A. 1998. "The Ministry of Popular Enlightenment and Propaganda and the Nazi Olympics of 1936." Pp. 33–47 in *Global and Cultural Critique: Problematizing the Olympic Games,* edited by R. K. Barney. London, ON: International Symposium for Olympic Research.

Mandell, R. D. 1982. *The Nazi Olympics.* London: Souvenir.

Mangan, J. A., ed. 2000. *Superman Supreme: Fascist Body as Political Icon.* London: Frank Cass.

Margolick, D. 2005. *Beyond Glory: Max Schmeling versus Joe Louis.* London: Bloomsbury.

Riordan, J., and A. Krüger, eds. 1998. *International Politics of Sport in the 20th Century: The Impact of Fascism and Communism on Sport.* London: Spon.

SQUADRISMO

The organized campaigns of intimidation and violence by the Fascist squads (often known as "Blackshirts" on account of their uniform) against their socialist, communist, and Catholic opponents in the provinces of northern and central Italy from the autumn of 1920

onward. The *squadristi,* comprising nuclei of former servicemen from World War I together with other younger elements, operated as armed paramilitary units not unlike the German *Freikorps* and performed the same counter-revolutionary function. Operating from bases in provincial towns, and often with the collusion of police and judicial authorities as well as of local garrison commanders, they systematically destroyed the physical centers of both Marxist and Catholic political parties, trades unions, and, above all, peasant organizations, intimidating their members and frequently murdering their leaders. This guerrilla activity in the countryside was essential to Mussolini's rise to power. By 1922 they were actually engaged in the seizure of political power from their opponents at a local level, a process that was the necessary prelude to Mussolini's bid for power at a national level, which he launched at the end of October 1922 in the March on Rome.

John Pollard

See Also: ANTIFASCISM; CATHOLIC CHURCH, THE; FARMERS; FASCIST PARTY, THE; FREIKORPS, THE; ITALY; MARCH ON ROME, THE; MARXISM; MUSSOLINI, BENITO ANDREA; PARAMILITARISM; SOCIALISM; TERROR; TRADES UNIONS; WAR VETERANS; WORLD WAR I

Reference

Lyttelton, A. 1973. *Seizure of Power: Fascism in Italy, 1919–1929,* London: Weidenfeld and Nicolson.

SQUADRISTI: See SQUADRISMO

SS, THE

Set up as a personal bodyguard for Hitler, the SS (*Schutzstaffel:* "Protection Squads") later developed into an army that formed the foundation of Nazi power. Like no other institution of the National Socialist dictatorship, the SS was the embodiment of the ideology and practice of its master-race worldview. The precursor had been the *Stabswache* (Staff Guard), banned after the Hitler coup in late 1923. In 1925 it was re-established, mainly in order to protect the party leadership and the party's meetings. Led in the early years of its existence by Julius Schreck, Joseph Berchthold, and Erhard Heiden, the SS gained growing importance after command had been handed over to Heinrich Himmler at the beginning of 1929. As the Reichsführer SS ("Reich Leader SS"), he not only multiplied membership numbers to some 52,000 in late 1932 (nearly 250,000 by 1939) but also set up the Rasse- und Siedlungsamt (Race and Settlement Office) and the Sicherheitsdienst (SD) as the NS-DAP's internal police. After the SS played a prominent role in the murder of the leadership of the SA in 1934, it was rewarded by Hitler with removal from subordination to the rival SA and placed under his direct command.

Members of the SS swore unquestioning loyalty to Hitler ("My honor is loyalty"). They were selected according to their height (above 6 feet) and had to submit an *Ariernachweis* (proof of Aryan descent), including an account of their ancestry back to the year 1750. It was Himmler's aim to give the SS the character of an elite community similar to an order. In 1931 he decreed that every SS member had to ask for a marriage allowance; by controlling the intimate partnerships of "Hitler's elite" he aimed at the creation of a German Nordic kinship group free of hereditary illness. The mentality of the SS was characterized by blind idealism toward its leadership, drastic discipline, loyalty and bonhomie, and by the exercise of brutal and merciless force against those classified as "racially inferior." Its members used symbols like the death's head and runes from the Old Teutonic World and wore black uniforms. The weekly publication of the SS, first published in early 1925 and entitled *Das Schwarzes Korps,* was an outspokenly racist and elitist paper with a circulation of 750,000 copies as late as 1944.

In the years following the National Socialist takeover, Himmler and Heydrich brought the police under their control step by step: Himmler became the *Reichsführer SS und Chef der deutschen Polizei* ("Reich leader SS and chief of German police") in June 1936, and he made the SS the most important instrument for the persecution of political opponents and the translation of racist beliefs into action. After 1939 the SS had twelve *Hauptämter* ("Departments"), their composition and tasks expressing two of the ideas basic to the National Socialist worldview: "extinction" and "selection." The *Hauptämter* headed a polyplike structure that was deeply involved in the intimidation, terrorization, and murder of the civilian population in the districts occupied by the German Wehrmacht, and also became responsible for the Holocaust. At the same time, they made efforts to strengthen Aryan-ness and to expand the German settlement areas; for example, in order to create a Greater German(ic) Reich, the SS Race and Settlement Office, following a Hitler order

from late 1939, organized the (re-)settlement of Germans in the occupied countries.

There was another sphere of activity in which the SS involved itself, the sphere of industry, for it came to be involved in running industrial concerns, and the operation of those concerns was often closely bound up with SS involvement in the implementation of Nazi racial policies. The Wirtschafts- und Verwaltungshauptamt (Economic and Administration Department) dealt mainly with economic affairs. In July 1938, SS-controlled companies that were active in industries like wood-processing, civil engineering, textiles, stones, and brickworks were merged into the Deutsche Wirtschaftsbetriebe GmbH (German Economic Industries). Most of the enterprises came from the exploitation of forced labor in the concentration camps. As part of the SS, the WVHA in particular—and with it the SS-Totenkopfverbände (SS Death's-Head Units)—were responsible for running the whole system of concentration camps, including the guarding, administration, and exploitation of the men and women taken into detention. Further acts of genocide and mass murder were undertaken by the Einsatzgruppen (Special Task Groups), highly mobile killing units that followed close behind the German Wehrmacht in the invasion of Poland and the Soviet Union. While the Einsatzgruppen consisted mainly of members of the SD and the Sicherheitspolizei (Security Police), many German army units as well as auxiliaries from the Ukraine and the Baltic states collaborated in the mass murder of Jews, communist politicians, and so-called saboteurs, a term used to legitimize the killing of civilians. As the war expanded, the Einsatzgruppen—which were responsible for killing more than half a million people—extended their area of operations into Greece, Romania, Slovakia, and Hungary. From these countries, too, hundreds of thousands of Jews and Gypsies were deported to the extermination camps controlled by the SS. Further parts of the SS included the Waffen-SS, which acted largely as elite combat units. Units of the Waffen-SS were subordinate to the commanders of the Wehrmacht on a tactical level but remained part of the SS in principle.

The International Military Tribunal in Nuremberg classified the entire SS as a criminal organization, only the Reiter-SS (Mounted SS) being exempted from the ban.

Fabian Virchow

See Also: AHNENERBE FORSCHUNGS- UND LEHRGEMEIN-SCHAFT; ANTI-SEMITISM; ARISTOCRACY; ARYANISM; CONCENTRATION CAMPS; ECONOMICS; ELITE THEORY; EUGENICS; FORCED LABOR; GERMANY; GREECE; HIMMLER,

HEINRICH; HEYDRICH, REINHARD; HITLER, ADOLF; HOLO-CAUST, THE; HUNGARY; INDUSTRY; NAZISM; NIGHT OF THE LONG KNIVES, THE; NORDIC SOUL, THE; NUREMBERG TRIALS, THE; PANGERMANISM; RACIAL DOCTRINE; ROMA AND SINTI, THE; ROMANIA; SA, THE; SCHÖNERER, GEORG RITTER VON; SD, THE; SLOVAKIA; TERROR; TIBET; TOLKIEN, JOHN RONALD REUEL; *UNTERMENSCHEN* ("SUBHUMANS"); WAFFEN-SS, THE; WEHRMACHT, THE; WORLD WAR II

References

Höhne, Heinz. 2000 [1967]. *The Order of the Death's Head. The Story of Hitler's SS.* London: Penguin.

Koehl, Robert Lewis. 1983. *The Black Corps: The Structure and Power Struggles of the Nazi SS.* Madison: University of Wisconsin Press.

Kogon, Eugen. 1950. *The Theory and Practice of Hell: The German Concentration Camps and the System Behind Them.* London: Secker and Warburg.

Lumsden, Robin. 2005. *Himmler's Black Order, 1923–1945.* Stroud: Sutton.

Reider, Frederic. 1981. *The Order of the Death's Head: A Pictorial History.* Slough: Foulsham.

Ziegler, Herbert F. 1989. *Nazi Germany's New Aristocracy: The SS-Leadership 1925–39.* Princeton: Princeton University Press.

STAB IN THE BACK, THE: *See* NOVEMBER CRIMINALS, THE

STAHLHELM ("STEEL HELMET")

Militant right-wing German nationalist association of war veterans established in 1918 by Franz Seldte. By 1923, Stahlhelm comprised 14,000 local groups, and membership was up to a million. Seldte's co-leader, Theodor Düsterberg, ran for the presidency in 1932 and won 2.5 million votes but withdrew in favor of Hitler. When Hitler became chancellor he appointed Seldte minister of labor, and Seldte put the Stahlhelm directly under the chancellor's control. Eventually, the organization was absorbed into the SA.

Cyprian Blamires

See Also: GERMANY; HITLER, ADOLF; NAZISM; SA, THE; WAR VETERANS; WEIMAR REPUBLIC, THE

References

Bessel, R. 1993. *Germany after the First World War.* Oxford: Clarendon.

Feuchtwanger, E. J. 1995. *From Weimar to Hitler, 1918–1933.* Basingstoke: Macmillan.

STALIN, IOSIF VISSARIONOVICH, known as "Josef" (real surname Dzhugashvili, 1878–1953)

General secretary of the Central Committee of the Communist Party from 1922 and, with varying official titles, autocrat of the Soviet Union from 1929 until his death. His adopted name, "Stalin," is derived from the Russian word *stal* ("steel"). While most observers agree that there were similarities between the institutional transformations, political styles, terror apparatuses, and foreign policies implemented by Stalin and Hitler (as well as, to a lesser degree, Mussolini), the ideological foundations of such parallels are contested. Although many pre-perestroika studies acknowledged the presence of Russian nationalist, xenophobic, anti-Semitic, traditionalist, and similar features in Stalin's political thought, mainstream scholarship has continued to conceptualize Stalinism as clearly left-wing. A number of post-Soviet Western and Russian studies, however, are lending support to the centrality of a cryptic but nevertheless virulent Russian organicist and imperialist nationalism to Stalin's thinking, and are thus casting doubt on unambiguous classifications of his worldview. Some commentators have gone as far as to call Stalin a fascist.

Born in the small Georgian town of Gori, Stalin grew up under poor circumstances. In spite of an underprivileged background, he managed to enter the reputed Tbilisi Theological Seminary, from where he was expelled in 1899 without having finished his course. After an apparent involvement with the Georgian nationalist movement, Stalin became a member of the Tbilisi branch of the Russian Social Democratic Workers Party upon its foundation in 1898. In spite of his earlier interest in Georgian nationalism, Stalin, in his first writings inspired by Marxism, denied the concept of a cultural identity of nations. At the same time, he expressed special appreciation for the Russians as a modern nation and a peculiar wrath against Jews as being uniquely reactionary. In doing so, he followed a distinction that had been introduced into Marxism by Friedrich Engels (1820–1895), who juxtaposed historical nations playing a progressive role with nonhistorical nations destined to disappear.

Ruthless Soviet dictator Iosif Stalin. Fear of Stalin and Soviet Bolshevism drove many into the arms of Hitler and Mussolini. (Library of Congress)

During the years preceding the 1917 revolution, Stalin gradually abandoned his nihilistic view of the nation and embraced partly Austro-Marxist approaches, acknowledging the continued relevance of national communities during the period of transition to world communism. Gradually, moreover, Stalin developed into the Bolshevik Party's expert on the national question and became the Soviet government's first people's commissar (that is, minister) of nationalities. Although insisting on the necessity of cultural autonomy for national republics, Stalin represented within the Soviet leadership a neoimperial solution to the nationalities question. His major opponent was initially Vladimir Lenin (1870–1924) himself, who accused Stalin of waging a "truly Great Russian nationalist campaign" and who, in 1922, resisted Stalin's proposal to incorporate the nominally independent Trans-Caucasian, Ukrainian, and Belorussian Soviet republics into the Russian Socialist Federal Soviet Republic. Instead, a new Union of Soviet Socialist Republics was created that, though de jure a hybrid between a federation and confederation, became an increasingly centralized unitary state largely along the lines imagined by Stalin.

Shortly before his death, Lenin became disillusioned about Stalin's qualities as a party functionary, and he demanded, in a famous letter, a limitation on his growing political power. As Lenin was seriously ill, however, Stalin managed to limit the circulation of this letter and to preserve his eminent position in the Soviet leadership. Although Stalin had assumed the party post of general secretary in 1922, that did not automatically secure unchallenged leadership after Lenin's death. Through a series of cunning political maneuvers and manipulation of cadre policies, Stalin gradually removed his political competitors, including Lev Trotskii, Grigorii Zinoviev (1883–1936), and Lev Kamenev (1883–1936), as well as, somewhat later, Nikolai Bukharin (1888–1938), from their leading posts. Subsequently, all of them were killed as "enemies of the people," on Stalin's orders.

In the course of the 1930s the Soviet Union went through a transformation amounting to a second social revolution "from above," marked by an agricultural collectivization campaign causing, among others, the deaths of 3 to 6 million mainly Ukrainian peasants in a famine in1932–1933, a particularly violent onslaught on a loosely defined category of, allegedly, better-performing anti-Soviet peasants labeled kulaks (*kulak*, "fist"; Russian term for peasant with midsize farm); an industrialization drive leading to a rise in urban population of about 30 million from 1926 to 1939; and the creation of an enormous forced labor camp and colonies system known under the Russian acronym GULag (Glavnoe upravlenie ispravitel'no-trudovykh lagerei: Chief Directorate of Corrective Labor Camps). Depending on widely varying estimates and the particular time period in question, the GULag had between 1.7 and 8 million inmates from the late 1930s until the early 1950s. Altogether, more than 20 million people probably went through Stalin's detention system. A part of the GULag population was provided as a result of a cardinal change in the composition of the Soviet administrative organs and large-scale purges at most party levels, governmental institutions, enterprises, and social organizations. Until the late 1920s, Soviet state terror had been applied primarily to presumed adversaries of communism, including priests, noblemen and -women, former czarist officials, or non-Bolshevik political activists. In contrast, among the victims of Stalin's "repressions" (a post-Stalinist Soviet euphemism denoting arrest, imprisonment, torture, and execution) in the 1930s were, to a disproportionately high degree, party functionaries including "Stalinists" as well as the staff of the highest echelons of the secret services and Red Army. Along with hundreds of thousands of ordinary citizens, tens of thousands of Soviet administrators, including most members of the so-called Old Bolshevik guard, were shot or tortured to death. Many more perished from malnutrition, cold, and disease in prisons, trains, and camps. The so-called Great Terror of 1937–1938 hit, also to a disproportionately high degree, representatives of a number of Soviet national minorities, including the Poles, Germans, Finns, Greeks, and Estonians. Some prominent personalities, among them highly placed party functionaries and representatives of the Soviet cultural establishment, committed suicide.

By the late 1930s, Stalin had transformed the Soviet political regime from a parto- and ideocracy (party rule informed by an ideology) into an auto- and logocracy (self-rule informed by the latest utterances of the supreme leader). While the Soviet state had, under its oligarchic government in the 1920s, been closer to the ideal-type of authoritarianism, it had acquired all the characteristics of totalitarianism and showed signs of sultanism by the late 1930s. As a result of the Soviet Union's victory over Nazi Germany and emergence as a superpower after World War II, Stalin's regime consolidated and preserved many of its core traits long after his death in 1953.

After Stalin had consolidated his power in the late 1920s, an increasingly orchestrated campaign affecting eventually all sectors of Soviet society aimed to create a new, isolated cultural community—the Soviet people—that would trace its roots to selected aspects of prerevolutionary Russian culture, traditions, and policies. The Russian nation was elevated to a leading position in Soviet society, and the Soviet people assigned the role of a collective messiah in world history. Both of these developments established a partial continuity with the ideological foundations of the czarist empires, and a substantive similitude between the USSR and the Third Reich.

Against the background of the New Economic Policy of the 1920s, novel and peculiarly Stalinist tendencies in the policies and political style of the Soviet leadership in the 1930s to 1950s included: replacement of class-sociological interpretations of historical events with traditional approaches to historical writing, in the early 1930s; an emphasis on the positive impact of national heroes—such as Ivan the Terrible and Peter the Great—and culture in the formation of a powerful Russian state; partial acknowledgement of the Soviet Union's role as a successor of the czarist empire, including justification of czarist imperialist and colonialist policies toward non-Russian nationalities; partial replacement of nativization-indigenization policies introduced in the 1920s with russification of non-Russian Soviet national-

ities in the late 1930s; juxtaposition of "healthy patriotism" against "rootless cosmopolitanism"; abstruse Russian chauvinist claims ascribing many inventions—including those of the radio and powered flight—to Russians; abandonment of egalitarian income policies in many sectors of the economy, science institutions, and cultural industry; resumption of preferred admission of students with a working-class background to higher education; replacement of various avant-garde styles in Russian cultural production (literature, film, music) with a uniform traditionalist "socialist realism"; illiberal family and gender policies including a recriminalization of male homosexuality, tightening of the divorce laws, prohibition of abortions, and so forth in the 1930s; temporary rapprochement with Nazi Germany and abandonment of anti-Nazi propaganda in 1939–1940; consideration of the USSR's possible participation in the Tripartite Pact between Germany, Italy, and Japan of 1940; various anti-Jewish campaigns, especially after World War II, such as the persecution of the members of the Jewish Anti-Fascist Committee, theater and literary critics of Jewish origin (accused of "cosmopolitanism"), and Stalin's mainly Jewish doctors, who were accused of a "plot" against him. Taken together, these and other similar measures amounted to a formidable amendment of not only the core ideas of Marxism but also important aspects of Leninism.

Many observers now agree that there were some striking similarities between important aspects of Stalin's and the czars' rule (for example, the two regimes' internal passport systems) as well as between certain traits of Stalinist and prerevolutionary Russian right-wing thought (such as messianism). Yet Stalin had only limited interest in the political ideas of the Slavophiles, Pan-Slavs, and Black Hundreds, or of such thinkers as Fëdor Tiutchev (1808–1873), Nikolai Danilevskii (1822–1885), Konstantin Pobedonostsev (1827–1907), and Konstantin Leont'ev (1831–1891). As Erik van Ree has shown, Stalin was well read only in Russian prerevolutionary left-wing and the varieties of international Marxist thought. Rather than creating an amalgam of Russian left- and right-wing ideologies—as post-Soviet Russia's Communist Party leader Gennadii Ziuganov (born 1943) has done recently—Stalin relied, in his revisions, on certain elitist and protonationalist aspects within international revolutionary thought that reached as far back as Jacobinism.

Andreas Umland

See Also: INTRODUCTION; ANTI-COMINTERN PACT, THE; ANTI-SEMITISM; ARENDT, HANNAH; AUTHORITARIANISM; BARBAROSSA, OPERATION; BOLSHEVISM; COMINTERN,

THE; CONCENTRATION CAMPS; CONSPIRACY THEORIES; CORPORATISM; COSMOPOLITANISM; DICTATORSHIP; ECONOMICS; EGALITARIANISM; ELITE THEORY; FAMILY, THE; FARMERS; FASCIST PARTY, THE; FILM; FORCED LABOR; GERMANY; HERO, THE CULT OF THE; HITLER, ADOLF; HITLER-STALIN PACT, THE; HOMOSEXUALITY; IMPERIALISM; INDUSTRY; ITALY; LEADER CULT, THE; *LEBENSRAUM;* MARXISM; MARXIST THEORIES OF FASCISM; MATERIALISM; *MEIN KAMPF;* MODERNISM; MODERNITY; MUSSOLINI, BENITO ANDREA; NATIONAL BOLSHEVISM; NATIONALISM; ORGANICISM; ORTHODOX CHURCHES, THE; POSTWAR FASCISM; RELIGION; ROOTLESSNESS; RURALISM; RUSSIA; SEXUALITY; SLAVS, THE (AND GERMANY); SOCIALISM; SOVIET UNION, THE; STATE, THE; TERROR; THEATER; THIRD REICH, THE; TOTALITARIANISM; TROTSKY, LEON; *UNTERMENSCHEN* ("SUBHUMANS"); *VOLKSGEMEINSCHAFT,* THE; WORLD WAR II; XENOPHOBIA

References

Besymenski, Lew. 2002. *Stalin und Hitler: Das Pokerspiel der Diktatoren.* Berlin: Aufbau.

Brent, Jonathan, and Vladimir P. Naumov. 2003. *Stalin's Last Crime: The Plot against the Jewish Doctors, 1948–1953.* New York: HarperCollins.

Bullock, Allan. 1991. *Hitler and Stalin: Parallel Lives.* London: HarperCollins.

Lewin, Moshe, and Ian Kershaw, eds. 1997. *Stalinism and Nazism: Dictatorships in Comparison.* Cambridge: Cambridge University Press.

Luks, Leonid, ed. 1998. *Der Spätstalinismus und die "jüdische Frage": Zur antisemitischen Wendung des Kommunismus.* Köln: Böhlau 1998.

Mehnert, Klaus. 1952. *Stalin versus Marx: The Stalinist Historical Doctrine.* London: George Allen and Unwin.

Oberländer, Erwin, ed. 1967. *Sowjetpatriotismus und Geschichte: Dokumentation.* Köln: Wissenschaft und Politik.

Perrie, Maureen. 2001. *The Cult of Ivan the Terrible in Stalin's Russia.* Basingstoke: Palgrave.

Service, Robert. 2005. *Stalin: A Biography.* Cambridge: Belknap.

Tucker, Robert C. 1990. *Stalin in Power: The Revolution from Above, 1928–1941.* New York: Norton.

Van Ree, Erik. 2002. *The Political Thought of Joseph Stalin: A Study in Twentieth-Century Revolutionary Patriotism.* London: RoutledgeCurzon.

Weitz, Eric D. 2002. "Racial Politics without the Concept of Race: Reevaluating Soviet Ethnic and National Purges." *Slavic Review* 61, no. 1: 1–29.

STALINGRAD, THE BATTLE OF

Legendary confrontation between Nazi and Soviet troops beginning in the autumn of 1942 and ending in February 1943 that was not merely the turning point in Hitler's conflict with the Soviet Union but also the turning point of World War II. Both sides endured terrible sufferings during the harsh winter conditions under which the battle for control of the city was fought. Although the German 6th Army under Field Marshal von Paulus nearly managed to take the whole city in September 1942, Russian resistance proved ultimately unbreakable, and von Paulus and 91,000 German soldiers were obliged to surrender (against the direct orders of Hitler) in February of the following year. It was a massive humiliation for the Third Reich, and it became a symbol for the Soviets of the superiority of their creed over fascism and their destiny to defeat Hitler.

Cyprian Blamires

See Also: BARBAROSSA, OPERATION; GERMANY; HITLER, ADOLF; *LEBENSRAUM;* MARXISM; *MEIN KAMPF;* SLAVS, THE (AND GERMANY); SOVIET UNION, THE; THIRD REICH, THE; *UNTERMENSCHEN* ("SUBHUMANS"); WEHRMACHT, THE; WORLD WAR II

References

Beevor, A. *Stalingrad.* London: Penguin.

Erickson, J. 2000. *The Road to Stalingrad.* London: Cassell and Co.

STARACE, ACHILLE (1889–1945)

Secretary of the Italian Fascist Party from 1931 to 1939, a longer period of time than any other secretary managed to stay in the post. Starace was celebrated for his fanatical loyalty to Mussolini, so extreme that it made him an object of amusement to many. The son of a wine merchant in Gallipoli (Puglia), he graduated from Lecce Technical Institute with a degree in accountancy. After (highly decorated) service in World War I, Starace moved north to Trento, where he became a member of the Fascist Party in 1920. His active involvement in asserting Fascist power over the South Tyrol brought him to Mussolini's notice, and in 1921 he was appointed deputy secretary of the Fascist Party. He took part in the March on Rome and was put on the executive committee of the party later in 1922. In 1924 he was elected to the Chamber of Deputies. As secretary of the National Fascist Party, Starace organized massive parades and marches, suggested the implementation of anti-Semitic measures, and labored to intensify the personality cult that had developed around the figure of Mussolini. His idol was reputed to have answered, when someone referred to Starace as "a cretin," that he was a "useful cretin." After the fall of Mussolini, Starace was arrested and, though released, he was later executed by anti-Fascist partisans in 1945. His body was hung up next to that of Il Duce.

Cyprian Blamires

See Also: ANTI-SEMITISM; CULTURE (ITALY); FASCIST PARTY, THE; ITALY; LEADER CULT, THE; MARCH ON ROME, THE; MUSSOLINI, BENITO ANDREA; SALÒ REPUBLIC, THE; WAR VETERANS; WORLD WAR I

References

Festorazzi, R. 2002. *Starace: il mastino della rivoluzione fascista.* Milan: Mursia.

Germino, D. 1959. *The Italian Fascist Party in Power.* Minneapolis: University of Minnesota Press.

STATE, THE

Both Italian Fascism and National Socialism envisaged a state that was to overcome the weaknesses of the prevailing democratic systems—fragile and unstable regimes and political alliances, internal divisions into competing parties and interest groups fighting among themselves, the endless search for parliamentarian majorities through debates, and impotence in the face of economic crises. The new fascist ideal of the state was the bringing together of the divergent groups under a single state leadership and the unification of society into a *Staatsvolk.* What was ultimately desired was the "total state" controlling all areas of civil life—what we understand today as "the totalitarian form of the state."

In actual fact, however, both Italian Fascism and National Socialism replaced the rule of parties by a dual hegemony of state and (state) party; consequently, in most areas there arose in practice a structural "chaos of powers" and overlap of responsibilities for tasks between the officials legitimized by the state (ministries, administrative bureaucracies) and the elite of the party and its organizations. In National Socialism a third power ultimately emerged in the shape of the SS apparatus of Heinrich Himmler with the Gestapo, the SD, and the Reich Security Service as a kind of "state within the state." The Duce and the Fuehrer both drew their unique power from their dual roles as head of state and head of the party. Both Italian Fascism and National Socialism after the "Roehm putsch" of 1934 experienced a conflict between the party, with its "revolutionary" ideology, and the increasing need to rely on traditional-conservative elites in the civil service, the justice department, and the military. Moreover, for all the theoretical domination of a strong, monolithic "Fuehrer state," the state and the legal authorities were constantly being undermined for the sake of ideological ends or at the behest of party elites whose powers were deliberately left unclear.

The Italian Fascists were strongly of the opinion (which was reinforced following the swift capitulation of the democratic constitutional state in the face of the somewhat dilettantish March on Rome) that they must do away with the old state. In the first years after 1922, the party showed particular aggressivity and revolutionary dynamism, dramatizing the power of Il Duce and promoting a cult of power, a permanent mobilization of the masses, and a state of emergency. At the same time, Justice Minister Alfredo Rocco inaugurated a phase of state institutionalization and legal "validation" of Fascism: now there was an overemphasis on the state apparatus, the extension of state administration, and invasive prescription in almost all areas of life. With the "special legislation" (*leggi fascistissime*) of 1925/1926, all non-Fascist parties were forbidden; freedoms of the press, of assembly, and of opinion were abolished; and police state reprisals were intensified—although the apparatus of state repression did not manifest the same degree of harshness as the Nazi state later.

The state now sought primarily to establish control and direction of the economy via long-term multiyear plans; measures embraced protection of the domestic market, control over banks and capital movements, state industrialization, housebuilding and trade policies, the gagging of labor representation through the banning of unions and works councils as well as enrollment of workers in Fascist organizations, a general ban on strikes, and the unification and centralization of wage agreements. The state was now to emerge as regulator in labor disputes, while "capital" and "labor" were to be in like measure "functional" components of a centrally directed state. The expansion of the state sector and a rapid increase in the number of state officials were to ensure the loyalty of the masses alongside the enrollment of women and young people in state organizations. With the extensive state, administrative, and constitutional reform of 1925/1926, the powers of Mussolini as president were widened; he ruled with the help of the "Grand Fascist Council," among others. All social groups and interest associations, but especially the individual branches of the economy, were brought together in corporations or "syndicates" and were to collaborate with the ends of state and party. A corporatist state emerged whose theoretical conception owed much to the "universalism" of Othmar Spann.

The world economic crises of the 1920s and later the requirements of war leadership at the side of Nazi Germany led, however, after the conclusion of a concordat with the Vatican, to a clear weakening of those modernistic-technocratic tendencies and measures that early Fascism had embraced. The reconciliation of Fascism and Catholicism led to a shift toward a strong politics of Christian-conservative order and to an involvement of conservative, traditionalist, and nationalistic forces on the side of the state. What emerged eventually was an Italian "National Fascism," a development favored by the mass integration of the traditionally conservative-Catholic population.

The National Socialists subjected the state apparatus to the ideological goals of the party more vigorously than the Italian Fascists, so that the main political objectives of the National Socialists—exclusion of Jews from public life, suppression of nonconformists, the militaristic and nationalistic education of the young, and later the euthanasia program and the genocide of the Jews—were implemented with the help of the state apparatus and the administrative bureaucracy. The precedence of the ideological in the National Socialist state had its roots in *völkisch* nationalism and racism, which Hitler had declared in *Mein Kampf* to be the foundation of the state. The state was not "an end in itself" but had to serve the "conservation and elevation of the race." States must be "*völkisch* states," since the "higher mission" of the state lay in "national character" and the "unity of blood." The error of previous state forms had lain in the toleration of "racial crossing" and "bastardization": the *völkisch* state had the task of supervising breeding, including the elimination of all the sick and "inferior." That must be the goal of all state political measures and the education of young persons, which must be education in "race understanding and race feeling" and state "selection of the capable." A true state leadership was possible only with "race homogeneity," and the goal was the "unified state" in which "everything is regulated from the center" (*Hitler's Monologues,* 16 November 1941).

In 1933 the National Socialists began to lay the foundations for the authoritarian "Fuehrer state" under cover of the ideology of a "legal revolution." State and society were to be transformed from the bottom up, but working with "legal means" through the appointment of Hitler as chancellor of the Reich, so that the "will of the German people" in its totality would find expression. Since the NSDAP was the only "state party," the NS leadership coined the formula "unity of party and state" (1933–1934). But the definition of the new National Socialist state proved rather imprecise, and the parallelism of powers between state and party posts soon led to persistent rivalries. The leading NS administration bureaucrats around Wilhelm Frick sought to establish a strong civil service state against the power of the party officials, but in the war years it was subjected to the brutal party and SS leadership around Goebbels, Himmler, and Bormann.

A special construct was the "Fuehrer state." Political theorists like Carl Schmitt and especially Ernst Forsthoff (*Der totale Staat,* 1933) constructed the "identification of leader and led," whereby the charismatically elevated person of the Fuehrer represented not only the will of state and party but also the totality of all Germans. According to the "Fuehrer principle," Hitler ruled not in the context of a constitution but as "the personification of the will of the people." Hitler stated: "The Fuehrer principle conditions a pyramid-style structure of organization in the details as in the whole. At the summit stands the Fuehrer. He appoints the necessary leaders for the individual areas of work of the leadership of the Reich, the party apparatus, and the administration of the state" (*Organisationsbuch der NSDAP,* 1943, p. 86).

Markus Hattstein
(translated by Cyprian Blamires)

See Also: ABSTRACTION; ANTI-SEMITISM; ARYANISM; BANKS, THE; BLOOD; BORMANN, MARTIN; CAPITALISM; CATHOLIC CHURCH, THE; COMMUNITY; CORPORATISM; COSMOPOLITANISM; DEMOCRACY; ECONOMICS; ELITE THEORY; EUGENICS; FASCIST PARTY, THE; FRICK, WILHELM; GERMANY; GESTAPO, THE; GOEBBELS, (PAUL) JOSEPH; GRAND COUNCIL OF FASCISM, THE; HIMMLER, HEINRICH; HITLER, ADOLF; HOLOCAUST, THE; INDIVIDUALISM; INDUSTRY; ITALY; LABOR FRONT, THE; LAW; LEADER CULT, THE; MARCH ON ROME, THE; MASSES, THE ROLE OF THE; MILITARISM; MUSSOLINI, BENITO ANDREA; NATIONALISM; NAZISM; NIGHT OF THE LONG KNIVES, THE; PALINGENETIC MYTH; PARLIAMENTARISM; RACIAL DOCTRINE; RACISM; REVOLUTION; ROCCO, ALFREDO; SCHMITT, CARL; SD, THE; SOCIOLOGY; SOCIALISM; SPANN, OTHMAR; SS, THE; THIRD REICH, THE; TOTALITARIANISM; TRADES UNIONS; *VOLK, VÖLKISCH; VOLKSGEMEINSCHAFT,* THE; WALL STREET CRASH, THE; WARRIOR ETHOS, THE; WOMEN; YOUTH

References

Burleigh, M., and W. Wippermann. 1991. *The Racial State: Germany 1933–45.* Cambridge: Cambridge University Press.

Gregor, A. James. 2005. *Mussolini's Intellectuals: Fascist Social and Political Thought.* Princeton: Princeton University Press.

Griffin, R. 1991. *The Nature of Fascism.* London: Routledge.

Linz, J. 2000. *Totalitarian and Authoritarian Regimes.* London: Lynne Rienner.
Payne, S. 1995. *A History of Fascism, 1914–1945.* London: University College London Press.

STAUFFENBERG, CLAUS SCHENK GRAF VON (1907–1944)

Prime mover of the July Plot, responsible for leaving the explosive in Hitler's headquarters that nearly killed the Fuehrer. Stauffenberg was born in a castle in Franconia into an aristocratic family. He was badly wounded in 1943 while serving in a cavalry regiment but survived to be appointed chief of staff of the Army Ordnance Department. His period of convalescence saw him turn against Hitler, and he joined the Kreisau Circle. Stauffenberg was executed later on the day of the abortive assassination attempt.

Cyprian Blamires

See Also: ANTI-FASCISM; CONSERVATISM; GERMANY; HITLER, ADOLF; JULY PLOT, THE; KREISAU CIRCLE, THE; WORLD WAR II

References
Baigent, M., and Richard Leigh. 1994. *Secret Germany: Claus von Stauffenberg and the Mystical Crusade against Hitler.* London: Cape.
Hoffmann, Peter. 2003. *Stauffenberg.* Montreal: McGill-Queens University Press.

STERILIZATION: *See* EUGENICS; HEALTH; SOCIAL DARWINISM

STOECKER, ADOLF (1835–1909)

German Lutheran theologian and court preacher, conservative anti-Semitic politician, and anticipator of some aspects of Nazism. In 1878 he founded the Christian-Social Workers' Party (after 1881 the Christian-Social Party), originally as a Christian conservative rival to Social Democracy. He used anti-Semitism as a weapon in the struggle against liberalism and Social Democracy and for a Christian-conservative Germany, without, however, reaching the workers as he hoped. He gained much more response from craftsmen and tradesmen, white-collar workers, and minor officials. Stoecker's party called for the exclusion of Jews from all official positions of authority and a prohibition on their immigration. Although Stoecker opposed the most radical anti-Semites in that he accepted that Jews could be changed by baptism, he did not always differ from them in his demands and in his choice of words. He played an important part in the spread of anti-Semitism in the German Lutheran Church.

Michael Schäbitz
(translated by Cyprian Blamires)

See Also: ANTI-SEMITISM; CHRISTIANITY; GERMANY; LIBERALISM; LUTHERAN CHURCHES, THE; NATIONALISM; PROTESTANTISM; SOCIALISM

References
Mosse, George L. 1964. *The Crisis of German Ideology: Intellectual Origins of the Third Reich.* London: Weidenfeld and Nicholson.
Pulzer, Peter. 1988 [1964]. *The Rise of Political Anti-Semitism in Germany and Austria.* London: Peter Halban.

STOJADINOVIĆ, MILAN (1888–1961)

Serbian politician and financial expert, prime minister of the Kingdom of Yugoslavia between 1935 and 1939, and founder of the profascist political party Jugoslovenska Radikalna Zajednica (Yugoslav Radical Union). Stojadinović began his political career in 1922 as a financial expert in the government of Nikola Pašić. In the 1920s and 1930s he intermittently held the office of finance minister before forming a government in 1935. While in office, he promoted closer ties with Hitler and Mussolini and modeled his government on the fascist regimes of Italy, Germany, and Romania. He founded the "Greenshirts," the Yugoslav equivalent of Hitler's "Brownshirts," introducing a fascist style salute and the title of *Vođa* ("Leader"). Sto-jadinović's government was dissolved by Prince Pavle Karađorđević in 1939.

Jovan Byford

See Also: FASCIST PARTY, THE; GERMANY; HITLER, ADOLF; ITALY; LEADER CULT, THE; LJOTIĆ, DIMITRIJE; MUS-SOLINI, BENITO ANDREA; NAZISM; ROMANIA; SALUTES; SERBS, THE; STYLE; YUGOSLAVIA

Reference
Rothschild, Joseph. 1974. *East Central Europe between the Two World Wars.* Seattle: University of Washington Press.

STORM TROOPERS: *See* SA, THE

STRASSER BROTHERS, THE

Leading advocates of an anticapitalist, but no less fascist and anti-Semitic, alignment of National Socialism. Gregor Strasser (1892–1934) reorganized the NSDAP after its unbanning in 1925 and served as the party's *Reichsorganisationsleiter* ("head of organization") from 1927. Following failed attempts to build an alliance with anticapitalist parts of the NSDAP, trades unions, and the army, he resigned from all party functions in December 1932 and was murdered by SS units in June 1934. His younger brother, Otto (1897–1974), left the NSDAP in 1930 to form national-revolutionary organizations, most notably the so-called Schwarze Front, and was exiled in 1933.

Stefan Vogt

See Also: ANTI-SEMITISM; CAPITALISM; CLASS; GERMANY; NAZISM; NIGHT OF THE LONG KNIVES, THE; REVOLU-TION; SOCIALISM; SS, THE; TRADES UNIONS

References
Reed, D. 1953. *The Prisoner of Ottawa: Otto Strasser.* London: Cape.
Smelser, Ronald, and Rainer Zitelmann. 1989. *The Nazi Elite.* Trans. Mary Fischer. Basingstoke: Macmillan.
Stachura, P. D. 1983. *Gregor Strasser and the Rise of Nazism.* London: Allen and Unwin.

STRASSERISM: *See* CLASS; STRASSER BROTHERS, THE

STRATEGY OF TENSION, THE: *See* TENSION, THE STRATEGY OF

STREICHER, JULIUS (1885–1946)

One of the most notorious Nazis, on account of the sheer degree of his obsessive hatred of Jews and his work as tabloid-style propagandist for Nazism. Streicher was one of the first NSDAP members (1922), and after taking part in the Munich Putsch of 1923 he was suspended from his job as a teacher. In 1923 he established the inflammatory anti-Semitic weekly newspaper *Der Stürmer* and became *Gauleiter* in the Bavarian district of Franken in 1925. After 1933, Streicher joined the Reich Parliament, distributed anti-Semitic children's books, and was leader of the Central Committee of the Boycott Movement, which organized economic boycotts against Jews in the 1930s. In 1940 he fell out with Goering but went on publishing *Der Stürmer.* Sentenced to death in the Nuremberg Trials, he was executed on 16 October 1946.

Fabian Virchow

See Also: ANTI-SEMITISM; GOERING, HERMANN; HOLO-CAUST, THE; MITFORD FAMILY, THE; MUNICH (BEER-HALL) PUTSCH, THE; NAZISM; NUREMBERG TRIALS, THE; PRESS, THE; PROPAGANDA; *STÜRMER, DER*

References
Bytwerk, Randall L. 2001. *Julius Streicher: Nazi Editor of the Notorious Anti-Semitic Newspaper Der Stürmer.* New York: Cooper Square.
Varga, William P. 1981. *The Number One Nazi Jew-Baiter: A Political Biography of Julius Streicher, Hitler's Chief Anti-Semitic Propagandist.* New York: Carlton.

STRENGTH THROUGH JOY: *See* LEISURE; TRADES UNIONS
STRIKES: *See* TRADES UNIONS
STROESSNER, ALFREDO: *See* PARAGUAY
STUDENTS: *See* EDUCATION; MEDICINE; YOUTH
STURMABTEILUNG: See SA, THE

STÜRMER, DER

Crude and semipornographic weekly publication established in 1923 by Julius Streicher to spread anti-Semitic propaganda. Its subtitle was *Nürnberger Wochenblatt zum Kampf um die Wahrheit* (*Nuremberg Weekly for the Battle for Truth*), the word *Nuremberg* being changed to *Deutsches* ("German") in 1933. It published reports of the "race shame" of Aryan women having sexual relations with Jewish men and tales of Jewish "ritual murder." It contained appeals to the readers to denounce "friends of the Jews." In the 1920s it sold 2,000 to 3,000 copies weekly, but in 1933 the circulation rose to 20,000; by 1944 it had reached 400,000.

Cyprian Blamires

See Also: ANTI-SEMITISM; ARYANISM; GERMANNESS (*DEUTSCHHEIT*); HOLOCAUST, THE; PRESS, THE; PROPAGANDA; RACIAL DOCTRINE; STREICHER, JULIUS

References
Bytwerk, Randall L. *Julius Streicher: Nazi Editor of the Notorious Anti-Semitic Newspaper "Der Stürmer."* Lanham, MD: Cooper Square.
Showalter, Dennis E. *Little Man, What Now?: "Der Stürmer" in the Weimar Republic.* North Haven, CT: Shoe String.

STURZO, LUIGI: *See* CLERICO-FASCISM; POLITICAL CATHOLICISM

STYLE

Since the 1970s many attempts to define *fascism* have broached the subject of a specifically fascist "style" of organization and politics. Juan J. Linz (1979) provided a definition that took into account style as one of the three main broad criteria (the other two being "negations" and "goals"). This tridimensional approach was emphatically restated in Stanley G. Payne's authoritative recent work on interwar fascism. In it, Payne produces an "ideal" checklist of fascist stylistic elements, including "political choreography," charismatic leadership, a cult of violence, glorification of youth, militarization, and a male-dominated social discourse. Beyond the obvious paradigms of Italian Fascism and National Socialism, the general fascination of sectors of the European Right with fascism as exemplified in interwar Italy and Germany resulted in the widespread appropriation, imitation, or adaptation of this fascist "style."

The fascist "style" of politics was much more than a set of pragmatic devices calculated to ensure more effective social control and political decision-making. It was an extension of fascist utopianism, reverberating its quest for a totally novel conception of societal life and political conduct. It also constituted a particular articulation of fascism's own brand of "totalitarianism," aiming to appeal to—and help promote—an "organic" and "holistic" vision of national life. It also provided crucial definitions and clarifications of what fascist utopianism meant by its organic hypernationalist discourse, and how it perceived the process of social transformation toward its own teleological vision. The Italian and German cases produced an informal blueprint for imitation that a number of interwar right-wing movements and regimes found hard to resist in their search for a "third" path to politics and a new populist framework for nationalist, antiliberal, and antisocialist mobilization.

The extent to which the stylistic elements of either the Italian Fascist or the National Socialist experience influenced our perceptions of fascist "style" is difficult to exaggerate. The "charismatic" authority of the two leaders, in terms of both their adulation by their movements' membership and the subsequent leader cult propagated by the regimes, was replicated in almost all interwar fascist movements and regimes. From the Iron Guard's mystical idolization of its leader Codreanu, to the similar glorification of Oswald Mosley in Britain and Antonio Primo de Reivera in Spain's Falange; from the official state cult of Ioannis Metaxas in Greece to the reluctant charismatization of Antonio Salazar in Portugal and Francisco Franco in post-1939 Spain, far-right leaders capitalized heavily on the appeal of charismatic rule as exemplified by Mussolini and Hitler. At the same time, the "sacralization" of politics—evidenced by the widespread use of rituals, emotional symbols, and a quasi-religious discourse of legitimation—spread across the continent as a reaction to the alleged rationality and agnosticism of liberal and socialist models. The balcony, the *piazza,* the popular rally, the choreographed march—often supported by symbols of total national reference—all revolved around and paid service to the alleged mystic union between leadership and nation. Youth, women's, and leisure organizations, employed in a coordinated way as devices for totalitarian, organic, controlled mobilization of the whole of society, became omnipresent in interwar Europe, not only in indisputably fascist cases but also in most authoritarian and parafascist regimes. Finally, the particular fascist-totalitarian mix of consensus and coercion allowed for the co-opting of trademark repressive elements, such as the overall model of "surveillance society," supported by secret police and an informal network of informants, geared toward eliminating any form of opposition and dissent from the allegedly organic discourse of the regime.

With the exception of a restricted sample of "neofascist" phenomena that unashamedly fetichize stylistic elements (insignia, marches) or idolize deceased fascist leaders, the bulk of the postwar experience of extreme right-wing politics manifests very little or no relevance to the interwar "style." Clearly, fundamental changes in the wider cultural and political environment of the postwar period have transformed the representation of extreme-right-wing politics, rendering many of its interwar stylistic features anachronistic or redundant. Contemporary fascism is still capable of transmitting its distinct message of rebirth with an aggressive ethno-exclusive discourse without having to seek recourse to the formalistic trappings of its discredited interwar precedents. This does not, however, mean that the interwar fascist "style" has been totally abandoned, or that there is no such distinct contemporary model for the extreme Right. Populist discourses of national mobilization supported by mass rallies and extensive use of national symbols, as well as strong leader-oriented parties—such as Vladimir Zhirinovsky's Liberal Democratic Party of Russia (LDPR) and Jean-Marie Le Pen's Front National in France—maintain links with the interwar fascist prototype, albeit on a fundamentally updated and eclectic basis. More respectable and adaptable, less ritualistic and mystical, having tactically abandoned its interwar fundamental opposition to democracy and liberalism, contemporary fascism continues to experiment with new communication strategies and organizational principles.

Aristotle Kallis

See Also: INTRODUCTION; ABSTRACTION; AUTHORITARIANISM; CODREANU, CORNELIU ZELEA; COMMUNITY; D'ANNUNZIO, GABRIELE; DEMOCRACY; FALANGE; FASCIST PARTY, THE; FIUME; FRANCE; FRANCO Y BAHAMONDE, GENERAL FRANCISCO; GERMANY; GOEBBELS, (PAUL) JOSEPH; GREAT BRITAIN; GREECE; HITLER, ADOLF; IRON GUARD, THE; ITALY; LE PEN, JEAN-MARIE; LEADER CULT, THE; LEISURE; LIBERALISM; MARXISM; MECHANISTIC THINKING; METAXAS, IOANNIS; MILITARISM; MOSLEY, SIR OSWALD; MUSSOLINI, BENITO ANDREA; MYSTICISM; NA-TIONAL FRONT, THE (FRANCE); NATIONALISM; NAZISM; NIHILISM; NUREMBERG RALLIES, THE; ORGANICISM; PALINGENETIC MYTH; PARAFASCISM; PORTUGAL; POSTWAR FASCISM; PRIMO DE RIVERA, JOSÉ ANTONIO; PROPAGANDA; RATIONALISM; RELIGION; RUSSIA; SALAZAR, ANTÓNIO DE OLIVEIRA; SALUTES; SOCIALISM; SPAIN; SPORT; *SQUADRISMO;* SWASTIKA, THE; SYMBOLS; TERROR; THIRD WAY, THE; TOTALITARIANISM; UTOPIA, UTOPIANISM; WOMEN; YOUTH

References

De Grand, A. J. 1995. *Fascist Italy and Nazi Germany: The "Fascist" Style of Rule.* London: Routledge.

Eatwell, Roger. 2002. "The Rebirth of Right-Wing Charisma? The Cases of Jean-Marie Le Pen and Vladimir Zhirinovsky." *Totalitarian Movements and Political Religions* 3, no. 3: 1–24.

Gentile, Emilio. 1996. *The Sacralization of Politics in Fascist Italy.* Cambridge: Harvard University Press.

Griffin, Roger. 2000. "Interregnum or Endgame? Radical Right Thought in the 'Post-fascist' Era." *Journal of Political Ideologies* 5: 163–178.

Larsen, Stein, ed. 2001 *Fascism outside Europe.* Boulder, CO: Social Science Monographs.

Linz, J. J. 1979. "Some Notes towards a Comparative Study of Fascism in Sociological Historical Perspective." Pp. 29–39 in *Fascism: A Reader's Guide: Analyses, Interpretations, Bibliography,* edited by W. Laqueur. Harmondsworth: Penguin.

O'Sullivan, N. 1983. *Fascism.* London: Dent.

Payne, Stanley G. 1980. "The Concept of Fascism." In *Who Were the Fascists: Social Roots of European Fascism,* edited by Stein Ugelvik Larsen, Bernt Hagtvet, and Jan Petter Myklebust. Bergen: Universitetsforlaget.

———. 1997. *A History of Fascism, 1918–1945.* London: UCL.

SUBHUMANS: *See UNTERMENSCHEN*

SUDETENLAND, THE

Prior to post–World War I settlement in 1919, a territory in Bohemia adjoining Germany that had been part of the Austro-Hungarian Empire. Its population included some 3 million German-speakers. Agitation by pro-Nazi elements led by Konrad Henlein resulted in its assignation to Germany by the terms of the Munich Pact in 1938. This event was a focal point in Hitler's drive to create a "greater Germany." After the war the German population was expelled from the Sudetenland, which was resettled by Czechs.

Cyprian Blamires

See Also: APPEASEMENT; AUSTRO-HUNGARIAN EMPIRE/
HABSBURG EMPIRE, THE; CZECHOSLOVAKIA; EXPANSION-
ISM; GERMANY; HENLEIN, KONRAD; HITLER, ADOLF;
IRREDENTISM; *MEIN KAMPF;* MUNICH AGREEMENT/PACT,
THE; PANGERMANISM; SLOVAKIA; VERSAILLES, THE
TREATY OF; WORLD WAR I

Reference
Smelser, R. M. 1975. *The Sudeten Problem.* Middletown, CT:
Wesleyan University Press.

SUPERMAN, THE: *See* NEW MAN, THE; NIETZSCHE, FRIEDRICH

SURVIVALISM

U.S. movement of the postwar era concerned with sur-
viving nuclear, environmental, or societal catastrophe
that contains a fascistic wing. Survivalists tend to be
united in their belief that modern society is on the
verge of collapse, that governments will be unable or
unwilling to protect them when such a collapse occurs,
and that, as a result, people must become self-sufficient
and able to look after themselves. Depending upon
their particular concerns, different survivalists prepare
for such impending crises in different ways: some construct fallout shelters; others learn how to hunt and
make their own clothes; some stockpile food and water
supplies, invest in gold and silver, or develop emergency communication networks; while others amass
weaponry and ammunition, or withdraw to fortified
compounds to prepare for the perceived conflict to
come. Survivalists can be found throughout the world,
but they have an especially strong presence in the
United States. The roots of survivalism are located in
anxieties about the creation and use of atomic weapons
during World War II, the military involvement of the
United States in Korea and Vietnam, and tensions with
the Soviet Union during the Cold War. Under the influence of magazines such as *American Survival Guide*
and *Soldier of Fortune,* the paramilitary aspects of survivalism came increasingly to the fore during the late
1970s and early 1980s. However, it is those elements of
the survivalist Right that have Christian Identity beliefs
(that white "Aryans" are the descendants of the lost
tribes of Israel, that Jews are children of Satan, and that
blacks and other minorities are "mud people," for ex-

ample), such as John Harrell's and Jack Mohr's Christian Patriots Defense League and James Ellison's
Covenant, Sword and Arm of the Lord, that have been
the cause of the greatest concern about the dangers
posed by survivalism to U.S. society.

Darren Mulloy

See Also: ANTI-SEMITISM; ARYAN NATIONS; ARYANISM;
CHRISTIAN IDENTITY; COLD WAR, THE; CONSPIRACY
THEORIES; DECADENCE; PARAMILITARISM; POSTWAR
FASCISM; RACISM; RADIO; UNITED STATES, THE (POST-
WAR); WORLD WAR II; ZIONIST OCCUPATION GOVERN-
MENT, THE (ZOG)

References
Barkun, Michael. 1994. *Religion and the Racist Right: The
Origins of the Christian Identity Movement.* Chapel Hill:
University of North Carolina Press.
Coates, James. 1995. *Armed and Dangerous: The Rise of the
Survivalist Right.* New York: Hill and Wang.
Lamy, Philip. 1996. *Millennium Rage: Survivalists, White
Supremacists and the Doomsday Prophecy.* New York:
Plenum.
Mitchell, Richard G. 2002. *Dancing at Armageddon:
Survivalism and Chaos in Modern Times.* Chicago: University
of Chicago Press.

SWASTIKA, THE

HISTORICAL BACKGROUND

An equilateral cross with its arms bent to the right,
used as their logo by the German Nazis. It is a very ancient and widespread ornamental symbol, found in the
fourth millennium B.C. on Persian pottery and later in
Greece, India, Tibet, Japan, and among the American
Indians. It is a very holy symbol in Hinduism, Jainism,
and Buddhism. It has wide currency in India, where
temples and festivals are often decorated with
swastikas, and its etymology is in fact Sanskrit (*svastika:*
"lucky"), where it was used of auspicious objects or of
marks meant to bring good fortune. Essentially, it
means something like "lucky charm." In the nineteenth
century the theorization of an Indo-European group of
languages led to a quest for links between modern Europeans and ancient Indo-Iranians ("Aryans"). Objects
decorated with the swastika were found in the ruins of
Troy, and this gave rise to the suggestion that it was a
symbol specific to the Indo-Europeans. The symbol
then became a popular one in the West. Its attraction

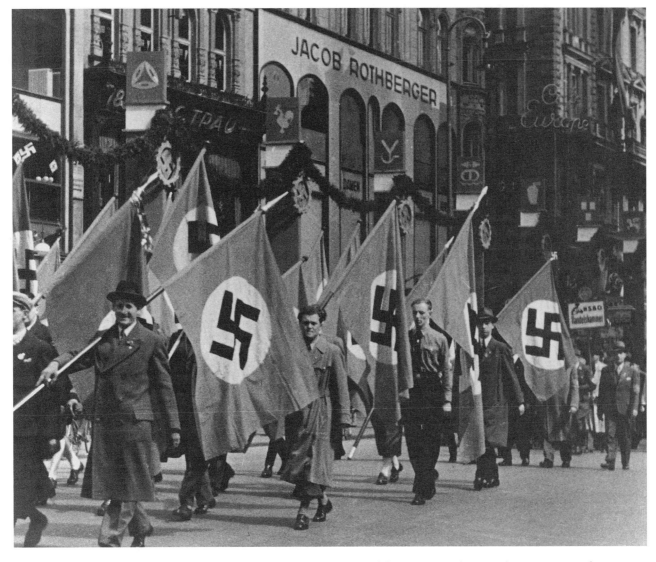

Flags bearing the swastika, the symbol of Nazism. It was in fact borrowed from Asian tradition and was seen as a reference to the 'superior' Aryan race which had originated in the East. (Library of Congress)

to the Nazis arose from the fact that their philosophy depended on an identification of modern Germanic peoples with an Aryan master race.

Cyprian Blamires

AS A SYMBOL OF NAZISM

When the swastika was adopted as an emblem by Adolf Hitler and the DAP in 1919, it was already associated with a pan-European, anti-Semitic discourse, constructed around fantasies of a superior "Aryan" race. The new insignia and flag made its first appearance at a rally of the new Nazi Party (NSDAP) in Mu-

nich in May 1920. Hitler's inclusion of the swastika symbol in his design for the flag was part of an attempt to redefine the Bismarckian concept of the German state according to the racial ideology and expansionist project" of a single party. The Nazi flag can therefore be regarded as a collage of elements serving a specific strategy of territorial conquest. In *Mein Kampf*, Hitler gives an account of the design of the swastika banner as a graphic synthesis of the black, white, and red colors of Bismarck's flag of 1866, with a symbol that could mark a distinction between the Nazi project and the values of earlier German nationalism, tarnished by the defeat of Germany in World War I. Hitler also saw other design advantages in the swastika as a visually distinctive device that would be clearly recognizable on posters, insignia, uniforms, armbands, and flags. Both the form of the Nazi flag and the direction of its critique indicate that the swastika was used to mark a set of differences—between Nazism and German nationalism, between Nazism and communism, and between the "Aryan" and the Jew. The anti-Semitic discourse around the swastika had developed in the nineteenth century in the writings of Aryanists such as Emile Burnouf, Michael Zmigrodski, and Lanz von Liebenfels and was characterized by an ahistorical and romantic appeal to purity of blood. The politicization and militarization of this discourse in Nazi propaganda also establishes differences between Nazism and its precursor, Italian Fascism. As the historian Ernst Nolte has observed, the Nazi flag, unlike the lictor's bundle of Italian Fascism, did not recall a particular historical era but a racial consciousness whose greatness was "lost" in history and whose ultimate victory lay in the future. Nolte's thesis is that Nazism was fascism in extremis, but it may also be suggested that Nazism was racist extremism in the form of a fascist political program. Nazism, in other words, may be thought of as fascism plus the swastika. The "afterlife" of the Nazi swastika in the visual lexicon of extreme racist groups, and the relative decline of the emblems of Italian Fascism, may support this conclusion.

Malcolm Quinn

See Also: INTRODUCTION; ANTI-SEMITISM; ARYANISM; BUDDHISM; EXPANSIONISM; FASCIO, THE; FASCIST PARTY, THE; GERMANNESS (*DEUTSCHHEIT*); GERMANY; HITLER, ADOLF; ITALY; MARXISM; *MEIN KAMPF;* NATIONALISM; NAZISM; NORDIC SOUL, THE; NOVEMBER CRIMINALS/ *NOVEMBERBRECHER*, THE; PROPAGANDA; RACIAL DOCTRINE; RACISM; SOCIALISM; SYMBOLS; TIBET; TRADITION; VERSAILLES, THE TREATY OF; WORLD WAR I

References
Burnouf, Emile. 1888. *The Science of Religions.* London: Swan, Sonnerschein, and Lowry.
Heller, Steven. 1992. "Symbol of the Century." *Print* 46: 39–49.
Hitler, Adolf. 1925–1927, 1992. *Mein Kampf.* London: Pimlico.
Goodrick-Clarke, Nicholas. 1985. *The Occult Roots of Nazism.* Wellingborough: Aquarian.
Kahn, Douglas. 1985. *John Heartfield: Art and the Mass Media.* New York: Tanam.
Memminger, Anton. 1922. *Hackenkreuz und Davidstern.* Würzburg: Gebruder Memminger.
Nolte, Ernst. 1965. *Three Faces of Fascism.* London: Encounter.
Quinn, Malcolm. 1994. *The Swastika: Constructing the Symbol.* London: Routledge.
Wilson, Thomas. 1896. *The Swastika, the Earliest Known Symbol and Its Migrations.* Washington, DC: U.S. National Museum.

SWEDEN

Sweden's first fascist party, the Swedish National Socialist Freedom Federation (Nationalsocialistiska Frihetsförbundet), was founded in 1924. Through a number of transformations, this party became the core of the Swedish National Socialist Party (Svenska Nationalsocialistiska Partiet; SNSP), which was led by Birger Furugård and which was to constitute one of two major Nazi parties in interwar Sweden. The second party, the National Socialist Workers Party (Nationalsocialistiska Arbetarepartiet; NSAP) under the leadership of Sven-Olov Lindholm, was founded in 1933 through a split within the SNSP. The cause of the split was both organizational and ideological. The SNSP advocated a more traditionalist path, while the NSAP had a much more radical political program. The SNSP was in addition more mimetic in regard to German Nazism, whereas the NSAP struggled to formulate its own indigenous Nazism, ideologically as well as organizationally independent from Germany. The more radical stance of the NSAP can partly be explained by the fact that many of its leaders had old ties to the only Italian-style fascist organization in Sweden, Sweden's Fascist Combat Organization (Sveriges Fascistiska Kamporganisation; SFKO). The SFKO was founded in 1926 as a radical and extremely activist militia that was modeled on the Italian *squadrismo.* In the late 1920s, however, the organization oscillated toward Nazism and eventually joined ranks with the SNSP.

Later in 1933 yet another alleged Nazi party was founded in the form of the National Socialist Bloc (Nationalsocialistiska Blocket; NSB), which had a strong upper-class following. Despite its name, the party should not be defined as ideologically fascist but radical right. It never became very successful, partly because of the total want of charisma of the party leader, Colonel Martin Ekström, and it vanished in 1936. The SNSP was also terminated in 1936, and its members were encouraged to join the NSAP. The immediate reason for the termination was its disastrous showing in the general election of 1936, in which the party, in coalition with the NSB, gained a mere handful of votes and only about one-sixth of the support of the NSAP.

Peaking in the mid-1930s, the Nazi parties could muster a following of around 30,000 members out of a population of 6.5 million. To that should be added the membership of the radical-right Sweden's National

Federation (Sveriges Nationella Förbund; SNF), which has been estimated at close to 40,000 in the mid-1930s. The history of the SNF goes back to 1915, when the organization was founded as an independent youth organization with close ties to the conservatives. In 1933, there was a split with the conservative party as a result of organizational problems and ideological conflicts regarding parliamentary rules and economic policies; during the 1930s the SNF can be characterized as radical-right, oscillating toward fascism proper around 1940. The reason for this ideological drift was a gradual loss of long-time and more traditionalist supporters, which paved the way for a more radical and gradually more fascistized fraction. This development was enhanced when the SNF in 1937 merged with the National Federation of the New Sweden (Riksförbundet det Nya Sverige; RNS) under the leadership of Per Engdahl (1909–1994). Engdahl started his political career in the SFKO, but when that organization turned to Nazism, Engdahl broke free and started his own movement. Like the NSAP, the Engdahl movement tried to steer clear of the German influence, formulating the idea of New Swedishness. Centered on the notion of a corporatist people's state, Engdahl's elaborated fascist vision differs from both Nazism and Italian-style Fascism, forming a specific variant of independent, indigenous fascism. The cooperation between the SNF and the Engdahl movement ended in 1942, when Engdahl started Swedish Opposition (Svensk Opposition), which was meant as an umbrella organization for the different ultranationalist groups in Sweden, but which was perceived as a competitor by the SNF.

Completing the ideological spectrum of interwar fascism is Sweden's Socialist Party (Sveriges Socialistiska Parti; SSP) under Nils Flyg. Originally communist in outlook and a former member of the Comintern, the party split in 1937 after a substantial part of its members had become increasingly critical of the Comintern in favor of an independent national communism. Initially trying to avoid fascism proper, the party appeared openly as a fascist party from 1941.

The NSAP, having changed its name to the Swedish Socialist Coalition (Svensk Socialistisk Samling; SSS) in 1938, went out of existence in 1950. The SNF and the Engdahl movement, which was renamed the New Swedish Movement (Nysvenska Rörelsen; NSR) after the war, still exist. After the war the SNF became an important advocate of Holocaust denial through its leader, Rütger Essén. Engdahl played an important part in the establishment of the MSI, also known as the Malmö Movement, in the 1950s. In the 1960s he became an ardent proponent of ecofascism, the merging of fascism and environmentalism. In the late 1980s, fascist movements started to gain momentum again, but in different forms from those of the interwar period. The organizations that survived the war saw little of this new wave of support. Instead, it was the militant White Power movement centered around the skinhead culture that started to grow, heavily influenced by British groups. One of many peaks of White Power activism in Sweden in the 1990s occurred in 1991–1992 and was centered on the group White Aryan Resistance (Vitt Ariskt Motstånd, VAM), which was heavily influenced by its U.S. counterpart and which made use of ZOG rhetoric.

Besides a strong White Power scene, Sweden has also, from the late 1980s onward, seen a growth in both political populism—mainly in the shape of New Democracy (Ny Demokrati), which held seats in parliament from 1991 to 1994—and ethnocratic semifascist groups similar to the Front National and the old MSI. The most successful of the latter are the Sweden Democrats (Sverigedemokraterna; SD), who have been increasingly successful in local elections from the 1990s onward but who still lack parliamentary representation.

Lena Berggren

See Also: COMINTERN, THE; CONSERVATISM; CORPORATISM; ECOLOGY; FASCIST PARTY, THE; GERMANY; HOLOCAUST DENIAL; IMMIGRATION; ITALY; MARXISM; MOVIMENTO SOCIALE ITALIANO, THE; NATIONAL FRONT, THE (FRANCE); NATIONALISM; NAZISM; NEO-NAZISM; POSTWAR FASCISM; RACISM; SKINHEAD FASCISM; SOCIALISM; *SQUADRISMO;* UNITED STATES, THE (POSTWAR); WHITE SUPREMACISM; XENOPHOBIA; ZIONIST OCCUPATION GOVERNMENT, THE (ZOG)

References

Berggren, Lena. 2002. "Swedish Fascism—Why Bother?" *Journal of Contemporary History* 37, no. 3: 395–417.
Lindström, Ulf. 1985. *Fascism in Scandinavia, 1920–1940.* Stockholm: Almqvist and Wiksell.

SWITZERLAND

Fascist organizations have emerged periodically in Switzerland since 1918. They reached their apogee at the beginning of the 1930s. Since World War II, right-wing radicalism has experienced several revivals. Anti-immigration parties have been more important than openly fascist organizations. The first protofascist tendencies were already registered in the antisocialist

Despite its benevolent and tolerant image, Switzerland has seen the emergence of numerous far-right groups in the postwar years. This is a poster for one of them, Nationale Aktion, founded in 1961; it calls for restrictions on immigration. (Library of Congress)

militias during and after the 1918 general strike. They came together in the Vaterlaendische Verband in 1919. In 1925, the anti-Semitic Heimatwehr was founded as the first clearly fascist organization. Numerous fascist groupings, the fronts, were created at the beginning of the 1930s. In 1933 they achieved several electoral successes (26.7 percent in Schaffhausen, 9 percent in Geneva, 7.8 percent in Zurich). After those initial successes, their numbers dropped dramatically, however. The Nationale Front, which existed from 1930 to 1940 under the leadership of Rolf Henne and Robert Tobler, was the strongest front in the German-speaking part of Switzerland. Tobler was a member of parliament between 1935 and 1939. Several smaller organizations split off—for instance, the Volksbund, the Eidgenoessische Soziale Arbeiter-Partei, and the Bund treuer Eidgenossen nationalsozialistischer Weltan-

schauung. In the French-speaking part of Switzerland, the Union Nationale in Geneva was the most important fascist organization. Its leader, Georges Oltramare, got financial support from Mussolini. Oltramare left the movement in 1939, after a failed attempt to merge with the Liberal Party. Afterward, the Union Nationale disappeared.

The borders between the traditional bourgeois parties and the fronts were fluid. Many antisocialists admired Mussolini as a victor over the labor movement. In 1937, he even received an honorary doctorate from the University of Lausanne. One Swiss intellectual sympathizing with fascism stands out from all the others: Gonzague de Reynold. Other politicians, prominent among them Catholic-conservative ministers Jean-Marie Musy, Giuseppe Motta, and Philipp Etter, embraced these ideas. The bourgeois parties and the fronts united against social democratic–dominated local governments in several elections. After the defeat of France in 1940, Swiss fascism reawakened. The Nationale Bewegung was created, whose representatives got an audience with President Marcel Pilet-Golaz in October 1940, and in November of that year, a petition of two hundred demanded measures against media hostile to Germany. Despite several prohibitions, the fascist organizations did not disappear until 1943. About 900 Swiss volunteers served in the Waffen-SS.

After World War II, right-wing extremism experienced several revivals. In 1951, Gaston-Armand Amaudruz created the racist Nouvel Ordre Européen and the short-lived Volkspartei der Schweiz. Several fascist organizations were founded during the 1970s: Europa-Burschenschaft Arminia in 1971; Nationale Basis Schweiz in 1974; and Volkssozialistische Partei in 1978. Starting in 1985, several short-lived fascist parties emerged: the Neue Nationale Front (1985 to 1987); the Volks-Aktiongegen zu viele Auslaender und Asylanten, which won a seat on the Basle Town Council in 1988, and whose leader obtained a share of 2.6 percent there in 2003; the Neue Front/Eidgenoessische Sozialisten (1988–1989); the Patriotische Front/Partei der Zukunft, which obtained a share of 6.4 percent in Canton Schwyz in 1991; the Nationalrevolutionaere Partei (1989–1990); the Nationale Initiative Schweiz (1996–1997); the Nationale Partei (2000 to 2003); the Partei National Orientierter Schweizer (founded in 2000); the Jeunesse Nationaliste Suisse et Européenne (founded in 2000); and the Nationale Ausserparlamentarische Opposition (founded in 2003). The Schweizer Hammerskins became the leading fascist network in the second half of the 1990s. In addition, the so-called revisionists who denied or played down the Holocaust have included Mariette Paschoud, Arthur Vogt, Juergen Graf, Bernhard Schaub, and Max Wahl. Some of them were organized in the esoteric circle "Avalon." More important than the open fascists were the parties fighting against so-called *Ueberfremdung* ("overforeignization"), which as pioneers of xenophobe parties in Western Europe exerted a considerable influence on migration politics. The Nationale Aktion (NA), founded in 1961, managed to send James Schwarzenbach as its first representative to parliament in 1967. In 1970, a popular initiative for the limitation of immigration obtained a share of 46 percent in the popular vote. A year later, the Republikaner, created by Schwarzenbach and the NA, received a share of 7.5 percent in national elections. In 1985, the anti-immigration movement Vigilance became the strongest party in Geneva, attaining a share of 18.9 percent in cantonal elections.

Since the 1980s, a diversification of the radical-right parties has taken place. Besides the NA (since 1990, Schweizer Demokraten), the Eidgenoessische Demokratische Union (founded in 1975), the Autopartei (founded in 1985, since 1994 the Freiheits-Partei), the Lega dei Ticinesi (founded in 1991), and the Katholische Volkspartei (founded in 1994) have emerged. During the 1990s, these parties became less and less important in view of the ascent of the populist and isolationist Schweizerische Volkspartei (SVP), which became the strongest party in Switzerland in 1999 (22.5 percent; 2003: 26.6 percent). Its leader, Christophe Blocher, became a member of the federal government in 2003.

Christian Koller

See Also: ANTI-SEMITISM; BANKS, THE; BOURGEOISIE, THE; FRANCE; HOLOCAUST DENIAL; IMMIGRATION; MUSSOLINI, BENITO ANDREA; NATIONALISM; POSTWAR FASCISM; RACISM; SOCIALISM; WAFFEN-SS, THE; WORLD WAR II; XENOPHOBIA

References
Braillard, P. 2001. *Switzerland and the Crisis of Dormant Assets and Nazi Gold.* London: Kegan Paul.
Cantini, Claude. 1992. *Les ultras: Extrême droite et droite extrême en Suisse: Les mouvements et la presse de 1921 à 1991.* Lausanne: Editions d'en bas.
Frischknecht, Juerg. 1991. *"Schweiz wir kommen": Die neuen Froentler und Rassisten.* Zurich: Limmat.
Gentile, Pierre, and Hanspeter Kriesi. 1998. "Contemporary Radical-Right Parties in Switzerland: History of a Divided Family." Pp. 125–142 in *The New Politics of the Right,* edited by Hans-Georg Betz and Stefan Immerfall. New York: St. Martin's.
LeBor, Adam. 1997. *Hitler's Secret Bankers: The Myth of Swiss Neutrality during the Holocaust.* Secaucus, NJ: Birch-Lane.
Mattioli, Aram, ed. 1995. *Intellektuelle von rechts: Ideologie und Politik in der Schweiz 1918–1939.* Zurich: Orell Fuessli.
Wolf, Walter. 1969. *Faschismus in der Schweiz: Die Geschichte der Frontenbewegungen in der deutschen Schweiz, 1930–1945.* Zurich: Flamberg.

SYMBOLS

Fascism was a political phenomenon with a consciously and deliberately high level of symbolic intensity deriving from its antirationalist conception of politics and the masses, which attributed an absolutely fundamental role to myth and ritual in collective life. All fascisms shared the conviction that aesthetic symbolism rather more than verbal symbolism was the political language most accessible to the masses, on account of the fundamentally irrational nature of their psychology, and the most effective instrument for the achievement of the fusion of the individual and the masses in the mystic totality of the national community. Hitler involved himself personally in the question of the form and color of the swastika as the symbol of the Nazi Party. The mystical and not merely instrumental essence of fascist symbolism seems evident in the mythical origin of the emblems of the principal fascist movements, such as the Italian lictors' fasces and the swastika, products of a modernistic redevelopment of ancient symbols to be adopted as sacred emblems of the national or racial community, regenerated by a movement of new men, artificers of a new state, in which the movement identified with and incarnated the totality of the nation. In this sense the symbolism of the fascist movements was not just an artifice of propaganda but also the coherent expression of a conception of life founded on mythical thought, and it played a crucial part in conferring on the fascist phenomenon the features of a political religion.

Emilio Gentile
(translated by Cyprian Blamires)

See Also: INTRODUCTION; ABSTRACTION; COMMUNITY; FASCIO, THE; FASCIST PARTY, THE; GERMANIC RELIGION; GERMANNESS; HITLER, ADOLF; ITALY; LE BON, GUSTAVE; MATERIALISM; MECHANISTIC THINKING; MUSSOLINI, BENITO ANDREA; MYSTICISM; MYTH; NAZISM; NEW AGE,

THE; NEW MAN, THE; NIHILISM; NORDIC SOUL, THE; PALINGENETIC MYTH; PROPAGANDA; RATIONALISM; RELIGION; ROME; SALUTES; SOUL; STATE, THE; SWASTIKA, THE; TOTALITARIANISM; TRADITION; *VOLKSGEMEINSCHAFT,* THE

References
Gentile, E. 1996. *The Sacralization of Politics in Fascist Italy.* London: Harvard University Press.
Goodrick-Clarke, Nicholas. 1985. *The Occult Roots of Nazism.* Wellingborough: Aquarian.

SYNDICALISM

The word *syndicat* in French, or *sindacato* in Italian, denotes a labor organization or trades union, and syndicalism emerged as a revolutionary political ideology within the left wing of the socialist and labor movements in Italy and France early in the twentieth century. Although syndicalism did not possess a rigidly defined set of ideas, its program being somewhat amorphous, syndicalist thinkers tended to concentrate on the concepts of the "general strike" and "direct action": methods intended to bring about the rapid overthrow of capitalism by paralyzing the economy and fostering the necessity of spontaneous acts of violence against the bourgeois parliamentary state in order to achieve working-class political power. Syndicalism criticized conventional Marxism for having become bureaucratic, and for having lost its revolutionary appeal because it concentrated on narrow economic considerations at the expense of revolutionary idealism. These perceived shortcomings were described as the tendency toward oligarchy by the German-Italian syndicalist theoretician Roberto Michels. For syndicalism, the revolution was not a legalistic matter; it had to express a spontaneous and aggressive instinctual vitalism.

Technically, the father of French revolutionary syndicalism was the French labor leader Fernand Pelloutier (1867–1901), but in 1906, with the publication of *Reflections on Violence* by Georges Sorel, revolutionary syndicalism acquired a more sophisticated ideological formulation, and the book came to be considered the representative statement of revolutionary syndicalism. Sorel was an important writer in France, but he also decisively influenced the formation of Italian syndicalism. In Sorel, one can detect the movement away from purely Marxist goals and the early formulation within

syndicalist theory of fascistic ideas. For Sorel, the general strike would lead not to the total destruction of capitalism but rather to a strengthening of the national community. In Social Darwinian terms, most likely derived from the popular writings of the German zoologist Ernst Haeckel (1834–1919), Sorel praised the beneficial social effects to be realized from an ongoing struggle between the proletariat and the middle class, a conflict that would lend a heroic character to society and serve to strengthen the major social classes that composed the community. A communist utopia, Sorel believed, would therefore never emerge according to the way it had been conceived by Marxism, as a society in which conflict and class struggle could be overcome. For Sorel, peaceful social conditions, parliamentary democracy, and democratic ideas could serve only to weaken a vigorous and healthy society. The power of aggressive instinct and the myth of unity and social cohesion should be cultivated to rally the energies of the proletariat in their eternal struggle with the bourgeoisie. In this way, Sorel comes close to the idea of fascism—that is, the revolution integrating the entire community, the nation, and not one particular social class being the focus of ideological concern.

Mussolini and other fascist leaders in Italy, such as Sergio Panunzio and Edmondo Rossoni (1884–1965), acknowledged ties to syndicalism. Under Italian Fascism, syndicalism continued to play an ideological and practical role in the hierarchical organization of society. But its activities were clearly subordinated to the power of the state, and its program was remote from its former call for proletarian revolutionary zeal.

Daniel Gasman

See Also: ABSTRACTION; BOURGEOISIE, THE; CAPITALISM; CLASS; CORPORATISM; ECONOMICS; FASCIST PARTY, THE; FRANCE; FRENCH REVOLUTION, THE; ITALY; LABOR FRONT, THE; MARXISM; MARXIST THEORIES OF FASCISM; MATERIALISM; MICHELS, ROBERTO; MUSSOLINI, BENITO ANDREA; PANUNZIO, SERGIO; PARLIAMENTARISM; SOCIAL DARWINISM; SOCIOLOGY; SOREL, GEORGES; STATE, THE; TRADES UNIONS; UTOPIA, UTOPIANISM; VITALISM; *VOLKSGEMEINSCHAFT,* THE

References
Dahl, Ottar. 1999. *Syndicalism, Fascism, and Post-Fascism in Italy, 1900–1950.* Oslo: Soum.
Jennings, Jeremy. 1990. *Syndicalism in France: A Study of Ideas.* New York: St. Martin's.
Roberts, D. D. 1979. *The Syndicalist Tradition in Italian Fascism.* Manchester: Manchester University Press.
Roth, J. J. 1967. "The Roots of Italian Fascism: Sorel and *Sorelismo." Journal of Modern History* 39, no. 1, pp. 30–45.

SZÁLASI, FERENC (1897–1946)

Major figure of Hungarian fascism who took power on 15 October 1944, Szálasi was the only chief ideologue of the Arrow Cross movement who did not recant during his trials in 1945. Born of a mixed Hungarian, Austrian, Slovak, and Armenian family, Szálasi was one of the most prominent and controversial figures of Hungarian fascism. He finished military academy and served thirty-six months in World War I and even achieved some fame for being an excellent military policy-maker but a "dangerous" politician. A close confidant of Prime Minister Gyula Gömbös during the early 1930s, Szálasi appeared on the scene in 1935 as a major political figure. He invented his own brand of fascist ideology, Hungarism—loosely, the ideology to create the Great Hungarian Fatherland under the leadership of the Great Leader. During the 1935 elections he refused to throw in his lot with Gömbös's party, instead creating his own Party of National Will, which carried his Hungarist idea and its slogan "Soil, Blood, Work."

Failing to enter official politics, Szálasi then created the Hungarist Movement in 1937, but his extremism earned him a two-year jail sentence between 1938 and 1940. After becoming prime minister, he ordered the "death-trains" for the Jews, which lasted until the end of December, and the creation of the Budapest ghetto. At the end of the war he was sentenced to death by hanging.

László Kürti

See Also: ANTI-SEMITISM; ARROW CROSS, THE; BLOOD AND SOIL; EXPANSIONISM; GHETTOS; GÖMBÖS, GYULA; HOLOCAUST, THE; HUNGARY; LEADER CULT, THE; WORLD WAR I

References
Ignotus, Paul. 1972. *Hungary.* New York: Praeger.
Lackó, M. *Arrow Cross Men, National Socialists, 1935–1944.* Budapest: Akadémiai Kiadó.
Macartney, C. A. 1961. *October Fifteenth.* Edinburgh: Edinburgh University Press.
Nagy-Talavera, M. M. 1970. *The Green Shirts and Others.* Stanford: Stanford University Press.
Rothschild, Joseph. 1974. *East-Central Europe between the Two World Wars.* Seattle: University of Washington Press.
Seton-Watson, Hugh. 1964. *Nationalism and Communism.* London: Methuen.

TECHNOLOGY

Scholarly understanding of the relationship between fascism and technology has changed significantly in the past twenty years. Today it is recognized that enthusiasm for modern technology is an integral part of the fascist phenomenon. It should be noted, however, that the fascists interpreted modern technology in a particular, one-dimensional way. German and Italian attitudes toward modern technology were once seen as separated by a wide gulf. Aware of the Italian Fascists' affinity for modernism and modernity, scholars in the 1960s and 1970s believed that German National Socialism centered instead on backward-looking ideologies such as "blood and soil" and a preindustrial, racist utopia that rejected technological society. Along with the different attitudes toward race, eugenics, and anti-Semitism that distinguished Nazi Germany from Fascist Italy, the alleged German-Italian split over modernity and technology cast doubt on the value of making generalizations and contributed to a devaluation of the fascist paradigm in the 1980s.

The long-held assumption that the Nazis were hostile to modernity first came under attack in the 1980s, however, when detailed studies of Nazi science policy and attitudes toward technology began to show a more nuanced picture. It became evident that scientific rationality existed side by side with antimodern impulses in Hitler's Germany, and that its familiar rhetoric of an-

ticapitalist, antidemocratic Romanticism included a passion for modern technology, engineering, and invention. Jeffrey Herff has described this phenomenon, which represented an embrace of the Enlightenment's instrumental rationality while rejecting its liberal, capitalist, and universal dimensions, as "reactionary modernism." The concept of reactionary modernism was intended to account for Germany's historical peculiarity vis-à-vis other Western nations. But it can also serve to align Nazi Germany with Fascist Italy as regards their attitudes toward modern technology. Both countries appropriated those aspects of modernity that could be recombined with what Robert Paxton calls the "mobilizing passions" of societies in crisis. In the post–World War I era, those passions centered on a mythic narrative of victimhood, populist hypernationalism, heroic leadership, collectivism, solidarity, violence, renewal, and redemption in Darwinian struggle. Modern technology and technological progress were said to spring from the same sources that powered the fascist phenomenon: heroic genius and artlike, antirationalistic, antibureaucratic creativity. In politics, those energies manifested themselves in the charismatic leadership of the Fuehrer and Il Duce. In technology, they took the form of a zeal for invention and innovation—for the "creative destruction" (Joseph Schumpeter) of older, ossifying technological systems by the authors of newer, more vibrant, and modern technologies. Folded into the mobilizing passions, technology thus defined produced a bend of brutality, efficiency, ruthlessness, productivism, and modernism. This was reflected in the affinities between fascism and modernism noted by scholars such as the art historian Mark Antliff, and in such seemingly unrelated projects as the SS's universe of labor and death camps, Albert Speer's monumental architecture, Mussolini's technocratic aspirations and urban planning, dreams of a "people's car," aeronautics and space rocketry, Futurism, motorways, "rationalized" industrial relations, and Hitler's grandiose designs of conquest and resettlement in the East.

The heroic interpretation of modern technology can be seen most clearly in National Socialism's conception of inventing and its policies toward inventors. The Nazis borrowed their view of inventing from a long-standing debate on the causes of technological progress. They rejected arguments that inventing was the product of systematic research and development in laboratories, siding instead with those who portrayed inventions as the work of individual genius and the inventor as "an image of the Creator, a being in which God has placed a spark of His own creative power" (Max Eyth, as quoted in Gispen 2002, 91). The exponents of this view, which went back to the nineteenth century, were mainly engineers and inventors themselves. They (over)emphasized the flash of genius to invalidate big business arguments that inventions resulted from the routine application of professional knowledge and company organization—which turned their authors into ordinary, fungible labor. Hitler in the 1920s made the engineers' perspective his own, writing in *Mein Kampf* that "it is not the mass that invents and the majority that organizes and thinks, but in everything always only the individual human being, the person" (quoted in ibid., 94).

In power, the Nazis also sided with inventors, both for ideological reasons and to encourage invention and innovation. If Nazi Germany had an overarching technology policy, promoting the inventor was its unifying theme. The regime institutionalized the heroic view of inventing in the new Patent Code of 1936, which strengthened the inventor's legal position vis-à-vis capital. From 1934 to 1941, the regime gave assistance to small and independent inventors (*Erfinderbetreuung*), in the mistaken belief that this group represented a vast untapped reservoir of Aryan inventive genius. In 1942–1943, armaments minister Speer introduced statutory rewards for employed inventors, in the unrealized hope that providing the fuel of interest to spark their fire of genius would help to win World War II.

With the defeat of the Axis powers in 1945, the fascist technological style went out of fashion. Significantly, however, it did not disappear completely. Ele-ments of it continued in the postwar period and, in some instances, survive today. Industrial firms nationalized under Mussolini in the context of his regime's technocratic ambitions grew into vast state-owned conglomerates with enormous financial power, such as IRI (Istitute per la Riconstruzione Industriale, founded in 1933) and ENI (Ente Nazionale Idrocarburi, the state oil company, established in 1926 as AGIP). National Socialism created institutional structures that gave preferential treatment to national champions, which helps to explain the striking postwar success of companies such as Daimler-Benz and, especially, Volkswagen. Some aesthetic and environmental aspirations survived in city planning and highway design. Nazi wartime wage-calculation methods transferred directly to West Germany, and the fascist emphasis on productivism mutated into the thriving field of industrial psychology. The aborted beginnings of a technology-based mass consumer society came to fruition in the 1950s. Finally, Nazism's pro-inventor reforms of the German patent code and Speer's imposition of mandatory, graduated rewards for employed inventors survive in modified form in Germany's legal system and influence its technological culture to this day.

Kees Gispen

See Also: INTRODUCTION; ANTI-SEMITISM; ARCHITECTURE; ART; ARYANISM; AXIS, THE; AUTOBAHNS; BLITZKRIEG; BLOOD AND SOIL; CAPITALISM; CONCENTRATION CAMPS; EUGENICS; FASCIST PARTY, THE; FUTURISM; GERMANY; HERO, THE CULT OF THE; HITLER, ADOLF; INDUSTRY; ITALY; LEADER CULT, THE; *LEBENSRAUM;* LIBERALISM; *MEIN KAMPF;* MODERNISM; MODERNITY; MUSSOLINI, BENITO ANDREA; NATIONALISM; NAZISM; PALINGENETIC MYTH; POSTWAR FASCISM; PRODUCTIVISM; PROGRESS; RACIAL DOCTRINE; RACISM; RATIONALISM; SCIENCE; SOCIAL DARWINISM; SPEER, ALBERT; SS, THE; UTOPIA, UTOPIANISM; VOLKSWAGEN; WORLD WAR II

References

Allen, Michael Thad. 2002. *The Business of Genocide: The SS, Slave Labor, and the Concentration Camps.* Chapel Hill: University of North Carolina Press.

Antliff, Mark. 2002. "Fascism, Modernism and Modernity." *Art Bulletin (The State of Art History Series)* (March): 148–169.

Gispen, Kees. 2002. *Poems in Steel: National Socialism and the Politics of Inventing from Weimar to Bonn.* New York: Berghahn.

Herff, Jeffrey. 1986. *Reactionary Modernism: Technology, Culture, and Politics in Weimar and the Third Reich.* Cambridge: Cambridge University Press.

Maier, Charles S. 1970. "Between Taylorism and Technocracy: European Ideologies and the Vision of Industrial Productivity in the 1920s." Reprinted on pp. 22–53 in Maier, *In Search of Stability: Explorations in Historical Political Economy.* Cambridge: Cambridge University Press.

Paxton, Robert O. 2004. *The Anatomy of Fascism.* New York: Alfred A. Knopf.

Reich, Simon. 1990. *The Fruits of Fascism: Postwar Prosperity in Historical Perspective.* Ithaca: Cornell University Press.

Siegel, Tilla. 1994/1995. "It's Only Rational: An Essay on the Logic of Social Rationalization." *International Journal of Political Economy* 24, no. 4 (winter): 35–70.

TEENAGERS: *See* SEXUALITY; YOUTH

TENSION, THE STRATEGY OF

An elaborate and relatively systematic campaign of terrorism and subversion carried out by neofascist paramilitary groups in Italy between the mid-1960s and the early 1980s. Subsequent judicial, parliamentary, and journalistic investigations revealed that the neofascist perpetrators had received covert aid and assistance from hardline factions within various Western security and intelligence agencies, diverse conservative and anticommunist groups, and even elements within the Italian political establishment. The seriousness of neofascist terrorism in Italy was reflected statistically in Italian police records, which attributed 83 percent of the 4,384 officially registered acts of political violence between 1969 and 1975 to the extreme Right. (Contrary to popular perceptions, left-wing terrorism did not become predominant in Italy until the latter half of the 1970s.) In addition to hundreds of acts of smaller-scale neofascist violence, the "strategy of tension" was marked by a series of terrorist atrocities that were at that time unprecedented in their indiscriminate brutality and precipitation of large numbers of casualties. These consisted mainly of a series of powerful bombings in public locales that were carefully selected to cause the maximum number of civilian casualties: the Agricultural Bank on Milan's Piazza Fontana in December 1969; the Piazza della Loggia in Brescia during a political rally in August 1974; the "Italicus" express train in December 1974; and Bologna's crowded central train station in August 1980. These acts of mass-casualty terrorism were interspersed with a succession of abortive "coups" involving both civilian extremists and high-ranking military personnel, including the so-called De Lorenzo coup of 1964, the December 1970 Borghese coup in Rome, and a series of overlapping

plots in 1973 and 1974 that were linked to the Rosa dei Venti ("Compass Rose") group and to former noncommunist partisans such as Edgardo Sogno and Carlo Fumagalli. The total casualty toll of this "strategy of tension" amounted to more than 200 deaths and well over 1,000 wounded, many of whom were horribly mutilated. In postwar Europe, only Northern Ireland, the Basque country, and Turkey were subjected to bloodier and more extensive campaigns of terrorism.

The individuals who carried out these attacks were members of the most important and radical neofascist groups at the time. During the first phase of the "strategy of tension," from the mid-1960s until 1975, the primary culprits were affiliated with the clandestine apparatus of Giuseppe ("Pino") Rauti's Ordine Nuovo (ON; New Order); Stefano delle Chiaie's Avanguardia Nazionale (AN; National Vanguard); ON's radical offshoot, Clemente Graziani's Movimento Politico Ordine Nuovo (MPON; New Order Political Movement); and Giorgio ("Franco") Freda's series of front groups based in the Padua and Veneto areas. Key personnel from these groups had previously received training in sophisticated French counterinsurgency techniques from elements of the so-called Black International, a loosely interconnected network of right-wing paramilitary groups then centered on Aginter Presse. In reality, this Lisbon-based "press agency," which had been established by former members of the Organisation de l'Armée Secrète (OAS; Secret Army Organization), the mixed military-civilian terrorist group that had violently resisted President Charles De Gaulle's efforts to grant Algeria independence, functioned as a training center for anticommunist covert action, subversion, and terrorism. These same Italian neofascist groups also received "cover" and covert logistical aid from various top secret parallel security apparatuses, including the Ufficio Affari Riservati (UAR; Covert Operations Section) of the Italian Ministry of the Interior, factions within the Italian Servizio Informazioni Difesa (SID; Defense Intelligence Service), the Portuguese secret police, the post-1967 Greek secret services, and elements of the Spanish security services, all of which were actively engaged in "plausibly deniable" destabilization operations against the Left. In the end, however, these neofascist radicals were "burned" by their erstwhile covert state "handlers" when they became more of a liability than an asset.

Indeed, these "first generation" neofascist terrorist groups had been systematically manipulated by their secret sponsors from the very beginning. They were encouraged to carry out a series of terrorist provocations designed to incriminate the far Left, above all the anarchists. However, the ultimate effects of their actions, far from laying the groundwork for a coup d'etat and a revolutionary fascist transformation of society, served only to strengthen the U.S.-dominated Atlantic Alliance and the corrupt *partitocrazia* in Italy that they themselves had sought to overthrow. What the international and national sponsors of the "strategy of tension" were actually conducting was a complex strategy designed to keep the communists and crypto-communists from entering the corridors of power on a national level and, in the process, ensure Italy's continued fidelity to the Atlantic Alliance. These sponsors were themselves divided into two main factional groupings, those who sought to preserve the existing political structure from which they derived tangible benefits, and those who sought to replace that dysfunctional system with a "presidentialist" arrangement that would strengthen the executive branch at the expense of the parliament. To accomplish their objectives, however, these rival factions both employed the tactics of destabilization by making instrumental use of right-wing radicals. What they were really engaged in all along was "destabilizing in order to stabilize," as many knowledgeable insiders and observers later revealed. In that sense, the participating neofascists were also victims of political manipulation. In the end, with some noteworthy exceptions, they did not benefit any more from the "strategy of tension" than their counterparts on the extraparliamentary Left. The beneficiaries were almost invariably their sub rosa state sponsors.

As a result, during the latter half of the 1970s a new generation of clandestine neofascist groups was founded by younger radicals who recognized that earlier neofascist terrorist organizations had been systematically manipulated by the hated "bourgeois" state. These included Terza Posizione (Third Position), Costruiamo l'Azione (Let's Take Action!), and the Nuclei Armati Rivoluzionari (NAR; Armed Revolutionary Nuclei). These "second generation" terrorist groups soon embarked upon a new strategy of "armed spontaneity" designed to undermine the state itself and to prevent its agents from destroying their new and more decentralized organizations. However, having declared open war on the state itself, thereby repudiating the covert institutional protection that had previously been provided by certain of its factions, they were suppressed fairly quickly and easily by the forces of order—but not before NAR members Giuseppe ("Giusva") Fioravante and Francesca Mambro had, according to investigating magistrates, carried out the devastating 1980 Bologna train station bombing.

This terrorist "strategy of tension" took an unusually large toll of human life by Euro-terrorist standards, played a significant role in heightening political tensions and social conflicts in Italy, further corrupted the already dysfunctional political system in that country, and included the worst single act of terrorism in Europe prior to the 11 March 2004 Madrid train station bombings. It also constituted a microcosm of a much broader pattern of covert state manipulation of right-wing terrorism, both elsewhere in Europe (including Turkey) and in parts of Latin America. Despite this, outside of Italy it has yet to receive the sort of journalistic and scholarly attention that has long been focused on the much less important acts of left-wing terrorism that occurred during that same period. Only the 1978 murder of Italian prime minister Aldo Moro by the Brigate Rosse (BR; Red Brigades) had as much political impact as the "strategy of tension," and it, too, ended up serving the interests of the pro-Atlantic political establishment far more than those of its radical opponents.

Jeffrey M. Bale

See Also: COLD WAR, THE; ITALY; MARXISM; PARAMILITARISM; POSTWAR FASCISM; RAUTI, GIUSEPPE ("PINO"); SOCIALISM; TERROR; THIRD POSITIONISM; TURKEY

References

Bale, Jeffrey M. 1994. "The 'Black' Terrorist International: Neo-Fascist Paramilitary Networks and the 'Strategy of Tension' in Italy, 1968–1974." Ph.D. dissertation, University of California at Berkeley, Department of History.

———. 1996. "The May 1973 Terrorist Attack at Milan Police Headquarters: Anarchist 'Propaganda of the Deed' or 'False Flag' Provocation?" *Terrorism and Political Violence* 8, no. 1: 132–166.

———. 2001. "Terrorism, Right-Wing." Pp. 1238–1240, vol. 2, in *Europe since 1945: An Encyclopedia,* edited by Bernard A. Cook. New York: Garland.

Cingolani, Giorgio 1996. *La destra in armi: Neofascisti italiani tra ribellismo ed eversione, 1977–1982.* Rome: Riuniti.

Corsini, Paolo, and Roberto Chiarini. 1983. *Da Salò a Piazza della Loggia: Blocco d'ordine, neofascismo, radicalismo di destra a Brescia, 1945–1974.* Milan: Angeli.

Corsini, Paolo, and Laura Novati, eds. 1985. *L'eversione nera: Cronache di un decennio, 1974–1984.* Milan: Angeli.

De Lutiis, Giuseppe. 1998. *Storia dei servizi segreti in Italia: Dal fascismo alla seconda Repubblica.* Rome: Riuniti.

Ferraresi, Franco. 1996. *Threats to Democracy: The Radical Right in Italy after the War.* Princeton: Princeton University Press (esp. chs. 3–7).

———, ed. 1984. *La destra radicale.* Milan: Feltrinelli.

Flamini, Gianni. 1981–1985. *Il partito del golpe: Le strategie della tensione e del terrore dal primo centrosinistra organico al sequestro Moro, 1964–1978.* 4 vols. Ferrara: Bovolenta.

Laurent, Frédéric. 1978. *L'orchestre noir.* Paris: Stock.

Vinciguerra, Vincenzo. 1989. *Ergastolo per la libertà: Verso la verità sulla strategia della tensione.* Florence: Arnaud.

Willan, Philip. 1991. *Puppetmasters: The Political Use of Terrorism in Italy.* London: Constable.

TERRA'BLANCHE, EUGÈNE (born 1941)

A brilliant speaker in the style of Hendrick Verwoerd (1901–1965) and the flamboyant leader of the Afrikaner Weerstandsbeweging (AWB; Afrikaner Resistance Movement), founded in 1971 to resist what was seen as government appeasement of black nationalism. The movement stages highly theatrical marches and events displaying a red and black flag with three interlinked 7s resembling the swastika. After serving a six-year jail term for attempted murder, Terra'Blanche was released in 2004 and renounced violence while still affirming his commitment to Afrikaner cultural survival.

Irving Hexham

See Also: PROPAGANDA; SOUTH AFRICA; WHITE SUPREMACISM; SWASTIKA, THE

˙TERROR

Whereas Marxists, while assuming that political violence was inevitable until the class war had been won, looked to a utopia in which conflict had been transcended and peaceful human relations established, interwar fascists, under the influence of Social Darwinism, took a much bleaker view of the potential for human progress. They accepted that the rule of the weak by the strong was a permanent fact of human existence (as Aristotle and Machiavelli, among others, had done before them) and assumed a need to retain power by the application of whatever force was necessary. More than that, they actually glorified violence as a means of keeping materialistic and hedonistic tendencies at bay and actively promoted a warrior cult as a means of preserving their power. Their brazen employ-ment of terror tactics was not, therefore, simply a matter of pragmatism, but a necessary feature of their philosophy of life. Pacifism, internationalism, and parliamentarism were all, in their view, symptoms of weakness and decadence, danger signs of societies about to collapse. That conviction was reinforced by the writings of publicists like Oswald Spengler, whose *Decline of the West* fed the pessimism of Hitler and Mussolini alike. The application of terror tactics to political opponents was a sign of the emergence of a powerful warlike new humanity, unafraid to assert its superiority over the degenerates who had been allowed by sinister forces such as the Jews or the Freemasons or the plutocrats to take the reins of society. Their frank espousal of conspiracy theories of this kind also enabled them to claim that they were performing a task necessary to social well-being in forcibly rooting out society's enemies. In the case of the Nazis there was a further motive: convinced as they were that Germany had been betrayed by the "November Criminals," they believed it their sacred duty to take revenge on the betrayers.

An additional influence on the fascist "philosophy of violence" was to be found in the theory of Georges Sorel, who preached a mystique of violent revolutionary action as the only way to provoke a revolution. This was a particular influence on Mussolini and Italian Fascism. Mussolini relied on the violence of the *squadristi* to achieve electoral success and intimidate his opponents. But long before that, he had turned from classical socialist internationalism to interventionism, calling for Italy to enter World War I, because he thought that the violence unleashed by the war would create an instability favorable to a revolutionary overthrow of the existing order, and in that he proved to be correct.

Cyprian Blamires

See Also: ANTI-SEMITISM; ARYANISM; CONCENTRATION CAMPS; CONSPIRACY THEORIES; COSMOPOLITANISM; DECADENCE; DEGENERACY; FREEMASONRY, FREEMASONS; HITLER, ADOLF; HOLOCAUST, THE; INTERVENTIONISM; MACHIAVELLI, NICCOLÒ; *MEIN KAMPF;* MUSSOLINI, BENITO ANDREA; NATIONALISM; NAZISM; NEW MAN, THE; NOVEMBER CRIMINALS/*NOVEMBERBRECHER*, THE; PACIFISM; PARAMILITARISM; PLUTOCRACY; PROGRESS; SOCIAL DARWINISM; SOCIALISM; SOREL, GEORGES; SPENGLER, OSWALD; *SQUADRISMO*, THE; STALIN, IOSIF VISSARIONOVICH; SYNDICALISM; TENSION, THE STRATEGY OF; UTOPIA, UTOPIANISM; WAR; WARRIOR ETHOS, THE; WORLD WAR I

References
Benewick, Robert. 1969. *Political Violence and Public Order: A Study of British Fascism.* London: Allen Lane.

Bullock, A. 1990 [1952]. *Hitler: A Study in Tyranny.* London: Penguin.

Cobley, Evelyn. 2002. *Temptations of Faust: The Logic of Fascism and Postmodern Archaeologies of Modernity.* Toronto: University of Toronto Press.

Hawkins, Mike. 1997. *Social Darwinism in European and American Thought, 1860–1945: Nature as Model and Nature as Threat.* Cambridge: Cambridge University Press.

Jaskot, P. B. 2000. *The Architecture of Oppression: The SS Forced Labour and Nazi Monumental Building Economy.* London: Routledge.

Mack Smith, Denis. 1981. *Mussolini.* London: Weidenfeld and Nicholson.

Traverso, E. 2003. *The Origins of Nazi Violence.* London: New Press.

Waite, R. 1977. *The Psychopathic God: Adolf Hitler.* New York: Basic.

Williamson, G. 1998. *The SS: Hitler's Instrument of Terror.* London: Sidgwick and Jackson.

TEUTONIC KNIGHTS: *See* HIMMLER, HEINRICH; WAGNER, RICHARD

THADDEN, ADOLF VON (1921–1996)

Adolf von Thadden was the chairman of the Nationaldemokratische Partei Deutschlands (NDP), founded in 1964. Under his chairmanship (1967 to 1971), the strong electoral showing made by the NPD during the late 1960s led to widespread fears that the party was on the cusp of gaining parliamentary representation. In 1962 von Thadden, then chairman of the Deutsche Reichspartei, attempted to found a pan-European fascist party at the Conference of Venice with other fascist leaders, including Oswald Mosley. Von Thadden left the NPD in 1975. For decades he was the pivotal figure in German and international fascism. In 2002, however, it was revealed that while head of the NPD, von Thadden had spied for MI6, the British intelligence service.

Graham Macklin

See Also: EUROFASCISM; EUROPE; EUROPEANIST FASCISM/RADICAL RIGHT, THE; GERMANY; INTERNATIONAL FASCISM; MOSLEY, SIR OSWALD; POSTWAR FASCISM

References

Hooper, J. 2002. "Neo-Nazi Leader Was MI6 Agent." *Guardian,* 13 August.

Long, W. 1968. *The New Nazis of Germany.* Philadelphia: Chilton.

THEATER

Given the essentially middle-class nature of established theater, many contemporary historians consider the only truly fascist performances to have taken place beyond traditional playhouses, in mass rituals. Such theatrical events as the Nuremberg Rallies provided an annual opportunity for the reinforcement of group solidarity through ritual. Such occasions were aesthetically conceived, defined the crowds of participants as actor-spectators, and often entailed triumphant narrative speeches by politicians and the recitation of original catechisms of fascist fidelity. Italian theater could not compete with these enormous outdoor spectacles and suffered initially from indecisive policies. In 1927, Mussolini claimed that theater was one of the most direct means of reaching the heart of the people, but in 1932 he refused to fund new theater buildings. Yet one year later, speaking in a theater in Rome, he declared the need to prepare a theater of the masses to house 15,000 or 20,000 people. The regime, meanwhile, attempted to reorganize existing Italian theater by controlling the Italian Society of Authors and Publishers and, in 1930, setting up the Corporazione dello Spettacolo. In 1931 a new censorship law meant that all play texts had to be submitted to the Ministry of the Interior for approval, and then, from 1935, to the Ministry of Press and Propaganda, which two years later became the Ministry for Popular Culture. Leopoldo Zurlo acted as chief censor, and, of the 17,330 plays submitted, only 630 were rejected outright. A General Theater Inspectorate, set up in 1935, controlled the repertory and selected theater companies for subsidy. This led to the prohibition of many foreign plays and drama in dialect. However, state intervention also led to a certain stability for those working in the theater. In 1938, state-designated companies sold 33 percent of all tickets.

The Italian Fascist regime provided financial support for a number of ventures, the most important of which were Luigi Pirandello's *Teatro d'Arte* in the 1920s (although, by 1934, the playwright was arguing directly against committed theater); two experimental companies run by Anton Giulio Bragaglia; the National Institute of Ancient Drama; the Royal Academy of Dramatic Arts acting school; Theatrical Saturdays (when ticket prices were reduced); amateur groups (developed by the Opera Nazionale Dopolavoro to a total of 1,901 by 1930); traveling dramatic and, later, operatic theater called, respectively, the *Carri di Tespi* (which reached more than 300,000 spectators in the first season in 1929) and the *Carri Lirici;* and university theater companies.

Despite this subsidy, there was no preponderance of performed political dramas in the period. Salvator Gotta made a claim to have written the first Fascist play, *The Martyrs' Congress,* a twenty-minute-long piece premiered in 1923. Mussolini himself collaborated with Giovacchino Forzano on three dramas—about Napoleon, Julius Caesar, and Cavour—and there was a plentiful supply of amateur scripts lauding Il Duce, the Fascist Party, and Italian exploits in Africa, the Spanish Civil War, and World War II. Of 354 new plays premiered between 1934 and 1940, only 5 percent had explicitly Fascist themes; a typical show was a romantic comedy by a writer like Aldo De Benedetti. Indeed, the theatrical undertakings backed by the state rarely promoted an ideological repertory. One exception was the production entitled *18 BL,* a heroic vision of a truck caught up in Fascist history and staged on the banks of the River Arno in Florence in 1934. Involving 2,000 amateur actors performing in front of 20,000 spectators, it did not evoke a favorable response, and everybody at the time agreed that this attempt at a theater of the masses was a failure. Toward the end of the regime some officials would voice the same opinion about the entirety of experiments in Fascist drama.

There had been Nazi theatrical projects and protest groups in the 1920s, so that the start of Hitler's chancellorship witnessed an immediate impact on theatrical life in Germany. Nazis forcibly took over theaters, dismissed personnel considered politically or racially suspect, and installed party members in positions of control. More than 4,000 theater practitioners were forced into exile while the regime subsumed existing professional organizations into the new order. Joseph Goebbels's Propaganda Ministry (created on 13 March 1933) had a theater section within a month, and the Reich Chamber of Culture (formed in September 1933) included a theater chamber of which all professionals had to be a member in order to work. Because of the Nuremberg Laws of 1935, non-Aryans and those married to non-Aryans were excluded from the cham-

ber. A decree of 1938 forbade Jews from attending concerts, cabarets, cinemas, circuses, lectures, and theaters. (The only refuge for Jews was the Jüdischer Kulturbund, the officially sanctioned organization for Jewish performance in front of exclusively Jewish audiences.)

Rainer Schlösser, the national *Reichsdramaturg* and, in effect, the chief censor following the Reich Theatre Act of May 1934, carried out an equivalent purification of the repertory. As well as rejecting playwrights on racial and political grounds, Nazi censorship virtually eliminated an entire period of drama: German plays of the Weimar Republic, which had constituted roughly 30 percent of the total repertory during 1929–1933, dropped to 5.56 percent in the first full season of Hitler's regime (1933–1934). Another major nail in the coffin of free expression was the banning of theater criticism (in favor of reporting) in November 1936. It looked as though the country with the most theaters in Europe had become a cultural prison.

In contrast to these prohibitive measures, there were large-scale participatory initiatives. Alfred Rosenberg's Nationalsozialistische Kulturgemeinde (with a membership of 1.5 million by 1935) organized performances with a strictly defined Nazi ethos, but it was absorbed into Robert Ley's Kraft durch Freude in 1937. Ley's association arranged cultural events with discounted tickets and mass subscriptions. Innovations in dramatic form were more controversial. A plan to build 400 outdoor venues for a new genre, the *Thingspiel,* was abandoned within three years of the Nazi takeover, but not before many mass cultic productions had taken place on the stages that had been completed; they often involved hundreds of actors in front of thousands of spectators, and the plays told simplistic stories of the defeat of Weimar decadence and poverty by a united and reborn German *Volk.* More consistent in traditional theaters were Nazi plays on historical themes by writers such as Hanns Johst and Eberhard Wolfgang Möller. In other dramas, a heroic acting style contributed to trumpet the values of "Blood and Soil" ideology, but contemporary authors also provided plenty of conservative escapist comedies. Moreover, the censor curbed overt anti-Semitism on stage, since Jewish influence was already meant to have been eliminated. The Nazi salute and even references to politics were later forbidden in the theater. Although the amount of foreign drama was considerably reduced, George Bernard Shaw remained popular, and the total number of Shakespearean productions during the period (sometimes in nazified versions and, very rarely, in oppositional styles) came second only to stagings of Schiller's plays. Theater was the most privileged of all the activities subsidized by the Propaganda Ministry, and the fact that theaters tended to be full, even during the war, can be considered a sign of success. As part of the total war effort, Goebbels ordered that all the theaters of the Reich should be shut down on 1 September 1944.

In Spain the dramatic theories of Giménez Caballero and Torrente Ballester were never followed systematically, notwithstanding some minor fascist propaganda plays put on during the Spanish Civil War and spectacular productions of Corpus Christi plays (*autos sacramentales*) staged outdoors. There was a competition for modern *autos,* sympathetic to the Spanish version of fascism, which was won by Torrente. In the early Francoist period (until 1945), the state-subsidized national theaters mounted a few triumphalist shows that articulated the ethos of the reformed Spanish fascist party, the Falange.

John London

See Also: INTRODUCTION; ANTI-SEMITISM; ART; ARYANISM; BLOOD AND SOIL; DECADENCE; ETHIOPIA; FALANGE; FILM; FRANCOISM; FUTURISM; GERMANY; GOEBBELS, (PAUL) JOSEPH; HERO, THE CULT OF THE; HITLER, ADOLF; ITALY; LEISURE; LEY, ROBERT; MASSES, THE ROLE OF THE; MODERNISM; MUSSOLINI, BENITO ANDREA; NAZISM; NUREMBERG LAWS, THE; NUREMBERG RALLIES, THE; PALINGENETIC MYTH; PROPAGANDA; RACIAL DOCTRINE; RELIGION; ROSENBERG, ALFRED; SALUTES; SPAIN; SPANISH CIVIL WAR, THE; SYMBOLS; TOTALITARIANISM; TRADITION; *VOLK, VÖLKISCH;* WEIMAR REPUBLIC, THE; WORLD WAR II

References

Berezin, Mabel. 1994. "Cultural Form and Political Meaning: State-subsidized Theater, Ideology, and the Language of Style in Fascist Italy." *American Journal of Sociology* 99: 1237–1286.

Berghaus, Günter, ed. 1996. *Fascism and Theater: Comparative Studies on the Aesthetics and Politics of Performance in Europe, 1925–1945.* Providence, RI: Berghahn.

London, John, ed. 2000. *Theatre under the Nazis.* Manchester: Manchester University Press.

Pedullà, Gianfranco. 1994. *Il teatro italiano nel tempo del fascismo.* Bologna: Il Mulino.

Schnapp, Jeffrey T. 1996. *Staging Fascism: 18BL and the Theater of the Masses.* Stanford: Stanford University Press.

THEOLOGY

Both Mussolini and Hitler allowed themselves to be feted by a few sympathetic theologians as "Savior of the West from Bolshevism" with messianic characteristics, but Hitler in particular emphasized that his "positive Christianity" stood above all confessions, dogmas, and theologies. On the other hand the *völkisch* race theorists, with their crude pseudo- and "counter-theologies" so beloved by the Nazis, had a much stronger relation to theological thought. The sharpening church struggle and the massive attacks on the Christian central message by the Nazis both encouraged elements in the church leadership in Germany to hold the regime at a distance after 1933 and also brought about a theological rethink—especially among the "young theologians" of the Lutheran Church. Already in the nineteenth century some *völkisch*-national ideologues used a discourse and a terminology having a clearly theological and prophetic resonance. This was true in particular of the writings of the Orientalist and cultural philosopher Paul de Lagarde, who proposed to call in theology as "Queen of the Sciences" to resolve confessional differences and establish a national "German-Christian faith." Houston Stewart Chamberlain's program for a "Germanization of Christendom" and the *Alldeutsche Bewegung* of Georg von Schönerer involved an appeal to theology to undergird anti-Semitism. The clearest plan of a *völkisch* "counter-theology" was, however, drawn up by the former monk Jorg Lanz von Liebenfels, who in his journal *Ostara* (1905–1931) spoke frequently of the "blond master race" and who had a huge influence on the racial thinking of the young Adolf Hitler. Lanz himself spoke of his race teaching as a "zootheology" and developed a theory that was a complete alternative account to the historical meaning of Christian theology. In opposition to the Christian historical sequence—paradise, fall, era after the fall (preparation for the Redeemer), emergence of the Redeemer (Jesus Christ), era of the Church, world judgment of the Redeemer with separation of mankind for heaven and hell—he advocated his "zootheological" model: paradise was the "era of racial purity"; the fall took place through the sodomy of the "blondes" with the "dark races," the "little apes" (called later by Hitler "apemen" or "subhumans"); this was followed by the era of the "mixing of races" until the Redeemer, "Frauja-Christ," emerged as the "prophet of racial purity" and established a "Church of racial purity"; finally, there would be a "world judgment by the blondes of the little apes," ending with the eternal lordship of the blondes ("Arioheroes") and the liquidation of the lower races (*Tschandalen*). Lanz constantly insisted that everything ugly and evil stemmed from "racial mixing," claiming that "Race is God, God is the purified race."

Lanz represents what was undoubtedly the most extreme expression of *völkisch* theology, but other groups, too, in part emerging from the Lutheran Church in Germany, reinterpreted Jesus Christ as a "Nordic-Aryan hero" and the Bible as a "work of the Germanic-Nordic spirit." The so-called German-Christian movements like the Bund für Deutsche Kirche (Association for German Church) of Kurd Niedlich (1884–1928) or the Geistchristliche Religionsgemeinschaft (Spiritual Christian Religious Community), founded in 1927 by Artur Dinter, demanded that God be sought "in a German way," that Jesus be proclaimed as the "Aryan hero," and that existing confessional divisions be abandoned. For Dinter, Christ had been the one most like God, and so the most "Aryanic man," who came down to earth so that through his example the Aryans might be helped to racial purity. The Glaubensbewegung Deutsche Volkskirche (Faith Movement of the German People's Church), founded in 1933 (later the Deutsche Glaubensfront [German Faith Front]), professed the "free gospel of the heroic Savior" and the "divine revelation of the *Volk* community rooted in blood and soil," and demanded that the crucifix be replaced by a rider on a white horse as the "fulfiller of Christendom" (following Revelation 10, 11ff). Even more radical were the Deutschgläubigen Bewegungen (German Faith Movements), which proposed an overcoming of Christendom in favor of "Germanic religion" and put forward the alternative "Wotan or Jehovah" (the title of a piece by Joseph Weber from 1906). The best known and most public was the *Tannenbergbund* (renamed in 1937 the *Bund für Deutsche Gotteserkenntnis*) of Mathilde Ludendorff, widow of Hitler's earlier comrade-in-arms General Erich Ludendorff, who wanted to gather into the "German *Volk*" all those "freed from Christian ideas."

THE REACTION OF CHRISTIAN THEOLOGIANS

Christian theologians were spurred to rethink and resist in the years 1933–1934, especially in response to the *Mythus des 20. Jahrhunderts* (1930) by Alfred Rosenberg, who voiced most insistently the hostility to the church to be found among the National Socialist leaders. He spoke, for example, of the "filthy moral theology" of Alphonsus Liguori, which in combination with "the creation of dishonor by Jesuitism" had destroyed everything great in European culture; according to Rosenberg, everything really great in European culture had "sprung from the anti-church spirit." Church leaders and theologians of both confessions began to counterattack against what they prudently called "the New

Heathenism" (rather than specifically naming National Socialism) with its obsessive focus on the idea of race. On the Catholic side the point was made that "the glorification of race overlooks the fact that the German race is as much a fallen creation as every other" (*Aussiger Deutsche Presse,* 8 March 1934). The "exclusion of the sense of sin" was condemned alongside the fact that the teaching of the "heroic Christ" overstressed human "heroic values." Even more outspoken was the bishop of Munster, Clemens August Graf von Galen, who in his Lenten pastoral letter of 1934 complained that race had been raised above morality and that the idea of God had been downgraded to that of "a function of race"; "moral" did not mean "what served the weal of the *Volk*" but only what "corresponded to the will of God." The placing of Rosenberg's *Mythus* on the Index of Forbidden Books on 7 February 1934 by the Holy Office sent out a clear signal as to the position of the Catholic Church. In 1934–1935 the *Studien zum Mythus des 20. Jahrhunderts* appeared as publications of the Episcopal Ordinariate of Berlin, as an expression of the hostility of Catholic theologians toward Rosenberg's book, and the *Studien* were distributed in many German dioceses.

The Lutheran churches had compromised themselves more with "the newly heathen state," so that a very much more fundamental reassessment was required on their part. The formation of the Pfarrernotbund (so-called Clerical Emergency Alliance) by Martin Niemöller in September 1933 and the "Confessing Church" that came out of it in 1934 were the signal for "young theologians" of the Lutheran Confession to raise the flag of spiritual resistance. In 1935, Walter Künneth published his highly respected critique of Rosenberg's work, which he entitled *Antwort auf den Mythus (Reply to the Myth)*, with the subtitle *Entscheidung zwischen dem nordischen Mythus und dem biblischen Christus (Choice between Nordic Myth and the Biblical Christ)*; Rosenberg reacted aggressively, with *An die Dunkelmänner unserer Zeit (To the Obscurantists of Our Time)*. In his *Table Talk,* Hitler later remarked that the attacks on Rosenberg by the churches had done him nothing but good, for they had been responsible for pushing sales of his book dramatically upward.

The most important thinker of the Confessing Church was Karl Barth (1886–1968), who since the 1930s had emerged as the most significant Lutheran fundamental theologian in the German-speaking world. Barth's 1933 writing *Theologische Existenz heute! (Theological Life Today)* was his response to the dramatic events of that year. Avoiding direct confrontation, he challenged his church "to pursue theology and

Karl Barth, the most celebrated Protestant theologian of the twentieth century. He was an inspiration for many in the German Confessing Church which opposed Hitlerism. (Library of Congress)

only theology," which meant speaking only about God's revelation in Christ. Christ alone was "Lord of the Church," and there could be "no second source of revelation" apart from him, whether it called itself "law, history, national character, natural order or culture." At this time Barth formulated his opposition to "natural theology," which referred to "natural orders" like national character, national law, history, or race to strengthen the "natural heathendom" of man. Barth contrasted with this his "revelation theology." This stimulated the Protestant tradition of refusal of obedience to incursions by the secular authorities and of resistance to every order of power that did not appeal to Christ alone. Karl Barth was also the theological brain behind the Barmen *Theologischen Erklärung zur gegenwärtigen Lage der Deutschen Evangelischen Kirche* (*Theological Clarification of the Present Situation of the German Lutheran Church*) of 31 May 1934, which formulated a cautious rejection of the National Socialist transformation of Germany. It denied that there was

any other revelation but the revelation of God in Christ (first thesis). The testimony of Christ was claimed as the model for behavior in the world (second thesis, "of Jesus Christ as God's strong claim on our whole life"). With this statement the two-kingdom teaching of the Reformation, according to which the (political) realm of this world could follow its own laws, was de facto suspended, and the "kingship of Christ" demanded not just for the spiritual but also for the secular world. In this way the Barmen theologians hoped to be able to make the model of Christ binding in the secular arena, and to counter the claim of an authoritarian-dictatorial and ultimately "new heathen" state to be entitled to dictate to the church.

As the struggles of the churches against the regime intensified, theologians in both confessions worked on theological justifications for resistance to the coercive measures of the "total state," opposing the sterilization laws of 1933–1934, euthanasia (1939–1941), and the "idolization of the state," which prejudiced the "totality claim of the kingdom of God." Individual theologians of both churches also spoke out bravely against the persecution of the Jews and pointed to the Jewish roots of Christendom, although there can be no easy rebuttal of the claim that a majority of theologians reacted too timidly or indifferently to the unfolding of the Holocaust. After the war, the Lutheran Church, among others, admitted the "moral denial" and the guilt of a majority of its leaders in the "Stuttgart Confession of Guilt" of 19 October 1945. The "theology of reconciliation" propounded there was again to a large extent indebted to the thought of Karl Barth. In Catholic theology, too, the idea became embedded that a "theology after Auschwitz" of the suffering of innocent men in the world must take on a political responsibility. The Second Vatican Council (1962–1965) denied that there was any legitimate basis in Christian theology for hatred of the Jews (the repudiation of the condemnation of Jews as "Christ-killers"), and called for Christian dialogue with the Jews, whom Pope John XXIII called "our elder brothers."

Markus Hattstein
(translated by Cyprian Blamires)

See Also: ANTI-SEMITISM; ARYANISM; AUSCHWITZ (-BIRKENAU); BLOOD; BLOOD AND SOIL; BOLSHEVISM; BONHOEFFER, DIETRICH; CATHOLIC CHURCH, THE; CHAMBERLAIN, HOUSTON STEWART; CHRISTIANITY; CONFESSING CHURCH, THE; COSMOPOLITANISM; DINTER, ARTUR; ECKHART, "MEISTER" JOHANN; EUGENICS; EUTHANASIA; GALEN, CLEMENS AUGUST GRAF VON; GERMAN CHRISTIANS, THE; GERMAN FAITH MOVEMENT, THE; HERO, THE CULT OF THE; HITLER, ADOLF; HOLOCAUST,

THE; JESUITS, THE; LAGARDE, PAUL DE; LIBERALISM (IN THEOLOGY); LIEBENFELS, JÖRG ADOLF JOSEF LANZ VON; LUDENDORFF, ERICH; LUDENDORFF, MATHILDE; LUTHERAN CHURCHES, THE; MATERIALISM; MUSSOLINI, BENITO ANDREA; MYSTICISM; NAZISM; NIEMOELLER, MARTIN; NORDIC SOUL, THE; OCCULTISM; PACIFISM; PIUS XI, POPE; PIUS XII, POPE; PROTESTANTISM; RACIAL DOCTRINE; RATIONALISM; RELIGION; ROSENBERG, ALFRED; SCHMITT, CARL; SCHÖNERER, GEORG RITTER VON; SOUL; SPANN, OTHMAR; TOTALITARIANISM; *UNTERMENSCHEN* ("SUBHUMANS"); *VOLK, VÖLKISCH;* WORLD WAR II

References

Fasching, Darrell J. 1991. *Narrative Theology after Auschwitz: From Alienation to Ethics.* Minneapolis, MN: Fortress.

Feige, Franz G. M. 1990. *The Varieties of Protestantism in Nazi Germany: Five Theopolitical Positions.* Lewiston: Edwin Mellen.

Lindsay, Mark R. 2001. *Covenanted Solidarity: The Theological Basis of Karl Barth's Opposition to Anti-Semitism and the Holocaust.* New York: Peter Lang.

Rubenstein, Richard L. *After Auschwitz: History, Theology, and Contemporary Judaism.* Baltimore, MD: Johns Hopkins University Press.

Schuttke-Scherle, Peter. 1989. *From Contextual to Ecumenical Theology? Dialogue between Minjung Theology and "Theology after Auschwitz."* Berne: Peter Lang.

Steigmann-Gall, Richard. 2003. *The Holy Reich: Nazi Conceptions of Christianity, 1919–1945.* Cambridge: Cambridge University Press.

Winter, Julie M. 1998. *Luther Bible Research in the Context of Volkish Nationalism in the Twentieth Century.* Berne: Peter Lang.

THIRD POSITIONISM

Variant of postwar fascism that rejects the stylistic trappings of "classic" interwar fascism, particularly its statism and corporate economics, seeking instead a "third way" between the twin materialistic poles of "capitalist greed and Marxist servitude." Third Positionism espouses a leftist, though not socialist, brand of anticapitalism, exemplified in the 1930s by conservative revolutionary thinkers like Ernst Jünger and Armin Mohler, as well as "martyrs" like José Antonio Primo de Rivera and Corneliu Codreanu. This "leftist" tradition, always a marginal influence on interwar fascism, is most frequently identified, however, with the anti-Semitic anticapitalism of the Strasser brothers, leading luminaries in the Nazi party prior to 1933. When Gregor was murdered in 1934 during the Night of the Long Knives, Otto fled into exile, where he became a vehement source of anti-Nazi anti-Semitism and an important ideological source nominally devoid of the taint of Nazism.

In Britain during the 1980s this tendency manifested itself within a faction of the National Front that sought to reinvent their anti-Zionist Strasserism as "patriotic socialism." In doing so they absorbed the abhorrence of the consequences of the Industrial Revolution prevalent in the writings of Victorian socialists like William Morris and Robert Blatchford, to situate themselves within what they claimed was a native Anglo-Saxon *völkisch* tradition.

The rampant ideological eclecticism of Third Position ideology also allows it to absorb the ideas of the French Nouvelle Droite, which argues that liberalism is deliberately fostering mass immigration, miscegenation, and material culture as a means of destroying the cultural and racial "ethno-plurality" of the European race. This intellectualized advocacy of a racial apartheid is often refined by the Third Position with reference to Julius Evola, whose esoteric Traditionalism led him to ascribe a spiritual, transcendental quality to white racial identity. This exclusive Indo-European identity is to be defended through a framework of decentralized regionalism embodied in the slogan "Europe of a Hundred Flags." In Britain this system was to be politically governed according to "popular rule" as outlined in the *Green Book* of Libyan leader Colonel Qadhafi. Third Positionism has lost none of its potency with the collapse of "really existing socialism" in 1989. Several groups have sought to maintain their ideological relevance by absorbing contemporary anarchist theories regarding the bipolar nature of the anticapitalist struggle (that is, centralists versus decentralists) in order to position themselves in the vanguard of the antiglobalization movement.

Graham Macklin

See Also: ANTI-SEMITISM; CAPITALISM; CODREANU, CORNELIU ZELEA; COMMUNITY; CORPORATISM; ECONOMICS; EUROPEAN NEW RIGHT, THE; EVOLA, JULIUS; GERMANY; GLOBALIZATION; IMMIGRATION; JÜNGER, ERNST; LIBERALISM; MARXISM; MATERIALISM; MOHLER, ARMIN; NATIONAL FRONT (UK), THE; NATIONALISM; NAZISM; NIGHT OF THE LONG KNIVES, THE; POSTWAR FASCISM; PRIMO DE RIVERA, JOSÉ ANTONIO; QADHAFI (GADDHAFI), MU'AMMAR: RACIAL DOCTRINE; SOCIALISM; STATE, THE; STRASSER BROTHERS, THE; THIRD WAY, THE; TRADITIONALISM; *VOLK, VÖLKISCH; VOLKSGEMEINSCHAFT,* THE; ZIONISM

References

Cheles, L., R. Ferguson, and M. Vaughan, eds. 1991. *Neo-Fascism in Europe.* London: Longman.

Eatwell, R. 1995. *Fascism: A History.* London: Chatto and Windus.

Griffin, R. 1993. *The Nature of Fascism.* London: Routledge.

———. 1995. *Fascism.* Oxford: Oxford University Press.

———. 1998. *"Ce n'est pas Le Pen":* The MSI/AN's Estrangement from the Front National's Immigration Policy." In *Racism, Ideology and Political Organization,* edited by Charles Westin London: Routledge.

———. 1999. "GUD Reactions: The Patterns of Prejudice of a Neo-fascist *Groupuscule." Patterns of Prejudice* 33, no. 2, pp. 31–50.

———. 2000a. "Between Metapolitics and *Apoliteía:* The New Right's Strategy for Conserving the Fascist Vision in the 'Interregnum.'" *Contemporary French Studies* 8, no. 2, pp. 35–53.

———. 2000b. "Interregnum or Endgame? Radical Right Thought in the 'Post-fascist' Era." *Journal of Political Ideologies* 5, no. 2, pp. 163–178.

Lee, M. 1997. *The Beast Reawakens.* London: Little, Brown.

Merkl, P. H., and L. Weinberg. 1997. *The Revival of Right-wing Extremism in the Nineties.* London: Frank Cass.

THIRD REICH, THE

Initially advocated in 1924 by "conservative revolutionary" Arthur Moeller van den Bruck in a book of the same name, and subsequently taken up as a Nazi slogan under the Weimar Republic. The term draws upon a number of historical precedents, particularly the Holy Roman Empire inaugurated by Charlemagne (Charles the Great) on Christmas Day, A.D. 800. This first Reich, or empire, lasted until 1806, when Napoleon Bonaparte introduced the Confederation of the Rhine and forced Francis II to abandon the historical title of "Holy Roman Emperor." This "thousand year Reich" was romanticized by German nationalists and was consciously evoked with the advent of the "Second Reich" under Kaiser (German for "Caesar") Wilhelm II following the Franco-Prussian War of 1870 and the unification of Germany in 1871. This Second Reich lasted until defeat in World War I; German ultranationalists and Nazis championed Imperial Germany during the Weimar Republic as the second instance of a dominant legacy and the promise of future European hegemony. Generally understood to have moved from ideological ideal to political reality with the rise of Hitler to the chancellorship of Germany on 30 January 1933, the term *Third Reich* is often used interchangeably with the term *Nazi Germany.*

Matt Feldman

See Also: BARBAROSSA, FREDERICK, HOLY ROMAN EMPEROR; GERMANY; HIMMLER, HEINRICH; HITLER, ADOLF; HOLY ROMAN EMPIRE, THE; *MEIN KAMPF;* MOELLER VAN DEN BRUCK, ARTHUR; NATIONALISM; NAZISM; TRADITION; WEIMAR REPUBLIC, THE; WORLD WAR I

References

Burleigh, Michael. 2000. *The Third Reich.* London: Macmillan.

Kershaw, Ian. 2002. *The Nazi Dictatorship: Problems of Perspective and Interpretation.* London: Hodder Arnold.

Leitz, Christian, ed. 1999. *The Third Reich: The Essential Readings.* Oxford: Blackwell.

Stackelberg, Roderick, and Sally A. Winkle. 2002. *The Nazi Germany Sourcebook.* London: Routledge.

THIRD WAY, THE

In the thinking of interwar fascist ideologues and some of their postwar successors, their doctrine was often presented as a "third way" between capitalism and socialism—whether of the Marxian or moderate Bernsteinian variety. In their way of thinking, both of these social philosophies were flawed. In the first place, both were varieties of "internationalism," which fascists were inclined to dismiss contemptuously as "cosmopolitanism." In other words, they both represented transnational networks that paid little or no attention to what in the fascist understanding was the fundamental issue (and source of value)—the nation. Early-twentieth-century financiers already operated in a global market; in their eyes profit was the main concern, the welfare of particular nations mattering not a jot. In fascist rhetoric the global activities of international banking and finance were stylized as "plutocracy." In the case of the Nazis and sometimes in Italian Fascist propaganda, this term was also a code for "Jews." Against this international plutocracy the fascist philosophy argued for economic autarky, or self-sufficiency. Fascists were hypernationalists, and for them the national interest was to be paramount. They were involved in a relentless war of attrition with other nations, with the survival of the fittest at stake, and so it was important to minimize dependence on rival nations. Like capitalism, socialism too was a transnational creed in which the interests of one class of person, the working man, was given primacy over the interests of all others—as in the celebrated slogan "Workers of the World Unite!" So both capitalism and classic socialism were found wanting by fascism.

A second grounds for rejecting capitalism and socialism alike was their association with materialism; fascists saw their creed as a noble creed of the higher values—courage, honor, pride, and the martial virtues. Communism was likewise dismissed as materialistic because of the Marxist theory of dialectical materialism with its conviction that changes in the social relations of production were the motive force of historical development and its resolute reduction of all social issues to financial ones.

These two themes—the subservience of national interests in both capitalism and socialism, and the materialism inherent in both that had dragged Germany and Italy down into the mire of decadence—were major reasons why fascists claimed to be rejecting both (classic) socialism and capitalism. Instead, they argued for an associative system known as corporatism that (they hoped) would involve representatives of the different elements in society cooperating in the national interest, rather than fighting for their sectional interests against those of the whole nation. They believed that the productive of the nation had so much in the way of common interest that the employee/boss polarity could be transcended; it was reminiscent of the protosocialism of Claude-Henri Saint-Simon, who had argued for an alliance of the productive in society against the "drones"—the aristocracy or the financial speculators. Their ideal was of a powerful, aggressive, and united nation ready to take on all comers. In the case of the Nazis there was the additional element that the nation meant not primarily a totality of citizens but a racially purified body; they were campaigning for the German nation as they wanted it to be, expanded to cover all linguistically and racially pukka Germans, rather than Germany as it was.

Left-wing critics of fascism quite rightly questioned what lay behind fascist rhetoric. Marxists flatly denied that fascism was anything but capitalist, as one would have expected of them. They thought of fascism as the most extreme form of capitalism yet encountered. All critics have discounted the claim of the Nazis in particular (but also of the Italian Fascists) that they were socialists of a new kind, *national* socialists, perhaps more out of a sense of horror that socialism could be associated with the historical horrors of fascism—especially of Nazism—rather than out of any logic. In truth there seems no reason to deny that in some sense fascists *did* represent a middle way, and indeed that this was one of the reasons for their success. The fact that they patently failed to implement their "middle way" policies effectively does not necessarily mean that they never intended to do so, since it is a rare phenomenon for politicians to implement their ideologies perfectly. In the end fascists clearly made compromises with capitalism, but equally they pursued measures for state control of industry such as would normally be considered "socialist."

Cyprian Blamires

See Also: INTRODUCTION; ABSTRACTION; ANTI-SEMITISM; BANKS, THE; CAPITALISM; CORPORATISM; COSMOPOLITANISM; DECADENCE; ECONOMICS; *EHRE* ("HONOR"); EXPANSIONISM; FASCIST PARTY, THE; GERMANY; INDUSTRY; ITALY; MARXISM; MARXIST THEORIES OF FASCISM; MATERIALISM; NATIONALISM; NAZISM; PERONISM; PLUTOCRACY; PRODUCTIVISM; RACIAL DOCTRINE; SOCIAL DARWINISM; SOCIALISM; SPANN, OTHMAR; STATE, THE; THIRD POSITIONISM; WARRIOR ETHOS, THE; WORK

References

Bastow, S. 2002. "A Neo-Fascist Third Way: The Discourse of Ethno-Differentialist Revolutionary Nationalism." *Journal of Political Ideologies* 7, no. 3: 351–368.
Bastow, S., and J. Martin. 2003. *Third Way Discourse: European Ideologies in the Twentieth Century.* Edinburgh: Edinburgh University Press.
Camus, Jean-Yves. 1998. *L'extrême droite aujourd'hui.* Toulouse: Milan.
Finocchiaro, Maurice A. 1999. *Beyond Right and Left: Democratic Elitism in Mosca and Gramsci.* New Haven: Yale University Press.
Sternhell, Z. 1986. *Neither Right, nor Left.* Princeton: Princeton University Press.

THOUSAND-YEAR REICH, THE: *See* THIRD REICH, THE

THULE SEMINAR, THE

A dominant constellation and network important for the rise of the "New Right" in Germany in the 1990s. Led by Pierre Krebs, it recycles ideas from the "conservative revolution" and adds in harsh anti-Americanism and anti-Zionism. The recurrent themes are "Europeanism," neopaganism, and SS esotericism. One main slogan is "ethno-pluralism"—that is, the primacy of the *Volk* over individuals and the common rights of every *Volk* to protect its own culture and history; in the end, this means something not far from apartheid. The seminar publishes the journals *Metapo* and *Elemente*. Its name alludes to the Thule Society.

Göran Dahl

See Also: AMERICANIZATION; EUROPEAN NEW RIGHT, THE; EUROPEANIST FASCISM/RADICAL RIGHT, THE; GLOBALIZATION; MYSTICISM; MYTH; NATIONALISM; NEO-NAZISM; POSTWAR FASCISM; SS, THE; *VOLK, VÖLKISCH*; ZIONISM

Reference
Harris, G. 1990. *The Dark Side of Europe. The Extreme Right Today.* Edinburgh: Edinburgh University Press.

THULE SOCIETY, THE

German esoteric order, often regarded as the political faction of the German Order, founded in 1912 by Rudolf von Sebottendorff (1875–1945). He also purchased the paper the *Beobachter* and renamed it the *Völkischer Beobeachter.* The context of the order was the short-lived Soviet regime in Bavaria in 1919, and it was actively involved in the overthrowing of that regime. It used the swastika as its logo, and among its members were Anton Drexler, Rudolf Hess, Gottfried Feder, Alfred Rosenberg, Julius Streicher, and Dietrich Eckart. In 1919, one of its meetings was attended by Adolf Hitler.

Göran Dahl

See Also: DREXLER, ANTON; ECKART, DIETRICH; FEDER, GOTTFRIED; GERMANY; HESS, RUDOLF; HIMMLER, HEINRICH; HITLER, ADOLF; MYSTICISM; NAZISM; OCCULTISM; RÓSENBERG, ALFRED; STREICHER, JULIUS; TIBET; *VOLKISCHER BEOBACHTER*, THE; SWASTIKA, THE

References
Goodrick Clarke, Nicholas. 1994. *The Occult Roots of Nazism: Secret Aryan Cults and Their Influence on Nazi Ideology.* New York: New York University Press.
Schwartzwaller, Wulf. 1990. *The Unknown Hitler: His Private Life and Fortune.* New York: Berkley.
Sklar, D. 1977. *The Nazis and the Occult.* New York: Dorset.

THUNDER CROSS, THE

The major extremist nationalist group in Latvia. It was founded in 1933 after its predecessor, Fire Cross (*Ugunskrusts*), was banned. Led by Gustavs Celmiň̌s

(1899–1968), Thunder Cross adopted certain paramilitary attributes and the slogan "Latvia for the Latvians." It was most popular among young, urban, educated men who resented the predominance of Germans and Jews in the professions. After declaring martial law in 1934, Prime Minister Kārlis Ulmanis arrested their leaders. Thunder Cross cells, nevertheless, continued to operate underground. Some former members collaborated with the Nazis when they invaded in 1941. Since Latvia's recovery of independence, a militant group of nationalists has revived the name.

Andres Kasekamp

See Also: ANTI-SEMITISM; LATVIA; NATIONALISM; NAZISM; ULMANIS, KĀRLIS

Reference
Ezergailis, Andrew. 1996. *The Holocaust in Latvia: The Missing Center.* Riga: Historical Institute of Latvia.

THYSSEN, FRITZ (1873–1951)

Wealthy industrialist and supporter of Hitler in the early 1930s. He invited Hitler to speak at a meeting of Düsseldorf industrialists on 27 January 1932, the first time that Hitler had an opportunity to meet German industry chiefs. They responded to him as a champion who was resolutely pro-private property and anti-Bolshevik. From that point on they became a source of funds for the Nazi Party. In 1933, Hitler put Thyssen in charge of an institute of studies for research on the corporate state, and he took on the mantle of an economics expert in the party. However, Thyssen soon developed doubts about the movement, and on 28 December 1939 he left Germany for Switzerland. He was later arrested in France and incarcerated in concentration camps until 1945. He died in Argentina some years after the war.

Cyprian Blamires

See Also: BOLSHEVISM; CONCENTRATION CAMPS; CORPORATISM; FINANCE; GERMANY; HITLER, ADOLF; INDUSTRY; NAZISM

Reference
Thyssen, Fritz. 1941. *I Paid Hitler.* London: Hodder and Stoughton.

TIBET

In 1938 the Ahnenerbe mounted an expedition to Tibet, one of the main purposes of which was to seek for scientific evidence regarding the origins of the Aryan race, believed by some to have originated there. Heinrich Himmler was a member of the Thule Society, named after the mythical land of Hyperborea-Thule, and some argued that the inhabitants of ancient Thule had survived to become a subterranean super-race. A nineteenth-century science fiction novel (Edward Bulwer-Lytton's *The Coming Race,* 1871) had portrayed them as potential world conquerors possessed of a special psychokinetic power that he called *Vril.* Professor Karl Haushofer founded the Vril Society, which sought contacts with these subterranean supermen in order to find out from them the secrets of ancient Thule. The Vril Society hypothesized that the Aryan race had a central Asian origin—hence the interest in Tibet, which in Haushofer's opinion held the key to discovering the power of *vril.* (Hitler himself had studied Haushofer's writings during his imprisonment and had subsequently been introduced to Haushofer by Rudolf Hess.)

It so happened that the Tibetan government was making overtures at the time to Germany and Japan as potential allies against the threat from China, and the Germans were invited to send a delegation to attend the Tibetan New Year celebrations of 1939. The expedition took the opportunity to do scientific research on the Tibetan people, and anthropologist Bruno Beger examined a large number of skulls from the region, recording their physical characteristics with great care. He came to the conclusion that the Tibetans were an intermediary between the Mongol and the European races, and he believed that the Tibetan aristocracy showed particularly strong European racial elements.

Cyprian Blamires

See Also: AHNENERBE; ANTHROPOLOGY; ARYANISM; HAUSHOFER, KARL ERNST; HESS, RUDOLF; HIMMLER, HEINRICH; HITLER, ADOLF; SS, THE; THULE SOCIETY, THE

References
Hale, C. 2003. *Himmler's Crusade: The True Story of the 1938 Nazi Expedition into Tibet.* London: Bantam.
Pringle, H. 2006. *The Master Plan: Himmler's Scholars and the Holocaust.* New York: Fourth Estate.

TISO, MGR. JOSEF (1887–1947)

President of the first Slovak Republic, 1939–1945. He was the natural successor when Msgr. Andrej Hlinka, leader of the Slovak People's Party, died in 1938. Prime minister of the autonomous region of Slovakia from October 1938, Tiso became president of the Slovak Republic when it became independent in March 1939. As a moderate, he sought to resist German Nazi encroachments on Slovak independence, in particular adherence to the Anti-Comintern Pact and the deportations of Slovak Jews to Auschwitz. He was tried for treason against the Czechoslovak state and executed on 18 April 1947.

John Pollard

See Also: ANTI-COMINTERN PACT, THE; ANTI-SEMITISM; AUSCHWITZ (-BIRKENAU); CATHOLIC CHURCH, THE; CLERICO-FASCISM; CZECHOSLOVAKIA; GERMANY; HOLOCAUST, THE; NAZISM; POLITICAL CATHOLICISM; SLOVAKIA

TOKYO ROSE: *See* RADIO

TOLKIEN, JOHN RONALD REUEL (1892–1973)

South African–born Oxford professor of Anglo-Saxon and subsequently of English language and literature; one of the most celebrated fiction writers of the twentieth century, whose plots and symbolism have been given fascistic interpretations in recent decades. In the late 1970s the Movimento Sociale Italiano (MSI), founded to perpetuate the values of Mussolini's Italian Social Republic, organized a summer camp in the Abruzzi mountains in Italy for its Youth Front under the name "Camp Hobbit." The title chosen for the book marking the foundation of the Italian New Right was *Hobbit/Hobbit;* it was published under the imprint "The Rock of Erec," another allusion to the Tolkien mythological universe. Moreover, the president of the Italian Tolkien Society in this period was the prominent neofascist intellectual and admirer of Julius Evola, Gianfranco de Turris, who has been a prominent spokesman of the Tolkien cult in Italy ever since the 1970s. In the early 2000s material on Tolkien was still to be found on the websites of Third Positionists, such as the "Synthesis" site of Troy Southgate (former organizer of the United Kingdom's National Front) and of the European New Right, such as Russia's "Eurasianist" Arctogaia organization, led by Alexander Dugin.

Four decades before its transformation into a hugely successful cinematic trilogy in 2003, *The Lord of the Rings* had become one of the "prescribed texts" of the international leftist counterculture of the 1960s, along with works by William Blake, Carl Jung, Carlos Castaneda, and Hermann Hesse, one of the hippie slogans being "Frodo Lives." The genesis of an extreme-right reading of Tolkien lies in the special political climate that emerged in Italy in the 1970s as a result of the failure of the MSI to break out of the political ghetto. This led some of its leading intellectuals to look to the French New Right as a role model for achieving "cultural hegemony" by creating a "right-wing culture" capable of emulating the powerful youth-oriented left-wing culture that had arisen all over Europe against the background of the hippie movement and an international wave of student militancy directed against both Soviet and U.S. imperialism as embodied in the arms race and the Vietnam War. These postwar fascists tapped into the deep fascination with things esoteric found in prewar fascism and particularly in Nazism. The early Nazi Party had links to the Thule Society, which based its cosmology on a merger of occultism and racism called Ariosophy. The Third Reich deliberately associated itself with the overtly antirationalist worldviews of such figures as Paracelsus, Wagner, and Nietzsche, while Himmler wove a number of mythic, pagan, and occultist notions into the elite training program of the SS in the training academies called Ordensburgen. A parallel to this esoteric strand of fascism in Nazism was the alternative philosophy of history that the Italian cultural "philosopher" Julius Evola elaborated in the 1930s out of Hindu, alchemical, and occultist currents of thought. These became the basis of a stream of publications through which he attempted to influence both Mussolini's regime and postwar fascism. In Spain, Romania, and South Africa, fascists, despite the fundamentally pagan orientation of their revolution, attempted to inject their ultranationalist movements with the spirituality of organized Christianity, which

in the case of the Romanian Iron Guard was blended with a cult of death and sacrifice with strong cultic and esoteric elements.

It is consistent with this urge to sacralize and metapoliticize reality that some contemporary right-wing intellectuals have produced a reading of *The Lord of the Rings* as the evocation of the higher values necessary to rebel against contemporary decadence and achieve a cultural and political rebirth. It involves what could be called a "Gnostic" reading, based on the assumption that Tolkien has (even subliminally) encoded spiritual truths that only those attuned to a higher realm of values are able to decipher. "Properly" understood (that is, in terms of a revolutionary nationalist or racist worldview), his epic can evoke a magical world whose fate is still decided by the outcome of metaphysical conflicts determined by the ability of chivalry and heroism to overcome a moral evil embodied in physical degeneracy. It can even be read as a moral legend bringing into stark relief the moral bankruptcy of modernity, in which the imperialism of liberal and communist societies represents the true evil, reducing man to a spiritual dwarf in the thrall of materialism and cut off from "magic consciousness." At the height of the new wave of Tolkien-mania unleashed by the film trilogy in 2003, Dr. Stephen Spencer, English lecturer at Warwick University, was warning in interviews to the press and on websites that *The Lord of the Rings* contained a deep subtext of racist alarm at the rise of a multicultural and materialist society. A year later the website of the neo-Nazi magazine *Spearhead* was claiming Tolkien to have been a regular reader of A. K. Chesterton's extreme-right-wing *Candour*, and was recommending his texts to its readers with the assertion that "the moral imperatives of the Northern European shine through in this great saga."

Roger Griffin

See Also: INTRODUCTION; CHESTERTON, ARTHUR KENNETH; CHRISTIANITY; CULTS OF DEATH; DECADENCE; DEGENERACY; DUGIN, ALEKSANDR GEL'EVICH; EUROPEAN NEW RIGHT, THE; EVOLA, JULIUS; FASCIST PARTY, THE; HIMMLER, HEINRICH; IRON GUARD, THE; ITALY; LIBERALISM; MARXISM; MATERIALISM; MODERNITY; MOVIMENTO SOCIALE ITALIANO, THE; MULTICULTURALISM; MUSSOLINI, BENITO ANDREA; MYSTICISM; MYTH; NATIONALISM; NAZISM; NIETZSCHE, FRIEDRICH; OCCULTISM; PALINGENETIC MYTH; POSTWAR FASCISM; RACISM; RELIGION; ROMANIA; SALÒ REPUBLIC, THE; SOUTH AFRICA; SPAIN; SS, THE; THIRD POSITIONISM; THIRD REICH, THE; THULE SOCIETY, THE; TIBET; WAGNER, (WILHELM) RICHARD; WARRIOR ETHOS, THE

References

Galli, Giorgio. 1983. "La componente magica della cultura di destra." In *Nuova destra e cultura reazionaria negli anni ottanta: Atti del Convegno—Cuneo 19–21 novembre 1982,* edited by P. Bologna and E. Mana. Notiziario dell'Istituto storico della Resistenza in Cuneo, no. 23.

Goodrick-Clarke, N. 1985. *The Occult Roots of Nazism.* Wellingborough: Aquarian.

———. 2002. *Black Sun: Aryan Cults, Esoteric Nazism and the Politics of Identity.* New York: New York University Press.

Griffin, R. 1985. "Revolts against the Modern World: The Blend of Literary and Historical Fantasy in the Italian New Right." *Literature and History* 11, no. 1, pp. 101–124.

Jesi, F. 1979. *Cultura di destra.* Milan: Garzanti.

Porrelli, A. 1983. "Tradizione e meta-tradizione: appunti su *Il Signore degli anelli.*" In *Nuova destra e cultura reazionaria negli anni ottanta, Atti del Convegno—Cuneo 19–21 novembre 1982,* edited by P. Bologna and E. Mana. Notiziario dell'Istituto storico della Resistenza in Cuneo, no. 23.

Sheehan, T. 1981. "Myth and Violence: The Fascism of Julius Evola and Alain de Benoist." *Social Research* 48, no. 1, pp. 45–73.

TOTALITARIANISM

"TOTALITARIAN" AND "TOTALITARIANISM"

The terms *totalitario* and *totalitarismo* were first introduced into political language in Italy in the 1920s. They were invented by the enemies of Italian Fascism shortly after the rise to power of Benito Mussolini at the end of 1922 to define the arbitrary and violent methods used by the Fascist Party to eliminate opposition and to win the monopoly of power. It seems that the man who coined the term *totalitarian* was the liberal antifascist Giovanni Amendola. He first used it in April 1923 to define the new electoral system that the Fascist government planned to exploit to guarantee control over the Chamber of Deputies, together with its subversion of the parliamentary regime by the superimposition on organs of state such as the Council of Ministers and the police of its own party organs—such as the Grand Council of Fascism and the Voluntary Militia for National Security, which legalized the armed Fascist squads. A few months later, when Fascism celebrated its first year in government, Amendola denounced "the totalitarian spirit" that motivated Fascism's claim to be entitled to impose itself on all Italians by means of a "religious war" to control not only their political activity but also their conscience, obliging them to conform to its style and ideology. The term *totalitarian* began to be used by Italian anti-

Fascists between 1923 and 1925 in conjunction with the terms *regime* and *state party* to define the integralist mentality and the violent methods used by the Fascist Party to destroy opposition and conquer the state. Early in 1924 the priest Luigi Sturzo, founder of the Italian Popular Party, analyzed the new Fascist conception of the "state party" as involving the total transformation of every moral, cultural, political, and religious force. In May 1924 another Catholic anti-Fascist, the writer Igino Giordani, criticized the attitude of the Church as too favorable to the Fascist government, claiming that the "totalitarian soul" of the "Fascist religion" was incompatible with Christian doctrine. Later, on the very day before Mussolini's speech of 3 January 1925, which marked the formal beginning of the Fascist dictatorship, the term *totalitarismo* was used by a Marxist anti-Fascist named Lelio Basso to describe the subordination of state institutions to the Fascist political monopoly.

After 1925, Fascists themselves began to use the term *totalitarian* and its derivatives to parade their decision to impose their own domination over the state and society. The Fascist philosopher Giovanni Gentile applied the term to indicate the religious character (in the sense of a secular religion) of Fascism and its conception of politics and the state. Mussolini used the term *totalitarian* for the first time in a speech of 25 June 1925 at the conclusion of the Congress of the Fascist Party, declaring openly that Fascism would no longer tolerate dissensions and opposition and aimed to "fascistize the nation": "We want . . . to fascistize the nation, so that tomorrow Italian and Fascist will be the same thing." In the years that followed, Fascism adopted the term *totalitarian state* or *totalitarian regime* as its hallmark, to define the new regime established by the Fascist Party. From then on, anti-Fascists and Fascists commonly used *totalitarian, totalitarian state,* and *totalitarianism* to define the ideology and organization of the new one-party regime established by Fascism after 1925 and based on the command of Il Duce as invested with an undisputed dictatorial power, on a system of police repression, and on a network of mass organizations that placed all of the population under the control of the Fascist Party.

THEORY OF TOTALITARIANISM

The advent to power of Nazism in 1933 and the spread of dictatorial regimes in Europe in the 1930s inspired the first attempts at a theoretical definition of totalitarianism through comparative analysis of

fascism, Bolshevism, and National Socialism. These were made between 1935 and 1945 by antifascist and anticommunist scholars like C. Hoover, H. Kohn, L. Sturzo, A. Cobban, F. Borkenau, E. Lederer, and S. Neumannn, to highlight the novelty of the new dictatorial regimes in comparison with traditional authoritarian governments—that is, the single party that monopolized power and organized and mobilized the masses, indoctrinating them according to an ideology transformed into a secular religion, established the leader cult, and applied a repressive terroristic practice with respect to persons and groups considered internal enemies. After 1946, with the beginning of the Cold War, the concept of totalitarianism was developed by antifascist and anticommunist scholars like H. Arendt, C. J. Friedrich, and Z. Brzezinski, who tended to associate the Nazi regime in particular with the Stalinist regime; they focused on the omnicomprehensive ideology; the control by the party of the state, the means of propaganda, the economy, and the organization of the anonymous masses; plus the politics of terrorism culminating in the Stalinist gulags and the Nazi extermination camps.

The concept of totalitarianism fell out of fashion in academic research for a while, but in recent years there has been a renewal of theoretical reflection on it, liberating it from polemical prejudices and from the rigidity of theoretical models. Political scientists and historians like J. Linz and K. D. Bracher developed definitions of totalitarianism more adequate to cover the historical reality of the phenomena that gave rise to the concept. The reflection and research of recent decades has led to the elaboration of a new definition of totalitarianism along the following lines: an experiment in political domination implemented by a revolutionary movement that is organized into a rigidly disciplined party with a totalizing conception of politics, which aspires to the monopoly of power and which, after having obtained it (whether by legal or by extralegal means), destroys or transforms the existing regime and constructs a new state, founded on a one-party regime, with the main objective of achieving the conquest of society—that is, the subordination, integration, and homogenization of the governed on the basis of the principle of the integral political nature of the existence of the individual and the collective, interpreted according to the categories, myths, and values of a sacralized ideology in the form of a political religion, with the purpose of molding the individual and the masses through an anthropological revolution, to regenerate the human being and create a new man, devoted body and soul to the realization of the revolutionary and imperialistic projects of the totalitarian party, with the aim of creating a new civilization of a supranational character.

FASCIST TOTALITARIANISM

Hitler and the Nazi chiefs did not apply the term *totalitarian* to the Third Reich, but the "totalitarian" affinities of the German and Italian regimes are evident in the structure of the political system and in the mass politics; in the militarization of politics through a rigid hierarchical organization of party and state; in the sacralization of the nation and the single party through the adoption of a liturgical style founded on rites and symbols; in the transformation of ideology into a secular religion that claimed to be defining the meaning and scope of earthly life for the individual and the masses; in the emergence of the figure of the leader made into the object of a collective cult; in the utilization of the means provided by technological and organizational modernization to mobilize the masses and develop an intense and constant activity of collective indoctrination; in the police repression of dissent and discrimination against groups considered harmful to the national community, down to persecution and (in the case of Nazism) to extermination; in the conservation of private property alongside an extension of state intervention and control over the economy; in the subordination of the trades unions to the state and the extension of welfare policy; in the ambition to subject society to permanent massive control by the single party, to achieve the creation of a new type of human being through indoctrination, physical education, and family policy, inspired by eugenic concepts of the protection and improvement of the race, with the predominant aim of demographic growth for the requirements of military power. Coherently with their conception of life, of politics, and of the nation, both regimes pursued a belligerent imperialist vocation on the international level to conquer new vital spaces and to create a New Europe and a New Order modeled on their own.

A fundamental aspect of fascist totalitarianism that distinguished it clearly from traditional authoritarianism was the constant mobilization of the masses through a network of men's and women's organizations, which included every category and every age, and tended to embrace every aspect of individual and collective life, from political activity to working activity, from leisure activity to specialized activity. Youth organizations like l'Organizzazione Nazionale Balilla and the Fasci Giovanili (later unified into the Gioventù Italiana del Littorio in 1937) and the Hitler Youth were objects of special attention as laboratories for the rearing of the "New Man." Alongside the properly political organizations of the party, reserved to men, the two regimes developed the organization of women, like the Fasci Femminili and the Nationalsozialistische Frauenschaft, and these manifested a notable variation with respect to the antifeminist model predominant in fascist culture of the woman as wife and mother; they promoted the mobilization of women outside the family and in the public arena of welfare and participation in the activity of physical education for the improvement of the race. Also very important in the two regimes were the leisure organizations like the Organizzazione nazionale Dopolavoro and Kraft durch Freude, which were concerned with sports and holidays for workers; they had no explicit ideological dimension, but nonetheless played an important role in helping to integrate the masses into the politics of the regime. The institution of a new calendar, making the year begin with the advent to power of the single party, together with the celebration of regular or occasional collective rites, helped with the process of the integration and indoctrination of the masses. The extent to which the indoctrination process was successful is a highly controverted subject, but of course the level of effectiveness varied according to the social class and type studied. What we can say for sure, however, is that the experience of fascism looks substantially different from that of authoritarian regimes that never took as their primary objective the mobilization of the masses and the anthropological revolution for the creation of a new type of human being.

Fascist totalitarianism as described above did not represent a monolithic, homogenous bloc, but rather a complex reality made up of tensions, contrasts, rivalries, contradictions, successes, and failures. Dualism between party and state at all levels—political, bureaucratic, and military—was a persistent feature of the fascist regimes in Italy and Germany, though it was more marked in Italy because of the presence of the monarchy. Having said that, recent historical researches have demonstrated that the so-called dyarchy between Il Duce and the king, as retroactively theorized by Mussolini after the end of the regime, was in reality a fiction, as fictional as the subordination of the party to the state officially declared by Mussolini in 1927. In reality, effective power in both countries was concentrated in the hands of the party chief, while the increasingly invasive and overbearing presence of the party in state and society was a factor of ongoing disorder and subversion that contributed not a little to weaken the very structure of the regime. The same applies to relations between the totalitarian fascist regimes and the Catholic Church in Italy and Germany, for the Concordat policies followed by both regimes was frequently in difficulties because of their totalitarian character. Putting forward their own total interpretation of the significance and goal of human existence on earth, they did not hesitate to enter into conflict with the traditional religion to claim the absolute primacy of politics and the monopoly of the education of the individual and the masses in accordance with the principles of their own secular ideology.

Of the other dictatorial regimes similar in type to fascism, only the regime of General Francisco Franco defined itself for some time as "authoritarian and totalitarian," but in its organization and structure and its mass politics there was little similarity with fascist totalitarianism—so little, in fact, that in the course of World War II the term *totalitarian* disappeared from the self-definition of the Franco regime. But even if they did not habitually describe themselves as totalitarian, all of the revolutionary nationalist movements that resembled fascism contained the idea of "totality" as expressing their conception of politics and their will to realize the unity and homogeneity of the nation by transforming it into a mystical community based on the sacralization of politics.

Emilio Gentile

See Also: INTRODUCTION; ANTI-SEMITISM; ARENDT, HANNAH; AUTHORITARIANISM; BODY, THE CULT OF THE; BOLSHEVISM; CALENDAR, THE FASCIST; CATHOLIC CHURCH, THE; CHRISTIANITY; COLD WAR, THE; COMMUNITY; CONCENTRATION CAMPS; CONFESSING CHURCH, THE; DEMOGRAPHIC POLICY; ECONOMICS; EDUCATION; EUGENICS; FAMILY, THE; FASCIST PARTY, THE; FRANCO Y BAHAMONDE, GENERAL FRANCISCO; FRANCOISM; GENTILE, GIOVANNI; GERMANY; GRAND COUNCIL OF FASCISM, THE; HITLER, ADOLF; HOLOCAUST, THE; IMPERIALISM; ITALY; LAW; *LEBENSRAUM;* LEADER CULT, THE; LEISURE; MASSES, THE ROLE OF THE; MILITARISM; MILIZIA VOLONTARIA PER LA SICUREZZA NAZIONALE; MUSSOLINI, BENITO ANDREA; MYTH; NAZISM; NEW MAN, THE; NIHILISM; PARLIAMENTARISM; PIUS XI, POPE; PIUS XII, POPE; PROPAGANDA; RACIAL DOCTRINE; RELIGION; REVOLUTION; ROMA AND SINTI, THE; SALUTES; SOVIET UNION, THE; SPAIN; *SQUADRISMO;* STALIN, IOSIF VISSARIONOVICH; STATE, THE; SYMBOLS; TERROR; TRADES UNIONS; VICTOR EMMANUEL/VITTORE EMANUELE III, KING; *UNTERMENSCHEN* ("SUBHUMANS"); *VOLKSGEMEINSCHAFT,* THE; WELFARE; WOMEN; WORLD WAR II; YOUTH

References

Arendt, H. 1986. *The Origins of Totalitarianism.* London: Deutsch.

Baehr, Peter, and Melvin Richter, eds. 2004. *Dictatorship in History and Theory: Bonapartism, Caesarism, and*

Totalitarianism. Washington, DC: German Historical Institute.

Gentile, E. 1996. *The Sacralization of Politics in Fascist Italy.* Cambridge: Harvard University Press.

Halberstam, M. 1999. *Totalitarianism and the Modern Conception of Politics.* London: Yale University Press.

Linz, J. 2000. *Totalitarian and Authoritarian Regimes.* London: Lynne Rienner.

TRADE

The political economy of interwar fascism was based around two central concepts: nation and state. The main belief was that the state is the instrument of the nation, and has a duty to protect it. This core assumption gives rise to other beliefs. It is the role of the state, by means of a giant bureaucratic machine, to control, direct, and "plan" the nation's economy. This does not imply ownership, as in the communist model, but it does imply intervention in a broad sense. Thus, there was a sizable gulf between the fascist conception of "state capitalism" and the traditional liberal-capitalist belief in the free market and free trade. Fascist officials held that state intervention in the economy speeded up economic development, whatever "level" the economy was at to begin with. Mussolini's regime in Italy imposed protective tariffs, regulated credit, and coordinated a structured wages and prices policy. It also launched a series of Four Year Plans. In the modern era, movements like the British National Party and French Front National have made economic nationalism a central pillar of their programs. And as a result, they have both indicated their hostility to the European Union and the policy of recruiting immigrant workers.

It is a short step from economic protectionism to autarky, a policy aimed at national self-sufficiency and insulation in the economic sphere. This brand of economic nationalism (or economic isolationism) is a defining feature of fascism in power. And it is associated mainly with periods of diplomatic and military tension. Autarky also featured strongly in fascist propaganda campaigns, with slogans such as "Help Us Defend You!"; "German Jobs for German Workers!"; "Buy Italian Goods!" Hitler put a major emphasis on autarky. He argued that a country did not require myriad trade links and could survive and prosper alone, on "its own two feet." In practice, the industries that were most affected by autarkic policy were those connected with arms production. But autarky was not a Nazi invention—the truth was that it had become a prominent idea in the years following 1918, when military personnel and politicians alike began to think through why Germany had suffered during the Great War. One answer was that the country had lacked preparedness in the economic sphere. Hence the call for self-sufficiency on a massive scale. But even in Nazi Germany, complete autarky was unattainable, and all trade links did not just disappear. Rather, Germany changed her focus: away from the "big powers" she might soon be at war with (Britain, the USSR, and the United States) and toward more "peripheral" regions such as the Balkans and Central and South America.

P. J. Davies

See Also: AUTARKY; BRITISH NATIONAL PARTY, THE; CAPITALISM; ECONOMICS; FASCIST PARTY, THE; GERMANY; HITLER, ADOLF; IMMIGRATION; INDUSTRY; ITALY; MUSSOLINI, BENITO ANDREA; NATIONAL FRONT, THE (FRANCE); NATIONALISM; NAZISM; STATE, THE; WORLD WAR I

References

Abraham, D. 1981. *The Collapse of the Weimar Republic: Political Economy and Crisis.* Princeton: Princeton University Press.

Barkai, A. 1994. *Nazi Economics: Ideology, Theory and Policy.* Oxford: Berg.

Milward, A. S. 1965. *The German Economy at War.* London: Athlone.

Welk, W. G. 1938. *Fascist Economic Policy: An Analysis of Italy's Economic Experiment.* Cambridge: Harvard University Press.

Zamagni, G. 1993. *The Economic History of Italy, 1860–1990.* Oxford: Clarendon.

TRADE UNIONS

In general terms, interwar fascism viewed trades unions as "left-wing" and "dangerous." In many cases they were banned. New "fascist" trades unions emerged, but in many ways these were artificial, cosmetic entities; the real trades unions went underground. In Germany, Hitler's campaign against the trades unions was a crucial aspect of his rise to power. After he became chancellor in January 1933, he abolished the trades unions. Their offices were closed, their funds were sequestrated, and their leaders were harassed and sent to jail. The aim was to tie working people to the Nazi regime: hence the establishment of the German Labor Front (DAF), a pseudo-workers' body led by Robert Ley and the only "workers organization" allowed under the Third Reich. It had complete control over wages and income tax deductions: pay was frozen, and then reduced. The right to strike was taken away. It issued work-books that acted as a kind of employment "passport"—they recorded the employment record of the individual worker, and no one could gain employment without such a book. It ordered that a worker could not leave his job without the government's consent. The number of hours worked by an average worker rose from sixty to seventy-two per week (including overtime) by 1939. However, one benefit that Ley did bring to working people was not insignificant: they could not be fired on the spot.

William Shirer, a U.S. journalist working in 1930s Germany, observed the new state of play under Hitler: "Despite his harassed life, the businessman made good profits. The businessman was also cheered by the way the workers had been put in their place under Hitler. There were no more unreasonable wage demands. Actually, wages were reduced a little despite a 25 per cent rise in the cost of living. And above all, there were no costly strikes. In fact, there were no strikes at all. The Law Regulating National Labor of January 20, 1934, known as the Charter of Labor, had put the worker in his place and raised the employer to his old position of absolute master—subject, of course, to interference by the all-powerful State." In 2003, in the midst of contemporary political battles, *Searchlight* magazine also made reference to the German situation: "In 1928 the Nazis initiated an 'into the factories' campaign and used anti-capitalist rhetoric to neutralize the hostility of the labor movement towards them—just as the BNP are attempting to do now. On May Day in 1933 Hitler said, 'We are not dreaming—quite the contrary—of destroying the unions. No, worker, your institutions are sacred and inviolable.' The following day, all union offices were occupied by storm troopers, all trade union property was confiscated and union officials were jailed."

In this area, Hitler and Mussolini trod a similar path. In founding the corporate state, Il Duce reorganized the existing system of trades unions and employers' associations. In 1934, twenty-two Fascist corporations—each one representing a specific industry and combining workers and employers—were established; in 1938 their representatives, acting as the so-called Chamber of Corporations, replaced the Italian Parliament.

P. J. Davies

See Also: CORPORATISM; ECONOMICS; EMPLOYMENT; FASCIST PARTY, THE; FORCED LABOR; GERMANY; HITLER, ADOLF; INDUSTRY; ITALY; LABOR FRONT, THE; LABOR SERVICE, THE; LAW; LEY, ROBERT; NAZISM; PERONISM; SA, THE; STATE, THE; SYNDICALISM; THIRD REICH, THE; TOTALITARIANISM

References

Black, R. 1975. *Fascism in Germany: How Hitler Destroyed the World's Most Powerful Labour Movement.* London: Steyne.

Carsten, F. 1995. *The German Workers and the Nazis.* Aldershot: Scolar.

Crew, D. 1994. *Nazism and German Society 1933–1945.* London: Routledge.

Farquarson, J. E. 1976. *The Plough and the Swastika: The NSDAP and Agriculture in Germany, 1928–1945.* London: Sage.

Fisher, C., ed. 1996. *The Rise of National Socialism and the Working Classes in Weimar Germany.* Oxford: Bergbahn.

Roberts, D. D. 1979. *The Syndicalist Tradition in Italian Fascism.* Manchester: Manchester University Press.

Smelser, Ronald. 1992. *Robert Ley: Hitler's Labour Front Leader.* Oxford: Berg.

TRADITION

The outstanding feature of interwar fascism's appeal to tradition was that it was nationalistic. The tradition that Mussolini referred to was that of Roman Antiquity; the tradition that Nazism referred to was Germanic. As the years of his dictatorship passed, Mussolini increasingly promoted the idea that he was responsible for the creation of a new Roman Empire. The language of Italian Fascism was from the beginning imbued with references to Roman Antiquity, from the *fascio,* which inspired its name to the *quadrumvirs* who led the March on Rome. Sarfatti's celebrated biography of Mussolini presented Il Duce as heir to the Roman Caesars. Nazism defined itself as the era of the Third Reich, consciously proposing to re-create the great empires of Germany's past: the medieval and the Wilhelmine.

The need to appeal to past traditions of greatness is suggestive of a present sense of weakness, and in their appeal to their heroic pasts, Italian Fascists and Nazis both played on the widespread disillusionment prevalent in their countries in the aftermath of World War I. At the same time, the obsession with the idea of "empire" reflected both countries' failure to play the role in the nineteenth-century adventure of European imperialism that had so aggrandized Britain and France, whose sense of national pride and self-importance had been greatly inflated by their conquests in Africa and Asia. The fascist concern with revival of their imperial traditions could be seen as the final act in the drama of imperial conquest that had brought so much of the nonindustrialized Southern Hemisphere under the control of two European nations. Italy's march into Ethiopia was in this sense merely anticipatory of Hitler's march into the Soviet Union in 1941, for Hitler was fascinated by the way in which Britain ruled India with a relatively small number of men, planning to deal with the Ukraine in the same way.

Both Italian Fascism and German Nazism consciously chose to emphasize their connectedness to a non-Christian tradition. By deliberately reconnecting with Ancient Rome, Mussolini was opting to go back to a pre-Christian pagan Italian past, implicitly denying Italy's Catholic centuries any value. His establishment of a new *Era fascista,* proclaiming the inauguration of a new Fascist epoch beginning with the March on Rome, was designed to replace the traditional A.D. chronological measurement founded by Christian Europe based on the birth of Christ as the determining moment in a new era of history. Symbolic of this attitude was Mussolini's promotion of extensive archaeological activities in the city of Rome to bring back to prominence the ruins of antiquity: this recuperation of pre-Christian Rome was carried out at the price of destroying a quantity of medieval and baroque buildings. In Nazi thinking the Aryan myth played a similar role, for it created a non-Christian (and non-Jewish) past for the contemporary citizens of Germany to be proud of. The Nazis also venerated the Holy Roman Empire in its early phase; this they interpreted in the fashion of many historians as a powerful, intransigent, and necessary counterweight to the supposedly overweening power of the Roman popes. It was highly significant that Hitler chose to name his invasion of Soviet Russia in 1941 Operation Barbarossa in memory of the Emperor Frederick Barbarossa.

The way that fascism used tradition was one of the features that marked it out from classic authoritarian conservatism. Conservatives in the classic mold aspire to preserve the best in the country's inherited traditions, whereas interwar fascists aspired to turn the myths of their national past into fuel for the creation of an entirely new order. This exploitation of national traditions also distinguished interwar fascism from the various socialisms, which had no investment in national traditions and sought to create a new world order based on an international alliance of the worldwide proletariat.

Cyprian Blamires

See Also: INTRODUCTION; ARYANISM; BARBAROSSA, FREDERICK, HOLY ROMAN EMPEROR; BARBAROSSA, OPERATION; CALENDAR, THE FASCIST; CHRISTIANITY; CONSERVATISM; COUNTERREVOLUTION; ETHIOPIA; *FASCIO*, THE; FASCIST PARTY, THE; HITLER, ADOLF; HOLY ROMAN EMPIRE, THE; IMPERIALISM; MARCH ON ROME, THE; MARXIST THEORIES OF FASCISM; MUSSOLINI, BENITO ANDREA; NATIONALISM; NAZISM; NEW ORDER, THE; NIHILISM; PALINGENETIC MYTH; PAPACY, THE; QUADRUMVIRS, THE; RELIGION; REVOLUTION; ROME; SECULARIZATION; THIRD REICH, THE; TRADITIONALISM; WORLD WAR I

References

Blinkhorn, Martin, ed. 1990. *Fascists and Conservatives: The Radical Right and the Establishment in Twentieth-century Europe.* London: Unwin Hyman.

Eley, G. 1980. *Reshaping the German Right.* London: Yale University Press.

Hermand, Jost. 1992. *Old Dreams of a New Reich: Volkish Utopias and National Socialism.* Trans. Paul Levesque and Stefan Soldovieri. Bloomington: Indiana University Press.

Mack Smith, Denis. 1979. *Mussolini's Roman Empire.* Harmondsworth: Penguin.

Painter, Borden. 2005. *Mussolini's Rome: The Fascist Transformation of the Eternal City.* Basingstoke: Palgrave Macmillan.

Sarti, R. 1970. "Fascist Modernisation in Italy: Traditional or Revolutionary?" *American Historical Review* 75, no.4.

TRADITIONALISM

Apart from its meaning in general parlance of "love of tradition," this term has at least two more specific technical senses in the politico-religious sphere, both of which derive from a particular current of counter-revolutionary thought that developed in France after 1789 and spread to other European countries, a current that influenced certain protofascist ideologues. The main names associated with traditionalism in its first phase in the aftermath of the French Revolution were those of Joseph de Maistre (1754–1821), L. G. A. de Bonald (1754–1840), and Hugues-Félicité Robert de Lamennais (1782–1854). Lamennais, who later abandoned the traditionalist standpoint, was mainly influential in the development of theology; it was Maistre and Bonald who had the biggest impact in the political arena. All three writers rebelled against the French Revolution in the name of tradition, arguing that subjecting national traditions ("the national reason") to rational critique was tantamount to placing the individual above society and exalting rebellion into a social principle, so that the murderous climax to the revolution was a predictable outcome of its philosophy. They blamed the revolution on "individualism," which claimed that the individual citizen had the right to assess the worth of social and political institutions—a claim that led to anarchy on account of the resulting variety and mutual incompatibility of the critiques. This analysis owed much to the celebrated *Reflections on the Revolution in France* (1790) by the Irish writer and politician Edmund Burke (1729–1797). In place of what they saw as modish anarchic individualism stemming from the unhealthy principles of the Enlightenment, these thinkers looked to long-established institutions such as the Catholic Church and the hierarchical society of the ancien regime as bearers of the wisdom of the ages and of the collectivity.

This principle of searching for the laws of the social order in a wisdom expressed in existing traditions, customs, and institutions was seminal in the development of the study of sociology: two of its founding fathers, Saint-Simon and Comte, were huge admirers of Maistre. It also inspired a counter-revolutionary tradition in France that persisted in rejecting the principles of 1789, including the set of ideas known as "integral nationalism," and it was into this tradition that Charles Maurras tapped at the end of the nineteenth century. But while this current of thought either adhered to the Catholicism of Maistre, Bonald, and Lamennais, or at least approved of it as of value to the social order, others concluded that the wisdom of the ages must be sought through the study of global rather than solely Western or French sources; this other kind of traditionalism came to refer to a syncretistic type of thinking that based itself on the wisdom it discovered in the traditions of Eastern as well as Western cultures. Many of those who went down this route became convinced of the old Gnostic belief that there is an occult stream of global wisdom that is available only to initiates; a parallel conviction held that it has been forcibly suppressed by those in authority. The former conviction could lead, for example, to adherence to a movement like Freemasonry, whereas the latter led to a fondness for conspiracy theories in which Freemasonry very frequently figured by contrast as an occult force for the suppression of truth.

While postrevolutionary Catholic traditionalism impacted very strongly on French integral nationalism and the Action française—considered by some scholars to be the first manifestation of fascism—it was "global" traditionalism that fed into Nazism. The whole Aryan myth rested on the idea of a specially gifted race that brought an ancient global wisdom from East to West. The Nazis believed themselves to be building a new world on the basis of this ancient wisdom, which had been submerged by Christianity. While many of them probably had little or no knowledge of the Eastern cultures that were held to be the cradle of the Aryan race, ideologues such as Chamberlain, Hauer, Lanz von Liebenfels, and Rosenberg took a great interest in Buddhism and Hinduism. In Italy the main sympathizer with Fascism, who was also a propagandist for this kind of "global" traditionalism, was Julius Evola, but it did not seriously impact on Mussolini or his followers in their development of their creed. Evola has, however, been a figure of huge importance in the development of postwar fascism.

There is a direct line from the postrevolutionary traditionalist prioritization of the collectivity over the individual to the core ideas of Italian Fascism. Postrevolutionary traditionalism diagnosed the ills resulting from the revolution as being caused by a weak political authority that allowed individuals unbridled license to criticize the existing order, and that certainly fed into both Italian Fascism and German Nazism. In addition, Joseph de Maistre (along with others, such as Barruel and Robison) helped popularize the idea that the revolution, far from being the result of intolerable oppression of one class by another, was in fact the result of nothing less than a deliberate conspiracy. But whereas Maistre, who had himself been a Freemason before the revolution, identified Protestants, Jansenists and philosophes as the conspirators, Barruel focused on the Freemasons; later publicists turned the spotlight on the Jews. Furthermore, the postrevolutionary French traditionalists followed Burke in attacking the "abstraction," rationalism, and intellectualism of the revolutionaries, which they attributed to the pernicious influence of the famous philosophes. Even while interwar fascists were creating their own new revolutionary order, they too attacked these targets because they equated intellectualism with socialism, internationalism, pacifism, and "antinationalist" values. Neither Hitler nor Mussolini was overly concerned about winning over the intelligentsia, for they valued above all men of action.

Cyprian Blamires

See Also: INTRODUCTION; ABSTRACTION; ACTION FRANÇAISE; "ANTI-" DIMENSION OF FASCISM, THE; ANTI-SEMITISM; ARYANISM; *BHAGAVADGITA,* THE; BODY, THE CULT OF THE; BUDDHISM; CATHOLIC CHURCH, THE; CHAMBERLAIN, HOUSTON STEWART; CONSPIRACY THEORIES; COSMOPOLITANISM; COUNTERREVOLUTION; ENLIGHTENMENT, THE; EVOLA, JULIUS; FRANCE; FREEMASONRY, FREEMASONS, THE; FRENCH REVOLUTION, THE; HAUER, JAKOB WILHELM; INDIVIDUALISM; INTEGRAL NATIONALISM; LIEBENFELS, JÖRG ADOLF JOSEF LANZ VON;

MARXISM; MUSSOLINI, BENITO ANDREA; NATIONALISM; NAZISM; NEW AGE, THE; NEW ORDER, THE; MAURRAS, CHARLES; ORGANICISM; PACIFISM; PROTOFASCISM; RATIONALISM; RELIGION; REVOLUTION; ROSENBERG, ALFRED; SOCIALISM; TRADITION

References

Davies, Peter. 2002. *The Extreme Right in France, 1789 to the Present: From de Maistre to Le Pen.* London: Routledge.

Drake, Richard H. 1986. "Julius Evola and the Ideological Origins of the Radical Right in Contemporary Italy." In *Political Violence and Terror: Motives and Motivations,* edited by Peter H. Merkl. Berkeley: University of California Press.

Goodrick Clarke, Nicholas. 2003. *Black Sun: Aryan Cults, Esoteric Nazism and the Politics of Identity.* New York: New York University Press.

Mayer, Arno J. 1971. *Dynamics of Counterrevolution in Europe, 1870–1956: An Analytical Framework.* New York: Harper and Row.

McClelland, J. S. 1970. *The French Right: From de Maistre to Maurras.* London: Cape.

Sedgwick, M. J. 2004. *Against the Modern World: Traditionalism and the Secret Intellectual History of the Twentieth Century.* Oxford: Oxford University Press.

Weiss, J. 1977. *Conservatism in Europe 1770–1945: Traditionalism, Reaction, and Counter-revolution.* London: Thames and Hudson.

TRAPP FAMILY, THE: *See* ANTIFASCISM
TRAVELERS: *See* ROMA

TRIUMPH OF THE WILL

The documentary *Triumph des Willens (Triumph of the Will)* was the most infamous movie made by German filmmaker Leni Riefenstahl, released in 1935. It depicts the 1934 Nuremberg Rally, one of the annual propagandistic events staged by the National Socialists. It was highly innovative in its film technique, but Riefenstahl has ever since been seen as one of the prime propagandists for the Nazi regime. *Triumph of the Will* was preceded by *Der Sieg des Glaubens (Victory of Belief)* about the 1933 Nuremberg Rally. Recently, internationally successful pop bands like U2 and Rammstein have used images from *Triumph of the Will* for their stage shows.

Christoph H. Müller

See Also: BERLIN OLYMPICS, THE; BODY, THE CULT OF THE; FILM; GOEBBELS, (PAUL) JOSEPH; NAZISM; NUREMBERG RALLIES, THE; PROPAGANDA; RIEFENSTAHL, LENI; SPORT; VOLUNTARISM

References

Barsam, Richard Meran. 1975. *Triumph of the Will.* Bloomington: Indiana University Press.

Snyder, Louis L. 1976. *Encyclopedia of the Third Reich.* London: Blandford.

TROTSKY, LEON (1879–1940)

Leading spokesman of the Russian Revolution and founder of the Red Army, who made two important contributions to left-wing antifascist theory. In contrast to the main spokesmen of the Communist International, he insisted that fascism was not merely a conspiracy of the rich but a mass movement, which because of its popular support was capable of wreaking untold damage. Second, he argued for socialists and communists to ally against fascism in a "united front."

David Renton

See Also: INTRODUCTION; ABSTRACTION; ANTIFASCISM; BODY, THE CULT OF THE; BOLSHEVISM; COMINTERN, THE; DEMOCRACY; MARXIST THEORIES OF FASCISM; MASSES, THE ROLE OF THE; SOCIALISM; SOVIET UNION, THE

Reference

Lynch, M. J. 1995. *Trotsky: The Permanent Revolutionary.* London: Hodder and Stoughton.

TROTT ZU SOLZ, ADAM VON (1909–1944)

Leading member of the German anti-Nazi Kreisau Circle. After studies in law, philosophy, and economics, Trott entered the diplomatic service in 1940. Having joined the NSDAP as a cover, he became (in 1943–1944) adviser to Stauffenberg on foreign affairs. He spoke up for an immediate end to the war, to be followed by far-reaching democratic and social reforms. His attempts to convince British diplomats of the seriousness of his peace offers failed because he included the Soviet Union in the negotiations, made territorial claims unacceptable to the Allies, and was in general distrusted as a diplomat in the service of Nazi Germany. This distrust was in spite of the fact that Trott had visited England before the war and was well known at the University of Oxford, among other places. His name occurs frequently in English autobiographical accounts or correspondence from the period. Trott was arrested in late July 1944 and executed for his part in the July Plot.

Fabian Virchow

See Also: ANTIFASCISM; GERMANY; JULY PLOT, THE; KREISAU CIRCLE, THE; NAZISM; STAUFFENBERG, CLAUS SCHENK GRAF VON; WORLD WAR I

References
MacDonogh, G. 1994. *A Good German: Adam von Trott zu Solz.* London: Quartet.
Schott, Andreas. 2001. *Adam von Trott zu Solz: Jurist im Widerstand.* Paderborn: Schöningh.

TUKA, DR. VOJTECH (1880–1946)

Leader of the radical wing of the Slovak People's Party, Tuka was sentenced to fifteen years' imprisonment for "treason" against the Czechoslovak state in 1929 but released in 1937. He became prime minister of the independent Slovak Republic in 1939 and sought to pursue national socialist policies under German patronage in conflict with Mgr. Tiso, the president. As minister of the interior, he ordered the deportation of Slovakian Jews to Auschwitz, and as foreign minister he adhered to the Anti-Comintern Pact. He died in prison in 1946 awaiting trial on war crimes charges.

John Pollard

See Also: ANTI-COMINTERN PACT, THE; ANTI-SEMITISM; AUSCHWITZ (-BIRKENAU); CATHOLIC CHURCH, THE; CZECHOSLOVAKIA; POLITICAL CATHOLICISM; SLOVAKIA; TISO, MGR. JOSEF

Reference
Kirschbaum, S. J., ed. 1999. *Historical Dictionary of Slovakia.* London: Scarecrow.

TURANISM

A political ideology based on the idea of the unification of all Turkic peoples (pan-Turkism) or, more ambitiously, the unification of Turks with Hungarians, Mongolians, and Finns.

Cyprian Blamires

See Also: EXPANSIONISM; HUNGARY; IRREDENTISM; PANGERMANISM; TURKEY

Reference
Landau, J. 1995. *Pan-Turkism.* Bloomington: Indiana University Press.

TURKEY

Considered by some to have had a fascistic-style regime in the interwar years. The constituent set of ideals behind the Turkish Republic was Janus-faced. Kemalism (the philosophy of the followers of Kemal Atatürk, modernizing president of Turkey, 1923–1938) retained recondite yet profound misgivings about modernity. However, it also aimed at rebuilding the old mythic society with a modern constitutive enthusiasm. Culture and populism were the core Kemalist armatures that were deployed for the aspired rebirth of society. The new nation was defined around a particularistic conception of Turkish culture, and populism provided the discourse for the organic unity of this new nation. The essential driving force that was used to mobilize the masses bound for the new regime was an extreme form of nationalism. This nationalism played the leading role in the conservative Turkish revolution, and brought the Kemalist endeavor of rebuilding society into close relation with fascism, most particularly in the 1930s.

Revolting against both the foreign powers and the old regime, the Kemalist movement established a semidictatorial system of government that claimed to speak on behalf of the people as a whole, in order to attain economic development in an unindustrialized country. The Kemalist regime and the path it followed—especially in the years between 1931 and

Kemal Atatürk, president of Turkey from 1923 to 1938. There were some parallels between the ideology of his Republican People's Party and Italian Fascism. (Library of Congress)

1945—had some obvious features overlapping with fascism, such as: a single party; a strong reaction against the old regime; the existence of solidarist and corporatist and later on, totalitarian tendencies; coalescence of state with party; adoption of a national leader system; and increasing state interventionism in the economy. The Kemalist Republican People's Party was not all that dissimilar in essence from Mussolini's Fasci di Combattimento when its authoritarian character and political program are taken into account. Six basic principles of Kemalism were laid down in the party program in 1931, and then incorporated into the Turkish Constitution in 1937. Republicanism was a salute to the new regime, outlawing political activity in favor of the old monarchic rule. Nationalism was the main instrument for the construction of a new national identity whose roots were found in history through a process of intensive myth creation. Secular-

ism was employed to remove religion totally from public life and to establish complete state control over the remaining religious institutions. Populism, as an adhesive element of the nationalist policies, became the tool for creating and maintaining national solidarity and unity on the one hand, and more decisively, denying class interests and suppressing class-based politics on the other. Statism affirmed the priority of the state over the economy.

For all the parallels, there were also a number of dissimilarities between Kemalism and fascism. The social accounts of Kemalism and Italian Fascism were comparatively the same, since Kemalism tried to create a national bourgeoisie and consolidate emergent capitalism at the expense of the working classes, while nationalizing foreign companies, railways, and some institutions in the banking sector. Fascist-style paramilitary forces were not deployed in disciplining the masses. Instead, Kemalism tried to use the People's Houses as a mass education organization to disseminate its set of ideals. Kemalism's expectations regarding international peace were not compatible with fascism's aggressive foreign policies. Furthermore, it abandoned the old regime's education and justice systems, deemed civilization to be universal, and thus strove for a secularized contemporary civilized society. Most important, Kemalism was a pragmatic ideology. In contrast to fascism, it did not have thoroughgoing totalitarian pretensions. Besides, the complex compound that made fascism possible in Italy was not really present in Turkey. The Kemalist one-party state should be understood in conjunction with the spirit and conditions of the 1930s. Kemalism never set the single-party regime as an aim in itself. Its declared goal was to reach the level of contemporary civilization, which was regarded as best represented by Western democracy. The Kemalist regime lacked political democracy and was authoritarian in character, but in the long run it also paved the way for the objective conditions of political democracy with its modernizing zeal.

Although the postwar state regime in Turkey cannot be described as fascist, it accommodates some fascistic elements, such as the prevalence of the state of emergency and exceptionism. Contemporary Turkey has inherited an authoritarian state regime from the Kemalist constitutive period that ideologically and structurally includes some totalitarian aspects, and those features occasionally present a quasi-fascist character. The state itself as the sacred value of the official ideology inspires fascist impulses with its unquestionable reason, ritual performance, and claim of being a metaphysical entity calling for total dedication. Nationalism functions as the backbone of this official ideology, with its power of assimilating almost all other ideologies. Since the end of World War II, fascist aspects of the state regime have usually been present as a method of governance, periodically articulating in a coherent manner, as in the aftermath of the 12 September 1980 coup d'etat, rather than as a result of an ideological orientation.

Since the early 1960s, the Nationalist Action Party (NAP, also known as Grey Wolves) has been the conduit of fascism as a sociopolitical and ideological movement in Turkey. Ideologically, it stems from the 1930s and 1940s pan-Turkist current, which was racist, nationalist-mystical in an irreligious manner, openly antidemocratic with a militarist-corporatist view of society, and which had a pan-Turanist tendency aimed at uniting the various Turkic peoples. The nationalist mysticism was abandoned after the party's adoption of a Sunni Islamic character, and the pan-Turanist ideal of the early pan-Turkist current was not manifest in an irredentist manner as a call for a greater Turkey, but instead as a call for freedom for the Turkic peoples living under Soviet rule. The NAP came of age in the 1970s with an imagery of a counterorder in which divine social harmony was to be established, turning back to the essentials of the sacred state by a cleansing of the vermin in the organism.

Özgür Gökmen

See Also: INTRODUCTION; AUTHORITARIANISM; BANKS, THE; CAPITALISM; CIVILIZATION; CORPORATISM; DEMOCRACY; ECONOMICS; EXPANSIONISM; FASCIST PARTY, THE; GERMANY; IRREDENTISM; ITALY; LEADER CULT, THE; MASSES, THE ROLE OF THE; MILITARISM; MODERNITY; MONARCHISM; MONARCHY; MYSTICISM; MYTH; NATIONALISM; NATIONALIZATION; NAZISM; ORGANICISM; PALINGENETIC MYTH; PARAMILITARISM; POSTWAR FASCISM; RACISM; RELIGION; REVOLUTION; SECULARIZATION; STATE, THE; TOTALITARIANISM; TURANISM

References

Adanir, Fikret. 2001. "Kemalist Authoritarianism and Fascist Trends in Turkey during the Interwar Period." Pp. 313–361 in *Fascism outside Europe*, edited by Stein Ulgevik Larsen. Boulder: Social Science Monographs.

Bora, Tanil. 1999. *Türk Saginin Üç Hâli: Milliyetçilik, Muhafazakârlik, Islâmcilik* [*Three Phases of the Turkish Right: Nationalism, Conservatism, Islamism*]. Istanbul: Birikim Yayinlari.

———. 2000. "Fasizmin Hâlleri [States of Fascism]." *Birikim* 133: 21–34.

Landau, Jacob M. 1982. *Pan Turkism: A Study of Turkish Irredentism*. Archon.

Toprak, Zafer. 1995. "Das Einparteiensystem und der autoritare Modernismus in der Türkie zwischen den Weltkriegen." *Comparativ—Macht und Geist Intellektuelle in der Zwischenkreigszeit* 5, no. 6: 119–134.

Zürcher, Erik J. 1998. *Turkey: A Modern History.* London: I. B. Tauris.

TURNER DIARIES, THE

A novel written pseudonymously in the 1970s by leading neo-Nazi William Pierce, it describes a terrorist campaign involving attacks on the FBI headquarters, the *Washington Post,* and the Israeli embassy. In the closing pages of the book, the "hero," Earl Turner, is killed crashing a nuclear-armed aircraft into the Pentagon, but the Jewish power-structure that Pierce portrays as controlling the United States is overthrown, the nation is ethnically cleansed, and a ruthless Aryan elite is installed in power. The name that Pierce chose for his fictional group, the Order, was subsequently adopted by a racist terrorist group in the 1980s.

Martin Durham

See Also: ANTI-SEMITISM; ARYAN NATIONS; ARYANISM; CONSPIRACY THEORIES; NEO-NAZISM; PIERCE, WILLIAM; POSTWAR FASCISM; UNITED STATES, THE (POSTWAR); WHITE SUPREMACISM; ZIONIST OCCUPATION GOVERNMENT, THE

Reference

Durham, M. 2004. "The Upward Path: Palingenesis, Political Religion and the National Alliance." *Totalitarian Movements and Political Religions* 5, no. 3, pp. 454–468.

TYNDALL, JOHN (1934–2005)

John Tyndall was the founder of the British National Party (BNP) and editor of *Spearhead.* He was a leading member of the National Socialist Movement (NSM) and was jailed in 1962 for organizing a paramilitary group. Despite his overtly Nazi past, Tyndall succeeded in joining the National Front in 1968. He became chairman in 1973, leading the organization to its 1974 peak. When the party began fragmenting after the 1979 general election debacle, Tyndall resigned and founded the BNP in 1982. He was ousted as chairman by Nick Griffin in September 1999.

Graham Macklin

See Also: BRITISH NATIONAL PARTY, THE; GREAT BRITAIN; GRIFFIN, NICHOLAS; NATIONAL FRONT (UK), THE; NEO-NAZISM; POSTWAR FASCISM

Reference
Walker, Martin. 1977. *The National Front.* London: Fontana/Collins.

ÜBERMENSCH, **THE:** *See* **NEW MAN, THE; NIETZSCHE, FRIEDRICH;** *UNTERMENSCHEN*

UK, THE: *See* **GREAT BRITAIN**

UKRAINE: *See* **ORTHODOX CHURCHES, THE; SLAVS, THE; SOVIET UNION, THE**

ULMANIS, KĀRLIS (1877–1942)

First prime minister of Latvia, creator of an authoritarian regime in the late 1930s. As leader of the conservative Farmers' Union, he was the foremost statesman of independent Latvia. Following the Estonian example, he declared martial law on 15 May 1934 and arrested the leaders of the fascist Thunder Cross and communists. While claiming to be saving democracy from the threat of extremism, Ulmanis erected his own authoritarian regime. In 1936 he united the office of president and prime minister in his own person. In 1940 the USSR annexed Latvia, and Ulmanis was deported to Russia, where he died in captivity.

Andres Kasekamp

See Also: AUTHORITARIANISM; ESTONIA; LATVIA; THUNDER CROSS, THE

ULTRANATIONALISM: *See* **NATIONALISM**

UN, THE: *See* **UNITED NATIONS, THE**

UNITED NATIONS, THE

International organization founded after World War II to further the quest for world peace and stability in succession to the discredited League of Nations. Its foundation was stimulated by a desire to counterbalance permanently the threat to world order posed by extreme nationalism of the fascist variety. It is suspected by some U.S. far-right movements of being a conspiracy to establish a (Jewish) world government and subvert U.S. sovereignty.

Cyprian Blamires

See Also: ANTI-SEMITISM; CONSPIRACY THEORIES; COSMOPOLITANISM; LEAGUE OF NATIONS, THE; NATIONALISM; UNITED STATES, THE (POSTWAR); UNIVERSALISM; WORLD WAR II; ZIONIST OCCUPATION GOVERNMENT, THE (ZOG)

Reference
Knight, Peter. 2003. *Conspiracy Theories in American History: An Encyclopedia.* Santa Barbara, CA: ABC-CLIO.

UNITED STATES, THE (pre-1945)

Many movements appeared fascist in the interwar years in the United States but were really something else. The Ku Klux Klan had an ideology that involved racism, extreme nationalism, and a mystique of violence, but it also stressed a return to traditional cultural values, not radical political or economic change; it sought to "purify" the United States by reasserting rule by white, Protestant, rural, native-born elites. In much of the public mind, Henry Ford was also perceived as a proto-fascist, particularly inasmuch as his weekly magazine, the *Dearborn Independent* (1919–1922), espoused a vehement form of anti-Semitism. Yet, though admired by Adolf Hitler, he never called for radical transformation of the U.S. social, political, or economic system. The same holds true for the Reverend Gerald Winrod, whose monthly magazine the *Defender* mixed endorsements of the *Protocols of the Learned Elders of Zion* with a "dispensationalist" theology centering on biblical "prophesies" outlined in the *Scofield Reference Bible.* Aside, however, from his anti-Semitism, Winrod's attacks on the New Deal differed little from those emanating from mainstream conservative Republicans, as both entities stressed economic individualism, not a centralized corporate state.

Far more visible was the Share Our Wealth program, launched by Louisiana governor Huey Pierce Long in January 1934 and lasting through his assassination in September 1935. Long's political platform centered on a radical redistribution of income and opposition to Franklin D. Roosevelt's New Deal. At its height the movement possessed a mailing list of 7.5 million names, located primarily in the U.S. South. Long administered his state as a personal fiefdom, bullying the legislature and turning the state guard against political opponents. Yet he made no effort to control the press or block elections, and he denounced anti-Semitism and the Klan. In the mid-1940s, however, the Reverend Gerald L. K. Smith, who had been national director of the Share Our Wealth clubs, organized the Christian Nationalist Crusade and published the monthly *Cross and the Flag,* both of which expressed hostility toward Jews and called for segregation of blacks. During the 1930s, press czar William Randolph Hearst, often accused of fascist leanings, backed mainstream Republican Alf Landon for president. Furthermore, he strongly denounced anti-Semitism and in the early 1940s actually supported the more militant faction of the Zionist movement.

The Black Legion, a group led by Virgil Effinger, was a body that broke with the Klan in 1925 and organized itself into a secret nativist band that engaged in vigilante killings in the Detroit area. With an estimated membership in 1935 of as many as 40,000 men, the legion spoke of seizing Washington, D.C., and exterminating American Jewry. Unlike any European counterparts, the legion lacked an economic doctrine. Investigations by the Detroit police soon resulted in its demise. To an observer of the 1930s, the Silver Shirts, led by William Dudley Pelley, represented a European-style fascism. Here one finds a uniformed, anti-Semitic cadre devoted to a leader who claimed to have experienced "seven minutes in eternity." Pelley's vague ideology drew, however, far less from *Mein Kampf* than from Edward Bellamy's utopian novel *Looking Backward* (1888), with its vision of a Christian commonwealth. There were similar groups, smaller in size, including the James True Associates; George E. Deatherage's Knight of the White Camelia and American Nationalist Confederation; Harry A. Jung's American Vigilant Intelligence Federation; Joseph E. McWilliams's Christian Mobilizers; and George W. Christians's Crusader White Shirts (after 1936, Crusaders for Economic Liberty). Historian Morris Schonbach notes that probably a majority of the native "fascist" organizations never got past a pretentious title, a mailing list, and an effort by the leader to make a living by dubious means.

Political writers Lawrence Dennis and Seward Collins both advocated forms of fascism, the former stressing a corporate state, the latter a return to the medieval guild system. Several groups deliberately aped foreign movements. In 1925 the Italian government established the Fascist League of North America, which claimed a membership of 12,000 and which was replaced in 1929 by a proliferation of smaller bodies, including the Dante Alighieri Society, the Lictor Federation, and the Sons of Italy. The German-American Bund was a paramilitary group limited to German-Americans. The Bund espoused the doctrine that National Socialism was the solution to America's problems. Eventually, it said, the United States would be cleansed of Jews, communists, and other alleged "parasites." Membership never passed 15,000, two-thirds of

German nationality and the rest naturalized Americans. From the outset the Bund was riddled with factionalism and drew little support from Germany's Nazi Party, the German state, or Hitler himself. German-American propagandist George Sylvester Viereck cast a much wider net in his efforts to promote Hitler's Germany, particularly after war broke out in Europe in 1939.

When in December 1941 the United States entered World War II, most such action groups disappeared. In April 1944 some thirty individuals stood trial for sedition, the specific charge being that they were part of a conspiratorial "worldwide Nazi movement" extending from Berlin to the District of Columbia. They were accused of having the specific aim of disseminating "systematic propaganda" to undermine morale in the armed forces and having the ultimate aim of bringing about an armed revolt. Among the defendants were McWilliams, Pelley, True, Winrod, Dennis, Deatherage, and Viereck. The judge died that November, after which a mistrial was proclaimed. Viereck was independently sentenced for failing to comply with the foreign agents registration act of 1938.

Fascist movements always remained tangential to the U.S. political landscape, but during the 1920s, Mussolini's brand of fascism held a surprising appeal for many U.S. intellectuals. Former muckraking journalists S. S. McClure, Lincoln Steffens, and Ida Tarbell found a kind of strenuous idealism in Il Duce himself, something that reminded them of Theodore Roosevelt. Herbert Croly, editor of the reformist weekly *New Republic,* admired the supposed dynamism of the Italian system, while activist historian Charles A. Beard expressed fascination with the concept of corporatism. Financial and industrial groups almost unanimously endorsed the Mussolini regime while labor united in opposition. Originally, many Americans believed that Mussolini's regime would become more democratic once the Italian economy improved. In June 1933, Breckinridge Long, U.S. ambassador to Italy, found the advent of Italian Fascism on a par with the framing of the U.S. Constitution in 1789, while President Franklin D. Roosevelt in July referred to Mussolini as "the admirable Italian gentleman." The dictator reciprocated, declaring in June 1933 that FDR's policies would end the Depression. But when Italy invaded Ethiopia in 1935, U.S. opinion was almost unanimously opposed, and soon U.S. business started using the word "fascist" as a negative term with which to flay the New Deal. Until Mussolini's death in 1945, both administration and public remained hostile to Italy's ruler and his regime. Only a few die-hard intellectuals, such as poet Ezra Pound, backed the man and the movement.

In contrast, the broad spectrum of U.S. public opinion never expressed sympathy for Adolf Hitler's National Socialism. In the popular mind, the Nazi regime was always seen as the epitome of police-state brutality. Certain administration diplomats thought it possible to negotiate positively with Hitler, among them Ambassador to Germany Hugh Wilson, Ambassador to Britain Joseph P. Kennedy, and Under Secretary of State Sumner Welles. The Roosevelt government, however, never indicated that it found Germany's domestic policies other than abhorrent. After the *Kristallnacht* of 10 November 1938, when the Nazis launched a full-scale rampage against the Jews, FDR recalled Ambassador Wilson. All diplomacy was thereafter conducted by lower-echelon officials. Once the United States entered the war in December 1941 as a full-scale belligerent, even the legal pretense of "neutrality" was over.

Justus Doenecke

See Also: AMERICANIZATION; ANTI-SEMITISM; BOOKS, THE BURNING OF THE; CHRISTIANITY; COLLINS, SEWARD; CONSPIRACY THEORIES; CORPORATISM; COUGHLIN, FR. CHARLES EDWARD; DEMOCRACY; DENNIS, LAWRENCE; ETHIOPIA; EUGENICS (USA); FASCIST PARTY, THE; FORD, HENRY; GERMAN-AMERICAN BUND, THE; GERMANY; GREAT BRITAIN; HEARST, WILLIAM RANDOLPH; HITLER, ADOLF; INTERVENTIONISM; ITALY; JAPAN AND WORLD WAR II; *KRISTALLNACHT;* KU KLUX KLAN, THE; LEAGUE OF NATIONS, THE; MUSSOLINI, BENITO ANDREA; NAZISM; PEARL HARBOR; PELLEY, WILLIAM DUDLEY; POUND, EZRA; *PROTOCOLS OF THE ELDERS OF ZION, THE;* RACISM; ROOSEVELT, FRANKLIN DELANO; SARFATTI-GRASSINI, MARGHERITA; U.S. CORPORATIONS; UNITED STATES, THE (POSTWAR); VIERECK, GEORGE SYLVESTER; WALL STREET CRASH, THE; WHITE SUPREMACISM; WINROD, GERALD BURTON; WORLD WAR II; ZIONISM; ZIONIST OCCUPATION GOVERNMENT, THE (ZOG)

References

Amann, Peter H. 1986. "Dog in the Nighttime Problem: American Fascism in the 1930s." *History Teacher* 19 (August): 559–584.

Brinkley, Alan. 1982. *Voices of Protest: Huey Long, Father Coughlin, and the Great Depression.* New York: Knopf.

Carter, John Boothe. 1953. "American Reaction to Italian Fascism, 1919–1933." Ph.D. diss., Columbia University.

Chalmers, David M. 1981. *Hooded Americanism: The History of the Ku Klux Klan.* 3d ed. New York: New Viewpoints.

Diamond, Sander A. 1974. *The Nazi Movement in the United States, 1924–1941.* Ithaca, NY: Cornell University Press.

Diggins, John P. 1972. *Mussolini and Fascism: The View from America.* Princeton: Princeton University Press.

Nasaw, David. 2000. *The Chief: The Life of William Randolph Hearst.* Boston: Houghton Mifflin.

Offner, Arnold A. 1969. *American Appeasement: United States Foreign Policy and Germany, 1933–1938.* Cambridge: Harvard University Press.

Ribuffo, Leo P. 1983. *The Old Christian Right: The Protestant Far Right from the Great Depression to the Cold War.* Philadelphia: Temple University Press.

———. 1992. "Henry Ford and the International Jew." Pp. 70–105 in *Right Center Left: Essays in American History,* edited by Ribuffo. New Brunswick, NJ: Rutgers University Press.

Schonbach, Morris. 1985. *Native American Fascism during the 1930s and 1940s: A Study of Its Roots, Its Growth and Its Decline.* New York: Garland.

Wallace, Max. 2003. *The American Axis.* New York: St. Martin's Griffin.

UNITED STATES, THE (postwar)

Few of the U.S. fascist groups of the 1930s survived World War II, and the main group that emerged in its immediate aftermath, the National Renaissance Party, received little support for its combination of National Socialism and occultism. In the early 1950s, however, the furor over the proposed desegregation of schools gave white supremacism a renewed impetus. Many of the most militant segregationists were organized in rival fragments of the Ku Klux Klan, whose terrorist campaigns against African Americans were sometimes accompanied by anti-Semitism. But white backlash also appeared in more clearly fascist forms. One group, the National States Rights Party, emerged in 1958. Another, the American Nazi Party, was launched the following year. Where the first grouping sought to identify itself with U.S., and particularly Southern, tradition, the American Nazi Party argued that only the politics of Hitler's *Mein Kampf* could secure a white America. Large-scale battles between uniformed storm troopers and opponents ensured the American Nazi Party considerable press attention. But while the National States Rights Party was eclipsed by its rival, the American Nazi Party was itself to crumble. In 1967, shortly after its renaming as the National Socialist White People's Party, its leader, George Lincoln Rockwell, was assassinated by a former member. Several different claimants to his mantle emerged. Where the National Socialist White People's Party proved unable to regain its former prominence, another group, the National Socialist Party of America, was devastated when its leader, Frank Collin, was imprisoned for sex with young boys. Another former Rockwell follower, Joseph

Tommasi, set up the openly terrorist National Socialist Liberation Front in 1974, only to be killed shortly afterward by a member of a rival faction.

But while overt National Socialism proved unsuccessful, an approach that drew on it but that avoided the use of Nazi symbolism was to prove more effective. Previously the editor of the American Nazi Party's theoretical journal, *National Socialist World,* William Pierce broke with its successor organization in 1970. Becoming leader of the National Youth Alliance, subsequently renamed the National Alliance, Pierce sought to popularize his ideas through a variety of media. Two novels written by him have attracted attention: the first, *The Turner Diaries,* portrayed a successful racist terrorist campaign to overthrow the U.S. government; the second, *Hunter,* depicts an individual who carries out attacks on mixed-race couples but who is brought to believe that the only effective way of waging race war is through membership in an organization. Pierce also promulgated his message through radio broadcasts, comic books, and, from the late 1990s, ownership of the main U.S. distributor of "white power music," Resistance Records. By the time of Pierce's death in 2002, the Alliance was the best-known fascist organization in the United States. It was not, however, the only such group. One rival was Aryan Nations, the principal exponent of Christian Identity, a doctrine that emerged in the immediate aftermath of World War II. Where extreme rightists had often professed Christianity, Christian Identity took the entanglement of religion and racism further by adopting the nineteenth-century idea that the original inhabitants of Israel had been dispersed to Europe and then to the other sites of European settlement. But where the originators of what had once been called Anglo-Israelism had held that the British Empire was God's instrument, Identity believers saw the United States as the new Israel. Many also held that Jews are literally the product of a sexual liaison between Eve and Satan in the Garden of Eden, and in the Aryan Nations' case, the sacralization of anti-Semitism that resulted took an explicitly pro-Nazi manifestation. Other Identity groupings have also sprung up, while other racists, unpersuaded by the contention that Christianity is truly Aryan, looked elsewhere for a racial faith.

Pierce himself rejected Christianity, constructing his own religion, Cosmotheism, in its place. National Alliance members did not have to embrace his religion, however. Another grouping that first emerged in the early 1980s, the Church of the Creator, insisted that its members reject Christianity and embrace Creativity, a religion that denounced any belief in divine beings

American Nazi Party leader George Lincoln Rockwell and followers next to a bus they used to travel the United States and disseminate their message of hatred for racial mixing, Jews, and communists. (Bettmann/Corbis)

while calling for Rahowa, Racial Holy War. Others, however, turned to what were seen as the ancestral gods of the white race and became adherents of Odinism. Early sympathy for this stance came from White Aryan Resistance, a particularly militant group formed in the 1970s by former Klansman (and former Identity adherent) Tom Metzger, while in the 1980s the leading role in white supremacist Odinism (some Odinists were nonracist) was taken up by a newly founded group, Wotansvolk.

If American fascists were divided over religion, they were divided too over tactics. Some prioritized the production of printed propaganda. One group formed in the late 1950s, Liberty Lobby, was particularly important in that regard, publishing from the mid-1970s the most widely circulated of the movement's periodicals, the weekly *Spotlight,* and pioneering the systematic denial of the Holocaust. (Ironically, a bitter court case between Liberty Lobby and the group that it initiated in the late 1970s, the Institute for Historical Review, was to lead at the end of the 1990s to the demise of the *Spotlight.*) The Liberty Lobby also supported electoral candidates, of whom one was to prove particularly im-

portant. In the 1970s, David Duke, a former student Nazi organizer, emerged as the leader of the Knights of the Ku Klux Klan, the most important Klan fragment. After concluding that the Klan would never lead a mass white backlash, he left it and created the National Association for the Advancement of White People. (He would later create another grouping, the European-American Unity and Rights Organization.) While unsuccessful as a presidential candidate, in 1989 he was elected as a Republican member of the Louisiana state legislature, in a seeming vindication of an electoral strategy that other extreme rightists also tried, unsuccessfully, to pursue. Other extreme rightists, however, looked toward terrorism. Most notably, in the early 1980s, supporters of the National Alliance and Aryan Nations came together with others to create the Order, named after the fictional organization that masterminded the terrorism portrayed in Pierce's first novel. After several robberies and two murders, a large number of members of the Order were caught and its leader killed during a siege by federal agents. The imprisoned former members continued to wield an influence on sections of the movement, but it was to be the arguments of another figure, former Texas Klan organizer Louis Beam, that were to prove particularly important. Published first in the 1980s, then again in the 1990s, Beam's most influential article held that centralized organizations were doomed to defeat. Instead, those who wished to fight the state should operate either individually or in small cells, following what Beam described as leaderless resistance.

American fascism is a divided and disputatious phenomenon. Two of its historically most important strands appear to be in crisis. One is the uniformed National Socialism pioneered by Rockwell in the 1960s. While some groups continue to adopt the trappings of the Third Reich, for many racists such an approach appears deeply unsuited to the United States. An older movement, the Ku Klux Klan, has always been rooted in American soil. But despite its existence in many U.S. states, it remained associated with resentment of the "Yankees" who had defeated the Confederacy in the 1860s. There were disputes, too, about the caliber of the recruits the Klan tended to attract. But if both the Klan and overt National Socialism appear to have run aground, other forms of American fascism are also problematic. The Church of the Creator, for instance, has been hard hit—first by losing control of its name in a copyright battle, and then by the conviction of its leader for soliciting the murder of the judge who had ruled against it. White Aryan Resistance lost a multi-million-dollar lawsuit following a racial murder carried out by supporters in Portland, Oregon. Aryan Nations has experienced splits and lost the compound on which it held its annual congresses as a result of a violent attack on a woman and her son by its security guards. Pierce's approach has proved more successful. This has not meant a moderation of what he long argued for as a Nazi activist. (In one National Alliance article, for instance, he expressed concern that some of those who espoused Holocaust revisionism appeared unwilling to defend the necessity of genocide.) But the Alliance's approach did mean garbing Nazi arguments in recognizably American clothing. Even here, however, there are problems. Before Pierce's death, others on the extreme Right had been appalled at his reported contempt for racists who did not accept the Alliance's leadership. Since his death, bitter quarrels have broken out over his successor's leadership.

If the main organizations were in disarray, leaderless resistance also seemed to offer little hope. While the short-lived Aryan Republican Army of the mid-1990s and the 1995 bombing of an Oklahoma federal building can be seen as examples of leaderless resistance, there were also individual "lone wolf" attacks. In July 1999, Ben Smith, a supporter of the Church of the Creator, committed suicide at the end of a series of racial attacks, while the following month Buford Furrow, an Aryan Nations supporter, attacked a Jewish community center before killing a Filipino-American postal worker. But none of this was likely to generate sympathy for white supremacism, any more than the declarations of admiration emanating from some on the extreme Right following the September 11 attacks on the World Trade Center and the Pentagon. In the sixty years since the beginnings of the battle against desegregation, the extreme Right has taken numerous forms in the United States. Some, notably sections of the Klan, have appeared more ultraconservative than fascist, although the credibility often given to theories of Jewish conspiracy and recurring examples of cooperation with or influence by Nazi groupings has made it difficult to be certain when the reactionary Right ends and the revolutionary Right begins. But even with the most generous estimate of who is to be included within its ranks, it is notable how divided American fascism remains. Rockwell's original party apparently never had more than 200 members. The Klan, some 55,000 strong in the late 1960s, was a tenth of that size by the 1990s, and at both points members were dispersed among a number of rival groups. Even the National Alliance at its peak in the late 1990s achieved only some 1,500 members. There have been numerous Christian Identity congregations, and, in recent years, it has been

suggested that as Identity has declined, Odinism has been enjoying an upsurge. But neither belief is hegemonic among extreme rightists. Nor have the disputes about elections or terrorism been settled. Where some on the American extreme Right seek to repeat Duke's success, others hope for a rebirth of the Order or for the spread of decentralized violence.

Martin Durham

See Also: AMERICANIZATION; ANTI-SEMITISM; ARYAN NATIONS, THE; ARYANISM; AUTHORITARIANISM; CHRISTIAN IDENTITY; CHRISTIANITY; CONSERVATISM; CONSPIRACY THEORIES; DUKE, DAVID; GROUPUSCULES; HITLER, ADOLF; HOLOCAUST DENIAL; INSTITUTE FOR HISTORICAL REVIEW, THE; KU KLUX KLAN, THE; KÜHNEN, MICHAEL; MCVEIGH, TIMOTHY; *MEIN KAMPF;* NAZISM; NEO-NAZISM; OCCULTISM; OKLAHOMA BOMBING, THE; PIERCE, WILLIAM; POSTWAR FASCISM; RACISM; RADIO; ROCK MUSIC; ROCKWELL, GEORGE LINCOLN; SURVIVALISM; THIRD REICH, THE; TRADITION; UNITED STATES, THE (PRE-1945); *TURNER DIARIES, THE;* WHITE SUPREMACISM; WORLD WAR II; ZIONISM; ZIONIST OCCUPATION GOVERNMENT, THE

References
Blee, K. P. 2002. *Inside Organized Racism: Women in the Hate Movement.* Berkeley: University of California Press.
Dobratz, B. A., and S. L. Shanks-Meile. 2000. *The White Separatist Movement in the United States.* Baltimore, MD: Johns Hopkins University Press.
Gardell, M. 2003. *Gods of the Blood: The Pagan Revival and White Separatism.* Durham, NC: Duke University Press.
Kaplan, J., ed. 2000. *Encyclopedia of White Power: A Sourcebook on the Radical Racist Right.* Walnut Creek, CA: Altamira.
Levitas, D. 2002. *The Terrorist Next Door: The Militia Movement and the Radical Racist Right.* New York: Thomas Dunne.

UNIVERSALISM

Negative term in the vocabulary of interwar fascism. It was taken to designate styles of thinking that placed the human race above the nation, the ultimate source of value for fascists. It was used similarly to *cosmopolitanism,* but that latter term had additional overtones of a metropolitan-style "decadence," the threat of Americanization, shallowness, and immorality. In the 1920s there was in many circles a massive revulsion from war after the final conclusion to the four years of harrowing bloodshed and agony of what had been the first global war known to history, and that was the motivation behind the creation of the League of Nations and the development of pacifism. At the same time Christianity had its own brand of universalism, since it preached universal brotherhood and peace, and socialism meanwhile called for a global union of the workers to oppose the capitalists. But fascists drew an entirely different lesson from World War I. Many war veterans in particular felt that such a bloodbath could only be legitimated and the sacrifices made worthwhile by the acquisition of appropriate spoils at the end, and they were left feeling either totally betrayed, as in the case of Germany, where many believed that they had not actually been defeated militarily at all, or profoundly disappointed, as in the case of Italy, for she did not gain much for her pains. Hardened and inured to war by their experience in the trenches, the former servicemen chose to continue the battle by other means, channeling their aggressive energies into the promotion of the nationalism they thought held hope of righting the balance and restoring to them the national greatness that should by rights be theirs. To them, therefore, calls for universal brotherhood or for a global union of the proletariat or for the recognition of universal "human rights" were at best a distraction and a delusion and at worst a deliberate policy to keep them permanently in the place of humiliation in which they had been left in 1918. Postwar fascists have sought to promote a different kind of universalism from the one embodied, for example, in the United Nations, claiming that it can be or indeed is being manipulated by forces behind the scenes. Unlike the more enthusiastic proponents of the European Union, who are working to erase the frontiers between the nations of Europe, they want to strengthen countries' individual identities; these identities they see as being threatened by immigration from outside Europe and by such contemporary trends as the Americanization and homogenization of culture.

Cyprian Blamires

See Also: INTRODUCTION; ABSTRACTION; AMERICANIZATION; CATHOLIC CHURCH, THE; CHRISTIANITY; COSMOPOLITANISM; DECADENCE; ENLIGHTENMENT, THE; EUROPE; EUROPEAN NEW RIGHT, THE; EUROPEANIST FASCISM/RADICAL RIGHT, THE; FRENCH REVOLUTION, THE; GERMANY; GLOBALIZATION; HITLER, ADOLF; IMMIGRATION; INDIVIDUALISM; ITALY; JESUITS, THE; LEAGUE OF NATIONS, THE; *MEIN KAMPF*; MUSSOLINI, BENITO ANDREA; NATIONALISM; NOVEMBER CRIMINALS/*NOVEMBERBRECHER*, THE; PACIFISM; POSTWAR FASCISM; SOCIALISM; TRADITION; TRADITIONALISM; UNITED NATIONS, THE; VERSAILLES TREATY, THE; WAR VETERANS; WORLD WAR I

References

Bessel, R. 1993. *Germany after the First World War.* Oxford: Clarendon.
Childers, T., ed. 1986. *The Formation of the Nazi Constituency, 1919–1933.* London: Croom Helm.
De Grand, Alex. 1978. *The Italian Nationalist Association and the Rise of Fascism in Italy.* London: University of Nebraska Press.
Eatwell, Roger. 1995. *Fascism: A History.* London: Chatto and Windus.
Feuchtwanger, E. J. 1995. *From Weimar to Hitler, 1918–1933.* Basingstoke: Macmillan.
Snyder, Louis L. 1978. *Roots of German Nationalism.* New York: Barnes and Noble.

UNIVERSITIES (Italy)

On 8 October 1931 the *Gazzetta Ufficiale del Regno d'Italia* published new Regulations on Higher Education. Article 18 laid down that university teachers must take the following oath: "I swear to be faithful to the King, to his royal successors and to the Fascist regime, to observe the statute faithfully, and the other laws of the state, to exercise the office of teacher and fulfill all academic duties, with the intention of forming diligent, upright citizens devoted to the Fatherland and to the Fascist Regime. I swear that I do not belong nor will I belong to associations or parties whose activity is not reconcilable with the duties of my office." It was not the first time that university teachers had been called on to swear loyalty to the state. But they had never before been told to swear loyalty to a particular government, and certainly not to an ideology. Almost all of them either signed up or submitted. A tiny band of twelve—one per thousand of the teaching body of the time—decided to refuse. Others took different paths, such as retirement, in order to escape the oath, while some younger ones deliberately opted for a different career. In this latter group were two important Jewish antifascist intellectuals, later leaders of the Resistance, both killed by the Nazis: Eugenio Colorni and Leone Ginzburg.

The imposition of the oath represented an acceleration in the process of the fascistization of the university as promoted and defended personally by Giovanni Gentile even against the doubts of Il Duce. Mussolini, in fact, feared a very different reaction on the part of the university world: a few years earlier, university teachers had taken up a public position against Fascism in support of the "antimanifesto" inspired by Benedetto Croce in answer to the *Manifesto of Fascist Intellectuals* promoted by Giovanni Gentile and published on

21 April 1925. But since then the regime had undergone consolidation and had definitively suppressed almost all freedom and scope for legal opposition. Croce was still around but now feared the damage to academe that would result from the loss of the best teachers. One force alone could have promoted widespread opposition: the Catholic Church. The Vatican, however, deferred to the principle of "giving to Caesar that which is Caesar's"—which in this case was interpreted as affirming the legitimacy of the requirement for an oath for professors at state universities, though not for those at private universities, who were to be left free to choose. The Catholic University of Milan welcomed Mario Rotondi, lecturer in commercial law, who had asked for a transfer from Pavia so as not to have to swear, while at the same time contributing to the fascistization of the Italian academy. Fifty-four of its fifty-eight teachers took the oath.

Many argued—and many still argue—that it was a good thing that the great majority of teachers decided to take the oath and continue their important mission. However, an almost unique opportunity was missed to cause embarrassment and perhaps even something worse to the dictatorship, while the precedent was created for an acquiescent attitude on the part of the Italian university world to the wishes of Fascism. The disastrous consequences of this emerged when it led to the passive acceptance of the anti-Semitic legislation of 1938. The effect of this legislation was that at least 386 "Jews" (many of them of Jewish family but no longer part of the Jewish community) were ejected from the ranks of full professors, lecturers, freelance teachers, auxiliaries, and assistants, amounting to about 7 percent of the entire Italian university teaching body. The silence in the academic community was resounding, and the posts vacated were filled with shameless alacrity, although even a Fascist periodical pointed out that "it will not be easy to fill all the chairs with well-qualified personnel; and perhaps in some subjects it will not be possible for some years" (*Vita universitaria*, 5 October 1938). The writer suggested that temporary stopgap appointments might be made and competitions avoided, for they could be exploited by fraudsters and unqualified individuals—as if to say: "It would be a good thing, provisionally, to avoid using the resources put at our disposal by the racial laws." Serious damage was done to the Italian universities, which lost scholars of the highest stature in many fields, from the history of antiquity to the history of philosophy, from physics to biology, from psychology to economics.

Roberto Finzi (translated by Cyprian Blamires)

See Also: ANTI-SEMITISM; CATHOLIC CHURCH, THE; CROCE, BENEDETTO; EDUCATION; FASCIST PARTY, THE; GENTILE, GIOVANNI; HOLOCAUST, THE; ITALY; LAW; MANIFESTO OF FASCIST INTELLECTUALS, THE; MEDICINE; MUSSOLINI, BENITO ANDREA; NAZISM; RACIAL DOCTRINE; SCIENCE; UNIVERSITIES (GERMANY)

References
Koon, Tracy H. 1985. *Believe, Obey, Fight: Political Socialization of Youth in Fascist Italy 1922–1943*. Chapel Hill: University of North Carolina Press.
Tannenbaum, Edward R. 1973. *Fascism in Italy: Society and Culture, 1922–1945*. London: Allen Lane.

UNIVERSITIES (Germany)

Their totalitarian pretensions inevitably prompted the National Socialists to try to revolutionize the universities and colleges along with all other scientific institutions. The "liberalistic," "Jewish," and "internationalist" universities and their science had to become National Socialist. However, the Nazis were not very successful in this enterprise. There was no clear policy on academic matters, and the many offices and groups that involved themselves competed with one another for influence. The Nazi "worldview" was in any case too crude and sketchy to permit any clear directives for universities and scholarship to be extrapolated from them. Moreover, Hitler's deep mistrust of anything even remotely academic, his low opinion of scholarly achievements, and the superficiality of his own education meant that he himself issued no directives that his followers could have used as guidelines.

For the duration of the Nazi dictatorship there was no real center from which universities and sciences could have been directed and controlled. The nearest to it was the Reich Ministry of Education, but that was an institution with little support in state and party. The universities managed to retain a certain freedom of movement, and the general nazification of science—whatever that might have meant—never happened. Consequently, the National Socialist Party often complained about a general lack of acceptance and support from the universities. Policies like the nurturing of a so-called German physics or German mathematics soon proved to be mistaken, and that greatly strengthened the distaste of the party for academics. Even research and publications by professors close to the Nazis did not succeed in lessening this distance and succeeded mainly in damaging the reputations of their authors as academics among their colleagues.

Only a few (mostly new) disciplines can be categorized under the heading of "Nazi scholarship." Those included military sciences—though it was never clear what exactly that meant—and the study of races or racial theory. Apart from these deadly disciplines only the study of folklore, prehistory, and early history were valued and encouraged by the Nazis, who were hoping to discover the old Germanic customs, ways, and attitudes that were to be imitated to realize the new type of person and state.

After the Nazis came to power in 1933, autonomy and corporate self-administration were replaced by authoritarianism along the lines of the Fuehrer state. The vice chancellor as Fuehrer, the deans as the Fuehrers of their various faculties, were to impose authority and guarantee the loyalty of their colleagues. The fact that older ideas and ways of behaving frequently undermined the new decrees made possible the preservation of an inner free space, freedom of research, and sometimes even freedom of teaching at many universities. Overt resistance was, however, rare. Even with the so-called Law to Re-Establish the Career Civil Service of 7 April 1933 there was no opposition nor any sign of solidarity with those affected. This "law" was the exact opposite of what its name suggests; it led to the most flagrant injustices imaginable: the expulsion of political opponents and scholars of Jewish origin. At some universities one-third of the lecturers had to leave (amounting to 2,000 to 3,000 individuals), being forced to emigrate or ending up (mostly some years later) in concentration camps. This led to a hemorrhage of scholarly competence, and it profoundly damaged the reputation of the German universities. Even more serious was the fact that professors, scientists, and intellectuals surrendered any claim they might have had to be intellectual and moral leaders.

If most academics initially felt a certain affinity with the Third Reich, the root cause lay in their alienation from the Weimar Republic, their basically national-conservative outlook, and their reverence for the empire of 1870. So it was that in 1933 most university lecturers were in favor of a strong state and strong political leadership. However, only about 2 percent were actual supporters of National Socialism. It was mainly among the students that Nazi supporters were to be found in the universities, though that changed after 1937, when many students withdrew from politics and party, while lecturers (especially the younger ones) increasingly joined the party or its organizations. This did not, however, mean that they were convinced National Socialists. Pressure on lecturers had very greatly intensified. At the end of the war about two-thirds of the lecturers were members of the NSDAP, though only about a third of them were real Nazis, as was established by the denazification tribunals.

Notker Hammerstein

See Also: ABSTRACTION; ANTI-SEMITISM; BOOKS, THE BURNING OF THE; CONCENTRATION CAMPS; COSMOPOLITANISM; DENAZIFICATION; EDUCATION; GERMANY; HITLER, ADOLF; LAW; LEADER CULT, THE; LIBERALISM; MEDICINE; NAZISM; NEW MAN, THE; RACIAL DOCTRINE; RATIONALISM; SCIENCE; STATE, THE; THIRD REICH, THE; TOTALITARIANISM; UNIVERSITIES (ITALY); WEIMAR REPUBLIC, THE; WHITE ROSE; YOUTH

References

Hartshorne, Edward Yarnall, Jr. 1937. *The German Universities and National Socialism*. London: George Allen and Unwin.
Noakes, Jeremy, and Geoffrey Pridham, eds. 2000. *A Documentary Reader: Nazism, 1919–1945*. Vol. 2: *State, Economy and Society, 1933–1939*. Exeter: Exeter University Press.

UNTERMENSCHEN ("SUBHUMANS")

Expression used by Nazi ideologues to label the Slavs, who, according to Nazi racial doctrine, were a "subhuman" race destined to be dominated and enslaved by the German *Herrenvolk*. The purpose of Hitler's invasion of the Soviet Union was to make possible the establishment of German colonies all over Russia in which the Slavs would serve as forced labor. For all the lowliness of their position in the racial hierarchy, however, the Slavs were still rated by the Nazis above the Jews, whose corrupting powers were considered so inherently dangerous and threatening to the Germanic race that the only way to deal with them was by mass murder.

Cyprian Blamires

See Also: INTRODUCTION; ANTI-SEMITISM; ARYANISM; CONCENTRATION CAMPS; FORCED LABOR; GERMANNESS; HITLER, ADOLF; HITLER-STALIN PACT, THE; HOLOCAUST, THE; LIEBENFELS, JÖRG ADOLF JOSEF LANZ VON; NAZISM; RACIAL DOCTRINE; SLAVS, THE (AND GERMANY)

References
Billig, M. 1979. *Psychology, Racism, and Fascism*. Birmingham: A. F. and R. Publications. Burleigh, M., and W. Wippermann. 1991. *The Racial State: Germany 1933–1945*. Cambridge: Cambridge University Press.

U.S. CORPORATIONS

Some U.S. corporations played a very important role in resourcing the Nazi war effort up to the declaration of war on the United States by Hitler in early 1942. On 2 October 1930, Henry Ford had gone to Cologne to open a new plant for the Ford subsidiary Ford Motor Company Aktiengesellschaft. This had been manufacturing trucks and Model T vehicles with great success. In 1936, Hitler had made a point of praising Ford's assembly-line methods as a model that German industry should follow. In 1939 the German army began manufacturing large quantities of military troop carriers, and Ford's business with the German government expanded hugely. By the time of the outbreak of war in Europe with Hitler's invasion of Poland in September 1939, Ford had become crucial to the German war effort. (Ford troop carriers served the German invaders particularly well on their journey into France.) The company was then asked to go into the business of munitions production for the Wehrmacht as well. To avoid potential embarrassment, a front company was set up under the name of Arendt to carry out this work, but in reality it was German Ford. Arendt carried on supplying armaments for the Nazi war machine throughout the war. As late as 1941 the U.S. parent company sent vital machinery to Cologne to make possible the expansion of the plant's military capacity.

Once in control of continental Western Europe, the Nazis were also in control of all Ford plants in the area—for example, Ford France, which had begun manufacturing trucks and engines for the French army since 1939. This capacity became available to the Germans, while at the same time Henry Ford was vetoing a contract to supply Britain with airplane engines. During the war Ford Germany, like other corporations, availed itself of slave labor. Evidence has been discovered which shows that slave labor was being used by the German subsidiary as early as September 1940, at a time when it was still controlled from the United States.

Other subsidiaries of U.S. corporations operating in Nazi Germany included GM's subsidiary Opel. This was manufacturing heavy vehicles for the Wehrmacht from 1935, and it has been claimed that its contribution to the German war effort dwarfed that of Ford. Opel, too, employed forced labor in its plants. GM spokesmen have said that control of the German subsidiary was lost after Pearl Harbor. IBM's German subsidiary developed the information technology that was used by Hitler in the efficient identification of Jews, so that they could be consigned to the Holocaust. Heinrich Albert, attorney for Ford-Werke, also served as IBM's German attorney.

In October 1942 the U.S. government seized all assets of the Union Banking Corporation of New York, which was accused of operating as a front for "enemy nationals." A federal government investigation concluded that Union Banking was in fact a cloak operation, laundering money for the Thyssens, who were helping to finance the Nazi regime. One of the partners of the Union Banking Corporation was Prescott Bush, grandfather of U.S. president George W. Bush.

Cyprian Blamires

See Also: ANTI-SEMITISM; FORCED LABOR; FORD, HENRY; HITLER, ADOLF; HOLOCAUST, THE; INDUSTRY; INTERVENTIONISM; NAZISM; PEARL HARBOR; UNITED STATES, THE (PRE-1945); WEHRMACHT, THE; WORLD WAR II

References
Black, Edwin. 2001. *IBM and the Holocaust: The Strategic Alliance between Nazi Germany and America's Most Powerful Corporation*. London: Little, Brown.
Wallace, Max. 2003. *The American Axis*. New York: St. Martin's Griffin.

USSR, THE: *See* SOVIET UNION, THE

USTASHA

An extreme nationalist and terrorist movement that ruled Croatia between 1941 and 1945. The ideology of Ustasha (*Ustaše:* "insurgents"), influenced by Italian Fascism and German Nazism, was also rooted in an extreme form of Croatian nationalism exemplified by the teachings of nineteenth-century political thinkers Ante

Starcević and Josip Frank. The guiding ideology of the Ustashas included the idealization of the peasant way of life, violence, and patriarchal family life. They desired a greater Croatia, ethnically homogeneous and cleansed of all "alien" groups: Jews, Gypsies, and, above all, Serbs, for whom the Ustashas harbored a visceral hatred. The Ustashas are notorious for their cruelty when they ruled Croatia. As well as a campaign of genocide against Serbs, Gypsies, and Jews, the Ustashas also established a series of death camps, such as Jasenovac, where 100,000 inmates were murdered. After the state collapsed in 1945, some supporters of the Ustashas were handed over to the communist government in Yugoslavia and executed. Others escaped abroad and thus avoided retribution, while others assimilated into the new Yugoslav society.

In the wake of the assassination of the Croatian peasant leader Stjepan Radić, the Ustasha Croatian Revolutionary Organization was established in 1929 by Ante Pavelić, a deputy for the nationalist Croatian Party of Rights, from student organizations at the University of Zagreb. Having issued a declaration calling for the independence of Croatia, Pavelić and his followers fled abroad. Under the protection of Fascist Italy and latterly Nazi Germany, they established terrorist camps and sent supporters back to Yugoslavia to carry out attacks. They also had clandestine cells that worked within Croatia, and the movement itself had popular appeal, especially to high school and university youth. With the collapse of the Yugoslav state in April 1941, Ustasha supporters declared Croatia and Bosnia-Herzegovina the Independent State of Croatia (Nezavisna Država Hrvatska; NDH), with Pavelić as a Fuehrer figure.

In common with other fascist states in Europe, public institutions of the NDH were brought in line with the ideology of the Ustashas. Jews and Gypsies, as well as antifascist Croatians and Bosnian Muslims, were discriminated against, subjected to persecution, and summarily executed. However, it was the Serbs of Croatia and Bosnia who were the main focus of Ustasha fury. During the months of May to August 1941, Ustasha officials gave speeches at rallies in which Serbs were portrayed as racially inferior. Officials demanded that they be expelled from the NDH; some officials even publicly threatened them with extermination. Ustasha officials also began to expropriate their property and expel them from cities and place them in ghettos. Meanwhile, Ustasha militias launched a campaign of genocide against ethnic Serbs in villages and smaller towns, using a brutality that shocked even the

Ante Pavelić, head of the 'independent state of Croatia' for a few years during World War II and founder of the Ustasha Croatian Revolutionary Organization. This pro-Nazi movement was responsible for a genocidal crusade against ethnic Serbs as well as against Jews, gypsies, and others. (AFP/Getty Images)

Nazis. In case genocide failed to have the desired effect, Ustasha ideologues attempted to eradicate the Serbian identity by forcibly converting the Orthodox Serbs to Catholicism and thus making them Croatian. The Catholic Church took an active role in these conversions and hence was later accused of being complicit in genocide, especially since some priests actively participated in Ustasha military units. Concentration camps, the most infamous of which was Jasenovac, were also established. However, increasingly, Croatian citizens rose up against the cruelty of the state and joined the main antifascist guerrilla movement in the NDH, the Partisans.

The NDH would probably have collapsed by 1942 had it not been for the support of the German army. From that point onward, the proportion of territory under the control of the Ustashas steadily decreased, and by 1945 the Ustasha regime hardly even controlled the capital. Despite this, support for the Ustashas in some regions remained strong. With the collapse of the NDH in May 1945, hundreds of thousands of Croatian civilians tried to flee abroad, but many were turned back and handed over to the Yugoslav authorities. A large number were interned or executed by the communists shortly afterward. Despite the fact that some high-ranking Ustasha officials were subjected to show trials after World War II, most important Ustashas, including Pavelić, evaded justice.

Rory Yeomans

See Also: ANTIFASCISM; ANTI-SEMITISM; CATHOLIC CHURCH, THE; CLERICO-FASCISM; COMMUNITY; CROATIA; FASCIST PARTY, THE; GERMANY; HOLOCAUST, THE; ITALY; NATIONALISM; NAZISM; ORTHODOX CHURCHES, THE; PALINGENETIC MYTH; PAPACY, THE; PARAMILITARISM; PAVELIĆ, DR. ANTE; PIUS XII, POPE; POLITICAL CATHOLICISM; RACIAL DOCTRINE; ROMA AND SINTI, THE; SERBS, THE; TERROR; WORLD WAR II; YUGOSLAVIA

References

Jelinek, Yeshayahu. 1985. "Nationalities and Minorities in the Independent State of Croatia." *Nationalities Papers* 7, no. 2: 195–206.

Paris, Edmond. 1961. *Genocide in Satellite Croatia: A Record of Racial and Religious Persecutions and Massacres.* Chicago: American Institute for Balkan Affairs.

Reinhartz, Dennis. 1986. "Aryanism in the Independent State of Croatia, 1941–1945: The Historical Basis and Cultural Questions." *South Slav Journal* 9, nos. 3–4 (autumn/winter): 19–25.

Sadkovich, James J. 1987. *Italian Support for Croatian Separatism, 1927–1937.* New York: Garland.

UTILITARIANISM

Term of abuse in interwar fascist vocabulary. It signified a crassly materialistic approach to life that ignored noble ideals and the heroic dimension. It was associated with the Anglo-American mind-set, with its alleged predilection for commerce rather than for the pursuit of the higher human values. Although the term was often applied in fascist propaganda to the general notion of treating life purely as a scene for the pursuit of personal advantage and pleasure, it did sometimes carry overtones of the philosophical doctrine of utilitarianism as propounded by the nineteenth-century English thinkers Jeremy Bentham and John Stuart Mill.

Cyprian Blamires

See Also: CIVILIZATION; CULTURE; FASCIST PARTY, THE; ITALY; MATERIALISM; NAZISM; NORDIC SOUL, THE; ORGANICISM; PALINGENETIC MYTH; REVOLUTION; SOUL; TERROR; WARRIOR ETHOS, THE

UTOPIA, UTOPIANISM

Most commentators—understanding utopianism as a deviation from socialism; as an idealist's vision of the good society too perfect to be realized in the historical circumstances of the time—have baulked at associating fascism and utopia. Nonfascists, who are almost inevitably also antifascists, have more readily identified fascism with dystopia—as, for example, in Katharine Burdekin's *Swastika Night* (1937). Utopia has achieved a certain place in the conceptual armory of the humanities and social sciences, but here, too, it has rarely been coupled with fascism. Karl Mannheim's (1936) sociology of the historical development of knowledge posited a series of dialectical stages whereby dominant "ideology" was challenged by "utopia." In this scheme fascism was judged to be a variant of bourgeois ideology, rather than a distinctive radical project. More recently utopian studies have seen significant conceptual development, but fascism, where it has been mentioned at all, has continued to be understood as intellectually void or as a pathological form of ultraconservatism.

Whatever pragmatic compromises fascists might make with the ruling classes on the way to power, they invariably regarded these as effete and their society as decadent. Fascism claimed to be inaugurating a new time, a new era of history, to be creating a "new man" and a dynamic and harmonious organic state-society. In reality, the boasts of fascist rhetoric were often undermined by the stubborn realities of self-interest, the old allegiances of class, and their unstable syncretism generally. Nonetheless, the scope of its ambitions, and the ruthlessness with which it pursued them, mark out fascism as one of the most utopian movements of the modern period.

Fascism in Germany engendered a rich vein of utopian prose fiction, and the utopian desire motivating many Nazis has been brought out by Peter Merkl (1975). Although the Third Reich survived for only twelve years of its new millennium, it made considerable progress toward its aim of transforming a class society into one stratified according to race. As a prerequisite of this process, National Socialism sought the comprehensive grasp of state and society characteristic of modern utopianism. Its plans for racial engineering reached an advanced stage of fulfillment through the extermination of so-called racial minorities and the killing or sterilization of other unwanted people. At the same time, racially acceptable Germans were subject to a battery of measures to prepare them to play their part in the national community. The negative process of "clearing away" is a prerequisite for almost all utopia-building, and the German armies functioned to create space for "Aryan" Germans to become the rulers of the helot masses of a new empire.

The centrality of racism in its utopia distinguishes Nazism from Mussolini's regime, but Italian ambitions to create a "new Fascist man," to solve the dysfunctions of liberal capitalism with a corporate state and to recover the spirit of Ancient Rome in a new empire, were similarly utopian. Even the supposedly "moderate" British Union of Fascists had a detailed blueprint for a "Greater Britain" that, it was hoped, would bring together the spirit of Tudor England with the modern potentialities of science, industry, and state planning.

Philip Coupland

See Also: INTRODUCTION; "ANTI-" DIMENSION OF FASCISM, THE; ANTIFASCISM; ARYANISM; COMMUNITY; CONSER-VATISM; CORPORATISM; DECADENCE; EUGENICS; EUTHANASIA; FASCIST PARTY, THE; GERMANY; GREAT BRITAIN; HITLER, ADOLF; INDUSTRY; ITALY; *LEBENSRAUM;* MARXISM; *MEIN KAMPF;* MUSSOLINI, BENITO ANDREA; NAZISM; NEW AGE, THE; NEW MAN, THE; NEW ORDER, THE; NIHILISM; ORGANICISM; ORGANICISM AND NAZISM; PALINGENETIC MYTH; PROGRESS; RACIAL DOCTRINE; RELIGION; REVOLUTION; SCIENCE; SOCIALISM; SOCIOLOGY; STATE, THE; THIRD REICH, THE; TOTALITARIANISM; TRADITION; *VOLKSGEMEINSCHAFT,* THE

References

Berezin, Mabel. 1997. *Making the Fascist Self: The Political Culture of Interwar Italy.* Ithaca: Cornell University Press.

Coupland, Philip M. 1998. "The Blackshirted Utopians." *Journal of Contemporary History* 33, no. 2 (April): 255–272.

Griffin, Roger. 1991. *The Nature of Fascism.* London: Routledge.

Hermand, Jost. 1992. *Old Dreams of a New Reich: Volkish Utopias and National Socialism.* Bloomington: Indiana University Press.

Herzenstein, Robert Edwin. 1982. *When Nazi Dreams Come True.* London: Sphere.

Levitas, Ruth. 1990. *The Concept of Utopia.* Hemel Hempstead: Philip Allen.

Mannheim, Karl. 1936. *Ideology and Utopia.* London: Routledge and Kegan Paul.

Merkl, Peter H. 1975. *Political Violence under the Swastika.* Princeton: Princeton University Press.

Vidler, Alec R. 1940. *God's Judgement on Europe.* London: Longmans.

VACHER DE LAPOUGE, GEORGES (1854–1936)

Former public prosecutor turned librarian, an uncompromising racial theorist who is seen by some as a precursor of the racial theory underpinning German National Socialism. A law graduate and sometime militant in the socialist Parti Ouvrier, for which he stood in municipal elections from 1888 to 1892, Lapouge gave up his career as a magistrate to focus on the study of anthropology, subsequently taking up posts at various French universities. Lapouge considered himself the founder of the science of anthropo-sociology. This aimed at a "scientific explanation of the historical development of civilizations by showing them to depend upon the processes of biological evolution" (Hawkins 1997, 198). Lapouge articulated a form of Social Darwinism that depicted evolution as based solely on heredity and selection. These two factors created and maintained different racial types into which humans could be classified. Different racial types possessed different physical, physiological, and psychic characteristics. The biological basis for racial difference meant that racial differences were innate and ineradicable. Racial interbreeding could modify racial character, but always in the negative direction (that is, the new racial product would possess the racial characteristics of the inferior race of the pairing). The idea of unifying and integrating races was specious, Lapouge argued. Moreover, for Lapouge, such a process of racial integration now predominated, as a result of the gradual replacement of natural selection by social selection, uniting different racial types within social groups against a common enemy. Social selection had perverted evolution, allowing the weakest to survive, and now threatened to destroy modern European civilization.

Lapouge argued that there were three major racial groups in Europe: *Homo Europaeus,* the "Aryan," who was tall, pale-skinned, and long-skulled; *Homo Alpinus,* who was smaller and darker than the Aryan, possessed a shorter skull, and was a product of racial interbreeding; and the *Mediterranean* type, who was long-headed but had the smallness and darkness of *Alpinus.* Alongside the physical differences between these races could be found psychological differences as well. Aryans, Lapouge suggested, were natural leaders and innovators and excelled in intellectual work. This fitted them to be natural conquerors and promoters of progress. *Homo Alpinus,* on the other hand, was naturally inferior, and had an innate desire for a master. Such characteristics were reflected in a "natural" division of labor, with the Aryans on the top. This natural division, however, had been perverted by social selection, subverting the Aryan and promoting *Alpinus.* Features that had promoted this subversion included democracy (because it is too leveling), modern war (which kills the best of the race, leaving the weakest at home), and religion, particularly Catholicism (which encourages moral conformity and intolerance). Lapouge produced three major works: *Les sélections sociales* (1896), *L'Aryen: son role social* (1899), and *Race et milieu social* (1909). Hawkins suggests that his work had little impact on the French radical Right, largely, he suggests, as a result of his criticisms of French culture and the French race, which he saw as mostly of an inferior racial type. Sternhell, however, places him as a key figure in the revolutionary Right, which was the precursor of French fascism.

Steve Bastow

See Also: ANTHROPOLOGY; ARISTOCRACY; ARYANISM; CATHOLIC CHURCH, THE; CHAMBERLAIN, HOUSTON STEWART; CHRISTIANITY; DEMOCRACY; ELITE THEORY; FRANCE; GERMANY; GOBINEAU, JOSEPH ARTHUR COMTE DE; NAZISM; PROTOFASCISM; RACIAL DOCTRINE; RELIGION; ROSENBERG, ALFRED; SOCIAL DARWINISM; WAR

References

Hawkins, M. 1997. *Social Darwinism in European and American Thought, 1860–1945: Nature as Model and Nature as Threat.* Cambridge: Cambridge University Press.
Nolte, E. 1969. *Three Faces of Fascism: Action Française, Italian Fascism, National Socialism.* New York: Signet.
Sternhell, Z. 1978. *Le Droit révolutionaire. Les origines françaises du fascisme.* Paris: Editions du Seuil.

VALOIS, GEORGES (real name Alfred Georges Gressent, 1878–1945)

Founder of the first French fascist party, Le Faisceau, whose political career spanned the gamut of political ideologies. An early attraction to anarchism was followed by a shift to a nationalism colored with xenophobia and anti-Semitism, after a period spent as a tutor in Russia. Valois subsequently became one of the economic and social experts of the Action Française. He left the movement in 1925 to found the Faisceau, having become unhappy with a perceived immobilism of the AF, and particularly its leader, Maurras. Increasing tensions within the Faisceau as Valois shifted the rhetoric of the movement leftward (for example, claiming that the "national revolution" would be but the

continuation and radicalization of the French Revolution), together with the stabilization of the economic and political situation, eventually led to the folding of the movement in 1928. Valois subsequently moved increasingly to the left, agitating for a syndicalist Republic. He supported economic sanctions against Nazi Germany, participated in the resistance, and died in Bergen-Belsen.

Steve Bastow

See Also: ACTION FRANÇAISE; ANTI-SEMITISM; ECONOMICS; FINANCE; FRANCE; FRENCH REVOLUTION, THE; GERMANY; INTEGRAL NATIONALISM; MAURRAS, CHARLES; NATIONALISM; NAZISM; SYNDICALISM; XENOPHOBIA

References

Douglas, A. 1992. *From Fascism to Libertarian Communism.* Berkeley: University of California Press.
Soucy, R. 1986. *French Fascism: The First Wave, 1924–1933.* New Haven: Yale University Press.
Sternhell, Z. 1986. *Neither Right nor Left.* Berkeley: University of California Press.

VAPS

The League of Veterans of the Estonian War of Independence (Eesti Vabadussõjalaste Liit), known as the Vaps movement, was founded in 1929. It was led by General Andres Larka (1879–1943) and the lawyer Artur Sirk (1900–1937). In October 1933 amendments to the constitution creating a strong presidency put forward by the veterans were approved in a referendum by 73 percent of voters. On 12 March 1934, prior to elections, Prime Minister Konstantin Päts proclaimed martial law and arrested the veterans' leaders. The league was declared a danger to public safety. In 1935, veterans' leaders plotted to overthrow the government, but the conspiracy was uncovered and the plotters were imprisoned.

Andres Kasekamp

See Also: ESTONIA; LATVIA; PÄTS, KONSTANTIN; WAR VETERANS

Reference

Kasekamp, Andres. 2000. *The Radical Right in Interwar Estonia.* London: Macmillan.

VARGAS, GETÚLIO DORNELLES (1882–1954)

Seized the presidency of Brazil with the help of the military in 1930 and established a corporatist dictatorship that he called Estado Novo, in imitation of Salazar's regime in Portugal. He combined repressive trade union legislation, paternalistic social measures, and a drive to modernize Brazil through a combination of private and state capitalism.

Cyprian Blamires

See Also: BRAZIL; CAPITALISM; CORPORATISM; DICTATORSHIP; ESTADO NOVO; MODERNITY; PORTUGAL; PROGRESS; SALAZAR, ANTÓNIO DE OLIVEIRA; SOCIALISM; STATE, THE; TRADES UNIONS

Reference
Rose, R. S. 2000. *One of the Forgotten Things: Getulio Vargas and Brazilian Social Control, 1930–1954.* Westport: Greenwood.

VATICAN, THE: *See* PAPACY, THE
VENEREAL DISEASE: *See* HEALTH; SEXUALITY

VENEZUELA

Fascist influence in Venezuela originated from both Germany and Spain. The German version was promulgated by Arnold Margerie, who founded the Groupo Regional de Venezuela del Partido Nazi to promote Nazi influence among the more than 2,000 German residents in Venezuela. Although membership was never more than 90, Margerie's group had an inordinate amount of influence, as it controlled Nazi front organizations, such as the Centro Cultural Alemán, that were funded by the German legation. The German school in Caracas proved to be fertile ground for recruitment for German youth groups directed by the fervent Nazi Kurt Riesch. It was not uncommon to ob-

serve the swastika and other symbols of Nazism in Venezuela in the late 1930s. Another venue for Nazi influence was the Ibero-American Institute, headed by the German general Wilhelm von Faupel. This element differed from Margerie's and Riesch's organization, as it was directed at Venezuelans of Spanish descent and played on themes of Spain's Falange movement. Faupel's wife, Edith von Faupel, was tasked with promoting the idea that the Spanish Empire should be restored in Venezuela and other Latin American nations.

Spain also attempted to promote fascist concepts in Venezuela by extolling *Hispanidad,* the idea of a common Spanish culture based on race and Roman Catholicism. The organization that promoted *Hispanidad* in Venezuela was the Falange Española. However, Venezuelan recognition of the Franco regime does not appear to have been linked to the influence of the Falange Española. While these groups achieved some attention, they did not resonate well with average Venezuelans. Nazi racial attitudes were simply unacceptable in a society that contained many people of non-Aryan or mixed racial backgrounds. Thus, fascism in Venezuela was confined almost exclusively to the German expatriate community and a handful of proponents of *Hispanidad.* Eventually, Venezuela supported the policy of hemispheric unity and broke relations with the Axis powers.

George Lauderbaugh

See Also: ARYANISM; CATHOLIC CHURCH, THE; EXPANSIONISM; FALANGE; FRANCO Y BAHAMONDE, GENERAL FRANCISCO; GERMANY; NATIONALISM; NAZISM; SPAIN; SWASTIKA, THE

Reference
Liss, Shelton. 1978. *Diplomacy & Dependency: Venezuela, the United States, and the Americas.* Salisbury, NC: Documentary Publications.

VERSAILLES, THE TREATY OF

Following a negotiated armistice to halt the fighting between the World War I adversaries on 11 November 1918, the Versailles Treaty was signed into force between Germany and the Allied Powers on 28 June 1919 to bring a definitive end to the conflict. The punitive terms of the treaty have often been seen by historians to contain both "material" and "psychological" burdens on the politics, economy, and even democratic legitimacy of interwar Germany. In terms of territorial settlements, for example, Germany lost all overseas colonies, as well as all of the land gained at the Treaty of Brest Litovsk in March 1918 with the fledgling Soviet Union. Worse still, some 13 percent of Germany's pre-1914 territory was lost to neighboring countries like France, Belgium, and Poland. This included a 12 percent loss in population, important industries along the Franco-Belgian border—including nearly half of all iron production—and large demilitarized zones across the Rhine.

Constraints on perceived German militarism also included a nonconscripted army limited in numbers to just 104,000, a naval fleet restricted to 20 percent of its prewar strength, and a ban on all offensive weapons (especially heavy artillery, airplanes, submarines, and tanks). These stipulations derived from the main "psychological" burden of the Versailles Treaty: Article 231, or the "War Guilt Clause," essentially blamed Germany for undertaking aggressive invasions in 1914. In consequence, maintaining German weakness took a number of forms beyond military restriction. Key cities such as Danzig were to be administered by the League of Nations, an organization barred to Germany; *Anschluss* with Austria was forbidden; and financial restitution was imposed. These economic reparations were ultimately fixed at 132 billion marks in 1921—a sum that Germany (and the British economist J. M. Keynes) quickly pointed out was unpayable. Legacies of the Versailles Treaty were both numerous and academically debated. Revanchism and the rise of revolutionary nationalism were immediate; longer-term effects are often traced to hyperinflation in 1923, antidemocratic propaganda and agitation; strained international relations; even the rise of Nazism in the wake of the 1929 Great Depression. Indeed, the Third Reich's 1935 reintroduction of conscription and rearmament, remilitarization of the Rhineland on 7 March 1936, and even *Anschluss* with Austria in March 1938—all were explicitly aimed at overturning the terms of the Versailles Treaty, which the Nazis regarded as the embodiment of Germany's "betrayal." The Nazis spoke not of the "Versailles Treaty" but of the *Versailles Diktat* (and of the "November criminals" who had signed it), and Hitler exploited the slogan in his call for national regeneration.

Matt Feldman

See Also: *ANSCHLUSS*, THE; FREEDOM; GERMANY; HITLER, ADOLF; INFLATION; *MEIN KAMPF;* NATIONALISM; NAZISM; NIHILISM; NOVEMBER CRIMINALS/*NOVEMBERBRECHER,* THE; PALINGENETIC MYTH; PANGERMANISM; POLAND AND NAZI GERMANY; REPARATIONS; THIRD REICH, THE; WALL STREET CRASH, THE; WAR VETERANS; WORLD WAR I

References

Absalom, A. N. L. 1969. *Mussolini and the Rise of Italian Fascism.* London: Methuen.

Bessel, R. 1993. *Germany after the First World War.* Oxford: Clarendon.

Boemeke, Manfred E., et al., eds. 1998. *The Treaty of Versailles: A Reassessment after 75 Years.* Cambridge: Cambridge University Press.

Childers, T., ed. 1986. *The Formation of the Nazi Constituency, 1919–1933.* London: Croom Helm.

De Grand, Alex. 1991. *The Italian Nationalist Association and the Rise of Fascism in Italy.* London: University of Nebraska Press.

Kleine-Ahlbrandt, William Laird. 1995. *The Burden of Victory: France, Britain and the Enforcement of the Versailles Treaty, 1919–1925.* Washington, DC: University Press of America.

Lederer, Ivo J. 1965. *The Versailles Settlement: Was it Foredoomed to Failure?* Boston: D. C. Heath.

MacMillan, Margaret. 2002. *Paris 1919: Six Months that Changed the World.* New York: Random House.

Treaties of Peace 1919–1923. 1924. New York: Carnegie Endowment for International Peace.

VICHY

Temporary French capital during German occupation (June 1940–August 1944); by extension, the name for the collaborationist regime that governed France from there. The French government evacuated Paris as German troops approached on 10 June 1940 and withdrew in stages to Bordeaux. It accepted armistices with Italy (24 June) and Germany (25 June). German occupation of Bordeaux made it move again (temporarily, it believed) to Vichy, where hotel space was abundant. Thereafter, because the Germans vetoed any return to Paris, it remained in makeshift hotel accommodations until the occupation ended. The Vichy regime began officially when the French National Assembly, at Pierre Laval's urging, voted full powers to Marshal Pétain on 10 July 1940. This vote empowered Pétain to draft a new constitution and, until its ratification by the French people, to govern by decree. Parliament was prorogued (though not formally abolished). Pétain decreed himself head of state and was widely regarded as a national savior.

Many authors consider the Vichy regime the ineluctable outcome of French defeat, as if submission

Poster supporting the French Vichy collaborationist government in 1944 for its punishment of Resistance fighters; the legend ridicules their claim to be 'liberators' and brands most of them as Jews. (Leonard de Selva/Corbis)

had no alternative. In truth, Vichy reflected two choices. The first was accepting an armistice rather than continuing the war from French North Africa. This choice was influenced by the memory of the catastrophic bloodletting in 1914–1918, and awe before German power. The second choice concerned reform of French institutions and values. Although Pétain could have awaited German departure, he and his advisors preferred immediate change. That option was influenced by the Third Republic's deep discredit following the Depression and scandals of the 1930s and the defeat of 1940, and also by the window of opportunity its fall offered to the French Right. Under the armistice agreement Germany occupied northern France (including Paris) and the Atlantic Coast; Italy occupied no territory but oversaw the application of the armistice

along its frontier and in French North Africa. The Armistice Agreement entitled the French government to administer the whole country but gave Germany extensive police and economic powers in occupied areas. At first, anticipating Britain's imminent defeat, German (and, even less, Italian) authorities intervened relatively little in French internal affairs.

Without direct Axis pressure, though surely influenced by the dictators' success, Pétain and his cabinet undertook a "national revolution" intended to eliminate the liberal and democratic values they blamed for French defeat. They sought to make France authoritarian, hierarchical, corporatist, anti-Semitic, and Catholic. Vichy purged the civil service of Jews, Marxists, and Freemasons, and promoted discipline, obedience, and order in schools and youth organizations. It abolished independent labor unions and the right to strike. It controlled culture and censored the press. "Organization Committees" under the supervision of businessmen managed each branch of trade, industry, and agriculture within a regulated economy. Vichy promoted large families, aided Catholic schools, and tried to restrict women to the hearthside. It abolished divorce and guillotined a woman abortionist. It replaced the republican motto "Liberty, Equality, Fraternity" by "Work, Family, Homeland." Busts of Pétain replaced busts of Marianne, symbol of the republic, in public buildings.

The most striking departure from French legal tradition was the Jewish Statute of 3 October 1940. It defined Jewishness and excluded Jewish citizens from public employment and cultural influence, and restricted their access to the professions. Another decree (4 October) authorized Vichy to intern foreign Jews. Pétain announced a policy of collaboration after meeting Hitler at Montoire-sur-le-Loir on 24 October 1940. Vichy warned the Allies that it would forcibly oppose any attempt to violate French neutrality and draw French colonies into their camp. Pétain's surprise dismissal of his chief minister Laval (13 December 1940) did not alter Vichy policies of neutrality, collaboration, and national revolution. Laval's successors, Pierre-Etienne Flandin (January–February 1941) and Admiral François Darlan (February 1941–April 1942), kept seeking better conditions for France within Hitler's Europe, which they regarded as definitive. In May–June 1941, Darlan offered Germany base rights in the Middle East and French North and West Africa in exchange for eased armistice obligations (Protocols of Paris). By then Hitler, preoccupied by his plans to invade Russia, refused concessions to France. Darlan also contracted to manufacture aircraft for the Germans, helped supply Rommel's force in North Africa, and broadened anti-Jewish measures to include sequestration of business property.

As the Armistice lasted far longer than expected, and especially after Germany invaded the USSR on 22 June 1941, triggering communist resistance, the Germans intervened more directly in French internal affairs. They shot fifty French citizens for every German assassinated by the Resistance. They sought to harness for their growing war effort the entire economy of France, the richest country they occupied. They paid for requisitions and contracts by levying "occupation costs" on France, as specified in the Armistice but at an artificially favorable exchange rate. "Occupation Costs" absorbed 58 percent of French national income (the French had exacted similar payments from Germany under the 1918 Armistice). By early 1942, Darlan had failed to alleviate the worst burdens of occupation: the Demarcation Line that obstructed travel between occupied and unoccupied France, and economic spoliation. When Pétain sought a new prime minister, the Germans required the return of Laval on 26 April 1942. Laval maneuvered vainly for German concessions. He offered to deploy French police against "enemies of the Germans" (Jews and communists) in exchange for German recognition of French police autonomy (Oberg-Bousquet Accords). When the Nazis began to deport Jews from the occupied zone in the summer of 1942, Vichy voluntarily handed over 10,000 foreign Jews interned in the unoccupied zone. Vichy assisted the German deportation of Jews to the end.

When the Germans demanded French workers for German war plants, Laval tried to enlist volunteers, then resorted to Obligatory Labor Service (STO, February 1943). Bitterly resented, the STO propelled many young Frenchmen into the Resistance. Despite Vichy's armed opposition to the Allied landing in Algeria and Morocco in November 1942, the Germans occupied the rest of France and abolished Vichy's small armed force. Italy occupied a zone east of the Rhône River. When the Germans tried to seize French naval vessels at Toulon, Vichy officers scuttled them (27 November 1942). Thus Vichy lost the main supports of its limited autonomy: an unoccupied zone, a mothballed but powerful navy, and its colonies. Germany now held Tunisia, the Allies the rest of Africa and the Caribbean, and the Japanese Indochina. By early 1943, Vichy appeared a mere Axis puppet. Even then, the crusade against communism and dreams of a compromise peace, which Vichy might help mediate, afforded Laval

some following. About 6,000 French anticommunist volunteers fought in Nazi uniforms on the Soviet Front.

Vichy did not govern through a single party, with a single youth organization, but through the traditional administrative and business elite, supported by the church and the army. It thus resembled authoritarian rule more closely than fascism, though it collaborated with fascism. Vichy's following was broad, at least early. It included most conservatives (except a few anti-Nazi patriots like Charles De Gaulle), technicians eager for greater state efficiency, and even the anticommunist and pacifist Left. Pétain and most ministers came from the nationalist Right. Their motivation was not ideological sympathy for Nazism (though they accepted cooperation with it), but collaboration d'état—pragmatic deals in hope of concessions, for "reasons of state." Most French ideological profascists remained in Paris on the Nazi payroll and criticized Vichy lukewarmness about the "new Europe." In 1944, as traditional conservatives grew hesitant and Vichy was reduced to a police state, two fascists became ministers: Marcel Déat and Joseph Darnand.

By the time the Allies landed in Normandy on 6 June 1944, most French people blamed Vichy for their sufferings. During the liberation, about 9,000 alleged collaborators were killed without trial or after summary justice. Women overly friendly with German soldiers had their heads shaved. As Free French general De Gaulle established his authority, the purge process became regularized. All Vichy ministers were tried by a special high court of justice; other collaborators were tried in lower courts. A total of 124,750 faced trial. About 1,600 were executed, 38,000 imprisoned, and thousands demoted or deprived of civic rights ("national indignity"). Amnesty laws in 1951–1952 ended punishment of collaborators. Most French people believed that Vichy had been imposed by German pressure, and that the nation had largely resisted. After the youth revolt of 1968 and the appearance of such works as the film *The Sorrow and the Pity* (1971), many younger French people understood that Vichy reflected indigenous influences, and that it had enjoyed popular support. An important shift of public opinion in the 1990s encouraged French courts to sentence two French citizens (the official Maurice Papon and the supplementary policeman Paul Touvier) to prison for crimes against humanity, for their share in the deportation or murder of Jews.

Robert O. Paxton

See Also: ANTIFASCISM; ANTI-SEMITISM; AUTHORITARIAN-ISM; BLANCHOT, MAURICE; CATHOLIC CHURCH, THE; CORPORATISM; DEAT, MARCEL; EDUCATION; FARMERS, THE; FRANCE; FREEMASONRY, FREEMASONS, THE; GERMANY; HITLER, ADOLF; HOLOCAUST, THE; INDUSTRY; ITALY; JAPAN AND WORLD WAR II; LAVAL, PIERRE; MARXISM; NATIONALISM; NAZISM; PACIFISM; PALINGENETIC MYTH; PETAIN, MARSHAL HENRI PHILIPPE; POLITICAL CATHOLICISM; REBATET, LUCIEN; REVOLUTION; SOCIALISM; TRADE; TRADES UNIONS; WALL STREET CRASH, THE; WORLD WAR I; WORLD WAR II; YOUTH

References
Burrin, Philippe. 1996. *France under the Germans: Collaboration and Compromise.* New York: New Press.
Jackson, Julian. 2001. *France: The Dark Years, 1940–1944.* Oxford: Oxford University Press.
Gildea, Robert. 2002. *Marianne in Chains.* London: Macmillan.
Paxton, Robert O. 2001. *Vichy France: Old Guard and New Order.* Rev. ed. New York: Columbia University Press.
Rousso, Henry. 1991. *The Vichy Syndrome: History and Memory in France since 1944.* Cambridge: Harvard University Press.
Sweets, John. 1986. *Choices in Vichy France: The French under Nazi Occupation.* New York: Oxford University Press.

VICTOR EMMANUEL/ VITTORIO EMANUELE III, KING (1869–1947)

King of Italy, 1900–1946, played a decisive role at key points in the history of Italian Fascism. During the March on Rome of October 1922, he refused to order martial law and appointed Mussolini prime minister. During the Matteotti Crisis of 1926 he ignored allegations of Mussolini's complicity in the murder of the opposition leader. Thereafter he acquiesced in the legislation constructing the Fascist dictatorship, including restrictions of his own prerogative. But on the day after the Fascist Grand Council's vote against Mussolini in July 1943, the king dismissed him and had him arrested.

John Pollard

See Also: FASCIST PARTY, THE; GRAND COUNCIL OF FASCISM, THE; ITALY; MARCH ON ROME, THE; MATTEOTTI, GIACOMO; MONARCHISM; MONARCHY; MUSSOLINI, BENITO ANDREA; SALÒ REPUBLIC, THE

Reference
Mack Smith, D. 1989. *Italy and Its Monarchy:* New Haven: Yale University Press

VIERECK, GEORGE SYLVESTER (1884–1962)

Leading fascist propagandist in the United States in the interwar years. Viereck was born in Munich, Germany, immigrating to the United States in 1897. Graduating in 1906 from the College of the City of New York, he wrote works of poetry and pursued a career in journalism. From 1914 through 1929 he edited a weekly-turned-monthly that until 1917 was entitled *The Fatherland;* it was subsequently renamed *Viereck's* and in 1920 *American Monthly.* In the 1920s and 1930s he produced books of contemporary history, served intermittently as special correspondent for the Hearst newspaper chain, and wrote often for the weekly *Liberty* magazine. Beginning in 1933, Viereck resumed his pro-German propaganda activities, this time for a nation under Nazi rule. In 1933–1934 he gave editorial assistance to the *German-American Economic Bulletin.* In 1939 he helped launch the bimonthly *Today's Challenge,* published by the German-financed American Fellowship Forum. From 1939 to 1941 he edited the weekly propaganda newsletter *Facts in Review,* published by the German Library of Information. Secret activities included the writing of pamphlets under various pseudonyms and supplying German funds for a front group, the arch-isolationist Make Europe Pay War Debts Committee. Arrested in 1941 on a charge of violating the Foreign Agents Registration Act, he was sentenced a year later and remained in prison until 1947. After his release he wrote two novels and a prison memoir.

Justus Doenecke

See Also: GERMAN-AMERICAN BUND, THE; GERMANY; HEARST, WILLIAM RANDOLPH; INTERVENTIONISM; NAZISM; UNITED STATES, THE (PRE-1945)

References
Gertz, Elmer. 1978. *Odyssey of a Barbarian: The Biography of George Sylvester Viereck.* Buffalo, NY: Prometheus.
Johnson, Niel M. 1972. *George Sylvester Viereck: German-American Propagandist.* Urbana: University of Illinois Press.

VIOLENCE: *See* TERROR

VITALISM

The popularity and spread of vitalistic beliefs in the nineteenth century deeply influenced many of the nationalistic creeds that anticipated National Socialist and fascistic ideas. Vitalism suggests the existence of forms of energy, spirit, or soul beyond the realm of the material world. Some adherents of vitalism confine their analyses to the organic world, maintaining that spirit is the force that engenders life. Other advocates of vitalism suggest a more heterodox view of material reality, arguing that there is no absolute boundary between the organic and the inorganic; still other thinkers, espousing even more unconventional positions, hold to the belief that because of the omnipresence of spirit, the inorganic world does not, strictly speaking, exist according to the usual meaning of the term. During the second half of the nineteenth century, after a long period when materialism had dominated most scientific thought, vitalistic theories began to reappear and could be seen influencing many branches of the sciences and playing a conspicuous role as well in popular culture, where occultism and belief in the viability of magic began to attract a great deal of attention. Under the influence of evolutionary ideas, vitalism became a major theme in the philosophical writings of Henri Bergson (1859–1941), the biological theories of Hans Driesch (1867–1941), and in the Monism of Germany's greatest zoologist of the nineteenth century, Ernst Haeckel (1834–1919), who postulated a unified cosmos resting on pan-psychic foundations. The entire universe, Haeckel argued, is suffused with soul; therefore there is no clear dividing line between the organic and the inorganic world.

Vitalism often led the way in rejecting traditional Western values and religious beliefs, arguing that it is not via the powers of a transcendent God or a Christian soul, but by the worship of a spiritually endowed nature that one can find true salvation. "National soil" defined in vitalistic terms assumed virtually divine attributes, and the ostensible racial identity of a people was viewed in terms of the existence of a racial soul. A healthy society, völkisch nationalists taught, turns away from the Christian heaven and aligns itself with the spiritual forces of the cosmos. Egalitarian ideologies like those of the Enlightenment, the French Revolution, and democratic socialism are, according to this mystically oriented approach, false mythologies; rather, all social and political norms are reducible to the antiegalitarian, Social Darwinian–inspired laws that are inherent in spiritualized nature and racially determined biology. With the victory of Italian Fascism and National Socialism in the twentieth century, the völkisch vitalism of the nineteenth century was re-energized. Fascism and National Socialism defined themselves as movements in harmony with living nature and as revolutionary creeds in rebellion against soulless materialism.

Daniel Gasman

See Also: ABSTRACTION; "ANTI" DIMENSION OF FASCISM, THE; CHRISTIANITY; CULTS OF DEATH; COMMUNITY; DEMOCRACY; EGALITARIANISM; ENLIGHTENMENT, THE; FASCIST PARTY, THE; FRENCH REVOLUTION, THE; GERMANY; ITALY; MATERIALISM; MYSTICISM; MYTH; NATIONALISM; NATURE; NAZISM; NIHILISM; NORDIC SOUL, THE; ORGANICISM; PALINGENETIC MYTH; RACIAL DOCTRINE; RELIGION; REVOLUTION; SOCIAL DARWINISM; SOCIALISM; SOUL; *VOLK, VÖLKISCH;* WARRIOR ETHOS, THE

References
Bossi, L. 2003. *Histoire naturelle de l'âme.* Paris: PUF.
Hughes, S. H. 1961. *Consciousness and Society.* New York: Vintage.
Mosse, G. L. 1966. *The Crisis of German Ideology: Intellectual Origins of the Third Reich.* London: Weidenfeld and Nicolson.

VITTORIO EMANUELE: *See* VICTOR EMMANUEL

VLAAMS BLOK

Belgian Flemish nationalist far-right political party (1979–2004). After World War II a new Flemish nationalist party was founded that broke with the fascist legacy of the Flemish National League. The Volksunie (VU) aimed for a peaceful regionalization of the Belgian state and for a democratization of Flemish society. The VU gained the support of the Flemish middle class and developed a left wing. But within and at the edges of the VU a far-right undertow continued to defend the antidemocratic concepts of the prewar and wartime periods. When in 1977 the VU took part in the Belgian government, the extreme-right undertow surfaced in two new parties that came together in the

Vlaams Blok (VB) in 1978. The party aimed for a Flemish independent state and thus the dismantling of the Belgian state. It supported a more authoritarian Flemish state against Belgian party politics, social conservatism against a liberal society, and Flemish monoculturalism against immigrant workers. In the 1980s the VB gained limited support (less than 3 percent of Flemish votes). It won popular support in the 1990s, however, when a new and young leadership gave the VB a clear xenophobe and racist profile against Moroccan and Turkish immigrants. The VB leadership had loose contacts with the Italian Lega Nord of Umberto Bossi, the Austrian Freiheitliche Partei Österreichs of Jörg Haider, and the French Front National of Jean-Marie Le Pen. With the latter the VB formed a parliamentary group (1989–1994) in the European Parliament. Flemish electoral support increased from 10 percent in 1991 to 15 percent in 1999; in 2004, the VB got 24 percent and became the largest Flemish party. The VB won votes from the VU, which was dissolved in 1999, and from all of the other traditional political parties, especially in urban regions. Despite its remarkable advantage, however, the VB could never gain executive power, as all of the other Flemish parties made an agreement not to make coalitions with the VB. In November 2004 the Belgian High Court condemned the VB for racism. To avoid prohibition, the party leadership moderated the VB's program and style. Officially the VB was dissolved, and a new party was formed under the name Vlaams Belang ("Flemish Interest"). Whether or not this is a mere window-dressing policy or an acceleration of an ongoing evolution inside the VB toward a more classic right-wing neoconservative party acceptable to other Flemish political groups remains to be seen.

Bruno de Wever

See Also: AUSTRIA; BELGIUM; CONSERVATISM; FRANCE; HAIDER, JÖRG; IMMIGRATION; ITALY; LE PEN, JEAN-MARIE; LIBERALISM; MULTICULTURALISM; NATIONAL FRONT, THE (FRANCE); NATIONALISM; POSTWAR FASCISM; RACISM; WORLD WAR II; XENOPHOBIA

References

Swyngedouw, Marc. 1998. "The Extreme Right in Belgium: Of a Non-existing Front National and an Omnipresent Vlaams Blok." Pp. 59–75 in *The New Politics of the Right: Neo-Populist Parties and Movements in Established Democracies,* edited by H. G. Betz and S. Immerfall. New York: St. Martin's.

Vos, L. 1998. "The Extreme Right in Post War Belgium: From Nostalgia to Building for the Future." Pp. 1344–1388 in *Modern Europe after Fascism,* edited by S. U. Larsen and B. Hagtvet. New York: Columbia University Press.

VOLK, VÖLKISCH

Related German terms popular among right-wing extremists with quite distinct ranges of meaning. While the noun *Volk* designates a concept important to recent and past right-wing extremism, but also to communist and democratic discourse, the adjective *völkisch* is almost exclusively linked to historical phenomena of the extreme Right. *Volk* is usually translated by the term "people," but there is more meaning and affection attached to the German term. *Völkisch* is even harder to translate. Originally it meant "folksy," but from the end of the nineteenth century it was propagated as an indigenous equivalent to the term *national,* and in the same instance loaded with racist connotations. In the Scandinavian languages, *folk* is quite close to the German counterpart *Volk,* but the corresponding adjectives *folklig/folkelig* usually reflect outspoken democratic notions. In Germany the attempt has been made to capture such notions with the adjective *volklich,* which has been advocated in contrast to the problematic *völkisch,* but this other word sounds artificial and has not gained general recognition.

The term *Volk* has a broad background of meanings ranging from a political unit, to a community of common descent, and to the common people (compare the Greek and Latin terms *demos, ethnos, populus, gens, natio*). Characteristically for German political culture—with political unity as a constant problem—the notions of the *Volk* as an ethnic community and as state citizens have been interrelated, and attempts to distinguish them have remained purely theoretical. Institutionally, this dualistic foundation has been underpinned by the idea of *ius sanguinis* ("descent") as the guiding principle upon which all German citizenship legislation rests. Different from these concepts, the notion of the *Volk* as "populace" in contrast to the elite, which can be referred to both in a pejorative and in an affirmative sense, has maintained a high degree of autonomy. In this connection, it might refer either to the lower classes or to the middle classes. Before the mid-twentieth century, the concept was also associated with the peasantry. In all, there is an ambiguous ethnic or political concept of the *Volk* on the one hand, and a rather vague social concept on the other.

Most important for the semantic development of the concept of *Volk* were the ideas of the philosopher Johann Gottfried von Herder in the second half of the eighteenth century. Herder was interested in revaluating local linguistically and historically defined cultures, the *Völker* (pl. of *Volk*), which he researched by collecting their folk songs and folk poetry. Not only did Herder give an unprecedented depth of meaning to the *Volk,* a term he used synonymously with *nation,* but also a sort of organic life of its own. At the same time, the revolutions in France and the United States established the principle of national political representation—with lasting consequences for German political thought on the *Volk.* In the nineteenth century increasingly reactionary notions developed, claiming for the German *Volk* not only precedence over its individual members but also supremacy over other nations. By the turn of the twentieth century, a *völkisch* concept of *Volk* had evolved, combining integral nationalism with Social Darwinism and other elements of racial thinking. The term *völkisch* became the overall label for the movement advocating such a fusion, basically an array of political sects on the margins of society (most prominent was the Alldeutscher Verband, the Pan-German League). The Nazis frequently used the word *völkisch* in an affirmative way and can be regarded as the movement's ideological heirs who implemented their program, but at the same time they distanced themselves from the sectarianism of these groups and from their unprofessional appearance in public. It is probably on account of a certain "backwoods" feel to the term *völkisch* even in the eyes of Nazis themselves that it has generally been avoided by neo-Nazi groups since the war.

The period from 1914 to 1945 became the heyday of the concept of *Volk* in German political thought across the political dividing lines. The *Volk* was now turned into "a final authority in moral-religious, political-social and historical respect, which was seemingly unsurpassable" (Gschnitzer et al. 1992, 389). Nazi ideology revolved around the notion of the *Volk,* in contrast to the doctrine of the Italian Fascists with their state-centered approach. This had far-reaching consequences for everyday communication in the Third Reich. As a contemporary observer noticed in the spring of 1933: "The term '*Volk* (people)' is now as customary in spoken and written language as salt at table, everything is spiced with a soupçon of *Volk*: *Volksfest* ('festival of the people'), *Volksgenosse* ('comrade of the people'), *Volksgemeinschaft* ('community of the people'), *volksnah* ('one of the people'), *volksfremd* 'alien to the people'), *volksentstammt* ('descended from the people')" (Klemperer 2000, 30). This quotation from a published English translation transmits a telling impression of the difficulty of finding adequate translations of notions in connection with *Volk* into other languages.

It is a peculiarity of Nazi ideology that it explicitly claimed that any abstract concept of the *Volk* was pointless, even if such a tendency might be considered as inherent to all notions claiming the supremacy of one particular nation. For the Nazis, only concrete examples of the *Volk* were accepted as categories making any sense, so that the *Volk* was comprehensible only as narrowed down to a specific singular. It goes without saying that the most relevant example in this respect was the German *Volk,* which was conceived as a *Volk ohne Raum* ("nation without room"). Propaganda Minister Joseph Goebbels, in particular, used the word *Volk* as an ever-repeated legitimizing key concept in his work and in his speeches. In spite of the prominence of the concept, it was characteristic of him and of other Nazi ideologists that the *Volk,* on closer look, was merely given the status of a ward of the Nazi movement. Hitler himself preferred the more politicized term *Volksgemeinschaft* and hardly tried to hide his contempt for the *Volk* as such. The *Volk* was in his view a "great stupid sheep's herd of patient lamblike people" (Hitler 1996, 555) that yearned to be manipulated by a leader. Moreover, in Nazi Germany racial doctrine began to dominate the notion of the *Volk* in such a way that it was transformed into an ahistorical category that, at least in theory, was defined by supposedly "hard" natural science.

Norbert Götz

See Also: INTRODUCTION; ABSTRACTION; ANTI-SEMITISM; ARYANISM; COMMUNITY; ELITE THEORY; EXPANSIONISM; FASCIST PARTY, THE; GERMANNESS (*DEUTSCHHEIT*); GERMANY; GOEBBELS, (PAUL) JOSEPH; HITLER, ADOLF; INTEGRAL NATIONALISM; ITALY; *LEBENSRAUM;* MASSES, THE ROLE OF THE; NATIONALISM; NAZISM; NEO-NAZISM; NORDIC SOUL, THE; PANGERMANISM; RACIAL DOCTRINE; RACISM; SCIENCE; SOCIAL DARWINISM; STATE, THE; THIRD REICH, THE; TRADITION; UNIVERSALISM; *VOLKSGEMEINSCHAFT,* THE

References

Cobley, Evelyn. 2002. *Temptations of Faust: The Logic of Fascism and Postmodern Archaeologies of Modernity.* Toronto: University of Toronto Press.

Götz, Norbert. 1997. "Modernisierungsverlierer oder Gegner der reflexiven Moderne? Rechtsextreme Einstellungen in Berlin." *Zeitschrift für Soziologie* 26: 393–413.

Gschnitzer, Fritz, et al. 1992. "Volk, Nation, Nationalismus, Masse." Pp. 141–431 in *Geschichtliche Grundbegriffe,* vol. 7: *Verw-Z,* edited by Otto Brunner, Werner Conze, and Reinhart Koselleck. Stuttgart: Klett-Cotta.

Hermand, Jost. 1992. *Old Dreams of a New Reich: Volkish Utopias and National Socialism.* Bloomington: Indiana University Press.

Hitler, Adolf. 1996. *Mein Kampf.* With an introduction by Cameron Watt. Trans. Ralph Manheim. London: Pimlico.

Klemperer, Victor. 2000. *The Language of the Third Reich: LTI, Lingua Tertii Imperii: A Philologist's Notebook.* London: Athlone.

Mosse, George L. 1981. *The Crisis of German Ideology: Intellectual Origins of the Third Reich.* New York: Schocken.

Noll, Richard. 1997. *The Aryan Christ: The Secret Life of Carl Gustav Jung.* London: Macmillan.

Winter, Julie M. 1998. *Luther Bible Research in the Context of Volkish Nationalism in the Twentieth Century.* Berne: Peter Lang.

VÖLKISCHER BEOBACHTER, THE

Translates from German as "People's Observer": the central party mouthpiece of National Socialism. A provincial weekly entitled the *Münchener Beobachter* from its 1887 inception until its renaming in 1919, the *Völkischer Beobachter* was purchased by the NSDAP in December 1920 (with financial assistance from the Reichswehr) and published twice weekly until becoming a daily from 8 February 1923. Under the editorship of Alfred Rosenberg, the paper was perpetually in financial straits prior to the Nazi assumption of power, and thereafter the most notable organ of propaganda for National Socialist Germany. The *Völkischer Beobachter* reflects Nazism's own program and development, from provincial racialist party to mainstream notoriety and ultimate dominion of the state.

Matt Feldman

See Also: GERMANY; NAZISM; PRESS, THE; PROPAGANDA; ROSENBERG, ALFRED; *VOLK, VÖLKISCH*

Reference
Muhlberger, Detlef. 2005. *Hitler's Voice: The Völkischer Beobachter.* 2 vols. Peter Lang: Berne.

VOLKSGEMEINSCHAFT, THE

One of the key concepts of National Socialist and neo-Nazi thought in Germany, describing and transfiguring the desired cohesive, classless, and racially pure society of the Nazi utopia. The term originates in the age of romanticism, and it has also been used in democratic contexts: in religious or socialist notions of the term,

Nazi propaganda poster emphasizing the idea of the German 'Volksgemeinschaft' ('national community'), a key concept in Nazism. It represented the notion of a reborn and united German people cleansed of 'alien' elements. (Library of Congress)

racist connotations have largely been omitted, and the aspect of general solidarity has been stressed. There are direct matches to the term *Volksgemeinschaft* in other tongues—for example, in the Scandinavian languages—but there is no English equivalent. Among the translations usually offered are "national community," "people's community," and "folk community." The difficulty is that *Volksgemeinschaft* is a compound of *Volk* and *Gemeinschaft* ("cohesive community"), two terms that are both hard to translate into English. In fact, the *Volk* in German is usually thought of as a *Gemeinschaft,* and the explicit combination of both concepts results in an inflationary effect that goes along with particularly seductive political implications and a sacral touch.

The breakthrough of the term *Volksgemeinschaft* in German ordinary political language dates to the time of World War I, with its experience of national solidarity transcending class boundaries. In the Weimar Republic, all major democratic parties advocated *Volksgemeinschaft*, adding their own flavor to the term. With the political Right eventually developing discursive hegemony, the term was overloaded with nationalist connotations. When the Nazis came to power in 1933, *Volksgemeinschaft* was launched as a symbol for the new order that had supposedly been created and that was further to be realized. *Volksgemeinschaft* was one of Adolf Hitler's favorite concepts, extensively used in his propaganda. Typical Nazi or nazified institutions such as the NSDAP, the Hitler Youth, the labor service, or the Winterhilfe were promoted as the vanguards of the *Volksgemeinschaft*, practicing a new solidarity of ethnic compatriots that was to transform the whole of society according to Nazi intentions. At the same time, the term *Volksgemeinschaft* was increasingly used in the social sciences and introduced and widely used in legal and administrative language. Nazi policies in the social and other fields, to a large degree, were designed as implementations of the goal to further what was perceived as the *Volksgemeinschaft*.

The basic feature of the Nazi concept of *Volksgemeinschaft* was its homogenous racial character. This perceived community transcended existing state boundaries and thereby comprised the German irredenta but excluded certain groups in the interior—in particular, persons with Jewish background. This notion was modified in two respects. First, there was a grading according to racial quality. The *Volksgemeinschaft* could even comprise the handicapped and persons of racially mixed origin, but these were seen as belonging to clearly inferior and precarious categories with a particular duty to sacrifice for the sake of the whole. Second, the privilege of belonging to the *Volksgemeinschaft* was seen as a question of behavior. There was not any demanding expectation as regards adherence to Nazi ideology. However, political dissent or deviant social behavior were considered and treated as treason and self-exclusion from the *Volksgemeinschaft*, frequently with fatal consequences.

Norbert Götz

See Also: INTRODUCTION; ABSTRACTION; ANTI-SEMITISM; CLASS; COMMUNITY; COSMOPOLITANISM; EUGENICS; EUTHANASIA; EXPANSIONISM; FAMILY, THE; GERMANNESS (*DEUTSCHHEIT*); GERMANY; HEALTH; HITLER, ADOLF; INDIVIDUALISM; IRREDENTISM; LABOR SERVICE, THE; NATIONALISM; NAZISM; NEW ORDER, THE; NIHILISM; NORDIC SOUL, THE; ORGANICISM; PALINGENETIC MYTH; PANGERMANISM; RACIAL DOCTRINE; RELIGION; SECULARIZATION; TRADITION; UNIVERSALISM; UTOPIA, UTOPIANISM; *VOLK, VÖLKISCH*; WEIMAR REPUBLIC, THE; WELFARE; WORLD WAR I; YOUTH

References
Götz, Norbert. 2001. *Ungleiche Geschwister: Die Konstruktion von nationalsozialistischer Volksgemeinschaft und schwedischem Volksheim*. Baden-Baden: Nomos.
———. 2005. "German Speaking People and the German Heritage: Nazi Germany and the Problem of Volksgemeinschaft." In *The Heimat Abroad: The Boundaries of Germanness*, edited by Renate Bridenthal, Krista Molly O'Donnell, and Nancy Reagin. Ann Arbor: University of Michigan Press.
Jurgens, Ernst Friedrich. 1938. *The Concept of Volksgemeinschaft in Representative German Novels between 1918 and 1933*. Iowa City: University of Iowa.
Mason, Tim. 1993. *Social Policy in the Third Reich: The Working Class and the "National Community" 1918–1939*. Providence, RI: Berg.

VOLKSGERICHT ("PEOPLE'S COURT"), THE

Court set up in Berlin to deal out summary justice to persons accused of being traitors to the Third Reich. The tribunal comprised two professional judges together with five others who were chosen from the ranks of the armed forces, party officials, and the SS. The presiding officer harangued and abused defendants in threatening language. Sessions were held in secrecy, and no appeals were permitted. The courtroom was demolished by Allied bombing in February 1945.

Cyprian Blamires

See Also: GERMANY; LAW; NAZISM; SS, THE; THIRD REICH, THE; TOTALITARIANISM

References
Koch, H. W. 1997. *In the Name of the Volk: Political Justice in Hitler's Germany*. London: I. B. Tauris.
Stolleis, M. 1998. *The Law under the Swastika*. Chicago: Chicago University Press.

VOLKSWAGEN

The Volkswagen emerged as a key symbol of the Nazi era in Germany. In some ways it was one of the "successes" of the period, along with the construction of the

Nazi chief Hermann Goering and officials around a Volkswagen convertible. The construction of a modern road network and the introduction of a 'people's car' (the meaning of 'Volkswagen') were part of Hitler's vision for a reborn Germany. (Library of Congress)

autobahns and achievements in other key industries. The VW Beetle was born in 1930s Germany. In the same way that the Nazi organization *Kraft durch Freude*—offered ordinary people cut-price holidays and leisure activities, Hitler's stated desire was that every German person should be able to own his or her own car. "People's Cars" is a literal translation of Volkswagen—and also a pertinent observation about the social and political significance of the vehicle. It is clear that one of the ways in which the Nazis could consolidate power and make themselves popular was to placate and impress ordinary German people, and offering them consumer goods such as Volkswagen cars was a perfect strategy. So important was the Volkswagen to Hitler that he created a town especially to house Volkswagen factories and the workers who staffed them. This was Wolfsburg in Lower Saxony, and today the town's population stands at around 125,000. By the end of 1942, 70,000 Volkswagens had been produced, and in 1945, in a swift recovery

following the war, Volkswagen produced almost 2,000 vehicles for Allied Forces and the new German Post Office. In 1998, Volkswagen announced that it would set up a fund to give humanitarian aid to victims of slave labor in its factories during the Nazi era. A company spokesman said that about 7,000 people had been forced into unpaid labor for Volkswagen, which was among several German companies using slave labor during World War II.

P. J. Davies

See Also: AUTOBAHNS, THE; FORCED LABOR; GERMANY; INDUSTRY; LEISURE; NAZISM; PROGRESS; TECHNOLOGY; U.S. CORPORATIONS; WORLD WAR II

References

Bracher, K. D. 1973. *The German Dictatorship.* Harmondsworth: Penguin.
Burleigh, M. 2000. *The Third Reich: A New History.* London: Macmillan.
Nelson, Walter Henry. 1971. *Small Wonder: The Story of the Volkswagen.* London: Hutchinson.

VOLPE, GIOACCHINO (1876–1971)

Major Italian advocate of Fascism in the field of scholarship and culture. Volpe was a medieval historian with a training in economics and law, a nationalist, and a monarchist. He gave his support to Fascism in the 1920s and then worked for the daily *Il Popolo d'Italia* and the Mussolinian review *Gerarchia*. Along with Gentile, he played a fundamental role in the field of cultural organization within the regime. He directed the *Rivista Storica Italiana* and important institutions such as the Institute for the Study of International Politics and the School of Modern Contemporary History. In his works, and in particular in *L'Italia in cammino* (1927) and *Storia del movimento fascista* (1934), he presented Fascism as the historical realization of the national aspirations of Italy. Out of loyalty to the monarchy, he refused to support the Salò Republic.

Alessandro Campi (translated by Cyprian Blamires)

See Also: CULTURE; FASCIST PARTY, THE; GENTILE, GIOVANNI; ITALY; MONARCHISM; MONARCHY; MUSSOLINI, BENITO ANDREA; NATIONALISM; SALÒ REPUBLIC, THE; SARFATTI-GRASSINI, MARGHERITA; VICTOR EMMANUEL/VITTORIO EMANUELE III, KING

References

Belardelli, G. 1988. *Il mito della "nuova Italia": Gioacchino Volpe tra guerra e fascismo.* Rome: Lavoro.
Tannenbaum, Edward R. 1971. "Gioacchino Volpe." In *Historians of Modern Europe*, edited by Hans A. Schmitt. Baton Rouge: Louisiana State University Press.

VOLUNTARISM

Term for those philosophies that uphold the primacy of the will and the emotional capacities over the intellect and its apprehension of rational truths; a potent ingredient in the philosophical brew of fascism. Mussolini and Hitler both seem to have been indebted to this kind of thinking, which was mediated through such figures as Nietzsche and Schopenhauer. It was also a characteristic of actualism in Italy. Voluntarism was a natural companion for the cult of the hero. This was promoted as an antidote to the determinism inherent in Marxism. Marx believed himself to have discovered the "iron laws" that govern historical development, and he expounded them in his philosophy of dialectical materialism. Communists believed that they knew where history was headed, and they claimed that their only task was to hasten its inevitable goal—the utopian postcapitalist society that would arise following the end of the prevailing class war. In their philosophy, history moved according to its own inner laws; the individual could do little but help it on its way. For fascists, espousing the "heroistic" rhetoric of a Carlyle or a Nietzsche, fed by the Schopenhauerian current, the role of the iron-willed warrior was paramount, and he could achieve mighty deeds. They looked at the history of civilizations differently, reading them through Spenglerian eyes as reflecting the biological development of human beings on an expanded level: nations had their infancy and their maturity and then their senescence. Like the Marxists, who did, after all, believe in vigorous revolutionary action to help the iron laws along, fascists never quite resolved the issue of how energetic, virile men could interfere with the workings of these biological laws of societies. Untroubled by the seeming contradiction, fascists spoke as though the heroic figures of history could buck the laws of nature and bring about the needful changes.

Cyprian Blamires

See Also: ABSTRACTION; ACTUALISM; CARLYLE, THOMAS; FASCIST PARTY, THE; GENTILE, GIOVANNI; HERO, THE CULT OF THE; GENTILE, GIOVANNI; GERMANY; ITALY; MARXISM; MARXIST THEORIES OF FASCISM; MATERIALISM; MUSSOLINI, BENITO ANDREA; NAZISM; NIETZSCHE, FRIEDRICH; ORGANICISM; SCHOPENHAUER, ARTHUR; SPENGLER, OSWALD; TRADITION; WARRIOR ETHOS, THE

References

Magee, Bryan. 1997. *The Philosophy of Schopenhauer.* Oxford: Clarendon.
Rosenberg, P. 1975. *The Seventh Hero: Thomas Carlyle and the Theory of Radical Activism.* Cambridge: Harvard University Press.
Simmel, Georg. 1991. *Schopenhauer and Nietzsche.* Urbana: University of Illinois Press.
Young, Julian. 2005. *Schopenhauer.* London: Routledge.

VOLUNTARY MILITIA FOR NATIONAL SECURITY: *See* MILIZIA VOLONTARIA PER LA SICUREZZA NAZIONALE (MVSN)

WAFFEN-SS, THE

The military arm of the SS. It was set up by Hitler because he did not wholly trust the Wehrmacht leadership. The Waffen-SS were schooled in Nazi ideology and blind obedience to Hitler. The SS as formed by Hitler in 1925 had two militarized sections, and these were combined to form the Waffen-SS. The relationship between the Waffen-SS and the Wehrmacht was fixed by Hitler in a secret order in August 1938 which stated that it was neither part of the Wehrmacht nor the police, instead being at his personal disposal. In wartime the Waffen-SS should be deployed within the framework of the army, but still subordinated to the SS-Führungshauptamt (SS Operations Administration) and having its own jurisdiction.

The Waffen-SS, numbering 150,000 in 1940, often had more, and more modern, weapons and armament than Wehrmacht units, and cultivated an elitist self-promotion. It acted ruthlessly against the enemy and against civilian populations. A long list of war crimes has to be attributed to its members—for example, the massacre of British soldiers in Le Paradis (1940), the murder of French civilians in Oradour-sur-Glane, and the illegal shooting of U.S. POWs in Malmédy (both in 1944). Units also participated in guard duties in the concentration camps and in the extermination of the Jews—for example, in Minsk or when the Warsaw Ghetto was razed and the remaining inhabitants deported to Treblinka (1943).

While in its beginnings the Waffen-SS had been a small unit, its esprit de corps molded by the fact that only volunteers who could prove their "Aryan origin" for several generations could join, its character changed as a result of the war and the high numbers of losses. To have some 900,000 Waffen-SS members in late 1944 was possible only by neglecting the principle of voluntariness and "racial purity." Further fighting units had been deployed besides the original SS divisions, in this case consisting of ethnic Germans and foreign volunteers from nearly all European countries, such as the SS Division Nordland, comprising Norwegian, Danish, and Baltic volunteers. The International Military Tribunal in Nuremberg classified the Waffen-SS as a criminal organization. In 1961 its former members succeeded in being accepted as regular members of the Wehrmacht, thereby securing financial maintenance. Today's German neo-Nazis often express their admiration for the Waffen-SS in their rallies.

Fabian Virchow

See Also: ARYANISM; CONCENTRATION CAMPS; GERMANY; GHETTOS; HITLER, ADOLF; HOLOCAUST, THE; MUSLIM VOLUNTEERS IN THE WAFFEN-SS; NAZISM; NEO-NAZISM; NUREMBERG TRIALS, THE; RACIAL DOCTRINE; SS, THE; WEHRMACHT, THE; WORLD WAR II

References
Lucas, James, and Matthew Cooper. 1990. *Hitler's Elite: Leibstandarte SS 1933–45.* London: Grafton.
Matthaeus, Juergen, et al. 2003. *Ausbildungsziel Judenmord? "Weltanschauliche Erziehung" von SS, Polizei und Waffen-SS im Rahmen der "Endloesung."* Frankfurt am Main: Fischer.

Mueller-Tupath, Karla. 1999. *Reichsfuehrers gehorsamster Becher. Eine deutsche Karriere.* Berlin: Aufbau.

Wegner, Bernd. 1990. *The Waffen-SS: Organization, Ideology and Function.* Oxford: Basil Blackwell.

Whiting, Charles. 1981. *Massacre at Malmédy: The Story of Jochen Peiper's Battle Group, Ardennes, December, 1944.* London: Arrow.

WAFFEN-SS, MUSLIM VOLUNTEERS IN: *See* MUSLIM VOLUNTEERS IN THE WAFFEN-SS

WAGNER, (WILHELM) RICHARD (1813–1883)

Celebrated nineteenth-century German composer Richard Wagner, whose operas were infused with his concept of Germanic superiority. They were naturally very popular with the Nazis. (The Illustrated London News Picture Library)

Controversy has raged ever since operatic composer Richard Wagner's lifetime over his vociferous and megalomaniacal personality as well as over his heterogeneous and rich variety of musical and written work, given the racist overtones detected in both and the eventual association of his music and ideas with Hitler and the National Socialist regime in Germany, with its elevation of Wagner to the status of a kind of "cultural patron." Wagner was born in Leipzig on 22 May 1813 to the family of a police actuary who died six months after his son's birth. Shortly afterward his mother remarried. Her new husband, Ludwig Geyer, was a Jewish artist and actor who was said by Nietzsche and others to be his actual biological father. In 1831, Wagner enrolled at Leipzig University to study music, and in the following year he turned to the composition of operas, leaving behind classical instrumental music. His first completed stage work was *Die Feen,* which was followed in chronological order by *Das Liebesverbot, Rienzi, Der Fliegende Holländer, Tannhäuser, Lohengrin, Der Ring des Nibelungen* (comprising *Das Rheingold, Die Walküre, Siegfried, Götterdämmerung*), *Tristan und Isolde, Die Meistersinger von Nürnberg,* and *Parsifal.* Wagner was also a writer who produced a large output of theoretical works on aesthetics, politics, and other subjects, the principal one being *Oper und Drama* (1851); in addition, he wrote an autobiography.

From 1842 he was Royal *Kapellmeister* in Dresden, where he witnessed the revolution of 1849. He was actively sympathetic to the revolutionary cause, though he later played down his involvement. In Dresden he embarked on the study of medieval Teutonic mythology that was to become the distinctive kernel of his *Ring* cycle and began to develop his aestheticized politics of a spiritualized redemption with a particular focus on the symbol of the Holy Grail (a sublimated adaptation of Christian Easter). In 1848 he started combining the medieval *Nibelungenlied* with Nordic *Edda,* forming the distinctive epic style of his "musical dramas" (like the *Ring, Tristan und Isolde, Die Meistersinger,* and *Parsifal*), as opposed to the other "romantic operas," musically expressing the innovative use of a leitmotif technique and the style of "infinite (or continuous) melody." Nazi commentators later saw in his works the exaltation of a Germanic race whose mission was to save the world.

In exile because of his active participation in the 1848 Revolution in Dresden, Wagner first fled to

Switzerland, then to and fro to Paris, Zurich, London (where he met Queen Victoria), then Venice, Vienna, and other European cities until in, Munich in 1864, he met Ludwig II, the new (and eventually mentally erratic) king of Bavaria, who became his patron and financial backer until Wagner's death. In 1870, his first wife having died in 1866, he married his long-term mistress, Cosima, wife of his friend, the eminent conductor and pianist Hans von Bülow and daughter of Franz Liszt. Cosima, a strong personality herself, was to play a seminal role in Wagner's own life and in the direction of the Bayreuth Festival, Wagner's realized operatic dream where the theater, house, and so forth were designed by himself as an actualization of his own thought.

Schopenhauer's philosophy of "pessimism" and "will" was undoubtedly the single most important constant influence on Wagner's thought after he first started studying it in 1854. He was further influenced by Schopenhauer's elevated aesthetic (and metaphysical) concept of music as "absolute music," the true essence of the world and powerfully effective on human sensibility (something that the Nazis were quick to realize). In 1868, Wagner met Nietzsche, but the two soon fell out; though Nietzsche's thought, too, was to be posthumously associated with fascism, he had a more ambivalent stance toward the Jews that would permit him to say, unjustly but revealingly, of Wagner that his anti-Semitism was Schopenhauerian. Wagner's most widely known concept of the *Gesamtkunstwerk* ("Total or Integrated Art Work"), the "Art Work of the Future," or complete musical drama that his operas were meant to create, signifies the synthesis of musical, literary, and dramatic art forms. Scholars have seen here a Hegelian idea of a "completed" higher stage of art where the erstwhile separate art forms are *aufgehoben,* or overcome, yet synthesized into a higher form that unites them without dissolving them completely.

The recurrent themes in the litany of charges against Wagner the composer and ideologue are, on the one hand, that he championed explicitly anti-Semitic ideas and proposals, and on the other that his prose writings, autobiography, libretti, style of music no less than his personality were all things that Hitler, his "disciple," was attracted to, making no bones about it himself: Wagner was, for Hitler, one of the triptych (along with Luther and Frederick the Great) of the great fathers of the German nation. The fact that Hitler actually possessed some of Wagner's manuscripts and that he was an invitee of Wagner's family, in charge of the Bayreuth Festival, the use of Wagner preludes for the Nuremberg

Rallies, or stories of young Hitler getting exhilarated upon hearing Wagner's music in Vienna—these are part of the evidence linking Wagner to Nazism no less than the relations of the composer's descendants with Hitler and the marriage of his daughter to the proto-Nazi English writer Houston Stewart Chamberlain. The choral piece "Germans awake! Soon will dawn the day" at the end of *Die Meistersinger* with its obvious mass-arousing tonality was made into the anthem of the Nazi Party by Goebbels.

In the case of Wagner, later Nazi elements and ideas have been projected back on the basis of conceptual associations with his writings and operatic music (for example, calling *Rienzi* a "fascist opera" because of the Fuehrer idea that some see in it), as well as on the basis of the Nazi appropriation of Wagner, itself the result of carefully orchestrated cultural politics usurping past thinkers' ideas for the benefit of the Nazis' own glorification, greatly helped by the filtering of Wagnerian aesthetics through the lens of protofascist aestheticists. This selective Nazi exploitation of Wagner's music and ideas and Hitler's own admiration for it were enhanced by parallels they thought they found in the Teutonic mythopoieia of the operas, or in the composer's belief that art (and principally his own, or a sublimated purified "German" one) should take over as a redeemer of humankind once the Christian religion was admitted to be in crisis and its true meaning lost because of degenerating "Judaizing" influences.

Siegfried in the *Ring* could be read as the true "Germanic" authentic and uncontaminated hero-vehicle of redemption emancipating mankind through self-sacrifice (like Jesus) or through love (the analog to the Schopenhauerian concept of "compassion") from the moral degradation and cultural distortion brought about by "Judaizing" bourgeois-capitalist values and racial miscegenation. This was tied up with a belief in an Aryan race or even a non-Jewish historical Jesus of whom both Wagner and Hitler spoke. Hostility to "Judaism" as equated with certain cultural and sociopolitical values that Wagner and others (romantics or young *Kultur*-conservatives or Fichtean and Herderian nationalists) felt deep antipathy to, though not identical to genetic or blood racism, corresponded to similar hostile feelings that undergirded Nazi atrocities in the next century.

More concretely, Nazi cultural politics began being promoted in earnest through the reopening of the Bayreuth Festival after it had remained closed for ten years after the outbreak of World War I. A number of consciously designed elements make up this "nazification" that combined the promotion of Wagner as the "spiritual godfather of the party" with anti–Weimar Republic propaganda: the many publications that linked the operas with racist ideas, the bracketing of Wagner with Hitler as the "redeemers" of Germanic values, and the performances bringing out obvious connotations of Nazi values and attuned to Nazi aesthetics. An example of this was a 1933 staging of *Die Meistersinger*, the much-exploited and "nazified" operatic music for the Nuremberg Rallies, which paralleled the actual events outside the theater. Although some modicum of independence was achieved in Bayreuth, after 1939 the festival turned officially into a "War Festival" attended by war veterans.

The tangible link (rather than simply the supposed parallelism or formal analogue alluded to) between the anti-Semitic resonance or expressions allegedly to be found in the musical scores and the actual music itself has started being explicitly studied only recently. Although no Jewish dramatis personae as such appear in Wagner's operas, detractors have usually pointed to the stereotypical loathsome bodily or vocal portrayal of some of the "evil" characters and cliches associated with the type of "Jew-hatred" rampant in Wagner's (and our own) time. This direct correlation of music and racist ideas was exploited by certain directors during the Nazi era in Germany. Negative associations of Wagner's operatic music, performances, and essays have ever since been blended with a number of emotionally debated issues, apologia, and polemics alike, as well as current state politics—as attested by recent events in Israel, where the Jewish-Argentinean conductor Daniel Barenboim had to apologize for agreeing to conduct a Wagner opera there.

Byron Kaldis

See Also: ANTI-SEMITISM; ARYANISM; BAYREUTH; BOURGEOISIE, THE; CAPITALISM; CHAMBERLAIN, HOUSTON STEWART; CHRISTIANITY; COSMOPOLITANISM; *DEUTSCHLAND ERWACHE!*; FREDERICK II, THE GREAT; GOEBBELS, (PAUL) JOSEPH; GERMANNESS (*DEUTSCHHEIT*); GERMANY; HITLER, ADOLF; LUTHER, MARTIN; MATERIALISM; MITFORD, FAMILY, THE; MUSIC (GERMANY); MYTH; NATIONALISM; NAZISM; NIETZSCHE, FRIEDRICH; NORDIC SOUL, THE; NUREMBERG RALLIES, THE; PROPAGANDA; PROTOFASCISM; RACIAL DOCTRINE; SCHOPENHAUER, ARTHUR; SOUL; VOLUNTARISM; WAGNER AND GERMANIC SUPERIORITY; WAGNER, WINIFRED; WAR VETERANS; WEIMAR REPUBLIC, THE

References

Rose, P. L. 1992. *Wagner: Race and Revolution.* New Haven: Yale University Press.
Tanner, M. 1996. *Wagner.* London: Harper Collins.
Weiner, M. A. 1995. *Richard Wagner and the Anti-Semitic Imagination.* London: University of Nebraska Press.

WAGNER AND GERMANIC SUPERIORITY

Wagner was a pioneer of the notion of the superiority of the Germanic races in the sphere of music. He considered it his vocation to extricate German music from the "chaos" of "cosmopolitan confusion," to free it from all "alien" influences and to raise it to its fullest potential on the basis of the heroic figures of German myth and legend. It was an article of faith with him that previously no such thing as a German style had existed, even despite his respect for Beethoven and Bach. His prose works were full of praise for the German spirit with its earnestness, its solidity, its naturalness, and its depth. He venerated modern German dramatists like Goethe and Schiller as worthy successors to Aeschylus and Euripides. He called for the erection of a German political system that would embody this magnificent German spirit in a truly German state. The Germans, in fact, had in his view a global obligation, a universal mission to teach the world to turn away from "French" materialism. Wagner called for the emergence of a German hero who would spearhead this German mission, and Hitler undoubtedly saw himself as fulfilling that role. Corresponding to his reverence for all things aesthetically German was Wagner's contempt for all things aesthetically Jewish. He laughed at the way the German language was "distorted" in the mouths of Jewish speakers, he scoffed at synagogue music, and he condemned the works of Jewish composers as a hotchpotch of styles taken from others without any individual genius or creativity. He also associated the Jews with egoism, claiming that Jewish egoism made it impossible for them to espouse noble ideals or to understand the ideal of self-sacrifice for a higher cause.

Cyprian Blamires

See Also: ANTI-SEMITISM; COSMOPOLITANISM; GERMANNESS (*DEUTSCHHEIT*); HERO, THE CULT OF THE; HITLER, ADOLF; INDIVIDUALISM; MATERIALISM; NATIONALISM; NORDIC SOUL, THE; RELIGION; SCHÖNERER, GEORG RITTER VON; SOUL; WAGNER, (WILHELM) RICHARD

References

Köhler, Joachim. 2004. *Richard Wagner, the Last of the Titans.* Trans. Stewart Spence. New Haven: Yale University Press.
Salmi, H. 1999. *Imagined Germany: Richard Wagner's National Utopia.* New York: P. Lang.

Wagner, Richard. 1995. *Judaism in Music and Other Essays.* Trans. William Aston Ellis. Lincoln: University of Nebraska Press.

WAGNER, WINIFRED (1897–1980)

Daughter-in-law of Richard Wagner who kept alive the cult of her father-in-law's music, much favored by Hitler, through her direction of the Bayreuth Festivals. She was English by birth and her maiden name was Williams, but she was in fact the adopted daughter of Karl Klindworth, a pupil of Franz Liszt. In 1915 she married Richard Wagner's son Siegfried and became a close personal friend of Hitler's, especially after the death of Siegfried in 1930.

Cyprian Blamires

See Also: BAYREUTH; WAGNER, (WILHELM) RICHARD

Reference

Hamann, B. 2005. *Winifred Wagner: A Life at the Heart of Hitler's Bayreuth.* London: Granta.

WALL STREET CRASH, THE

Defining moment and nadir in interwar world economics, and, in consequence, also its politics. Many high school history texts argue the existence of a direct link between the Wall Street Crash and the rise of Nazism. While undoubtedly there is a general link between the state of international finance and the rise of political extremism, the impact of a bear market in the 1930s was a worldwide phenomenon; the Great Depression hit many countries in similar ways, not always leading to a fascist regime. Therefore, its effects should be seen as more complex, and as one among many factors that contributed to create the sense of generalized national crisis that encouraged the growth and acceptance of fascist ideologies.

The crash was caused firstly by the massive growth of investment by private individuals in the United States in a flourishing securities market, especially from 1927, creating a seemingly effortless economic boom. Increasing corruption set in, and many companies began to issue shares that would not be able to meet the overstated expectations placed upon them by these new and less economically savvy consumers. Secondly, by October 1929, stock market professionals believed that they could generate further profits, for themselves at least, by switching from a bull market to a bear market. Consequently, 24 October 1929, "Black Thursday," saw the first shocks of the bursting financial bubble, when the number of shares sold increased massively; by the following Tuesday, "Black Tuesday," the financial system was in chaos, with the share prices of corporations such as General Electric collapsing. Ten billion dollars was wiped from share values and bankruptcies became widespread. The impact of this financial crisis was global, as investors sought to recoup foreign loans; the 1930s saw a generalized downturn in world trade that impacted on many national economies. The crash and the Great Depression that followed should be seen as the gloomy backcloth that set the stage for a decade of crises that formed the grim backdrop to later interwar politics. Further, for those fearful of the rise of world communism, the crash suggested for many that while capitalism appeared deeply flawed, communism seemed to be "working." This both suggested that existing capitalist systems needed radical restructuring to prevent further instabilities and augmented the intellectual case for communist revolution, all of which helped to polarize political debate throughout the 1930s.

In Europe all countries felt its impact. The only fascist state at the time, Italy, suffered greatly between 1929 and 1933. For example, stock prices lost 39 percent of their value, unemployment rose dramatically, and the Bank of Italy's reserves fell by around a third. In response, Fascism presented itself as the political "third way" between New York and Moscow, and the regime responded by developing the policy of autarky as a demonstration of the state's independence and superiority toward the vagaries of international finance. The impact of the crash thus created the political space for the country to pursue a radical policy of protectionism and also aided the regime's experiment with corporatism; the former at least, to a greater or lesser extent, was a widespread phenomenon as nations sought to protect their economies. Other responses implemented across Europe as a result of the economic crisis were deflationary economic policies combined with the cutting of public spending on welfare provisions, all of which intensified a subjective cultural sense of a world in decline.

A typical case was Hungary, which suffered from a loss of large-scale foreign investments while short-term loans were no longer available. Further, existing debts were called in, and an agrarian economic crisis soon ensued. As a consequence, falling revenues led to drastic cuts in the state's civil service, radicalizing the educated classes. Ultimately, Horthy realized the need for a strong government; he appointed Gömbös as "Depression prime minister" in 1932. However, historians should be careful not to generalize. The Scandinavian countries were particularly hard hit by the Depression, especially their farming communities, leading to a proliferation of new single-issue parties, some of which were fascistic. Yet overall fascism was not successful in those countries, and the older agrarian and conservative parties were able to weather the political and economic storm of the Depression. On the other hand, in Spain, where the tensions already present between landowners and a radicalized agrarian workforce were amplified by the Depression, these frictions stymied attempts to push through land reforms in the early 1930s by the center-left reforming coalitions of the new republic. Ultimately, these tensions exploded in the Spanish Civil War from 1936.

Finally, in Germany the impact of the crash became the latest chapter in the Weimar Republic's failing history, sparking both an economic crisis in agriculture and massive urban unemployment. Further, the crisis paralyzed the political process, largely because of the weaknesses inherent in the country's fledgling liberal-democratic political system, which ultimately led to the emergence of Nazi rule. As in other Westernized countries, when businesses failed a sense of national crisis welled up. In Germany this was particularly emotive, because it appeared to be the latest chapter in a long string of national humiliations inflicted on the country by "external" forces since 1918, which augmented the *Los-von-Weimar* ("out of Weimar") mood. Against the backcloth of the Depression, ultranationalist arguments could more plausibly convey the idea that Germans had lost their sense of a psychological homeland essentially on account of liberal democratic policies, and that they were in the most desperate need of a strong leader to lead them into a new society in which they could construct a new and stable national identity, making tropes of the crisis, such as the unemployment queues, a thing of the past.

Paul Jackson

See Also: ANTI-SEMITISM; AUTARKY; BANKS, THE; CORPORATISM; DECADENCE; DEMOCRACY; ECONOMICS; FARMERS; FASCIST PARTY, THE; FRANCO Y BAHAMONDE, GENERAL FRANCISCO; FRANCOISM; GERMANY; GÖMBÖS, GYULA; HORTHY DE NAGYBÁNYA, MIKLÓS; HUNGARY; INDUSTRY; INFLATION; ITALY; LEADER CULT, THE; LIBERALISM; MARXISM; MARXIST THEORIES OF FASCISM; NATIONALISM; NAZISM; NOVEMBER CRIMINALS/*NOVEMBERBRECHER,* THE; PACIFISM; PALINGENETIC MYTH; PARLIAMENTARISM; PLUTOCRACY; REVOLUTION; SOCIALISM; SPAIN; SPANISH CIVIL WAR, THE; SPENGLER, OSWALD; TRADES UNIONS; VERSAILLES, THE TREATY OF; WAR VETERANS; WEIMAR REPUBLIC, THE; WORLD WAR I

References

Broch, Hermann. 1996. *The Sleepwalkers: A Trilogy.* New York: Vintage International.

De Grand, Alexander. 2000. *Italian Fascism: Its Origins and Development.* Lincoln: University of Nebraska Press.

Griffin, Roger. 1991. *The Nature of Fascism.* London: Routledge.

Morgan, Phillip. 2003. *Fascism in Europe 1919–1945.* London: Routledge.

Thomas, Gordon, and Max Morgan-Witts. 1979. *The Day the Bubble Burst: A Social History of the Wall Street Crash of 1929.* London: H. Hamilton.

WANDERVÖGEL, THE

Groups of students and other young persons in Germany in the early twentieth century who protested against industrialization by going to hike in the country and commune with nature in the woods together. From first beginnings in 1901 the *Wandervögel* ("Birds of Passage") grew rapidly, and by 1914 they numbered 25,000. Their philosophy focused on the revival of old Teutonic values and involved a strong emphasis on nationalism and anti-Semitism; this was fertile terrain for the sowing of National Socialist ideas.

Cyprian Blamires

See Also: ANTI-SEMITISM; ECOLOGY; GERMANNESS (*DEUTSCHHEIT*); GERMANY; NATIONALISM; NATURE; NAZISM; NORDIC SOUL, THE; RURALISM; WAGNER, (WILHELM) RICHARD; WAGNER AND GERMANIC SUPERIORITY; YOUTH

References

Laqueur, Walter. 1994. *Young Germany: A History of the German Youth Movement.* London: Transaction.

Mosse, George L. 1964. *The Crisis of German Ideology: Intellectual Origins of the Third Reich.* London: Weidenfeld and Nicholson.

Strachura, Peter D. 1981. *The German Youth Movement 1900–1945: An Interpretative and Documentary History.* London: Macmillan.

WANNSEE CONFERENCE, THE

Held on 20 January 1942 overlooking Lake Wannsee, the Wannsee Conference was decisive in coordinating and implementing the "final solution of the Jewish question"—that is, the systematic destruction of European Jewry in the Holocaust. Attended by fourteen Nazi functionaries and chaired by Reinhard Heydrich, this secret meeting defined and determined the number of Jews in Europe by country (based on the 1935 Nuremberg Laws), and established the blueprint for future actions directed at "evacuating" (that is, murdering) the estimated 11,000,000 designated enemies of Nazi Germany. Details of the Wannsee Conference emerged in 1947 with the unearthing of the only extant minutes of the meeting—the Wannsee Protocol—which have since that time remained a central indictment of planned genocide undertaken by the Third Reich.

Matt Feldman

See Also: ANTI-SEMITISM; ASOCIALS; EUGENICS; EUTHANA-SIA; GERMANY; GHETTOS; GYPSIES; HEYDRICH, REINHARD; HITLER, ADOLF; HOLOCAUST, THE; HOMOSEXUALITY; NUREMBERG LAWS, THE; ROMA AND SINTI, THE; THIRD REICH, THE

Reference
Roseman, Mark. 2003. *The Wannsee Conference and the Final Solution: A Reconsideration.* London: Picador.

WAR

A positive assessment of war lies at the heart of interwar fascism. The turning point in Mussolini's career was his decision to abandon his colleagues on the Left, for whom the only war that mattered was the class war, and call for Italy to enter World War I. It was this call to arms that signified his shift away from the traditional Left and toward what was to become Fascism. It was the moment when nationalism overtook universalism in his thinking. This was an ideological development followed by many of his contemporaries, but one distinctive thing at least about Mussolini's interventionism was that he actually welcomed the disruption of the war experience because he thought it would open the door to revolution—an assumption that proved to be correct. Mainline socialism saw the war as a diversion from the business of the emancipation of the proletariat, whereas Mussolini saw it as an opportunity. It would be fair to say that Fascism was born out of the call to war. The horrors of war that Mussolini and Hitler both endured did not, however, lead them to pacifism; far from it. They were left, at the end of World War I, with an overwhelming sense of disappointment and bitterness, because they felt that the sacrifices they and their comrades had made in the trenches had been for nothing; in this they undoubtedly represented the feelings of many other war veterans. While the reaction of many to the experience of war was to throw themselves into the creation of organizations for international cooperation such as the League of Nations, so as to ensure that such a catastrophic conflict would never flare up again, Mussolini and Hitler and their supporters were unashamedly working out a philosophy of war. As the *Enciclopedia italiana* article on the doctrine of Fascism (published under Mussolini's own byline but written by Gentile) put it: "Fascism, insofar as it considers and observes the future and the development of humanity quite apart from the political considerations of the moment believes neither in the possibility nor in the utility of perpetual peace. It thus repudiates the doctrine of pacifism—born of a renunciation of the struggle and an act of cowardice in the face of sacrifice. War alone brings up to their highest tension all human energies and puts the stamp of nobility upon the peoples who have the courage to meet it. All other trials are substitutes which never really put a man in front of himself in the alternative of life and death."

In German Nazism the myth of the German warrior knights of old held a fascination for many, and the mass rallies at Nuremberg were displays of military might as well as of national unity. Hitler, too, had a doctrine of development of character through struggle. But although the propagandists of fascism liked to portray themselves as advocates of the warrior spirit against the feeble, unmanly defenders of pacifism on the Left, the truth is, of course, that the Left also glorified struggle—but in their case the war in question was the class war. Fascists glorified war as traditionally waged between nations, a kind of struggle that the Left saw as an internal matter for the bourgeoisie, the workers having no stake in national boundaries or conflicts, but only in solidarity with each other against their oppressors. So it would be misleading to propose the belligerent glorification of war as a unique hallmark of fascism, making it stand out from the peace-loving doctrines around it. The Left, too, glorified war—the class war—and put forward a pantheon of heroes and martyrs of this conflict. The Left, too, exalted the character-building qualities of the experience of hostilities in their class war. The "different" reality behind the fascist attitude here was simply extreme nationalism, which argued that the interests of their nation were to be advanced with shameless belligerence against other nations, that the interests of the nation far outweighed the general interest in peace. The issue between fascism and the Left was not between lovers of war and lovers of peace, but between proponents of two types of war: the nationalist war and the class war. On the other hand it can be argued that while communists and some other socialists have always held to a vision of an ultimate utopia of peace at the conclusion of the class war, the interwar fascists assumed no such happy ending, believing "neither in the possibility nor in the utility of perpetual peace." As believers in Social Darwinism, they held that it is impossible to buck nature's laws: conflict and struggle are endemic to existence. For them, any other conclusion would have been "unscientific."

Cyprian Blamires

See Also: BOURGEOISIE, THE; CAPITALISM; FASCIST PARTY, THE; FREDERICK II, THE GREAT; GENTILE, GIOVANNI; GERMANY; HERO CULT, THE; HITLER, ADOLF; INTERVENTIONISM; ITALY; LEAGUE OF NATIONS, THE; LIBERALISM; MARXISM; MARXIST THEORIES OF FASCISM; MATERIALISM; *MEIN KAMPF;* MUSSOLINI, BENITO ANDREA; NATIONALISM; NUREMBERG RALLIES, THE; PACIFISM; PALINGENETIC MYTH; REVOLUTION; SCIENCE; SOCIAL DARWINISM; SOCIALISM; TERROR; UNIVERSALISM; WAR VETERANS; WARRIOR ETHOS, THE; WORLD WAR I; WORLD WAR II

References

Eksteins, Modris. 2000. *Rites of Spring: The Great War and the Birth of the Modern Age.* London: Papermac.
Kershaw, I. 1998. *Hitler, 1889–1936: Hubris.* London: Allen Lane.
Mosse, George L. 1990. *Fallen Soldiers: Reshaping the Memory of the World Wars.* New York: Oxford University Press.
Payne, Stanley G. 1995. *A History of Fascism, 1914–1945.* London: University College Press.
Stromberg, Roland. 1982. *Redemption by War: The Intellectuals and 1914.* Lawrence: Regents Press of Kansas.
Weinberg, G. L. 1994. *A World at Arms: A Global History of World War II.* Cambridge: Cambridge University Press.

WAR CRIMES: *See* NUREMBERG TRIALS, THE

WAR VETERANS

Veterans of World War I were, in varying degrees, among the rank and file of many fascist paramilitary organizations; the ideology of the front-line experience was part and parcel of the self-description of these organizations. In Italy, Mussolini called Fascism a *trincerocrazia,* or "trenchocracy," a government of war veterans. The Fascist newspaper *Gerarchia* declared in 1922: "Fascism is a child of the War" (Reichardt 2002, 366). Not only fascists themselves but also early socialist and liberal observers or theorists of fascism from Austria, France, and Germany like Julius Braunthal or Lucie Varga asserted that Italian Fascism and National Socialism were a protest movement of military desperados, uprooted by the war experience and the failure of social and psychological demobilization.

The empirical evidence about membership in fascist paramilitary organizations allows for discrimination as to these claims. For Italy, samples of *squadristi* from Bologna and Florence indicate that, in 1921/1922, only 47.5 and 45.4 percent, respectively, of the members were war veterans. Roughly the fourth part of these veterans had been officers, and between 14 and 21 percent of all veterans had been members of the Italian shock troop units, the Arditi. The large majority of the war veterans among the *squadristi* belonged to the age cohort born between 1890 and 1900. The proportion of veterans in the Italian Fascist Party was slightly higher. Among 151,644 members of the Partito Nazionale Fascista polled in November 1921, 57 percent claimed to be former servicemen. Therefore, war veterans supplied a large part, although not the majority, of the paramilitary activists of *squadrismo* in Italy. In Germany, they accounted for only a small minority of the storm troopers in the Sturmabteilungen (SA) in the years after 1930, when the SA had become a mass movement. In a variety of regional samples the age cohort born prior to 1900—that is, those men eligible for conscription during World War I—represented only 20 percent or even less of all SA members. Exact quantitative data for the Austrian Heimwehr is not available, but it is estimated that veterans constituted a significant part of their rank and file, and former officers a large part of their leadership.

This quantitative evidence requires a revision of older arguments, which had stated a direct causal relationship between the alleged "brutalization" of the whole war generation suffering in the trenches from 1914 to 1918, and their readiness to participate in fascist paramilitary movements after 1918. The results of "brutalization" and violence-prone identification with wartime combat were largely confined to the experiences of members of the Arditi and similar shock troop units in Germany, of whom many became Freikorps members in 1919, and later part of the SA leadership. Not the former servicemen's experiences, but rather the mythological interpretation of the front line experience in ideologies, symbols, and rituals of World War I veterans were important for the social integration of fascist paramilitary groups. The cult of the "unknown soldier" in Italian Fascism and in the National Socialist mass movement, the glorification of the "comradeship of the trenches" among both the *squadristi* and the storm troopers, and the theme of a "redemption" of the veterans from moral corruption in postwar society through paramilitary activism point, among others, to the importance of the cult of the war veterans for fascist mass mobilization. The enemy images and the glorification of violence in the plethora of autobiographical accounts of fascist war veterans were of particular importance for the appeal of fascism among the victory-watchers of the war youth generation—that is, those men born after 1900, both in Italy and in Germany.

Benjamin Ziemann

See Also: INTRODUCTION; DECADENCE; FASCIST PARTY, THE; FREIKORPS, THE; GERMANY; HEIMWEHR, THE; HITLER, ADOLF; ITALY; MUSSOLINI, BENITO ANDREA; MYTH; NAZISM; PACIFISM; PALINGENETIC MYTH; PARAMILITARISM; SA, THE; *SQUADRISMO;* SYMBOLS; WAR; WARRIOR ETHOS, THE; WORLD WAR I; WORLD WAR II

References

Field, Frank. 1975. *Three French Writers and the Great War: Studies in the Rise of Communism and Fascism.* Cambridge: Cambridge University Press.

Hüppauf, Bernd. 2004. "The Birth of Fascist Man from the Spirit of the Front." Pp. 264–291, vol. 3, in *Fascism: Critical Concepts,* edited by Roger Griffin with Matthew Feldman. London: Routledge.

Krassnitzer, Patrick. 2002. "Die Geburt des Nationalsozialismus im Schützengraben. Formen der Brutalisierung in den Autobiographien von nationalsozialistischen Frontsoldaten." Pp. 119–148 in *Der verlorene Frieden. Politik und Kriegskultur nach 1918,* edited by Jost Düffer and Gerd Krumeich. Essen: Klartext.

Reichardt, Sven. 2002. *Faschistische Kampfbünde. Gewalt und Gemeinschaft im italienischen Squadrismus und in der deutschen SA.* Köln: Böhlau.

Suzzi Valli, Roberta. 2000. "The Myth of *Squadrismo* in the Fascist Regime." *Journal of Contemporary History* 35: 131–150.

Ziemann, Benjamin. 2003. "Germany after the First World War—A Violent Society? Results and Implications of Recent Research on Weimar Germany." *Journal of Modern European History* 1: 80–95.

WARRIOR ETHOS, THE

The chief instigators of fascism were men who had served in the most bloody and destructive war in known history and who had returned home to feel that the courage and heroism they had seen in battle were neither to be found among their current rulers nor even respected by those rulers. The regimes that Hitler and Mussolini instituted in their respective nations owed a great deal to their military experiences and to the "warrior ethos" they had developed at the front. Disillusioned with the results of World War I, they did not blame those who started the hostilities, but what they perceived as the cowardice, treachery, and weakness of the politicians and the malign international forces such as Bolsheviks, Freemasons, pacifists, Jews, the international plutocracy, clerics, and so forth putting pressure on them and manipulating them. What the fascist ideologues called for was not a peaceable solution to the world's problems but a revival and reassertion of the "warrior ethos." They saw themselves as facing an armed struggle to subdue the malign forces that would undermine and subvert this ethos. Instead of respecting the values of peaceful conflict-resolution and negotiated dispute-settlement on which the League of Nations was intended to be based, they abused and condemned it in the name of "virile" militaristic values. Influenced by Machiavellian and Social Darwinistic theories, they were firm believers in the rule of the strong and the survival of the fittest. They had nothing but contempt for parliamentary "talk-shops" and preached strong leadership as the only way to create and foster national unity. In promoting paramilitary associations and in using violent tactics to deal with opposing forces, they were putting into practice the "warrior ethos" that undergirded their philosophy. In the long run they believed this to be for the good of society, in that the rooting out of elements that enfeebled the social order was a necessary purgation that would only benefit the health of the nation. In this respect they were entirely different from traditional mafia-style groups who used power simply to maintain their wealth or status in society. However, they were not so different from the Bolsheviks, who were also convinced that the violent suppression of resistance to their rule was essential to rid the social order of damaging elements. The difference is that the Bolsheviks were pursuing the aim of a worldwide proletarian revolution while the fascists were motivated by hypernationalism.

It was a logical consequence of this philosophy that Fascism in Italy and Nazism in Germany embarked on a militarization of society, enrolling most sections of the population into military-style organizations and consciously aiming to instill a military-style discipline. This is reflected powerfully in many photographs and newsreels showing large masses of individuals acting in unison, as in military parades, rallies, or women's gymnastics. Again this was an echo of manifestations of Bolshevism, but again the difference lay in the purpose: exaltation of the values of a greater Germany/Italy/Hungary/Croatia/Albania on the one hand, the "dictatorship of the proletariat" on the other. And whereas the utopia of the Bolsheviks was egalitarian, that of the fascists was elitist. The spoils would always go to the strong, the vigilant, and the ruthless; the bravest warriors would always come out on top. Their class would dominate the structures of the new hierarchical order, and their values would be replicated throughout society.

As part of his strategy for imposing Nazism on the world, Hitler founded three grades of academy for training future leaders. The elite academies for the upper echelons were the *Ordensburgen* ("order castles"), four of which were established; they were intended for students in their mid-twenties. The name was a reference to the medieval castles built by the Teutonic Knights. These were residential schools accommodating 1,000 students each, although they were not always full in practice. Discipline was of the severest, punishments draconian, and physical training paramount. The purpose of these institutions was to breed an inner core of hard, brutal, and warlike leaders who would crush the enemies of the Germanic race mercilessly. This new generation of merciless knights were the antithesis of the medieval knights with their ethos of chivalrous defense of the weak and vulnerable and their courtly ideas, as embodied in the Knights of the Round Table.

This ideal of energetic warlike action was felt by Hitler and Mussolini and their followers to be at the opposite pole from the purely verbal energies expended in parliamentary debates. They felt nothing but contempt for "talking shops" in which dynamic measures and determined political strategies became bogged down in discussion involving a range of typical parliamentary figures they stereotyped as pacifists, internationalists, socialists, liberals, and so forth. Needless to say, the Nazis in particular also contrasted the heroic Nordic and Teutonic warrior spirit with the materialistic preoccupations they attributed to the Jews. This idea was nourished by a widespread myth that associated the Jews with desk and backroom jobs during the Great War.

Cyprian Blamires

See Also: INTRODUCTION; ALBANIA; "ANTI-" DIMENSION OF FASCISM, THE; ANTI-SEMITISM; ARYANISM; BODY, THE CULT OF THE; BOLSHEVISM; COMMUNITY; COSMOPOLITANISM; CROATIA; DEMOCRACY; ELITE THEORY; FASCIST PARTY, THE; GERMANNESS (*DEUTSCHHEIT*); GERMANY; HERO, THE CULT OF THE; HITLER, ADOLF; HUNGARY; ITALY; LEADER CULT, THE; LEAGUE OF NATIONS, THE; LIBERALISM; MARXISM; *MEIN KAMPF;* MILITARISM; MUSSOLINI, BENITO ANDREA; NATIONALISM; NAZISM; NEW MAN, THE; NIHILISM; NORDIC SOUL, THE; NOVEMBER CRIMINALS/*NOVEMBERBRECHER*, THE; PACIFISM; PALINGENETIC MYTH; PARAMILITARISM; PARLIAMENTARISM; RELIGION; SOCIAL DARWINISM; SOCIALISM; SOUL; SS, THE; TERROR; TOTALITARIANISM; UTOPIA, UTOPIANISM; WAFFEN-SS, THE; WAGNER, (WILHELM) RICHARD; WAR; WAR VETERANS; WOMEN; WORLD WAR I; YOUTH

References

Bartov, Omer. 1985. *The Eastern Front 1941–45: German Troops and the Barbarisation of Warfare.* London: Macmillan.

Cook, Stephen, and Stuart Russell. 2000. *Heinrich Himmler's Camelot: Pictorial/Documentary, The Wewelsberg, Ideological Center of the SS 1934–1945.* Andrews, NC: Kressmann Backmeyer.

Hüppauf, Bernd. 2004. "The Birth of Fascist Man from the Spirit of the Front." Pp. 264–291, vol. 3, in *Fascism: Critical Concepts,* edited by Roger Griffin with Matthew Feldman. London: Routledge.

Mangan, J. A. 1999. *Shaping the Superman: Fascist Body as Political Icon.* London: Frank Cass.

Mosse, George L. 1990. *Fallen Soldiers: Reshaping the Memory of the World Wars.* New York: Oxford University Press.

———. 1996. *The Image of Man: The Creation of Modern Masculinity.* Oxford: Oxford University Press.

Spackman, B. 1996. *Fascist Virilities: Rhetoric, Ideology and Social Fantasy in Italy.* Minneapolis: University of Minnesota Press.

WARSAW GHETTO: *See* GHETTOS

WEBSTER, NESTA (1876–1960)

Prominent and influential English anti-Semite and conspiracy theorist of the first half of the twentieth century. Born Nesta Bevan, she was educated at Westfield College and married Captain Arthur Webster, superintendent of the English police in India. In *The French Revolution: A Study in Democracy* (1919), she alleged that the French Revolution had been planned and implemented by the Freemasons and the Jews, to whom she also attributed responsibility for the Bolshevik Revolution. Her ideas impressed both Lord Kitchener and Winston Churchill. She attacked Continental Freemasonry as atheistic and revolutionary but distinguished it from what she considered to be the benign British version. In 1924 she published *Secret Societies and Subversive Movements* and two years later *The Need for Fascism in Great Britain*. She was a member of the first British fascist movement, the British Fascisti. In 1938 in *Germany and England* she hailed Adolf Hitler as the man who had blocked the Jewish ambition to take over the world, but her enthusiasm for the German dictator did not survive his pact with Stalin. Her ideas were influential in the development of racism and anti-Semitism in Great Britain and also in the United States.

Cyprian Blamires

See Also: ANTI-SEMITISM; BRITISH FASCISTI/BRITISH FASCIST PARTY, THE; CONSPIRACY THEORIES; FREEMASONRY/FREEMASONS, THE; FRENCH REVOLUTION, THE; GERMANY; GREAT BRITAIN; HITLER, ADOLF; HITLER-STALIN PACT, THE; NAZISM; RACISM

References

Linehan, Thomas. 2000. *British Fascism 1919–1939: Parties, Ideology and Culture.* Manchester: Manchester University Press.
Webster, Nesta. 2003. *Secret Societies and Subversive Movements:* Whitefish, MT: Kessinger.

WEHRMACHT, THE

Official name for the military forces (army, navy, and air force) of the Third Reich; from 1935 it replaced the term Reichswehr, which had been used of Germany's army—strictly limited by the terms of the Versailles Treaty to 100,000 men. The most important lesson that Hitler learned from the failed Putsch of 9 November 1923 was the conviction that National Socialism would never come to power with the army against it and that its radically racist and expansionist program could not be carried through without army support. He therefore tolerated the "apolitical" line of the army, independent of party politics, under the Weimar Republic. He knew that the army agreed with him on central issues—the rejection of parliamentarism and the desire for a strong leader state, the battle against the Versailles Treaty and for the recovery of the territories ceded, the heightening of war readiness and the elimination of "pacifism" as embodied by the Left and by the Jews. This common ground shared by Hitler and the army meant that the Reichswehr approved of Hitler's access to power on 30 January 1933. It could feel itself affirmed by his policies: Hitler declared that the new state rested on the "twin pillars" of party and Wehrmacht. He dealt with competition from the SA by having its chief of staff, Roehm, and its leadership murdered; he introduced general military service, and he occupied the demilitarized Rhineland. The armed forces showed their gratitude to Hitler by the adoption of the swastika as national emblem on uniforms and orders, by the introduction of a specially composed oath of personal devotion to Hitler, and by the exclusion of all Jews from the ranks. Just as the Wehrmacht became politically a part of the National Socialist state through these measures, likewise it became so on the ideological level through an extensive education program.

The leadership of the Wehrmacht first strove to introduce the officer corps to the Nazi worldview, and then from 1938 with the assumption of supreme command by Hitler, the fanaticization of the troops became the foremost aim. In a training manual introduced in 1939 the troops were taught that they had to lead the battle against the "poisonous parasite" of world Jewry: in Jewry would be found "not just an enemy of our people, but a plague for all peoples." It was during the attack on Poland that the Wehrmacht leadership was first informed of Heydrich's program to eliminate the Polish intelligentsia and Jews, which did arouse a few generals to protest. When it came to the attack on the Soviet Union, Hitler personally informed those in command that this was not a normal war but a "battle between two worldviews," in which the international rules of war did not apply (30 March 1941). Orders issued subsequently called for all political commissars to be shot, declared that prisoners of war were subversive criminals, and allowed the troops to proceed by armed courts martial against the civilian population; Jews were to be transferred onto the murder program of the Einsatzgruppen. Each individual soldier was told who his enemy was and against whom he was to proceed with "utter ruthlessness": "Bolshevik agitators, irregulars, saboteurs, Jews." More than 10,000 commissars were "eliminated" on the spot; out of 5.7 million prisoners of war, 3.3 million died while in the hands of the Wehrmacht, and a million civilians were either shot as suspected partisans or in reprisal, or else deported to Germany as slave laborers. The Wehrmacht played a role in the murder of some 2 million Jews: in the course of the invasion they carried out an important work of identifying and ghettoizing the Jews, and they then gave logistical support to the ensuing massacres by the Einsatzgruppen and police battalions.

The annihilation ghettos of Riga and Minsk would have been impossible without their help; likewise the mass murder at Babi Yar. This transformation of the Wehrmacht into "Hitler's army" (Bartov 1991) was the sum of numerous factors, including rabid anti-Semitic and anti-Slav racism and a fanatical belief in the Fuehrer and his world historical mission. Above all, it was a result of the actual experience of war on the Russian Front: the powers of resistance and sheer doggedness of the enemy, and the strains and stresses of the invasion. Their own high losses were, for the war-seasoned troops, explicable only as a result of the "Asiatic malice" of the Russians founded in their national character and years of agitation among the people and the army by "Jewish Bolshevism." This "insight," supported by propaganda, provoked the soldiers into breaking through all existing moral boundaries and eventually resulted in the fanaticization that Hitler had wanted. Now appeared the type of the political warrior, "bearer of an inexorable *völkisch* idea," "avenger of all the bestialities" of Jewish Bolshevism against the German people, who abandoned the time-honored traditions of soldiery. With the growth of armed resistance in the rest of Occupied Europe, and especially after the landing of the Allied troops, this kind of soldier came to predominate everywhere. Hence the massacres of civilians, the shooting of prisoners of war, and the deportations of Jews all over Europe. A few military men, including *Abwehr* chief admiral Canaris, had raised objections against the criminal orders of 1941. But seeing that their protest had had no effect, they carried these orders out. Only as the war developed, in the face of the daily practice of genocide, and with military defeat looming, did an organized resistance develop, made up mostly of younger staff officers, joined by a few generals, including the then chief of staff, General Ludwig Beck, and Field Marshal Erwin von Witzleben. The uprising they plotted on 20 July 1944 under the leadership of Colonel Claus Schenk von Stauffenberg failed, not just because of an unfortunate combination of circumstances, but above all because there was no support for it in Hitler's Wehrmacht.

Hannes Heer
(translated by Cyprian Blamires)

See Also: ANTI-SEMITISM; BARBAROSSA, OPERATION; BOLSHEVISM; CANARIS, ADMIRAL WILHELM; EXPANSIONISM; GERMANY; GHETTOS; HERO, THE CULT OF THE; HEYDRICH, REINARD; HITLER, ADOLF; HOLOCAUST, THE; JULY PLOT, THE; KREISAU CIRCLE, THE; LEADER CULT, THE; MARXISM; *MEIN KAMPF;* MILITARY DICTATORSHIP; MUNICH (BEER-HALL) PUTSCH, THE; NAZISM; NIGHT OF THE LONG KNIVES, THE; NOVEMBER CRIMINALS/ *NOVEMBERBRECHER*, THE; PACIFISM; PARLIAMENTARISM; POLAND AND NAZI GERMANY; RACISM; SA, THE; SLAVS, THE (AND GERMANY); SOCIALISM; SOVIET UNION, THE; STAUFFENBERG, CLAUS SCHENK GRAF VON; SWASTIKA, THE; TERROR; *UNTERMENSCHEN* ("SUBHUMANS"); VERSAILLES TREATY, THE; *VOLK, VÖLKISCH;* WAFFEN-SS, THE; WAR; WARRIOR ETHOS, THE; WEIMAR REPUBLIC, THE; WORLD WAR II

References

Bartov, Omer. 1991. *Hitler's Army: Soldiers, Nazis, and War in the Third Reich.* Oxford: Oxford University Press.

Deist, W. 1981. *The Wehrmacht and German Rearmament.* London: Macmillan.

De Zayas, A. 1989. *The Wehrmacht War Crimes Bureau 1939–1945.* Lincoln: University of Nebraska Press.

Heer, H., and K. Naumann, eds. 2000. *War of Extermination: The German Military in World War II, 1941–1944.* Oxford: Berghahn.

WEIMAR REPUBLIC, THE

Period of parliamentary democracy in Germany between 1918 and 1933, in between the Wilhelmine Empire and the Third Reich, whose liberal structure, social democratic predominance, and supposed "Jewish" character, made it a central and frequent target of Nazi propaganda and Nazi violence. It was often referred to as the Weimar "System" by the Nazis, for whom parliamentary pluralism remained an implacable ideological enemy with which no compromise was possible. Moreover, the litany of crises faced by interwar German democracy contributed to the increasingly antidemocratic voting patterns of the electorate (in terms of support for the revolutionary Right and Left); and more specifically, to the trans-class popularity of Nazism.

Because of unrest in the German capital, Berlin, the elected National Assembly met in the town of Weimar on 6 February 1919—hence the name given to the republic constitutionally enacted by the first president, Friedrich Ebert, on 11 August 1919. However, even those important dates are historically controversial in demarcating the Weimar Republic: prior to the armistice concluding World War I on 11 November 1918, a parliamentary monarchy was briefly established under Prince Max von Baden in October 1918; on 9 November 1918, Kaiser Wilhelm II abdicated the throne, and a liberal-democratic state was declared on 9 November 1918. Any of these dates may be given as the inception of the Weimar Republic. Similarly, the appointment of Hitler as German chancellor on 30 January 1933 is often understood to represent the end of the German republic, although parliamentary democracy was effectively curtailed with the resignation of the last elected government on 27 March 1930; it has also been viewed as persisting in form (if not substance) until Hitler's amalgamation of the offices of Reich president and chancellor on 2 August 1934. Historians continue to debate many central features of the Weimar Republic, including its birth pangs, culture (symbolized by the Bauhaus milieu and artistic modernism), degree of popular and institutional support (for example, by the army), liberal character (epitomized by Hugo Preuss's 1919 constitution), and the reasons for its demise.

The final months of World War I indicated that dramatic changes were inevitable in Germany, especially considering the reverses suffered on the Western Front and the refusal by the Allies (Britain, France, and the United States) to negotiate peace with a German monarch. The ensuing year witnessed the construction of representative democracy (as opposed to the participatory *Räte,* or councils, enacted in late 1918) with elections ending the Provisional Government on 19 January 1919; acceptance of the Weimar constitution and the Treaty of Versailles (the latter on 28 June 1919); and participation of autonomous groups like the army, civil service, and aristocracy. However, despite a policy of "fulfilling" treaty obligations by successive governments, the 1923 occupation of the Ruhr—the German industrial heartland—by French and Belgian troops over the issue of financial reparations led to hyperinflation and economic meltdown in Germany. That was largely mitigated in 1924 by the introduction of overseas loans, restructured war indemnities, and a new currency, as well as by the skillful diplomacy of Gustav Stresemann (principally in attempting to normalize international relations)—all helping to stabilize the Weimar Republic, if only temporarily. During these years the Weimar Republic enjoyed real successes based on arguably illusory foundations, subsequently clarified during the massive unemployment and hardships engendered by the 1929 World Economic Crisis, perhaps felt most severely in Germany.

Radicalization of the populace was a major consequence of German sociopolitical breakdown after 1929, exemplified by the Nazis' jump in the national polls from 2.6 percent to 37.4 percent between elections on 20 May 1928 and 31 July 1932. Despite its previous profile as yet another extremist organization with failed revolutionary pretensions, the restructuring of the NSDAP in 1925 and the dissolution of electoral politics after 1929 both contributed to the enormous popular support for Nazism by the early 1930s. Moreover, the ascendancy of openly revolutionary parties (like the nationalists and communists) in later Weimar elections meant that coalition governments—always a necessity—under prodemocratic parties (like the Social Democrats, Center Party, and German Democratic Party) became untenable and increasingly identified with the "November criminals" held responsible for German travails under the Weimar Republic. One product of this electoral polarization was the antagonism of most moderates to communism, making many conservatives bedfellows of National Socialism.

Matt Feldman

See Also: ANTI-SEMITISM; ARCHITECTURE; ART; BOLSHEVISM; CENTER PARTY, THE; CONSERVATISM; ECONOMICS; GERMANY; HITLER, ADOLF; INFLATION; LIBERALISM; NAZISM; MUNICH (BEER-HALL) PUTSCH, THE; NOVEMBER CRIMINALS/*NOVEMBERBRECHER*, THE; PARLIAMENTARISM; REPARATIONS; SOCIALISM; THIRD REICH, THE; VERSAILLES TREATY, THE; WALL STREET CRASH, THE; WEHRMACHT, THE; WORLD WAR I

References
Evans, Richard. 2003. *The Coming of the Third Reich.* London: Routledge.
Kaes, Anton, Martin Jay, and Edward Dimendberg, eds. 1994. *The Weimar Republic Sourcebook.* Berkeley: University of California Press.
Peukart, Detlef. 1991. *The Weimar Republic.* London: Penguin.

WELFARE

Over the last century, fascist and far-right political movements have had a paradoxical and slightly confused attitude toward welfare. On the one hand, they have vehemently opposed the social welfare state. In Germany, for example, the Weimar system of state welfare was criticized for being too bureaucratic, arbitrary, and overambitious. On the other hand, fascists and neofascists have glorified their own brand of "welfare." In one of its early manifestos, the Nazi Party stated: "We demand an expansion on a large scale of old age welfare." In power, Hitler created a state infrastructure that blended charity, volunteerism, and massive Nazi Party involvement. It was about the individual submitting to the good health of the collective. Significant organizations emerged, including People's Welfare (founded 1933) and Winterhilfe (which mimicked a Weimar creation of 1931). Welfare organizations took on a significant Nazi complexion and performed a major role in the Nazi welfare state. The German Red Cross was thoroughly nazified, and was controlled by leading SS doctors. The Protestant Innere Mission and some Catholic welfare experts condoned sterilization. The Nationalsozialistische Volkswohlfahrt (National Socialist Peoples Welfare Organization) came to play a major role in organizing the voluntary sector.

In France, the Vichy administration (1940–1944) made great play of its special payments to mothers. In February 1941, Marshal Pétain increased family allowance rates, for he and his colleagues at the apex of the regime regarded reproduction as one of the most noble of roles—and their goal was for women to feel wanted and appreciated. Was this a horribly reactionary policy, as many historians have intimated? Or was it a progressive, forward-thinking welfare measure that presaged modern-day family allowance payments? In postwar France, Jean-Marie Le Pen's Front National is very proud of its policy of "national preference"—a policy which says that French "natives" should get priority treatment in the sphere of welfare. As one newspaper put it: "To combat France's high unemployment and poverty, the FN's manifesto has several suggestions. First, that "French employment should be reserved for French citizens," that any employer not complying would be sanctioned, and that all unemployed foreigners be "placed in transit camps before being deported." Second, that social welfare—unemployment benefits, healthcare benefits, and rights to education, housing, and child benefits—be reserved for French citizens. Third, that immigration, other than in "exceptional cases," be banned, all ten-year residence permits be withdrawn, and foreigners convicted of more than one criminal offense be expelled without appeal. Fourth, that police powers be extended to allow them "to check and to arrest immigrant delinquents on French soil." For some—aware of the "bounty" available for children born to "French families"—this policy is tantamount to institutionalized racism; to Le Pen and his colleagues, it is *le bon sens* ("common sense").

Some commentators now feel that Mussolini's corporate state was a welfare state in embryo, or perhaps a prototype. He undertook a major expansion of public works and significant improvements in social insurance measures. He established the Dopolavoro organization, which provided workers with cheap relaxation and entertainment possibilities. He made advances in public health with an attack on TB and the foundation of a huge maternal and child welfare organization, which led to a dramatic fall in the incidence of TB and a lowering of the infant mortality rate by more than 20 percent. He oversaw improvements in education and in the general public infrastructure. And it could be argued that he helped to create one of the most advanced welfare states in the world of his day.

P. J. Davies

See Also: BODY, THE CULT OF THE; CATHOLIC CHURCH, THE; COMMUNITY; CORPORATISM; DEMOGRAPHIC POLICY; EDUCATION; FAMILY, THE; FASCIST PARTY, THE; FRANCE; GERMANY; HEALTH; HITLER, ADOLF; IMMIGRATION; INDIVIDUALISM; ITALY; LE PEN, JEAN-MARIE; LEISURE; MEDICINE; MUSSOLINI, BENITO ANDREA; NATIONAL FRONT, THE (FRANCE); NAZISM; PERONISM; PETAIN, MARSHAL HENRI PHILIPPE; SEXUALITY; SPORT; SS, THE; STATE, THE; TOTALITARIANISM; TRADES UNIONS; VICHY; WEIMAR REPUBLIC, THE; WINTERHILFE; WOMEN; YOUTH

References

Bracher, K. D. 1973. *The German Dictatorship.* Harmondsworth: Penguin.

Bridenthal, R. 1984. *When Biology became Destiny: Women in Weimar and Nazi Germany.* New York: Monthly Review.

Harvey, E. 1993. *Youth and the Welfare State in Weimar Germany.* Oxford: Clarendon.

Quine, Maria. 2002. *Italy's Social Revolution: Charity and Welfare from Liberalism to Fascism.* Basingstoke: Palgrave.

Welk, W. G. 1938. *Fascist Economic Policy.* Cambridge: Harvard University Press.

WELTANSCHAUUNG/ WORLDVIEW

In National Socialism the term *Weltanschauung* (which in the nineteenth century had been a synonym for "beliefs, convictions, ideology") came to mean "total ideology," implying, of course, the claim to an all-embracing validity that excluded all other philosophies. As a quasi-religious-mystical confession propagated in numerous "enlightenment writings," the National Socialist *Weltanschauung* called for unconditional acceptance: it was not something one could understand; it had to be "felt." It was one of a trio of slogans (the others being *Führer* and *Kampfform,* "form of struggle,") that were to guide the Germans to the accomplishment of the "national community." This would be a community of the truly "blood-bound" (that is, "bound by ties of race/blood"), "natural," "organic," "living," and "integrated."

In *Philosophie—Werkzeug und Waffe* (1940), the philosopher Ferdinand Weinhandl, National Socialist and SA member, attempted to revitalize the inflationary *Weltanschauung* concept for philosophy, contrasting it with *Ideologie.* For Weinhandl, *Weltanschauung* stood for the recognition of the *völkisch* order of life as naturally given reality over "abstract" values that were the product of mere thinking. Like Spengler, Weinhandl drew on Goethe's morphology and physiognomics for the justification of his anti-intellectualism; he also made use of Goethe's concept of *Gestalt* in arguing for the "racial" conditioning of philosophy.

In *Vom Wesen der deutschen Philosophie,* published in 1941, the German Nationalist Hegelian scholar Hermann Glockner also sought to achieve the reintegration of the concept into academic thinking. Like Weinhandl, Glockner wanted to show the "organic" connection between *Weltanschauung* and philosophy and to rehabilitate German philosophers as *Volksgenossen* ("national comrades") "ready for action" who knew themselves to be free in "leadership and discipleship."

The answer to the question of how *Weltanschauung* could have come to be a key word in the language of the Third Reich was located by the Jewish philologist and literature specialist Victor Klemperer in the hostility of Nazism toward philosophy. In *Lingua Tertii Imperii* (1946), Klemperer observed, in an essay on the theatrical scenarios beloved of the Nazi leadership, the inner connection between *Weltanschauung* and *Schau* (also in the sense of the English "show"), ultimately expressing their deep yearning for mystical revelation and religious ecstasy as the opposite to clear thinking.

Susanne Pocai
(translated by Cyprian Blamires)

See Also: ABSTRACTION; ARYANISM; BLOOD AND SOIL; CHAMBERLAIN, HOUSTON STEWART; COMMUNITY; COSMOPOLITANISM; GERMANNESS (*DEUTSCHHEIT*); GERMANY; INDIVIDUALISM; MYSTICISM; NATIONALISM; NAZISM; NORDIC SOUL, THE; ORGANICISM AND NAZISM; RACIAL DOCTRINE; RATIONALISM; RELIGION; SA, THE; SCHOPENHAUER, ARTHUR; SOUL; SPENGLER, OSWALD; VITALISM; VOLUNTARISM; *VOLK, VÖLKISCH; VOLKSGEMEINSCHAFT,* THE; WAGNER, (WILHELM) RICHARD

References
Jäckel, E. 1981. *Hitler's World View: A Blueprint for Power.* Cambridge: Harvard University Press.
Klemperer, Victor. 2000. *Language of the Third Reich.* Trans. Martin Brady. London: Athlone.
Weinhandl, Ferdinand. 1940. *Philosophie—Workzeug und Waffe.* Neumünster in Holstein: Karl Wachholz.

WESSEL, HORST (1907–1930)

Author of the lyrics of what became an additional German national anthem together with the traditional *Deutschland über Alles.* As a youth, Wessel became a member of nationalist and militarist organizations (Bismarck-Jugend, 1922; Wiking-Bund, 1923); later he joined the NSDAP and the SA (1926). Promoted by Goebbels, in 1929 he became leader of SA-Sturm 5 in Berlin-Friedrichshain, a communist stronghold, provoking clashes with leftist workers. After he was shot as a result of a dispute with his lessor, Goebbels made a martyr of him. That same year the *Horst-Wessel-Song* ("Raise the flag high! Close the ranks tight! Storm troopers march, . . .") became the official party anthem.

Fabian Virchow

See Also: GERMANNESS (*DEUTSCHHEIT*); GERMANY; GOEBBELS, (PAUL) JOSEPH; NATIONALISM; NAZISM; SA, THE

References
Baird, Jay W. 1982. "Goebbels, Horst Wessel, and the Myth of Resurrection and Return." *Journal of Contemporary History* 17: 633–650.

Brownlow, Donald Grey. 1997. *Life and Times of Horst Wessel.* Hanover, MA: Christopher.

Knobloch, Heinz. 1993. *Der arme Epstein: wie der Tod zu Horst Wessel kam.* Berlin: Links.

Oertel, Thomas. 1988. *Horst Wessel: Untersuchung einer Legende.* Cologne: Böhlau.

WHITE NOISE

Term commonly used to denote neo-Nazi rock music. The phrase entered common parlance in the early 1980s when British far-right band Skrewdriver recorded their *White Power* single for White Noise Records, which had been formed by Ian Stuart Donaldson and the Young National Front to organize concerts and release records boycotted by the mainstream record industry. Quickly realizing the potential of music as a recruiting tool, the National Front began producing the *White Noise* "fanzine" in 1986, overseeing the organization of a truly international "white noise" music scene—ironically, just as it was beginning to dissipate in Britain.

John Pollard

See Also: BLACK METAL; GREAT BRITAIN; NATIONAL FRONT, THE; NEO-NAZISM; POSTWAR FASCISM; ROCK MUSIC; SKINHEAD FASCISM; SKREWDRIVER

Reference

Lowes, Nick, and Steve Silver, eds. 1998. *White Noise: Inside the International Nazi Skinhead Scene.* London: Searchlight.

WHITE POWER: *See* WHITE SUPREMACISM

WHITE ROSE

Student movement of resistance to the Nazis established at the University of Munich by Hans and his sister Sophie Scholl. They began by distributing a small anti-Nazi newsletter at the university, where Hans was studying medicine. Others joined them, notably Christoph Probst and Alexander Schmorell; also Karl Muth and Theodor Häcker, a Catholic writer and philosopher. The group was advised by Professor Huber, a Catholic conservative opponent of Nazism. By August 1942 both Scholl and Schmorell were serving on the Eastern Front. Scholl returned to Munich in November of that year, and by the following January he and Willi Graf began distributing leaflets in central German towns. These called for democracy, social justice, and a federal constitution for Germany. The following month, Hans and Sophie started handing out leaflets openly and were arrested and executed after being tried by the People's Court.

Cyprian Blamires

See Also: ANTI-FASCISM; CATHOLIC CHURCH, THE; GERMANY; NAZISM; UNIVERSITIES (GERMANY); *VOLKS-GERICHT*, THE

References

Mommsen, Hans. 2003. *Alternatives to Hitler: German Resistance under the Third Reich.* Trans. Angus McGeoch. London: I. B. Tauris.

Scholl, Inge. *The White Rose, Munich 1942–1943.* Trans. Arthur R. Schultz. Middletown, CT: Wesleyan University Press.

WHITE SUPREMACISM

Doctrine according to which the "white" races are superior to all others, which has been commonplace in theories about racial origins, going back at least to the Enlightenment. It was nineteenth-century doctrines about the superiority of "Aryan" peoples over others that motivated Nazism's racial beliefs. In the postwar era, it is the superiority of whites in general over blacks and Asians that is trumpeted by fascists, chiefly in response to European concerns about immigration. In the United States, white supremacist language represents a renewal of a long-established antiblack racism and is often found in combination with anti-Semitism. The Southern states of the United States have long been recognized as the stronghold of this thinking, and it took federal government action in the decades after World War II to bring the force of the law to bear against antiblack racism. Federal government measures to coerce individual U.S. states into combating discrimination against blacks are part of the reason for hostility to the U.S. federal government among many white supremacists.

Cyprian Blamires

See Also: ARYANISM; IMMIGRATION; KU KLUX KLAN, THE; NEO-NAZISM; POSTWAR FASCISM; RACIAL DOCTRINE; RACISM; RHODESIA; SKINHEAD FASCISM; SOUTH AFRICA; SWEDEN; UNITED STATES, THE (POSTWAR); WELFARE; ZIONIST OCCUPATION GOVERNMENT, THE

Reference
Dobratz, Betty A., and Stephanie L. Shanks-Meile. 2000. *The White Separatist Movement in the United States: White Power, White Pride!* Baltimore, MD: Johns Hopkins University Press.

that he was acting as a self-appointed "Nazi hunter" and "avenger" of the Jewish people, he wrote his Memoirs in 1988 with the title *Recht, nicht Rache.*

Markus Hattstein
(translated by Cyprian Blamires)

See Also: ANTI-SEMITISM; AUSTRIA; CONCENTRATION CAMPS; CONSERVATISM; DENAZIFICATION; EICHMANN, OTTO ADOLF; GERMANY; HOLOCAUST, THE; NAZISM; NUREMBERG TRIALS, THE; ODESSA; WAFFEN-SS, THE; WEHRMACHT, THE

Reference
Pick, H. 1996. *Simon Wiesenthal: A Life in Search of Justice.* London: Weidenfeld and Nicolson.

WIESENTHAL, SIMON (1908–2005)

Leading figure in the unmasking of Nazi war criminals in the postwar years. The son of a Jewish businessman, Wiesenthal studied architecture in Prague and Lemberg and from 1932 worked in a Lemberg architect's office, until he was arrested after the German invasion in 1941. He was in twelve different concentration camps up to 1945, and was the only one of his family to survive the Holocaust; he was freed from Mauthausen in May 1945. Wiesenthal was then given the task by the Allies of hunting down Nazi war criminals, and in 1947 he established a Documentation Centre about the Jewish Holocaust victims and their persecutors in Linz, Austria. From 1961, he headed up the Jewish Documentation Centre in Vienna.

The author of numerous books (*Ich jagte Eichmann* (1960); *Doch die Mörder leben* (1967); *Die Sonnenblume* (1969), Wiesenthal was a leading participant in the tracking down of Holocaust Organizer Adolf Eichmann in Argentina, as well as of other prominent Nazi culprits (Treblinka commandant Franz Stangl in 1967, Deputy Sobibor commandant Gustav Wagner in 1978). On account of his determination to deal with the past and name Nazi culprits, he came into conflict with conservative forces in Austria, especially in 1975–1976 over the issue of Vice Chancellor Friedrich Peter's Waffen-SS past, and in 1986–1987 over the Wehrmacht past of President Kurt Waldheim. In answer to the accusation by National Conservative circles

WINDSOR, EDWARD DUKE OF (1894–1972)

As Prince of Wales, and then in his year as King Edward VIII of England, the Duke of Windsor showed much sympathy for Nazi Germany. Then, between the abdication and the war, an ill-conceived visit to Germany gave rise to further doubts about his judgment. There is much controversy about his attitudes after the fall of France. The future Edward VIII had become Prince of Wales in 1910. In that role he presented a very different image from that of his somewhat straight-laced father. In the years 1933–1935, observers noted Edward's increasing sympathy for Nazi Germany, his admiration for dictatorship, and his dislike of the Foreign Office's alignment with France, which he described to the German ambassador as far too one-sided. These opinions were shared by his brother George, Duke of Kent. In January 1936, Edward acceded to the throne. Although his Abdication in December of the same year was directly caused by his wish to marry Mrs. Wallis Simpson, an American divorcee, the Establishment clearly had other reasons for wishing him to go. He had shown himself unreliable in a variety of ways. In particular, he had committed a number of indiscretions in relation to Germany, and his violently pro-German views had been freely expressed in the social circles in which he moved. His first activities as Duke of Windsor were ill-advised. Under the influence of Charles Bedaux, a French-American entrepreneur, he undertook a visit to Nazi

Germany in 1937 to "study housing and working conditions." Pictures of him associating with Nazi leaders caused a furor in Britain and the United States. The naivete shown in this case, and Edward's misplaced trust in Bedaux, may also be the explanation of his indiscreet comments (when attached to the British military mission in Paris during the first months at the war) about Allied military preparedness, uttered at dinner parties attended by Bedaux, who was by then almost certainly a German spy.

At the fall of France the Windsors managed to get to neutral Spain, then to neutral Portugal. Here the duke became the center of a German plot to make use of him as a potential British Pétain. Opinions are divided as to how much he went in with such plans, and he certainly seems to have seen domestic matters, such as his wife's title, as far more important. His acceptance of the governorship of the Bahamas appeared to put an end to the matter. He did, however, send a telegram to his contacts on at least one occasion thereafter, attempting to keep the lines open. Like many in the summer of 1940, he appears to have believed that British defeat was inevitable, and he seems to have considered himself as a possible intermediary in that eventuality. The German documents on this question were to cause some embarrassment to the British royal family after the war.

Richard Griffiths

See Also: FRANCE; GERMANY; GREAT BRITAIN; MITFORD FAMILY, THE; NAZISM; PETAIN, MARSHAL HENRI PHILIPPE; VICHY; WORLD WAR II

References
Allen, Martin. 2000. *Hidden Agenda: How the Duke of Windsor Betrayed the Allies*. London: Macmillan.
Donaldson, Frances. 1974. *Edward VIII*. London: Weidenfeld and Nicolson.

WINROD, GERALD BURTON (1900–1957)

Leading U.S. anti-Semite and pro-German sympathizer in the interwar years. Born in Wichita, Kansas, Winrod left school after the fifth grade, underwent a conversion experience at age eleven, and soon became an itinerant evangelist. In 1925 he helped to organize the Defenders of the Christian Faith, and in 1926 he launched a monthly journal, *The Defender*. At first

Winrod harped on the evils of Darwinism, divorce, "loose living," Protestant "Modernism," and Roman Catholicism. By 1934, however, his attacks increasingly centered on Franklin Roosevelt's New Deal, which he claimed was controlled by a secret Jewish "world conspiracy" that was unknown even to fellow Jews. To Winrod, who believed that the *Protocols of the Learned Elders of Zion* revealed the unfolding of biblical prophecy, Hitler's Germany was the world's single bulwark against occultism, communism, and high finance, all of which he saw as instruments of Jewish power. In 1938, Winrod ran the Kansas Republican primary election for U.S. senator but drew less than a fourth of the vote. When, in 1939, World War II broke out in Europe, Winrod called for "rigid neutrality"; three years later he was indicted for sedition. By 1947, when the case had been dropped, he had returned to Wichita, where he continued to publish *The Defender* while dabbling in unorthodox medicine.

Justus Doenecke

See Also: ANTI-SEMITISM; BOLSHEVISM; CATHOLIC CHURCH, THE; CHRISTIANITY; CONSPIRACY THEORIES; FAMILY, THE; GERMAN-AMERICAN BUND, THE; GERMANY; HITLER, ADOLF; INTERVENTIONISM; LIBERALISM (IN THEOLOGY); OCCULTISM; PLUTOCRACY; PROTESTANTISM; *PROTOCOLS OF THE ELDERS OF ZION, THE*; ROOSEVELT, FRANKLIN DELANO; SEXUALITY; UNITED STATES, THE (PRE-1945); U.S. CORPORATIONS; WORLD WAR II

References
Ribuffo, Leo P. 1983. *The Old Christian Right: The Protestant Far Right from the Great Depression to the Cold War*. Philadelphia: Temple University Press.
Sindell, Gail Ann. 1973. "Gerald Winrod and the 'Defender': A Case Study of the Radical Right." Ph.D. diss. Cleveland, OH: Case Western Reserve University.

WINTERHILFE

Annual charity collection whose proceeds were to go to the National Socialist People's Welfare Organization, which was the official private charity run by the Nazis. On one Sunday each year Nazi organizations were expected to make their staff available for street collections. Party officers and stage and screen celebrities made appearances in city centers as collectors.

Cyprian Blamires

See Also: COMMUNITY; GERMANY; NAZISM; WELFARE

WOMEN

An understanding of the relationship between fascism and women involves a consideration both of the role women have played in the fascist movement and their role in fascist states. Fascism has long been associated with an assignment of the sexes to separate spheres in which women are predominantly mothers. This was exemplified in Fascist Italy and Nazi Germany but is also evident in neofascist pronouncements. There has, however, been considerable disagreement among fascists over the role of women. While only a few women were present at the founding meeting of the Italian Fascist movement in early 1919, Fascist women's groups began to emerge the following year, and in 1924 a Fascist women's congress was held. In the years that followed, however, the party leadership purged those women they saw as insufficiently accepting of male prerogatives, and while the party recruited large numbers of women during the 1930s, it ensured that they were answerable to a male hierarchy. In Germany, while women were present within the Nazi Party from its inception, they were specifically forbidden to run as electoral candidates. In addition to individual women's membership, some branches had women's groups attached to them, and while at the national level a pro-Nazi women's organization, the German Women's Order, was established in 1923, another grouping, the Newland movement, moved from conservatism to Nazism. The resultant tensions between different Nazi women led to the creation in 1931 of one organization, the National Socialist Women's Organization (NSF). In 1932, less than 8 percent of Nazi Party members were women, but thousands of others were organized supporters; after the party came to power, both women's party membership and the NSF grew massively.

If in both the Italian and German cases, the party was led by men and predominantly made up of men, their policies in power also favored men. For Italian Fascism, women's most important function was as mother. In 1927, Mussolini gave a speech on the urgent need to reverse Italy's falling birthrate. The regime had already banned the sale of contraceptives and the carrying out of abortions, while in 1925 it had set up the Opera nazionale per la maternità ed infanzia (National Agency for Maternity and Infancy), which sought to provide improved prenatal and postnatal care and gave monetary awards for marriages and births. Mussolini also expressed hostility toward women's role

1932 Nazi propaganda poster urging women to vote for Hitler. Though women were not allowed any political power under Italian Fascism or German Nazism, large numbers of them did support these movements. (Library of Congress)

in the economy. In a 1934 article, he blamed women workers for male unemployment. What was needed, he declared, was an "exodus of women from the work force." In 1938 the regime formulated plans to reduce the number of women drastically in most sectors of the economy. These plans, however, were overtaken by the outbreak of war.

Nazi Germany was equally committed to emphasizing women's domestic role. In a 1934 speech to Nazi women, Hitler declared that while man's world was the larger world of the state, woman's was the smaller world of "her husband, her family, her children, and her home." In June 1933 a law was passed introducing interest-free loans for couples in which the woman had given up her job before marriage, and the regime subsequently gave the Honor Cross of the German Mother to women who bore four or more children. For the Nazis, however, pronatalism did not apply to all potential mothers. In part, this was implicit in its racism. Thus in 1935 the government forbade sex between an Aryan and a Jew. But the regime also discriminated among those it classified as Aryan. "We must," its minister of the interior declared, "have the courage again to grade our people according to its genetic values." Nearly 200,000 women are thought to have been compulsorily sterilized.

In a period in which women were entering the workforce in large numbers, there was widespread resentment on the side of men, particularly at times of high unemployment, and fascist parties sought to argue that their victory would restore the natural order within the labor market. In Italy, Fascism was associated with male veterans, concerned to gain access to jobs, while in Germany, the Nazi Party denounced what were termed "double earners"—women who worked when their husbands were already employed. In national elections in 1928 and 1930, the Nazi electorate was predominantly male. In 1932, however, the gender gap closed so that approximately half of the party's nearly 14 million votes came from women.

In the postwar period, the French Front National has both individual women members and an affiliated National Circle of Women of Europe. It opposes abortion, calls for the defense of the family, and emphasizes the centrality of raising the birth-rate. Mothers who stay at home, it holds, should both be honored and receive an income. Likewise in Britain, the dominant group of recent years, the British National Party (BNP), has long campaigned against abortion. Opposed to sexual relationships between whites and nonwhites, the BNP has also opposed the rise of the career woman, believing that home-making is women's "highest vocation." Unlike the FN or the main interwar movements, it does not organize women in their own groupings, but does recruit women individually and has selected some of them as municipal and parliamentary candidates. In addition to a reluctance to identify with interwar movements, those postwar extreme rightists who envisage an electoral road to power have also tended to avoid arguing that women must play a purely domestic role. Instead, they claim, a maternal income would make it possible for women to be able to choose to stay at home. This argument can be traced back to the 1930s, when the British Union of Fascists declared that it would not force women out of the workplace; even the Nazis, during the 1932 elections, announced that they would not do so.

Martin Durham

See Also: ANTI-SEMITISM; ARYANISM; BRITISH FASCISTI, THE; BRITISH NATIONAL PARTY, THE; DEMOGRAPHIC POLICY; EDUCATION; EUGENICS; FAMILY, THE; FEMINISM; FÖRSTER-NIETZSCHE, ELISABETH; FASCIST PARTY, THE; GERMANY; GOEBBELS, MAGDA; GREAT BRITAIN; HEALTH; HOMOSEXUALITY; ITALY; LE PEN, JEAN-MARIE; LINTORN-ORMAN, ROTHA; LUDENDORFF, MATHILDE; MITFORD FAMILY, THE; MOSLEY, SIR OSWALD; NATIONAL FRONT, THE (FRANCE); NAZISM; POSTWAR FASCISM; RACIAL DOCTRINE; RIEFENSTAHL, LENI; SARFATTI-GRASSINI, MARGHERITA; SCHOLTZ-KLINK, GERTRUD; SEXUALITY; TOTALITARIANISM; WEBSTER, NESTA; WELFARE; YOUTH

References

Bacchetta, Paola, and Margaret Power. 2002. *Right-Wing Women: From Conservatives to Extremists around the World.* London: Routledge.

Blee, Kathleen M. 2002. *Inside Organized Racism: Women in the Hate Movement:* Berkeley: University of California Press.

Durham, Martin. 1998. *Women and Fascism.* London: Routledge.

Gori, Gigliola. 2004. *Female Bodies, Sport, Italian Fascism.* London: Frank Cass.

Gottlieb, Julie V. 2000. *Feminine Fascism: Women in Britain's Fascist Movement 1923–1945.* London: I. B. Tauris.

Passmore, Kevin. 2003. *Women, Gender and Fascism in Europe, 1919–45,* Manchester: Manchester University Press.

Richmond, Kathleen. 2003. *Women and Spanish Fascism: The Women's Section of the Falange 1934–1959.* London: Routledge.

Stephenson, Jill. 1981. *The Nazi Organization of Women.* London: Croom Helm.

WORK

The creation of a new work ethic and of a new understanding of work played a crucial role in interwar fascist movements and societies. Three general tendencies can be noted: the fascist conception of work had strong nationalistic, militaristic, and (in the case of Nazism) racist connotations. According to the nationalistic dimension, work derived its value only from its usefulness to the national community. Generally, "work" is seen as an activity giving meaning to life and legitimizing the existence of the individual. Contrary to liberal conceptions, the individual is regarded as important only if serving the national community. Consequently, fascist ideologies glorified and sometimes even sacralized work. This was especially true for simple, manual labor. The nationalistic dimension emphasized that all kinds of work be regarded as equally valuable, as long as they serve the national interest. Fascist movements and states therefore upgraded manual labor symbolically. With a combination of anti-Marxist and anticapitalist arguments, they especially attempted to court the working classes. But despite all ambivalences and inner-fascist controversies over the right notion of work, in social and economic practice fascist societies did not change the distribution of property fundamentally or break radically with the capitalist economic system. On the other hand, since it was the fascist movement or state that defined the national interest, this conception of "work" provided an opening for broad state intervention in the labor market and the economy, even if the exact degree of interference varied.

Second, fascism stands for a militarization of the conception of work. On the one hand, the semantic fields of labor and the military sphere were connected or even merged. In fascist movements and societies, work activities were frequently described by using military terms and metaphors—for example, *battaglia del grano* ("fight for grain") or *Erzeugungsschlacht* ("battle of production"). Fascists saw work and warfare as the two forms that the struggle for existence can take. A military ethos with ideas such as duty and sacrifice, hierarchy and courage was ingrained into the conception of work. Work was to serve as a means to create social discipline. There was also a tendency to militarize labor relations. In Nazi Germany, for example, the free change of workplace was more and more restricted, and regular employment was interpreted as service in analogy to military duties.

In Nazism, "work" often had a racist and anti-Semitic dimension. In Nazi Germany all those excluded from the national community were also barred from the sphere of work. At the same time, the very idea of work was interpreted as an Aryan characteristic, whereas Jews were seen as a people unwilling and unable to undertake proper work. Thus work not only had a highly integrative side by glorifying national projects and the people performing it but also a highly exclusive and aggressive dimension.

Kiran Patel

See Also: ANTI-SEMITISM; ARYANISM; ECONOMICS; EMPLOYMENT; FASCIST PARTY, THE; FORCED LABOR; GERMANY; INDUSTRY; ITALY; LABOR FRONT, THE; LABOR SERVICE, THE; MASSES, THE ROLE OF THE; MILITARISM; NATIONALISM; NAZISM; PLUTOCRACY; PRODUCTIVISM; RACISM; SOCIAL DARWINISM; TRADES UNIONS; *VOLKSGEMEINSCHAFT*, THE; WAR; WARRIOR ETHOS, THE

References

Campbell, Joan. 1989. *Joy in Work, German Work: The National Debate, 1800–1945.* Princeton: Princeton University Press.
Eatwell, Roger. 1995. *Fascism: A History.* London: Chatto and Windus.
Griffin, Roger. 1991. *The Nature of Fascism.* London: Routledge.
Patel, Kiran Klaus. 2005. *"Soldiers of Work": Labor Services in New Deal America and Nazi Germany, 1933–1945.* New York: Cambridge University Press (esp. ch. IV.2.1).
Payne, Stanley G. 1995. *A History of Fascism, 1914–1945.* London: University College London Press.

WORKERS, THE: *See* EMPLOYMENT; MARXIST THEORIES OF FASCISM; MASSES, THE ROLE OF THE; SOCIALISM; TRADES UNIONS; WORK

WORLD WAR I

World War I led to a number of factors that, together, contributed to the growth of fascist ideology in Europe. Most important, the war placed enormous pressure on all the political systems of the belligerent countries, creating a mass politicization of society and a polarization of left- and right-wing politics that undermined European liberal-democratic traditions. In Britain and France, well-established liberal-democratic systems were able to cope with the war crisis through "national union" governments. That was not the case in Southern, Central, and Eastern Europe, however, where such traditions were far weaker. Germany's younger and more fragile democratic system was placed under strain, and the country was effectively under military command by 1916. Italy was forced into combat by the "interventionist campaign," which lacked widespread support and undermined the Giolittian liberal parliamentary system. Autocratic Russia was torn apart by the conflict and in 1917 collapsed into successive revolutions, communist one-party rule, and then civil war. And this was not true only for the Great Powers. For example, both the government and the monarchy in Greece were overthrown before she joined the Allies in 1917. After Portugal entered the war, political instability led to the formation of a semiauthoritarian charismatic leadership under Sidonia Pais, portending future fascist regimes. Neutral Spain had to put down three

Italian troops after their catastrophic defeat at Caporetto in 1917. Both the Italian Fascists and the German Nazis contrasted the 'heroism' of the frontline soldiers with the 'treacherous' and 'mercenary' behavior of the politicians, whom they blamed for military disasters like this one. (Hulton Archive/Getty Images)

attempted uprisings in 1917 alone, highlighting the war's impact on nonbelligerent European nations.

This political instability continued after the war, and it was not ameliorated by the reordering of Europe at Versailles. The Habsburg Empire was transformed from a multiracial kingdom with a tradition as a key European power into the emasculated rump state of Austria. The breakup of Austro-Hungary led to the further division of the Balkans and Eastern Europe into unstable nation-states, which included the creation of Yugoslavia, a considerably enlarged Romania, and the formation of Poland as an independent state; the latter also divided Germany from East Prussia. The German defeat and revolution in 1918 ended the Second Reich and the Hohenzollern monarchy and brought the ultimately unworkable Weimar Republic into being. Italy felt betrayed by the agreement because she did not receive all of the European land promised upon her entry

into the war; although she ended up on the winning side, many Italians saw it as a "mutilated victory." This widespread sense of experiencing a national humiliation was inflicted on many European states by the peace settlement.

Much of postwar Europe was made up of a number of nation-states at fundamentally different stages of development toward liberal parliamentary systems, and many of these nations—Germany, Austria, Finland, Lithuania, Poland, Yugoslavia, Hungary, and Romania—were operating with new and seemingly alien liberal-democratic constitutions. Furthermore, it is difficult to overstate the importance of the emergence of Communist Russia in describing the postwar European political dynamic. That system presented a highly desirable alternative to capitalism for many on the European Left, while materializing the worst fears of the European Right. Also of great importance were the ways in which wartime experiences had fundamentally altered the way in which "ordinary people" of Europe viewed themselves in relation to the state. World War I was the first "total war," requiring the mobilization of the productive and human resources of entire countries. Consequently, the war politicized national populations through extreme propaganda campaigns that increasingly demonized the Other and exposed citizens to new state bureaucracies that augmented the populist nationalism increasingly "in the air" across Europe in the run-up to 1914. This encouraged the postwar construction of identities conceived on populist and nationalized "us versus them" dichotomies, and this "nationalization of the masses" also created a greater expectation and dependency on the state. The wartime model of a powerful executive power coupled with an effective bureaucracy that intervened in economic affairs and civil rights in order to protect national interests was seen by many as still desirable in the postwar crisis years, when liberal political elites seemed so weak and out of touch. The war had opened up a new sociopolitical space whereby contingent factors such as economic crisis coupled with the sense of social anomie were highly conducive to the development of radical ultranationalist political ideologies.

Further strains were created as each nation had to demobilize hundreds of thousands of troops and reintegrate them into civil societies across Europe. After the war that led to the development of networks of civilian veterans groups, and consequently to a widespread "paramilitarization" of European society. This was to become a major characteristic of interwar fascist movements, and was a factor that arose directly from the experiences of the trenches. After the war had ended, political violence thus often seemed a natural solution and even became normalized. Further, the trench experiences had helped to forge a psychological dynamic whereby significant sections within European societies developed an interest in chauvinistic and egoistical fantasies that were bolstered with sense of mission, sacrifice, and duty to the national cause. This predisposed many of the war generation to be vulnerable to appeals to view themselves as vanguards of new political elites capable of forging new political orders. Mussolini dubbed the Italian permutation of this phenomenon "trenchocracy."

The Enlightenment idea of the "progress" of humanity from savage ancestors to civilized Europeans was shattered, and European culture and society began to labor under a widespread sense of crisis and decline—though shot through with new visions of hope. A text such as Oswald Spengler's *Decline of the West* was

typical of that form of discourse. The whole Enlightenment tradition of the progressive elimination of the irrational by the advance of "reason" was felt to be in crisis, and a new politics of emotion and action was often perceived as required in response to the contingency of postwar Europe's political crises. Sometimes this was imbued with a renewed sense of the sacred and desire for rebirth, a mind-set that Roger Griffin has identified as fascism's palingenetic quality. The new mass propaganda—which always contained the subtext "Once the suffering of today is over, a better world will come tomorrow!"—allowed ideologues to exploit the general sense of unrealized hopes that resulted from the war and that were often assumed to be symptomatic of the incapacity of liberal-democratic politics to deliver. In this context, radical authoritarian alternatives could appear to be genuinely progressive in comparison to liberal democracy or communism.

The war was also crucial in turning myriad protofascist movements into unified ideological forces that could exercise a genuine influence over political events, transforming them from esoteric and sometimes conservative forces into radically modern ideologies. For example, in Italy the various protofascist intellectuals and movements became unified around Italian intervention in the war as a means for Italy to secure new territories, gain international prestige, and establish authoritative political leadership that would kill off revolutionary socialism. This "interventionist campaign" consisted of a highly diverse grouping of organizations such as the Associazione Nazionale Italiana; periodicals such as *La Voce* and *L'Idea Nazionale*; elements of the revolutionary Left, especially the neosyndicalist movement; politicians, including Prime Minister Antonio Salandra; and key intellectuals such as Filippo Marinetti, Gabriele D'Annunzio, and Benito Mussolini. This campaign was also marked by many key tropes of fascist politics, "*piazza* politics" and crowd power, the glorification of violence and of the heroism of war, and a commingling between utopian visions of a "new Italy" with a pragmatic agenda in an ideological synthesis that rejected "rational" for charismatic politics. Despite a lack of mass popular support, Italy entered the war in 1915 to a war fever dubbed "the radiant days of May."

The war did gain popular support, paradoxically, after the defeat at the Battle of Caporetto in 1917. Across Italy local patriotic groupings (*Fasci*) emerged, generated widespread animosity against neutralists and socialists, and promoted the patriotic cause. This new populist-nationalist fervor was also reflected on a national level, and a prowar lobby consisting of a cross-party selection of deputies was formed. By this time Mussolini's nationalist organ, *Il Popolo d'Italia,* had established itself as the primary journal of the interventionist movement. After the war he sought to build on the new nationalistic and belligerent political dynamic, *combattentismo,* and the "spirit of the trenches," *trincerismo,* with his new organization, Fasci di combattimento. Other *Fasci* included those of the Political Futurists, the ANI's Sempre Pronti, and Captain Vecchi's Arditi. Thus in Italy the war not only gave birth to the budding ideology of Fascism but also unified and radicalized the "protofascist" elements in Italy, and forged a political and social dynamic highly conducive to Fascist politics.

Many arguably protofascist currents existed in Germany before the war, this time drawing on *völkisch* tradition of an "organic" nation and radicalized by war experiences. The outbreak of the war led to hopes of a rebirth of a healthy German *Kultur* triumphing over the degenerate *Zivilisation,* which in turn would result in a "reawakened" German *Volksgemeinschaft.* The fact that, even in the summer of 1918, Germany was still expecting victory in the war only enhanced the terrible shock and humiliation felt across Germany when Friedrich Ebert unconditionally surrendered in November of that year. This in turn led to the *Dolchstoss,* or "stab in the back," myth, which became a central aspect of many postwar German nationalisms and which was absolutely central to Nazi propaganda. The myth claimed that the peace-mongering socialist politicians who negotiated the end of the war were essentially national traitors, and further that Germany had not actually been defeated on the battlefield but simply betrayed by left-wing politicians. Also of significance during the war was a growing perception that associated "Jewishness" with safe bureaucratic positions rather than military roles (and therefore with cowardice), and also with left-wing politics in general. This forged a widespread misconception of a lack of German-Jewish patriotism and commitment to the war, on which could be erected myriad racist constructions.

In the immediate postwar milieu the socialist coalition government faced attack from communist revolutionaries and relied on paramilitary squads, Freikorps, to prevent the very real threat of revolution. This demonstrates not only the postwar dynamic of paramilitarized politics but also the significance of the Russian Revolution of 1917—lighting beacons of left-wing revolutionary hope across Europe and also fermenting equally radicalized right-wing responses to the threat. After German emasculation was enshrined in the Ver-

sailles Treaty and the Weimar Republic, *völkisch* movements proliferated in German civil society. These often glorified in the war, fostered the *Dolchstoss* myth, and developed the *Los-von-Weimar,* or "out of Weimar," mood. This attitude was key to Nazi success. Hitler often drew on his own war experiences—for example, in *Mein Kampf* he described that on hearing of the outbreak of war he was overtaken "by stormy enthusiasm, I fell down on my knees and thanked Heaven from an overflowing heart for granting me the good fortune of being permitted to live at this time. . . . There now began the greatest and most unforgettable time of my earthly existence" (Kershaw 1998, 70). Once in power the Nazi regime also repeatedly played on the power of World War I in its attempts to generate a "new man," drawing on a semiotic of war that formed what G. L. Mosse has dubbed a "civic religion" of heroism and faith in the nation.

Finally, the Armenian Massacres (1915–1923) were another significant event that emerged from the war and also one that directly impacted upon the history of fascism, and especially the Holocaust. The murder of some 1 million Armenians by the Turks was the twentieth century's first great genocide, and the event set a grisly precedent for future "projects" of systematic mass murder. Hitler was alleged to have said on the eve of World War II: "Who now remembers the massacre of the Armenians?"

Paul Jackson

See Also: INTRODUCTION; ANTI-SEMITISM; AUSTRIA; AUSTRO-HUNGARIAN/HABSBURG EMPIRE, THE; BOLSHEVISM; CAPITALISM; CAPORETTO; CIVILIZATION; COSMOPOLITANISM; CULTURE; D'ANNUNZIO, GABRIELE; DECADENCE; DEMOCRACY; ECONOMICS; ENLIGHTENMENT, THE; FASCIO, THE; FASCIST PARTY, THE; FINLAND; FIUME; FREIKORPS, THE; FUTURISM; GERMANY; GREECE; HERO, THE CULT OF THE; HITLER, ADOLF; HOLOCAUST, THE; HUNGARY; INFLATION; INTERVENTIONISM; ITALY; LEAGUE OF NATIONS, THE; LIBERALISM; LITHUANIA; MARINETTI, FILIPPO TOMMASO; MARXISM; MARXIST THEORIES OF FASCISM; *MEIN KAMPF;* MILITARISM; MUSSOLINI, BENITO ANDREA; MYTH; NATIONALISM; NAZISM; NIHILISM; NORDIC SOUL, THE; NOVEMBER CRIMINALS/*NOVEMBERBRECHER,* THE; PACIFISM; PALINGENETIC MYTH; PARAMILITARISM; PARLIAMENTARISM; POLAND; POLAND AND NAZI GERMANY; PORTUGAL; PROGRESS; PROTOFASCISM; RATIONALISM; REPARATIONS; REVOLUTION; ROMANIA; SLAVS, THE (AND GERMANY); SOCIALISM; SOVIET UNION, THE; SPENGLER, OSWALD; TOTALITARIANISM; TURKEY; UNIVERSALISM; UTOPIA, UTOPIANISM; VERSAILLES, THE TREATY OF; *VOLK, VÖLKISCH; VOLKSGEMEINSCHAFT,* THE; WALL STREET CRASH, THE; WAR; WAR VETERANS; WARRIOR ETHOS, THE; WEIMAR REPUBLIC, THE; WORLD WAR II; YUGOSLAVIA

References

Cassels, Alan. 1975. *Fascism.* Arlington Heights, Il: Harlan Davidson.

Eksteins, Modris. 2000. *Rites of Spring: The Great War and the Birth of the Modern Age.* London: Papermac.

Griffin, Roger. 1991. *The Nature of Fascism.* London: Routledge.

Hüppauf, Bernd. 2004. "The Birth of Fascist Man from the Spirit of the Front." Pp. 264–291, vol. 3, in *Fascism: Critical Concepts,* edited by Roger Griffin with Matthew Feldman. London: Routledge.

Kershaw, Ian. 1998. *Hitler 1889–1936: Hubris.* London: Penguin.

Linz, Juan J. 1980. "Political Space and Fascism as a Late-Comer: Conditions Conducive to the Success or Failure of Fascism as a Mass Movement in Inter-War Europe." Pp. 153–189 in *Who Were the Fascists: Social Roots of European Fascism,* edited by S. U. Larsen, B. Hagtvet, and J. P. Myklebust. Bergen: Universitetsforlaget.

Mosse, George L. 1990. *Fallen Soldiers: Reshaping the Memory of the World Wars.* New York: Oxford University Press.

Payne, Stanley G. 1995. *A History of Fascism, 1914–1945.* London: University College Press.

Stromberg, Roland. 1982. *Redemption by War: The Intellectuals and 1914.* Lawrence: Regents Press of Kansas.

WORLD WAR II

The origins of World War II lay in the ideological drive for expansion manifest in the Nazi worldview. The basic goal was to create an expanded Germany to the east, thereby recapturing German *Lebensraum* in order to form a new superpower: the Thousand-Year Reich. In so doing, Hitler envisaged destroying the USSR and eliminating France as a continental power. Further, this would be combined with an ethnic revolution in the region, promoted by the Nazis as being a defense of German-speaking peoples. It was this racial aspect that distinguished Nazi policy from older forms of German expansionism. As far back as 1934, Hitler ordered his generals to be ready for war "within eight years." This policy of rearmament was given a substantial fillip by the failure of the West to react to Hitler's remilitarization of the Rhineland in 1936. Hitler believed that he could forge allegiances with Great Britain and the Soviet Union in order to gain the time to fulfill this plan. With regard to the latter, Nazi diplomacy resulted in the Molotov-Ribbentrop Pact, signed on 23 August 1939. Hitler believed that despite the lack of a formal alliance, this promise of nonaggression by the USSR would deter Britain from fighting. The pact itself was mutually beneficial. For Stalin, not only did a secret protocol allow for westward territorial expansion, but it would also very likely result in a war between Germany and the imperial powers that would engender favorable conditions for the wider spread of communism in Europe. Hitler's Germany was, therefore, a "friend" of communism—though not an "ally"—and Soviet terminology dubbed Hitler the "icebreaker of the revolution."

Hitler had offered the Polish government status as a satellite state at the beginning of 1939. When this was turned down, Hitler decided to destroy Poland. It took less than two weeks for the rest of the country to be overrun by the German forces, and this was followed by a Soviet invasion. Initially the German public did not have a great enthusiasm for the offensive. This was a period when the Nazi Party was in decline in the popular consciousness, despite the fact that Hitler's own standing remained high. However, morale was improved by the swift victory. Unprecedented Blitzkrieg tactics allowed for a new form of warfare, far removed from the trenches of World War I, to be implemented. The combination of modern technology with a belief that the "spirit" of the Teutonic warriors of old was working with them in winning breathtakingly rapid and decisive victories was typical of the Nazi idealization of modern warfare. Following this victory, the ethnic cleansing programs that would develop into the Holocaust began to evolve. For example, Himmler was given the role of "Reich commissariat for the strengthening of Germandom," and under his governance 1,000,000 Poles were removed from western Polish provinces and replaced with German immigrants. The majority of Poland was placed under the rule of a Nazi governorship, which formed the "Government of Central Poland," and the Reich directly annexed Upper Silesia, West Prussia, Poznan, and Danzig.

Following the invasion of Poland, German attention turned to Denmark and Norway in the spring of 1940. These invasions were pragmatic, as the supply of Swedish iron ore was essential for the German war machine. A British-occupied Norway might have halted this flow of raw materials. Again, easy victories followed, despite British and French intervention. Attention then switched to Western Europe, and May 1940 saw the Blitzkrieg sweep across Belgium, Holland, and France. In the previous winter, Germany had developed a plan to attack France at the north of the defensive barrier, the Maginot Line, via the Ardennes Mountains. This proved highly effective and split the Allied armies; the French capitulated because of poor morale, and 300,000 British troops were forced into a legendary evacuation via the port of Dunkirk. On 16 June, Marshal Pétain became the new French head of state, and peace negotiations were signed. Hitler toured Paris in triumph and returned to Germany to a genuine excitement at the dramatic victories in Western Europe, fueling National Socialist propaganda of a virile "people's Germany" that was triumphant over Western decadence. The British, now under the new leadership of Winston Churchill, declared that there would be "no surrender"—this despite high-level British discussions for a negotiated peace. Goering's plan to defeat Britain in 1940 via Luftwaffe bombing raids—the Battle of Britain—failed to remove Britain from the war or crush the RAF. Both countries maintained aerial bombing raids on civilian and military targets.

Instead of invading Britain, Hitler decided to fulfill a greater objective: the destruction of the Soviet Union. This was an ideological "war of racial annihilation," as Hitler informed his generals, rather than a battle for expansion. Hitler was convinced that the Red Army had been emasculated as a result of the Great Purges, a belief greatly encouraged by the Soviets' poor performance in the invasion of Finland in November 1939. After some delays in the spring of 1941, Operation Barbarossa was launched on 22 June. Some 147 divisions were allocated to the invasion, initially joined by Romanian and Finnish troops. Despite warnings of an attack, the invasion came as a surprise to Stalin. Consequently, the Soviets lost most of their air force, and Germany soon made vast gains, taking a huge number of prisoners of war. However, by the winter the German forces had failed in their initial aspiration of knocking out the Red Army in five months, and they were ill prepared for the freezing conditions of the Russian winter. To compound these logistical problems, German supply lines had become increasingly overstretched by Hitler's decision to split the attack between Moscow and the Ukraine. The occupied Soviet territories were chaotically administered, and it is difficult to overstate the brutality that the Germans unleashed on the local populations, which served to unify the Soviet forces in the defense of "Mother Russia." Logistical difficulties were compounded by the Japanese attack on Pearl Harbor in December. Not only did this draw Germany into a state of war with the United States, thereby demoralizing the home front, but it also freed up experienced Soviet troops from the Siberian Front to fight the Nazi invasion: it was clear that Japan would be too busy with South Asian expansion to nurture designs against the Soviet Union.

In 1942, Albert Speer was promoted to minister for armaments and war production, and he brought about dramatic increases in the construction of wartime materials, more than trebling production in three years. This was often achieved through the use of foreign prisoners and slave labor in the concentration camps. From its peak at the start of Operation Barbarossa, enthusiasm in Germany for the war began to dwindle. Optimism was still very much "in the air" in Germany during 1942, especially with news of Rommel's victories in North Africa and U-boat supremacy over British shipping in the North Atlantic. However, 1942 also saw the suspension of Nazi reforms to the state welfare and insurance schemes, and so the redistributive aspect of Nazi "socialism" and plans for a massive increase in social housing were shelved in favor of the essential war economy.

The war turned decisively against Germany in 1943. In February, German forces were defeated at Stalingrad—a battle that Hitler swore he would never lose—and in May, Rommel was defeated in North Africa. By the summer the U-boat campaign was turning in favor of the Allies, and in July the Germans were defeated at the famous tank battle around Kursk. Consequently, it was not until 1943 that the Goebbels propaganda machine reached its height in order to counter the increasingly gloomy news of the war's progress, compounded by rising prices and intensified Allied bombing campaigns. By this time, Hitler's health—mental and physical—had begun to decline. Often meetings with military personnel led to histrionics from the Fuehrer and sometimes to major disputes over tactical matters. Hopes for avoiding a German defeat were dwindling, and they now lay either in the possibility that the Red Army would not be able to maintain its unique ability to absorb a truly colossal rate of attrition, or with the idea that an increased Soviet conquest of Eastern Europe would lead to a squabble that would destroy the Allies unity. Such hopes were finally dashed with the D-Day landings in Normandy in June 1944. The success of this invasion was made possible by the massive industrial capacity of the United States to produce war materials, in combination with the fact that the Allies had cracked Enigma, the German codes. Although the initial battles were by no means certain, the Allies soon proved successful and began moving eastward.

By 1944 the Nazi regime had become increasingly unstable. The July Plot against Hitler's life augmented the power base of the SS and its leader, Himmler, in whom Hitler now placed a deep trust. He gave the former chicken farmer the position of "commander-in-chief of the reserve army and supreme commander of the Army Group Vistula," the sort of promotion that is indicative of a wider characteristic of the Nazi war machine—placing people in positions for which they had no real training. This gave Himmler prime responsibility for defending Germany from the onslaught of the Red Army, a task in which he failed spectacularly. In these final months, Martin Bormann rose, too, and plotted against Himmler and other high-ranking Nazis, a development that was symptomatic of the fact that the upper echelons of the Nazi Party were shot through with infighting. In the shadow of imminent defeat, Himmler and Goering both sought peace settlements, the latter, incredibly, acting under the false belief that he was now Germany's de facto leader. Hitler, however, was determined that Germany would not surrender. In his final words, written in a Berlin bunker, he expressed no contrition for the frightful destruction he had unleashed, and prophesied that a new National Socialist Germany would one day rise again from the ruins. It was here, on 29 April, that he married Eva Braun, and later committed suicide. Before doing so, he promoted Goebbels to chancellor, Bormann to party secretary, and Admiral Dönitz to Reich president and supreme commander of the armed forces. On 7 May 1945, German representatives signed an initial peace and unconditional surrender order, and the following day they signed an unconditional surrender to all the Allies in Berlin.

For Italy, too, the war followed a tragic path. Although war was central to Fascist ideology, it is clear that initially Mussolini had no intention of involving Italy in such a great conflagration. Italy lacked the military infrastructure to mount a major war against Western powers, and Mussolini was happy to limit himself to piecemeal expansionist policies in Africa and the Balkans. Despite the "Pact of Steel" of May 1939, Mussolini did not enter the war immediately. In fact, he regarded the Molotov-Ribbentrop Pact as criminal, backed Finland after the Soviet invasion of that country, and sold weapons, including airplanes, to France until May of 1940. On 10 June 1940, when France was on the verge of defeat, Italy entered on the side of Germany in hopes of territorial gains. Mussolini wanted only a partial association with Nazi expansionism. Therefore, he decided to fight a "parallel war" in Italy's interests, basically to make Italy the key regional power in the Mediterranean and North Africa. In October 1940, Mussolini ordered an invasion of Greece that quickly ran into difficulties because of the military strength built up under the Metaxas regime in the in-

terwar years. Italian troops were forced into retreat. Mussolini was rescued in April 1941 when Hitler overran Yugoslavia and Greece, delaying Operation Barbarossa. This was due to an anti-German coup in Yugoslavia and a British military expedition supporting Greece. After that Italy was stripped of her military independence. Italian troops were sent to aid the invasion of the Soviet Union and also to Rommel's campaign in Africa. The latter sat awkwardly with the Italian's self-image, at least at a rhetorical level, of performing a civilizing form of imperialism, emancipating indigenous populations from British and French rule. However, despite their own atrocities committed in Africa, it is worth noting that the Italians did not comply with the Nazi Jewish policy, and maintained the second highest survival rate of Jewish populations among occupied countries.

The hostilities highlighted the fact that the Italian Fascist war machine was a weak force, negating the ideals of the Fascist new man. Further, it became increasingly obvious that the Italian Fascist Party and its associated militia, the MVSN, were both ineffective and corrupt. By 1943 public confidence in the regime collapsed, as it seemed to many that the war was contrary to any Italian interests. Mussolini, however, could see no way out and felt that Italy's destiny was tied inextricably to Germany. Following the Allied invasion of Sicily on 9 July 1943, a meeting of the Fascist Grand Council was called for 24 July. There Dino Grandi collected signatures supporting a resumption of rule by King Victor Emmanuel III. Mussolini was deposed, and a new government was created under Marshal Pietro Badoglio. Mussolini was placed under arrest, and the new government signed peace terms on 8 September, the eve of the Allied invasion of Italy.

German forces then invaded, and the peninsula became the site of civil war between anti-Fascists and a combination of German and Fascist forces. Mussolini was rescued on 12 September and was coerced by Hitler into running a puppet state. Installed in a villa near Salò, Mussolini was essentially a prisoner of the SS. The Italian Social Republic, or the Salò Republic as it was popularly known, initially attempted to introduce a new "socialization" scheme that would reorder the economy along more corporatist lines. The German Reich terminated these reforms, as it was fearful of a drop in essential wartime production. The republic did gain a genuine minority support, however, and it founded a new army of around 500,000 men and a new militia, the National Republican Guard. However, the Allied invasion was too powerful, and the republic was eventually defeated. Partisans captured Mussolini at the end of April 1945. He was executed, and his body was hung in a square in Milan.

In other invaded territories Hitler preferred to set up satellite regimes that, in the main, drew on local conservative forces, rather than either drawing on indigenous fascist forces or governing annexed regions directly from Berlin. The Scandinavian countries were given somewhat lenient treatment, and Denmark, Norway, and Holland were allowed relatively autonomous governance. This stemmed from a belief that Scandinavians, the Dutch and the Flemish were considered "racially redeemable." The most notorious of these was the regime of Norway's Vidkun Quisling, who ruled in Germany's interests for most of the war, and whose name became synonymous with such a relationship. Holland, Denmark, and Belgium also developed collaborationist regimes. However, because of contingencies of administration, indigenous fascists did gain more significant positions of power in some invaded countries. In Romania, Hitler's main concern was to make the country a stable satellite and bulwark in support of the invasion of the USSR. The Iron Guard did, however, briefly seize power. In 1940, King Carol realigned Romanian allegiance from Britain to Germany and offered Horia Sima and others from the Iron Guard places in the government. However, when Germany transferred Transylvania to Hungary, Carol's popularity dropped. Carol put in General Ion Antonescu as dictator, and the latter then forced the king to abdicate in favor of his son Prince Michael. Other parties were unwilling to form a grand coalition, so Antonescu relied on the Iron Guard to back his pro-German Romanian nationalism. Thereafter, the Iron Guard became the only political party in Romania, and Sima became vice premier. "Romanianization" commissars from the Iron Guard peppered the country, and even gained new powers over industry. Overall, this simply resulted in bad (and increasingly unpopular) administration. Antonescu attempted to appropriate the Iron Guard, emulating Franco's tactics with the Falange—a policy that Hitler backed. However, amid increasing political tension, on the 21 January 1941 the legion carried out a full revolt, seized local government offices, and enacted a vicious Jewish pogrom. This rebellion was crushed, however, and the Iron Guard was banned. Antonescu remained in power, and Romanian forces were sent to the Eastern Front in return for territorial gains. Antonescu also presided over Romania's own Jewish genocide, the largest by non-German forces during the war.

Hungary was also reinvented as a Nazi satellite state in which the Arrow Cross, led by Ferenc Szálasi, eventually secured power. The regent, Admiral Horthy, initially resisted the fascist party. He favored the rise of the new radical-right party, Hungarian Renewal, under Bela Imredy. Hitler, too, initially resisted Szálasi, and preferred to give power to Imredy after Hungary entered the war as a German ally. The Arrow Cross held representatives in the Hungarian parliament and set up a biological racial office in 1942. The advance of Soviet forces in 1943 led to a full German occupation in March, and Horthy was forced to put a more radical-right government into office; yet Szálasi refused to be a party to this coalition. By the autumn of 1944, German authorities wanted to put Szálasi and the Arrow Cross in power. They seized the existing government, and Szálasi was installed. By this time half of the Jewish population had been transported to death camps, and under Szálasi the rest were deported. Szálasi developed an ideological project for a new "Hungarian Order," and a "Corporate Order of the Working Nation" comprising a nationalized and "controlled" economy. By March 1945 the country was under full Soviet occupation, and Szálasi was captured and executed for war crimes.

After invading Yugoslavia, Hitler dismantled the country, following which the Ustasha rose to power in Croatia. The leader of the Ustasha, Dr. Ante Pavelić, was put at the head of the new Independent State of Croatia (NDH), and remained there throughout the war. He developed a charismatic leadership and "mystical bond" with the nation. Under this administration chaos reigned, and a culture of very high ethnic violence developed. That resulted in the attempted extermination of a large proportion of the Orthodox Serb population, some 1,000,000 strong. The regime also spontaneously executed around 40,000 Jews.

After the French defeat, Marshal Pétain headed what was the most independent of the satellite states, Vichy France. Comprising southeastern and central France, the regime maintained official sovereign status and formal diplomacy throughout the war and was allowed to keep France's colonial empire. Essentially, this was an authoritarian, right-wing dictatorship modeled on Franco rather than Hitler or Mussolini. It did, however, respond to widespread desires for patriotic reform, and announced a "national revolution." This involved the promotion of conservative values, the reintroduction of religious instruction in schools, and the modernization of industry along corporatist lines. Also, new youth and veterans' organizations were formed. Anti-Semitic policies were introduced in 1940, and the French police ended up deporting tens of thousands of Jews to Germany and beyond. In August 1941 the regime became more authoritarian when Pétain suppressed political parties, formed new courts, and created a new national police force. Mandatory labor was introduced in 1942, basically to ensure that the youth worked for German interests. However, by 1942 the Vichy zone was under direct German occupation, which blocked further constitutional reform. From that point onward Pétain was a mere figurehead. Marcel Déat and other indigenous French fascists were given positions in the assembly. After the Allied invasion the government was moved to Sigmaringen in Germany, in order to organize guerrilla tactics opposing the liberation.

As the war progressed it developed an increasingly international aspect. There was a significant Europewide, rather than exclusively German, input into the German armed forces, reflective of the way that for many across Europe the war took on the face of a genuine ideological conflict between "European Civilization" and "Asian Bolshevism." For example, the Waffen-SS drew on not only non-national *Volksdeutche* ("ethnic Germans") but also other volunteers from Northern, Eastern, and Western Europe, and even non-Europeans (*see* Muslim Volunteers in the Waffen-SS). This was often constructed in terms of a somewhat convoluted Nietzschean ideal of the emergence of European "supermen." However, it was more likely that these recruits were inspired by deeply felt anticommunist sentiments that allowed any Nazi atrocities to be justified in the greater good of defeating Bolshevism. Typical of this fusion between increasing Nazification and anti-Bolshevism was the leader of the Belgian Rex movement, Léon Degrelle, who spent a great deal of time on the Eastern Front. He also developed a "Eurofascism" that argued that Nazi-style racism must become manifest in all nationalisms, which would result in a unified European community of nations after the war.

World War II was devastating for the fascist worldview. Inherent to fascism—especially Nazism—was the idea that war was the ultimate test of the nation and of the new fascist men created in its name. Consequently, the comprehensive defeat of Nazi expansionism, which drew other forms of fascism and authoritarian right politics into its hurricane, revealed the inherently self-destructive nature of fascist ideologies. In the postwar dynamic this has meant that fascist ideology has sought to build ideological constructions that either attempt to transcend this history through sophisticated metapolitical discourses of "organic nationalism," or else fetishize

these experiences, often in esoteric paramilitary groupuscules.

Paul Jackson

See Also: ANTI-COMINTERN PACT, THE; ANTI-SEMITISM; ANTONESCU, GENERAL ION; APPEASEMENT; ARYANISM; AUSCHWITZ (-BIRKENAU); AUTHORITARIANISM; BADOGLIO, PIETRO; BARBAROSSA, OPERATION; BATTLE OF BRITAIN, THE; BELGIUM; BLITZKRIEG; BORMANN, MARTIN; BOLSHEVISM; CATHOLIC CHURCH, THE; CHURCHILL, SIR WINSTON LEONARD SPENCER; CIVILIZATION; CONCENTRATION CAMPS; CONSERVATISM; CORPORATISM; CROATIA; DEAT, MARCEL; DECADENCE; DEGRELLE, LEON; DENMARK; DUNKIRK; D-DAY LANDINGS, THE; DOENITZ, ADMIRAL KARL; ECONOMICS; EL ALAMEIN; ETHIOPIA; EUROFASCISM; EXPANSIONISM; FALANGE; FASCIST PARTY, THE; FINLAND; FRANCE; FRANCO Y BAHAMONDE, GENERAL FRANCISCO; FRANCOISM; FREEDOM; *GENERALGOUVERNEMENT*/GENERAL GOVERNMENT, THE; GERMANNESS (*DEUTSCHHEIT*); GERMANY; GOEBBELS, (PAUL) JOSEPH; GOERING, HERMANN; GRAND COUNCIL OF FASCISM, THE; GRANDI, DINO; GREAT BRITAIN; GREECE; GROUPUSCULES; HERO, THE CULT OF THE; HIMMLER, HEINRICH; HITLER, ADOLF; HITLER-STALIN PACT, THE; HOLOCAUST, THE; HORTHY DE NAGYBÁNYA, MIKLÓS; HUNGARY; INDUSTRY; IRON GUARD, THE; ITALY; JAPAN AND WORLD WAR II; JULY PLOT, THE; LEADER CULT, THE; *LEBENSRAUM;* LIBYA; LUFTWAFFE, THE; MARXISM; METAXAS, GENERAL IOANNIS; *MILIZIA VOLONTARIA PER LA SICUREZZA NAZIONALE* (MVSN); MITFORD FAMILY, THE; MOSLEY, SIR OSWALD; MUSLIM VOLUNTEERS IN THE WAFFEN-SS; MUSSOLINI, BENITO ANDREA; NATIONALISM; NATIONALIZATION; NAZISM; NETHERLANDS, THE; NEW MAN, THE; NEW ORDER, THE; NIETZSCHE, FRIEDRICH; NORDIC SOUL, THE; NORWAY; ORTHODOX CHURCHES, THE; PACIFISM; PANGERMANISM; PAPACY, THE; PAVELIĆ, DR. ANTE; PEARL HARBOR; PETAIN, MARSHAL HENRI PHILIPPE; PIUS XII, POPE; POLAND AND NAZI GERMANY; POSTWAR FASCISM; PROPAGANDA; QUISLING, VIDKUN; RACIAL DOCTRINE; REXISM; ROMANIA; ROME; ROOSEVELT, FRANKLIN DELANO; SALÒ REPUBLIC, THE; SERBS, THE; SIMA, HORIA; SKORZENY, OTTO; SLAVS, THE (AND GERMANY); SLAVS, THE (AND ITALY); SOCIALISM; SOVIET UNION, THE; SPAIN; SPEER, ALBERT; SS, THE; STALIN, IOSIF VISSARIONOVICH; STALINGRAD; STATE, THE; SWEDEN; SZÁLASI, FERENC; TERROR; UNITED STATES, THE (PRE-1945); *UNTERMENSCHEN* ("SUBHUMANS"); U.S. CORPORATIONS; USTASHA; VICHY; VICTOR EMMANUEL/VITTORIO EMANUELE III, KING; WAFFEN-SS, THE; WAR; WARRIOR ETHOS, THE; WEHRMACHT, THE; WELFARE; WINDSOR, EDWARD DUKE OF; WORLD WAR I; YUGOSLAVIA

References
Bartov, Omer. 1985. *The Eastern Front 1941–45: German Troops and the Barbarisation of Warfare.* London: Macmillan.
Burleigh, Michael. 2000. *The Third Reich: A New History.* London: Pan Macmillan.
Deakin, F. W. 1962. *The Brutal Friendship: Mussolini, Hitler, and the Fall of Italian Fascism.* London: Weidenfeld and Nicolson.

Eatwell, Roger. 1996. *Fascism: A History.* London: Vintage.

Griffin, Roger. 1993. *The Nature of Fascism.* London: Routledge.

Payne, Stanley G. 1995. *A History of Fascism 1914–45.* London: UCL.

Rich, Norman. 1973. *Hitler's War Aims.* 2 vols. London: André Deutsch.

Weinberg, G. L. 1994. *A World at Arms: A Global History of World War II.* Cambridge: Cambridge University Press.

XENOPHOBIA

One of the central features of fascism is the emphasis on nationalism, race, and, in particular, an "ethnic conception of the nation" (Davies and Lynch 2002, 116). This concept of the nation is exclusionary, and it can lead to a form of xenophobia in which the Other is seen as being not only an outsider but eventually a threat. Prior to the end of World War II, this xenophobia manifested itself first and foremost as anti-Semitism, but since 1945 fascist aggression has focused more on immigrants and other groups who are considered outside of the nation. The leader of the French National Front, Jean-Marie Le Pen, uses the slogan "France for the French" and "the French first," indicating that political rights and social benefits should be reserved for those who are French (that is, not given to immigrants). Jörg Haider of the Austrian Freedom Party has stated that Austria is not a country of immigration, and his party has continually linked immigrants to crime. Fascist skinheads continue to target Jews as well as foreigners and ethnic minorities, leading to the desecration of Jewish cemeteries, the fire bombing of synagogues and mosques, and physical attacks on immigrants.

Terri Givens

See Also: ANTI-SEMITISM; ARYANISM; AUSTRIA; COMMUNITY; FRANCE; HAIDER, JÖRG; IMMIGRATION; LE PEN, JEAN-MARIE; NATIONAL FRONT, THE (FRANCE); NATIONALISM; NEO-NAZISM; POSTWAR FASCISM; RACIAL DOCTRINE; RACISM; SKINHEAD FASCISM; WELFARE; WHITE SUPREMACISM; WORLD WAR II

References
Davies, Peter, and Derek Lynch. 2002. *The Routledge Companion to Fascism and the Far Right.* London: Routledge.
Sully, Melanie A. 1997. *The Haider Phenomenon.* New York: Columbia University Press.

YEATS, WILLIAM BUTLER (1865–1939)

Celebrated Irish poet and man of letters and friend of Ezra Pound who was attracted to fascism in the mid-1930s. Both World War I and the celebrated Easter Rising in Dublin in 1916 had a profound effect on Yeats, and they served to complicate his views of Irish nationalism and the function of politics within a civic society. Significantly, Yeats was horrified by the effect of violence on society, yet he applauded the insurgents of 1916 for their promotion of advanced nationalism. Throughout the decades of the twentieth century in which he lived, he became increasingly pessimistic about politics and the virtue of democracy. During the later 1920s he spent increasing amounts of time touring Europe, and he witnessed firsthand both the chaos of failing democracies and what he saw as the opportunities offered by new systems of government. At the opening of the Tailteann Games, a major state-building initiative put on by the Irish Free State government, Yeats used his welcoming address to praise the work of Mussolini. With the emergence of the Blueshirts in Ireland in 1933, Yeats saw what he thought was the Irish manifestation of a worldwide movement. He met, through his friend Frank Mac-Manus, the leader of the Blueshirts, General Eoin O'Duffy. He was persuaded to write some marching songs for the movement but quickly despaired at the parochial nature of the Blueshirt campaign and disassociated himself from it. Although frequently dismissed by contemporaries and commentators, including George Orwell, as a fascist, Yeats was no such thing. While he undoubtedly had an eclectic mix of interests—mysticism, the occult, eugenics—he appears as one of many who were deeply uneasy about the state of the post–World War I democracies and fearful of Soviet communism. Elitism rather than fascism was the creed of Yeats.

Mike Cronin

See Also: ARISTOCRACY; BOLSHEVISM; DECADENCE; DEMOCRACY; ELITE THEORY; EUGENICS; IRELAND; ITALY; MARXISM; MUSSOLINI, BENITO ANDREA; MYSTICISM; OCCULTISM; O'DUFFY, EOIN; ORWELL, GEORGE; POUND, EZRA; SPENGLER, OSWALD; WORLD WAR I

References

Cronin, M. 1997. *The Blueshirts and Irish Politics.* Dublin: Four Courts.

Cullingford, E. *Yeats, Ireland and Fascism.* New York: New York University Press.

Foster, R. F. 2003. *W. B. Yeats, A Life: Arch-Poet, 1915–1939.* Oxford: Oxford University Press.

YOCKEY, FRANCIS PARKER (1917–1960)

Onetime U.S. lawyer and war-crimes prosecutor, Yockey remains best known for his book *Imperium*, first published in London in 1948. In it, Yockey argued that the postwar European Right must abandon nationalism and fight for a united European superstate. Only such an imperium could free Europe from U.S. and Russian domination. Yockey further insisted that the United States, not Russia, posed the greatest threat to future European unity. His fierce anti-Americanism and clandestine lifestyle caught the attention of the U.S. government, which spent years trying to locate him. A few weeks after his arrest in California on multiple passport violation charges, Yockey committed suicide by swallowing a cyanide capsule in his jail cell.

Kevin Coogan

See Also: AMERICANIZATION; EUROFASCISM; EUROPE; EUROPEANIST FASCISM/RADICAL RIGHT, THE; NATIONALISM; NUREMBERG TRIALS, THE; POSTWAR FASCISM

References
Coogan, Kevin. 2000. *Dreamer of the Day: Francis Parker Yockey and the Postwar Fascist International.* Cambridge, MA: Semiotext, MIT Press.
Yockey, F. P. 1962. *Imperium: The Philosophy of History and Politics.* Torrance, CA: Noontide.

YOUTH

The interwar fascist movements laid great emphasis on the youthfulness of their outlook. They saw themselves as rebelling against the "old" liberalism, parliamentarism, and Christianity that they believed had been at best complicit in and at worst a prime cause of the decadence of their nations. They tended to see in World War I the culmination and result of the antiquated failed attitudes and policies of the older generation. Hitler's love of fast cars and Mussolini's love of airplanes were symptomatic of this philosophy, which chimed with their cult of the body and encourage-

ment of sporting achievement. The mass youth movements that they encouraged and indeed forced young people to join were one of the most striking outward manifestations of the power and energy of their regimes. When Mussolini was elected to parliament in 1921, he was at thirty-seven years of age the "old man" of the thirty-five-strong Fascist parliamentary grouping.

Cyprian Blamires

See Also: BERLIN OLYMPICS, THE; BODY, THE CULT OF THE; CHRISTIANITY; HERO, THE CULT OF THE; HITLER, ADOLF; LIBERALISM; MUSSOLINI, BENITO ANDREA; PARLIAMENTARISM; PROGRESS; PROPAGANDA; SCIENCE; SPORT; TECHNOLOGY; WAR VETERANS; WORLD WAR I; YOUTH MOVEMENTS

YOUTH MOVEMENTS (Germany)

BOYS

The Hitler Youth (Hitler-Jugend, HJ) was the overall name of the National Socialist youth organization in Germany between 1926 and 1945. At the same time it became the name of the branch reserved for fourteen- to eighteen-year-old boys, the other boys' branch being the Deutsches Jungvolk, for the 10- to 14-year-olds. The predecessors of the organization date back to 1922. In the early 1930s, the Hitler Youth rose from being a marginal factor to holding a position of some importance, but the largest increase in its membership occurred in the wake of the Nazi rise to power in 1933. Mainly because of the incipient *Gleichschaltung* of other youth organizations, total membership rose, according to official Nazi statistics, from about 0.1 million at the end of 1932 to 2.3 million at the end of 1933. Membership is said to have risen further, to more than 7 million, in 1938. In the following year a general "youth service duty" for German teenagers was introduced that nominally made all Germans in the age group from ten to eighteen (about 9 million young people) members of the Hitler Youth.

In the Weimar Republic the Hitler Youth had the character of an anti-intellectual and social revolutionary combat organization; for many years it was subordinated to the SA. In 1932 the Hitler Youth became independent, and in the Third Reich it was turned into an organization that comprised elements of both party and state character. Alongside the home and the school, it was regarded as the third source of education, with the particular task of establishing the Volksgemeinschaft. The Hitler Youth was uniformed and primarily taken up with physical culture and the cult of the body, and only secondarily with ideological matters in a narrow sense. It offered a number of special-interest groups—for instance, in the fields of aviation, the navy, machines, and the health services. During World War II, the concept of the "youth state" was gradually replaced by a youth directly involved in the military endeavors of the larger state. This development is in some respect symbolized by the shift in leadership from Baldur von Schirach, with his aristocratic background and his mother coming from a wealthy U.S. family, to the down-to-earth son of the working class Arthur Axmann in 1940.

Norbert Götz

GIRLS

The notorious Hitler Youth was for boys. For girls there was a parallel movement comprising the Bund deutscher Mädel (BdM) for those aged fourteen to eighteen, and the Jungmädelbund for those aged ten to fourteen. By 1936 these two organizations had a total membership of more than 2 million. There were 125,000 leaders who were trained for their task in thirty-five area schools. The girls were taught to be promoters of the Nazi worldview, and the values instilled into them were of comradeship, service, and physical fitness, essential for their eventual motherhood. There was also a branch of the BdM for older girls between the ages of seventeen and twenty-one; it was called Glaube und Schönheit ("Faith and Beauty") and was intended to prepare girls for marriage by instructing them in domestic science and fashion design.

Cyprian Blamires

See Also: BODY, THE CULT OF THE; COMMUNITY; EDELWEISS PIRATES, THE; EDUCATION; FAMILY, THE; GERMANY; *GLEICHSCHALTUNG*; HITLER, ADOLF; LEISURE; MILITARISM; NATIONALISM; NAZISM; PROGRESS; REVOLUTION; SA, THE; SCHIRACH, BALDUR VON; SEXUALITY; SPORT; THIRD REICH, THE; *VOLKSGEMEINSCHAFT*, THE; *WANDERVÖGEL*, THE; WELFARE; WOMEN; YOUTH

References

Koch, Hannsjoachim W. 2000. *The Hitler Youth: Origins and Development 1922–1945*. New York: Cooper Square.

Rupprecht, Nancy E. 1982. *Ideology and Socialization in the Pre-war Hitler Youth*. Ann Arbor, MI: Microfilms.

Stachura, Peter D. 1975. *Nazi Youth in the Weimar Republic*. Santa Barbara, CA: ABC-CLIO.

Walker, Lawrence D. 1970. *Hitler Youth and Catholic Youth 1933–1936: A Study in Totalitarian Conquest*. Washington, DC: Catholic University of America Press.

YOUTH MOVEMENTS (Italy)

Fascist regimes placed great emphasis on enrolling young people into uniformed youth organizations, where they would receive paramilitary training as well as participate in athletic activities. In 1926, Mussolini gave Under Secretary for Education Renato Ricci the task of "reorganizing youth from the moral and physical point of view." Among those Ricci consulted was the English founder of the Scout Movement, Baden-Powell, who gave him "valuable advice." The result of Ricci's labors was the establishment of the Opera Nazionale Balilla (ONB) by a law passed in April 1926. The name was chosen as a reminder of an eighteenth-century Genoese lad whose heroism in the anti-Austrian cause was legendary. Balilla in the Genoese parlance of the day was a diminutive for the name Giovan Battista, or Giambattista, and the boy in question was Giovan Battista Perasso. The story was that on 5 December 1746 he had thrown the first stone to incite a riot against occupying Austrian troops. The Fascist organization named after Balilla was to take in hand the physical and moral education of young persons from eight to eighteen years of age; it was to instill in the youth a military sense of discipline, national pride, and a consciousness that they would be "the Fascists of tomorrow." Progressively, other non-Fascist youth organizations were prohibited, although the Catholic movement Gioventù Italiana Cattolica was able to continue albeit at a reduced level of activity. Not even the Scout Movement escaped the ax (despite Ricci's contact with Baden-Powell), for in 1927–1928 all Scout and Guide units were "invited to close." Nonetheless, movements were formed secretly in some place to perpetuate the spirit of scouting.

Typical parade of interwar fascist youth, in this case young women in Italy in 1932. Italian Fascists and German Nazis sought to indoctrinate young people through their coerced membership in official youth movements. (Keystone/Getty Images)

The ONB was not conceived simply as an extracurricular movement but was entrusted with physical education in schools, and head teachers were told to welcome ONB initiatives and encourage students to participate in them. In addition, by 1937 the organization was actually running more than 6,000 rural schools. It also held professional training courses, and for women there were courses in childcare and domestic science. It was initially subdivided into four uniformed groups: Balilla was for boys eight to fourteen; Piccole italiane was for girls of the same age range; Avanguardisti was for boys between fourteen and eighteen; Giovani Italiane was for girls of that same age range; and a fifth group was added later, the Figli della Lupa, for six- to eight-year-olds. For those aged eighteen to twenty-two there were separate organizations outside the ambit of the ONB. There were drills after school and "Fascist Saturdays," as well as camps during the holidays. But in spite of governmental pressure, the numbers of those enrolled in the youth movements never reached 50 percent of the total Italian youth population.

Cyprian Blamires

See Also: BODY, THE CULT OF THE; CATHOLIC CHURCH, THE; EDUCATION; FAMILY, THE; FASCIST PARTY, THE; ITALY; LEISURE; MILITARISM; MUSSOLINI, BENITO ANDREA; NATIONALISM; SPORT; TOTALITARIANISM; WOMEN; YOUTH MOVEMENTS (GERMANY)

Reference
Koon, T. A. 1985. *Believe, Obey, Fight: Political Socialization of Youth in Fascist Italy, 1922–1943.* London: University of North Carolina Press.

YUGOSLAVIA

Serb, Croat, and Slovene state that emerged in 1918 from the ruins of the Austro-Hungarian Empire by virtue of the World War I peace settlement but that was to be broken up into its constituent parts sixty years later after a long civil war (1999); in the interwar years it was the home of an extreme nationalist terrorist movement known as Orjuna (see below).

Cyprian Blamires

References
Burgwyn, H. James. 2005. *Empire on the Adriatic: Mussolini's Conquest of Yugoslavia, 1941–1943.* New York: Enigma.
Lampe, John R. 2000. *Yugoslavia as History: Twice There Was a Country.* Cambridge: Cambridge University Press.

ORJUNA

The foremost fascistic movement in interwar Yugoslavia was Orjuna, a nationalist terrorist organization founded in 1922 with official backing as an anticommunist force aggressively promoting the idea of a united Yugoslav nation. Extremely violent, its increasingly independent and militant actions as well as disagreements among its members eventually led to its prohibition and collapse in 1929. Orjuna originated in a 1919 congress of Yugoslav youth organized by youth activists of the Democratic Party. It called for youth to mobilize against all those who threatened the unity of the Kingdom of the Serbs, Croats, and Slovenes, and it also had the support of veterans' groups. In 1920 strikes in Serbia and Vojvodina and rebellion in Montenegro erupted, and national guards were created to crush them. In 1921, after the assassination of government minister Milan Drašković by a communist, these disparate groups formed the Yugoslav Progressive Nationalist Youth (JNNO) in Split to fight communist insurgency and Croat separatism. The JNNO was divided into regional branches and enjoyed the support of some famous writers and artists. It was particularly influential in areas of Slovenia and Croatia that were the subject of Italian and Austrian irredentism and also tended to be popular in areas where an ethnic minority were perceived to be powerful or separatist—for example, in the Vojvodina, prosperous Germans and "separatist" Hungarians were targeted. Its membership was young and ethnically mixed.

In May 1922 the JNNO became Orjuna, and it held its first congress in November of that year. The regional nature of the JNNO was maintained, and that led to a great deal of independence in individual Orjuna branches. Orjuna also ran its own newspapers, an academic club, a labor organization, a section for high school students—Young Yugoslavia—and a paramilitary wing, the Action Section. Especially in its military expeditions, Orjuna was highly independent, and on a number of occasions, despite the displeasure of the Yugoslav authorities, it launched operations on the Austrian and Italian borders to liberate "oppressed" Slav populations with bloody consequences. Despite this, it was itself accused of having a fascist political program and style of politics. Like the fascists, it believed in a corporate state, the abolition of democracy, and the destruction of "Jewish" capital. However, it was genuinely Yugoslavist: not only did it attack "separatist" minorities, but it also attacked Serbian nationalists. This made it the enemy of the Serb nationalist Radical Party of Nikola Pašić. When the Radical Party came to power in 1923, it used Croatian nationalist groups to persecute and harass Orjuna.

By 1925 the persecution of Orjuna had led to an irreversible decline, and its membership shrank. In 1929, with the declaration of King Alexander's dictatorship and a unitarist Yugoslav state, it appeared that the aims of Orjuna had been achieved, but the fact that the dictatorship banned all political organizations signaled the final demise of Orjuna. Its members, such as Edo Bulat, Ivo Mogorovic, and Marko Kranjec, joined successor Yugoslavist organizations, such as the Zbor movement, or else other extreme political movements such as the communists, Chetnik organizations, or the Ustasha movement.

Rory Yeomans

See Also: ANTI-SEMITISM; AUSTRIA; CORPORATISM; CROATIA; DALMATIA; DEMOCRACY; EXPANSIONISM; FIUME; FREEDOM; GERMANY; HUNGARY; IRREDENTISM; ITALY; LJOTIĆ, DIMITRIJE; NATIONALISM; PANGERMANISM; PARAMILITARISM; SERBS, THE; SLAVS, THE (AND ITALY); STOJADINOVIĆ, MILAN; USTASHA; WAR VETERANS; WORLD WAR I; WORLD WAR II; YOUTH

References

Banac, Ivo. 1984. *The National Question: Origin, History, Politics*. Ithaca: Cornell.

Gligorjević, Branislav. 1965. "Organizacija jugoslovenskih nacionalista (Orjuna)." *Istorija xx veka: zbornik radova* 5: 314–393.

ZBOR: See SERBS, THE
ZENTRUMSPARTEI: See CENTER
PARTY, THE

ZHIRINOVSKII, VLADIMIR VOL'FOVICH (born 1946)

Leader of the ultranationalist (misnamed) Liberal-Democratic Party of Russia founded in 1990, and winner of post–Soviet Russia's first multiparty parliamentary elections in December 1993 (with 22.92 percent). Of partly Jewish descent, Zhirinovskii grew up in Almaty and studied Turkology and law at Moscow State University. After entering Moscow's political scene in the late 1980s, most probably as a KGB provocateur, he became a noted political figure when taking third place in Russia's first presidential elections of June 1991 (with 7.81 percent). In spite of his scandalous public behavior, Zhirinovskii has remained an important player in Russian parliamentary politics since 1993.

Andreas Umland

See Also: NATIONALISM; POSTWAR FASCISM; RUSSIA

Reference
Klepikova, Elena, and Vladimir Solovyov. 1995. *Zhirinovsky: The Paradoxes of Russian Fascism*. Trans. Catherine A. Fitzpatrick. Harmondsworth, Middlesex: Penguin.

ZIMBABWE: See RHODESIA/ZIMBABWE

ZIONISM

The Jewish nationalist movement known as Zionism, a product of European political currents, included in its ranks in Israel in the 1930s some who favored rapprochement with Mussolini and his allies. Theodor Herzl at the close of the nineteenth century argued that the essence of the Jewish dilemma was not individual but national: the lack of a state. The development of ethnically based theories of nationalism and self-determination had left the Jews, a diaspora people, with no choice but to pursue their historical claim to *Eretz Yisrael,* the Land of Israel or Zion, otherwise known as Palestine. Although expelled two millennia earlier, they had managed, he asserted, to retain religious, cultural, and social ties to the "promised land." The goal of the World Zionist Organization, which Herzl founded in

A Zionist propaganda poster. Some interwar Zionists admired Mussolini and Italian Fascism. (Library of Congress)

August 1897, was to create for the Jewish people a national home in Palestine. On 2 November 1917 the British government issued the Balfour Declaration, which promised support for the project. It was included in the League of Nations mandate for Palestine granted to Great Britain on 24 July 1922, allowing for Jewish immigration and a measure of internal self-government. However, two months later London decided that these provisions would not apply to the area east of the Jordan River, which eventually became the Hashemite Kingdom of Jordan.

Although a majority of Zionists were members of socialist or liberal ideological streams, the right of the spectrum was represented by the followers of Vladimir (Ze'ev) Jabotinsky, the founder of Zionist Revisionism, a movement that opposed any partition of Palestine and advocated the inclusion of Transjordan as

well. Jabotinsky also harbored few hopes for coexistence with the Palestinian Arab population and demanded the creation of an "iron wall" of Jewish military might to prevent the Arabs from blocking the establishment of a Jewish state. In 1925, Jabotinsky founded the Union of Zionists-Revisionists (Hatzohar); he broke with the official Zionist movement ten years later, forming the New Zionist Organization (NZO), after his political program calling for the immediate establishment of a Jewish state was rejected. Jabotinsky admired Benito Mussolini and spoke favorably of Fascist Italy's policies, and his movement repeatedly sought assistance from Rome. His brown-shirted youth wing, Betar (Brit Trumpeldor), named after Joseph Trumpeldor, a pioneer who had died in 1920 defending the settlement of Tel Hai against Arab attack, established a naval training academy at Civitavecchia, Italy, in 1934. Jabotinsky, who preferred that private capital investment support Jewish economic development in Palestine, objected to the formation of kibbutzim (agricultural collectives) and the growth of the Histadrut, the Jewish trade union federation, since both provided a powerful political base for socialist Zionism. Two Revisionists were accused of killing labor leader Chaim Arlosoroff in 1933, and the Revisionist movement was condemned as fascist in its ideology and political methods by its opponents. Such criticism became more pronounced when Jabotinsky, before the start of World War II, proposed a policy of alliances with countries in Central and Eastern Europe, including the fascistic governments of Italy and Poland, in order to gain their support for his plan to rescue millions of East European Jews by thwarting British restrictions on Jewish entry to Palestine through "illegal" mass immigration.

The followers of Jabotinsky, who died in August 1940, organized their own armed units in Palestine to fight the British and the Palestinian Arab majority. The Irgun Zvai Leumi (National Military Organization), founded in 1937, operated after 1943 under the direction of Menachem Begin; further to its right was the Lohamei Herut Yisrael (or Lehi, Fighters for the Freedom of Israel), formed in 1940 by Abraham Stern, which engaged in anti-British terrorism. Stern rejected any compromises with the British and demanded the creation of a Greater Israel. He even opposed Jews joining the British army to fight Nazism. The Lehi was responsible for the killing of Lord Moyne, the British minister resident for the Middle East, on 6 November 1944. With the end of the war, the Irgun also stepped up its anti-British activities, bombing the King David

Hotel in Jerusalem, the site of the British military command, on 22 July 1946, killing ninety-one people.

Determined to leave Palestine, the British placed the issue before the United Nations, and on 29 November 1947 the General Assembly voted for partition of the country into Arab and Jewish entities. The state of Israel was proclaimed on 14 May 1948, but armed conflict between the two communities had already commenced. The main Zionist fighting force was the Haganah (Defense), the future Israeli army. However, the Irgun and Lehi forces continued to operate independently and were responsible for a massacre of Palestinian Arab villagers in Deir Yassin, near Jerusalem, on 9 April 1948, precipitating a flight of Palestinians from the country. The Lehi also assassinated Count Folke Bernadotte, the UN special mediator on Palestine, on 17 September 1948. The coalition government led by the new Mapai (Land of Israel Labor Party) outlawed right-wing political militias and drove the point home by sinking the *Altalena,* a vessel that was bringing arms to the Irgun, off Tel Aviv on 22 June 1948, killing sixteen Irgun fighters. Prime Minister David Ben-Gurion argued that the Irgun had planned a fascist revolt. One month later, Begin helped to found the Herut (Freedom) Party, which he led until 1983, though he did not succeed in winning power until the election of 17 May 1977, as head of the Likud (Unity) coalition. Yitzhak Shamir, active in both the Irgun and the Lehi in the prestate period, Benjamin Netanyahu, and Ariel Sharon are the other Likud leaders who have governed the country since. While Labor has been ready, as the price of peace, to cede sovereignty to the Palestinians in much of the area occupied after the 1967 Arab-Israeli War, the Likud has insisted that control of such territory is vital to Israel's security and sense of nationhood. Its ideology remains irredentist, and it continues to uphold, in principle, the right of Jews to exercise sovereignty over all of *Eretz Yisrael,* including Gaza and the West Bank (Judea and Samaria), although it has reconciled itself to an independent Jordan.

Henry Srebrnik

See Also: ANTI-SEMITISM; FASCIST PARTY, THE; GREAT BRITAIN; HOLOCAUST, THE; IRREDENTISM; ITALY; LEAGUE OF NATIONS, THE; MIDDLE EAST, THE; MUSSOLINI, BENITO ANDREA; NATIONALISM; NAZISM; PALESTINE; POLAND; SOVIET UNION, THE; STATE, THE; UNITED NATIONS, THE; WORLD WAR II; ZIONIST OCCUPATION GOVERNMENT, THEM(ZOG)

References
Heller, Joseph L. 1995. *The Stern Gang: Ideology, Politics, and Terror, 1940–1949.* London: Frank Cass.
Perlmutter, Amos. 1987. *The Life and Times of Menachem Begin.* Garden City, NY: Doubleday.
Sarig, Mordechai, ed. 1998. *The Political and Social Philosophy of Ze'ev Jabotinsky: Selected Writings.* London: Vallentine Mitchell.
Shindler, Colin. 2001. *The Land beyond Promise: Israel, Likud and the Zionist Dream.* London: I. B. Tauris.
Stanislawski, Michael. 2001. *Zionism and the Fin de Siècle: Cosmopolitanism and Nationalism from Nordau to Jabotinsky.* Berkeley: University of California Press.

ZIONIST OCCUPATION GOVERNMENT, THE (ZOG)

Term used by far-right Americans opposed to the U.S. federal government since the late twentieth century to imply that their government is under the control of "Zionists." The latter term may connote a person sympathetic with the idea of a Jewish state, or any Jew pure and simple. The expression first came to public notice in 1984 when a *New York Times* journalist, writing about robberies committed by a white supremacist group named the Order, stated that the members of this group regarded the federal authorities as a Zionist occupation government. In the mid-1990s the Aryan Nations used the expression publicly in an "Aryan Declaration of Independence" posted on the Internet, and many other anti-Semitic groups have taken it up. The concept embodied in this particular conspiracy theory illustrates a specifically U.S. far-right preoccupation—that of the perceived threat to the traditional rugged individualism of rural America, viewed as the backbone of the nation, from a remote and centralized power-hungry metropolitan elite corrupted by "alien" influences. However, there is nothing new, as such, about the belief by far-right citizens that their own government is controlled by Jews: the British fascist Arnold Spencer Leese, for example, was in the habit of referring to the "Jewish government" of his own nation in the interwar and postwar decades, while the Nazis under the Weimar Republic detected the "Jewish" hand behind that regime. In late-nineteenth-century France, the insinuation that the French government was in the power of the Jews was a commonplace claim in nationalist discourse.

Cyprian Blamires

See Also: ANTI-SEMITISM; ARYAN NATIONS, THE; ARYANISM; CONSPIRACY THEORIES; LEESE, ARNOLD SPENCER; NAZISM; RACIAL DOCTRINE; RADIO; UNITED STATES, THE (POSTWAR); WEIMAR REPUBLIC, THE; ZIONISM

References
Burnett, Thom. 2005. *Conspiracy Encyclopedia: The Encyclopedia of Conspiracy Theories.* Easthampton, MA: Chamberlain.
Knight, Peter. 2003. *Conspiracy Theories in American History: An Encyclopedia.* Denver, CO: ABC-CLIO.

ZOG: *See* ZIONIST OCCUPATION GOVERNMENT, THE

ZYKLON-B

Notorious as the gas used to carry out mass killings in Nazi death camps. Because killing by shooting or by hanging was found to be too slow (and too disturbing for at least some of those responsible) as a means of large-scale murder, large-scale gassing was resorted to. It was found that one or two opened tins of Zyklon-B, based on prussic acid and made by a subsidiary of IG Farben, could kill 250 persons within half an hour.

Cyprian Blamires

See Also: AUSCHWITZ (-BIRKENAU); CONCENTRATION CAMPS; HOLOCAUST, THE; IG FARBEN; SS, THE; WORLD WAR II

References
Kogon, E. 1992. *Zyklon B: Nazi Mass Murder by Poison Gas.* Washington, DC: U.S. Holocaust Memorial Museum.

Chronology of Fascism

1861   Italy was proclaimed as a Kingdom.

1871   Germany was unified and the Second German Empire was founded under Otto von Bismarck.

   In America the Ku Klux Klan was formed, followed by a U.S. congressional inquiry.

1875   In Germany, the Socialist Workers Party was founded.

1879   Austria and Germany signed the 'Dual Alliance'.

1883   Mussolini was born on 29 July.

1886   In France, Boulanger became Minister for War.

   Drumont's *La France Juive* was published.

1888   In Germany, Friedrich Wilhelm Viktor Albert von Preußen became Kaiser.

1889   Adolf Hitler was born on 20 April in Braunau am Inn.

1890   Langbehn's *Rembrandt as Teacher* was published.

   In Germany, Bismarck was dismissed as Chancellor.

1891   In Germany, the Socialist Party became the Social Democratic Party and adopted a Marxist program.

   The Russo-Franco Alliance was signed.

1893   The Pan-German League was founded.

   The Gobineau Society was founded.

1895   Le Bon's *Psychology of Crowds* was published.

1898   In France, the term 'socialist nationalism' was first coined by Maurice Barrès.

   Germany began a program of naval expansion.

1899   Houston Stewart Chamberlain's *Foundations of the Nineteenth Century* was published.

   In France, the *Action Française* was founded by Charles Maurras.

1903   In Italy, Giovanni Giolitti became Prime Minister.

   In Germany, The *Wandervögel* movement was founded.

1907   The 'Triple Entente' between Britain, France, and Russia was formed in August.

1908   Sorel's *Reflections on Violence* was published.

   Austria annexed Bosnia on 5 October.

   In France, the *Action Française* launched their newspaper.

1909   Marinetti's 'Futurist Manifesto' was published.

1910   In Italy, the Italian Nationalist Association was founded by Corradini and Federzoni.

1911–
1912   The *Cercle Proudhon* met.

1911   A German gunboat was sent to Agadir in French-controlled Morocco, creating an international crisis.

1912   In Germany, the SDP became the largest party in the Reichstag.

         In Italy, Mussolini became editor of *Avanti*.

1914   In Bosnia, Archduke Franz Ferdinand was assassinated by Gavrilo Princip of the Young Bosnia movement in Sarajevo on 28 June.

         Austro-Hungary declared war on Serbia on 28 July.

         Germany declared war on Russia on 1 August.

         Germany declared war on France on 3 August.

         Britain declared war on Germany on 4 August.

         The German Army was defeated at the Battle of the Marne on 10 September, marking the failure of the Schlieffen Plan that was designed to secure a quick German victory.

         The Italian Socialist Party ousted Mussolini from the editorship of *Avanti* and from the party after he began to campaign for the entry of Italy into World War I.

         In Italy, the *Fasci di Azione Rivoluzionaria* was founded in October.

1915   Italy entered the war on the side of the Allies in May.

         In the United States, the Ku Klux Klan was reconstituted.

1916   In Germany, Field Marshall Paul von Hindenburg became the Commander-in-Chief of the German Forces in August, and General Erich Ludendorff became his Chief of Staff.

1917   In Russia, Czar Nicholas II abdicated on 16 March after a period of revolutionary fervor.

         The United States declared war on Germany on 6 April.

         In Germany, the Fatherland Party was founded in September.

         Italians suffered hugely traumatic but galvanizing defeat at the Battle of Caporetto between October and November.

         In Russia, the Bolsheviks took power on 7 November.

         The 'Peace Decree' was issued by Lenin on 8 November.

         Russia and Germany agreed an armistice on 16 December.

1918   President Wilson announced his 'Fourteen Points' in January.

         In Argentina, the University Reform movement emerged.

         In South Africa, the *Broederbond* movement was founded.

         The peace treaty of 'Brest-Litovsk' was signed by the USSR and Germany on 14 March.

         In the USSR, civil war broke out in May and the Allied forces sided with the counterrevolutionaries.

         Germany began to negotiate peace with the Allies in October.

         In Germany, sailors based in Kiel revolted.

         In Bavaria, a Republic was declared on 7 November after the Bavarian monarchy was overthrown.

In Germany, Kaiser Wilhelm's abdication was announced on 9 November and the German Republic was proclaimed.

The German government signed an armistice at Compiègne on 11 November, ending World War I.

In Germany, the German Communist Party was founded in December.

1919   The Paris Peace Conference began in January.

In Germany, the 'Spartacist' rising of communists was suppressed by *Freikorps* in January.

In Germany, the National Constitutional Assembly convened in Weimar in February, and Friedrich Ebert became President.

The Comintern was founded in March.

In Hungary, a Soviet Republic was formed in March.

In Italy, Mussolini formed the *Fasci di Combattimento* on 23 March.

In Germany, a Bavarian Soviet regime was proclaimed in April.

The Soviet regime in Bavaria was suppressed in May by both the army and *Freikorps*.

The Treaty of Versailles was signed on the 28 June.

In Germany, the Weimar Constitution was adopted on 31 July.

In Hungary, the Hungarian Soviet Republic was defeated in August by Yugoslav, Romanian, and Czech forces alongside nationalist counterrevolutionaries.

Gabriele D'Annunzio began his occupation of Fiume in September.

In Germany, Hitler joined the German Workers' Party based in Munich on 12 September.

In Italy, Mussolini was defeated in national elections in November.

1920   The Covenant of the League of Nations was agreed in February.

In Germany, the German Workers' Party was renamed the National Socialist German Workers' Party in February, and the '25 Point Program' was adopted by the party on 24 February.

In Germany, the Kapp Putsch attempt occurred in Berlin in March.

In Italy, the 'Red Two Years' reached its pinnacle, and was marked by worker occupation of factories in the summer.

In Italy, Fascism spread into the countryside in the autumn, and *Squadristi* violence escalated.

In the USSR, the civil war ended after an armistice with Poland was signed on 6 October.

In Hungary, Admiral Horthy was elected head of state in December.

D'Annunzio's occupation of Fiume was ended in December.

1921   In Italy, the Italian Communist Party was formed in January.

In Italy, after national elections in May, Mussolini, alongside thirty-five other fascists, was elected to the Italian parliament.

In Italy, the *Arditi del Popolo* was formed in the spring.

The 'Little Entente' between Czechoslovakia, Romania, and Yugoslavia was completed in June.

In Germany, the National Socialist German Workers' Party (NSDAP) or Nazi Party appointed Hitler as party chairman on 29 July.

In Italy, the Italian Fascist Party was formed in November.

1922   In Finland, the Academic Karelia Society was founded.

In the United States, Texas returned a Ku Klux Klan representative to the U.S. Senate.

In Italy, Mussolini was made Prime Minister of Italy on 30 October after the 'March on Rome'.

1923   The French and Belgian armies began their occupation of the industrialized Ruhr region of Germany on 11 January.

In Italy, the Italian Grand Council was created in January.

In Romania, the National Christian Defense League was founded.

In Germany, the Nazi Party held its first Congress in Munich on 27 January.

In Italy, the Italian Nationalists merged with the Fascist Party in March.

Germany experienced a period of hyper-inflation from June, and Gustav Stresemann became Chancellor on 12 August and ended the policy of passive resistance to France.

In Hungary, Gömbös alongside others formed the Party of Racial Defense in August.

The Greek island of Corfu was occupied briefly by the Italian regime in August.

In Spain, Miguel Primo de Rivera successfully mounted a military coup in September.

In Germany, Bavaria broke off diplomatic relations with the central German government in Berlin on 20 October.

In Germany, Hitler led the Nazi Party's failed 'Beer-Hall Putsch' in Munich on 9 November.

In Germany, the inflationary crisis was ended after the introduction of a new currency on 15 November.

In Italy, the Fascist government, Italian industrialists, and Fascist syndicates established the 'Palazzo Chigi' agreement in December.

1924   Fiume was annexed by Italy on 16 March.

Hitler was convicted of high treason on 1 April and sentenced to five years' imprisonment, eligible for parole after six months.

Italian Fascists gained 374 seats, an overwhelming majority in the Italian parliament, in April as a result of the Acerbo electoral law.

The Dawes Plan to revise German reparations was agreed.

In Italy, the Socialist deputy Matteotti was abducted and murdered by Italian Fascists because of his critique of Fascist violence during the April elections.

In Italy, the Aventine Secession began.

In Sweden, the National Socialist League of Freedom and the National Unity Movement were formed.

In Germany, Hitler was released from prison on 20 December.

1925   In Italy, Mussolini resolved the Matteotti crisis by announcing the beginning of the Fascist dictatorship in January.

In France, George Valois founded *Le Faisceau*.

In Germany, the Nazi Party was re-established in February.

In Germany, Hindenburg was elected president on 25 April.

The first volume of Hitler's *Mein Kampf* was published in July.

In Italy, the 'Battle for Grain' was launched in October.

In Germany, the SS protection squad was formed on 9 November.

In Italy, Mussolini gained total executive powers in December.

1926   In Austria, the Nationalist Socialist German Workers' Party formed in April.

In Italy, Syndical Laws were approved by the Fascist regime in April.

In Poland, Josef Pilsudsky staged a military coup in May.

In Portugal, General Gomes de Costa staged a military coup in May.

In Romania, the National Christian Defense League gained six parliamentary seats.

In Italy, the Ministry of Corporations was formed in June.

Germany entered the League of Nations in September.

1927   In France, an Anti-Fascist congress was held in Paris in April.

In Romania, Codreanu formed the Legion of the Archangel Michael in June.

1928   In France, Valois ended *Le Faisceau* in April.

In Germany, the Nazi party polled 2.6 percent of the national vote in May, gaining only 12 seats in the Reichstag.

In France, the *Croix de Feu* (CF) was founded.

In Britain, the Imperial Fascist League was established.

In Italy, the Fascist Grand Council was made into a constitutional organ in December.

1929   In Yugoslavia, King Alexander staged a royal coup in January.

In Estonia, the Vaps movement was formed.

In Sweden, the National Rural Association was formed.

The Italian Fascist Regime and the Vatican signed the Lateran Agreements in February.

The Young Plan was issued in June.

The Wall Street Crash inflicted a worldwide economic downturn from October.

In Finland, the Lapua movement was founded in November.

1930   In Germany, Chancellor Heinrich Brüning (who took office in March) began governing by decree under article 48 of the Weimar Constitution on 16 July.

In Denmark, the Danish National Socialist Workers Party was founded.

In Britain, Oswald Mosley founded his 'New Party'.

In Romania, the Iron Guard was founded by Codreanu to work alongside the Legion of the Archangel Michael.

In Sweden, the Swedish Religious People's Party was established.

In Spain, the *Partido Nacionalista Español* was founded.

In Portugal, the *União Nacional* was established.

In Romania, King Carol returned from exile in June.

In Germany, the Nazis experienced an electoral breakthrough and won over 18 percent of the national vote in the parliamentary elections in September.

1931   In Spain, the monarchy was replaced by a parliamentary republic in January.

In the Netherlands, the Dutch National Socialist Movement was founded.

In Norway, Quisling established the Nordic Folk Awakening movement.

In Spain, the Redondo-Ramos JONS and *La Conquista del Estado* movements were founded.

In Britain, Mosley published his *A National Policy* in March.

In Britain, the 'National Government' was formed in August and the Gold Standard was abandoned in September.

Japan invaded Manchuria in September.

In Britain, Mosley's New Party failed to win a seat in the British General Election.

In Hungary, the Scythe cross movement was formed in December.

In the Netherlands, the Dutch National Socialist Party was formed in December.

In Germany, unemployment rose to 5.6 million.

1932   In Finland, after an attempted Lapua coup in February, the movement was banned and it evolved into the People's Patriotic Movement (IKL).

In Germany, Hitler was defeated by Hindenburg in German presidential elections in March and April.

In Germany, the SA and the SS were prohibited by Brüning in April.

In Germany, von Papen became Chancellor of Germany, replacing Brüning, in May.

In Germany, the ban on the SA and SS was lifted by von Papen.

In Chile, the *Movimiento Nacional Socialista de Chile* (MNS) was founded.

In the Netherlands, the General Dutch Fascist Union was founded.

In France, the *Cartel des Gauches* won the national elections in May.

In Finland, the People's Patriotic Movement was formed in June.

In Yugoslavia, the Ustasha movement was founded.

In Germany, the Nazis won over 37 percent of the national vote in parliamentary elections.

In Portugal, the National Syndicalist movement was founded by Rolão Preto in September.

In Hungary, Horthy appointed Gömbös as Prime Minister in October.

In Britain, after dissolving his New Party in April, Mosley established the British Union of Fascists (BUF) in October.

In Italy, Fascists celebrated the ten year anniversary of the 'March on Rome', which included the famous exhibition of the Fascist Revolution.

In Germany, the Nazis won 33 percent of the national vote in parliamentary elections in November and Communists increased their share of the vote, after which von Papen resigned as Chancellor.

In Germany, von Schleicher became chancellor in December.

1933   In Germany, Hitler was appointed Chancellor on 30 January, von Papen was made his vice-chancellor.

In Germany, the Reichstag was destroyed by fire on 27 February, and, blaming the Communists, Hitler suspended many basic civil liberties the following day.

In Austria, Dollfuss suspended the parliament in March in order to rule by decree.

In Germany, Goebbels launched his Ministry of Popular Enlightenment and Propaganda in March.

In Germany, the first Nazi concentration camp was opened on 20 March in Dachau.

In Germany, Hitler was given full dictatorial powers on 23 March after the Reichstag passed the Enabling Act.

In Finland, *Lapua* gained fourteen seats in the general election.

In France, the *Franciste* movement was formed.

In Germany, *Gleichschaltung* began on 31 March.

In Portugal, Salasar's 'New State' constitution came into effect in April.

In Germany, Nazis organized for Jewish businesses to be boycotted on 1 April.

In Germany, Jews, communists, social democrats, and miscellaneous other political opponents were expelled from the civil service by the Nazis on 7 April.

In Norway, Vidkun Quisling's National Union movement was formed.

In Mexico, the Mexican Revolutionary Action movement was founded.

In Germany, the German Labour Front was established on 2 May.

In Germany, 'un-German' books were burned on 10 May.

In Germany, Nazis became the only legal party on 14 July.

Germany signed a concordat with the Vatican on 20 July.

Germany left the League of Nations and disarmament conference on 14 October.

In Belgium, the Flemish National Front was formed in October.

In Estonia, the Estonian War of Independence Veterans' League received 73 percent of the national vote in a referendum.

In Spain, the *Falange* was formed in October by José Antonio Primo de Rivera.

In the United States, Pelley's Silver Shirts movement was formed.

1934   Germany signed a non-aggression pact with Poland in January.

Mussolini and Hitler met in Venice in June.

In Germany, a purge directed at Ernst Roehm and the SA left over 120 dead on 30 June.

In Britain, the BUF held its Olympia Rally.

In Austria, Dollfuss was murdered by the Austrian Nazis in a failed coup in July.

In Germany, Hitler became *Führer* after the death of Hindenburg in August gave him the opportunity to consolidate the role of President and Chancellor.

The USSR joined the League of Nations in September.

In Switzerland, the Montreux meeting of international fascist movements was held in December.

In Latvia, the Fascist Peasants Union gained power.

1935   In Hungary, Szálasi formed the Party of National Will in January.

In Bolivia, the *Falange Socialista Boliviana* was founded.

In Germany, universal military training was introduced by Hitler on 1 March, in defiance of the Treaty of Versailles.

In Serbia, the *Zbor* movement was founded.

The Franco-Soviet treaty was signed in May.

In Ireland, the National Corporate Party was founded by Eoin O'Duffy in June.

The 'Popular Front' strategy was agreed upon by the USSR at a meeting of the Comintern in August.

In Germany, the Nuremberg Racial Laws that denied Jews political rights were announced in September.

Italy invaded Ethiopia in October, causing the League of Nations to impose sanctions.

In Belgium, the Rex movement was formed.

1936   In Spain, a 'Popular Front' government was formed in February.

The Nazis entered and remilitarized the Rhineland in March.

In France, a 'Popular Front' government was formed in May.

In Italy, Mussolini proclaimed the birth of the Italian Empire after victory in Ethiopia in May.

In Spain, civil war broke out on 31 July after a right wing rising against the Spanish Republic led by Francisco Franco. Later, both Hitler and Mussolini intervened on the side of Franco.

In Germany, the Berlin Olympics began on 1 August.

In Germany in September, Hitler announced the 'Four Year Plan' to prepare Germany's armed forces and economy for war.

The 'Axis' Italo-German treaty was created in October.

The German-Japanese Anti-Comintern Pact was created in November.

In Germany, the Hitler Youth program was made mandatory from December.

1937   The Papal encyclical on 'The Church in Germany' was issued on 14 March.

Hitler and Mussolini met in Vienna.

In Romania, the Legion of the Archangel Michael gained 16 percent of the vote and Antonescu was appointed Chief of General Staff.

Italy joined Germany and Japan in the Anti-Comintern Pact in November.

Under the policy of appeasement, Lord Halifax went to Germany in November seeking a British-German agreement.

1938   In Romania, King Carol abolished the country's parliamentary system in February.

In Argentina, the Argentinian Fascist Party was founded.

Germany annexed Austria in March, Mussolini supported the action.

In Germany and Austria, a plebiscite in April gave over 99 percent approval to the Austrian *Anschluss*.

In Italy, anti-Semitic legislation was introduced in July.

The Sudetenland was transferred from Czechoslovakia to Germany after the Munich Agreement on 29 September.

In Germany, the Nazi *Kristallnacht* pogrom terrorized Jewish communities on 9 November, leaving 267 synagogues and 815 Jewish shops destroyed.

1939   The new Franco regime was officially recognized by Britain on 27 February.

In Romania, Codreanu was killed in a purge of the Legion of the Archangel Michael.

German forces occupied Prague and the whole of Czechoslovakia in March, violating the Munich Agreement.

Albania was occupied by Italy in April.

In response to unauthorized German aggrandisement, the British Prime Minister Neville Chamberlain pledged military support for Poland.

The Anglo-German Naval Treaty and the Non-Aggression Treaty with Poland were both renounced by Germany in May.

In Hungary, the Arrow Cross gained 25 percent of the national vote in elections in May.

The 'Pact of Steel' between Italy and Germany was signed on 22 May.

Danzig (Gdansk) was demanded by the Germans from Poland on 16 August.

The Nazi-Soviet Non-Aggression Pact was agreed on 23 August.

Germany invaded Poland on 1 September, beginning World War II.

Britain declared war on Germany on 3 September.

Warsaw surrendered to Germany on 27 September.

The Nazi euthanasia program was authorised by Hitler in October.

France and Britain declined Hitler's peace offer of accepting the legitimacy of Germany's conquest of Poland on 6 October, and continued the war against Nazi expansionism.

1940   Construction began on the Auschwitz concentration camp in February.

Germany occupied Norway and invaded Denmark in April.

Germany attacked Holland, Belgium, Luxembourg, and France in May.

Italy entered the war on the side of Germany on 10 June.

The French signed an armistice with Germany at Compiègne on 22 June, following which the Vichy regime was established and Pétain became head of state.

Hungary reclaimed Transylvania from Romania in August.

Germany began the 'Battle of Britain' on 13 August.

In Romania, King Carol abdicated and the Iron Guard jointly took power to form the 'National Legionary State' in September.

The Tripartite Pact was signed by Italy, Germany, and Japan in September.

Italy invaded Greece in October.

Soviet Foreign Minister Molotov visited Berlin and met with Hitler in November.

1941   In Romania, Antonescu dissolved the Iron Guard in January after their attempted coup. German forces invaded Greece and Yugoslavia in April.

Rudolf Hess flew to Scotland in May, ostensibly in a bid to bring about peace between Britain and Germany. Replacing him with Bormann, Hitler declared Hess 'mad.'

Hitler issued the 'Commissar Order' on 6 June that called for the liquidation of all Communists in the forthcoming Operation Barbarossa.

Operation Barbarossa commenced and German forces began the invasion of the USSR on 22 June.

In Germany, the Ministry for the Occupied Eastern Territories was created under the leadership of Alfred Rosenberg in July.

In Croatia, the Ustasha came to power.

In Occupied France, foreign Jews began to be rounded up.

The Atlantic Charter was signed by Churchill and Roosevelt in August.

At Auschwitz, the Nazis began experiments with Zyklon-B from September.

In the USSR, Leningrad was surrounded on 4 September.

In Germany, from 19 September Jews were forced to wear a yellow Star of David.

At Chlemno, Nazis began to gas Jews in December.

The Japanese bombed Pearl Harbor on 7 December.

War on the United States was declared by Italy and Germany on 11 December.

In Germany, after the dismissal of Field Marshal Walther von Brauchitsch, Hitler assumed operational command of the German armed forces on 19 December.

1942   The Wannsee Conference was held with the aim of coordinating the genocide programs of the Holocaust on 20 January.

In Norway, Quisling became prime minister in February.

In Czechoslovakia, Heydrich was assassinated on May 27 in Prague.

In Poland, Jews began to be deported from the Warsaw Ghetto to Treblinka from June.

At Auschwitz, mass gassing of Jews began in June.

In the USSR, German forces reached Stalingrad in September.

At El Alamein in Egypt, Rommel's Afrika Korps were forced into retreat in October.

British and American troops landed in North Africa in November.

In Vichy France, German forces occupied the country on 11 November.

In the USSR, the German Sixth Army was encircled at Stalingrad on 23 November.

1943   In the USSR, the German Sixth Army surrendered at Stalingrad on 31 January.

In Poland, the Warsaw Ghetto uprising began in April.

In North Africa, the Afrika Korps surrendered on 12 May.

In Poland, the Warsaw Ghetto uprising was crushed by 16 May and the ghetto was destroyed.

Allied forces landed in Sicily on July 10, leading to Mussolini's removal as head of state and later arrest on 25 July.

Allied forced landed on the Italian mainland on 3 September.

An armistice with Allied forces was announced by the new Italian regime on 8 September.

Mussolini was rescued on 12–13 September by German forces from Gran Sasso, following which the birth of the Italian Social Republic was announced by Mussolini at Salò.

Italy declared war on Germany on 13 October.

1944   In Hungary, German forces occupied the country and Eichmann began a roundup of Hungarian Jews.

Rome was liberated by Allied forces on 4 June.

The D-Day landings began on 6 June.

Colonel Stauffenberg attempted to assassinate Hitler on 20 July.

In Romania, Antonescu's pro-German government fell in August.

The Red Army reached the German borders in East Prussia on 18 August.

Paris was liberated by the Allies on 25 August.

The Anglo-American forces reached Germany's western borders by 15 September.

The German counteroffensive, the Battle of the Bulge, began on 16 December in the Ardennes.

1945   Auschwitz was liberated by the Red Army in January.

In Germany, Hitler made his last broadcast to the German people on 30 January.

At Yalta in the Crimea, Churchill, Roosevelt, and Stalin met on 11 February and decided on the temporary post-war arrangements for Germany.

In Germany, Hitler issued his 'Nero Command' or scorched earth policy on March 19.

In Italy, after the liberation of northern Italy in April, Mussolini was captured by partisans on 26 April and executed on 28 April in Milan.

Hitler committed suicide on 30 April.

Germany unconditionally surrendered on 8 May.

Japan unconditionally surrendered on 2 September after atomic bombs were dropped on Hiroshima and Nagasaki.

In Germany, the Nuremberg War Crimes trials began on 20 November.

1946   In Argentina, Juan Perón was elected President.

In Germany, Nazi war criminals were executed at Nuremberg in October.

In Italy, the *Movimento Sociale Italiano* (MSI) was founded in December.

1947   George Marshall announced the European Recovery Program in June.

1948   In Italy, the Italian Republic was officially proclaimed on 1 January, and its constitution outlawed a return of the Fascist Party.

The USSR blocked land access to Berlin in June in protest at the creation of the separate West German state.

In Ecuador, the *Alianza Revolucionaria Nacionalista Ecuatoriana* (ARNE) was founded.

In South Africa, apartheid was established.

1949   The Soviet blockade of Berlin ended in May.

The Federal Republic of Germany (FRG) was established on 23 May, and Konrad Adenauer became Chancellor on 15 September.

The German Democratic Republic (GDR) was established on 12 October, led by Walter Ulbricht.

Salazar's Portugal entered NATO.

In South Africa, the National Party was created.

1950   In Belgium, the *Mouvement Social Belge* was founded.

Nation Europa was founded.

In West Germany, the far-right *Sozialistiche Reichspartei* was founded.

1951   The European Social Movement was formed at Malmö.

1952   Eva Perón died.

The Federal Republic of Germany (FRG–West Germany) agreed to restitution payments with Israel to the Jewish people.

1953   In the Netherlands, the Dutch National European Socialist Movement was founded.

Evola's *Men Standing among the Ruins* was published.

1954   In France, the *Parti Patriotique Révolutionnaire* was created.

In Britain, the League of Empire Loyalists was founded by A. K. Chesterton.

1955   The Paris Agreements allowed FRG to rearm, though without developing weapons of mass destruction, and also gave full sovereignty to the new state.

The USSR formed the Warsaw Pact in response to FRG rearmament and the rise of NATO.

1956   In Austria, the Freedom Party of Austria (FPÖ) was formed.

1960   In Britain, the British National Party (BNP) was founded.

1961   In Israel, Eichmann was tried and convicted.

The German Democractic Republic (GDR–East Germany) began building the Berlin Wall.

Evola's *To Ride the Tiger* was published.

1962   The World Union of National Socialists was formed.

In Britain, the National Socialist Movement was founded.

1964   In France, *Occident* was founded.

In Germany, the National Democratic Party of Germany was founded.

1966   In Portugal, the Portuguese National Revolutionary Front was formed.

1967   In Britain, the British National Front was established.

In the United States, the leading Nazi sympathizer George Lincoln Rockwell was assassinated; the U.S. government published a report investigating contemporary activities of the Ku Klux Klan.

1968   In France, *Occident* was banned.

In Portugal, Salazar left office.

The Group for Research and Studies on European Civilization (GRECE) was founded.

1969   In France, the *Ordre Nouveau* was born.

In Italy, Almirante became leader of the MSI.

In the United States, the Posse Comitatus movement was founded.

In West Germany, the National Democratic Party gained 4 percent of the vote.

1970   In the United States, Christian Identity ideologue Wesley Smith died.

1971   In the FRG, the *Deutsche Volks Union* was founded.

In the GDR, Walter Ulbricht was replaced by Erich Honecker as head of state.

1972   In Italy, the MSI gained 8.7 percent of the vote in national elections.

In France, Le Pen's *Front National* was founded.

1973   In Belgium, the Flemish *Vlaams-Nationale Raad* was founded.

In Argentina, Perón returned to the position of President.

In Germany, *Wehrsportgruppe Hoffmann* was created.

In South Africa, the African Resistance Movement was formed.

Thies Christopherson's *The Auschwitz Lie* was published.

1974   In Portugal, the dictatorship collapsed.

In France, the *Parti des Forces Nouvelles* (PNF) was formed.

1975   In Spain, the death of Franco ended his dictatorship.

In Cambodia, the Khmer Rouge came to power.

1976   In Belgium, the Belgian Nationalist Student Confederation was created.

1977   In the United States, the Christian Patriot's Defense League was founded.

In Greece, the National Alignment (EP) movement was founded.

In Belgium, the Flemish *Vlaams-Nationale Partij* (VNP) and the *Vlaamse Volkspartij* (VVP) were formed.

In Portugal, the *Movimento Independente para a Reconstrucão Nacional* (MIRN) was founded.

In Germany, the neo-Nazi movement *Aktionsfront Nationaler Sozialisten* (ANS) was formed.

1978   William Pierce's *The Turner Diaries* was published.

Arthur Butz's *The Hoax of the Twentieth Century* was published.

In France, the *Légitime Défence* was created.

In Belgium, the *Vlaams Blok* (VB) and the *Union Démocratique pour le Respect du Travail* (UDRT) were formed.

1979   In Cambodia, after a sustained program of genocide the Khmer Rouge fell from power.

In France, *Securité et Liberté* was formed.

In Greece, the United Nationalist Movement was founded.

1980   In Germany, the Thule Seminar was founded.

In Austria, Norbert Burger of the National Democratic Party gained 3.2 percent of the presidential vote.

In the United States, National Socialist sympathizer Harold Covington won 43 percent of the vote in North Carolina.

1982   In Belgium, the Belgian Nationalist Young Students Association was created.

In Britain, the BNP was re-constituted.

1983   In FRG, the *Republikaner* party was founded.

In France, Le Pen's National Front made an electoral breakthrough.

In the United States, the Order movement was founded.

1984   In France, Le Pen's National Front gained over 10 percent in European elections.

1985   In Spain, the *Junta Coordinatora de Fuerzas Nacionales* was created.

In Belgium, the *Front National-Nationaal Front* was formed.

1986   In France, the National Front won thirty-five seats in parliamentary elections.

In Yugoslavia, Milošević issued the SANU Memorandum.

In Austria, Kurt Waldheim ran a controversial election campaign, while Haider took over leadership of the FPÖ.

1987   Klaus Barbie was tried for war crimes.

In Austria, far-right ideologues held 'summit talks' with Haider.

1988   In France, Le Pen received 14.6 percent of the vote in the presidential election.

Fred Leuchter published *The Leuchter Report*, a revisionist history of the Nazi gas chambers.

1989   In Belgium, the Agir movement was founded.

In France, the National Front won a seat in the Dreux parliamentary by election.

In Germany, the Berlin Wall fell, providing a symbolic historical reference point marking the end of the Cold War.

In FRG, the *Republikaner* party won eleven seats in West Berlin in national elections, and six seats in European elections. Also the *Deutsche Alternative, Freundeskreis Freiheit für Deutschland,* and *Nationale List* movements were created.

In Greece, the Nationalist Youth Front was founded.

In Portugal, the *Força National-Nova Monarquia* was formed.

1990   GDR and FRG were united under the West German constitution.

In Denmark, the Party of Well-Being was founded.

In the United States, white supremacist candidate David Duke won 44 percent in a Louisiana election.

In Romania, the Romanian Cradle movement was formed.

In Austria, the FPÖ received over 15 percent in elections.

In Germany, the *Republikaner* party lost its eleven seats in Berlin, and Schönhuber resigned the leadership in May, and was re-elected leader in June.

In Italy, Rauti replaced Fini as leader of the MSI after the party gained a mere 4 percent in local elections.

1991   In Austria, in Vienna local elections the FPÖ won 23 percent of the vote.

In Germany, the *Deutscher Kameradschaftsbund, Nationaler Bloc,* and *Deutsche Liga für Volk und Heimat* were founded.

In South Africa, Apartheid ended.

In the United States, David Duke won 39 percent of the vote in Louisiana governor elections.

In Italy, Fini was re-instated as leader of MSI.

In Romania, the Movement for Romania was formed.

1992   In Croatia, the Croatian Party of Pure Rights and the Croatian Party of Rights Youth Group were founded.

In Romania, the Romanian Party of the National Right was formed.

In Baden–Württemberg in Germany, the *Republikaner* party received 11 percent of the vote.

1993   In Britain, the BNP gained its first councillor in the Isle of Dogs after winning 34 percent of the vote in local elections.

In Italy, the MSI's Fini stood for Mayor of Rome and Alessandra Mussolini stood for the Mayor of Naples.

In Austria, dissenters left the FPÖ, while Haider published *Freiheitlichen Thesen.*

1994   In Austria, the FPÖ polled 22 percent in parliamentary elections.

In Italy, Fini launched Alleanza Nazionale (AN) in January, and in May the AN won 13.5 percent in Italian elections gaining five seats in Berlusconi's cabinet.

In European elections, the French National Front and the German Republikaner party won 10.5 percent and 3.9 percent of the vote respectively.

1995   In Denmark, the Danish People's Party was founded.

In Russia, the *Derzhava* movement was formed.

In the United States, Timothy McVeigh exploded a massive bomb in government offices in Oklahoma.

In France, Le Pen won fifteen percent of the vote in French presidential elections.

1996   In Austria, the FPÖ polled 28 percent in European elections.

In Italy, the AN won 15.7 percent in Italian parliamentary elections and 150,000 attended an AN rally in September in Milan.

1998   In India, Bharatiya Janata made an electoral breakthrough.

1999   In France, friends of Bruno Mégret formed the *Mouvement National Républicain* after splitting with Le Pen's National Front.

In Britain, David Copeland exploded a series of nail bombs in London.

In European elections, the FPÖ in Austria won five seats in the European parliament; elsewhere the *Republikaner* party in Germany polled 1.7 percent, and in France the National front gained 5.7 percent of the vote.

2000   In Italy, Fini became Berlusconi's Deputy Prime Minister.

2001   In Britain, the BNP exploited race riots in Oldham, Burnley, and Bradford.

In Denmark, the Danish People's Party won 22 parliamentary seats.

2002   In France, Le Pen gained 17 percent in the first round of the presidential elections and went through to the second round.

In Britain, the BNP won three council seats in Burnley.

In the Netherlands, the far-right leader Pim Fortuyn was assassinated.

2003   In Italy, Alessandra Mussolini left AN after disagreeing with Fini over his denunciation of fascism.

2004   In Italy, Alessandra Mussolini was elected to the European parliament.

Bibliography

KEY SECONDARY SOURCES ON GENERIC FASCISM

Allardice, G. ed. 1971. *The Place of Fascism in European History.* Englewood Cliffs, NJ: Prentice-Hall.

Almog, S. 1990. *Nationalism and Anti-Semitism in Europe.* Oxford: Pergamon Press.

Bessel, R. 1996. *Fascist Italy and Nazi Germany: Comparison and Contrasts.* Cambridge: Cambridge University Press.

Billig, M. 1978. *Fascists: A Social-psychological View of the National Front.* London: Academic Press in co-operation with European Association of Experimental Social Psychology.

Billig, M. 1979. *Psychology, Racism and Fascism.* Birmingham: A. F. & R. Publications.

Blinkhorn, M. ed. 1990. *Fascists and Conservatives.* London: Unwin Hyman.

Blinkhorn, Martin. 2001. *Fascism and the Right in Europe; 1919–1945.* Harlow: Longman.

Blum, G. 1998. *The Rise of Fascism in Europe.* London: Greenwood Press.

Brooker, P. 1991. *The Faces of Fraternalism: Nazi Germany, Fascist Italy, Imperial Japan.* Oxford: Clarendon Press.

Carsten, F. L. 1971. *The Rise of Fascism.* Berkeley, CA: University of California Press.

Cassels, A. 1975. *Fascism.* Arlington Heights, IL: Harlan Davidson.

Chakotin, S. 1934. *The Rape of the Masses: The Psychology of Totalitarian Propaganda.* London: Routledge.

Cheles, L., Ferguson, R., Vaughan, M. eds. 1991. *Neo-Fascism in Europe.* London: Longman.

Clark, T. 1997. *Art and Propaganda in the Twentieth Century: The Political Image in the Age of Mass Culture.* New York, NY: Harry N. Abrams.

Cohen, Carl.1972. *Communism, Fascism, Democracy: The Theoretical Foundations.* New York, NY: Random House.

Cullen, S. M. 1986. 'Leaders and Martyrs: Codreanu, Mosley and José Antonio', in *History,* vol. 71.

Davies, P., Lynch, D. 2002. *Routledge Companion to Fascism and the Far Right.* London: Routledge.

De Felice, R. 1977 *Interpretations of Fascism.* London: Harvard University Press.

De Felice, R., Ledeen, M. 1976. *Fascism: An Informal Introduction to its Theory and Practice.* New Brunswick, NJ: Transaction Books.

Deakin, F. W. 1962. *The Brutal Friendship: Mussolini, Hitler and the Fall of Italian Fascism.* London: Weidenfeld and Nicolson.

Delzell, C. F. 1970. *Mediterranean Fascism, 1919–1945.* London: Macmillan.

Durham, M. 1998. *Women and Fascism.* London: Routledge.

Eagleton, T. 1991. *Ideology: An introduction.* London: Verso.

Eatwell, Roger. 2003. *Fascism: A History.* London: Pimlico.

Eatwell, R., Write, A. eds. 1993. *Contemporary Political Ideologies.* London: Pinter.

Eksteins, M. 1989. *Rites of Spring: The Great War and the Birth of the Modern Age.* London: Bantam.

Elliott, W. Y. 1968. *The Pragmatic Revolt in Politics: Syndicalism, Fascism, and the Constitutional State.* New York, NY: Howard Fertig.

Farquharson, J. E. 1976. *The Plough and the Swastika: the NSDAP and Agriculture in Germany, 1928–45.* London: Sage.

Feuer, L. S. 1975. *Ideology and the Ideologists.* Oxford: Blackwell.

Foreman, J. D. 1974. *Fascism: The Meaning and Experience of Reactionary Revolution.* New York, NY: F. Watts.

Fraser, L. 1957. *Propaganda*. London: Oxford University Press.

Gentile, E. 2000. 'The Sacralization of Politics: Definitions, Interpretations and Reflections on the Question of Secular Religion and Totalitarianism,' *Totalitarian Movements and Political Religions* vol. 1, no. 1.

Germani, G. 1978. *Authoritarianism, Fascism and National Populism*. New Brunswick, NJ: Transaction Books.

Golsan, R. ed. 1992. *Fascism, Aesthetics and Culture*. London: University Press of New England.

Greene, N. ed. 1968 *Fascism: An Anthology*. Arlington Heights, IL: Harlan Davidson.

Gregor, A. J. 1969. *The Ideology of Fascism: The Rationale of Totalitarianism*. New York, NY: Free Press.

Gregor, A. J. 1979. *Italian Fascism and Developmental Dictatorship*. Princeton, NJ: Princeton University Press.

Gregor, A. J. 1999. *Phoenix: Fascism in Our Time*. London: Transaction Publishers.

Griffin, R. D. 1991. *The Nature of Fascism*. London: Routledge.

Griffin, R. D. ed. 1995. *Fascism*. Oxford: Oxford University Press.

Griffin, R. D. ed. 1998. *International Fascism: Theories, Causes and the New Consensus*. London: Arnold.

Griffin, R. D., Feldman, M. eds. 2004. *Fascism: Critical Concepts in Social Science* (5 volumes) London: Routledge.

Griffiths, R. 2005. *Fascism*. London: Continuum.

Hainsworth, P. 1992. *The Extreme Right in Europe and the USA*. London: Pinter.

Hamilton, A. 1971. *The Appeal of Fascism. A Study of Intellectuals and Fascism, 1919–1945*. New York, NY: Macmillan.

Hamilton, B. 1987. 'The Elements of the Concept of Ideology,' in *Political Studies*, vol. 35.

Hayes, P. 1973. *Fascism*. London: Allen & Unwin.

Hoffmann, H. 1996. *The Triumph of Propaganda: Film and National Socialism, 1933–1945*. Oxford: Berghahn Books.

Kallis, A. A. 2000. *Fascist Ideology: Territory and Expansionism in Italy and Germany, 1922–1945*. London: Routledge.

Kallis, A. A. ed. 2003. *The Fascism Reader*. London: Routledge.

Kedward, H. R. 1971. *Fascism in Western Europe*. New York, NY: New York University Press.

Kitchen, M. 1976. *Fascism*. London: Macmillan.

Laclau, E. 1977. *Politics and Ideology in Marxist Theory: Capitalism, Fascism, Populism*. London: NLB.

Laqueur, W. ed. 1976. *Fascism: A Reader's Guide: Analyses, Interpretations, Bibliography*. Harmondsworth: Penguin Books.

Larsen, S. U, Hagtvet, B., Myklebust, J. P. eds. 1980. *Who Were the Fascists? Social Roots of European Fascism*. Bergen: Universitetsforlaget.

Lubas, H. ed. 1973. *Fascism: Three Major Regimes*. New York, NY: J. Wiley.

Mangan, J. A. ed. 2000. *Superman Supreme: Fascist Body as Political Icon—Global Fascism*. London: Frank Cass.

Michaelis, M. 1989. 'Fascism, Totalitarianism and the Holocaust. Reflections on Current Interpretations of National Socialist Anti-Semitism,' in *European History Quarterly*, vol. 19.

Milfull, J. ed. 1990. *The Attractions of Fascism: Social Psychology and Aesthetics of the 'Triumph of the Right.'* Oxford: Berg.

Miller, E. A. ed. 1989. *The Legacy of Fascism: Lectures Delivered at the University of Glasgow*. Glasgow: University of Glasgow.

Morgan, P. 2003. *Fascism in Europe, 1919–1945*. London: Routledge.

Mosse, G. L. 1966. 'The Genesis of Fascism', in *Journal of Contemporary History*, vol. 1, no. 1.

Mosse, G. L. 1980. *Masses and Man: Nationalist and Fascist Perceptions of Reality*. New York: H. Fertig.

Mosse, G. L. 1990. *Fallen Soldiers. Reshaping the Memory of the World Wars*. Oxford: Oxford University Press.

Mosse, G. L. 1999. *The Fascist Revolution: Towards a General Theory of Fascism*. New York, NY: H. Fertig.

Mosse, G. L., Laqueur, W. eds. 1966 *International Fascism 1920–1945*. New York, NY: Harper & Row.

Mühlberger, D. ed. 1987. *The Social Basis of European Fascist Movements*, London: Croom Helm.

Nathan, P. W. 1943. *The Psychology of Fascism*. London: Faber and Faber.

Nolte, E. 1965. *Three Faces of Fascism: Action Française, Italian Fascism, National Socialism*. London: Weidenfeld and Nicolson.

O'Sullivan, N. 1983. *Fascism*. London: J. M. Dent.

Passmore, K. 2002. *Fascism: A Very Short Introduction*. Oxford: Oxford University Press.

Passmore, K. ed. 2003. *Women, Gender and Fascism in Europe, 1919–1945*. Manchester: Manchester University Press.

Paxton, R. O. 2005. *The Anatomy of Fascism*. London: Penguin.

Payne S. G. 1980. *Fascism: Comparison and Definition*. London: University of Wisconsin Press.

Payne, S.G. 1995. *A History of Fascism, 1914–1945*. London: UCL Press.

Pratkin, A., Aronson, E. 2001. *The Age of Propaganda: The Everyday Use and Abuse of Persuasion*. New York, NY: W.H. Freeman.

Pronay, N., Spring, D. eds. 1982. *Propaganda, Politics, and Film*. London: Macmillan.

Pulzer, P. 1964. *The Rise of Political Anti-Semitism in Germany and Austria.* New York, NY: Wiley.

Rees, R. 1985. *Fascism and Pre-fascism in Europe 1890–1945: A Bibliography of the Extreme Right.* (2 vols.) Brighton, Sussex: Harvester Press.

Renton, D.1999. *Fascism: Theory and Practice.* London: Pluto Press.

Ridley, F. A. 1988. *Fascism Down the Ages: From Caesar to Hitler.* London: Romer.

Robinson, R. A. H. 1995. *Fascism: The International Phenomenon.* London: Historical Association.

Rogger, H., Weber, E. eds. 1965. *The European Right: A Historic Profile.* London: Weidenfeld and Nicolson.

Schueddekopf, O.E. 1973. *Revolutions of Our Time: Fascism.* London: Weidenfeld & Nicolson.

Sternhell, Z. 1994. *The Birth of Fascist Ideology: From Cultural Rebellion to Political Revolution.* Princeton, NJ: Princeton University Press.

Turner, H. A. ed. 1975. *Reappraisals of Fascism.* New York, NY: New Viewpoints.

Turner, S. P., Käsler, D. eds. 1992. *Sociology Responds to Fascism.* London: Routledge.

Weber, E. 1964. *Varieties of Fascism: Doctrines of Revolution in the Twentieth Century.* Princeton, NJ: Van Nostrand.

Weber, E. 1982. 'Decadence on Private Income,' in *Journal of Contemporary History,* vol. 17, no. 1.

Wolff, R. J., Hoensch, J. K. 1987. *Catholics, the State, and the European Radical Right, 1919–1945.* Cambridge: Cambridge University Press.

Woolf, S. J. ed. 1981. *Fascism in Europe.* London: Methuen.

KEY SECONDARY WORKS ON THE INTERWAR FASCIST REGIMES

Italy

Absalom, A.N.L. 1969. *Mussolini and the Rise of Italian Fascism.* London: Methuen.

Adamson, W. L. 1992. 'The Language of Opposition in Early 20th Century Italy: Rhetorical Continuities between Pre-war Florentine Avant-gardism and Mussolini's Fascism,' in *Journal of Modern History,* vol. 64, no. 1.

Adamson, W. L. 1993. *Avant-Garde Florence: From Modernism to Fascism.* London: Harvard University Press.

Anderson, W. L. 1989. 'Fascism and Culture: Avant-Gardes and Secular Religion in the Italian Case,' in *Journal of Contemporary History,* vol. 24.

Antliff, M., Affron, M. 1997. *Fascist Visions: Art and Ideology in Italy and France.* Princeton, NJ: Princeton University Press.

Appollionio, V. ed. 1973. *Futurist Manifestos.* New York, NY: Viking Press.

Baer, G. 1967. *The Coming of the Italo-Ethiopian War.* Cambridge, MA: Harvard University Press.

Binchy, D. A. 1941. *Church and State in Fascist Italy.* London: Oxford University Press.

Bosworth, R. 1998. *The Italian Dictatorship. Problems and Perspectives in the Interpretation of Mussolini's Italy.* London: Arnold.

Braun, M. 2000. *Mario Sironi and Italian Modernism: Art and Politics under Fascism.* Cambridge: Cambridge University Press.

Cannistraro, P. V. 1972. 'Mussolini's Cultural Revolution: Fascist or Nationalist,' in *Journal of Contemporary History,* vol. 7.

Cannistraro, P. V. ed. 1982. *A Historical Dictionary of Fascism.* Westport, CN: Greenwood Press.

Cassels, A. 1969. *Fascist Italy.* London: Routledge & Kegan Paul.

Clark, M. 1984. *Modern Italy, 1871–1982.* London: Longman.

De Grand, A. 1972. 'Curzio Malaparte: The Illusion of the Fascist Revolution,' in *Journal of Contemporary History,* vol. 7, nos 1–2.

De Grand, A. 1976. 'Women Under Italian Fascism,' in *The Historical Journal,* vol. 19.

De Grand, A. 1978. *The Italian Nationalist Association and the Rise of Fascism in Italy.* London: University of Nebraska Press.

De Grand, A. 1982. *Italian Fascism: Its Origins and Development.* London: University of Nebraska Press.

De Grand, A. 1991. 'Cracks in the Facade: The Failure of Fascist Totalitarianism in Italy 1935–1939,' in *European History Quarterly,* vol. 21.

De Grazia, V. 1981. *The Culture of Consent: 'Mass Organizations of Leisure in Fascist Italy.'* Cambridge: Cambridge University Press.

De Grazia, V. 1992. *How Fascism Ruled Women: Italy, 1922–1945.* Berkeley, CA: University of California Press.

Deakin, F. W. 1962. *The Brutal Friendship: Mussolini, Hitler and the Fall of Italian Fascism.* London: Weidenfeld and Nicolson.

Di Scala, Spencer M. 2004. *Italy from Revolution to Republic: 1700 to the Present.* Oxford: Westview.

Ebenstein, W. 1939. *Fascist Italy.* Chicago, IL: American Book Company.

Elwin, W. 1934. *Fascism at Work.* London: M. Hopkinson.

Etlin, R. 1991. *Modernism in Italian Architecture, 1890–1940.* London: MIT Press.

Falasca-Zamponi, S. 1997. *Fascist Spectacle: The Aesthetics of Power in Fascist Italy.* London: University of California Press.

Finer, 1964. *Mussolini's Italy.* London: Frank Cass.

Forgacs, D., ed. 1986. *Rethinking Italian Fascism: Capitalism, Populism and Culture.* London: Lawrence and Wishart.

Forgacs, D. 1990. *Italian Culture in the Industrial Era. 1880–1980. Cultural Industries, Politics and the Public.* Manchester: Manchester University Press.

Gallo, M. 1974. *Mussolini's Italy. Twenty Years of the Fascist Era.* London: Abelard-Schuman.

Gentile, E. 1984. 'The Problem of the Party in Italian Fascism,' in *Journal of Contemporary History,* vol. 19, no. 2.

Gentile, E. 1990. 'Fascism as Political Religion,' in *Journal of Contemporary History,* vol. 25.

Gentile, E. 1996. *The Sacralization of Politics in Fascist Italy.* London: Harvard University Press.

Germino, D. L. 1971. *The Italian Fascist Party in Power: A Study in Totalitarian Rule.* Minneapolis, MN: University of Minnesota Press.

Ginsborg, P. 1990. *A History of Contemporary Italy: Society and Politics, 1943–1988.* Harmondsworth: Penguin.

Gregor, A. J. 1979. *The Young Mussolini and the Intellectual Origins of Fascism.* Berkeley, CA: University of California Press.

Gregor, A. J. 1979. *Italian Fascism and Developmental Dictatorship.* Princeton, NJ: Princeton University Press.

Halperin, S. 1971. *The Separation of Church and State in Italian Thought from Cavour to Mussolini.* New York, NY: Octagon Books.

Halperin, W. 1964. *Mussolini and Italian Fascism.* Princeton, NJ: Van Nostrand.

Hay, J. 1987. *Popular Film Culture in Fascist Italy: The Passing of the Rex.* Bloomington, IN: Indiana University Press.

Hite, J., Hinton, C. 1998. *Fascist Italy.* London: John Murray.

Horn, D. G. 1994. *Social Bodies: Science, Reproduction and Italian Modernity.* Princeton, NJ: Princeton University Press.

Ipsen, C. 1996. *Dictating Demography: The Problem of Population in Fascist Italy.* Cambridge: Cambridge University Press.

Jensen, R.1995. 'Futurism and Fascism,' in *History Today,* vol. 45 no. 11.

Joll, J. 1965. *Three Intellectuals in Politics.* New York, NY: Harper & Row.

Kent, P. 1981. *The Pope and the Duce: The International Impact of the Lateran Agreements.* London: Macmillan Press.

Knight, P. 2003. *Mussolini and Fascism.* London: Routledge.

Knox, M. 2000. *Common Destiny. Foreign Policy and War in Fascist Italy and Nazi Germany.* Cambridge: Cambridge University Press.

Koon, T. 1985. *Believe, Obey, Fight. Political Socialization of Youth in Fascist Italy, 1922–43.* London: University of North Carolina Press.

Landy, M. 2000. *Fascist Film.* Cambridge: Cambridge University Press.

Ledeen, M. A. 1969. 'Italian Youth and Fascism,' in *Journal of Contemporary History,* vol. 4.

Ledeen, M. A. 1971. 'Fascism and the Generation Gap,' in *European Studies Review Quarterly,* vol. 1, no. 3.

Ledeen, M. A. 1976. 'Women under Italian Fascism,' in *Historical Journal,* vol. 19.

Ledeen, M. A. 1976. 'Renzo de Felice and the Controversy over Italian Fascism,' in *Journal of Contemporary History,* vol. 11.

Ledeen, M. A. 1977. *The First Duce: D'Annunzio at Fiume.* London: Johns Hopkins University Press.

Liehm, M. 1984. *Passion and Defiance. Film in Italy from 1942 to the Present.* London: University of California Press.

Lyttleton, A. ed. 1973. *Italian Fascisms from Pareto to Gentile.* London: Cape.

Lyttleton, A. 2004. *The Seizure of Power: Fascism in Italy, 1919–1929.* London: Routledge.

Mack Smith, D. 1979. *Mussolini's Roman Empire.* Harmondsworth: Penguin.

Mack Smith, D. 1981. *Mussolini.* London: Weidenfeld and Nicolson.

Mallett, R. 2003. *Mussolini and the Origins of the Second World War, 1933–1940.* Basingstoke: Palgrave Macmillan.

Matteotti, G. 1969. *The Fascisti Exposed: A Year of Fascist Domination.* London: Independent Labour Party Publication Department.

Melograni, P. 1976. 'The Cult of the Duce in Mussolini's Italy,' in *Journal of Contemporary History,* vol. 11, vol. 4.

Michaelis, M.1978. *Mussolini and the Jews: German-Italian Relations and the Jewish Question in Italy, 1922–1945.* New York, NY: Oxford University Press.

Minio-Paluello, L. 1946. *Education in Fascist Italy.* London: Oxford University Press.

Morgan, P. 1995. *Italian Fascism 1919–1945.* Basingstoke: Macmillan.

Mosse, G. L.1990. 'The Political Culture of Italian Futurism: A General Perspective,' in *Journal of Contemporary History,* vol. 25, nos. 2–3.

Pollard, J. F. 1985. *The Vatican and Italian Fascism 1929–1932.* Cambridge: Cambridge University Press.

Pollard, J. F. 1998. *The Fascist Experience in Italy.* London: Routledge.

Quine, M. 1996. *Population Politics in Twentieth Century Europe: Fascist Dictatorships and Liberal Politics.* London: Routledge.

Quine, Maria. 2002. *Italy's Social Revolution: Charity and Welfare from Liberalism to Fascism.* Basingstoke: Palgrave.

Redman, T. 1991. *Ezra Pound and Italian Fascism.* Cambridge: Cambridge University Press.

Reich, J., Garofalo, P. eds. 2002. *Re-viewing Fascism: Italian Cinema, 1922–43.* Bloomington, IN: Indiana University Press.

Rhodes, A. 1973. *The Vatican in the Age of the Dictators, 1922–1945.* London: Hodder and Stoughton.

Rittner, C., Roth, J. eds. 2002. *Pope Pius XII and the Holocaust.* London: Leicester University Press.

Roberts, D. D. 1979. *The Syndicalist Tradition in Italian Fascism.* Manchester: Manchester University Press.

Robertson, E. M. 1977. *Mussolini as Empire Builder. Europe and Africa, 1932–36.* London: Macmillan.

Robertson, E. M. 1988. 'Race as a Factor in Mussolini's Policy in Africa and Europe,' in *Journal of Contemporary History,* vol. 23, no. 3.

Robson, M. 2000. *Italy: Liberalism and Fascism, 1870–1945.* London: Hodder & Stoughton.

Roth, J. J. 1967. 'The Roots of Italian Fascism: Sorel and Sorelismo,' in *Journal of Modern History,* vol. 39, no. 1.

Salomone, W. ed. 1971. *Italy from the Risorgimento to Fascism: An Enquiry into the Origins of the Totalitarian State.* Newton Abbot: David & Charles.

Sarti, R. 1970. 'Fascist Modernisation in Italy: Traditional or Revolutionary?' in *American Historical Review,* vol. 75, no. 4.

Sbacchi, A. 1985. *Ethiopia under Mussolini. Fascism and the Colonial Experience.* London: Zed.

Segre, C. G. 1987. *Italo Balbo: A Fascist Life.* London: University of California Press.

Settembrini, D. 1976. 'Mussolini and the Legacy of Revolutionary Syndicalism,' in *Journal of Contemporary History,* vol. 11.

Snowden, F. 1989. *The Fascist Revolution in Tuscany, 1919–1922.* Cambridge: Cambridge University Press.

Sorlin, P. 1996. *Italian National Cinema 1896–1996.* London: Routledge.

Stone, M. 1998. *The Patron State. Culture and Politics in Fascist Italy.* Princeton, NJ: Princeton University Press.

Tannenbaum, E. R. 1969. 'The Goals of Italian Fascism,' in *The American Historical Review,* vol. 74.

Tannenbaum, E. R. 1972. *Fascism in Italy: Italian Society and Culture 1922–1945.* London: Allen Lane.

Thompson, D. 1991. *State Control in Fascist Italy: Culture and Conformity.* Manchester: Manchester University Press.

Togliatti, P. 1976. *Lectures on Fascism.* London: Lawrence and Wishart.

Turner, H. A. Jnr. ed. 1975. *Reappraisals of Fascism.* New York, NY: New Viewpoints.

Valli, R. S. 2000. 'The Myth of Squadrismo in the Fascist Regime,' in *Journal of Contemporary History,* vol. 35 no. 2.

Villari, L. 1956. *Italian Foreign Policy Under Mussolini.* London: Holborn Pub. Co.

Visser, R. 1992. 'Fascist Doctrine and the Cult of *Romanità*,' in *Journal of Contemporary History,* vol .27, no. 1.

Vivarelli, R. 1991. 'Interpretations of the Origins of Fascism,' in *Journal of Modern History* , vol. 63, no. 1.

Wanrooij, B. 1987. 'The Rise and Fall of Italian Fascism as Generational Revolt,' in *Journal of Contemporary History,* vol. 22, no. 3.

Webster, R. 1961. *Christian Democracy in Italy, 1860–1960.* London: Hollis & Carter.

Wiskemann, E. 1969. *Fascism in Italy: Its Development and Influence.* London: Macmillan.

Wolff, R, Hoensch, J. 1987. *Catholics, the State and the European Radical Right, 1919–1945.* Boulder, CO: Social Science Monographs.

Germany

Abraham, D. 1981. *The Collapse of the Weimar Republic: Political Economy and Crisis.* Princeton, NJ: Princeton University Press.

Allen, W. S. 1989. *The Nazi Seizure of Power: The Experience of a Single German Town, 1922–1945.* Harmondsworth: Penguin.

Altner, A. 2002. *Berlin Dance of Death.* Staplehurst: Spellmount.

Aschheim, S. E. 1992. *The Nietzsche Legacy in Germany, 1890–1990.* London: University of California Press.

Ashkenasi, A. 1976. *Modern German Nationalism.* London: Wiley.

Aycoberry, P. 1981. *The Nazi Question: An Essay on the Interpretations of National Socialism, 1922–1975.* London: Routledge and Kegan Paul.

Bankier, D. 1992. *The Germans and the Final Solution: Public Opinion under Nazism.* Oxford: Blackwell.

Barkai, A. 1990. *Nazi Economics: ideology, theory, and policy.* Oxford: Berg.

Barnett, V. 1992. *For the Soul of the People: Protestant Protest against Hitler.* Oxford: Oxford University Press.

Barnouw, D. 1988. *Weimar Intellectuals and the Threat of Modernity.* Bloomington, IN: Indiana University Press.

Bartov, O. 1991. *Hitler's Army: Soldiers, Nazis and War in the Third Reich.* Oxford: Oxford University Press.

Bartov, O. 2001. *The Eastern Front: German Troops and the Barbarisation of Warfare.* Basingstoke: Palgrave.

Bartov, O., ed. 2000. *The Holocaust: Origin, Interpretations, Aftermath.* London: Routledge.

Bauer, Y. 1982. *A History of the Holocaust.* New York, NY: F. Watts.

Bauman, Z. 1989. *Modernity and the Holocaust.* Cambridge: Polity Press.

Bendersky, J. 1983. *Carl Schmitt: Theorist for the Reich.* Princeton, NJ: Princeton University Press.

Bessel, R. 1993. *Germany after the First World War.* Oxford: Clarendon Press.

Bethell, N. 1972. *The War Hitler Won: September 1939.* London: Allen Lane.

Beyerchen, A. D. 1977. *Scientists under Hitler: Politics and the Physics Community in the Third Reich.* London: Yale University Press.

Birken, L. 1995. *Hitler as Philosophe: Remnants of the Enlightenment in National Socialism.* London: Praeger.

Black, R. 1975. *Fascism in Germany: How Hitler Destroyed the World's Most Powerful Labour Movement.* London: Steyne Publications.

Blackbourn, D.1984. *The Peculiarities of German History: Bourgeois Society and Politics in Nineteenth Century Germany.* Oxford: Oxford University Press.

Bracher, K. D. 1973. *The German Dictatorship: The Origins, Structure, and Consequences of National Socialism.* Harmondsworth: Penguin University Books.

Bramsted, E. K. 1965. *Goebbels and National Socialist Propaganda, 1925–1945.* London: Cresset Press.

Bramwell, A. 1985. *Blood and Soil: Walther Darré and Hitler's Green Party.* Bourne End: The Kensal Press.

Breitman, R. 2004. *The Architect of Genocide: Himmler and the Final Solution.* London: Pimlico.

Bridenthal, R. 1984. *When Biology became Destiny. Women in Weimar and Nazi Germany.* New York, NY: Monthly Review Press.

Broszat, M., 1966. *German National Socialism, 1919–45.* Santa Barbara, CA: Clio Press.

Broszat, M., 1981. *The Hitler State.* London: Longman.

Browder, G. C. 1990. *Foundations of the Nazi Police State: The Formation of Sipo and SD.* Lexington, KY: University Press of Kentucky.

Brustein, W. 1996. *The Logic of Evil: The Social Origins of the Nazi Party, 1925–1933.* London: Yale University Press.

Bullock, A., 1990 [1952]. *Hitler: A Study in Tyranny.* London: Penguin Books.

Burden, H. 1967. *The Nuremberg Party Rallies, 1923–39.* London: Pall Mall Press.

Burleigh, M. ed. 1996. *Confronting the Nazi Past: New Debates on Modern German History.* London: Collins & Brown.

Burleigh, M. 2000. *The Third Reich: A New History.* London: Macmillan.

Burleigh, M., Wippermann, W. 1991. *The Racial State: Germany, 1933–1945.* Cambridge: Cambridge University Press.

Burrin, P. 1994. *Hitler and the Jews: The Genesis of the Holocaust.* London: Edward Arnold.

Campbell, B. 1998. *The SA Generals and the Rise of Nazism.* Lexington, KY: University Press of Kentucky.

Carsten, F. 1995. *The German Workers and the Nazis.* Aldershot: Scolar.

Chickering, R. 1984. *We Men Who Feel Most German: A Cultural Study of the Pan-German League, 1886–1914.* London: George Allen & Unwin.

Childers, T. ed. 1986. *The Formation of the Nazi Constituency 1919–1933.* London: Croom Helm.

Crew, D. ed. 1994. *Nazism and German Society, 1933–1945.* London: Routledge.

Deakin, F. W. 1962. *The Brutal Friendship: Mussolini, Hitler and the Fall of Italian Fascism.*

Eley, G. 1980. *Reshaping the German Right.* London: Yale University Press.

Eley, G. 1983. 'What Produces Fascism: Pre-industrial Traditions or the Crisis of the Capitalist State,' in *Politics and Society,* vol. 12, no. 1.

Evans, R. 2003. *The Coming of the Third Reich.* London: Allen Lane.

Fest, J. 1987. *Hitler.* London: Weidenfeld and Nicolson.

Fischer, K. P. 1995. *Nazi Germany: A New History.* London: Constable.

Fisher, C. ed. 1996. *The Rise of National Socialism and the Working Classes in Weimar Germany.* Oxford: Berghahn Books.

Fuechtwanger, E. J. 1995. *From Weimar to Hitler, 1918–1933.* Basingstoke: Macmillan.

Fuechtwanger, E. J. ed. 1973. *Upheaval and Continuity: A Century of German History.* London: Wolff.

Gailus, M. 2003. "Overwhelmed by Their Own Fascination with the 'Ideas of 1933': Berlin's Protestant Social Milieu in the Third Reich," in *German Studies Review,* vol. 26, no. 3.

Giles, G.L. 1985. *Students and National Socialism.* Princeton, NJ: Princeton University Press.

Gregor, N. 1998. *Daimler-Benz in the Third Reich.* London: Yale University Press.

Gregor, N. ed. 2000. *Nazism.* Oxford: Oxford University Press.

Grunberger, R. 1971. *A Social History of the Third Reich.* London: Weidenfeld and Nicolson.

Hake, S. 1993. *The Cinema's Third Machine—Writing on Film in Germany, 1907–1933.* London: University of Nebraska Press.

Harvey, E. 1993. *Youth and the Welfare State in Weimar Germany.* Oxford: Clarendon Press.

Hauner, M. 1978. 'Did Hitler Want a World Dominion?' in *Journal of Contemporary History,* vol. 13.

Herf, J. 1984. *Reactionary Modernism: Technology, Culture and Politics in Weimar and the Third Reich.* Cambridge: Cambridge University Press.

Herzstein, R. E. 1982. *When Nazi Dreams Come True: The Third Reich's Internal Struggle over the Future of Europe after a German Victory: A Look at the Nazi Mentality, 1939–45.* London: Abacus.

Hildebrand, K., 1984. *The Third Reich.* London: Allen & Unwin.

Hinz, B. 1979. *Art in the Third Reich.* Oxford: Basil Blackwell.

Hitler, A. 2003. *Mein Kampf.* New York, NY: Fredonia Classics.

Housden, M. 1997. *Resistance and Conformity in the Third Reich.* London: Routledge.

Hughes, M., Mann, C. 2000. *Fighting Techniques of a Panzergrenadier, 1941–1945: Training, Techniques, and Weapons.* London: Cassell.

James-Chakraborty, K. 2000. *German Architecture for a Mass Audience.* London: Routledge.

Jaskot, P. B. 2000. *The Architecture of Oppression: The SS Forced Labour and Nazi Monumental Building Economy.* London: Routledge.

Jones, L. E. 1998. *German Liberalism and the Dissolution of the Weimar Party System, 1918–1933.* London: University of North Carolina Press.

Kershaw, I. 1987. *The Hitler Myth.* Oxford: Oxford University Press.

Kershaw, I. ed. 1990. *Weimar: Why Did German Democracy Fail?* London: Weidenfeld and Nicolson.

Kershaw, I. 1998. *Hitler, 1889–1936: Hubris.* London: Allen Lane.

Kershaw, I. 2000. *Hitler, 1936–1945: Nemesis.* London: Allen Lane.

Koch, H. 1975. *The Hitler Youth—Origins and Development, 1922–45.* London: Macdonald and Jane's.

Koonz, C. 1986. *Mothers in the Fatherland: Women, the Family and Nazi Politics.* London: Jonathan Cape.

Lane, B. M. 1968 *Architecture and Politics in Germany, 1918–1945.* Cambridge, MA: Harvard University Press.

Laqueur, W. 1962. *Young Germany: A History of the German Youth Movement.* London: Routledge and Kegan Paul.

Lauryssens, S. 2002. *The Man Who Invented the Third Reich: The Life and Times of Moeller van den Bruck.* Stroud : Sutton.

Merkl, P. 1980. *The Making of a Stormtrooper.* Princeton, N.J: Princeton University Press.

Milfull, J. ed. 1990. *The Attractions of Fascism: Social Psychology and Aesthetics of the 'Triumph of the Right.'* New York: Berg.

Mommsen, H. 1996. *The Rise and Fall of Weimar Democracy.* London: University of North Carolina Press .

Mosse, G. L. 1966. *The Crisis of German Ideology.* London: Weidenfeld and Nicolson.

Mosse, G. L. 1978. *Nazism: A Historical and Comparative Analysis of National Socialism.* Oxford: Basil Blackwell.

Mühlberger, D., 1987. *The Social Basis of European Fascist Movements.* London: Croom Helm.

Mühlberger, D. 1991. *Hitler's Followers. Studies in the Sociology of the Nazi Movement.* London: Routledge.

Mühlberger, D. 2003. *Hitler's Voice: The Völkischer Beobachter, 1920–1933.* Oxford: Peter Lang.

Noakes, J., Pridham, G. 1998. *Nazism, 1919–1945* (4 volumes) Exeter: University of Exeter Press.

Orlow, D. 1967. 'The Conversion of Myths into Political Power: The Case of the Nazi Party, 1925–26,' in *The American Historical Review,* no. 72.

Peukert, D. J. K. 1987. *Inside Nazi Germany: Conformity, Opposition and Racism in Everyday Life.* Harmondsworth: Penguin.

Poliakov, L. 1974. *The Aryan Myth.* London: Chatto & Windus.

Pulzer, P. 1964. *The Rise of Political Anti-Semitism in Germany and Austria.* New York, NY: Wiley.

Rabinbach, A. 1976. 'The Aesthetics of Production in the Third Reich,' in *Journal of Contemporary History,* vol. 11, no. 4.

Rauschning, H. 1939. *Hitler Speaks: A Series of Political Conversations with Adolph Hitler on His Real Aims.* London: Thornton Butterworth.

Reimer, R. ed. 2000. *Cultural History through a National Socialist Lens: Essays on the Cinema of the Third Reich.* Woodbridge, Suffolk: Camden House.

Rempel, G. 1989. *Hitler's Children—The Hitler Youth and the SS.* London: University of North Carolina Press.

Rittner, C., Roth, J. eds. 2002. *Pope Pius XII and the Holocaust.* London: Leicester University Press.

Roberts, S. 1938. *The House that Hitler Built.* London: Methuen.

Rogger, H., Weber, E. eds. 1966. *The European Right.* Berkeley, CA: University of California Press.

Rosenbaum, R. 1980. *Explaining Hitler: The Search for the Origins of his Evil.* London: Macmillan.

Rozett, R., Spector, S. 1990. *Encyclopedia of the Holocaust.* New York, NY: Macmillan Library Reference USA.

Schulte-Sass, L. 1996. *Entertaining the Third Reich: Illusions of Wholeness in the Nazi Cinema.* London: Duke University Press.

Shand, J. D. 1984. 'The *Reichsautobahn:* Symbol for the New Reich,' in *Journal of Contemporary History,* vol. 19, no. 2.

Shirer, W. L. 1960. *The Rise and Fall of the Third Reich: A History of Nazi Germany.* New York, NY: Simon and Schuster.

Snyder, Louis L. 1976. *Encyclopedia of the Third Reich.* London: Cassell.

Stachura, P. D. 1975. *Nazi Youth in the Weimar Republic.* Oxford: Clio.

Stachura, P. D. 1983. *Gregor Strasser and the Rise of Nazism.* London: Allen & Unwin.

Stachura, P. D. ed. 1983. *The Nazi Machtergreifung.* London: Allen & Unwin.

Stackelberg, R. 1999. *Hitler's Germany: Origins, Legacies, Interpretations.* London: Routledge.

Stephenson, J. 1975. *Women in Nazi Society.* London: Croom Helm.

Stern, F. 1961. *The Politics of Cultural Despair: A Study in the Rise of the Germanic Ideology.* Berkeley, CA: University of California Press.

Struve, W. 1973. *Elites against Democracy: Leadership Ideals in Bourgeois Political Thought in Germany, 1890–1933.* Princeton, NJ: Princeton University Press.

Taylor, J., W. Shaw. 1987. *A Directory of the Third Reich.* London: Grafton.

Taylor, R. 1974. *The Word in Stone: The Role of Architecture in the National Socialist Ideology.* London: University of California Press.

Taylor R. 1998. *Film Propaganda: Soviet Russia and Nazi Germany.* London: I.B. Tauris.

Traverso, E. 2003. *The Origins of Nazi Violence.* London: New Press.

Vondung, K. 1979. 'Spiritual Revolution and Magic: Speculation and Political Action in National Socialism,' in *Modern Age,* vol. 23, part 4.

Waite, R. 1977. *The Psychopathic God: Adolf Hitler.* New York, NY: Basic Books.

Weber, E., 1964. *Varieties of Fascism: Doctrines of Revolution in the Twentieth Century.* Princeton, NJ: Van Nostrand.

Weindling, P. 1989. *Health, Race and German Politics between National Unification and Nazism, 1870–1945.* Cambridge: Cambridge University Press.

Welch, D. 2002. *The Third Reich: Politics and Propaganda.* London: Routledge.

Williamson, D. G. 1982. *The Third Reich.* Harlow: Longman.

Williamson, G. 1998. *The SS. Hitler's Instrument of Terror.* London: Sidgwick & Jackson.

Zeman, Z. 1973. *Nazi Propaganda.* London: Oxford University Press.

KEY SECONDARY WORKS ON EUROPEAN INTERWAR FASCIST MOVEMENTS BY REGION

The Balkans

Banac, Ivo. 1984. *The National Question: Origin, History, Politics.* Cornell, NY: Ithaca.

Dragnich, A. 1974. *Serbia, Nicola Pasic, and Yugoslavia.* New Brunswick, NJ: Rutgers University Press.

Fischer, Berndt J. 1999. *Albania at War, 1941–1945.* London: Hurst and Company.

Higham, R., Veremis, T. eds. 1993. *The Metaxas Dictatorship: Aspects of Greece, 1936–1940.* Athens: Hellenic Foundation for Defense and Foreign Policy and Speros Basil Vryonis Center for the Study of Hellenism.

Hoptner, J. B. 1962. *Yugoslavia in Crisis, 1934–1941.* New York, NY: Columbia University Press.

Irvine, J. A. 1993. *The Croat Question: Partisan Politics in the Formation of the Yugoslav Socialist State.* Oxford: Westview.

Jelinek, Yeshayahu. 1985. 'Nationalities and Minorities in the Independent State of Croatia,' in *Nationalities Papers,* 7: 2.

Kofas, J. 1981. *Authoritarianism in Greece: The Metaxas Regime.* New York, NY: Eastern European Monographs: Columbia University Press.

MacKensie, D. 1989. *Apis: The Congenial Conspirator.* Boulder, CO: East European Monographs.

Malcolm, Noel. 1995. *Kosovo: A Short History.* London: MacMillan.

Martic, Miloš. 1980. 'Dimitrije Ljotić and the Yugoslav National Movement Zbor, 1935–1945,' in *East European Quarterly,* vol. 16, no. 2.

Mavrogordatos, G. 1983. *Stillborn Republic: Social Conditions and Party Strategies in Greece, 1922–1936.* Berkeley, CA: University of California Press.

Milazzo, M. J. 1975. *The Chetnik Movement and the Yugoslav Resistance.* Baltimore, MD: Johns Hopkins University Press.

Paris, Edmond. 1961. *Genocide in Satellite Croatia: A Record of Racial and Religious Persecutions and Massacres.* Chicago, IL: American Institute for Balkan Affairs.

Perry, D. M. 1988. *The Politics of Terror: The Macedonian Revolutionary Movements, 1893–1903.* London: Duke University Press.

Reinhartz, Dennis. 1986. 'Aryanism in the Independent State of Croatia, 1941–1945: The Historical Basis and Cultural Questions,' in *South Slav Journal,* vol. 9, nos. 3–4.

Sadkovich, James J. 1987. *Italian Support for Croatian Separatism, 1927–1937.* New York, NY: Garland Publishing.

Tomasevich, J. 1975. *War and Revolution in Yugoslavia: The Chetniks.* Stanford, CA: Stanford University Press.

Vatikiotis, P. J. 1998. *Popular Autocracy in Greece, 1936–1941: A Political Biography of General Ioannis Metaxas.* London: Frank Cass.

Vickers, Miranda. 1998. *Between Serb and Albanian: A History of Kosovo.* London: Hurst and Company.

Benelux, France, and Switzerland

Baker, D. N. 1976. 'Two Paths to Socialism: Marcel Déat and Marceau Pivert,' in *Journal of Contemporary History,* vol. 11, no. 1.

Conway, M. 1994. *Collaboration in Belgium. Léon Degrelle and the Rexist Movement.* London: Yale University Press.

Curtis, M. 1959. *Three Against the Third Republic.* Princeton, NJ: Princeton University Press.

Douglas, A.1984. 'Violence and Fascism: The Case of the Faisceau,' in *Journal of Contemporary History,* vol. 19, no. 4.

Gentile, P., Hanspeter, K. 1998. 'Contemporary Radical-Right Parties in Switzerland: History of a Divided Family,' in Betz, H. G., Immerfall, S. eds. *The New Politics of the Right.* New York, NY: St. Martin's Press.

Griffiths R. 1978. 'Anticapitalism and the French Extra—Parliamentary Right, 1870–1940,' in *Journal of Contemporary History,* vol. 13, no. 4.

Hansen, E. 1981. 'Depression Decade Crisis: Social Democracy and Planisme in Belgium and the Netherlands, 1929–1939,' in *Journal of Contemporary History,* vol. 16, no. 2.

Hutton, P. H. 1976. 'Popular Boulangism and the Advent of Mass Politics in France, 1886–90,' in *Journal of Contemporary History,* vol. 11, no. 1.

LeBor, Adam. 1997. *Hitler's Secret Bankers: The Myth of Swiss Neutrality During the Holocaust.* Secaucus, NJ: Birch Lane Press.

Mazgaj, P. 1979. *The Action Française and Revolutionary Syndicalism.* Chapel Hill, NC: University of North Carolina Press.

Mazgaj, P. 1982. 'The Young Sorelians and Decadence,' in *Journal of Contemporary History,* vol. 17, no. 1.

Müller, K. J. 1976. 'French Fascism and Modernisation,' in *Journal of Contemporary History,* vol. 11.

Paxton, R. O. 1982. *Vichy France: Old Guard and New Order, 1940–1944.* New York, NY: Columbia University Press.

Pels, D. 1987. 'Hendrik de Man and the Ideology of Planism,' in *International Review of Social History,* vol. 32.

Shorrock, W. I. 1975. 'France and the Rise of Fascism in Italy,' in *Journal of Contemporary History,* vol. 10.

Soucy, R. J. 1966. 'The Nature of Fascism in France,' in *Journal of Contemporary History,* vol. 1, no. 1.

Soucy, R. J. 1972. *Fascism in France: The Case of Maurice Barrès.* Berkeley, CA: University of California Press.

Soucy, R. J. 1974. 'French Fascist Intellectuals in the 1930s: an Old New Left?' in *French Historical Studies,* vol. 8, no. 3.

Soucy, R. J. 1979. *Fascist Intellectual: Drieu la Rochelle.* Berkeley, CA: University of California Press.

Soucy, R. J. 1980. 'Drieu la Rochelle and the Modernist Anti—Modernism in French Fascism,' in *Modern Language Notes,* vol. 95, no. 4.

Soucy, R. J. 1986. *French Fascism: The First Wave, 1924–33.* London: Yale University Press.

Sternhell, Z. 1973. 'National Socialism and Antisemitism: The Case of Maurice Barrès,' in *Journal of Contemporary History,* vol. 8, no. 4.

Sternhell, Z. 1987. "The 'Anti-materialist' Revision of Marxism as an Aspect of the Rise of Fascist Ideology," in *Journal of Contemporary History,* vol. 22, no. 3.

Sternhell, Z. 1995. *Neither Right nor Left: Fascist Ideology in France.* Princeton, NJ: Princeton University Press.

Sutton, M. 1982. *Nationalism, Positivism and Catholicism: The Politics of Charles Maurras and French Catholics, 1890–1914.* Cambridge: Cambridge University Press.

Central and Eastern Europe

Aczél, T. ed. 1966. *Ten Years After.* London: MacGibbon and Kee.

Batkay, W. M. 1982. *Authoritarian Politics in a Transitional State: Istvan Bethlen and the Unified Party in Hungary.* Boulder, CO: East European Monographs.

Bell, J. D. 1977. *Peasants in Power: Alexander Stamboliski and the Bulgarian Agrarian Union, 1899–1923.* Princeton, NJ: Princeton University Press.

Bischof, G., Pelinka, A., Lassner, A. 2003. *The Dollfuss/Schuschnigg Era in Austria: A Reassessment* (Contemporary Austrian Studies). Somerset, NJ: Transaction Publishers.

Bukey, E. B. 1986. *Hitler's Home Town: Linz, Austria, 1908–1945.* Bloomington, IN: Indiana University Press.

Butnaru, I. C. 1992. *The Silent Holocaust: Romania and its Jews.* London: Greenwood.

Carsten, F. L. 1977. *Fascist Movements in Austria from Schönerer to Hitler.* London: Sage.

Fischer-Galati, S. 1970. *Twentieth Century Rumania.* New York, NY: Columbia University Press.

Gross, J. T. 2001. *Neighbors: The Destruction of the Jewish Community in Jedwabne, Poland.* Princeton, NJ: Princeton University Press.

Hitchins, K. 1994. *Rumania, 1866–1947.* Oxford: Clarendon Press.

Hoebelt, L. 2003. *Defiant Populist: Joerg Haider and the Politics of Austria.* West Lafayette, IN: Purdue University Press.

Innes, A. 2001. *Czechoslovakia: The Short Goodbye.* West Lafayette, IN: Purdue University Press.

Ioanid, R. 1990. *The Sword of the Archangel: Fascist Ideology in Romania.* Boulder, CO: East European Monographs.

Jászi, O. 1921. *Revolution and Counter-revolution in Hungary.* London: P. S. King.

Jellinek, Y. 1976. *The Parish Republic: Hlinka's Slovak People's Party.* Boulder, CO: East European Monographs.

Kelly, D. D. 1995. *The Czech Fascist Movement, 1922–1942.* New York, NY: Columbia University Press.

Kirschbaum, S. J. 1983. *Slovak Politics: Essays on Slovak History in Honour of J. Kirschbaum.* Cleveland, OH: Slovak Institute .

Kirschbaum, S. J. ed. 1999. *Historical Dictionary of Slovakia.* London: Scarecrow Press.

Kitchen, M. 1980. *The Coming of Austrian Fascism.* Montreal: McGill Queens University Press.

Kürti, L. 2003. 'The Uncivility of a Civil Society: Skinhead Youth in Hungary,' in Kopecky, P., Mudde, C. eds. *Uncivil Society? Contentious Politics in Post-communist Europe.* London: Routledge.

Maas, W. B. 1972. *Assassination in Vienna.* New York, NY: Charles Scribner's Sons.

Macartney, C. A. 1937. *Hungary and Her Successors.* London: Royal Institute of International Affairs .

Macartney, C. A. 1957. *October Fifteenth: A History of Modern Hungary.* Edinburgh: Edinburgh University Press.

Mann, M. 2004. *Fascists.* Cambridge: Cambridge University Press.

Mastny, V. 1971. *The Czechs under Nazi Rule: The Failure of National Resistance, 1939–1942.* New York, NY: Columbia University Press.

Miller, M. 1975. *Bulgaria During the Second World War.* Stanford, CA: Stanford University Press.

Nagy-Talavera M. 1970. *The Green Shirts and Others: A History of Fascism in Hungary and Rumania.* Stanford, CA: Hoover Institution Press.

Oliver, H. 1998. *We Were Saved: How the Jews in Bulgaria Were Kept from the Death Camps.* Sofia: Sofia Press.

Parkinson, F. ed. 1989. *Conquering the Past: Austrian Nazism Yesterday and Today.* Detroit, MI: Wayne State University Press.

Pauley, B. 1981. *Hitler and the Forgotten Nazis: A History of Austrian National Socialism.* Chapel Hill, NC: University of North Carolina Press.

Sugar, P. 1971. *Native Fascism in the Successor States, 1918–1945.* Santa Barbara CA: ABC-Clio.

Sugar, P. ed. 1990. *A History of Hungary.* London: Tauris.

Volovici, L. 1976. *Nationalist Ideology and Antisemitism: the Case of Romanian Intellectuals in the 1930s.* Oxford: Pergamon Press.

Great Britain and Ireland

Allen, M. 2000. *Hidden Agenda: How the Duke of Windsor Betrayed the Allies.* London: Macmillan.

Baker, D. 1996. *Ideology of Obsession: A. K. Chesterton and British Fascism.* London: I.B. Tauris.

Benewick, R. 1969. *Political Violence and Public Order: A Study of British Fascism.* London: Allen Lane.

Cronin, M. 1997. *The Blueshirts and Irish Politics.* Dublin: Four Courts Press.

Cross, C. 1966. *The Fascists in Britain.* London: Barrie and Rockliff.

Durham, M. 1992. 'Gender and the British Union of Fascists,' in *Journal of Contemporary History,* vol. 27.

Griffiths, R. 1980. *Fellow Travellers of the Right: British Enthusiasts for Nazi Germany, 1933–9.* London: Constable.

Lewis, D. S. 1987. *Illusions of Grandeur: Mosley, Fascism and British Society, 1931–1981.* Manchester: Manchester University Press.

Linehan, T. 1996. *East End for Mosley.* London: Frank Cass.

Linehan, T. 2000. *British Fascism: Parties, Ideology and Culture.* Manchester: Manchester University Press.

Lunn, K., Thurlow, R. 1980. *British Fascism: Essays on the Radical Right in Inter-war Britain.* London: Croom Helm.

McGarry, F. 1999. *Irish Politics and the Spanish Civil War.* Cork: Cork University Press.

Stone, D. 2002. *Breeding Superman: Nietzsche, Race and Eugenics in Edwardian and Interwar Britain.* Liverpool: Liverpool University Press.

Renton, D. 1998. *Fascism and Anti-Fascism in Britain in the 1940s.* London: Macmillan.

Thurlow, R. 1998. *Fascism in Britain: From Mosley's Blackshirts to the National Front.* London: I.B. Tauris.

Thurlow, R. 2001. *Fascism in Modern Britain.* Stroud: Sutton.

Walker, M. 1981. *The National Front.* London: Routledge and Kegan Paul.

The Iberian Peninsula

Ben-Ami, S. 1983. *Fascism from Above: The Dictatorship of Primo de Rivera in Spain, 1923–1930.* Oxford: Clarendon Press.

Brenan, G. 1960. *The Spanish Labyrinth: An Account of the Social and Political Background of the Civil War.* Cambridge: Cambridge University Press.

Carr, R. 1966. *Spain, 1808–1939.* Oxford: Clarendon Press.

Carr, R., Fusi, J. P. 1979. *Spain: Dictatorship to Democracy.* London: Allen & Unwin.

Coverdale, J. 1975. *Italian Intervention in the Spanish Civil War.* Princeton, NJ: Princeton University Press.

De Blaye, E. 1974. *Franco and the Politics of Spain.* Harmondsworth: Penguin.

Delzell, C. F. ed.1970. *Mediterranean Fascism: 1919–1945.* London: Macmillan.

Foard, D. W. 1975. 'The Forgotten Falangist: Ernesto Gimenez Caballero,' in *Journal of Contemporary History,* vol. 10, no. 1.

Gallo, M. 1973. *Spain under Franco.* London: Allen & Unwin.

Payne, S. G. 1961. *Falange: A History of Spanish Fascism.* London: Oxford University Press.

Payne, S. G. 1999. *Fascism in Spain, 1923–1977.* Madison, WI: University of Wisconsin Press.

Pinto, A. C. 2000. *The Blueshirts: Portuguese Fascists and the New State.* Boulder, CO: Social Science Monographs.

Pinto, A. C. ed. 2003. *Contemporary Portugal: Politics, Society and Culture.* Boulder, CO: Social Science Monographs.

Preston, P. 1994. *The Coming of the Spanish Civil War 1931–1939: Reaction and Revolution in the Second Republic.* London: Routledge.

Preston, P. 1995. *The Politics of Revenge: Fascism and the Military in Twentieth-Century Spain.* London: Routledge.

Preston, P. ed. 1976. *Spain in Crisis: The Evolution and Decline of the Franco Regime.* Hassocks: Harvester.

Preston, P. ed. 1984. *Revolution and War in Spain.* London: Methuen.

Robinson, R.A.H. 1970. *The Origins of Franco's Spain: The Right, the Republic and Revolution, 1931–1936.* Newton Abbot: David & Charles.

Thomas, H. S. 1977. *The Spanish Civil War.* Harmondsworth: Penguin.

Russia, the Soviet Union and the Baltic States

Abramovitch, R. 1962. *The Soviet Revolution, 1880–1963.* London: Allen & Unwin.

Agursky, M. 1987. *The Third Rome: National Bolshevism in the USSR.* Boulder, CO: Westview Press.

Brandenberger, D. 2002. *National Bolshevism: Stalinist Mass Culture and the Formation of Modern Russian National Identity, 1931–1956.* Cambridge, MA: Harvard University Press.

Brent, J., Naumov, V. P. 2003. *Stalin's Last Crime: The Plot Against the Jewish Doctors, 1948–1953.* New York, NY: HarperCollins.

Brudny, Y. 1998. *Reinventing Russia: Russian Nationalism and the Soviet State, 1953–1991.* Cambridge, MA: Harvard University Press.

Bullock, A. 1991. *Hitler and Stalin: Parallel Lives.* London: HarperCollins.

Daniels, R. V. ed. 1965. *The Stalin Revolution: foundations of Soviet totalitarianism.* Lexington, MA: Heath.

Dunlop, J. B. 1976. *The New Russian Revolutionaries.* Belmont, MA: Nordland Publishing Company.

Dunlop, J. B. 1984. *The Faces of Contemporary Russian Nationalism.* Princeton, NJ: Princeton University Press.

Eidintas, A., Zalys, V. 1998. *Lithuania in European Politics: The Years of the First Republic, 1918–1940.* New York, NY: St. Martin's.

Ezergailis, A. 1996. *The Holocaust in Latvia: The Missing Center.* Riga: Historical Institute of Latvia.

Haslam, J. 1984. *The Soviet Union and the Struggle for Collective Security in Europe, 1933–1939.* London: Macmillan.

Kasekamp, A. 1999. 'Radical Right-Wing Movements in the North-East Baltic,' in *Journal of Contemporary History,* vol. 34, no. 4.

Kasekamp, A. 2000. *The Radical Right in Interwar Estonia.* Basingstoke: Macmillan.

Kostyrchenko, G. 1995. *Out of the Red Shadows: Antisemitism in Stalin's Russia.* Amherst, NY: Prometheus.

Laqueur, W. 1994. *Black Hundred: The Rise of the Extreme Right in Russia.* New York, NY: HarperPerennial.

Lewin, M., Kershaw, I. eds. 1997. *Stalinism and Nazism: Dictatorships in Comparison.* Cambridge: Cambridge University Press.

Mastny, V. 1979. *Russia's Road to the Cold War: Diplomacy, Warfare, and the Politics of Communism, 1941–1945.* New York, NY: Columbia University Press.

Mehnert, K. 1952. *Stalin versus Marx: The Stalinist Historical Doctrine.* London: George Allen & Unwin.

Parming, T. 1975. *The Collapse of Liberal Democracy and the Rise of Authoritarianism in Estonia.* London: Sage Publications.

Rauch, G. 1995. *The Baltic States: The Years of Independence, 1970–1940.* London: Hurst.

Rossman, V. 2002. *Russian Intellectual Antisemitism in the Post-Communist Era.* Jerusalem: The Vidal Sassoon International Center for the Study of Antisemitism.

Shenfield, S. D. 2001. *Russian Fascism: Traditions, Tendencies, Movements.* Armonk, NY: M.E. Sharpe.

Stephan, J. J. 1978. *The Russian Fascists: Tragedy and Farce in Exile, 1925–1945.* New York, NY: HarperCollins.

Tucker, R. C. 1990. *Stalin in Power: The Revolution from Above, 1928–1941.* New York, NY: Norton.

Van Ree, E. 2002. *The Political Thought of Joseph Stalin: A Study in Twentieth-Century Revolutionary Patriotism.* London: Routledge.

Weitz, E. D. 2002. 'Racial Politics without the Concept of Race: Reevaluating Soviet Ethnic and National Purges,' in *Slavic Review,* no. 61 (1).

Yanov, A. 1987. *The Russian Challenge and the Year 2000.* New York, NY: Basil Blackwell.

Scandinavia

Berggren, L. 2002. 'Swedish Fascism—Why Bother?' in *Journal of Contemporary History,* vol. 37.

Dahl, H. F. 1995. *Quisling. A Study of Treachery.* London: Cambridge University Press.

Hoidal, O. K. 1999. *Quisling: A Study in Treason.* Cambridge: Cambridge University Press.

Karvonen, L. 1988. *From White to Blue and Black: Finnish Fascism in the Interwar Era.* Helsinki: Finnish Society of Sciences and Letters.

Lindström, U. 1985. *Fascism in Scandinavia, 1920–1940.* Stockholm: Almqvist & Wiksell International.

Milward, A. 1972. *The Fascist Economy in Norway.* Oxford: Clarendon Press.

Rintala, M. 1962. *Three Generations: The Extreme Right Wing in Finnish Politics.* Bloomington, IN: Indiana University.

KEY SECONDARY WORKS ON FASCISM OUTSIDE EUROPE BY REGION

Asia

Berger, G. M. 1977. *Parties out of Power in Japan, 1931–1941.* Princeton, NJ: Princeton University Press.

Chander, J. P. ed. 1943. *Gandhi Against Fascism.* Lahore: Free India Publications.

Chang, M. H. 1985. *The Chinese Blue Shirt Society: Fascism and Developmental Nationalism.* Berkeley, CA: University of California, Berkeley, Institute of East Asian Studies.

Chang, M. H. 2001. *Return of the Dragon: China's Wounded Nationalism.* Boulder, CO: Westview Press.

Crowley, J. 1966. *Japan's Quest for Autonomy: Security and Foreign Policy, 1930–1938.* Princeton, NJ: Princeton University Press.

Eastman, L. E. 1974. *The Abortive Revolution: China Under Nationalist Rule, 1927–1937.* Cambridge, MA: Harvard University Press.

Elst, K. 2001. *The Saffron Swastika, The Notion of Hindu 'Fascism.'* New Delhi: Voice of India.

Etcheson, C. In Press. *After the Killing Fields: Lessons from the Cambodian Genocide.* New York, NY: Praeger.

Fletcher, W. M. 1982. *The Search for a New Order: Intellectuals and Fascism in Pre-war Japan.* Chapel Hill, NC: University of North Carolina Press.

Golwalkar, M.S. 1945. *We or Our Nationhood Defined.* 3rd Edition. Nagpur: M. N. Kale.

Gordon, A. 1991. *Labor and Imperial Democracy in Pre-war Japan.* Oxford: University of California Press.

Hauner, M. 1981. *India in Axis Strategy: Germany, Japan, and Indian Nationalists in the Second World War.* Stuttgart: Klett-Cotta.

Havens, T. R. H. 1974. *Farm and Nation in Modern Japan: Agrarian Nationalism, 1870–1940.* Princeton, NJ: Princeton University Press.

Jackson, K. ed. 1989. *Cambodia 1975–78: Rendez-vous with Death.* Princeton, NJ: Princeton University Press.

Krishna, C. ed. 2003. *Fascism in India: Faces, Fangs and Facts.* New Delhi: Manak Publications.

Maruyama, M. 1969. *Thought and Behavior in Modern Japanese Politics.* London: Oxford University Press.

Mitchell, R. H. 1976. *Thought Control in Pre-war Japan.* Ithaca, NY: Cornell University Press.

Morris, I. ed. 1963. *Japan, 1931–1945: Militarism, Fascism, Japanism?* Boston, MA: Heath.

Oka, Y. 1983. *Konoe Fumimaro: A Political Biography.* Tokyo: University of Tokyo Press.

Scalapino, R. A. 1953. *Democracy and the Party Movement in Pre-war Japan: The Failure of the First Attempt.* Berkeley, CA: University of California Press.

Shillony, B. 1973. *Politics and Culture in Wartime Japan.* Oxford: Clarendon Press.

Wilson, G. M. 1969. *Radical Nationalist in Japan: Kita Ikki, 1883–1937.* Cambridge, MA: Harvard University Press.

Africa

2000. *The Middle East and North Africa 2000: A Survey and Reference Book.* London: Europa Publications.

Bloomberg, C. 1989. *The Afrikaner Broederbond.* Bloomington, IN: Indiana University Press.

Bunting, B. 1969. *The Rise of the South African Reich.* Harmondsworth: Penguin.

Davenport, T.R.H. 1966. *The Afrikaner Bond.* Oxford: Oxford University Press.

Furlong, P. J. 1991. *Between Crown and Swastika.* Middletown, CT: Wesleyan University Press.

Godwin, P. 1993. *"Rhodesians Never Die:" The Impact of War and Political Change on White Rhodesia, c. 1970–1980.* Oxford: Oxford University Press.

Hexham, I. 1981. *The Irony of Apartheid.* Toronto: Edwin Mellen.

Liddell Hart, B. H., ed. 1953. *The Rommel Papers.* London: Collins.

Mockley, A. 1984. *Haile Selassie's War: The Italian-Ethiopian Campaign, 1935–1941.* Oxford: Oxford University Press.

Montgomery, V. 1958. *The Memoirs of Field-Marshall the Viscount Montgomery of Alamein, K.G.* London: Collins.

Moodie, D. 1975. *The Rise of Afrikanerdom.* Berkeley, CA: University of California Press.

Simpson, H. 1980. *The Social Origins of Afrikaner Fascism and Its Apartheid Policy.* Stockholm: Almqvist & Wiksell International.

Van Jaarsveld, F. A. 1961. *The Awakening of Afrikaner Nationalism.* Cape Town: Human & Rousseau.

Vatcher, W. H., Jr. 1965. *White Laager: The Rise of Afrikaner Nationalism.* London: Pall Mall Press.

Australia and New Zealand

Greason, D. 1994. *I Was a Teenage Fascist.* Ringwood, Victoria: McPhee Gribble.

Leach, M., Stokes, G., Ward, I. eds. 2000. *The Rise and Fall of One Nation.* St Lucia, Queensland: University of Queensland Press.

Moore, A. 1989. *The Secret Army and the Premier: Conservative Paramilitary Organisations in New South Wales 1930–32.* Kensington, New South Wales: New South Wales University Press.

Moore, A. 1995. *The Right Road: A History of Right-Wing Politics in Australia.* Oxford: Oxford University Press.

Middle East

2000. *The Middle East and North Africa 2000: A Survey and Reference Book.* London: Europa Publications.

Abu Jaber, K. 1966. *The Arab Ba'th Socialist Party: History, Ideology, and Organization.* Syracuse, NY: Syracuse University.

Adanir, F. 2001. 'Kemalist Authoritarianism and Fascist Trends in Turkey during the Interwar Period,' in Larsen, S. U. ed. *Fascism Outside Europe.* Boulder, CO: Social Science Monographs.

Al-Khalil, S. 2003. *The Monument: Art, Vulgarity and Responsibility in Iraq.* London: I. B. Tauris.

C.A.R.D.R.I. 1989. *Saddam's Iraq: Revolution or Reaction?* London: Zed Books.

Choueiri, Y. M. 2000. *Arab Nationalism: A History.* Oxford: Blackwell.

Cleveland, W. L. 1994. *A History of the Modern Middle East.* Oxford: Westview Press.

Farouk-Sluglett, M., P. Sluglett, 2001. *Iraq since 1958: From Revolution to Dictatorship.* London: I. B. Tauris.

Genocide in Iraq: The Anfal Campaign Against the Kurds. 1993. New York, NY: Middle East Watch.

Hirszowicz, L. 1966. *The Third Reich and the Arab East.* London: Routledge and Kegan Paul.

Hovannisian, R. G. ed. 1987. *The Armenian Genocide in Perspective.* New Brunswick, NY: Transaction Books.

Jankowski, J. P. 1975. *Egypt's Young Rebels: 'Young Egypt,' 1933–1952.* Stanford, CA: Hoover Institution Press.

Kienle, E. 1990. *Ba'th v Ba'th: The Conflict Between Syria and Iraq, 1968–1989.* London: I. B. Tauris.

Makiya, A. 1989. *Republic of Fear: The Inside Story of Saddam's Iraq.* Berkeley, CA: University of California Press.

Mansfield, P. 1992. *A Modern History of the Middle East.* London: Penguin.

Marr, P. 2004. *The Modern History of Iraq.* Cambridge, MA: Westview Press.

Melson, R. 1992. *Revolution and Genocide: On the Origins of the Armenian Genocide and the Holocaust.* London: University of Chicago Press.

Olson, R. 1982. *The Ba'th and Syria, 1947–1982: The Evolution of Ideology, Party and State.* Princeton, NJ: Kingston.

Schultze, R. 2000. *A Modern History of the Muslim World.* London: I. B. Tauris .

Seale, P. 1986. *The Struggle for Syria.* London: Yale University Press.

Tibi, B. 1990. *Arab Nationalism: A Critical Inquiry.* New York: St. Martin's.

Tripp, C. 2000. *A History of Iraq.* Cambridge: Cambridge University Press.

Zürcher, E. J. 1998. *Turkey: A Modern History.* London: I.B. Tauris.

South and Central America

Alexander, R. J. 1951. *The Perón Era.* London: Gollancz.

Alexander, R. J. 1982. *Bolivia: Past, Present, and Future of Its Politics.* New York, NY: Praeger.

Chomsky, N., Herman, E. 1979. *The Washington Connection and Third World Fascism.* Boston, MA: South End Press.

Collier, D. ed. 1979. *The New Authoritarianism in Latin America.* Princeton, NJ: Princeton University Press.

Crassweller, R. D. 1987. *Perón and the Enigmas of Argentina.* New York, NJ: Norton.

Deutsch, S. M. 1999. *Las Derechas. The Extreme Right in Argentina, Brazil, and Chile, 1890–1939.* Stanford, CA: Stanford University Press.

Falcoff, M., Pike, F. 1982. *The Spanish Civil War: American Hemispheric Perspectives.* Lincoln, NE: University of Nebraska Press.

Hilliker, G. 1971. *The Politics of Reform in Peru: The Aprista and Other Mass Parties of Latin America.* Baltimore, MD: Johns Hopkins Press.

James, D. 1988. *Resistance and Integration. Peronism and the Argentine Working Class, 1946–1976.* Cambridge: Cambridge University Press.

Johnson, J. 1958. *Political Change in Latin America. The Emergence of the Middle Sectors.* Stanford, CA: Stanford University Press.

Jordan, D. 1996. *Nationalism in Contemporary Latin America.* New York: New Press.

Klarén, P. F. 2000. *Peru: Society and Nationhood in the Andes.* Oxford: Oxford University Press.

Klein, H. 1969. *Parties and Political Change in Bolivia, 1880–1952.* Cambridge: Cambridge University Press.

Klein, H. 1982. *Bolivia: The Evolution of a Multi-Ethnic Society.* New York, NY: Oxford University Press.

Klein, H. 2003. *A Concise History of Bolivia.* Cambridge: Cambridge University Press.

Lewis, P. H. 1980. *Paraguay under Stroessner.* Chapel Hill, NC: The University of North Carolina Press.

Malloy, J. M. ed. 1977. *Authoritarianism and Corporatism in Latin America.* Pittsburgh, PA: University of Pittsburgh Press.

Marett, S.R. 1969. *Peru.* New York, NY: Praeger Publishers.

Martz, J. D. 1972. *Ecuador: Conflicting Political Culture and the Quest for Progress.* Boston, MA: Allyn and Bacon, Inc.

McGee, D. S. 1986. *Counterrevolution in Argentina: The Argentine Patriotic League.* Lincoln, NE: University of Nebraska Press.

McGee D. S., Dolkart, R. H. eds. 1993. *The Argentine Right. Its History and Intellectual Origins.* Wilmington, DE: S. R. Books.

McKale, D. 1977. *The Swastika Outside Germany.* Kent, OH: The Kent State University Press.

Miranda, C. R. 1990. *The Stroessner Era: Authoritarian Rule in Paraguay.* Boulder, CO: Westview Press.

Payne, L. A. 2000. *Uncivil Movements. The Armed Right Wing and Democracy in Latin America.* London: The Johns Hopkins University Press.

Power, M. 2002. *Right-Wing Women in Chile. Feminine Power and the Struggle Against Allende, 1964–1973.* University Park, PA: Pennsylvania State University Press.

Rock, D. 1992. *Authoritarian Argentina: The Nationalist Movement, Its History and Impact.* Berkeley, CA: University of California Press.

Rouquié, A. 1987. *The Military and the State in Latin America.* Berkeley, CA: University of California Press.

Schuler, F. E. 1998. *Mexico Between Hitler and Roosevelt. Mexican Foreign Politics in the Age of Lázaro Cárdenas, 1934–1940.* Albuquerque: University of New Mexico Press.

Sherman, J. W. 1997. *The Mexican Right.* Westport CT: Praeger.

Silvert, K. 1961. *The Conflict Society: Reaction and Revolution in Latin America.* New Orleans, LA: The Hauser Press.

Skidmore, T. 1967. *Politics in Brazil, 1930–1964. An Experiment in Democracy.* Oxford: Oxford University Press.

Spektorowski, A. S. 2003. *The Origins of Argentina's Revolution of the Right.* Notre Dame, IN: University of Notre Dame Press.

United States

Barkun, M. 1997. *Religion and the Racist Right. The Origins of the Christian Identity Movement.* London: University of North Carolina Press.

Bell, L. V. 1973. *In Hitler's Shadow: The Anatomy of American Fascism.* Port Washington, NY: Kennikat Press.

Bennett, D. H. 1969. *Demagogues in the Depression: American Radicals and the Union Party, 1932–1936.* New Brunswick, NJ: Rutgers University Press.

Blee, K. M. 2002. *Inside Organized Racism. Women in the Hate Movement.* London: University of California Press.

Brinkley, A. 1982. *Voices of Protest: Huey Long, Father Coughlin, and the Great Depression.* New York, NY: Knopf .

Chalmers, D. M. 1965. *Hooded Americanism: The First Century of the Ku Klux Klan, 1865–1965.* Garden City, NY: Doubleday.

Diggins, J. P. 1972. *Mussolini and Fascism: The View from America.* Princeton, NJ: Princeton University Press.

Dobratz, B. A., Shanks-Meile, S. L. 2000. *The White Separatist Movement in the United States. White Power, White Pride.* Baltimore, MD: Johns Hopkins University Press.

Gardell, M. 2003. *Gods of the Blood. The Pagan Revival and White Separatism.* Durham, NC: Duke University Press.

Gossett, T. F. 1997. *Race: The History of an Idea in America.* London: Oxford University Press.

Handlin, O. 1957. *Race and Nationality in American Life.* Boston, MA: Little Brown.

Jackson, K. T. 1967. *The Ku Klux Klan in the City, 1915–1930.* London: Oxford University Press.

Kaplan, J. ed. 2000. *Encyclopedia of White Power. A Sourcebook on the Radical Racist Right.* Walnut Creek, CA: AltaMira Press.

Levitas, D. 2002. *The Terrorist Next Door. The Militia Movement and the Radical Racist Right.* New York, NY: Thomas Dunne Books.

Nasaw, D. 2000. *The Chief: The Life of William Randolph Hearst.* Boston, MA: Houghton, Mifflin.

Offner, A. A. 1969. *American Appeasement: United States Foreign Policy and Germany, 1933–1938.* Cambridge, MA: Harvard University Press.

Randel, W. P. 1965. *The Ku Klux Klan: A Century of Infamy.* London: H. Hamilton.

Ribuffo, L. P. 1983. *The Old Christian Right: The Protestant Far Right from the Great Depression to the Cold War.* Philadelphia: Temple University Press .

Ribuffo, L. P. ed. 1992. *Right Center Left: Essays in American History.* New Brunswick, NJ: Rutgers University Press.

Schonbach, M. 1985. *Native American Fascism during the 1930s and 1940s: A Study of Its Roots, Its Growth and Its Decline.* New York: Garland .

Sims, P. 1978. *The Klan.* New York: Scarbrough Books.

Stanton, B. 1992. *Klanwatch. Bringing the Ku Klux Klan to Justice.* Bergenfield, New Jersey: Mentor.

Wade, W. C. 1987. *The Fiery Cross. The Ku Klux Klan in America.* New York: Simon and Schuster .

KEY SECONDARY WORKS ON POST-WAR FASCISM

Akenson, D. H. 1992. *God's Peoples: Covenant and Land in South Africa, Israel, and Ulster.* Ithaca and London: Cornell University Press.

Barkun, M. 1997. *Religion and the Racist Right: The Origins of Christian Identity Movement.* Chapel Hill and London: The University of North Carolina Press.

Bar-On, T. 2001. 'The Ambiguities of the Nouvelle Droite, 1968–1999', in *The European Legacy* 6 (3).

Berlet, C. et al. *Right-wing Populism in America: Too Close for Comfort.* London: Guilford Press.

Cheles, L., Ferguson, R., Vaughan, M. eds. 1991. *Neo-Fascism in Europe.* London: Longman.

Cheles, L. et al. eds. 1995. *The Far Right in Western and Eastern Europe.* London: Longman.

Coogan, K. 1999. *Dreamer of the Day: Francis Parker Yockey and the Postwar Fascist International.* New York: Autonomedia.

Eatwell, R. 2003. *Fascism: A History.* London: Pimlico.

Ford, G. ed. 1992. *Fascist Europe. The Rise of Racism and Xenophobia.* London: Pluto Press.

Goodrick-Clarke, N. 2002. *Black Sun: Aryan Cults, Esoteric Nazism, and the Politics of Identity.* London: New York University Press.

Griffin, R. 1991. *The Nature of Fascism.* London: Routledge.

Griffin, R. ed. 1995. *Fascism.* Oxford: Oxford University Press.

Griffin, R. 1998. 'Ce n'est pas Le Pen: The MSI/AN's Estrangement from the Front National's Immigration Policy,' in Westin, C. ed. *Racism, Ideology and Political Organization.* London: Routledge.

Griffin, R. 1999. 'GUD Reactions: The Patterns of Prejudice of a Neo-Fascist *Groupuscule,*' in *Patterns of Prejudice,* vol. 33, no. 2.

Griffin, R. 2000. "Interregnum or Endgame? Radical Right Thought in the 'Post-fascist' Era," in *The Journal of Political Ideologies,* vol. 5, no. 2.

Griffin, R. 2000. "Between Metapolitics and *Apoliteía:* The New Right's Strategy for Conserving the Fascist Vision in the 'Interregnum,'" in *Contemporary French Studies* vol. 8 no. 2.

Griffin, R. 2000. 'Plus ça change! The Fascist Pedigree of the Nouvelle Droite,' in Arnold, E. ed. *The Development of the Radical Right in France.* London: Macmillan.

Griffin, R. 2000. "Interregnum or Endgame? The radical Right in the 'post-fascist' Era." Pp. 163–178 in *Journal of Political Ideologies,* vol. 5, no. 2.

Hainsworth, P. ed. 1992. *The Extreme Right in Europe and the USA.* London: Pinter.

Harris, G. 1990. *The Dark Side of Europe. The Extreme Right Today.* Edinburgh: Edinburgh University Press.

Hockenos, P. 1993. *Free to Hate: The Rise of the Right in Post-Communist Eastern Europe.* London: Routledge.

Kaplan, J. ed. 2000. *Encyclopedia of White Power. A Sourcebook on the Radical Racist Right.* Walnut Creek, CA: AltaMira Press.

Kaplan, J., Weinberg, L. 1998. *The Emergence of a Euro-American Radical Right.* New Brunswick, NJ: Rutgers University Press.

Kitschelt, H. 1995. *The Radical Right in Western Europe: A Comparative Analysis.* Ann Arbor: University of Michigan Press.

Landes, R. ed. 2000. *The Encyclopedia of Millennialism and Millennial Movements.* New York: Routledge.

Laqueur, W. 1996. *Fascism. Past, Present, Future.* Oxford: Oxford University Press.

Lee, M. 1997. *The Beast Reawakens.* London: Little, Brown.

Maclean, N. 1994. *Behind the Mask of Chivalry: The Making of the Second Ku Klux Klan.* Oxford: Oxford University Press.

Merkl, P. H., Weinberg, L. 1997. *The Revival of Right-wing Extremism in the Nineties.* London: Frank Cass.

O'Maolain, C. 1987. *The Radical Right: A World Directory.* Harlow: Longman.

Riboffo, L. P. 1983. *The Old Christian Right: The Protestant Far Right from the Great Depression to the Cold War.* Philadelphia, PA: Temple University Press.

Schmidt, M. 1993. *The New Reich: Violent Extremism in Unified Germany and Beyond.* London: Hutchinson.

Shenfield, S. 2001. *Russian Fascism: Tradition, Tendencies, Movements.* London: M. E. Sharpe.

Simmons, H. 1996. *The French National Front: The Extremist Challenge to Democracy.* Boulder, CO: Westview Press.

Skypietz, I. 1994. 'Right Wing Extremism in Germany', in *German Politics,* vol. 3, no. 1.

Sternhell, Z. et. al. 1994. *The Birth of the Fascist Ideology.* Princeton, NJ: Princeton University Press.

Sunic, T. 1990. *Against Democracy and Equality: The European New Right.* New York, NY: Peter Lang.

Thurlow, R. 1998. *Fascism in Britain: From Mosley's Blackshirts to the National Front.* London. I. B. Tauris.

Thurlow, R. 2001. *Fascism in Modern Britain.* Stroud: Sutton.

Special Issue on Right Wing Extremism in Western Europe. 1988. *West European Politics,* vol. 1, no. 2.

OTHER BOOKS RELATED TO THE STUDY OF FASCIST IDEOLOGY

Adamson, W. L. 1980. *Hegemony and Revolution: A Study of Antonio Gramsci's Political and Cultural Theory.* Berkeley, CA: University of California Press.

Adorno, T. et al. 1950. *The Authoritarian Personality.* New York, NY: Harper.

Albin, M. ed. 1980. *New Directions in Psycho-history: The Adelphi Papers in Honor of Erik H. Erikson.* Lexington, MA: Lexington Books.

Alexander, J. ed. 1989. *Durkheimian Sociology: Cultural Studies.* Cambridge: Cambridge University Press.

Apter, D. 1965. *The Politics of Modernisation.* London: University of Chicago Press.

Arendt, H. 1967. *The Origins of Totalitarianism.* London: Allen & Unwin.

Baradt, L. P. 1991. *Political Ideologies: Their Origins and Impact.* London: Prentice-Hall International.

Bauman, Z. 1991. *Modernity and Ambivalence.* Cambridge: Polity.

Billington, J. S. 1980. *Fire in the Minds of Men: Origins of Revolutionary Faith.* London: Temple Smith.

Cohn, N. 1993. *The Pursuit of the Millennium: Revolutionary Millenarians and Mystical Anarchists of the Middle Ages.* London: Pimlico.

Davies, P. D. Lynch. 2002. *The Routledge Companion to Fascism and the Far Right.* London and New York: Routledge.

Eliade, M. 1987. *The Sacred and the Profane: The Nature of Religion.* London: Harcourt Brace.

Hayes, C. J. H. 1960. *Nationalism: A Religion.* New York, NY: Macmillan.

Koestler, A. 1989. *The Ghost in the Machine.* London: Arkana.

Leed, E. J. 1979. *No Man's Land: Combat and Identity in World War I.* Cambridge: Cambridge University Press.

Rees, Philip. 1990. *Biographical Dictionary of the Extreme Right Since 1890.* New York, NY: Simon & Schuster.

Roshwald, A., Stites, R. eds. 2002. *European Culture in the Great War.* Cambridge: Cambridge University Press.

Scruton, R. 1982. *A Dictionary of Political Thought.* London: Macmillan.

Smith, A. 1979. *Nationalism in the Twentieth Century.* New York, NY: New York University Press.

Stromberg, R. 1966. *An Intellectual History of Modern Europe.* New York, NY: Appleton-Century-Crofts.

Stromberg, R. 1982. *Redemption by War: The Intellectuals and 1914.* Lawrence, KS: Regents Press of Kansas.

Theweleit, K. 1987–1989. *Male Fantasies* (2 Vols.) Cambridge: Polity.

Turner, V. 1975. *The Ritual Process: Structure and Antistructure.* Harmondsworth: Penguin.

Index

Page ranges for main entries appear in boldface type.

Editor's Biography

CYPRIAN BLAMIRES
MA (Oxon) D Phil

Cyprian Blamires is a freelance scholar, writer, editor, and translator based in the United Kingdom. He completed a doctoral thesis in the History of Ideas at the University of Oxford under the supervision of one of the most celebrated twentieth century intellectuals, the late Sir Isaiah Berlin. It was the research he did for this thesis—focussing on counter-revolutionary and proto-socialist reactions to the French Revolution—which first sparked his long-standing interest in the ideology of fascism. He has Oxford degrees in European Languages and Literature and in Theology, has taught at Oxford, London, and Leicester Universities, and has held research fellowships in London and Geneva. He has written extensively in English and in French on the history of European thought and is co-editor of two modern editions of works by English philosopher Jeremy Bentham. He has a working knowledge of seven languages, has translated books from Italian, German, and French in the fields of economics, and religion, philosophy and has also translated numerous entries written in these languages for this encyclopedia (as well as authoring numerous entries totalling more than 60,000 words). He is married to an ophthalmic surgeon and has one son, who is a lawyer.